Python and Tkinter Programming

Python and Tkinter Programming

JOHN E. GRAYSON

MANNING

Greenwich
(74° w. long.)

For online information and ordering of this and other Manning books,
go to www.manning.com. The publisher offers discounts on this book
when ordered in quantity. For more information, please contact:

Special Sales Department
Manning Publications Co.
32 Lafayette Place   Fax: (203) 661-9018
Greenwich, CT 06830   email: orders@manning.com

Manning Publications Co.   Copyeditor: Kristen Black
32 Lafayette Place   Typesetter: Dottie Marsico
Greenwich, CT 06830   Cover designer: Leslie Haimes

Printed in the United States of America
1 2 3 4 5 6 7 8 9 10 – CM – 03 02 01 00

To the memory of Backy, who taught me the value of language.

brief contents

contents

Part 3 *Putting it all together... 311*

preface

I first encountered Python in 1993 when I joined a small company in Rhode Island. Their primary product was a GUI-builder for X/Motif that generated code for C, C++, Ada and Python. I was tasked with extending the object-oriented interface for X/Motif and Python. In the past I'd become skeptical about the use of interpretive languages, so I began the task with little excitement. Two days later I was hooked. It was easy to develop interfaces that would have taken much more time and code to develop in C. Soon after, I began to choose interfaces developed using the Python interface in preference to compiled C code.

After I left the company in Rhode Island, I began to develop applications using Tkinter, which had become the preeminent GUI for Python. I persuaded one company, where I was working on contract, to use Python to build a code-generator to help complete a huge project that was in danger of overrunning time and budget. The project was a success. Four years later there are many Python programmers in that company and some projects now use Tkinter and Python for a considerable part of their code.

It was this experience, though, that led me to start writing this book. Very little documentation was available for Tkinter in the early days. The *Tkinter Life Preserver* was the first document that helped people pull basic information together. In 1997 Fredrik Lundh released some excellent documentation for the widget classes on the web, and this has served Tkinter programmers well in the past couple of years. One of the problems that I saw was that although there were several example programs available (the Python distribution contains several), they were mostly brief in content and did not represent a framework for a full application written with Tkinter. Of course, it is easy to connect bits of code together to make it do more but when the underlying architecture relies on an interpreter it is easy to produce an inferior product, in terms of execution speed, aesthetics, maintainability and extensibility.

So, one of the first questions that I was asked about writing Tkinter was "How do I make an XXX?" I'd usually hand the person a chunk of code that I'd written and, like most professional programmers, they would work out the details. I believe strongly that learning from full, working examples is an excellent way of learning how to program in a particular language and to achieve particular goals.

When I was training in karate, we frequently traveled to the world headquarters of Shukokai, in New Jersey, to train with the late Sensei Shigeru Kimura. Sensei Kimura often told us "I can't *teach* you how to do this (a particular technique)—you have to *steal* it." My approach to learning Tkinter is similar. If someone in the community has solved a problem, we need to steal it from them. Now, I am not suggesting that we infringe copyright and professional practice! I simply mean you should learn from whatever material is available. I hope that you will use the examples in the book as a starting point for your own creations. In a small number of cases I have used code or the ideas of other programmers. If this is the case I have given the original author an appropriate acknowledgment. If you use one of these pieces of code, I'd appreciate it if you would also acknowledge the original author. After all, what we "steal" has more value than what we produce ourselves—it came from the *Sensei!*

I was impressed by the format of Douglas A. Young's *The X Window System: Programming and Applications with Xt.* It is a little old now, but it had a high proportion of complete code examples, some of which made excellent templates upon which new applications could be built. *Python and Tkinter Programming* has some parallels in its layout. You will find much longer examples than you may be accustomed to in other programming books. I hope that many of the examples will be useful either as templates or as a source of inspiration for programmers who have to solve a particular problem.

One side effect of presenting complete examples as opposed to providing code fragments is that you will learn a great deal about *my* style of programming. During the extensive reviews for *Python and Tkinter Programming* some of the reviewers suggested alternate coding patterns for some of the examples. Wherever possible, I incorporated their suggestions, so that the examples now contain the programming styles of several people. I expect that you will make similar improvements when you come to implement your own solutions.

I hope that you find *Python and Tkinter Programming* useful. If it saves you even a couple of hours when you have an application to write, then it will have been worth the time spent reading the book.

special thanks

Writing *Python and Tkinter Programming* has been the collective effort of many people. Each of these persons contributed their time, expertise and effort to help make the book more effective. Many of the words are theirs and not mine—the book is now better.

I want to thank the team of technical reviewers: Fred L. Drake, Robin Friedrich, Alan Gauld, Bob Gibson, Lynn Grande, Doug Hellmann, Garrett G. Hodgson, Paul Kendrew, Andrew M. Kuchling, Cameron Laird, Gregory A. Landrum, Ivan Van Laningham, Burt Leavenworth, Ken McDonald, Frank McGeough, Robert Meegan, William Peloquin, Robert J. Roberts and Guido van Rossum. They provided detailed comments that resulted in significant improvements to the book's content, focus and accuracy.

Some of the code examples were derived from code written by others. I want to thank these authors for agreeing to allow me to use their code in this book.

Doug Hellman wrote an excellent module for Pmw, GUIAppD.py, which I adapted as App-Shell.py and used for many examples within the book. Doug agreed that I could use the code. If you find AppShell.py useful in your applications, please acknowledge the original author of this work.

Konrad Hinsen wrote TkPlotCanvas.py, which was intended to be used with NumPy, which uses extension modules optimized for numerical operations. I adapted it to run without NumPy and also added some additional graphical capabilities. Again, if you find it useful, please acknowledge Konrad Hinsen.

The Tree and Node classes used in chapter 8 are derived from code released by OpenChem for inclusion within their Open Source project. You might want to look at any future releases from this organization, since the tree-widget examples presented in this book are limited in their capability.

Appendix B uses the main pages for Tk as a starting point for documenting Tkinter. The copyright owners, the Regents of the University of California and Sun Microsystems allow derivative works to be made, provided that the original copyright is acknowledged.

I also want to thank Gordon Smith at General Dynamics for having confidence in the use of Python and Tkinter in some of the projects for which he was responsible; observing their use in real-world applications is one of the factors that prompted me to begin the task of writing the book. I was able to test some of the draft chapters by giving them to his staff and intern students to solve some of their programming tasks.

Next, I want to thank everyone at Manning Publications who turned my ideas into a book. I had many long conversations with the publisher, Marjan Bace, who led me through the somewhat complex task of writing a book that is going to be useful to its readers. Ted Kennedy coordinated the review process which produced much constructive criticism. Mary Piergies took care of the production of the book with Kristen Black, the copyeditor, and Dottie Marsico, the typesetter, who took my crude attempts to use FrameMaker and gave the book the professional edge it needed. Doug Hellman did a fine technical edit and corrected many code problems found in the final typeset copy.

Finally, I'd like to thank my wife, Allison, and my children, Nina, Chris, Jeff and Alana, for understanding that it wasn't so much losing a spouse and father but gaining an author.

about the reader

Python and Tkinter Programming is intended for programmers who already know Python or who are learning Python (perhaps using Manning's *Quick Python* as their guide) who wish to add graphical user interfaces (GUIs) to their applications. Because *Python and Tkinter Programming* presents many fully functional examples with lots of code annotations, experienced programmers *without* Python expertise will find the book helpful in using Python and Tkinter to solve immediate problems.

The book may also be used by Tcl/Tk script programmers as a guide to converting from Tcl/Tk to Python and Tkinter. However, I do not intend to get into a philosophical discussion about whether that would be a proper thing to do—I'm biased!

about the author

John Grayson is a consultant specializing in graphical user interfaces (GUIs). He has been supporting application design at a large U.S. communications company for several years, designing innovative interfaces and introducing Python and Object-Oriented Programming (OOP) to traditional development methods. Elsewhere, he has delivered real-world applications written in Python and Tkinter for commercial use.

He holds a Bachelor's degree in Applied Biology and a Ph.D. in Molecular Biology—but that has never been an impediment (especially because 90 percent of his thesis covered computer modeling of enzyme behavior).

Before specializing in user interfaces, he was an operating-system specialist and was later instrumental in developing support methodologies for UNIX at Stratus Computer, Inc., he built an F77 compiler and UNIX porting tools at Pacer Software, Inc. and he was an operating-system specialist at Prime Computer, Inc. both in the United States and Great Britain.

conventions

Example code plays a very important role in *Python and Tkinter Programming*. Many programming books feature short, simple examples which illustrate one or two points very well—but really do little. In this book, the examples may be adapted for your own applications or even used just as they are. Most of the examples are intended to be run *stand-alone* as opposed to being run *interactively*. Most examples include markers in the body of the code which correspond to explanations which follow. For example:

```
def mouseDown(self, event):
    self.currentObject = None                                        ❶
    self.lastx = self.startx = self.canvas.canvasx(event.x)
    self.lasty = self.starty = self.canvas.canvasy(event.y)
    if not self.currentFunc:
        self.selObj = self.canvas.find_closest(self.startx,          ❷
                                  self.starty)[0]
        self.canvas.itemconfig(self.selObj, width=2)

        self.canvas.lift(self.selObj)
```

Code comments

❶ The mouseDown method deselects any currently selected object. The event returns x and y coordinates for the mouse-click as screen coordinates. The canvasx and canvasy methods of the Canvas widget ...

❷ If no drawing function is selected, we are in select mode and we search to locate the nearest object on the canvas and select it. This method of ...

Occasionally, I have set portions of code in **bold** code font to highlight code which is of special importance in the code example.

In a number of examples where the code spans several pages I have interspersed code explanations within the code sequence so that the explanatory text appears closer to the code that is being explained. The marker numbering is continuous within any given example.

about the cover

The cover illustration of this book is from the 1805 edition of Sylvain Maréchal's four-volume compendium of regional dress customs. This book was first published in Paris in 1788, one year before the French Revolution. Its title alone required no fewer than 30 words:

Costumes Civils actuels de tous les peuples connus dessinés d'après nature gravés et coloriés, accompagnés d'une notice historique sur leurs coutumes, moeurs, religions, etc., etc., redigés par M. Sylvain Maréchal

The four volumes include an annotation on the illustrations: "gravé à la manière noire par Mixelle d'après Desrais et colorié." Clearly, the engraver and illustrator deserved no more than to be listed by their last names—after all they were mere technicians. The workers who colored each illustration by hand remain nameless.

The colorful variety of this collection reminds us vividly of how culturally apart the world's towns and regions were just 200 years ago. Dress codes have changed everywhere and the diversity by region, so rich at the time, has faded away. It is now hard to tell the inhabitant of one continent from another. Perhaps we have traded cultural diversity for a more varied personal life—certainly a more varied and exciting technological environment. At a time when it is hard to tell one computer book from another, Manning celebrates the inventiveness and initiative of the computer business with book covers based on the rich diversity of regional life of two centuries ago, brought back to life by Maréchal's pictures. Just think, Maréchal's was a world so different from ours people would take the time to read a book title 30 words long.

author online

Purchase of *Python and Tkinter Programming* includes free access to a private Internet forum where you can make comments about the book, ask technical questions and receive help from the author and other Python and Tkinter users. To access the forum, point your web browser to www.manning.com/grayson. There you will be able to subscribe to the forum. This site also provides information on how to access the forum once you are registered, what kind of help is available and the rules of conduct on the forum.

All source code for the examples presented in this book is available from the Mannng website. The URL www.manning.com/grayson includes a link to the source code files.

Basic concepts

In part 1, I'll introduce Python, Tkinter and application programming. Since I assume you're already somewhat familiar with Python, chapter 1 is intended to illustrate the most important features of the language that will be used throughout the book. Additionally, I'll discuss features of Python's support for object-oriented programming so that those of you familiar with C++ or Java can understand how your experience may be applied to Python.

Chapter 2 quickly introduces Tkinter and explains how it relates to Tcl/Tk. You will find details of mapping Tk to Tkinter, along with a brief introduction to the widgets and their appearance.

Chapter 3 illustrates application development with Tkinter using two calculator examples. The first is a simple no-frills calculator that demonstrates basic principles. The second is a partially finished application that shows you how powerful applications may be developed using Python's and Tkinter's capabilities.

C H A P T E R   1

Python

This chapter defines the key features of Python that make the language ideal for rapid proto-typing of systems and for fully-functional applications. *Python and Tkinter Programming* is not intended to be a learning resource for beginning Python programmers; several other publications are better-suited to this task: *Quick Python, Learning Python, Programming Python, Internet Programming in Python* and *The Python Pocket Reference* are all excellent texts. Further information is provided in the "References" section at the end of this book. In this chapter, the key features of Python will be highlighted in concise examples of code to illustrate some of the building blocks that will be used in examples throughout the book.

1.1 Introduction to Python programming and a feature review

As stated earlier, this book is not intended to be used to learn Python basics directly. Pro-grammers experienced in other languages will be able to analyze the examples and discover the key points to programming in Python. However, if you are relatively new to program-ming generally, then learning Python this way will be a tough, upward struggle.

This chapter is really not necessary for most readers, then, since the material will already be familiar. Its purpose is to provide a refresher course for readers who worked with Python in the early days and a map for Tcl/Tk programmers and those readers experienced with other languages.

Readers unfamiliar with object-oriented programming (OOP) may find section 1.3 useful as an introduction to OOP as it is implemented in Python. C++ or Java programmers who need to see how Python's classes operate will benefit as well.

I'm not going to explain the reasons why Python was developed or when, since this information is covered in every other Python book very well. I will state that Guido van Rossum, Python's creator, has been behind the language since he invented it at Stichting Mathematisch Centrum (CWI) in Amsterdam, The Nederlands, around 1990; he is now at the Corporation for National Research Initiatives (CNRI), Reston, Virginia, USA. The fact that one person has taken control of the growth of the language has had a great deal to do with its stability and elegance, although Guido will be the first to thank all of the people who have contributed, in one way or another, to the language's development.

Perhaps more important than any of the above information is the name of the language. This language has nothing to do with snakes. Python is named after *Monty Python's Flying Circus*, the BBC comedy series which was produced from 1969 to 1974. Like many university students around 1970, I was influenced by Monty Python, so when I started writing this book I could not resist the temptation to add bits of Python other than the language. Now, all of you that skipped the boring beginning bit of this book, or decided that you didn't need to read this paragraph are in for a surprise. Scattered through the examples you'll find bits of Python. If you have never experienced Monty Python, then I can only offer the following advice: if something about the example looks weird, it's probably Python. As my Yugoslavian college friend used to say "You find *that* funny"?

1.1.1   Why Python?

Several key features make Python an ideal language for a wide range of applications. Adding Tkinter to the mix widens the possibilities dramatically. Here are some of the highlights that make Python what it is:

- Automatic compile to bytecode
- High-level data types and operations
- Portability across architectures
- Wide (huge) range of supported extensions
- Object-oriented model
- Ideal prototyping system
- Readable code with a distinct C-like quality supports maintenance
- Easy to extend in C and C++ and embed in applications
- Large library of contributed applications and tools
- Excellent documentation

You might notice that I did not mention an interpreter explicitly. One feature of Python is that it is a bytecode engine written in C. The extension modules are written in C. With a little care in the way you design your code, most of your code will run using *compiled C* since many operations are built into the system. The remaining code will run in the bytecode engine.

The result is a system that may be used as a scripting language to develop anything from some system administration scripts all the way to a complex GUI-based application (using database, client/server, CORBA or other techniques).

1.1.2 Where can Python be used?

Knowing where Python can be used is best understood by learning where it might *not* be the best choice. Regardless of what I just said about the bytecode engine, Python has an interpretive nature, so if you can't keep within the C-extensions, there has to be a performance penalty. Therefore, real-time applications for high-speed events would be a poor match. A set of extensions to Python have been developed specifically for numerical programming (see "NumPy" on page 626). These extensions help support compute-bound applications, but Python is not the best choice for huge computation-intensive applications unless time *isn't* a factor. Similarly, graphics-intensive applications which involve real-time observation are not a good match (but see "Speed drawing" on page 271 for an example of what *can* be done).

1.2 Key data types: lists, tuples and dictionaries

Three key data types give Python the power to produce effective applications: two *sequence* classes—lists and tuples—and a *mapping* class—dictionaries. When they are used together, they can deliver surprising power in a few lines of code.

Lists and *tuples* have a lot in common. The major difference is that the elements of a list can be modified in place but a tuple is *immutable*: you have to deconstruct and then reconstruct a tuple to change individual elements. There are several good reasons why we should care about this distinction; if you want to use a tuple as the *key* to a dictionary, it's good to know that it can't be changed arbitrarily. A small advantage of tuples is that they are a slightly cheaper resource since they do not carry the additional operations of a list.

If you want an in-depth view of these data types take a look at chapters 6 and 8 of *Quick Python*.

1.2.1 Lists

Let's look at lists first. If you are new to Python, remember to look at the tutorial that is available in the standard documentation, which is available at www.python.org.

Initializing lists

Lists are easy to create and use. To initialize a list:

```
lst = []                             # Empty list
lst = ['a', 'b', 'c']                # String list
lst = [1, 2, 3, 4]                   # Integer list
lst = [[1,2,3], ['a','b','c']]       # List of lists
lst = [(1,'a'),(2,'b'),(3,'c')]      # List of tuples
```

Appending to lists

Lists have an append method built in:

```
lst.append('e')
lst.append((5,'e'))
```

Concatenating lists

Combining lists works well:

```
lst = [1, 2, 3] + [4, 5, 6]
print lst
[1, 2, 3, 4, 5, 6]
```

Iterating through members

Iterating through a list is easy:

```
lst = ['first', 'second', 'third']
for str in lst:
    print 'this entry is %s' % str

set = [(1, 'uno'), (2, 'due'), (3, 'tres')]
for integer, str in set:
    print 'Numero "%d" in Italiano: è "%s"' % (integer, str)
```

Sorting and reversing

Lists have built-in sort and reverse methods:

```
lst = [4, 5, 1, 9, 2]
lst.sort()
print lst
[1, 2, 4, 5, 9]

lst.reverse()
print lst
[9, 5, 4, 2, 1]
```

Indexing

Finding an entry in a list:

```
lst = [1, 2, 4, 5, 9]
print lst.index(5)
3
```

Member

Checking membership of a list is convenient:

```
if 'jeg' in ['abc', 'tuv', 'kie', 'jeg']:
    ...

if '*' in '123*abc':
    ...
```

Modifying members

A list member may be modified in place:

```
lst = [1, 2, 4, 5, 9]
lst[3] = 10
print lst
[1, 2, 3, 4, 10, 9]
```

Inserting and deleting members

To insert a member in a list:

```
lst = [1, 2, 3, 4, 10, 9]
lst.insert(4, 5)
print lst
[1, 2, 3, 4, 5, 10, 9]
```

To delete a member:

```
lst = [1, 2, 3, 4, 10, 9]
del lst(4)
print lst
[1, 2, 3, 4, 9]
```

1.2.2   Tuples

Tuples are similar to lists but they are *immutable* (meaning they cannot be modified). Tuples are a convenient way of collecting data that may be passed as a single entity or stored in a list or dictionary; the entity is then *unpacked* when needed.

Initializing tuples

With the exception of a tuple containing *one* element, tuples are initialized in a similar manner to lists (lists and tuples are really related sequence types and are readily interchangeable).

```
tpl = ()                            # Empty tuple
tpl = (1,)                          # Singleton tuple
tpl = ('a', 'b', 'c')               # String tuple
tpl = (1, 2, 3, 4)                  # Integer tuple
tpl = ([1,2,3], ['a','b','c'])      # Tuple of lists
tpl = ((1,'a'),(2,'b'),(3,'c'))     # Tuple of tuples
```

Iterating through members

```
for i in tpl:
    ...

for i,a in ((1, 'a'), (2, 'b'), (3, 'c')):
    ...
```

Modifying tuples

(But you said tuples were immutable!)

```
a = 1, 2, 3
a = a[0], a[1], 10, a[2]
a
(1, 2, 10, 3)
```

Note that you are not modifying the original tuple but you are creating a new name binding for a.

1.2.3 Dictionaries

Dictionaries are arrays of data indexed by *keys*. I think that they give Python the edge in designing compact systems. If you use lists and tuples as data contained within dictionaries you have a powerful mix (not to say that mixing code objects, dictionaries and abstract objects isn't powerful!).

Initializing dictionaries

Dictionaries may be initialized by providing key:value pairs:

```
dict = {}                           # Empty dictionary
dict = {'a'': 1, 'b': 2, 'c': 3}    # String key
dict = {1: 'a', 2: 'b', 3: 'c'}     # Integer key
dict = {1: [1,2,3], 2: [4,5,6]}     # List data
```

Modifying dictionaries

Dictionaries are readily modifiable:

```
dict['a'] = 10
dict[10] = 'Larch'
```

Accessing dictionaries

Recent versions of Python facilitate lookups where the key may not exist. First, the old way:

```
if dict.has_key('a'):
    value = dict['a']
else:
    value = None
```

or:

```
try:
    value = dict['a']
except KeyError:
    value = None
```

This is the current method:

```
value = dict.get('a', None)
```

Iterating through entries

Get the keys and then iterate through them:

```
keys = dict.keys()
for key in keys:
    ...
```

Sorting dictionaries

Dictionaries have arbitrary order so you must sort the keys if you want to access the keys in order:

```
keys = dict.keys().sort()
for key in keys:
    ...
```

1.3 Classes

I'm including a short section on Python classes largely for C++ programmers who may need to learn some of the details of Python's implementation and for Python programmers who have yet to discover OOP in Python.

1.3.1 How do classes describe objects?

A class provides the following object descriptions:

- The attributes (data-members) of the object
- The behavior of the object (methods)
- Where behavior is inherited from other classes (superclasses)

Having said all that, C++ programmers will probably be tuning out at this point—but hold on for a little longer. There are some valuable features of Python classes, some of which may come as a bit of a surprise for someone who is not fully up to speed with Python OOP.

Most of the examples of applications in this book rely heavily on building class libraries to create a wide range of objects. The classes typically create instances with multiple formats (see LEDs and Switches in chapter 7). Before we start building these objects, let's review the rules and features that apply to Python classes.

1.3.2 Defining classes

A Python class is a user-defined data type which is defined with a class statement:

```
class AClass:
    statements
```

Statements are any valid Python statements defining attributes and member functions. In fact, any Python statement can be used, including a `pass` statement, as we will see in the next section. Calling the class as a function creates an instance of the class:

```
anInstanceOfAClass = AClass()
```

1.3.3 Neat Python trick #10

A class instance can be used like a C structure or Pascal record. However, unlike C and Pascal, the members of the structure do not need to be declared before they are used—they can be created dynamically. We can use this ability to access arbitrary data objects across modules; examples using class instances to support global data will be shown later.

```
class DummyClass:
    pass

Colors = DummyClass()
Colors.alarm   = 'red'
Colors.warning = 'orange'
Colors.normal  = 'green'
```

If the preceding lines are stored in a file called programdata.py, the following is a possible code sequence.

```
from programdata import Colors
...
Button(parent, bg=Colors.alarm, text='Pressure\nVessel',
       command=evacuateBuilding)
```

Alternately, if you apply a little knowledge about how Python manages data internally, you can use the following construction.

```
class Record:
    def __init__(self, **kw):
        self.__dict__.update(kw)
Colors = Record(alarm='red', warning='orange', normal='green')
```

1.3.4 Initializing an instance

Fields (instance variables) of an instance may be initialized by including an `__init__` method in the class body. This method is executed automatically when a new instance of the class is created. Python passes the instance as the first argument. It is a convention to name it `self` (it's called *this* in C++). In addition, methods may be called to complete initialization. The `__init__` methods of inherited classes may also be called, when necessary.

```
class ASX200(Frame):
    def __init__(self, master=None):
        Frame.__init__(self, master)
        Pack.config(self)
        self.state = NORMAL
        self.set_hardware_data(FORE)
        self.createWidgets()
    ...
    ...
switch = ASX200()
```

> *Note* To use instance variables you must reference the containing object (in the previous example it is `switch.state`, not `self.state`). If you make a reference to a variable by itself, it is to a local variable within the executing function, not an instance variable.

1.3.5 Methods

We have already encountered the `__init__` method that is invoked when an instance is created. Other methods are defined similarly with `def` statements. Methods may take arguments: `self` is always the first or only argument.

You will see plenty of examples of methods, so little discussion is really necessary. Note that Python accepts named arguments, in addition to positional arguments, in both methods and function calls. This can make supplying default values for methods very easy, since omission of an argument will result in the default value being supplied. Take care when mixing positional and named arguments as it is very easy to introduce problems in class libraries this way.

1.3.6 Private and public variables and methods

Unless you take special action, all variables and methods are public and virtual. If you make use of name mangling, however, you can emulate private variables and methods. You mangle the name this way: Any name which begins with a double-underscore (__) is private and is not exported to a containing environment. Any name which begins with a single underscore (_) indicates *private by convention*, which is similar to *protected* in C++ or Java. In fact, Python usually is more intuitive than C++ or other languages, since it is immediately obvious if a reference is being made to a private variable or method.

1.3.7 Inheritance

The rules of inheritance in Python are really quite simple:

- Classes inherit behavior from the classes specified in their header and from any classes above these classes.
- Instances inherit behavior from the class from which they are created and from all the classes above this class.

When Python searches for a reference it searches in the immediate namespace (the instance) and then in each of the higher namespaces. The first occurrence of the reference is used; this means that a class can easily redefine attributes and methods of its superclasses. If the reference cannot be found Python reports an error.

Note that inherited methods are not automatically called. To initialize the base class, a subclass must call the __init__ method explicitly.

1.3.8 Multiple inheritance

Multiple inheritance in Python is just an extension of inheritance. If more than one class is specified in a class's header then we have multiple inheritance. Unlike C++, however, Python does not report errors if attributes of classes are multiple defined; the basic rule is that the first occurrence found is the one that is used.

1.3.9 Mixin classes

A class that collects a number of common methods and can be freely inherited by subclasses is usually referred to as a *mixin* class (some standard texts may use base, generalized or abstract classes, but that may not be totally correct). Such methods could be contained in a Python module, but the advantage of employing a mixin class is that the methods have access to the instance self and thus can modify the behavior of an instance. We will see examples of mixin classes throughout this book.

C H A P T E R   2

Tkinter

This chapter describes the structure of the Tkinter module and its relationship to Tcl/Tk. The mapping with Tcl/Tk constructs to Tkinter is explained in order to assist Tcl/Tk programmers in converting to Tkinter from Tcl/Tk. Native GUIs for UNIX, Win32 and Macintosh implementations will be discussed and key architectural differences will be highlighted. Font and color selection will be introduced, and I'll cover this topic in more detail in "Tkinter widgets" on page 31. For readers who are unfamiliar with Tkinter, this chapter illustrates its importance to Python applications.

2.1 The Tkinter module

2.1.1 What is Tkinter?

Tkinter provides Python applications with an easy-to-program user interface. Tkinter supports a collection of Tk widgets that support most application needs. Tkinter is the Python interface to Tk, the GUI toolkit for Tcl/Tk. Tcl/Tk is the scripting and graphics facility developed by John Ousterhout, who was originally at University of California at Berkeley and later at Sun Microsystems. Currently, Tcl/Tk is developed and supported by the Scriptics Corporation, which Ousterhout founded. Tcl/Tk enjoys a significant following with developers in a number of fields, predominantly on UNIX systems, but more recently on Win32 systems and MacOS. Ousterhout's *Tcl and the Tk Toolkit*, which was the first Tcl/Tk book, is still a viable, though old, reference document for Tcl/Tk. (You will find some excellent newer texts on the subject in the section "References" on page 625).

Tcl/Tk was first designed to run under the X Window system and its widgets and windows were made to resemble Motif widgets. The behavior of bindings and controls was also designed to mimic Motif. In recent versions of Tcl/Tk (specifically, release 8.0 and after), the widgets resemble native widgets on the implemented architecture. In fact, many of the widgets *are* native widgets and the trend to add more of them will probably continue.

Like Python extensions, Tcl/Tk is implemented as a C library package with modules to support interpreted scripts, or *applications*. The Tkinter interface is implemented as a Python module, Tkinter.py, which is bound to a C-extension (_tkinter) which utilizes these same Tcl/Tk libraries. In many cases a Tkinter programmer need not be concerned with the implementation of Tcl/Tk since Tkinter can be viewed as a simple extension of Python.

2.1.2 What about performance?

At first glance, it is reasonable to assume that Tkinter is not going to perform well. After all, the Python interpreter is utilizing the Tkinter module which, in turn, relies on the _tkinter interface which calls Tcl and Tk libraries and sometimes calls the Tcl interpreter to bind properties to widgets. Well, this is all true, but on modern systems it really does not matter too much. If you follow the guidelines in "Programming for performance" on page 348, you will find that Python and Tkinter have the ability to deliver viable applications. If your reason for using Python/Tkinter is to develop prototypes for applications, then the point is somewhat moot; you *will* develop prototypes quickly in Python/Tkinter.

2.1.3 How do I use Tkinter?

Tkinter comprises a number of components. _tkinter, as mentioned before, is the low level interface to the Tk libraries and is linked into Python. Until recently, it was the programmer's responsibility to add Tkinter to the Python build, but beginning with release 1.5.2 of Python, Tkinter, Tcl and Tk are part of the installation package—at least for the Win32 distribution. For several UNIX variants and Macintosh, it is still necessary to build Python to include Tkinter. However, check to see if a binary version is available for your particular platform.

Once a version of Python has been built and _tkinter has been included, as a shared library, dll or statically linked, the Tkinter module needs to be *imported*. This imports any other necessary modules, such as Tkconstants.

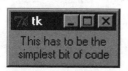

Figure 2.1 Trivial Example

To create a Tkinter window, type three lines into the Python command line (or enter them into a file and type "python filename.py").

```
from Tkinter import Label, mainloop                    ①
Label(text='This has to be the\nsimplest bit of code').pack()   ②
mainloop()                                              ③
```

Code comments

① First, we import components from the `Tkinter` module. By using `from module import Label, mainloop` we avoid having to reference the module to access attributes and methods contained in the module.

② We create a `Label` containing two lines of text and use the `Pack` geometry manager to *realize* the widget.

③ Finally, we call the Tkinter `mainloop` to process events and keep the display activated. This example does not react to any application-specific events, but we still need a mainloop for it to be displayed; basic window management is automatic.

What you will see is shown in figure 2.1. Now, it really cannot get much simpler than that!

2.1.4   Tkinter features

Tkinter adds object-oriented interfaces to Tk. Tcl/Tk is a command-oriented scripting language so the normal method of driving Tk widgets is to apply an operation to a widget identifier. In Tkinter, the widget references are *objects* and we drive the widgets by using object *methods* and their *attributes*. As a result, Tkinter programs are easy to read and understand, especially for C++ or Java programmers (although that is entirely another story!).

One important feature that Tk gives to any Tkinter application is that, with a little care in selecting fonts and other architecture-dependent features, it will run on numerous flavors of UNIX, Win32 and Macintosh without modification. Naturally, there are some intrinsic differences between these architectures, but Tkinter does a fine job of providing an architecture-independent graphics platform for applications.

It is the object-oriented features, however, that really distinguish Tkinter as an ideal platform for developing application frameworks. You will see many examples in this book where relatively little code will support powerful applications.

2.2   *Mapping Tcl/Tk to Tkinter*

Mapping of Tcl/Tk commands and arguments to Tkinter is really quite a simple process. After writing Tkinter code for a short time, it should be easy for a Tcl/Tk programmer to make the shift—maybe he will never go back to Tcl/Tk! Let's look at some examples.

Commands in Tk map directly to class constructors in Tkinter.

Txl/Tk	Tkinter
label .myLabel	myLabel = Label(master)

Parent widgets (usually referred to as *master* widgets) are explicit in Tkinter:

Tcl/Tk	Tkinter
label .screen.for	label = Label(form) (screen is form's parent)

For configuration options, Tk uses keyword arguments followed by values or configure commands; Tkinter uses either keyword arguments or a dictionary reference to the option of the configure method in the target widget.

Tcl/Tk	Tkinter
label .myLabel -bg blue	myLabel = Label(master, bg="blue")
.myLabel configure -bg blue	myLabel["bg"] = "blue"
	myLabel.configure(bg = "blue")

Since the Tkinter widget object has methods, you invoke them directly, adding arguments as appropriate.

Tcl/Tk	Tkinter
pack label -side left -fill y	label.pack(side=LEFT, fill=Y)

The following illustration demonstrates how we access an inherited method *pack* from the Packer. This style of programming contributes to the compact nature of Tkinter applications and their ease of maintenance and reuse.

Full mappings of Tk to Tkinter are provided in "Mapping Tk to Tkinter" on page 383.

2.3 *Win32 and* Unix *GUIs*

As I mentioned earlier, it is reasonable to develop Tkinter applications for use in Win32, Unix and Macintosh environments. Tcl/Tk is portable and can be built on the specific platform, as can Python, with its _tkinter C module. Using Pmw* (Python MegaWidgets), which provides a portable set of composite widgets and is 100% Python code, it is possible to use the bytecode generated on a Unix system on a Win32 or Macintosh system. What you cannot control is the use of fonts and, to a lesser extent, the color schemes imposed by the operating system.

---

* Pmw—Python MegaWidgets provide complex widgets, constructed from fundamental Tkinter widgets, which extend the available widgets to comboboxes, scrolled frames and button boxes, to name a few. Using these widgets gives GUI developers a rich palette of available input devices to use in their designs.

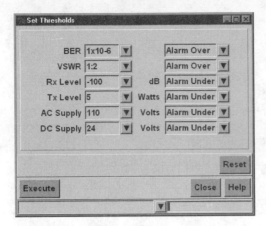

Figure 2.2 Tkinter and Pmw on win32

Figure 2.3 Tkinter and Pmw running on UNIX

Take a look at figure 2.2. This application uses Pmw combobox widgets along with Tkinter button and entry widgets arranged within frames. The font for this example is Arial, bold and 16 point. Apart from the obvious Win32 controls in the border, there is little to distinguish this window from the one shown in figure 2.3, which was run on UNIX. In this case, the font is Helvetica, bold and 16 point. The window is slightly larger because the font has slightly different kerning rules and stroke weight, and since the size of the widget is dependent on the font, this results in a slightly different layout. If precise alignment and sizing is an absolute requirement, it is possible to detect the platform on which the application is running and make adjustments for known differences. In general, it is better to design an application that is not sensitive to small changes in layout.

If you look closely, you may also notice a difference in the top and bottom highlights for the Execute and Close buttons, but not for the buttons on the Pmw widgets. This is because Tk is drawing Motif decorations for UNIX and Windows SDK decorations for Win32.

In general, as long as your application does not make use of very platform-specific fonts, it will be possible to develop transportable code.

2.4 *Tkinter class hierarchy*

Unlike many windowing systems, the Tkinter hierarchy is really quite simple; in fact, there really isn't a hierarchy at all. The WM, Misc, Pack, Place and Grid classes are mixins to each of the widget classes. Most programmers only need to know about the lowest level in the tree to perform everyday operations and it is often possible to ignore the higher levels. The notional "hierarchy" is shown in figure 2.4.

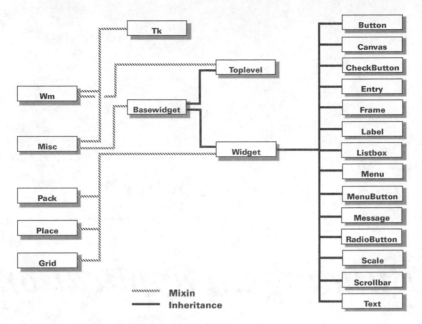

Figure 2.4 Tkinter widget "hierarchy"

Figure 2.5 Tkinter widgets: a collage

2.5 Tkinter widget appearance

To conclude this initial introduction to Tkinter, let's take a quick look at the appearance of the widgets available to a programmer. In this example, we are just looking at the basic configuration of the widgets and only one canvas drawing option is shown. I've changed the border on the frames to add some variety, but you are seeing the widgets with their default appearance. The widgets are shown in figure 2.5. The code is not presented here, but it is available online.

C H A P T E R   3

Building an application

Most books on programming languages have followed Kernigan and Ritchie's example and have presented the obligatory "Hello World" example to illustrate the ease with which that language may be applied. Books with a GUI component seem to continue this tradition and present a "Hello GUI World" or something similar. Indeed, the three-line example presented on page 13 is in that class of examples.

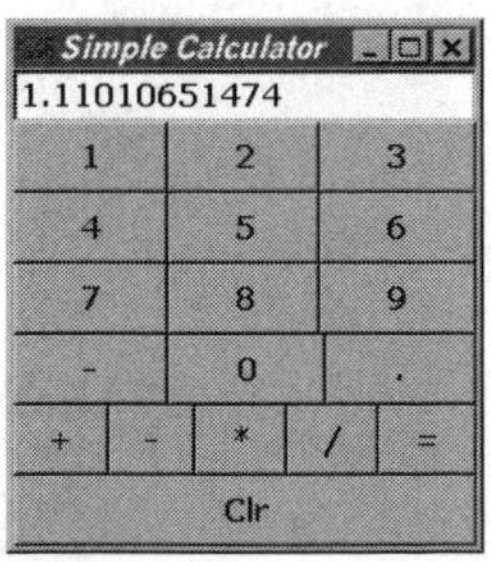

There is a growing trend to present a calculator example in recent publications. In this book I am going to start by presenting a simple calculator (you may add the word obligatory, if you wish) in the style of its predecessors. The example has been written to illustrate several Python and Tkinter features and to demonstrate the compact nature of Python code.

The example is not complete because it accepts only mouse input; in a full example, we would expect keyboard input as well. However, it does work and it demonstrates that you do not need a lot of code to get a Tkinter screen up and running. Let's take a look at the code that supports the screen:

Figure 3.1 A simple calculator

18

```python
from Tkinter import *

def frame(root, side):
    w = Frame(root)
    w.pack(side=side, expand=YES, fill=BOTH)
    return w

def button(root, side, text, command=None):
    w = Button(root, text=text, command=command)
    w.pack(side=side, expand=YES, fill=BOTH)
    return w


class Calculator(Frame):
    def __init__(self):
        Frame.__init__(self)
        self.pack(expand=YES, fill=BOTH)
        self.master.title('Simple Calculator')
        self.master.iconname("calc1")

        display = StringVar()
        Entry(self.master, relief=SUNKEN,
            textvariable=variable).pack(side=TOP, expand=YES,
                                    fill=BOTH)

        for key in ("123", "456", "789", "-0."):
            keyF = frame(self, TOP)
            for char in key:
                button(keyF, LEFT, char,
                  lambda w=display, s=' %s '%c: w.set(w.get()+s))

        opsF = frame(self, TOP)
        for char in "+-*/=":
            if char == '=':
                btn = button(opsF, LEFT, char)
                btn.bind('<ButtonRelease-1>',
                        lambda e, s=self, w=display: s.calc(w), '+')
            else:
                btn = button(opsF, LEFT, char,
                        lambda w=display, c=char: w.set(w.get()+' '+c+' '))

        clearF = frame(self, BOTTOM)
        button(clearF, LEFT, 'Clr', lambda w=display: w.set(''))

    def calc(self, display):
        try:
            display.set(`eval(display.get())`)
        except ValueError:
            display.set("ERROR")

if __name__ == '__main__':
    Calculator().mainloop()
```

Code comments

1 We begin by defining convenience functions to make the creation of frame and button widgets more compact. These functions use the `pack` geometry manager and use generally useful values for widget behavior. It is always a good idea to collect common code in compact functions (or classes, as appropriate) since this makes readability and maintenance much easier.

2 We call the `Frame` constructor to create the toplevel shell and an enclosing frame. Then, we set titles for the window and icon.

3 Next, we create the display at the top of the calculator and define a Tkinter variable which provides access to the widget's contents:

```
display = StringVar()
Entry(self.master, relief=SUNKEN,
    textvariable=variable).pack(side=TOP, expand=YES,
                                fill=BOTH)
```

4 Remember that character strings are sequences of characters in Python, so that each of the subsequences is really an array of characters over which we can iterate:

```
for key in ("123", "456", "789", "-0."):
    keyF = frame(self, TOP)
    for char in key:
```

We create a frame for each row of keys.

5 We use the convenience function to create a `button`, passing the frame, pack option, label and callback:

```
button(keyF, LEFT, char,
        lambda w=display, c=char: w.set(w.get() + c))
```

Don't worry about the `lambda` form of the callback yet, I will cover this in more detail later. Its purpose is to define an inline function definition.

6 The = key has an alternate binding to the other buttons since it calls the `calc` method when the left mouse button is released:

```
btn.bind('<ButtonRelease-1>',
        lambda e, s=self, w=display: s.calc(w))
```

7 The `calc` method attempts to evaluate the string contained in the display and then it replaces the contents with the calculated value or an ERROR message:

```
display.set(`eval(display.get())`)
```

Personally, I don't like the calculator, even though it demonstrates compact code and will be quite easy to extend to provide more complete functionality. Perhaps it is the artist in me, but it doesn't *look* like a calculator!

Let's take a look at a partly-finished example application which implements a quite sophisticated calculator. It has been left unfinished so that curious readers can experiment by adding functionality to the example (by the time you have finished reading this book, you will be ready to build a Cray Calculator!). Even though the calculator is unfinished, it can still be put to some use. As we will discover a little later, some surprising features are hidden in the reasonably short source code.

Let's start by taking a look at some of the key features of the calculator.

3.1 Calculator example: key features

The calculator example illustrates many features of applications written in Python and Tkinter, including these:

Figure 3.2
A better calculator

- *GUI application structure* Although this is a simple example, it contains many of the elements of larger applications that will be presented later in the book.
- *Multiple inheritance* It is simple in this example, but it illustrates how it may be used to simplify Python code.
- *Lists, dictionaries and tuples* As mentioned in chapter 1, these language facilities give Python a considerable edge in building concise code. In particular, this example illustrates the use of a dictionary to dispatch actions to methods. Of particular note is the use of lists of tuples to define the content of each of the keys. Unpacking this data generates each of the keys, labels and associated bindings in a compact fashion.
- *Pmw (Python megawidgets)* The scrolled text widget is implemented with Pmw. This example illustrates setting its attributes and gaining access to its components.
- *Basic Tkinter operations* Creating widgets, setting attributes, using text tags, binding events and using a geometry manager are demonstrated.
- *eval and exec functions* The example uses eval to perform many of the math functions in this example. However, as you will see later in this chapter, eval cannot be used to execute arbitrary Python code; exec is used to execute single or multiple lines of code (and multiple lines of code can include control flow structures).

3.2 Calculator example: source code

calc2.py

```
from Tkinter   import *
import Pmw                              ❶ Python MegaWidgets

class SLabel(Frame):
    """ SLabel defines a 2-sided label within a Frame. The
        left hand label has blue letters; the right has white letters. """
    def __init__(self, master, leftl, rightl):
        Frame.__init__(self, master, bg='gray40')
        self.pack(side=LEFT, expand=YES, fill=BOTH)
        Label(self, text=leftl, fg='steelblue1',
            font=("arial", 6, "bold"), width=5, bg='gray40').pack(
            side=LEFT, expand=YES, fill=BOTH)
        Label(self, text=rightl, fg='white',
            font=("arial", 6, "bold"), width=1, bg='gray40').pack(
```

```
                    side=RIGHT, expand=YES, fill=BOTH)

class Key(Button):
    def __init__(self, master, font=('arial', 8, 'bold'),
            fg='white',width=5, borderwidth=5, **kw):
        kw['font'] = font
        kw['fg'] = fg
        kw['width'] = width
        kw['borderwidth'] = borderwidth
        apply(Button.__init__, (self, master), kw)
        self.pack(side=LEFT, expand=NO, fill=NONE)

class Calculator(Frame):
    def __init__(self, parent=None):
        Frame.__init__(self, bg='gray40')
        self.pack(expand=YES, fill=BOTH)
        self.master.title('Tkinter Toolkit TT-42')
        self.master.iconname('Tk-42')
        self.calc = Evaluator()          # This is our evaluator
        self.buildCalculator()           # Build the widgets

        # This is an incomplete dictionary - a good exercise!
        self.actionDict = {'second': self.doThis, 'mode': self.doThis,
                    'delete': self.doThis, 'alpha':   self.doThis,
                    'stat':   self.doThis, 'math':    self.doThis,
                    'matrix': self.doThis, 'program': self.doThis,
                    'vars':   self.doThis, 'clear':   self.clearall,
                    'sin':    self.doThis, 'cos':     self.doThis,
                    'tan':    self.doThis, 'up':      self.doThis,
                    'X1':     self.doThis, 'X2':      self.doThis,
                    'log':    self.doThis, 'ln':      self.doThis,
                    'store':  self.doThis, 'off':     self.turnoff,
                    'neg':    self.doThis, 'enter':   self.doEnter,
                    }
        self.current = ""

    def doThis(self,action):
        print '"%s" has not been implemented' % action

    def turnoff(self, *args):
        self.quit()

    def clearall(self, *args):
        self.current = ""
        self.display.component('text').delete(1.0, END)

    def doEnter(self, *args):
        self.display.insert(END, '\n')
        result = self.calc.runpython(self.current)
        if result:
            self.display.insert(END, '%s\n' % result, 'ans')
        self.current = ""

    def doKeypress(self, event):
        key = event.char
        if key != '\b':
            self.current = self.current + key
```

❷

❸

❹

❺

❻

❼ ❽

```
        else:
              self.current = self.current[:-1]          7    8

  def keyAction(self, key):
      self.display.insert(END, key)
      self.current = self.current + key

  def evalAction(self, action):
      try:
            self.actionDict[action](action)
      except KeyError:
            pass
```

Code comments

1 Pmw (Python MegaWidgets) widgets are used. These widgets will feature prominently in this book since they provide an excellent mechanism to support a wide range of GUI requirements and they are readily extended to support additional requirements.

2 In the constructor for the Key class, we add key-value pairs to the kw (keyword) dictionary and then apply these values to the Button constructor.

```
def __init__(self, master, font=('arial', 8, 'bold'),
        fg='white',width=5, borderwidth=5, **kw):
    kw['font'] = font
    ...
    apply(Button.__init__, (self, master), kw)
```

This allows us a great deal of flexibility in constructing our widgets.

3 The Calculator class uses a dictionary to provide a *dispatcher* for methods within the class.

```
            'matrix': self.doThis, 'program': self.doThis,
            'vars':   self.doThis, 'clear':   self.clearall,
            'sin':    self.doThis, 'cos':     self.doThis,
```

Remember that dictionaries can handle much more complex references than the relatively simple cases we need for this calculator.

4 We use a Pmw ScrolledText widget, which is a composite widget. To gain access to the contained widgets, the component method is used.

```
self.display.component('text').delete(1.0, END)
```

5 When the ENTER key is clicked, the collected string is directed to the calculator's evaluator:

```
result = self.calc.runpython(self.current)
```

The result of this evaluation is displayed in the scrolled text widget.

6 The final argument in the text insert function is a text tag 'ans' which is used to change the foreground color of the displayed text.

```
self.display.insert(END, '%s\n' % result, 'ans')
```

7 doKeypress is a *callback* bound to all keys. The event argument in the callback provides the client data for the callback. event.char is the key entered; several attributes are available in the client data, such as x-y coordinates of a button press or the state of a mouse operation (see "Tkinter events" on page 98). In this case we get the character entered.

8 A simple exception mechanism to take action on selected keys is used.

```
def buildCalculator(self):
    FUN  = 1                  # A Function        ❾
    KEY  = 0                  # A Key
    KC1  = 'gray30'           # Dark Keys
    KC2  = 'gray50'           # Light Keys
    KC3  = 'steelblue1'       # Light Blue Key
    KC4  = 'steelblue'        # Dark Blue Key
    keys = [
        [('2nd',  '',    '',   KC3, FUN, 'second'),  # Row 1
         ('Mode', 'Quit', '',  KC1, FUN, 'mode'),
         ('Del',  'Ins',  '',  KC1, FUN, 'delete'),
         ('Alpha','Lock', '',  KC2, FUN, 'alpha'),
         ('Stat', 'List', '',  KC1, FUN, 'stat')],
        [('Math', 'Test', 'A', KC1, FUN, 'math'),    # Row 2
         ('Mtrx', 'Angle','B', KC1, FUN, 'matrix'),
         ('Prgm', 'Draw', 'C', KC1, FUN, 'program'),
         ('Vars', 'YVars','',  KC1, FUN, 'vars'),
         ('Clr',  '',    '',   KC1, FUN, 'clear')],
        [('X-1',  'Abs',  'D', KC1, FUN, 'X1'),      # Row 3
         ('Sin',  'Sin-1','E', KC1, FUN, 'sin'),
         ('Cos',  'Cos-1','F', KC1, FUN, 'cos'),
         ('Tan',  'Tan-1','G', KC1, FUN, 'tan'),
         ('^',    'PI',   'H', KC1, FUN, 'up')],
        [('X2',   'Root', 'I', KC1, FUN, 'X2'),      # Row 4
         (',',    'EE',   'J', KC1, KEY, ','),
         ('(',    '{',    'K', KC1, KEY, '('),
         (')',    '}',    'L', KC1, KEY, ')'),
         ('/',    '',     'M', KC4, KEY, '/')],
        [('Log',  '10x',  'N', KC1, FUN, 'log'),     # Row 5
         ('7',    'Un-1', 'O', KC2, KEY, '7'),
         ('8',    'Vn-1', 'P', KC2, KEY, '8'),
         ('9',    'n',    'Q', KC2, KEY, '9'),
         ('X',    '[',    'R', KC4, KEY, '*')],
        [('Ln',   'ex',   'S', KC1, FUN, 'ln'),      # Row 6
         ('4',    'L4',   'T', KC2, KEY, '4'),
         ('5',    'L5',   'U', KC2, KEY, '5'),
         ('6',    'L6',   'V', KC2, KEY, '6'),
         ('-',    ']',    'W', KC4, KEY, '-')],
        [('STO',  'RCL',  'X', KC1, FUN, 'store'),   # Row 7
         ('1',    'L1',   'Y', KC2, KEY, '1'),
         ('2',    'L2',   'Z', KC2, KEY, '2'),
         ('3',    'L3',   '',  KC2, KEY, '3'),
         ('+',    'MEM',  '"', KC4, KEY, '+')],
        [('Off',  '',    '',   KC1, FUN, 'off'),     # Row 8
         ('0',    '',    '',   KC2, KEY, '0'),
         ('.',    ':',   '',   KC2, KEY, '.'),
         ('(-)',  'ANS',  '?', KC2, FUN, 'neg'),
         ('Enter','Entry','',  KC4, FUN, 'enter')]]

    self.display = Pmw.ScrolledText(self, hscrollmode='dynamic',   ❿
                       vscrollmode='dynamic', hull_relief='sunken',
                       hull_background='gray40', hull_borderwidth=10,
```

```
                                      text_background='honeydew4', text_width=16,
                                      text_foreground='black', text_height=6,
                                      text_padx=10, text_pady=10, text_relief='groove',
                                      text_font=('arial', 12, 'bold'))
                self.display.pack(side=TOP, expand=YES, fill=BOTH)

                self.display.tag_config('ans', foreground='white')                    ⑪
                self.display.component('text').bind('<Key>', self.doKeypress)
                self.display.component('text').bind('<Return>', self.doEnter)

                for row in keys:
                    rowa = Frame(self, bg='gray40')
                    rowb = Frame(self, bg='gray40')
                    for p1, p2, p3, color, ktype, func in row:
                        if ktype == FUN:
                            a = lambda s=self, a=func: s.evalAction(a)
                        else:                                                          ⑫
                            a = lambda s=self, k=func: s.keyAction(k)
                        SLabel(rowa, p2, p3)
                        Key(rowb, text=p1, bg=color, command=a)
                    rowa.pack(side=TOP, expand=YES, fill=BOTH)
                    rowb.pack(side=TOP, expand=YES, fill=BOTH)

class Evaluator:
    def __init__(self):
        self.myNameSpace = {}
        self.runpython("from math import *")

    def runpython(self, code):
        try:
            return `eval(code, self.myNameSpace, self.myNameSpace)`             ⑬
        except SyntaxError:
            try:
                exec code in self.myNameSpace, self.myNameSpace                  ⑭
            except:
                return 'Error'

Calculator().mainloop()
```

Code comments (continued)

⑨ A number of constants are defined. The following data structure is quite complex. Using constants makes it easy to change values throughout such a complex structure and they make the code much more readable and consequently easier to maintain.

```
FUN = 1              # A Function
KEY = 0              # A Key
KC1 = 'gray30'       # Dark Keys
KC2 = 'gray50'       # Light Keys
```

These are used to populate a nested list of lists, which contains tuples. The tuples store three labels, the key color, the function or key designator and the method to bind to the key's cmd (activate) callback.

⑩ We create the Pmw ScrolledText widget and provide values for many of its attributes.

```
self.display = Pmw.ScrolledText(self, hscrollmode='dynamic',
```

```
            vscrollmode='dynamic', hull_relief='sunken',
            hull_background='gray40', hull_borderwidth=10,
            text_background='honeydew4', text_width=16,
```

Notice how the attributes for the hull (the container for the subordinate widgets within Pmw widgets) and the text widget are accessed by prefixing the widget.

⑪ We define a text tag which is used to differentiate output from input in the calculator's screen.

```
        self.display.tag_config('ans', foreground='white')
```

We saw this tag in use earlier in the text insert method.

⑫ Again, we must use a lambda expression to bind our callback function.

⑬ Python exceptions are quite flexible and allow simple control of errors. In the calculator's evaluator (runpython), we first run eval.

```
        try:
            return `eval(code, self.myNameSpace, self.myNameSpace)`
```

This is used mainly to support direct calculator math. eval cannot handle code sequences, however, so when we attempt to eval a code sequence, a SyntaxError exception is raised.

⑭ We trap the exception:

```
        except SyntaxError:
            try:
                exec code in self.myNameSpace, self.myNameSpace
            except:
                return 'Error'
```

and then the code is exec'ed in the except clause. Notice how this is enclosed by another try... except clause.

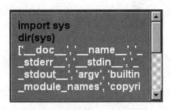

Figure 3.3 Python input

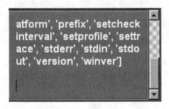

Figure 3.4 Output from dir()

Figure 3.2 shows the results of clicking keys on the calculator to calculate simple math equations. Unlike many calculators, this displays the input and output in different colors. The display also scrolls to provide a history of calculations, not unlike a printing calculator. If you click on the display screen, you may input data directly. Here is the surprise: you can enter Python and have exec run the code.

Figure 3.3 shows how you can import the sys module and access built-in functions within Python. Technically, you could do almost anything from this window (within the constraint of a very small display window). However, I don't think that this calculator is the much-sought Interactive Development Environment (IDE) for Python! (Readers who subscribe to the Python news group will understand that there has been a *constant* demand for an IDE for Python. Fortunately, Guido Van Rossum has now released IDLE with Python.)

When you press ENTER after dir(), you will see output similar to figure 3.4. This list of built-in symbols has scrolled the display over several lines (the widget is only 16 characters wide, after all).

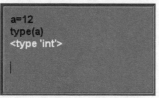

```
a=12
type(a)
<type 'int'>

|
```

Figure 3.5 Variables and built-in functions

Because we are maintaining a local namespace, it is possible to set up an interactive Python session that can do some useful work. Figure 3.5 shows how we are able to set variables within the namespace and manipulate the data with built-ins.

```
from math import pi
r = 5
d = pi * r * r
d
78.5398163397
```

Figure 3.6 Using the string module

Figure 3.6 is yet another example of our ability to gain access to the interpreter from an interactive shell. While the examples have been restricted to operations that fit within the limited space of the calculator's display, they do illustrate a potential for more serious applications. Note how Python allows you to create and use variables within the current namespace.

Note   When developing applications, I generally hide a button or bind a "secret" key sequence to invoke a GUI which allows me to execute arbitrary Python so that I can examine the namespace or modify objects within the running system. It is really a miniature debugger that I always have access to during development when something unusual happens. Sometimes restarting the application for a debug session just does not get me to the solution. An example of one of these tools is found in "A Tkinter explorer" on page 334.

3.3 Examining the application structure

The calculator example derives its compact code from the fact that Tkinter provides much of the structure for the application. Importing Tkinter establishes the base objects for the system and it only requires a little extra code to display a GUI. In fact, the minimal Tkinter code that can be written is just four lines:

```
from Tkinter import *
aWidget = Label(None, text='How little code does it need?')
aWidget.pack()
aWidget.mainloop()
```

In this fragment, the label widget is realized with the `pack` method. A `mainloop` is necessary to start the Tkinter event loop. In our calculator example, the application structure is a little more complex:

```
from Tkinter import *
...
define helper classes
...
class Calculator:
```

```
...
create widgets
...
Calculator.mainloop()
```

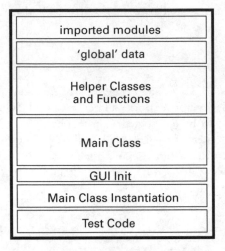

imported modules

'global' data

Helper Classes
and Functions

Main Class

GUI Init

Main Class Instantiation

Test Code

Figure 3.7 Application structure

Calling `Calculator.mainloop()` creates a calculator instance and starts the mainloop.

As we develop more applications, you will see this structure repeatedly. For those of us that tend to think spatially, the diagram shown in figure 3.7 may help.

All we have to do is fill in the blocks and we're finished! Well, nearly finished. I believe that the most important block in the structure is the last one: "Test Code." The purpose of this section is to allow you to test a module that is part of a suite of modules without the whole application structure being in place. Writing Python code this way will save a great deal of effort in integrating the components of the application. Of course, this approach applies to any implementation.

3.4 *Extending the application*

I leave you now with an exercise to extend the calculator and complete the functions that have been left undefined. It would be a simple task to modify the `keys` list to remove unnecessary keys and produce a rather more focused calculator. It would also be possible to modify the keys to provide a business or hex calculator.

In subsequent examples, you will see more complex manifestations of the application structure illustrated by this example.

## PART 2

Displays

In this section of the book we are going to examine the components that are used to build an application. We will begin with Tkinter widgets in chapter 4 and an explanation of their key features and their relationship to the underlying Tk widgets they are driving. Remember that Tkinter provides an object-oriented approach to GUIs, so that even though the behavior of the widgets is the same as those widgets created within a Tcl/Tk program, the methods used to create and manipulate them are quite different from within a Tkinter program.

Once we have looked at the widgets and examined Pmw (Python MegaWidgets), which provides a valuable library of application-ready widgets, we will discuss laying out the screen using the various geometry managers that are defined in chapter 5.

Chapter 6 explains how to make your application react to external events. This is an important chapter, since it covers a variety of methods for handling user input.

Chapter 7 shows the application of *classes* and *inheritance* as they apply to Tkinter. This is important for programmers new to object-oriented programming and it may be useful for those who are used to OOP as it applies to C++ and Java, since there are some notable differences. Then, in chapter 8, I will introduce more advanced techniques to drive a variety of dialogs and other interaction models.

Chapter 9 introduces panels and machines; this may be a new idea to some readers. It shows how to construct innovative user interfaces which resemble (in most cases) the devices that they control or monitor.

Chapter 10 gives information on building interfaces that permit the user to draw objects on a screen. It then explains methods to change their properties. You will also find some example code which illustrates how Tcl/Tk programs from the demonstration programs distributed with the software can be converted to Tkinter quite easily. Chapter 11 explains how to draw graphs using fairly conventional two-dimensional plots along with some alternative three-dimensional graphics.

C H A P T E R   4

Tkinter widgets

In this chapter I'll present the widgets and facilities available to Tkinter. Pmw Python Mega-Widgets, will also be discussed, since they provide valuable extensions to Tkinter. Each Tkinter and Pmw widget will be shown along with the source code fragment that produces the display. The examples are short and simple, although some of them illustrate how easy it is to produce powerful graphics with minimal code.

This chapter will not attempt to document all of the options available to a Tkinter programmer; complete documentation for the options and methods available for each widget is presented in appendix B. Similarly, Pmw options and methods are documented in Appendix C. Uses these appendices to determine the full range of options for each widget.

4.1   Tkinter widget tour

The following widget displays show typical Tkinter widget appearance and usage. The code is kept quite short, and it illustrates just a few of the options available for the widgets. Sometimes one or more of a widget's methods will be used, but this only scratches the surface. If you need to look up a particular method or option, refer to appendix B. Each widget also has references to the corresponding section in the appendix.

With the exception of the first example, the code examples have been stripped of the boilerplate code necessary to import and initialize Tkinter. The constant code is shown **bolded** in the first example. Note that most of the examples have been coded as *functions*, rather than *classes*. This helps to keep the volume of code low. The full source code for all of the displays is available online.

4.1.1 Toplevel

The `Toplevel` widget provides a separate container for other widgets, such as a Frame. For simple, single-window applications, the *root* `Toplevel` created when you initialize Tk may be the only shell that you need. There are four types of toplevels shown in figure 4.1:

1 The main toplevel, which is normally referred to as the *root*.

2 A *child* toplevel, which acts independently to the root, unless the root is destroyed, in which case the child is also destroyed.

3 A *transient* toplevel, which is always drawn on top of its parent and is hidden if the parent is iconified or withdrawn.

4 A `Toplevel` which is undecorated by the window manager can be created by setting the `overrideredirect` flag to a nonzero value. This creates a window that cannot be resized or moved directly.

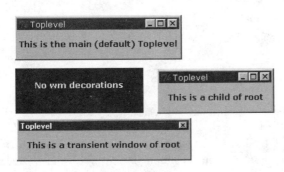

Figure 4.1
Toplevel widgets

```
from Tkinter import *
root = Tk()
root.option_readfile('optionDB')
root.title('Toplevel')

Label(root, text='This is the main (default) Toplevel').pack(pady=10)
t1 = Toplevel(root)
Label(t1, text='This is a child of root').pack(padx=10, pady=10)
t2 = Toplevel(root)
Label(t2, text='This is a transient window of root').pack(padx=10, pady=10)
t2.transient(root)
t3 = Toplevel(root, borderwidth=5, bg='blue')
```

```
Label(t3, text='No wm decorations', bg='blue', fg='white').pack(padx=10,
pady=10)
t3.overrideredirect(1)
t3.geometry('200x70+150+150')
```

`root.mainloop()`

Note The use of the `option_readfile` call in each of the examples to set application-wide defaults for colors and fonts is explained in "Setting application-wide
default fonts and colors" on page 49. This call is used to ensure that most examples have
consistent fonts and predictable field sizes.

Documentation for the `Toplevel` widget starts on page 539.

4.1.2 Frame

`Frame` widgets are *containers* for other widgets. Although you can bind mouse and keyboard
events to callbacks, frames have limited options and no methods other than standard widget
options.

One of the most common uses for a frame is as a *master* for a group of widgets which will
be handled by a geometry manager. This is shown in figure 4.2. The second frame example,
shown in figure 4.3 below, uses one frame for each row of the display.

Figure 4.2   Frame widget

```
for relief in [RAISED, SUNKEN, FLAT, RIDGE, GROOVE, SOLID]:
    f = Frame(root, borderwidth=2, relief=relief)
    Label(f, text=relief, width=10).pack(side=LEFT)
    f.pack(side=LEFT, padx=5, pady=5)
```

In a similar manner to buttons and labels, the appearance of the frame can be modified
by choosing a relief type and applying an appropriate borderwidth. (See figure 4.3.) In fact, it
can be hard to tell the difference between these widgets. For this reason, it may be a good idea
to reserve particular decorations for single widgets and not allow the decoration for a label to
be used for a button, for example:

```
class GUI:
    def __init__(self):
        of = [None]*5
        for bdw in range(5):
            of[bdw] = Frame(self.root, borderwidth=0)
            Label(of[bdw], text='borderwidth = %d  ' % bdw).pack(side=LEFT)
            ifx = 0
            iff = []
            for relief in [RAISED, SUNKEN, FLAT, RIDGE, GROOVE, SOLID]:
```

```
           iff.append(Frame(of[bdw], borderwidth=bdw, relief=relief))
           Label(iff[ifx], text=relief, width=10).pack(side=LEFT)
           iff[ifx].pack(side=LEFT, padx=7-bdw, pady=5+bdw)
           ifx = ifx+1
       of[bdw].pack()
```

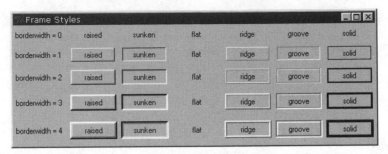

Figure 4.3 Frame styles combining relief type with varying borderwidths

A common use of the GROOVE relief type is to provide a labelled frame (sometimes called a *panel*) around one or more widgets. There are several ways to do this; figure 4.4 illustrates just one example, using two frames. Note that the outer frame uses the *Placer* geometry manager to position the inner frame and label. The widgets inside the inner frame use the *Packer* geometry manager.

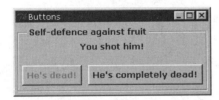

Figure 4.4 Using a Frame widget to construct a panel

```
f = Frame(root, width=300, height=110)
xf = Frame(f, relief=GROOVE, borderwidth=2)
Label(xf, text="You shot him!").pack(pady=10)
Button(xf, text="He's dead!", state=DISABLED).pack(side=LEFT, padx=5,
                                                    pady=8)
Button(xf, text="He's completely dead!", command=root.quit).pack(side=RIGHT,
                                                    padx=5, pady=8)
xf.place(relx=0.01, rely=0.125, anchor=NW)
Label(f, text='Self-defence against fruit').place(relx=.06, rely=0.125,
                                                    anchor=W)
f.pack()
```

Documentation for the Frame widget starts on page 491.

4.1.3 Label

`Label` widgets are used to display text or images. Labels can contain text spanning multiple lines, but you can only use a single font. You can allow the widget to break a string of text fitting the available space or you can embed linefeed characters in the string to control breaks. Several labels are shown in figure 4.5.

Figure 4.5 Label widget

Although labels are not intended to be used for interacting with users, you can bind mouse and keyboard events to callbacks. This may be used as a "cheap" button for certain applications.

```
Label(root, text="I mean, it's a little confusing for me when you say "
    "'dog kennel' if you want a mattress.  Why not just say 'mattress'?",
    wraplength=300, justify=LEFT).pack(pady=10)

f1=Frame(root)
Label(f1, text="It's not working, we need more!",
        relief=RAISED).pack(side=LEFT, padx=5)
Label(f1, text="I'm not coming out!", relief=SUNKEN).pack(side=LEFT,
                                                          padx=5)
f1.pack()

f2=Frame(root)
for bitmap,rlf in [ ('woman',RAISED),('mensetmanus',SOLID),
                    ('terminal',SUNKEN), ('escherknot',FLAT),
                    ('calculator',GROOVE),('letters',RIDGE)]:
    Label(f2, bitmap='@bitmaps/%s' % bitmap, relief=rlf).pack(side=LEFT,
                                                              padx=5)
f2.pack()
```

Documentation for the `Label` widget starts on page 495.

4.1.4 Button

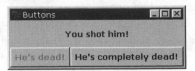

Figure 4.6 Button widgets

Strictly, *buttons* are *labels* that react to mouse and keyboard events. You bind a method call or callback that is invoked when the button is *activated*. Buttons may be *disabled* to prevent the user from activating a button. Button widgets can contain text (which can span multiple lines) or images. Buttons can be in the *tab group*, which means that you can navigate to them using the TAB key. Simple buttons are illustrated in figure 4.6.

```
Label(root, text="You shot him!").pack(pady=10)
Button(root, text="He's dead!", state=DISABLED).pack(side=LEFT)
Button(root, text="He's completely dead!",
        command=root.quit).pack(side=RIGHT)
```

Not all GUI programmers are aware that the relief option may be used to create buttons with different appearances. In particular, FLAT and SOLID reliefs are useful for creating toolbars where icons are used to convey functional information. However, some care must be exercised when using some relief effects. For example, if you define a button with a SUNKEN relief, the widget will not have a different appearance when it is activated, since the default behavior is to show the button with a SUNKEN relief; alternative actions must be devised such as changing the background color, font or wording within the button. Figure 4.7 illustrates the effect of combining the available relief types with increasing borderwidth. Note that increased borderwidth can be effective for some relief types (and RIDGE and GROOVE don't work unless borderwidth is 2 or more). However, buttons tend to become ugly if the borderwidth is too great.

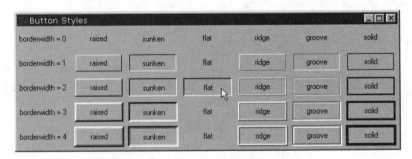

Figure 4.7 Combining relief and varying borderwidth

```
class GUI:
    def __init__(self):
        of = [None] *5
        for bdw in range(5):
            of[bdw] = Frame(self.root, borderwidth=0)
            Label(of[bdw], text='borderwidth = %d' % bdw).pack(side=LEFT)
            for relief in [RAISED, SUNKEN, FLAT, RIDGE, GROOVE, SOLID]:
                Button(of[bdw], text=relief,
                    borderwidth=bdw, relief=relief, width=10,
                    command=lambda s=self, r=relief, b=bdw: s.prt(r,b))\
```

```
                        .pack(side=LEFT, padx=7-bdw, pady=7-bdw)
                of[bdw].pack()
        def prt(self, relief, border):
            print '%s:%d' % (relief, border)
```

Documentation for the `Button` widget starts on page 453.

4.1.5   Entry

`Entry` widgets are the basic widgets used to collect input from a user. They may also be used to display information and may be disabled to prevent a user from changing their values.

Entry widgets are limited to a single line of text which can be in only one font. A typical entry widget is shown in figure 4.8. If the text entered into the widget is longer than the available display space, the widget scrolls the contents. You may change the visible position using the arrow keys. You may also use the widget's scrolling methods to bind scrolling behavior to the mouse or to your application.

Figure 4.8   Entry widget

```
Label(root, text="Anagram:").pack(side=LEFT, padx=5, pady=10)
e = StringVar()
Entry(root, width=40, textvariable=e).pack(side=LEFT)
e.set("'A shroe! A shroe! My dingkom for a shroe!'")
```

Documentation for the `Entry` widget starts on page 184.

4.1.6   Radiobutton

**Figure 4.9
Radiobutton widget**

The `Radiobutton` widget may need renaming soon! It is becoming unusual to see car radios with mechanical button selectors, so it might be difficult to explain the widget to future GUI designers. However, the idea is that all selections are *exclusive*, so that selecting one button deselects any button already selected.

In a similar fashion to `Button` widgets, `Radiobuttons` can display text or images and can have text which spans multiple lines, although in one font only. Figure 4.9 illustrates typical `Radiobuttons`.

You normally associate all of the radiobuttons in a group to a single variable.

```
var = IntVar()
for text, value in [('Passion fruit', 1), ('Loganber-
ries', 2),
        ('Mangoes in syrup', 3), ('Oranges', 4),
        ('Apples', 5),('Grapefruit', 6)]:
    Radiobutton(root, text=text, value=value, variable=var).pack(anchor=W)
var.set(3)
```

If the `indicatoron` flag is set to FALSE, the radiobutton group behaves as a button box, as shown in figure 4.10. The selected button is normally indicated with a SUNKEN relief.

```
var = IntVar()
for text, value in [('Red Leicester', 1), ('Tilsit', 2), ('Caerphilly', 3),
                    ('Stilton', 4), ('Emental', 5),
                    ('Roquefort', 6), ('Brie', 7)]:
    Radiobutton(root, text=text, value=value, variable=var,
                indicatoron=0).pack(anchor=W, fill=X, ipadx=18)
var.set(3)
```

Figure 4.10 Radiobuttons: indicatoron=0

Documentation for the `Radiobutton` widget starts on page 519.

4.1.7 Checkbutton

`Checkbutton` widgets are used to provide on/off selections for one or more items. Unlike radiobuttons (see "Radiobutton" on page 37) there is no interaction between checkbuttons. You may load checkbuttons with either text or images. Checkbuttons should normally have a variable (`IntVar`) assigned to the variable option which allows you to determine the state of the checkbutton. In addition (or alternately) you may bind a callback to the button which will be called whenever the button is pressed.

Note that the appearance of checkbuttons is quite different on UNIX and Windows; UNIX normally indicates selection by using a fill color, whereas Windows uses a checkmark. The Windows form is shown in figure 4.11.

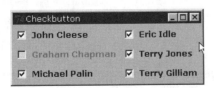

Figure 4.11 Checkbutton widget

```
for castmember, row, col, status in [
    ('John Cleese', 0,0,NORMAL), ('Eric Idle', 0,1,NORMAL),
    ('Graham Chapman', 1,0,DISABLED), ('Terry Jones', 1,1,NORMAL),
```

```
('Michael Palin',2,0,NORMAL), ('Terry Gilliam', 2,1,NORMAL)]:
    setattr(var, castmember, IntVar())
    Checkbutton(root, text=castmember, state=status, anchor=W,
        variable = getattr(var, castmember)).grid(row=row, col=col, sticky=W)
```

Documentation for the `Checkbutton` widget starts on page 481.

4.1.8   Menu

`Menu` widgets provide a familiar method to allow the user to choose operations within an application. Menus can be fairly cumbersome to construct, especially if the cascades *walk out* several levels (it is usually best to try design menus so that you do not need to walk out more than three levels to get to any functionality).

Tkinter provides flexibility for menu design, allowing multiple fonts, images and bitmaps, and checkbuttons and radiobuttons. It is possible to build the menu in several schemes. The example shown in figure 4.12 is one way to build a menu; you will find an alternate scheme to build the same menu online as altmenu.py.

Figure 4.12 Menu widget

Figure 4.13 illustrated adding Button commands to menu.

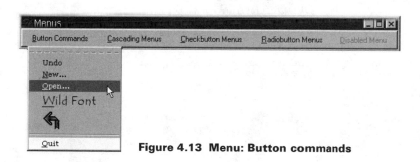

Figure 4.13 Menu: Button commands

```
mBar = Frame(root, relief=RAISED, borderwidth=2)
mBar.pack(fill=X)
CmdBtn = makeCommandMenu()
CasBtn = makeCascadeMenu()
ChkBtn = makeCheckbuttonMenu()
RadBtn = makeRadiobuttonMenu()
NoMenu = makeDisabledMenu()
mBar.tk_menuBar(CmdBtn, CasBtn, ChkBtn, RadBtn, NoMenu)
def makeCommandMenu():
    CmdBtn = Menubutton(mBar, text='Button Commands', underline=0)
```

```
CmdBtn.pack(side=LEFT, padx="2m")
CmdBtn.menu = Menu(CmdBtn)

CmdBtn.menu.add_command(label="Undo")
CmdBtn.menu.entryconfig(0, state=DISABLED)

CmdBtn.menu.add_command(label='New...', underline=0, command=new_file)
CmdBtn.menu.add_command(label='Open...', underline=0, command=open_file)
CmdBtn.menu.add_command(label='Wild Font', underline=0,
        font=('Tempus Sans ITC', 14), command=stub_action)
CmdBtn.menu.add_command(bitmap="@bitmaps/RotateLeft")
CmdBtn.menu.add('separator')
CmdBtn.menu.add_command(label='Quit', underline=0,
        background='white', activebackground='green',
        command=CmdBtn.quit)

CmdBtn['menu'] = CmdBtn.menu
return CmdBtn
```

Figure 4.14 shows the appearance of Cascade menu entries.

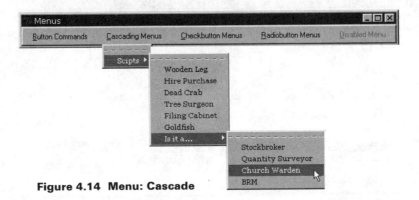

Figure 4.14 Menu: Cascade

```
def makeCascadeMenu():
  CasBtn = Menubutton(mBar, text='Cascading Menus', underline=0)
  CasBtn.pack(side=LEFT, padx="2m")
  CasBtn.menu = Menu(CasBtn)

  CasBtn.menu.choices = Menu(CasBtn.menu)
  CasBtn.menu.choices.wierdones = Menu(CasBtn.menu.choices)

  CasBtn.menu.choices.wierdones.add_command(label='Stockbroker')
  CasBtn.menu.choices.wierdones.add_command(label='Quantity Surveyor')
  CasBtn.menu.choices.wierdones.add_command(label='Church Warden')
  CasBtn.menu.choices.wierdones.add_command(label='BRM')
  CasBtn.menu.choices.add_command(label='Wooden Leg')
  CasBtn.menu.choices.add_command(label='Hire Purchase')
  CasBtn.menu.choices.add_command(label='Dead Crab')
  CasBtn.menu.choices.add_command(label='Tree Surgeon')
  CasBtn.menu.choices.add_command(label='Filing Cabinet')
```

```
CasBtn.menu.choices.add_command(label='Goldfish')
CasBtn.menu.choices.add_cascade(label='Is it a...',
menu=CasBtn.menu.choices.wierdones)
CasBtn.menu.add_cascade(label='Scipts', menu=CasBtn.menu.choices)
CasBtn['menu'] = CasBtn.menu
return CasBtn
```

Check buttons may be used within a menu, as shown in figure 4.15.

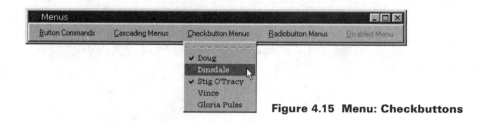

Figure 4.15 Menu: Checkbuttons

```
def makeCheckbuttonMenu():
   ChkBtn = Menubutton(mBar, text='Checkbutton Menus', underline=0)
   ChkBtn.pack(side=LEFT, padx='2m')
   ChkBtn.menu = Menu(ChkBtn)

   ChkBtn.menu.add_checkbutton(label='Doug')
   ChkBtn.menu.add_checkbutton(label='Dinsdale')
   ChkBtn.menu.add_checkbutton(label="Stig O'Tracy")
   ChkBtn.menu.add_checkbutton(label='Vince')
   ChkBtn.menu.add_checkbutton(label='Gloria Pules')

   ChkBtn.menu.invoke(ChkBtn.menu.index('Dinsdale'))
   ChkBtn['menu'] = ChkBtn.menu
   return ChkBtn
```

An alternative is to use Radiobuttons in a menu, as illustrated in figure 4.16.

```
def makeRadiobuttonMenu():
   RadBtn = Menubutton(mBar, text='Radiobutton Menus', underline=0)
   RadBtn.pack(side=LEFT, padx='2m')
   RadBtn.menu = Menu(RadBtn)

   RadBtn.menu.add_radiobutton(label='metonymy')
   RadBtn.menu.add_radiobutton(label='zeugmatists')
   RadBtn.menu.add_radiobutton(label='synechdotists')
   RadBtn.menu.add_radiobutton(label='axiomists')
   RadBtn.menu.add_radiobutton(label='anagogists')
   RadBtn.menu.add_radiobutton(label='catachresis')
   RadBtn.menu.add_radiobutton(label='periphrastic')
   RadBtn.menu.add_radiobutton(label='litotes')
   RadBtn.menu.add_radiobutton(label='circumlocutors')

   RadBtn['menu'] = RadBtn.menu
   return RadBtn
```

```
def makeDisabledMenu():
    Dummy_button = Menubutton(mBar, text='Disabled Menu', underline=0)
    Dummy_button.pack(side=LEFT, padx='2m')
    Dummy_button["state"] = DISABLED
    return Dummy_button
```

Documentation for the Menu widget starts on page 501.
Documentation for the Menubutton widget starts on page 506.
Documentation for the OptionMenu class starts on page 510.

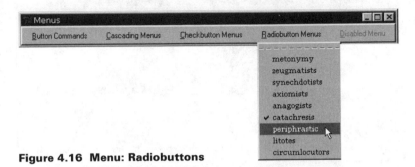

Figure 4.16 Menu: Radiobuttons

4.1.9 Message

The Message widget provides a convenient way to present multi-line text. You can use one font and one foreground/background color combination for the complete message. An example using this widget is shown in figure 4.17.

The widget has the standard widget methods.

```
Message(root, text="Exactly.  It's my belief that these sheep are laborin' "
    "under the misapprehension that they're birds.  Observe their "
    "be'avior. Take for a start the sheeps' tendency to 'op about "
    "the field on their 'ind legs.  Now witness their attempts to "
    "fly from tree to tree.  Notice that they do not so much fly "
    "as...plummet.", bg='royalblue', fg='ivory',
    relief=GROOVE).pack(padx=10, pady=10)
```

Documentation for the Message widget starts on page 508.

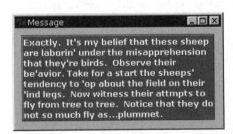

Figure 4.17 Message widget

4.1.10 Text

The Text widget is a versatile widget. Its primary purpose is to display text, of course, but it is capable of multiple styles and fonts, embedded images and windows, and localized event binding.

The Text widget may be used as a simple editor, in which case defining multiple tags and markings makes implementation easy. The widget is complex and has many options and methods, so please refer to the full documentation for precise details. Some of the possible styles and embedded objects are shown in figure 4.18.

Figure 4.18 Text widget with several embedded objects

```
text = Text(root, height=26, width=50)
scroll = Scrollbar(root, command=text.yview)
text.configure(yscrollcommand=scroll.set)

text.tag_configure('bold_italics', font=('Verdana', 12, 'bold', 'italic'))
text.tag_configure('big', font=('Verdana', 24, 'bold'))
text.tag_configure('color', foreground='blue', font=('Tempus Sans ITC', 14))
text.tag_configure('groove', relief=GROOVE, borderwidth=2)

text.tag_bind('bite', '<1>',
        lambda e, t=text: t.insert(END, "I'll bite your legs off!"))

text.insert(END, 'Something up with my banter, chaps?\n')
text.insert(END, 'Four hours to bury a cat?\n', 'bold_italics')
text.insert(END, 'Can I call you "Frank"?\n', 'big')
text.insert(END, "What's happening Thursday then?\n", 'color')
text.insert(END, 'Did you write this symphony in the shed?\n', 'groove')

button = Button(text, text='I do live at 46 Horton terrace')
text.window_create(END, window=button)
```

```
photo=PhotoImage(file='lumber.gif')
text.image_create(END, image=photo)

text.insert(END, 'I dare you to click on this\n', 'bite')
text.pack(side=LEFT)
scroll.pack(side=RIGHT, fill=Y)
```

Documentation for the Text widget starts on page 528.

4.1.11 Canvas

Canvases are versatile widgets. Not only can you use them to draw complex objects, using lines, ovals, polygons and rectangles, but you can also place images and bitmaps on the canvas with great precision. In addition to these features you can place any widgets within a canvas (such as buttons, listboxes and other widgets) and bind mouse or keyboard actions to them.

You will see many examples in this book where Canvas widgets have been used to provide a free-form container for a variety of applications. The example shown in figure 4.19 is a somewhat crude attempt to illustrate most of the available facilities.

One property of Canvas widgets, which can be either useful or can get in the way, is that objects are drawn on top of any objects already on the canvas. You can change the order of canvas items later, if necessary.

Figure 4.19 Canvas widget

```
canvas = Canvas(root, width =400, height=400)
canvas.create_oval(10,10,100,100, fill='gray90')
canvas.create_line(105,10,200,105, stipple='@bitmaps/gray3')
canvas.create_rectangle(205,10,300,105, outline='white', fill='gray50')
canvas.create_bitmap(355, 53, bitmap='questhead')

xy = 10, 105, 100, 200
canvas.create_arc(xy, start=0, extent=270, fill='gray60')
```

```
canvas.create_arc(xy, start=270, extent=5, fill='gray70')
canvas.create_arc(xy, start=275, extent=35, fill='gray80')
canvas.create_arc(xy, start=310, extent=49, fill='gray90')

canvas.create_polygon(205,105,285,125,166,177,210,199,205,105, fill='white')
canvas.create_text(350,150, text='text', fill='yellow', font=('verdana', 36))

img = PhotoImage(file='img52.gif')
canvas.create_image(145,280, image=img, anchor=CENTER)

frm = Frame(canvas, relief=GROOVE, borderwidth=2)
Label(frm, text="Embedded Frame/Label").pack()
canvas.create_window(285, 280, window=frm, anchor=CENTER)
canvas.pack()
```

Documentation for the Canvas widget starts on page 456.
Documentation for the Bitmap class starts on page 452.
Documentation for the PhotoImage class starts on page 512.

4.1.12 Scrollbar

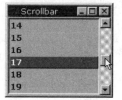

Figure 4.20
Scrollbar widget

Scrollbar widgets can be added to any widget that supports scrolling such as Text, Canvas and Listbox widgets.

Associating a Scrollbar widget with another widget is as simple as adding callbacks to each widget and arranging for them to be displayed together. Of course, there is no requirement for them to be co-located but you may end up with some unusual GUIs if you don't! Figure 4.20 shows a typical application.

```
list = Listbox(root, height=6, width=15)
scroll = Scrollbar(root, command=list.yview)
list.configure(yscrollcommand=scroll.set)
list.pack(side=LEFT)
scroll.pack(side=RIGHT, fill=Y)
for item in range(30):
   list.insert(END, item)
```

Documentation for the Scrollbar widget starts on page 525.

4.1.13 Listbox

Listbox widgets display a list of values that may be chosen by the user. The default behavior of the widget is to allow the user to select a single item in the list. A simple example is shown in figure 4.21. You may add additional bindings and use the selectmode option of the widget to allow multiple-item and other properties.

See "Scrollbar" above, for information on adding scrolling capability to the listbox.

```
list = Listbox(root, width=15)
list.pack()
for item in range(10):
    list.insert(END, item)
```

Documentation for the Listbox widget starts on page 497.

Figure 4.21 List box widget

4.1.14 Scale

The Scale widget allows you to set linear values between selected lower and upper values and it displays the current value in a graphical manner. Optionally, the numeric value may be displayed.

The Scale widget has several options to control its appearance and behavior; otherwise it is a fairly simple widget.

The following example, shown in figure 4.22, is an adaptation of one of the demonstrations supplied with the Tcl/Tk distribution. As such, it may be useful for programmers in Tcl/Tk to see how a conversion to Tkinter can be made.

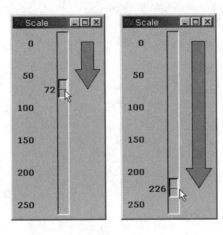

Figure 4.22 Scale widget: application

```
def setHeight(canvas, heightStr):
    height = string.atoi(heightStr)
    height = height + 21
    y2 = height - 30
    if y2 < 21:
        y2 = 21
    canvas.coords('poly',
        15,20,35,20,35,y2,45,y2,25,height,5,y2,15,y2,15,20)
```

```
canvas.coords('line',
     15,20,35,20,35,y2,45,y2,25,height,5,y2,15,y2,15,20)

canvas = Canvas(root, width=50, height=50, bd=0, highlightthickness=0)
canvas.create_polygon(0,0,1,1,2,2, fill='cadetblue', tags='poly')
canvas.create_line(0,0,1,1,2,2,0,0, fill='black', tags='line')

scale = Scale(root, orient=VERTICAL, length=284, from_=0, to=250,
     tickinterval=50, command=lambda h, c=canvas:setHeight(c,h))
scale.grid(row=0, column=0, sticky='NE')
canvas.grid(row=0, column=1, sticky='NWSE')
scale.set(100)
```

Documentation for the `Scale` widget starts on page 522.

4.2 Fonts and colors

The purpose of this section is to present the reader with an overview of fonts and colors as they apply to Tkinter. This will provide sufficient context to follow the examples that will be presented throughout the text.

4.2.1 Font descriptors

Those of us that have worked with X Window applications have become accustomed to the awkward and precise format of X window font descriptors. Fortunately, with release 8.0 and above of Tk, there is a solution: Tk defines *font descriptors*. Font descriptors are architecture independent. They allow the programmer to select a font by creating a tuple containing the family, pointsize and a string containing optional styles. The following are examples:

```
('Arial', 12, 'italic')
('Helvetica', 10)
('Verdana', 8, 'medium')
```

If the font family does not contain embedded spaces, you may pass the descriptor as a single string, such as:

```
'Verdana 8 bold italic'
```

4.2.2 X Window System font descriptors

Of course, the older font descriptors are available if you really want to use them. Most X Window fonts have a 14-field name in the form:

```
-foundry-family-weight-slant-setwidth-style-pixelSize-pointSize-
  Xresolution-Yresolution-spacing-averageWidth-registry-encoding
```

Normally, we only care about a few of the fields:

```
-*-family-weight-slant-*-*-*-pointSize-*-*-*-*-registry-encoding
```

These fields are defined as follows:

- `family`   A string that identifies the basic typographic style for example, `helvetica`, `arial`, etc.).

- weight   A string that identifies the nominal blackness of the font, according to the *foundry's* judgment (for example, medium, bold, etc.).
- slant   A code string that indicates the overall posture of the typeface design used in the font—one of roman (R), italic (I) or oblique (0).
- pointSize   An unsigned integer-string typographic metric in device-independent units which gives the body size for which the font was designed.
- encoding   A registered name that identifies the coded character set as defined by the specified registry.

An example of an X font descriptor might be:

```
'-*-verdana-medium-r-*-*-8-*-*-*-*-*-*-*'
```

This describes an 8-point Verdana font, medium weight and roman (upright). Although the descriptor is somewhat ugly, most programmers get used to the format quickly. With X-servers, not all fonts scale smoothly if a specific pointsize is unavailable in a font; unfortunately it is a trial-and-error process to get exactly the right combination of font and size for optimal screen appearance.

4.2.3 Colors

Tkinter allows you to use the color names defined by the X-server. These names are quite florid, and do not always fully describe the color: LavenderBlush1, LemonChiffon, LightSalmon, MediumOrchid3 and OldLace are just a few. Common names such as red, yellow, blue and black may also be used. The names and the corresponding RGB values are maintained in a Tk include file, so the names may be used portably on any Tkinter platform.*

It is often easier to precisely define colors using *color strings*:

#RGB	for 4-bit values (16 levels for each color)
#RRGGBB	for 8-bit values (256 levels for each color)
#RRRRGGGGBBBB	for 16-bit values (65526 levels for each color)

Here is an example of how one might set up part of a color definition table for an application (incomplete code):

```
# These are the color schemes for xxx and yyy front panels
#          Panel     LED off    ON             Active       Warning
COLORS = [('#545454','#656565','LawnGreen',  'ForestGreen','DarkOrange',\
#          Alarm     Display   Inside    Chrome     InsideP   Chassis
           '#ff342f','#747474','#343434','#efefef','#444444','#a0a0a0',\
#        DkChassis LtChassis VDkChassis VLtChassis Bronze
         '#767600','#848400','#6c6c00','#909000','#7e5b41'),
```

etc.

---

* X window color names are present in the standard X11 distribution but are not specified by the X11 Protocol or Xlib. It is permissible for X-server vendors to change the names or alter their intepretation. In rare cases you may find an implementation that will display different colors with Tkinter and X Window applications using the same color name.

4.2.4   Setting application-wide default fonts and colors

When designing an application, you may find that the default colors, fonts and font-sizes supplied by the system are not appropriate for the particular layout that you have in mind. At such times you must set their values explicitly. The values *could* be put right in the code (you will see several examples in the book where this has been done). However, this prevents end users or system administrators from tailoring an application to their particular requirements or business standards. In this case the values should be set in an *external* option database. For X window programmers this is equivalent to the *resource database* which is usually tailored using a .Xdefaults file. In fact the format of the Tk option database is exactly like the .Xdefaults file:

```
*font:                  Verdana 10
*Label*font:            Verdana 10 bold
*background:            Gray80
*Entry*background:      white
*foreground:            black
*Listbox*foreground:    RoyalBlue
```

The purpose of these entries is to set the font for all widgets *except* `Labels` to `Verdana 10` (regular weight) and `Labels` to `Verdana 10 bold`. Similarly we set the default colors for background and foreground, modifying `Entry` backgrounds and `Listbox` foregrounds. If we place these entries in a file called *optionDB*, we can apply the values using an `option_readfile` call:

```
root = Tk()
root.option_readfile('optionDB')
```

This call should be made *early* in the code to ensure that all widgets are created as intended.

4.3   *Pmw Megawidget tour*

Python megawidgets, *Pmw*, are composite widgets written entirely in Python using Tkinter widgets as base classes. They provide a convenient way to add functionality to an application without the need to write a lot of code. In particular, the `ComboBox` is a useful widget, along with the `Entry` field with several built-in validation schemes.

In a similar fashion to the Tkinter tour, above, the following displays show typical Pmw widget appearance and usage. The code is kept short and it illustrates some of the options available for the widgets. If you need to look up a particular method or option, refer to appendix C. Each widget also has references to the corresponding section in the appendix.

Pmw comes with extensive documentation in HTML format. Consequently this chapter will not repeat this information here. Additionally, there is example code for all of the widgets in the demos directory in the Pmw distribution. Most of the examples shown are simplifications derived from that code.

With the exception of the first example, the code examples have been stripped of the boilerplate code necessary to import and initialize Tkinter. The common code which is not shown in any sequences after the first is shown in **bold**. The full source code for all of the displays is available online.

4.3.1 AboutDialog

The `AboutDialog` widget provides a convenience dialog to present version, copyright and developer information. By providing a small number of data items the dialog can be displayed with minimal code. Figure 4.23 shows a typical `AboutDialog`.

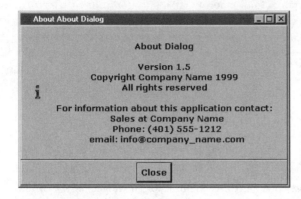

Figure 4.23 Pmw AboutDialog widget

```
from Tkinter import *
import Pmw
root = Tk()
root.option_readfile('optionDB')
Pmw.initialise()

Pmw.aboutversion('1.5')
Pmw.aboutcopyright('Copyright Company Name 1999\nAll rights reserved')
Pmw.aboutcontact(
    'For information about this application contact:\n' +
    '  Sales at Company Name\n' +
    '  Phone: (401) 555-1212\n' +
    '  email: info@company_name.com'
    )
about = Pmw.AboutDialog(root, applicationname='About Dialog')

root.mainloop()
```

This widget is used in the `AppShell` class which will be presented in "A standard application framework" on page 155 and it is used in several examples later in the book.

Documentation for the `AboutDialog` widget starts on page 542.

4.3.2 Balloon

The `Balloon` widget implements the now somewhat familiar *balloon help* motif (this is sometimes called *Tool Tips*). The purpose of the widget is to display help information when the cursor is placed over a widget on the screen, normally after a short delay. Additionally (or alternatively) information may be displayed in a status area on the screen. The information in this area is removed after a short delay. This is illustrated in figure 4.24.

Although balloon help can be very helpful to novice users, it may be annoying to experts. If you provide balloon help make sure that you provide an option to turn off output to the balloon and the status area, and make such choices persistent so that the user does not have to turn off the feature each time he uses the application.

```
balloon = Pmw.Balloon(root)
frame = Frame(root)
frame.pack(padx = 10, pady = 5)
field = Pmw.EntryField(frame, labelpos=W, label_text='Name:')
field.setentry('A.N. Other')
field.pack(side=LEFT, padx = 10)

balloon.bind(field, 'Your name', 'Enter your name')
check = Button(frame, text='Check')
check.pack(side=LEFT, padx=10)
balloon.bind(check, 'Look up', 'Check if name is in the database')
frame.pack()

messageBar = Pmw.MessageBar(root, entry_width=40,
                            entry_relief=GROOVE,
                            labelpos=W, label_text='Status:')
messageBar.pack(fill=X, expand=1, padx=10, pady=5)

balloon.configure(statuscommand = messageBar.helpmessage)
```

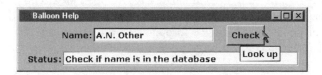

After a few seconds

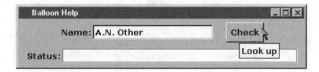

Figure 4.24 Pmw Balloon widget

Documentation for the Balloon widget starts on page 545.

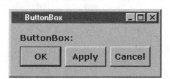

Figure 4.25 Pmw ButtonBox widget

4.3.3 ButtonBox

The ButtonBox widget provides a convenient way to implement a number of buttons and it is usually used to provide a *command area* within an application. The box may be laid out either horizontally or vertically and it is possible to define a default button. A simple ButtonBox is shown in figure 4.25.

```
def buttonPress(btn):
    print 'The "%s" button was pressed' % btn
def defaultKey(event):
    buttonBox.invoke()

buttonBox = Pmw.ButtonBox(root, labelpos='nw', label_text='ButtonBox:')
buttonBox.pack(fill=BOTH, expand=1, padx=10, pady=10)

buttonBox.add('OK',     command = lambda b='ok':     buttonPress(b))
buttonBox.add('Apply',  command = lambda b='apply':  buttonPress(b))
buttonBox.add('Cancel', command = lambda b='cancel': buttonPress(b))

buttonBox.setdefault('OK')
root.bind('<Return>', defaultKey)
root.focus_set()
buttonBox.alignbuttons()
```

Documentation for the `Buttonbox` widget starts on page 546.

4.3.4 ComboBox

The `ComboBox` widget is an important widget, originally found on Macintosh and Windows interfaces and later on Motif. It allows the user to select from a list of options, which, unlike an `OptionMenu`, may be scrolled to accommodate large numbers of selections. The list may be displayed permanently, such as the example at the left of figure 4.26 or as a dropdown list, shown at the right of figure 4.26. Using the dropdown form results in GUIs which require much less space to implement complex interfaces.

```
choice = None
def choseEntry(entry):
    print 'You chose "%s"' % entry
    choice.configure(text=entry)

asply = ("The Mating of the Wersh", "Two Netlemeng of Verona", "Twelfth
Thing", "The Chamrent of Venice", "Thamle", "Ring Kichard the Thrid")

choice = Label(root, text='Choose play', relief='sunken', padx=20, pady=20)
choice.pack(expand=1, fill='both', padx=8, pady=8)

combobox = Pmw.ComboBox(root, label_text='Play:', labelpos='wn',
                        listbox_width=24, dropdown=0,
                        selectioncommand=choseEntry,
                        scrolledlist_items=asply)
combobox.pack(fill=BOTH, expand=1, padx=8, pady=8)
combobox.selectitem(asply[0])

# ===========
combobox = Pmw.ComboBox(root, label_text='Play:', labelpos='wn',
                        listbox_width=24, dropdown=1,
...
```

Documentation for the `ComboBox` widget starts on page 549.

Figure 4.26 Pmw ComboBox widget

4.3.5 **ComboBoxDialog**

The ComboBoxDialog widget provides a convenience dialog to allow the user to select an item from a ComboBox in response to a question. It is similar to a SelectionDialog widget except that it may allow the user to type in a value in the EntryField widget or select from a permanently displayed list or a dropdown list. An example is shown in figure 4.27.

```
choice = None
def choseEntry(entry):
    print 'You chose "%s"' % entry
    choice.configure(text=entry)

plays = ("The Taming of the Shrew", "Two Gentelmen of Verona", "Twelfth
Night", "The Merchant of Venice", "Hamlet", "King Richard the Third")

dialog = Pmw.ComboBoxDialog(root, title = 'ComboBoxDialog',
        buttons=('OK', 'Cancel'), defaultbutton='OK',
        combobox_labelpos=N, label_text='Which play?',
        scrolledlist_items=plays, listbox_width=22)
dialog.tkraise()

result = dialog.activate()
print 'You clicked on', result, dialog.get()
```

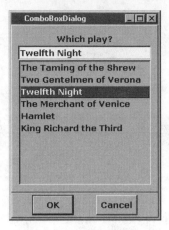

Figure 4.27 Pmw ComboBoxDialog widget

Documentation for the ComboBoxDialog widget starts on page 551.

4.3.6 Counter

The Counter widget is a versatile widget which allows the user to cycle through a sequence of available values. Pmw provides integer, real, time and date counters and it is possible to define your own function to increment or decrement the displayed value. There is no limitation on the value that is displayed as the result of incrementing the counter, so there is no reason that the counter cannot display "eine, zwei, drei" or whatever sequence is appropriate for the application. Some examples are shown in figure 4.28.

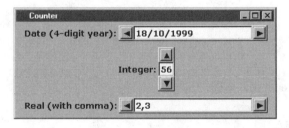

Figure 4.28 Pmw Counter widget

```
def execute(self):
    print 'Return pressed, value is', date.get()

    date = Pmw.Counter(root, labelpos=W,
        label_text='Date (4-digit year):',
        entryfield_value=time.strftime('%d/%m/%Y',
                    time.localtime(time.time())),
        entryfield_command=execute,
        entryfield_validate={'validator' : 'date', 'format' : 'dmy'},
        datatype = {'counter' : 'date', 'format' : 'dmy', 'yyyy' : 1})

real = Pmw.Counter(root, labelpos=W,
        label_text='Real (with comma):',
```

```
            entryfield_value='1,5',
            datatype={'counter' : 'real', 'separator' : ','},
            entryfield_validate={'validator' : 'real',
                'min' : '-2,0', 'max' : '5,0',
                'separator' : ','},
            increment= .1)

int = Pmw.Counter(root, labelpos=W,
            label_text='Integer:',
            orient=VERTICAL,
            entry_width=2,
            entryfield_value=50,
            entryfield_validate={'validator' : 'integer',
                'min' : 0, 'max' : 99})

counters = (date, real)
Pmw.alignlabels(counters)
for counter in counters:
    counter.pack(fill=X, expand=1, padx=10, pady=5)
    int.pack(padx=10, pady=5)
```

Documentation for the `Counter` widget starts on page 553.

4.3.7   CounterDialog

The `CounterDialog` widget provides a convenience dialog requesting the user to select a value from a `Counter` widget. The counter can contain any data type that the widget is capable of cycling through, such as the unlikely sequence shown in figure 4.29.

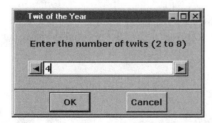

Figure 4.29 Pmw CounterDialog widget

```
choice = None
dialog = Pmw.CounterDialog(root,
            label_text='Enter the number of twits (2 to 8)\n',
            counter_labelpos=N, entryfield_value=2,
            counter_datatype='numeric',
            entryfield_validate={'validator': 'numeric', 'min': 2, 'max': 8},
            buttons=('OK', 'Cancel'), defaultbutton='OK',
            title='Twit of the Year')
dialog.tkraise()

result = dialog.activate()
print 'You clicked on', result, dialog.get()
```

Documentation for the `CounterDialog` widget starts on page 556.

4.3.8 Dialog

The `Dialog` widget provides a simple way to create a `toplevel` containing a `ButtonBox` and a child site area. You may populate the child site with whatever your application requires. Figure 4.30 shows an example of a `Dialog`.

Figure 4.30 Pmw Dialog widget

```
dialog = Pmw.Dialog(root, buttons=('OK', 'Apply', 'Cancel', 'Help'),
        defaultbutton='OK', title='Simple dialog')
w = Label(dialog.interior(), text='Pmw Dialog\nBring out your dead!',
        background='black', foreground='white', pady=20)
w.pack(expand=1, fill=BOTH, padx=4, pady=4)
dialog.activate()
```

Documentation for the `Dialog` widget starts on page 558.

4.3.9 EntryField

The `EntryField` widget is an `Entry` widget with associated validation methods. The built-in validation provides validators for integer, hexadecimal, alphabetic, alphanumeric, real, time and date data formats. Some of the controls that may be placed on the validation include checking conformity with the selected data format and checking that entered data is between minimum and maximum limits. You may also define your own validators. A few examples are shown in figure 4.31.

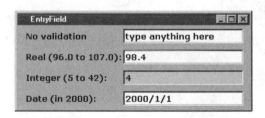

Figure 4.31 Pmw EntryField widget

```
noval = Pmw.EntryField(root, labelpos=W, label_text='No validation',
        validate = None)

real  = Pmw.EntryField(root, labelpos=W, value = '98.4',
        label_text = 'Real (96.0 to 107.0):',
        validate = {'validator' : 'real',
            'min' : 96, 'max' : 107, 'minstrict' : 0})
```

```
int   = Pmw.EntryField(root, labelpos=W, label_text = 'Integer (5 to 42):',
        validate = {'validator' : 'numeric',
            'min' : 5, 'max' : 42, 'minstrict' : 0},
        value = '12')

date = Pmw.EntryField(root, labelpos=W,label_text = 'Date (in 2000):',
        value = '2000/1/1', validate = {'validator' : 'date',
            'min' : '2000/1/1', 'max' : '2000/12/31',
            'minstrict' : 0, 'maxstrict' : 0,
            'format' : 'ymd'})

widgets = (noval, real, int, date)
for widget in widgets:
    widget.pack(fill=X, expand=1, padx=10, pady=5)
Pmw.alignlabels(widgets)

real.component('entry').focus_set()
```

Documentation for the EntryField widget starts on page 559.

4.3.10 Group

The Group widget provides a convenient way to place a labeled frame around a group of widgets. The label can be any reasonable widget such as a Label but it can also be an Entry-Field, RadioButton or CheckButton depending on the application requirements. It is also possible to use the widget as a graphic frame with no label. These examples are shown in figure 4.32.

Figure 4.32 Pmw Group widget

```
w = Pmw.Group(root, tag_text='place label here')
w.pack(fill=BOTH, expand=1, padx=6, pady=6)
cw = Label(w.interior(), text='A group with a\nsimple Label tag')
cw.pack(padx=2, pady=2, expand=1, fill=BOTH)

w = Pmw.Group(root, tag_pyclass=None)
w.pack(fill=BOTH, expand=1, padx=6, pady=6)
cw = Label(w.interior(), text='A group\nwithout a tag')
cw.pack(padx=2, pady=2, expand=1, fill=BOTH)

w = Pmw.Group(root, tag_pyclass=Checkbutton,
            tag_text='checkbutton', tag_foreground='blue')
```

```
w.pack(fill=BOTH, expand=1, padx=6, pady=6)
cw = Frame(w.interior(),width=150,height=20)
cw.pack(padx=2, pady=2, expand=1, fill=BOTH)
```

Documentation for the Group widget starts on page 564.

4.3.11 LabeledWidget

The LabeledWidget widget is a convenience container which labels a widget or collection of widgets. Options are provided to control the placement of the label and control the appearance of the graphic border. The child site can be populated with any combination of widgets. The example shown in figure 4.33 uses the widget as a frame which requires less code than using individual components.

Figure 4.33 Pmw LabeledWidget widget

```
frame = Frame(root, background = 'gray80')
frame.pack(fill=BOTH, expand=1)

lw = Pmw.LabeledWidget(frame, labelpos='n',
        label_text='Sunset on Cat Island')
lw.component('hull').configure(relief=SUNKEN, borderwidth=3)
lw.pack(padx=10, pady=10)

img = PhotoImage(file='chairs.gif')
cw = Button(lw.interior(), background='yellow', image=img)
cw.pack(padx=10, pady=10, expand=1, fill=BOTH)
```

Documentation for the LabeledWidget widget starts on page 565.

4.3.12 MenuBar

The `MenuBar` widget is a manager widget which provides methods to add menu buttons and menus to the menu bar and to add menu items to the menus. One important convenience is that it is easy to add balloon help to the menus and menu items. Almost all of the menu options available with Tkinter `Menu` widgets (see "Menu" on page 39) are available through the Pmw MenuBar. Figure 4.34 illustrates a similar menu to the one shown in figure 4.13 using discrete Tkinter widgets.

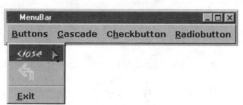

Figure 4.34 Pmw MenuBar widget

```
balloon = Pmw.Balloon(root)
menuBar = Pmw.MenuBar(root, hull_relief=RAISED,hull_borderwidth=1,
                      balloon=balloon)
menuBar.pack(fill=X)

menuBar.addmenu('Buttons', 'Simple Commands')
menuBar.addmenuitem('Buttons', 'command', 'Close this window',
                    font=('StingerLight', 14), label='Close')
menuBar.addmenuitem('Buttons', 'command',
                    bitmap="@bitmaps/RotateLeft", foreground='yellow')
menuBar.addmenuitem('Buttons', 'separator')
menuBar.addmenuitem('Buttons', 'command',
                    'Exit the application', label='Exit')

menuBar.addmenu('Cascade', 'Cascading Menus')
menuBar.addmenu('Checkbutton', 'Checkbutton Menus')
menuBar.addmenu('Radiobutton', 'Radiobutton Menus')
```

Documentation for the `MenuBar` widget starts on page 572.

4.3.13 MessageBar

The `MessageBar` widget is used to implement a status area for an application. Messages in several discrete categories may be displayed. Each message is displayed for a period of time which is determined by its category. Additionally, each category is assigned a priority so the message with the highest priority is displayed first. It is also possible to specify the number of times that the bell should be rung on receipt of each message category. Figure 4.35 shows how a `system error` would appear.

```
messagebar = box = None
def selectionCommand():
   sels = box.getcurselection()
   if len(sels) > 0:
```

```
                messagetype = sels[0]
                if messagetype == 'state':
                    messagebar.message('state', 'Change of state message')
                else:
                    text = messages[messagetype]
                    messagebar.message(messagetype, text)

messages = { 'help'        : 'Save current file',
             'userevent'   : 'Saving file "foo"',
             'busy'        : 'Busy deleting all files from file system ...',
             'systemevent': 'File "foo" saved',
             'usererror'   : 'Invalid file name "foo/bar"',
             'systemerror': 'Failed to save file: file system full',
             }

messagebar = Pmw.MessageBar(root, entry_width=40, entry_relief=GROOVE,
                                 labelpos=W, label_text='Status:')
messagebar.pack(side=BOTTOM, fill=X, expand=1, padx=10, pady=10)

box = Pmw.ScrolledListBox(root,listbox_selectmode=SINGLE,
        items=('state', 'help', 'userevent', 'systemevent',
                   'usererror', 'systemerror', 'busy',),
        label_text='Message type', labelpos=N,
        selectioncommand=selectionCommand)
box.pack(fill=BOTH, expand=1, padx=10, pady=10)
```

Documentation for the MessageBar widget starts on page 574.

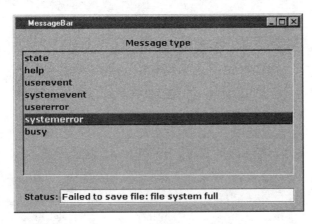

Figure 4.35 Pmw MessageBar widget

4.3.14 MessageDialog

The `MessageDialog` widget is a convenience dialog which displays a single message, which may be broken into multiple lines, and a number of buttons in a `ButtonBox`. It is useful for creating simple dialogs "on-the-fly." Figure 4.36 shows an example.

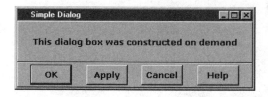

Figure 4.36 Pmw MessageDialog widget

```
dialog = Pmw.MessageDialog(root, title = 'Simple Dialog',
                  defaultbutton = 0,
                  buttons = ('OK', 'Apply', 'Cancel', 'Help'),
                message_text = 'This dialog box was constructed on demand')
dialog.iconname('Simple message dialog')

result = dialog.activate()
print 'You selected', result
```

Documentation for the `MessageDialog` widget starts on page 576.

4.3.15 NoteBookR

The `NoteBookR` widget implements the popular *property sheet* motif. Methods allow a number of pages or panes to be created. Any content may then be added to the panels. The user selects a panel by clicking on the tab at its top. Alternatively panels may be raised or lowered through instance methods. An example is shown in figure 4.37.

```
nb = Pmw.NoteBookR(root)

nb.add('p1', label='Page 1')
nb.add('p2', label='Page 2')
nb.add('p3', label='Page 3')

p1 = nb.page('p1').interior()
p2 = nb.page('p2').interior()
p3 = nb.page('p3').interior()

nb.pack(padx=5, pady=5, fill=BOTH, expand=1)
Button(p1, text='This is text on page 1', fg='blue').pack(pady=40)

c = Canvas(p2, bg='gray30')
w = c.winfo_reqwidth()
h = c.winfo_reqheight()
c.create_oval(10,10,w-10,h-10,fill='DeepSkyBlue1')
c.create_text(w/2,h/2,text='This is text on a canvas', fill='white',
        font=('Verdana', 14, 'bold'))
c.pack(fill=BOTH, expand=1)
```

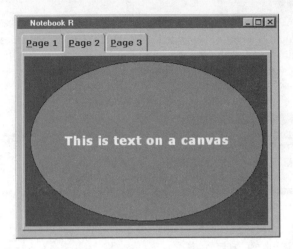

Figure 4.37 Pmw NoteBookR widget

Documentation for the NotebookR widget starts on page 580.

4.3.16 NoteBookS

The NoteBookS widget implements an alternative style of NoteBook. NoteBookS provides additional options to control the color, dimensions and appearance of the tabs. Otherwise it is quite similar to NoteBookR. Figure 4.38 illustrates a similar layout using NotebookS.

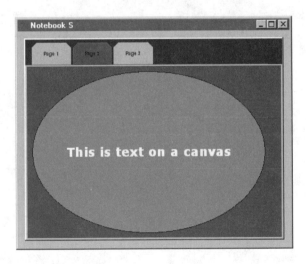

Figure 4.38 Pmw NoteBookS widget

```
nb = Pmw.NoteBookS(root)

nb.addPage('Page 1')
nb.addPage('Page 2')
nb.addPage('Page 3')
```

```
f1 = nb.getPage('Page 1')
f2 = nb.getPage('Page 2')
f3 = nb.getPage('Page 3')

nb.pack(pady=10, padx=10, fill=BOTH, expand=1)
Button(f1, text='This is text on page 1', fg='blue').pack(pady=40)

c = Canvas(f2, bg='gray30')
w = c.winfo_reqwidth()
h = c.winfo_reqheight()
c.create_oval(10,10,w-10,h-10,fill='DeepSkyBlue1')
c.create_text(w/2,h/2,text='This is text on a canvas', fill='white',
        font=('Verdana', 14, 'bold'))
c.pack(fill=BOTH, expand=1)
```

Documentation for the NotebookS widget starts on page 582.

4.3.17 NoteBook

Release 0.8.3 of Pmw replaces NoteBookR and NoteBookS with Notebook. While it is quite similar to the previous notebooks, there are some small changes. In fact, you will have to make changes to your code to use NoteBook with existing code. However, the changes are minor and the new form may be a little easier to use. Figure 4.39 illustrates the new widget.

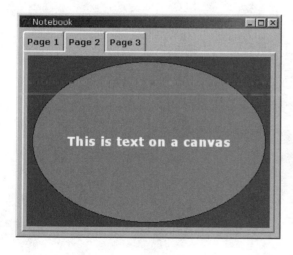

Figure 4.39 Pmw NoteBook widget (version 0.8.3)

```
from Tkinter import *
import Pmw

root = Tk()
root.option_readfile('optionDB')
root.title('Notebook')
Pmw.initialise()

nb = Pmw.NoteBook(root)
p1 = nb.add('Page 1')
```

```
p2 = nb.add('Page 2')
p3 = nb.add('Page 3')
nb.pack(padx=5, pady=5, fill=BOTH, expand=1)

Button(p1, text='This is text on page 1', fg='blue').pack(pady=40)
c = Canvas(p2, bg='gray30')
w = c.winfo_reqwidth()
h = c.winfo_reqheight()
c.create_oval(10,10,w-10,h-10,fill='DeepSkyBlue1')
c.create_text(w/2,h/2,text='This is text on a canvas', fill='white',
        font=('Verdana', 14, 'bold'))
c.pack(fill=BOTH, expand=1)

nb.setnaturalpagesize()
root.mainloop()
```

Documentation for the Notebook widget starts on page 578.

4.3.18 OptionMenu

The OptionMenu widget implements a classic popup menu motif familiar to Motif programmers. However, the appearance of the associated popup is a little different, as shown in figure 4.40. OptionMenus should be used to select limited items of data. If you populate the widget with large numbers of data the popup may not fit on the screen and the widget does not scroll.

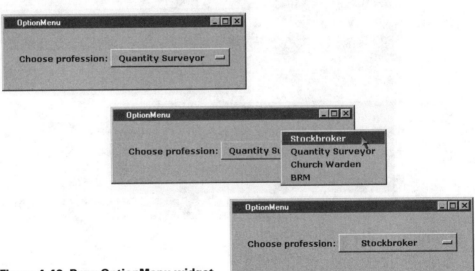

Figure 4.40 Pmw OptionMenu widget

```
var = StringVar()
var.set('Quantity Surveyor')
opt_menu = Pmw.OptionMenu(root, labelpos=W,
        label_text='Choose profession:', menubutton_textvariable=var,
```

```
                items=('Stockbroker', 'Quantity Surveyor', 'Church Warden', 'BRM'),
                menubutton_width=16)
    opt_menu.pack(anchor=W, padx=20, pady=30)
```

Documentation for the OptionMenu widget starts on page 584.

4.3.19 PanedWidget

The PanedWidget widget creates a manager containing multiple frames. Each frame is a container for other widgets and may be resized by dragging on its handle or separator line. The area within each pane is managed independently, so a single pane may be grown or shrunk to modify the layout of its children. Figure 4.41 shows an example.

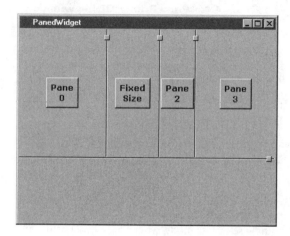

Figure 4.41 Pmw PanedWidget widget

```
pane = Pmw.PanedWidget(root, hull_width=400, hull_height=300)
pane.add('top', min=100)
pane.add('bottom', min=100)

topPane = Pmw.PanedWidget(pane.pane('top'), orient=HORIZONTAL)
for num in range(4):
    if num == 1:
        name = 'Fixed\nSize'
        topPane.add(name, min=.2, max=.2)
    else:
        name = 'Pane\n' + str(num)
        topPane.add(name, min=.1, size=.25)
    button = Button(topPane.pane(name), text=name)
    button.pack(expand=1)
topPane.pack(expand=1, fill=BOTH)

pane.pack(expand=1, fill=BOTH)
```

Documentation for the PanedWidget widget starts on page 586.

4.3.20　PromptDialog

The `PromptDialog` widget is a convenience dialog which displays a single `EntryField` and a number of buttons in a `ButtonBox`. It is useful for creating a simple dialog on-the-fly. The example shown in figure 4.42 collects a password from a user.

Figure 4.42　Pmw PromptDialog widget

```
dialog = Pmw.PromptDialog(root, title='Password', label_text='Password:',
            entryfield_labelpos=N, entry_show='*', defaultbutton=0,
            buttons=('OK', 'Cancel'))

result = dialog.activate()
print 'You selected', result
```

Documentation for the `PromptDialog` widget starts on page 587.

4.3.21　RadioSelect

The `RadioSelect` widget implements an alternative to the Tkinter `RadioButton` widget. `RadioSelect` creates a manager that contains a number of buttons. The widget may be configured to operate either in single-selection mode where only one button at a time may be activated, or multiple selection mode where any number of buttons may be selected. This is illustrated in figure 4.43.

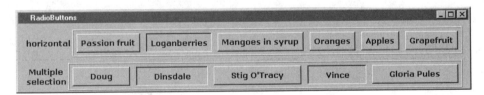

Figure 4.43　Pmw RadioSelect widget

```
horiz = Pmw.RadioSelect(root, labelpos=W, label_text=HORIZONTAL,
        frame_borderwidth=2, frame_relief=RIDGE)
horiz.pack(fill=X, padx=10, pady=10)

for text in ('Passion fruit', 'Loganberries', 'Mangoes in syrup',
            'Oranges', 'Apples', 'Grapefruit'):
    horiz.add(text)
```

```
horiz.invoke('Mangoes in syrup')

multiple = Pmw.RadioSelect(root, labelpos=W, label_text='Multiple\nselection',
        frame_borderwidth=2, frame_relief=RIDGE, selectmode=MULTIPLE)
multiple.pack(fill=X, padx=10)

for text in ('Doug', 'Dinsdale', "Stig O'Tracy", 'Vince', 'Gloria Pules'):
    multiple.add(text)
multiple.invoke('Dinsdale')
```

Documentation for the RadioSelect widget starts on page 589.

4.3.22   ScrolledCanvas

The ScrolledCanvas widget is a convenience widget providing a Canvas widget with associated horizontal and vertical scrollbars. An example is shown in figure 4.44.

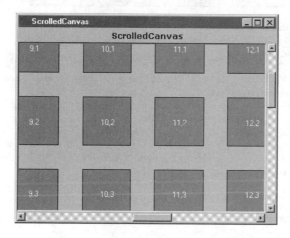

Figure 4.44 Pmw ScrolledCanvas widget

```
sc = Pmw.ScrolledCanvas(root, borderframe=1, labelpos=N,
                        label_text='ScrolledCanvas', usehullsize=1,
                        hull_width=400,hull_height=300)

for i in range(20):
    x = -10 + 3*i
    y = -10
    for j in range(10):
        sc.create_rectangle('%dc'%x,'%dc'%y,'%dc'%(x+2),'%dc'%(y+2),
                            fill='cadetblue', outline='black')
        sc.create_text('%dc'%(x+1),'%dc'%(y+1),text='%d,%d'%(i,j),
                        anchor=CENTER, fill='white')
        y = y + 3

sc.pack()
sc.resizescrollregion()
```

Documentation for the ScrolledCanvas widget starts on page 592.

4.3.23 ScrolledField

The `ScrolledField` widget provides a labeled `EntryField` widget with bindings to allow the user to scroll through data which is too great to be displayed within the available space. This widget should be reserved for very special uses, since it contravenes many of the commonly considered human factors for GUI elements. Figure 4.45 shows the effect of scrolling the field using the keyboard arrow keys.

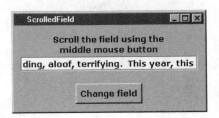 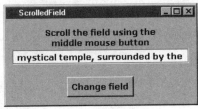

Figure 4.45 Pmw ScrolledField widget

```
lines = (
    "Mount Everest.  Forbidding, aloof, terrifying.  This year, this",
    "remote Himalayan mountain, this mystical temple, surrounded by the",
    "most difficult terrain in the world, repulsed yet another attempt to",
    "conquer it.  (Picture changes to wind-swept, snowy tents and people)",
    "This time, by the International Hairdresser's Expedition.  In such",
    "freezing, adverse conditions, man comes very close to breaking",
    "point.  What was the real cause of the disharmony which destroyed",
    "their chances at success?")

 global index
field = index = None
def execute():
    global index
    field.configure(text=lines[index % len(lines)])
    index = index + 1
field = Pmw.ScrolledField(root, entry_width=30,
            entry_relief=GROOVE, labelpos=N,
            label_text='Scroll the field using the\nmiddle mouse button')
field.pack(fill=X, expand=1, padx=10, pady=10)

button = Button(root, text='Change field', command=execute)
button.pack(padx=10, pady=10)

index = 0
execute()
```

Documentation for the `ScrolledField` widget starts on page 594.

4.3.24　ScrolledFrame

The `ScrolledFrame` widget is a convenience widget providing a `Frame` widget with associated horizontal and vertical scrollbars. An example is shown in figure 4.46.

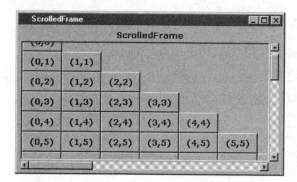

Figure 4.46　Pmw ScrolledFrame widget

```
global row, col
row = col = 0
sf = frame = None
def addButton():
    global row, col
    button = Button(frame, text = '(%d,%d)' % (col, row))
    button.grid(row=row, col=col, sticky='nsew')
    frame.grid_rowconfigure(row, weight=1)
    frame.grid_columnconfigure(col, weight=1)
    sf.reposition()
    if col == row:
        col = 0
        row = row + 1
    else:
        col = col + 1

sf = Pmw.ScrolledFrame(root, labelpos=N, label_text='ScrolledFrame',
        usehullsize=1, hull_width=400, hull_height=220)
sf.pack(padx=5, pady=3, fill='both', expand=1)
frame = sf.interior()

for i in range(250):
    addButton()
```

Documentation for the `ScrolledFrame` widget starts on page 595.

4.3.25   ScrolledListbox

The ScrolledListbox widget is a convenience widget providing a ListBox widget with associated horizontal and vertical scrollbars. Figure 4.47 shows a typical ScrolledListbox.

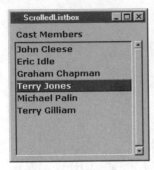

Figure 4.47 Pmw ScrolledListbox widget

```
box = None
def selectionCommand():
    sels = box.getcurselection()
    if len(sels) == 0:
        print 'No selection'
    else:
        print 'Selection:', sels[0]

box = Pmw.ScrolledListBox(root, listbox_selectmode=SINGLE,
            items=('John Cleese', 'Eric Idle', 'Graham Chapman',
                    'Terry Jones', 'Michael Palin', 'Terry Gilliam'),
            labelpos=NW, label_text='Cast Members',
            listbox_height=5, vscrollmode='static',
            selectioncommand=selectionCommand,
             dblclickcommand=selectionCommand,
                usehullsize=1, hull_width=200, hull_height=200,)
box.pack(fill=BOTH, expand=1, padx=5, pady=5)
```

Documentation for the ScrolledListbox widget starts on page 598.

4.3.26   ScrolledText

The ScrolledText widget is a convenience widget providing a Text widget with associated horizontal and vertical scrollbars, as shown in figure 4.48.

```
st = Pmw.ScrolledText(root, borderframe=1, labelpos=N,
        label_text='Blackmail', usehullsize=1,
        hull_width=400, hull_height=300,
        text_padx=10, text_pady=10,
        text_wrap='none')
st.importfile('blackmail.txt')
st.pack(fill=BOTH, expand=1, padx=5, pady=5)
```

Documentation for the ScrolledText widget starts on page 600.

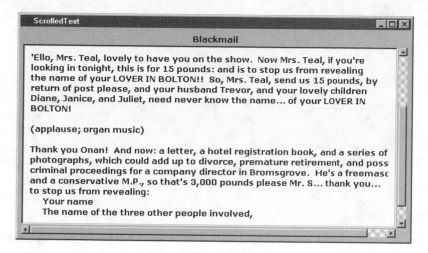

Figure 4.48 Pmw ScrolledText widget

4.3.27 SelectionDialog

The `SelectionDialog` widget provides a convenience dialog to allow the user to select an item from a `ScrolledList` in response to a question. It is similar to a `ComboBoxDialog` except that there is no provision for the user to type in a value. Figure 4.49 shows an example.

Figure 4.49 Pmw SelectionDialog widget

```
dialog = None
def execute(result):
    sels = dialog.getcurselection()
    if len(sels) == 0:
        print 'You clicked on', result, '(no selection)'
```

```
    else:
        print 'You clicked on', result, sels[0]
    dialog.deactivate(result)

dialog = Pmw.SelectionDialog(root, title='String',
    buttons=('OK', 'Cancel'), defaultbutton='OK',
    scrolledlist_labelpos=N, label_text='Who sells string?',
    scrolledlist_items=('Mousebat', 'Follicle', 'Goosecreature',
                'Mr. Simpson', 'Ampersand', 'Spong', 'Wapcaplet',
                'Looseliver', 'Vendetta', 'Prang'),
    command=execute)
dialog.activate()
```

Documentation for the `SelectionDialog` widget starts on page 603.

4.3.28 TextDialog

The `TextDialog` widget provides a convenience dialog used to display multi-line text to the user. It may also be used as a simple text editor. It is shown in figure 4.50.

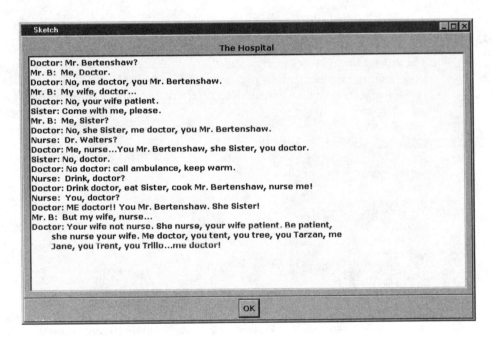

Figure 4.50 Pmw TextDialog widget

```
sketch = """Doctor: Mr. Bertenshaw?
Mr. B:  Me, Doctor.
# ------Lines removed----------
Jane, you Trent, you Trillo...me doctor!"""

dialog = Pmw.TextDialog(root, scrolledtext_labelpos='n',
```

```
            title='Sketch',
            defaultbutton=0,
            label_text='The Hospital')
dialog.insert(END, sketch)
dialog.configure(text_state='disabled')
dialog.activate()
dialog.tkraise()
```

Documentation for the `TextDialog` widget starts on page 605.

4.3.29 TimeCounter

The `TimeCounter` widget implements a device to set hours, minutes and seconds using up and down arrows. The widget may be configured to autorepeat so that holding down a button will slew the value displayed in the widget. Figure 4.51 shows the widget's appearance.

Figure 4.51 Pmw TimeCounter widget

```
time = Pmw.TimeCounter(root, labelpos=W, label_text='HH:MM:SS',
                       min='00:00:00', max='23:59:59')
time.pack(padx=10, pady=5)
```

Documentation for the `TimeCounter` widget starts on page 607.

4.4 *Creating new megawidgets*

In addition to supplying useful widgets, Pmw provides a simple mechanism to allow you to develop new megawidgets. The documentation supplied with Pmw describes the process of coding a megawidget. This description is an adaptation of that material.

4.4.1 Description of the megawidget

This widget will implement a simple gauge which tracks an integer value supplied by a `Scale` widget, which selects a number from a range. The gauge indicates the setting as a percentage of the range. The completed megawidget will look like the one shown in figure 4.52.

The scale widget will be a component of the megawidget since the range may be set by the programmer; the size and color of the gauge may similarly be changed, as appropriate for the application, so we make this a component, too.

Figure 4.52 Gauge widget

4.4.2 Options

In addition to the options for the scale and gauge components, we will need to define some options for the megawidget. First, we define min and max to allow the programmer the range supported by the widget. Secondly, we define fill and size to control the color and size of the gauge. Lastly, we define value to allow us to set the initial value of the megawidget.

4.4.3 Creating the megawidget class

Pmw megawidgets inherit from either Pmw.MegaWidget, Pmw.MegaToplevel or Pmw.Dialog. The gauge widget is intended to be used within other code widgets so it inherits from Pmw.MegaWidget. Here is the code for the megawidget.

pmw_megawindget.py

```
from Tkinter import *
import Pmw

class Gauge(Pmw.MegaWidget):
    def __init__(self, parent=None, **kw):
        # Define the options for the megawidget
        optiondefs = (
                ('min',        0,        Pmw.INITOPT),
                ('max',        100,      Pmw.INITOPT),
                ('fill',       'red',    None),
                ('size',       30,       Pmw.INITOPT),
                ('value',      0,        None),
                ('showvalue',  1,        None),
                )

        self.defineoptions(kw, optiondefs)

        # Initialize the base class
        Pmw.MegaWidget.__init__(self, parent)

        interior = self.interior()

        # Create the gauge component
        self.gauge = self.createcomponent('gauge',
                    (), None,
                    Frame, (interior,),
                    borderwidth=0)
        self.canvas = Canvas(self.gauge,
                width=self['size'], height=self['size'],
                background=interior.cget('background'))
        self.canvas.pack(side=TOP, expand=1, fill=BOTH)
        self.gauge.grid()

        # Create the scale component
        self.scale = self.createcomponent('scale',
                    (), None,
                    Scale, (interior,),
                    command=self._setGauge,
                    length=200,
```

❶ **❷** **❸** **❹** **❺**

```
                             from_ = self['min'],
                             to    = self['max'],
                             showvalue=self['showvalue'])
              self.scale.grid()

              value=self['value']
              if value is not None:
                  self.scale.set(value)

              # Check keywords and initialize options
              self.initialiseoptions(Gauge)

      def _setGauge(self, value):
          self.canvas.delete('gauge')
          ival = self.scale.get()
          ticks = self['max'] - self['min']
          arc = (360.0/ticks) * ival
          xy = 3,3,self['size'],self['size']
          start = 90-arc
          if start < 0:
              start = 360 + start
          self.canvas.create_arc(xy, start=start, extent=arc-.001,
                          fill=self['fill'], tags=('gauge',))

Pmw.forwardmethods(Gauge, Scale, 'scale')

root = Tk()
root.option_readfile('optionDB')
root.title('Gauge')
Pmw.initialise()

g1 = Gauge(root, fill='red', value=56, min=0, max=255)
g1.pack(side=LEFT, padx=1, pady=10)

g2 = Gauge(root, fill='green', value=60, min=0, max=255)
g2.pack(side=LEFT, padx=1, pady=10)

g3 = Gauge(root, fill='blue', value=36, min=0, max=255)
g3.pack(side=LEFT, padx=1, pady=10)

root.mainloop()
```

⑤ ⑥ ⑦

Code comments

❶ Options for the megawidget are specified by a three-element sequence of the option name, default value and a final argument. The final argument can be either a callback function, Pmw.INITOPT or None. If it is Pmw.INITOPT then the option may only be provided as an initialization option and it cannot be set by calling configure. Calling self.defineoptions includes keyword arguments passed in the widget's constructor. These values may override any default values.

❷ Having set the options we call the constructor of the base class, passing the parent widget as the single argument.

❸ By convention, Pmw defines an interior attribute which is the container for components.

④ We then create the gauge's indicator, which is going to be drawn on a `canvas` contained in a `frame`. The `createcomponent` method has five standard arguments (name, `aliases`, `group`, `class` and arguments to the constructor) followed by any number of keyword arguments.

⑤ Then, we construct the scale component in a similar manner.

⑥ Having completed the constructor, we first call `initialiseoptions` to check that all of the keyword arguments we supplied have been used. It then calls any option callbacks that have been defined.

⑦ Once the megawidget's class has been defined we call the `Pmw.forwardmethods` method to direct any method calls from other widgets to the scale component.

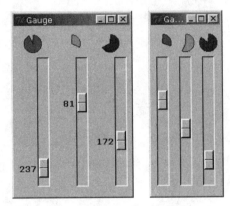

Figure 4.53 Using the gauge megawidget as a color mixer

Figure 4.53 illustrates a possible application of the gauge megawidget as a color mixer. The widget may be reconfigured to show or hide the current value of each slider. It is an easy task to add more options to the widget.

C H A P T E R   5

Screen layout

GUI layout is an often-misunderstood area; a programmer could conceivably waste a lot of time on it. In this chapter, the three geometry managers, Pack, Grid and Place are covered in detail. Some advanced topics, including approaches to variable-size windows and the attendant problems of maintaining visually attractive and effective interfaces, will be presented.

5.1 Introduction to layout

Geometry managers are responsible for controlling the size and position of widgets on the screen. In Motif, widget placement is handled by one of several manager widgets. One example is the Constraint Widget class which includes the XmForm widget. Here, layout is controlled by attaching the widget by one, or more, of the top, bottom, left or right sides to adjacent widgets and containers. By choosing the appropriate combinations of attachments, the programmer can control a number of behaviors which determine how the widget will appear when the window is grown or shrunk.

Tk provides a flexible approach to laying out widgets on a screen. X defines several manager class widgets but in Tk, three geometry managers may be used. In fact, it is possible to use the managers with each other (although there are some rather important rules about how one goes about this). Tk achieves this flexibility by exploiting the X behavior that says widget geometry is determined by the geometry managers and *not* by the widgets themselves. Like X, if you do not manage the widget, it will not be drawn on the screen, although it will exist in memory.

Geometry managers available to Tkinter are these: the Packer, which is the most commonly used manager; the Grid, which is a fairly recent addition to Tk; the Placer, which has the least popularity, but provides the greatest level of control in placing widgets. You will see examples of all three geometry managers throughout the book. The geometry managers are available on all architectures supported by Tkinter, so it is not necessary to know anything about the implementation of the architecture-dependent toolkits.

5.1.1 Geometry management

Geometry management is a quite complex topic, because a lot of negotiation goes on between widgets, their containers, windows and the supporting window manager. The aim is to lay out one or more *slave* widgets as subordinates of a *master* widget (some programmers prefer to refer to *child* widgets and *parents*). *Master* widgets are usually containers such as a `Frame` or a `Canvas`, but most widgets can act as masters. For example, place a button at the bottom of a frame. As well as simply locating slaves within masters, we want to control the behavior of the widget as more widgets are added or when the window is shrunk or grown.

The negotiation process begins with each slave widget requesting width and height adequate to display its contents. This depends on a number of factors. A button, for example, calculates its required size from the length of text displayed as the label and the selected font size and weight.

Next, the master widget, along with its geometry manager, determines the space available to satisfy the requested dimensions of the slaves. The available space may be more or less than the requested space, resulting in squeezing, stretching or overlapping of the widgets, depending on which geometry manager is being employed.

Next, depending on the design of the window, space within a master's *master* must be apportioned between all *peer* containers. The results depend on the geometry manager of the peer widgets.

Finally, there is negotiation between the toplevel widget (normally the toplevel shell) and the window manager. At the end of negotiations the available dimensions are used to determine the final size and location in which to draw the widgets. In some cases there may not be enough space to display all of the widgets and they may not be realized at all. Even after this negotiation has completed when a window is initialized, it starts again if any of the widgets change configuration (for example, if the text on a button changes) or if the user resizes the window. Fortunately, it is a lot easier to use the geometry managers than it is to discuss them!

A number of common schemes may be applied when a screen is designed. One of the properties of the Packer and to a lesser extent the Grid, is that it is possible to allow the geometry manager to determine the final size of a window. This is useful when a window is created dynamically and it is difficult to predict the population of widgets. Using this approach, the window changes size as widgets are added or removed from the display. Alternatively, the designer might use the Placer on a fixed-size window. It really depends on the effect that is wanted.

Let's start by looking at the Packer, which is the most commonly used manager.

5.2 Packer

The Packer positions slave widgets in the master by adding them one at a time from the outside edges to the center of the window. The Packer is used to manage rows, columns and combinations of the two. However, some additional planning may have to be done to get the desired effect.

The Packer works by maintaining a list of slaves, or the *packing list*, which is kept in the order that the slaves were originally presented to the Packer. Take a look at figure 5.1 (this figure is modeled after John Ousterhout's description of the Packer).

Figure 5.1(1) shows the space available for placing widgets. This might be within a frame or the space remaining after placing other widgets. The Packer allocates a parcel for the next slave to be processed by slicing off a section of the available space. Which side is allocated is determined by the options supplied with the pack request; in this example, the side=LEFT and fill=Y options have been specified. The actual size allocated by the Packer is determined by a number of factors. Certainly the size of the slave is a starting point, but the available space and any optional padding requested by the slave must be taken into account. The allocated parcel is shown in figure 5.1(2).

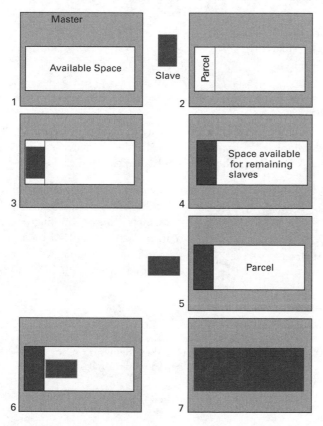

Figure 5.1 Packer operation

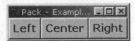

Figure 5.2 Pack geometry manager

Next, the slave is positioned within the parcel. If the available space results in a smaller parcel than the size of the slave, it may be squeezed or cropped, depending on the requested options. In this example, the slave is smaller than the available space and its height is increased to fill the available parcel. Figure 5.1(4) shows the available space for more slaves. In figure 5.1(5) we pack another slave with side=LEFT and fill=BOTH options. Again, the available parcel is larger than the size of the slave (figure 5.1(6)) so the widget is grown to fill the available space. The effect is shown in figure 5.1(7).

Here is a simple example of using the pack method, shown in figure 5.2:

Example_5_1.py

```python
from Tkinter import *

class App:
  def __init__(self, master):
      Button(master, text='Left').pack(side=LEFT)
      Button(master, text='Center').pack(side=LEFT)
      Button(master, text='Right').pack(side=LEFT)

root = Tk()
root.option_add('*font', ('verdana', 12, 'bold'))
root.title("Pack - Example 1")
display = App(root)
root.mainloop()
```

❶

Code comments

❶ The side=LEFT argument tells the Packer to start locating the widgets in the packing list from the left-hand side of the container. In this case the container is the default Toplevel shell created by the Tk initializer. The shell shrinks or expands to enclose the packed widgets.

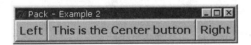

Figure 5.3 Packer accommodates requested widget sizes

Enclosing the widgets in a frame has no effect on the shrink-wrap effect of the Packer. In this example (shown in figure 5.3), we have increased the length of the text in the middle button and the frame is simply stretched to the requested size.

Example_5_2.py

```python
fm = Frame(master)
Button(fm, text='Left').pack(side=LEFT)
Button(fm, text='This is the Center button').pack(side=LEFT)
Button(fm, text='Right').pack(side=LEFT)
fm.pack()
```

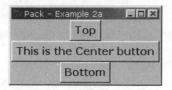

Figure 5.4 Packing from the top side

Packing from the top of the frame generates the result shown in figure 5.4. Note that the Packer centers the widgets in the available space since no further options are supplied and since the window is stretched to fit the widest widget.

```
Button(fm, text='Top').pack(side=TOP)
Button(fm, text='This is the Center button').pack(side=TOP)
Button(fm, text='Bottom').pack(side=TOP)
```

**Figure 5.5
Combining sides**

Combining `side` options in the Packer list may achieve the desired effect (although more often than not you'll end up with an effect you did not plan on!). Figure 5.5 illustrates how unusual layouts may be induced.

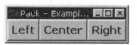

Figure 5.6 Effect of changing frame size

In all of these examples we have seen that the Packer negotiates the overall size of containers to fit the required space. If you want to control the size of the container, you will have to use *geometry* options, because attempting to change the `Frame` size (see example_5_4.py) has no effect as shown in figure 5.6.

Example_5_4.py

```
fm = Frame(master, width=300, height=200)
Button(fm, text='Left').pack(side=LEFT)
```

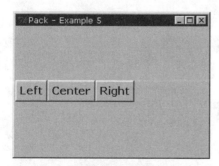

Figure 5.7 Assigning the geometry of the Toplevel shell

Sizing windows is often a problem when programmers start to work with Tkinter (and most other toolkits, for that matter) and it can be frustrating when there is no response as `width` and `height` options are added to widget specifications.

To set the size of the window, we have to make use of the `wm.geometry` option. Figure 5.7 shows the effect of changing the geometry for the root window.

Example_5_5.py

```
master.geometry("300x200")
```

5.2.1 Using the expand option

The expand option controls whether the Packer expands the widget when the window is resized. All the previous examples have accepted the default of expand=NO. Essentially, if expand is true, the widget *may* expand to fill the available space within its parcel; whether it does expand is controlled by the fill option (see "Using the fill option" on page 82).

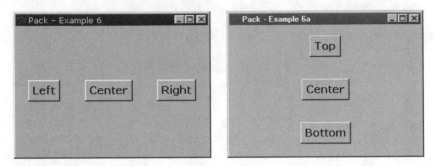

Figure 5.8 Expand without fill options

Example_5_6.py

```
Button(fm, text='Left').pack(side=LEFT, expand=YES)
Button(fm, text='Center').pack(side=LEFT, expand=YES)
Button(fm, text='Right').pack(side=LEFT, expand=YES)
```

Figure 5.8 shows the effect of setting expand to true (YES) without using the fill option (see Example_5_6.py). The vertical orientation in the second screen is similar to side=TOP (see Example_5_2a.py).

5.2.2 Using the fill option

Example_5_7.py illustrates the effect of combining fill and expand options; the output is shown in figure 5.9(1)

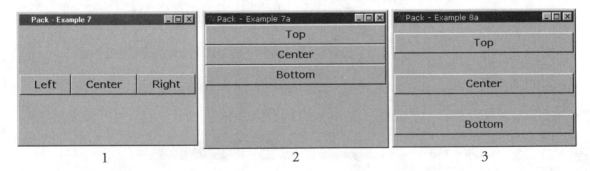

Figure 5.9 Using the fill option

CHAPTER 5   SCREEN LAYOUT

```
Button(fm, text='Left').pack(side=LEFT, fill=X, expand=YES)
Button(fm, text='Center').pack(side=LEFT, fill=X, expand=YES)
Button(fm, text='Right').pack(side=LEFT, fill=X, expand=YES)
```

If the fill option *alone* is used in Example_5_7.py, you will obtain a display similar to figure 5.9(2). By using fill and expand we see the effect shown in figure 5.9(3).

Varying the combination of fill and expand options may be used for different effects at different times. If you mix expand options, such as in example_5_8.py, you can allow some of the widgets to react to the resizing of the window while others remain a constant size. Figure 5.10 illustrates the effect of stretching and squeezing the screen.

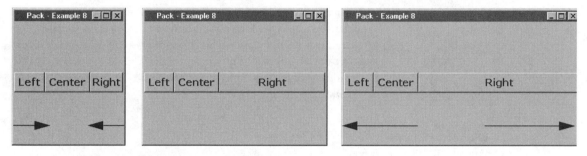

Figure 5.10 Allowing widgets to expand and fill independently

```
Button(fm, text='Left').pack(side=LEFT, fill=X, expand=NO)
Button(fm, text='Center').pack(side=LEFT, fill=X, expand=NO)
Button(fm, text='Right').pack(side=LEFT, fill=X, expand=YES)
```

Using fill=BOTH allows the widget to use all of its parcel. However, it might create some rather ugly effects, as shown in figure 5.11. On the other hand, this behavior may be exactly what is needed for your GUI.

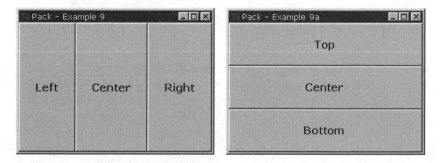

Figure 5.11 Using fill=BOTH

5.2.3 Using the padx and pady options

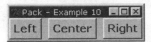

Figure 5.12 Using padx to create extra space

The `padx` and `pady` options allow the widget to be packed with additional space around it. Figure 5.12 shows the effect of adding `padx=10` to the pack request for the center button. Padding is applied to the specified left/right or top/bottom sides for `padx` and `pady` respectively. This may not achieve the effect you want, since if you place two widgets side by side, each with a `padx=10`, there will be 20 pixels between the two widgets and 10 pixels to the left and right of the pair. This can result in some unusual spacing.

5.2.4 Using the anchor option

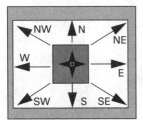

Figure 5.13 Anchoring a widget within the available space

The `anchor` option is used to determine where a widget will be placed within its parcel when the available space is larger than the size requested and none or one `fill` direction is specified. Figure 5.13 illustrates how a widget would be packed if an anchor is supplied. The option `anchor=CENTER` positions the widget at the center of the parcel. Figure 5.14 shows how this looks in practice.

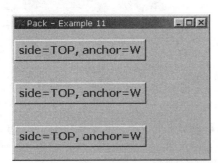
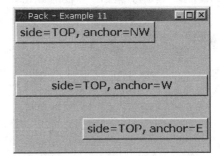

Figure 5.14 Using the anchor option to place widgets

5.2.5 Using hierarchical packing

While it is relatively easy to use the Packer to lay out simple screens, it is usually necessary to apply a hierarchical approach and employ a design which packs groups of widgets within frames and then packs these frames either alongside one other or inside other frames. This allows much more control over the layout, particularly if there is a need to fill and expand the widgets.

Figure 5.15 illustrates the result of attempting to lay out two columns of widgets. At first glance, the code appears to work, but it does not create the desired layout. Once you have packed a slave using `side=TOP`, the remaining space is below the slave, so you cannot pack alongside existing parcels.

Example_5_12.py

```
fm = Frame(master)
Button(fm, text='Top').pack(side=TOP, anchor=W, fill=X, expand=YES)
Button(fm, text='Center').pack(side=TOP, anchor=W, fill=X, expand=YES)
Button(fm, text='Bottom').pack(side=TOP, anchor=W, fill=X, expand=YES)
Button(fm, text='Left').pack(side=LEFT)
Button(fm, text='This is the Center button').pack(side=LEFT)
Button(fm, text='Right').pack(side=LEFT)
fm.pack()
```

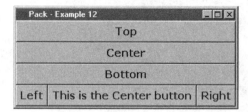

Figure 5.15 Abusing the Packer

All we have to do is to pack the two columns of widgets in separate frames and then pack the frames side by side. Here is the modified code:

Example_5_13.py

```
fm = Frame(master)
Button(fm, text='Top').pack(side=TOP, anchor=W, fill=X, expand=YES)
Button(fm, text='Center').pack(side=TOP, anchor=W, fill=X, expand=YES)
Button(fm, text='Bottom').pack(side=TOP, anchor=W, fill=X, expand=YES)
fm.pack(side=LEFT)
fm2 = Frame(master)
Button(fm2, text='Left').pack(side=LEFT)
Button(fm2, text='This is the Center button').pack(side=LEFT)
Button(fm2, text='Right').pack(side=LEFT)
fm2.pack(side=LEFT, padx=10)
```

Figure 5.16 shows the effect achieved by running Example_5_13.py.

This is an important technique which will be seen in several examples throughout the book. For an example which uses several embedded frames, take a look at Examples/chapter17/ Example_16_9.py, which is available online.

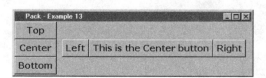

Figure 5.16 Hierarchical packing

5.3 Grid

Many programmers consider the Grid geometry manager the easiest manager to use. Personally, I don't completely agree, but you will be the final judge. Take a look at figure 5.17. This is a fairly complex layout task to support an image editor which uses a "by example" motif. Laying this out using the Packer requires a hierarchical approach with several nested Frames to enclose the target widgets. It also requires careful calculation of padding and other factors to achieve the final layout. It is much easier using the Grid.

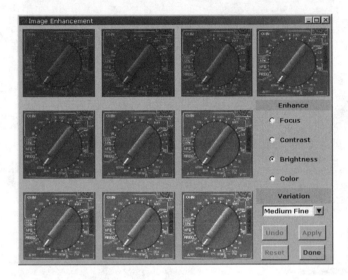

Figure 5.17 An image enhancer using Grid geometry management

Figure 5.18 A dialog laid out using Grid

Before we tackle laying out the image editor, let's take a look at a simpler example. We'll create a dialog containing three labels with three entry fields, along with OK and Cancel buttons. The fields need to line up neatly (the example is a change-password dialog). Figure 5.18 shows what the Grid manager does for us. The code is quite simple, but I have removed some less-important lines for clarity:

Example_5_14.py

```
class GetPassword(Dialog):
    def body(self, master):
        self.title("Enter New Password")

        Label(master, text='Old Password:').grid(row=0, sticky=W)          ❶
        Label(master, text='New Password:').grid(row=1, sticky=W)
        Label(master, text='Enter New Password Again:').grid(row=2, sticky=W)
```

```
self.oldpw    = Entry(master, width = 16, show='*')
self.newpw1   = Entry(master, width = 16, show='*')      ❷
self.newpw2   = Entry(master, width = 16, show='*')

self.oldpw.grid(row=0, column=1, sticky=W)
self.newpw1.grid(row=1, column=1, sticky=W)             ❸
self.newpw2.grid(row=2, column=1, sticky=W)
```

Code comments

❶ First, we create the labels. Since we do not need to preserve a reference to the label, we can apply the grid method directly. We specify the row number but allow the column to default (in this case to column 0). The sticky attribute determines where the widget will be attached within its cell in the grid. The sticky attribute is similar to a combination of the anchor and expand options of the Packer and it makes the widget look like a packed widget with an anchor=W option.

❷ We *do* need a reference to the entry fields, so we create them separately.

❸ Finally, we add the entry fields to the grid, specifying both row and column.

Let's go back to the image editor example. If you plan the layout for the fields in a grid it is easy to see what needs to be done to generate the screen. Look at figure 5.19 to see how the areas are to be gridded. The important feature to note is that we need to span both rows and columns to set aside the space for each of the components. You may find it convenient to sketch out designs for complex grids before committing them to code. Here is the code for the image editor. I have removed some of the code, since I really want to focus on the layout and not the operation of the application. The full source code for this example is available online.

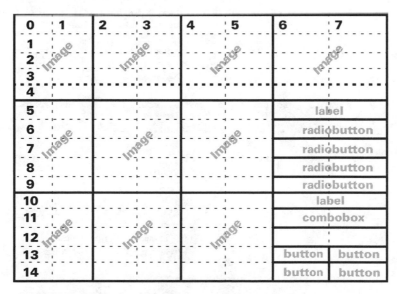

Figure 5.19 Designing the layout for a gridded display

imageEditor.py

```
from Tkinter import *
import sys, Pmw, Image, ImageTk, ImageEnhance                    ❶

class Enhancer:
    def __init__(self, master=None, imgfile=None):
        self.master = master
        self.masterImg = Image.open(imgfile)                     ❷
        self.masterImg.thumbnail((150, 150))

        self.images = [None]*9
        self.imgs   = [None]*9
        for i in range(9):                                       ❸
            image = self.masterImg.copy()
            self.images[i] = image
            self.imgs[i] = ImageTk.PhotoImage(self.images[i].mode,
                                         self.images[i].size)

        i = 0
        for r in range(3):
            for c in range(3):
                lbl = Label(master, image=self.imgs[i])          ❹
                lbl.grid(row=r*5, column=c*2,
                    rowspan=5, columnspan=2,sticky=NSEW,
                    padx=5, pady=5)
                i = i + 1

        self.original = ImageTk.PhotoImage(self.masterImg)
        Label(master, image=self.original).grid(row=0, column=6,
                            rowspan=5, columnspan=2)
                                                                 ❺
        Label(master, text='Enhance', bg='gray70').grid(row=5, column=6,
                            columnspan=2, sticky=NSEW)

        self.radio = Pmw.RadioSelect(master, labelpos = None,    ❻
                    buttontype = 'radiobutton', orient = 'vertical',
                    command = self.selectFunc)

        self.radio.grid(row=6, column=6, rowspan=4, columnspan=2)

# --- Code Removed --------------------------------------------------

        Label(master, text='Variation',
            bg='gray70').grid(row=10, column=6,
                    columnspan=2, sticky=NSWE)

        self.variation=Pmw.ComboBox(master, history=0, entry_width=11,
                    selectioncommand = self.setVariation,
                    scrolledlist_items=('Fine','Medium Fine','Medium',
                            'Medium Course','Course'))

        self.variation.selectitem('Medium')

        self.variation.grid(row=11, column=6, columnspan=2)
```

```
                   Button(master, text='Undo',
                          state='disabled').grid(row=13, column=6)

                   Button(master, text='Apply',
                          state='disabled').grid(row=13, column=7)
                   Button(master, text='Reset',
                          state='disabled').grid(row=14, column=6)
                   Button(master, text='Done',
                          command=self.exit).grid(row=14, column=7)

       # --- Code Removed --------------------------------------------------

       root = Tk()
       root.option_add('*font', ('verdana', 10, 'bold'))
       root.title('Image Enhancement')
       imgEnh = Enhancer(root, sys.argv[1])
       root.mainloop()
```

Code comments

1 This example uses the Python Imaging Library (PIL) to create, display, and enhance images. See "Python Imaging Library (PIL)" on page 626 for references to documentation supporting this useful library of image methods.

2 Although it's not important in illustrating the grid manager, I left some of the PIL code in place to demonstrate how it facilitates handling images. Here, in the constructor, we open the master image and create a thumbnail within the bounds specified. PIL scales the image appropriately.

```
       self.masterImg = Image.open(imgfile)
       self.masterImg.thumbnail((150, 150))
```

3 Next we create a copy of the image and create a Tkinter PhotoImage placeholder for each of the images in the 3x3 grid.

4 Inside a double `for` loop we create a `Label` and place it in the appropriate cell in the grid, adding rowspan and columnspan options.

```
       lbl = Label(master, image=self.imgs[i])
       lbl.grid(row=r*5, column=c*2,
                rowspan=5, columnspan=2,sticky=NSEW, padx=5,pady=5)
```

Note that in this case the `sticky` option attaches the images to all sides of the grid so that the grid is sized to constrain the image. This means that the widget will stretch and shrink as the overall window size is modified.

5 Similarly, we grid a label with a different background, using the `sticky` option to fill all of the available cell.

```
       Label(master, text='Enhance', bg='gray70').grid(row=5, column=6,
                                      columnspan=2, sticky=NSEW)
```

6 The Pmw `RadioSelect` widget is placed in the appropriate cell with appropriate spans:

```
       self.radio = Pmw.RadioSelect(master, labelpos = None,
                      buttontype = 'radiobutton', orient = 'vertical',
                      command = self.selectFunc)

       self.radio.grid(row=6, column=6, rowspan=4, columnspan=2)
```

7 Finally, we place the `Button` widgets in their allocated cells.

You have already seen one example of the ImageEditor in use (figure 5.17). The real advantage of the grid geometry manager becomes apparent when you run the application with another image with a different aspect. Figure 5.20 shows this well; the grid adjusts perfectly to the image. Creating a similar effect using the Packer would require greater effort.

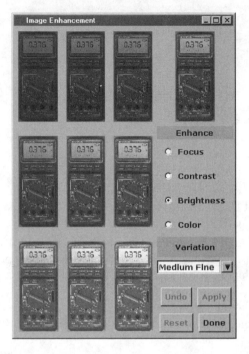

Figure 5.20 ImageEditor—scales for image size

5.4 *Placer*

Figure 5.21 A simple scrapbook tool

The Placer geometry manager is the simplest of the available managers in Tkinter. It is considered difficult to use by some programmers, because it allows precise positioning of widgets within, or relative to, a window. You will find quite a few examples of its use in this book so I could take advantage of this precision. Look ahead to figure 9.5 on page 213 to see an example of a GUI that would be fairly difficult to implement using pack or grid. Because we will see so many examples, I am only going to present two simple examples here.

Let's start by creating the simple scrapbook window shown in figure 5.21. Its function is to display some images, which are scaled to fit the window. The images are selected by clicking on the numbered buttons. It is quite easy to build a little application like this; again, we use PIL to provide support for images.

It would be possible to use pack to lay out the window (and, of course, grid would work if the image spanned most of the columns) but place provides some useful behavior when windows are *resized*. The Buttons in figure 5.21 are attached to *relative* positions, which means that they stay in the same relative position as the dimensions of the window change. You express relative positions as a real number with 0.0 representing *minimum* x or y and 1.0 representing *maximum* x or y. The minimum values for the axes are conventional for window coordinates with x0 on the left of the screen and y0 at the top of the screen. If you run scrapbook.py, test the effect of squeezing and stretching the window and you will notice how the buttons reposition. If you squeeze too much you will cause the buttons to collide, but somehow the effect using place is more acceptable than the clipping that occurs with pack. Here is the code for the scrapbook.

scrapbook.py

```
from Tkinter import *
import Image, ImageTk, os

class Scrapbook:
    def __init__(self, master=None):
        self.master = master
        self.frame = Frame(master, width=400, height=420, bg='gray50',
                    relief=RAISED, bd=4)

        self.lbl = Label(self.frame)                                    ❶
        self.lbl.place(relx=0.5, rely=0.48, anchor=CENTER)

        self.images = []                                                ❷
        images = os.listdir("images")

        xpos = 0.05
        for i in range(10):
            Button(self.frame, text='%d'%(i+1), bg='gray10',            ❸
              fg='white', command=lambda s=self, img=i: \
              s.getImg(img)).place(relx=xpos, rely=0.99, anchor=S)
            xpos = xpos + 0.08
            self.images.append(images[i])

        Button(self.frame, text='Done', command=self.exit,             ❹
          bg='red', fg='yellow').place(relx=0.99, rely=0.99, anchor=SE)
        self.frame.pack()
        self.getImg(0)

    def getImg(self, img):                                             ❺
        self.masterImg = Image.open(os.path.join("images",
                                    self.images[img]))
        self.masterImg.thumbnail((400, 400))
        self.img = ImageTk.PhotoImage(self.masterImg)
        self.lbl['image'] = self.img

    def exit(self):
        self.master.destroy()

root = Tk()
```

```
root.title('Scrapbook')
scrapbook = Scrapbook(root)
root.mainloop()
```

Code comments

1 We create the `Label` which will contain the image, placing it approximately in the center of the window and anchoring it at the center. Note that the relative placings are expressed as percentages of the width or height of the container.

```
self.lbl.place(relx=0.5, rely=0.48, anchor=CENTER)
```

2 We get a list of files from the `images` directory

3 `place` really lends itself to be used for *calculated* positioning. In the loop we create a `Button`, binding the index of the button to the `activate` callback and placing the button at the next available position.

4 We put one button at the bottom right of the screen to allow us to **quit** the scrapbook. Note that we anchor it at the `SE` corner. Also note that we `pack` the outer frame. It is quite common to pack a group of widgets placed within a container. The Packer does all the work of negotiating the space with the outer containers and the window manager.

5 `getImg` is the PIL code to load the image, create a thumbnail, and load it into the `Label`.

In addition to providing precise window placement, `place` also provides *rubber sheet* placement, which allows the programmer to specify the size and location of the slave window in terms of the dimensions of the master window. It is even possible to use a master window which is *not* the parent of the slave. This can be very useful if you want to track the dimensions of an arbitrary window. Unlike `pack` and `grid`, `place` allows you to position a window outside the master (or sibling) window. Figure 5.22 illustrates the use of a window to display some of an image's properties in a window above each of the images. As the size of the image changes, the information window scales to fit the width of the image.

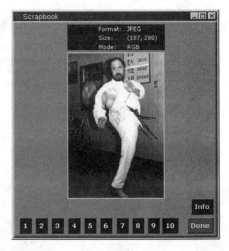

Figure 5.22 Adding a sibling window which tracks changes in attached window

The Placer has another important property: unlike the other Tkinter managers, it does not attempt to set the geometry of the master window. If you want to control the dimensions of container widgets, you must use widgets such as Frames or Canvases that have a config-ure option to allow you to control their sizes. Let's take a look at the code needed to implement the information window.

scrapbook2.py

```
from

Tkinter import *
import Image, ImageTk, os, string

class Scrapbook:
    def __init__(self, master=None):

# --- Code Removed ----------------------------------------------------

        Button(self.frame, text='Info', command=self.info,
          bg='blue', fg='yellow').place(relx=0.99, rely=0.90, anchor=SE)      ❶
        self.infoDisplayed = FALSE

    def getImg(self, img):

# --- Code Removed ----------------------------------------------------

        if self.infoDisplayed:
            self.info();self.info()                                           ❷

    def info(self):
        if self.infoDisplayed:
            self.fm.destroy()                                                 ❹
            self.infoDisplayed = FALSE
        else:
            self.fm = Frame(self.master, bg='gray10')                         ❸
            self.fm.place(in_=self.lbl, relx=0.5,                             ❺
                relwidth=1.0, height=50, anchor=S,
                rely=0.0, y=-4, bordermode='outside')
            ypos = 0.15
            for lattr in ['Format', 'Size', 'Mode']:
                Label(self.fm, text='%s:\t%s' % (lattr,
                    getattr(self.masterImg,
                        '%s' % string.lower(lattr))),
                    bg='gray10', fg='white',
                    font=('verdana', 8)).place(relx=0.3,                      ❻
                    rely= ypos, anchor=W)
                ypos = ypos + 0.35
            self.infoDisplayed = TRUE

# --- Code Removed ----------------------------------------------------
```

Code comments

1 We add a button to display the image information.

2 To force a refresh of the image info, we toggle the info display.

```
self.info();self.info()
```

3 The `info` method toggles the information display.

4 If the window is currently displayed, we destroy it.

5 Otherwise, we create a new window, placing it above the image and setting its width to match that of the image. We also add a negative increment to the *y* position to provide a little whitespace.

```
self.fm.place(in_=self.lbl, relx=0.5,
        relwidth=1.0, height=50, anchor=S,
        rely=0.0, y=-4, bordermode='outside')
```

6 The entries in the information window are placed programmatically.

5.5 *Summary*

Mastering the geometry managers is an important step in developing the ability to produce attractive and effective GUIs. When starting out with Tkinter, most readers will find `grid` and `pack` to be easy to use and capable of producing the best results when a window is resized. For very precise placement of widgets, `place` is a better choice. However, this does take quite a bit more effort.

You will see many examples of using the three managers throughout the book. Remember that it is often appropriate to combine geometry managers within a single window. If you do, you must be careful to follow some rules; if things are just not working out, then you have probably broken one of those rules!

C H A P T E R   6

Events, bindings and callbacks

GUI applications rely heavily on events and binding callbacks to these events in order to attach functionality to widgets. I anticipate that many readers may have some familiarity with this topic. However, this may be a new area for some of you, so I will go into some detail to make sure that the subject has been fully covered. Advanced topics will be discussed, including dynamic callback handlers, data verification techniques and "smart" widgets.

6.1 Event-driven systems: a review

It quite possible to build complex GUI applications without knowing anything about the underlying event-mechanism, regardless of whether the application is running in a UNIX, Windows or Macintosh environment. However, it is usually easier to develop an application that behaves the way *you* want it to if you know how to request and handle events within your application.

Readers familiar with events and event handlers in X or with Windows messages might wish to skip ahead to look at "Tkinter events" on page 98, since this information is specific to Tkinter.

6.1.1   What are events?

Events are notifications (*messages* in Windows parlance) sent by the windowing system (the X-server for X, for example) to the client code. They indicate that something has occurred or that the state of some controlled object has changed, either because of user input or because your code has made a request which causes the server to make a change.

In general, applications do not receive events automatically. However, you may not be aware of the events that have been requested by your programs indirectly, or the requests that widgets have made. For example, you may specify a *command callback* to be called when a button is pressed; the widget binds an `activate` event to the callback. It is also possible to request notification of an event that is normally handled elsewhere. Doing this allows your application to change the behavior of widgets and windows generally; this can be a good thing but it can also wreck the behavior of complex systems, so it needs to be used with care.

All events are placed in an event queue. Events are usually removed by a function called from the application's `mainloop`. Generally, you will use Tkinter's mainloop but it is possible for you to supply a specialized mainloop if you have special needs (such as a threaded application which needs to manage internal locks in a way which makes it impossible to use the standard scheme).

Tkinter provides implementation-independent access to events so that you do not need to know too much about the underlying event handlers and filters. For example, to detect when the cursor enters a frame, try the following short example:

Example_6_1.py

```
from Tkinter import *
root = Tk()

def enter(event):
   print 'Entered Frame: x=%d, y=%d' % (event.x, event.y)

frame = Frame(root, width=150, height=150)
frame.bind('<Any-Enter>', enter)            # Bind event
frame.pack()

root.mainloop()
```

The `bind` method of `Frame` is used to bind the `enter` callback to an `Any-Enter` event. Whenever the cursor crosses the frame boundary from the outside to the inside, the message will be printed.

Note   This example introduces an interesting issue. Depending on the speed with which the cursor enters the frame, you will observe that the x and y coordinates show some variability. This is because the x and y values are determined at the time that the event is processed by the event loop not at the time the actual event occurs.

6.1.2   Event propagation

Events occur relative to a *window*, which is usually described as the *source window* of the event. If no client has registered for a particular event for the source window, the event is propagated up the window hierarchy until it either finds a window that a client has registered with, it finds a window that prohibits event propagation or it reaches the root window. If it does reach the root window, the event is ignored.

Only device events that occur as a result of a key, pointer motion or mouse click are propagated. Other events, such as exposure and configuration events, have to be registered for explicitly.

6.1.3   Event types

Events are grouped into several categories depending on X event masks. Tk maps Windows events to the same masks when running on a Windows architecture. The event masks recognized by Tk (and therefore Tkinter) are shown in table 6.1.

Table 6.1   Event masks used to group X events

NoEventMask	StructureNotifyMask	Button3MotionMask
KeyReleaseMask	SubstructureNotifyMask	Button5MotionMask
ButtonReleaseMask	FocusChangeMask	KeymapStateMask
LeaveWindowMask	ColormapChangeMask	VisibilityChangeMask
PointerMotionHintMask	KeyPressMask	ResizeRedirectMask
Button2MotionMask	ButtonPressMask	SubstructureRedirectMask
Button4MotionMask	EnterWindowMask	PropertyChangeMask
ButtonMotionMask	PointerMotionMask	OwnerGrabButtonMask
ExposureMask	Button1MotionMask	

Keyboard events

Whenever a key is pressed, a KeyPress event is generated, and whenever a key is released, a KeyRelease event is generated. Modifier keys, such as SHIFT and CONTROL, generate keyboard events.

Pointer events

If buttons on the mouse are pressed or if the mouse is moved, ButtonPress, ButtonRelease and MotionNotify events are generated. The window associated with the event is the lowest window in the hierarchy unless a pointer grab exists, in that case, the window that initiated the grab will be identified. Like keyboard events, modifier keys may be combined with pointer events.

Crossing events

Whenever the pointer enters or leaves a window boundary, an EnterNotify or LeaveNotify event is generated. It does not matter whether the crossing was a result of moving the pointer or because of a change in the stacking order of the windows. For example, if a window containing the pointer is lowered behind another window, and the pointer now is in the top window, the lowered window receives a `LeaveNotify` event and the top window receives an `EnterNotify` event.

Focus events

The window which receives keyboard events is known as the *focus window*. `FocusIn` and `FocusOut` events are generated whenever the focus window changes. Handling focus events is a little more tricky than handling pointer events because the pointer does not necessarily have to be in the window that is receiving focus events. You do not usually have to handle focus events yourself, because setting `takefocus` to `true` in the widgets allows you to move focus between the widgets by pressing the TAB key.

Exposure events

Whenever a window or a part of a window becomes visible, an `Exposure` event is generated. You will not typically be managing `exposure` events in Tkinter GUIs, but you do have the ability to receive these events if you have some very specialized drawing to support.

Configuration events

When a window's size, position or border changes, `ConfigureNotify` events are generated. A `ConfigureNotify` event will be created whenever the stacking order of the windows changes. Other types of configuration events include `Gravity`, `Map/Unmap`, `Reparent` and `Visibility`.

Colormap events

If a new colormap is installed, a `ColormapNotify` event is generated. This may be used by your application to prevent the annoying colormap flashing which can occur when another application installs a colormap. However, most applications do not control their colormaps directly.

6.2 Tkinter events

In general, handling events in Tkinter applications is considerably easier than doing the same in X/Motif, Win32 or QuickDraw. Tkinter provides convenient methods to bind callbacks to specific events.

6.2.1 Events

We express events as strings, using the following format:

```
<modifier-type-qualifier>
```

- `modifier` is optional and may be repeated, separated by spaces or a dash.
- `type` is optional if there is a `qualifier`.
- `qualifier` is either a *button-option* or a `keysym` and is optional if `type` is present.

Many events can be described using just `type`, so the `modifier` and `qualifier` may be left out. The `type` defines the class of event that is to be bound (in X terms it defines the *event mask*). Many events may be entered in a shorthand form. For example, `<Key-a>`, `<Key-Press-a>`, and a are all acceptable event identifiers for pressing a lower-case a.

Here are some of the more commonly used events. You will find a complete list of events and keysyms in "Events and keysyms" on page 617

Event	Alt. 1	Alt2	Mod	Type	Qualifier	Action to generate event
`<Any-Enter>`			Any	Enter		Enter event regardless of mode.
`<Button-1>`	ButtonPress-1	1		Button	1	Left mouse button click.
`<Button-2>`	ButtonPress-2	2		ButtonPress	1	Middle mouse button click.
`<B2-Motion>`			B1	Motion		Mouse movement with middle mouse button down.
`<ButtonRelease-3>`				ButtonRelease	3	Release third mouse button 3.
`<Configure>`				Configure		Size stacking or position has changed.
`<Control-Insert>`			Control		Insert	Press INSERT key with CONTROL key down.
`<Control-Shift-F3>`			Control-Shift		F3	Press CONTROL-SHIFT and F3 keys simultaneously.
`<Destroy>`				Destroy		Window is being destroyed.
`<Double-Button-1>`			Double	Button	1	Double-click first mouse button 1.
`<Enter>`				Enter		Cursor enters window.
`<Expose>`				Expose		Window fully or partially exposed.
`<FocusIn>`				FocusIn		Widget gains focus.
`<FocusOut>`				FocusOut		Widget loses focus.
`<KeyPress>`	Key			KeyPress		Any key has been pressed.
`<KeyRelease-backslash>`				KeyRelease	backslash	Backslash key has been released.
`<Leave>`				Leave		Cursor leaves window.
`<Map>`				Map		Window has been mapped.
`<Print>`					Print	PRINT key has been pressed.
z					z	Capital Z has been pressed.

Let's take a look at some example code that allows us to explore the event mechanism as it's supported by Tkinter.

Example_6_2.py

```
from Tkinter import *
import Pmw

eventDict = {
```

```
             '2': 'KeyPress', '3': 'KeyRelease', '4': 'ButtonPress',
             '5': 'ButtonRelease', '6': 'Motion', '7': 'Enter',
             '8': 'Leave', '9': 'FocusIn', '10': 'FocusOut',
             '12': 'Expose', '15': 'Visibility', '17': 'Destroy',
             '18': 'Unmap', '19': 'Map', '21': 'Reparent',
             '22': 'Configure', '24': 'Gravity', '26': 'Circulate',
             '28': 'Property', '32': 'Colormap','36': 'Activate',
             '37': 'Deactivate',
}

root = Tk()

def reportEvent(event):
    rpt = '\n\n%s' % (80*'=')
    rpt = '%s\nEvent: type=%s (%s)' %  (rpt, event.type,
                          eventDict.get(event.type, 'Unknown'))
    rpt = '%s\ntime=%s'    %  (rpt, event.time)
    rpt = '%s  widget=%s' %  (rpt, event.widget)
    rpt = '%s  x=%d, y=%d'%  (rpt, event.x, event.y)
    rpt = '%s  x_root=%d, y_root=%d' % (rpt, event.x_root, event.y_root)
    rpt = '%s  y_root=%d' %  (rpt, event.y_root)
    rpt = '%s\nserial=%s' %  (rpt, event.serial)
    rpt = '%s  num=%s' %  (rpt, event.num)
    rpt = '%s  height=%s' %  (rpt, event.height)
    rpt = '%s  width=%s' %  (rpt, event.width)
    rpt = '%s  keysym=%s' %  (rpt, event.keysym)
    rpt = '%s  ksNum=%s' %  (rpt, event.keysym_num)

    #### Some event types don't have these attributes
    try:
        rpt = '%s  focus=%s' % (rpt, event.focus)
    except:
        try:
            rpt = '%s  send=%s' % (rpt, event.send_event)
        except:
            pass

    text2.yview(END)
    text2.insert(END, rpt)

frame = Frame(root, takefocus=1, highlightthickness=2)
text  = Entry(frame, width=10, takefocus=1, highlightthickness=2)
text2 = Pmw.ScrolledText(frame)

for event in eventDict.values():
    frame.bind('<%s>' % event, reportEvent)
    text.bind('<%s>' % event, reportEvent)

text.pack()
text2.pack(fill=BOTH, expand=YES)
frame.pack()
text.focus_set()
root.mainloop()
```

Code comments

1 `eventDict` defines all of the event types that Tkinter (strictly Tk) recognizes. Not all of the event masks defined by X are directly available to Tkinter applications, so you will see that the enumerated event type values are sparse.

```
'12': 'Expose', '15': 'Visibility', '17': 'Destroy',
```

The dictionary is also used to look up the event-type name when the event is detected.

2 `reportEvent` is our event handler. It is responsible for formatting data about the event. The event type is retrieved from `eventDict`; if an unrecognized event occurs, we will type it as `Unknown`.

```
def reportEvent(event):
    rpt = '\n\n%s' % (80*'=')
    rpt = '%s\nEvent: type=%s (%s)' % (rpt, event.type,
                          eventDict.get(event.type, 'Unknown'))
```

3 Not all events supply `focus` and `send_event` attributes, so we handle `AttributeErrors` appropriately.

4 Finally, we bind each of the events to the `reportEvent` callback for the `Frame` and `Entry` widgets:

```
for event in eventDict.values():
    frame.bind('<%s>' % event, reportEvent)
    text.bind('<%s>' % event, reportEvent)
```

Figure 6.1 shows the result of running Example_6_2.py. The displayed events show the effect of typing SHIFT-M. You can see the `KeyPress` for the SHIFT key, and the `KeyPress` for the M key, followed by the corresponding `KeyRelease` events.

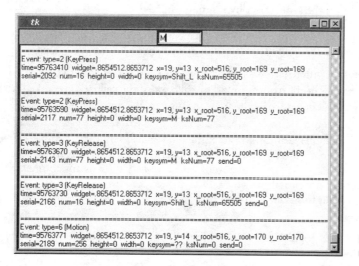

Figure 6.1 An event monitor

Note If you are new to handling events, you might find it useful to run Example_6_2.py to investigate the behavior of the system as you perform some simple tasks in the window. For example, holding the SHIFT key down creates a stream of events; moving the mouse creates a stream of motion events at an even greater frequency.

This may come as a surprise initially, since the events are normally invisible to the user (and to the programmer). It is important to be aware of this behavior and as you program to take account of how events will actually be generated. It is especially important to make sure that the callback does not do any intensive processing; otherwise, it is easy to cause severe performance problems.

6.3 *Callbacks*

Callbacks are simply functions that are called as the result of an event being generated. Handling arguments, however, can be problematic for beginning Tkinter programmers, and they can be a source of latent bugs, even for seasoned programmers.

The number of arguments depends on the type of event that is being processed and whether you bound a callback *directly* or *indirectly* to an event. Here is an example of an indirect binding:

```
btn = Button(frame, text='OK', command=buttonAction)
```

command is really a convenience function supplied by the Button widget which calls the buttonAction callback when the widget is activated. This is usually a result of a <Button-Press-1> event, but a <KeyPress-space> is also valid, if the widget has focus. However, be aware that many events have occurred as a result of moving and positioning the mouse before the button was activated.

We could get the same effect by binding directly:

```
btn.bind('<Button-1>', buttonAction)
btn.bind('<KeyPress-space>', buttonAction)
```

So what is the difference? Well, apart from the extra line of code to bind the events directly, the real difference is in the invocation of the callback. If the callback is invoked from the event, the event object will be passed as the first (in this case the only) argument of the callback.

Note Event handlers can be a source of latent bugs if you don't completely test your applications. If an event is bound (intentionally or erroneously) to a callback and the callback does not expect the event object to be passed as an argument, then the application could potentially crash. This is more likely to happen if the event rarely occurs or is difficult to simulate in testing.

If you want to reuse buttonAction and have it called in response to both direct and indirect events, you will have to write the callback so that it can accept variable arguments:

```
def buttonAction(event=None):
    if event:
        print 'event in: %s' % event.type
```

```
    else:
        print 'command in:'
```

Of course, this does increase complexity, particularly if the function already has arguments, since you will have to determine if the first argument is an event object or a regular argument.

6.4 Lambda expressions

Oh no! Not the *dreaded* lambda again!* Although lambda has been mentioned earlier in the book, and has been used extensively in examples, before we go on to the next section we must take another look at the use of `lambda`.

The term *lambda* originally came from Alonzo Church's *lambda calculus* and you will now find lambda used in several contexts—particularly in the functional programming disciplines. Lambda in Python is used to define an anonymous function which appears to be a statement to the interpreter. In this way you can put a single line of executable code where it would not normally be valid.

Take a look at this code fragment:

```
var   = IntVar()
value = 10
...
btn.bind('Button-1', (btn.flash(), var.set(value)))
```

A quick glance at the bolded line might not raise any alarms, but the line will fail at runtime. The intent was to flash the button when it was clicked and set a variable with some predetermined value. What is actually going to happen is that both of the calls will be called when the `bind` method executes. Later, when the button is clicked, we will not get the desired effect, since the callback list contains just the return values of the two method calls, in this case (`None`, `None`). Additionally, we would have missed the event object–which is always the first argument in the callback—and we could possibly have received a runtime error. Here is the correct way to bind this callback:

```
btn.bind('Button-1', lambda event, b=btn, v=var, i=value:
    (b.flash(), v.set(i)))
```

Notice the event argument (which is ignored in this code fragment).

6.4.1 Avoiding lambdas altogether

If you don't like lambda expressions, there are other ways of delaying the call to your function. Timothy R. Evans posted a suggestion to the Python news group which defines a command class to wrap the function.

```
class Command:
    def __init__(self, func, *args, **kw):
        self.func = func
        self.args = args
```

---

* "Cardinal Fang! Bring me the lambda!"

```
        self.kw = kw

    def __call__(self, *args, **kw):
        args = self.args + args
        kw.update(self.kw)
        apply(self.func, args, kw)
```

Then, you define the callback like this:

```
Button(text='label', command=Command(function, arg [, moreargs...] ))
```

The reference to the function and arguments (including keywords) that are passed to the Command class are stored by its constructor and then passed on to the function when the callback is activated. This format for defining the callbacks may be a little easier to read and maintain than the lambda expression. At least there are alternatives!

6.5 *Binding events and callbacks*

The examples so far have demonstrated how to bind an event handler to an instance of a widget so that its behavior on receiving an event will not be inherited by other instances of the widget. Tkinter provides the flexibility to bind at several levels:

1   At the *application* level, so that the same binding is available in all windows and widgets in the application, so long as one window in the application has focus.
2   At the *class* level, so that all instances of widgets have the same behavior, at least initially.
3   At the *shell* (Toplevel or *root*) level.
4   At the *instance* level, as noted already.

Binding events at the application and class level must be done carefully, since it is quite easy to create unexpected behavior in your application. In particular, indiscriminate binding at the class level may solve an immediate problem, but cause new problems when new functionality is added to the application.

Note   It is generally good practice to avoid creating highly nonstandard behavior in widgets or interfaces with which the user is familiar. For example, it is easy to create bindings which allow an entry field to fill in reverse (so typing **123** is displayed as **321**), but this is not typical entry behavior and it might be confusing to the user.

6.5.1   Bind methods

You will find more information on bind and unbind methods in "Common options" on page 425, so in this section, I will just illustrate bind methods in the context of the four binding levels.

Application level

Applications frequently use F1 to deliver help. Binding this keysym at the application level means that pressing F1, when any of the application's windows have focus, will bring up a help screen.

Class level

Binding at the class level allows you to make sure that classes behave uniformly across an application. In fact, Tkinter binds this way to provide standard bindings for widgets. You will probably use class binding if you implement new widgets, or you might use class binding to provide audio feedback for entry fields across an application, for example.

Toplevel window level

Binding a function at the root level allows an event to be generated if focus is in any part of a shell. This might be used to bind a print screen function, for example.

Instance level

We have already seen several examples of this, so we will not say any more at this stage.

The following hypothetical example illustrates all four of the binding modes together.

Example_6_3.py

```
from Tkinter import *
def displayHelp(event):

def displayHelp(event):
  print 'hlp', event.keysym                                    1

def sayKey(event):
  print 'say',event.keysym, event.char

def printWindow(event):
  print 'prt', event.keysym

def cursor(*args):
  print 'cursor'

def unbindThem(*args):                                      unbind all bindings
  root.unbind_all('<F1>')
  root.unbind_class('Entry', '<KeyPress>')                     2
  root.unbind('<Alt_L>')
  frame.unbind('<Control-Shift-Down>')
  print 'Gone...'

root = Tk()
frame = Frame(root, takefocus=1, highlightthickness=2)
text  = Entry(frame, width=10, takefocus=1, highlightthickness=2)

root.bind_all('<F1>', displayHelp)                                    3

text.bind_class('Entry', '<KeyPress>', lambda e, x=101: sayKey(e,x))  4
root.bind('<Alt_L>', printWindow)                    5

frame.bind('<Control-Shift-Down>' , cursor)             6

text.bind('<Control-Shift-Up>', unbindThem)
```

```
text.pack()
frame.pack()
text.focus_set()
root.mainloop()
```

___

Code comments

❶ First, the callbacks are defined. These are all simple examples and all but the last one take account of the event object being passed as the callback's argument, from which we extract the keysym of the key generating the event.

```
def displayHelp(event):
    print 'hlp', event.keysym
```

❷ Although the class-level binding was made with a method call to an `Entry` widget, `bind_class` is an inherited method, so any instance will work and `root.unbind_class` is quite acceptable. This is not true for an instance binding, which is local to the instance.

❸ We make an application-level binding:

```
root.bind_all('<F1>', displayHelp)
```

❹ In this class-level binding we use a lambda function to construct an argument list for the callback:

```
text.bind_class('Entry', '<KeyPress>', lambda e, x=101: sayKey(e,x))
```

❺ Here we make a toplevel binding for a print-screen callback:

```
root.bind('<Alt_L>', printWindow)
```

❻ Finally, we make instance bindings with double modifiers:

```
frame.bind('<Control-Shift-Down>', cursor)
text.bind('<Control-Shift-Up>', unbindThem)
```

___

Note Be prepared to handle multiple callbacks for events if you use combinations of the four binding levels that have overlapping bindings.

Tkinter selects the best binding at each level, starting with any instance bindings, then toplevel bindings, followed by any class bindings. Finally, application level bindings are selected. This allows you to override bindings at any level.

___

6.5.2 Handling multiple bindings

As I mentioned in the note above, you can bind events at each of the four binding events. However, because events are propagated, that might not result in the behavior that you intended.

For a simple example, suppose you want to override the behavior of a widget, and rather than have BACKSPACE remove the previous character, you want to insert \h into the widget. So you set up the binding like this:

```
text.bind('<BackSpace>', lambda e: dobackspace(e))
```

and define the callback like this:

```
def dobackspace(event):

    event.widget.insert(END, '\\h')
```

Unfortunately this doesn't work, because the event is bound at the application level. The widget still has a binding for BACKSPACE, so after the application level has been invoked and \h has been inserted into the widget, the event is propagated to the class level and the h is removed.

There is a simple solution: return "break" from the last event handler that you want to propagate events from and the superior levels don't get the event. So, the callback looks like this:

```
def dobackspace(event):

    event.widget.insert(END, '\\h')

    return "break"
```

6.6 Timers and background procedures

The `mainloop` supports callbacks which are not generated from events. The most important result of this is that it is easy to set up timers which call callbacks after a predetermined delay or whenever the GUI is idle. Here is a code snippet from an example later in the book:

```
if self.blink:
    self.frame.after(self.blinkrate * 1000, self.update)

def update(self):
  # Code removed
  self.canvas.update_idletasks()
  if self.blink:
      self.frame.after(self.blinkrate * 1000, self.update)
```

This code sets up to call `self.update` after `self.blinkrate * 1000` milliseconds. The callback does what it does and then sets up to call itself again (these timers are called once only—if you want them to repeat you must set them up again).

For more information on timers, see "Common options" on page 425.

6.7 Dynamic callback handlers

A single callback is frequently bound to an event for the duration of an application. However, there are many cases where we need to change the bindings to the widget to support application requirements. One example might be attaching a callback to remove reverse video (that was applied as the result of a validation error) on a field when a character is input.

Getting dynamic callbacks to work is simply a matter of binding and unbinding events. We saw examples of this in Example_6_3.py on page 105, and there are other examples in the source code.

Note If you find that you are constantly binding and unbinding events in your code, it may be a good idea to review the reasons why you are doing this. Remember that events can be generated in rapid succession—mouse movement, for example, generates a slew of events. Changing bindings during an event storm may have unpredictable results and can be very difficult to debug. Of course, we burn CPU cycles as well, so it can have a considerable effect on application performance.

6.8 *Putting events to work*

In several of the early chapters, we saw examples of setting widgets with data and of getting that data and using it in our applications. In "Dialogs and forms" on page 140, we will see several schemes for presenting and getting data. This is an important topic that may require some ingenuity on your part to devise correct behavior. In the next few paragraphs, I'll present some ideas to help you solve your own requirements.

6.8.1   Binding widgets to dynamic data

Tkinter provides a simple mechanism to bind a variable to a widget. However, it not possible to use an arbitrary variable. The variable must be subclassed from the `Variable` class; several are predefined and you could define your own, if necessary. Whenever the variable changes, the widget's contents are updated with the new value. Look at this simple example:

Example_6_4.py

```
from Tkinter import *
root = Tk()

class Indicator:
  def __init__(self, master=None, label='', value=0):
      self.var = BooleanVar()
      self.i = Checkbutton(master, text=label, variable = self.var,
                  command=self.valueChanged)
      self.var.set(value)
      self.i.pack()

  def valueChanged(self):
      print 'Current value = %s' % ['Off','On'][self.var.get()]

ind = Indicator(root, label='Furnace On', value=1)
root.mainloop()
```

This example defines `self.var` and binds it to the widget's variable; it also defines a callback to be called whenever the value of the widget changes. In this example the value is changed by clicking the checkbutton—it could equally be set programmatically.

Setting the value as a result of an external change is a reasonable scenario, but it can introduce performance problems if the data changes rapidly. If our GUI contained many widgets that displayed the status and values of components of the system, and if these values changed asynchronously (for instance, each value arrived in the system as SNMP traps), the overhead of constantly updating the widgets could have an adverse effect on the application's performance. Here is a possible implementation of a simple GUI to monitor the temperature reported by ten sensors.

Example_6_5.py

```
from Tkinter import *
import random
root = Tk()
```

```
class Indicator:
    def __init__(self, master=None, label='', value=0.0):
        self.var = DoubleVar()                              ❶
        self.s = Scale(master, label=label, variable=self.var,   ❷
                    from_=0.0, to=300.0, orient=HORIZONTAL,
                    length=300)
        self.var.set(value)                                 ❸
        self.s.pack()


def setTemp():
    slider = random.choice(range(10))                       ❹
    value  = random.choice(range(0, 300))
    slist[slider].var.set(value)                            ❺
    root.after(5, setTemp)                                  ❻


slist = []
for i in range(10):
    slist.append(Indicator(root, label='Probe %d' % (i+1)))
setTemp()                                                   ❼
root.mainloop()
```

Code comments

❶ First we create a Tkinter variable. For this example we store a real value:
```
        self.var = DoubleVar()
```

❷ We then bind it to the Tk variable:
```
        self.s = Scale(master, label=label, variable=self.var,
```

❸ Then we set its value. This immediately updates the widget to display the new value:
```
        self.var.set(value)
```

❹ The purpose of the setTemp function is to create a value randomly for one of the "sensors" at 5 millisecond intervals.

❺ The variable is updated for each change:
```
    slist[slider].var.set(value)
```

❻ Since after is a one-shot timer, we must set up the next timeout:
```
    root.after(5, setTemp)'
```

❼ The call to setTemp starts the simulated stream of sensor information.

The display for this example is not reproduced here (the code is available online, of course). However, the display's behavior resembles Brownian motion, with widgets constantly displaying new values. In a "real" application, the update rate would be annoying to the user, and it requires throttling to create a reasonable update rate. Additionally, constantly redrawing the widgets consumes an exceptionally high number of CPU cycles. Compare Example_6_5.py with the code for Example_6_6.py.

Example_6_6.py

```
from Tkinter import *
import random
root = Tk()

class Indicator:
    def __init__(self, master=None, label='', value=0.0):
        self.var = DoubleVar()
        self.s = Scale(master, label=label, variable=self.var,
                    from_=0.0, to=300.0, orient=HORIZONTAL,
                    length=300)
        self.value = value                              ❶
        self.var.set(value)
        self.s.pack()
        self.s.after(1000, self.update)                 ❷

    def set(self, value):                               ❸
        self.value = value

    def update(self):
        self.var.set(self.value)                        ❹
        self.s.update_idletasks()
        self.s.after(1000, self.update)

def setTemp():
    slider = random.choice(range(10))
    value  = random.choice(range(0, 300))
    slist[slider].set(value)                            ❺
    root.after(5, setTemp)

slist = []
for i in range(10):
    slist.append(Indicator(root, label='Probe %d' % (i+1)))
setTemp()
root.mainloop()
```

Code comments

❶ In addition to the Tkinter variable, we create an instance variable for the widget's current value:

```
self.value = value
```

❷ An `after` timeout arranges for the `update` method to be called in one second:

```
self.s.after(1000, self.update)
```

❸ The class defines a `set` method to set the current value.

④ The `update` method sets the Tkinter variable with the current value, updating the widget's display. To redraw the widgets, we call `update_idletasks` which processes events waiting on the event queue.

```
self.s.update_idletasks()
```

⑤ Now, when the value changes, we set the instance variable:

```
slist[slider].set(value)
```

The display now updates the widgets once a second, which results in a more relaxed display and noticeably lowers the CPU overhead. You can optimize the code more, if you wish, to further reduce the overhead. For example, the widgets could be updated from a single update timeout rather than from a one-per-widget call.

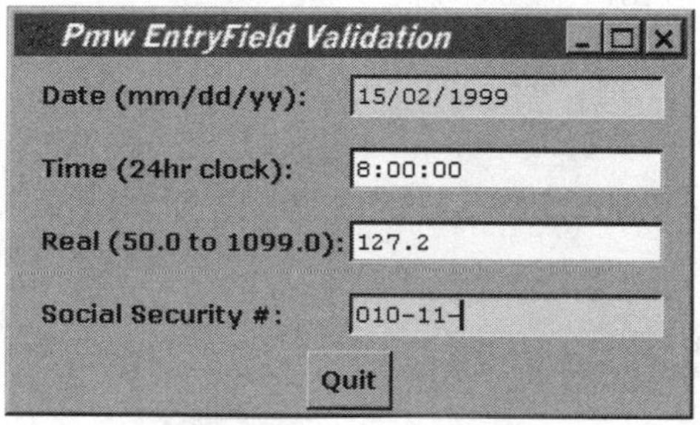

Figure 6.2 Validating entry fields (Example_6_7.py)

6.8.2 Data verification

An important part of a GUI, which performs data entry, is verifying appropriate input values. This area can consume a considerable amount of time and effort for the programmer. There are several approaches to validating input, but we will not attempt to cover all of them here.

Pmw `EntryField` widgets provide built-in validation routines for common entryfield types such as dates, times and numeric fields. Using these facilities can save you a considerable amount of time. Here is a simple example of using Pmw validation:

Example_6_7.py

```
import time, string
from Tkinter import *
import Pmw

class EntryValidation:
    def __init__(self, master):
        now = time.localtime(time.time())
        self._date = Pmw.EntryField(master,
                    labelpos = 'w', label_text = 'Date (mm/dd/yy):',
                    value = '%d/%d/%d' % (now[1], now[2], now[0]),
                    validate = {'validator':'date',
                            'format':'mdy', 'separator':'/'})    ❶
```

```
                self._time = Pmw.EntryField(master,
                        labelpos = 'w', label_text = 'Time (24hr clock):',
                        value = '8:00:00',
                        validate = {'validator':'time',                        ❷
                                'min':'00:00:00', 'max':'23:59:59',
                                'minstrict':0, 'maxstrict':0})

            self._real = Pmw.EntryField(master,
                        labelpos = 'w',value = '127.2',
                        label_text = 'Real (50.0 to 1099.0):',
                        validate = {'validator':'real',          ⬤  Setup real
                                'min':50, 'max':1099,                   field
                                'minstrict':0},
                        modifiedcommand = self.valueChanged)

            self._ssn = Pmw.EntryField(master,
                        labelpos = 'w', label_text = 'Social Security #:',
                        validate = self.validateSSN, value = '')  ❸

            fields = (self._date, self._time, self._real, self._ssn)
            for field in fields:
                field.pack(fill='x', expand=1, padx=12, pady=8)
                                                                   ❹
            Pmw.alignlabels(fields)
            self._date.component('entry').focus_set()

    def valueChanged(self):
        print 'Value changed, value is', self._real.get()
    def validateSSN(self, contents):
        result = -1
        if '-' in contents:                                        ❺
            ssnf = string.split(contents, '-')
            try:
                if len(ssnf[0]) == 3 and \
                   len(ssnf[1]) == 2 and \
                   len(ssnf[2]) == 4:                               ❻
                    result = 1
            except IndexError:
                result = -1
        elif len(contents) == 9:
            result = 1
        return result

if __name__ == '__main__':
  root = Tk()
  root.option_add('*Font', 'Verdana 10 bold')
  root.option_add('*EntryField.Entry.Font', 'Courier 10')         ❼
  root.option_add('*EntryField.errorbackground', 'yellow')
  Pmw.initialise(root, useTkOptionDb=1)

  root.title('Pmw EntryField Validation')
  quit = Button(root, text='Quit', command=root.destroy)
  quit.pack(side = 'bottom')
  top = EntryValidation(root)
  root.mainloop()
```

Code comments

1 The `date` field uses the built-in date validator, specifying the format of the data and the separators:

```
validate = {'validator':'date',
            'format':'mdy', 'separator':'/'})
```

2 The `time` field sets maximum and minimum options along with `minstrict` and `maxstrict`:

```
validate = {'validator':'time',
            'min':'00:00:00', 'max':'23:59:59',
            'minstrict':0, 'maxstrict':0})
```

Setting `minstrict` and `maxstrict` to `False` (zero) allows values outside of the `min` and `max` range to be set. The background will be colored to indicate an error. If they are set to `True`, values outside the range cannot be input.

3 The `Social Security` field uses a user-supplied validator:

```
validate = self.validateSSN, value = '')
```

4 Pmw provides a convenience method to align labels. This helps to reduce the need to set up additional formatting in the geometry managers.

```
Pmw.alignlabels(fields)
self._date.component('entry').focus_set()
```

It is always a good idea to set input focus to the first editable field in a data-entry screen.

5 The `validateSSN` method is simple; it looks for three groups or characters separated by dashes.

6 Since the entry is cumulative, the `string.split` call will fail until the third group has been entered.

7 We set the `Tk options database` to override fonts and colors in all components used in the Pmw widgets.

```
root.option_add('*Font', 'Verdana 10 bold')
root.option_add('*EntryField.Entry.Font', 'Courier 10')
root.option_add('*EntryField.errorbackground', 'yellow')
Pmw.initialise(root, useTkOptionDb=1)
```

This construct will be seen in many examples. However, this is a less-frequently used option to `Pmw.initialise` to force the use of the `Tk option database`.

Running Example_6_7 displays a screen similar to figure 6.2. Notice how the `date` and `Social Security fields` have a shaded background to indicate that they contain an invalid format.

Although validation of this kind is provided automatically by the Pmw `Entryfield` widget, it has some drawbacks.

1 There is no indication of the actual validation error. The user is required to determine the cause of the error himself.

2 Data which is valid, when complete, is indicated as being in error as it is being entered (the `Social Security` field in figure 6.2 is a good example).

3 Where validation requires complex calculations and access to servers and databases, etc,. the processing load can be high. This could be a source of performance problems in certain environments.

To circumvent these and other problems you may use alternative approaches. Of course, your application may not use Pmw widgets, so yet another approach may be required.

Note Personally, I prefer not to use the built-in validation in Pmw widgets. If the action of formatting the content of the widget requires a redraw, you may observe annoying display glitches, particularly if the system is heavily loaded; these may distract the user. The following method avoids these problems.

To avoid validating *every* keystroke (which is how the Pmw EntryField manages data input), we will arrange for validation to be done in the following cases:

1 When the user moves the mouse pointer out of the current field.

2 When the focus is moved from the field using the TAB key.

3 When the ENTER key is pressed.

Validating this way means that you don't get false errors as an input string is built up. In figure 6.3, for example, entering 192.311.40.10 would only raise a validation error when the field was left or if RETURN was pressed, thereby reducing operator confusion and CPU overhead..

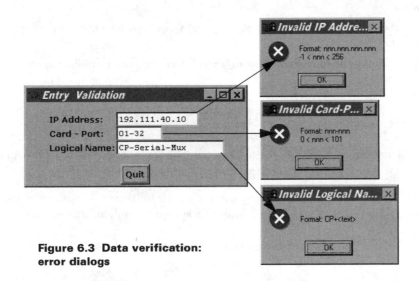

Figure 6.3 Data verification: error dialogs

Example_6_8.py

```
import string
from Tkinter import *
from validation import *
```

```
class EntryValidation:
    def __init__(self, master):
        self._ignoreEvent = 0
        self._ipAddrV = self._crdprtV = self._lnameV = ''

        frame = Frame(master)
        Label(frame, text='     ').grid(row=0, column=0,sticky=W)       ❶
        Label(frame, text='     ').grid(row=0, column=3,sticky=W)

        self._ipaddr = self.createField(frame, width=15, row=0, col=2,  ❷
                        label='IP Address:', valid=self.validate,
                        enter=self.activate)
        self._crdprt = self.createField(frame, width=8, row=1, col=2,
                        label='Card - Port:', valid=self.validate,
                        enter=self.activate)
        self._lname  = self.createField(frame, width=20, row=2, col=2,
                        label='Logical Name:', valid=self.validate,
                        enter=self.activate)

        self._wDict = {self._ipaddr: ('_ipAddrV', validIP),           ❸
                    self._crdprt: ('_crdprtV', validCP),
                    self._lname:  ('_lnameV',  validLName) }

        frame.pack(side=TOP, padx=15, pady=15)

    def createField(self, master, label='', text='', width=1,
                valid=None, enter=None, row=0, col=0):
        Label(master, text=label).grid(row=row,  column=col-1, sticky=W)
        id = Entry(master, text=text, width=width, takefocus=1)
        id.bind('<Any-Leave>', valid)
        id.bind('<FocusOut>', valid)                                   ❹
        id.bind('<Return>',    enter)
        id.grid(row=row, column=col, sticky=W)
        return id

    def activate(self, event):
        print '<Return>: value is', event.widget.get()

    def validate(self, event):
        if self._ignoreEvent:                                         ❺
            self._ignoreEvent = 0
        else:
            currentValue = event.widget.get()
            if currentValue:
                var, validator = self._wDict[event.widget]            ❻
                nValue, replace, valid = validator(currentValue)

                if replace:
                    self._ignoreEvent = 1
                    setattr(self, var, nValue)
                    event.widget.delete(0, END)
                    event.widget.insert(0, nValue)                    ❼
                if not valid:
                    self._ignoreEvent = 1
                    event.widget.focus_set()

root = Tk()
```

```
root.option_add('*Font', 'Verdana 10 bold')
root.option_add('*Entry.Font', 'Courier 10')
root.title('Entry  Validation')

top = EntryValidation(root)
quit = Button(root, text='Quit', command=root.destroy)
quit.pack(side = 'bottom')

root.mainloop()
```

Code comments

❶ The `grid` geometry manager sometimes needs a little help to lay out a screen. We use an empty *first* and *last* column in this example:

```
Label(frame, text='    ').grid(row=0, column=0,sticky=W)
Label(frame, text='    ').grid(row=0, column=3,sticky=W)
```

You cannot use the `Grid` manager's `minsize` option if the column (or row) is empty; you have to use the technique shown here. As an alternative, you can pack the gridded widget inside a `Frame` and use padding to add space at the sides.

❷ Since we are using native Tkinter widgets, we have to create a `Label` and `Entry` widget for each row of the form and place them in the appropriate columns. We use the `createField` method to do this.

❸ We create a dictionary to define a variable used to store the contents of each widget.

```
self._wDict = {self._ipaddr: ('_ipAddrV', validIP),
               self._crdprt: ('_crdprtV', validCP),
               self._lname:  ('_lnameV',  validLName) }
```

Using the dictionary enables us to use bindings to a single event-handler with multiple validators, which simplifies the code.

❹ The bindings for validation are when the cursor leaves the widget and when focus is lost (tabbing out of the field). We also bind the activate function called when the ENTER key is pressed.

```
id.bind('<Any-Leave>', valid)
id.bind('<FocusOut>', valid)
id.bind('<Return>',   enter)
```

❺ One of the complications of using this type of validation scheme is that whenever a field loses focus, its validator is called—including when we return to a field to allow the user to correct an error. We provide a mechanism to ignore one event:

```
if self._ignoreEvent:
    self._ignoreEvent = 0
```

❻ We get the `variable` and `validator` for the widget creating the event:

```
var, validator = self._wDict[event.widget]
nValue, replace, valid = validator(currentValue)
```

and call the `validator` to check the widget's contents—possibly editing the content, as appropriate.

❼ Finally, we react to the result of validation, setting the widget's content. In the case of a validation error, we reset focus to the widget. Here we set the flag to ignore the resulting focus event:

```
self._ignoreEvent = 1
```

6.8.3 Formatted (smart) widgets

Several data-entry formats benefit from widgets that format data as it is entered. Some examples include dates, times, telephone numbers, Social Security numbers and Internet (IP) addresses. Making this work may reintroduce some of the issues that were solved by the previous example, since the ideal behavior of the widget is to update the format continuously as opposed to the alternate scheme of reformatting the field after it has been entered. This introduces even more problems. Take entering a phone number, for example. Several number groupings are typical:

1	1-(401) 111-2222	Full number with area code
2	1-401-111-2222	Full number separated with dashes
3	401-111-2222	Area code and number without *1*
4	111-2222	Local number
5	017596-475222	International (United Kingdom)
6	3-1111-2222	International (Japan)

With so many combinations, it is important that the user is shown the format of the telephone number, or other data, in the label for the widget. If your application has requirements to accommodate a range of conflicting formats, it may be better to format the string after it has been entered completely or else leave the formatting to the user. For date and time fields, you might want to use Pmw widgets, which help the user get the input in the correct format.

For other formats, you are going to have to write code. This example demonstrates how to format phone numbers and Social Security numbers.

Example_6_9.py

```
import string
from Tkinter import *

class EntryFormatting:
    def __init__(self, master):
        frame = Frame(master)
        Label(frame, text='   ').grid(row=0, column=0,sticky=W)
        Label(frame, text='   ').grid(row=0, column=3,sticky=W)

        self._ipaddr = self.createField(frame, width=16, row=0, col=2,

                        label='Phone Number:\n(nnn)-nnn-nnn',
                        format=self.fmtPhone, enter=self.activate)
        self._crdprt = self.createField(frame, width=11, row=1, col=2,
                        label='SSN#:', format=self.fmtSSN,
                        enter=self.activate)
        frame.pack(side=TOP, padx=15, pady=15)

    def createField(self, master, label='', text='', width=1,
            format=None, enter=None, row=0, col=0):
        Label(master, text=label).grid(row=row, column=col-1,
                        padx=15, sticky=W)
        id = Entry(master, text=text, width=width, takefocus=1)
```

①

```
                    id.bind('<KeyRelease>', format)          ❷
                    id.bind('<Return>',    enter)
                    id.grid(row=row, column=col, pady=10, sticky=W)
                    return id

            def activate(self, event):
                print '<Return>: value is', event.widget.get()

            def fmtPhone(self, event):
                current = event.widget.get()
                if len(current) == 1:                        ❸
                    current = '1-(%s' % current
                elif len(current) == 6:
                    current = '%s)-' % current
                elif len(current) == 11:
                    current = '%s-' % current
                    event.widget.delete(0, END)
                    event.widget.insert(0, current)

            def fmtSSN(self, event):
                current = event.widget.get()
                if len(current) in [3, 6]:                   ❹
                    current = '%s-' % current
                event.widget.delete(0, END)
                event.widget.insert(0, current)

    root = Tk()
    root.title('Entry  Formatting')

    top = EntryFormatting(root)
    quit = Button(root, text='Quit', command=root.destroy)
    quit.pack(side = 'bottom')

    root.mainloop()
```

Code comments

❶ The createField method provides a wrapper to bind a formatting function that runs whenever the user presses a key.

❷ This is the binding that initiates the formatting.

❸ The fmtPhone method has to count the digits entered into the field to supply the additional separators.

❹ Similarly, fmtSSN inserts hyphens at the appropriate positions.

If you run Example_6_9.py, you will see output similar to figure 6.4.

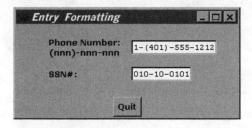

Figure 6.4 Simple formatted widgets

6.9 *Summary*

The material contained in this chapter is important to a GUI programmer. Almost all GUIs are event-driven and appropriate responses to what can be a deluge of events can be important for performance-sensitive applications.

The second half of the chapter introduced data input validation. This is also an important topic, since failure to identify values that are inappropriate can be infuriating to a user, especially if the user has to retype information into a data-entry screen.

C H A P T E R   7

Using classes, composites and special widgets

The Object-Oriented Programming (OOP) capabilities of Python position the language as an ideal platform for developing prototypes and, in most cases, complete applications. One problem of OOP is that there is much argument over the methodologies (Object-Oriented Analysis and Design—OOAD) which lead to OOP, so many developers simply avoid OOP altogether and stay with structured programming (or unstructured programming in some case). There is nothing really magical about OOP; for really simple problems, it might not be worth the effort. However, in general, OOP in Python is an effective approach to developing applications. In this chapter, we are making an assumption that the reader is conversant with OOP in C++, Java or Python, so the basic concepts should be understood. For an extended discussion of this subject, Harms' & McDonald's *Quick Python* or Lutz and Ascher's *Learning Python*.

7.1 Creating a Light Emitting Diode class

The following example introduces an LED class to define Light Emitting Diode objects. These objects have status attributes of on, off, warn and alarm (corresponding to typical network management alarm levels) along with the blink on/off state, which may be selected at instantiation. The LED class also defines the methods to set the status and blink state at run-time. Figure 7.1 demonstrates the wide range of LED formats that can be generated from this simple class.

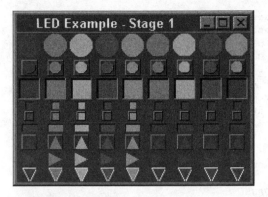

Figure 7.1 LED example

Example_7_1.py

```
from Tkinter    import *

SQUARE            = 1
ROUND             = 2
ARROW             = 3

POINT_DOWN        = 0
POINT_UP          = 1
POINT_RIGHT       = 2        ●   Define constants
POINT_LEFT        = 3

STATUS_OFF        = 1
STATUS_ON         = 2
STATUS_WARN       = 3
STATUS_ALARM      = 4
STATUS_SET        = 5

class StructClass:
   pass

Color  = StructClass()

Color.PANEL       =    '#545454'
Color.OFF         =    '#656565'
Color.ON          =    '#00FF33'
Color.WARN        =    '#ffcc00'
Color.ALARM       =    '#ff4422'

class LED:
   def __init__(self, master=None, width=25, height=25,
                       appearance=FLAT,
```

```
                              status=STATUS_ON, bd=1,
                              bg=None,
                              shape=SQUARE, outline="",
                              blink=0, blinkrate=1,
                              orient=POINT_UP,
                              takefocus=0):
    # Preserve attributes
        self.master  = master
        self.shape   = shape
        self.onColor  = Color.ON
        self.offColor  = Color.OFF
        self.alarmColor  = Color.ALARM
        self.warningColor = Color.WARN
        self.specialColor = '#00ffdd'
        self.status  = status
        self.blink   = blink
        self.blinkrate  = int(blinkrate)
        self.on      = 0
        self.onState  = None
        if not bg:
            bg = Color.PANEL

    ## Base frame to contain light
        self.frame=Frame(master, relief=appearance, bg=bg, bd=bd,
                    takefocus=takefocus)
        basesize = width
        d = center = int(basesize/2)
        if self.shape == SQUARE:
            self.canvas=Canvas(self.frame, height=height, width=width,
                        bg=bg, bd=0, highlightthickness=0)
            self.light=self.canvas.create_rectangle(0, 0, width, height,
                                    fill=Color.ON)
        elif self.shape == ROUND:
            r = int((basesize-2)/2)
            self.canvas=Canvas(self.frame, width=width, height=width,
                        highlightthickness=0, bg=bg, bd=0)
            if bd > 0:
                self.border=self.canvas.create_oval(center-r, center-r,
                                        center+r, center+r)
                r = r - bd
            self.light=self.canvas.create_oval(center-r-1, center-r-1,
                                    center+r, center+r, fill=Color.ON,
                                    outline=outline)
        else:  # Default is an ARROW
            self.canvas=Canvas(self.frame, width=width, height=width,
                        highlightthickness=0, bg=bg, bd=0)
            x = d
            y = d

            if orient == POINT_DOWN:        ❶
                self.light=self.canvas.create_polygon(x-d,y-d, x,y+d,
                                        x+d,y-d, x-d,y-d, outline=outline)
            elif orient == POINT_UP:
                self.light=self.canvas.create_polygon(x,y-d, x-d,y+d,
                                        x+d,y+d, x,y-d, outline=outline)
```

```
                    elif orient == POINT_RIGHT:
                        self.light=self.canvas.create_polygon(x-d,y-d, x+d,y,
                                             x-d,y+d, x-d,y-d, outline=outline)
                    elif orient == POINT_LEFT:
                        self.light=self.canvas.create_polygon(x-d,y, x+d,y+d,
                                             x+d,y-d, x-d,y, outline=outline)

            self.canvas.pack(side=TOP, fill=X, expand=NO)
            self.update()

        def turnon(self):        ❷
            self.status = STATUS_ON
            if not self.blink: self.update()
        def turnoff(self):
            self.status = STATUS_OFF
            if not self.blink: self.update()
        def alarm(self):
            self.status = STATUS_ALARM
            if not self.blink: self.update()
        def warn(self):
            self.status = STATUS_WARN
            if not self.blink: self.update()
        def set(self, color):
            self.status  = STATUS_SET
            self.specialColor = color
            self.update()
        def blinkon(self):
            if not self.blink:
                self.blink  = 1
                self.onState = self.status
                self.update()
        def blinkoff(self):
            if self.blink:
                self.blink  = 0
                self.status  = self.onState
                self.onState = None
                self.on      = 0
                self.update()

        def blinkstate(self, blinkstate):
            if blinkstate:
                self.blinkon()
            else:
                self.blinkoff()

        def update(self):
            # First do the blink, if set to blink
            if self.blink:
                if self.on:
                    if not self.onState:
                        self.onState = self.status
                    self.status  = STATUS_OFF
                    self.on      = 0
                else:
                    if self.onState:
```

```python
                    self.status = self.onState      # Current ON color
                self.on = 1

            if self.status == STATUS_ON:      ❸
                self.canvas.itemconfig(self.light, fill=self.onColor)
            elif self.status == STATUS_OFF:
                self.canvas.itemconfig(self.light, fill=self.offColor)
            elif self.status == STATUS_WARN:
                self.canvas.itemconfig(self.light, fill=self.warningColor)
            elif self.status == STATUS_SET:
                self.canvas.itemconfig(self.light, fill=self.specialColor)
            else:
                self.canvas.itemconfig(self.light, fill=self.alarmColor)
            self.canvas.update_idletasks()   ❹
            if self.blink:
                self.frame.after(self.blinkrate * 1000, self.update)

    if __name__ == '__main__':
        class TestLEDs(Frame):
            def __init__(self, parent=None):
                # List of Colors and Blink On/Off
                states = [(STATUS_OFF, 0),
                          (STATUS_ON, 0),
                          (STATUS_WARN, 0),
                          (STATUS_ALARM, 0),
                          (STATUS_SET, 0),
                          (STATUS_ON, 1),
                          (STATUS_WARN, 1),
                          (STATUS_ALARM, 1),
                          (STATUS_SET, 1)]
                # List of LED types to display,
                # with sizes and other attributes
                leds = [(ROUND, 25, 25, FLAT, 0, None, ""),
                        (ROUND, 15, 15, RAISED, 1, None, ""),
                        (SQUARE, 20, 20, SUNKEN, 1, None, ""),
                        (SQUARE,  8,  8, FLAT, 0, None, ""),
                        (SQUARE,  8,  8, RAISED, 1, None, ""),
                        (SQUARE, 16,  8, FLAT, 1, None, ""),
                        (ARROW, 14, 14, RIDGE, 1, POINT_UP, ""),
                        (ARROW, 14, 14, RIDGE, 0, POINT_RIGHT, ""),
                        (ARROW, 14, 14, FLAT, 0, POINT_DOWN, "white")]

                Frame.__init__(self)  # Do superclass init
                self.pack()
                self.master.title('LED Example - Stage 1')

                # Iterate for each type of LED
                for shape, w, h, app, bd, orient, outline in leds:
                    frame = Frame(self, bg=Color.PANEL)
                    frame.pack(anchor=N, expand=YES, fill=X)
                    # Iterate for selected states
                    for state, blink in states:
                        LED(frame, shape=shape, status=state,
                            width=w, height=h, appearance=app,
                            orient=orient, blink=blink, bd=bd,
```

```
                       outline=outline).frame.pack(side=LEFT,
                                      expand=YES, padx=1, pady=1)

TestLEDs().mainloop()
```

Code comments

1 We have some simple drawing constructs to draw a triangular area on the `canvas`.

2 The LED widget has a number of methods to change the appearance of the display, show several colors and turn blink on and off.

3 The selected state of the LED is updated:
```
if self.status == STATUS_ON:
        self.canvas.itemconfig(self.light, fill=self.onColor)
```

4 We always flush the event queue to ensure that the widget is drawn with the current appearance.

Note Throughout this book I will encourage you to find ways to reduce the amount of code that you have to write. This does not mean that I am encouraging you to write obfuscated code, but there is a degree of elegance in well-constructed Python. The TestLEDs class in Example_7_1.py is a good example of code that illustrates Python economy. Here I intended to create a large number of LEDs, so I constructed two lists: one to contain the various statuses that I want to show and another to contain the LED shapes and attributes that I want to create. Put inside two nested loops, we create the LEDs with ease.

This technique of looping to generate multiple instances of objects will be exploited again in other examples. You can also expect to see other rather elegant ways of creating objects within loops, but more of that later.

Example_7_1.py produces the screen shown in figure 7.1. Although this might not seem to be very useful at this point, it illustrates the ability of Tkinter to produce some output that might be useful in an application.

Unfortunately, it is not possible to see the LEDs flashing on a printed page, so you will have to take my word that the four columns on the right flash on and off (you can obtain the examples online to see the example in action).

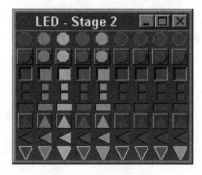

Figure 7.2 LED example (shorter code)

7.1.1 Let's try that again

One thing that most Python programmers quickly discover is that whenever they take a look at a piece of code they wrote some time before, it always seems possible to rewrite it in fewer lines of code. In addition, having written a segment of code, it is often possible to reuse that code in later segments.

To demonstrate the ability to reduce the amount of code required to support our example, let's take a look at how we can improve the code in it. First, we'll remove the constants that we defined at the start of the program and save the code in Common_7_1.py; I'm sure that we'll be using these constants again in later examples.

Common_7_1.py

```
SQUARE          = 1
ROUND           = 2
...
...
Color.WARN      = '#ffcc00'
Color.ALARM     = '#ff4422'
```

Now, we have an excellent opportunity to make the LED methods mixins, since we can readily reuse the basic methods of the LED class to construct other widgets.

GUICommon_7_1.py

```
from Common_7_1 import *

class GUICommon:
    def turnon(self):
        self.status = STATUS_ON
        if not self.blink: self.update()

    def turnoff(self):
        self.status = STATUS_OFF
        if not self.blink: self.update()

    def alarm(self):
        self.status = STATUS_ALARM
        if not self.blink: self.update()

    def warn(self):
        self.status = STATUS_WARN
        if not self.blink: self.update()

    def set(self, color):
        self.status       = STATUS_SET
        self.specialColor = color
        self.update()

    def blinkon(self):
        if not self.blink:
            self.blink   = 1
            self.onState = self.status
            self.update()
```

```
        def blinkoff(self):
            if self.blink:
                self.blink   = 0
                self.status  = self.onState
                self.onState = None
                self.on=0
                self.update()

        def blinkstate(self, blinkstate):        ❶
            if blinkstate:
                self.blinkon()
            else:
                self.blinkoff()

    def update(self):
        raise NotImplementedError

# The following define drawing vertices for various
# graphical elements
ARROW_HEAD_VERTICES = [
    ['x-d', 'y-d', 'x',   'y+d', 'x+d', 'y-d', 'x-d', 'y-d'],
    ['x',   'y-d', 'x-d', 'y+d', 'x+d', 'y+d', 'x',   'y-d'],    ❷
    ['x-d', 'y-d', 'x+d', 'y',   'x-d', 'y+d', 'x-d', 'y-d'],
    ['x-d', 'y',   'x+d', 'y+d', 'x+d', 'y-d', 'x-d', 'y'  ]]
```

Code comments

❶ Note that although we have added methods such as turnon and blinkoff, we have defined an update method that raises a NotImplementedError. Since every widget will use very different display methods, this serves as a reminder to the developer that he is responsible for providing a method to override the base class.

❷ The previous code used a four-case it-elif-else statement to process the arrow direction. I like to remove these whenever possible, so we'll take a different approach to constructing the code. Instead of breaking out the individual vertices for the arrow graphic, we are going to store them in yet another list, ARROW_HEAD_VERTICES, for later use.

Example_7_2.py

```
from Tkinter          import *
from Common_7_1       import *
from GUICommon_7_1    import *             ❶

class LED(GUICommon):                      ❷
    def __init__(self, master=None, width=25, height=25,
                       appearance=FLAT,
                       status=STATUS_ON, bd=1,
                       bg=None,
                       shape=SQUARE, outline='',
                       blink=0, blinkrate=1,
                       orient=POINT_UP,
                       takefocus=0):
        # Preserve attributes
        self.master  = master
```

```
        self.shape   = shape
        self.Colors  = [None, Color.OFF, Color.ON,
                        Color.WARN, Color.ALARM, '#00ffdd']
        self.status  = status
        self.blink   = blink
        self.blinkrate = int(blinkrate)
        self.on      = 0
        self.onState = None

        if not bg:
            bg = Color.PANEL

        ## Base frame to contain light
        self.frame=Frame(master, relief=appearance, bg=bg, bd=bd,
                         takefocus=takefocus)

    basesize = width
    d = center = int(basesize/2)

    if self.shape == SQUARE:
        self.canvas=Canvas(self.frame, height=height, width=width,
                           bg=bg, bd=0, highlightthickness=0)

        self.light=self.canvas.create_rectangle(0, 0, width, height,
                                                fill=Color.ON)
    elif self.shape == ROUND:
        r = int((basesize-2)/2)
        self.canvas=Canvas(self.frame, width=width, height=width,
                           highlightthickness=0, bg=bg, bd=0)
        if bd > 0:
            self.border=self.canvas.create_oval(center-r, center-r,
                                        center+r, center+r)
            r = r - bd
        self.light=self.canvas.create_oval(center-r-1, center-r-1,
                                        center+r, center+r,
                                        fill=Color.ON,
                                        outline=outline)
    else:  # Default is an ARROW
        self.canvas=Canvas(self.frame, width=width, height=width,
                           highlightthickness=0, bg=bg, bd=0)

        x = d
        y = d
        VL = ARROW_HEAD_VERTICES[orient] # Get the vertices for the arrow
        self.light=self.canvas.create_polygon(eval(VL[0]),
                        eval(VL[1]), eval(VL[2]), eval(VL[3]),
                        eval(VL[4]), eval(VL[5]), eval(VL[6]),
                        eval(VL[7]), outline = outline)

    self.canvas.pack(side=TOP, fill=X, expand=NO)
    self.update()

def update(self):
    # First do the blink, if set to blink
    if self.blink:
        if self.on:
```

```
        if not self.onState:
            self.onState = self.status
        self.status  = STATUS_OFF
        self.on      = 0
    else:
        if self.onState:
            self.status = self.onState   # Current ON color
        self.on = 1

    # Set color for current status
    self.canvas.itemconfig(self.light, fill=self.Colors[self.status])

    self.canvas.update_idletasks()

    if self.blink:
        self.frame.after(self.blinkrate * 1000, self.update)
```

Code comments

❶ First, we `import` the newly-created constants file and the GUI mixins.

❷ We inherit from the `GUICommon` mixin. This mixin does not have a constructor so we do not need to call it.

❸ We build a list of colors, which act as an enumeration when we key by current status.

❹ We extract the appropriate list of x/y coordinate data and `eval` each value to calculate the offset based on the current location.

7.1.2   What has changed?

Actually, we have not changed very much. We have removed some common code and created a mixin class to allow us to create a superclass to contain some of the reusable code. To eliminate at least one of the `if-elif-else` constructs we have made color attributes for the class into a list. The ugly code to draw arrowheads has been replaced by a list reference to the arrowhead vertices. Similarly, the references to statuses have been converted to a reference to a list. Finally, we've changed the appearance of some of the LEDs by changing sizes and outlines so that you know that we have not just copied figure 7.1!

If Example_7_2.py is run, we'll observe a screen similar to the one generated by the previous example (figure 7.2). I don't expect you to see any change in the execution of the example, but the Python code is somewhat more compact.

7.2   Building a class library

Now that we have seen the concept of mixin classes and subclassing at work, we can start to build our class library of useful objects for our GUIs. There is often a need to create a series of coordinated colors in our displays, so let's create a routine to create a range of coordinated shades from a base color.

First, we have to extend our `GUICommon` class to add some color transformation methods. Here are the mixin methods that we will add to GUICommon_7_1.py to create GUICommon_7_2.py:

```
# This routine modifies an RGB color (returned by winfo_rgb),
# applies a factor, maps -1 < Color < 255, and returns a new RGB string
  def transform(self, rgb, factor):
        retval = "#"
        for v in [rgb[0], rgb[1], rgb[2]]:
            v = (v*factor)/256
            if v > 255: v = 255
            if v < 0:   v = 0
            retval = "%s%02x" % (retval, v)
        return retval

# This routine factors dark, very dark, light, and very light colors
# from the base color using transform
  def set_colors(self):
        rgb = self.winfo_rgb(self.base)                    ❶
        self.dbase  = self.transform(rgb, 0.8)
        self.vdbase = self.transform(rgb, 0.7)             ❷
        self.lbase  = self.transform(rgb, 1.1)
        self.vlbase = self.transform(rgb, 1.3)
```

Code comments

❶ We calculate color variations derived from the base color. winfo_rgb returns a tuple for the RGB values.

❷ We set arbitrary values for each of the color transformations.

The following example illustrates the use of these routines:

Example_7_3.py

```
from Tkinter          import *
from GUICommon_7_2    import *

import string

class TestColors(Frame, GUICommon):
  def __init__(self, parent=None):
        Frame.__init__(self)              ● Init base class
        self.base = "#848484"             ● Set base color
        self.pack()
        self.set_colors()                 ● Spread colors
        self.make_widgets()

  def make_widgets(self):
        for tag in ['VDBase', 'DBase', 'Base', 'LBase', 'VLBase']:
            Button(self, text=tag, bg=getattr(self, '%s'% string.lower(tag)),
                fg='white', command=self.quit).pack(side=LEFT)

if __name__ == '__main__':
  TestColors().mainloop()
```

Running Example_7_3.py displays the screen shown in figure 7.3:

Figure 7.3 Transforming colors

7.2.1 Adding a hex nut to our class library

Now let's make use of the color transformations to add some visual effects to a drawn object. In this example we are going to create hex nuts. As you'll see later, these simple objects can be used in many different ways.

We will begin by extending some of the definitions in Common_7_1.py, which will be saved as Common_7_2.py:

Common_7_2.py

```
NUT_FLAT    = 0
NUT_POINT   = 1

Color.BRONZE      = '#7e5b41'
Color.CHROME      = '#c5c5b8'
Color.BRASS       = '#cdb800'
```

Here is the code for our HexNut class. This example is a little more complex and has options for instantiating a variety of nuts. The test routine illustrates some of the possible variations. Running this code displays the window shown in figure 7.4.

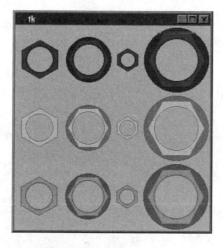

Figure 7.4 Basic nuts

Example_7_4.py

```
from Tkinter           import *
from GUICommon_7_2      import *
from Common_7_2         import *
```

```
class HexNut(GUICommon):
    def __init__(self, master, frame=1, mount=1, outside=70, inset=8,
            bg=Color.PANEL, nutbase=Color.BRONZE,
            top=NUT_FLAT, takefocus=0, x=-1, y=-1):
        points = [ '%d-r2,%d+r,%d+r2,%d+r,%d+r+2,%d,%d+r2,%d-r,\
                    %d-r2,%d-r,%d-r-2,%d,%d-r2,%d+r',
                   '%d,%d-r-2,%d+r,%d-r2,%d+r,%d+r2,%d,%d+r+2,\
                    %d-r,%d+r2,%d-r,%d-r2,%d,%d-r-2' ]
        self.base   = nutbase
        self.status = STATUS_OFF
        self.blink  = 0
        self.set_colors()
        basesize = outside+4
        if frame:
            self.frame = Frame(master, relief="flat", bg=bg, bd=0,
                        highlightthickness=0,
                        takefocus=takefocus)
            self.frame.pack(expand=0)
            self.canv=Canvas(self.frame, width=basesize,  bg=bg,
                        bd=0, height=basesize,
                        highlightthickness=0)
        else:
            self.canv = master      # it was passed in...
        center = basesize/2
        if x >= 0:
            centerx = x
            centery = y
        else:
            centerx = centery = center
        r = outside/2
        ## First, draw the mount, if needed
        if mount:
            self.mount=self.canv.create_oval(centerx-r, centery-r,
                                centerx+r, centery+r,
                                fill=self.dbase,
                                outline=self.vdbase)

        ## Next, draw the hex nut
        r  = r - (inset/2)
        r2 = r/2
        pointlist = points[top] % (centerx,centery,centerx,centery,
                        centerx,centery,centerx,centery,
                        centerx,centery,centerx,centery,
                        centerx,centery)

        setattr(self, 'hexnut', self.canv.create_polygon(pointlist,
            outline=self.dbase, fill=self.lbase))

        ## Now, the inside edge of the threads
        r = r - (inset/2)
        self.canv.create_oval(centerx-r, centery-r,
                        centerx+r, centery+r,
                        fill=self.lbase, outline=self.vdbase)
        ## Finally, the background showing through the hole
        r = r - 2
        self.canv.create_oval(centerx-r, centery-r,
```

```
                        centerx+r, centery+r,
                        fill=bg, outline="")
            self.canv.pack(side="top", fill='x', expand='no')

    class Nut(Frame, HexNut):
        def __init__(self, master, outside=70, inset=8, frame=1, mount=1,
                bg="gray50", nutbase=Color.CHROME, top=NUT_FLAT):
            Frame.__init__(self)
            HexNut.__init__(self, master=master, outside=outside,
                        inset=inset, frame=frame, mount=mount,
                        bg=bg, nutbase=nutbase, top=top)

    class TestNuts(Frame, GUICommon):
        def __init__(self, parent=None):
            Frame.__init__(self)
            self.pack()
            self.make_widgets()
        def make_widgets(self):
            # List of Metals to create
            metals = [Color.BRONZE, Color.CHROME, Color.BRASS]
            # List of nut types to display,
            # with sizes and other attributes
            nuts  = [(70, 14, NUT_POINT, 0), (70, 10, NUT_FLAT,  1),
                    (40,  8, NUT_POINT, 0), (100,16, NUT_FLAT,  1)]
            # Iterate for each metal type
            for metal in metals:
                mframe = Frame(self, bg="slategray2")
                mframe.pack(anchor=N, expand=YES, fill=X)
                # Iterate for each of the nuts
                for outside, inset, top, mount in nuts:
                    Nut(mframe, outside=outside, inset=inset,
                        mount=mount, nutbase=metal,
                        bg="slategray2",
                        top=top).frame.pack(side=LEFT,
                                expand=YES,
                                padx=1, pady=1)

    if __name__ == '__main__':
        TestNuts().mainloop()
```

Note *Another way of handling variable data:* In Example 7_2.py, we used a mechanism to allow us to draw the vertices of the polygon used for the arrowheads. In this example we employ another technique which will be used repeatedly in other examples. Because of the relative complexity of the polygon used to depict the hex nut and the fact that we have to calculate the vertices for both the point and flat forms of the nut, we use the setattr function. This allows us to set the value of an attribute of an object using a reference to the object and a string representation of the attribute.

7.2.2 Creating a switch class

It's time for something more interesting than LEDs and nuts. Once you get started creating classes it really is hard to stop, so now let's create some switches. Although these could be pretty boring, we can add some pizzazz to any GUI that represents any device which has on/off controls. We are also going to introduce some animation, albeit simple.

Note In subsequent examples, GUICommon.py and Common.py will be edited directly, rather than creating new versions each time.

We need to define two more constants in Common.py because switches point up when on in the U.S., but point down when on in the UK (I know that this is an arcane property of switches in these countries, but it is important to the locals!):

Common.py

```
MODE_UK     = 0
MODE_US     = 1
```

Here is the code to draw a toggle switch:

Example_7_5.py

```
from Tkinter       import *
from GUICommon     import *
from Common        import *
from Example_7_4 import HexNut

class ToggleSwitch(Frame, HexNut):
    def __init__(self, master, outside=70, inset=8, bg=Color.PANEL,
            nutbase=Color.CHROME, mount=1, frame=1,
            top=NUT_POINT, mode=MODE_US, status=STATUS_ON):
        Frame.__init__(self)
        HexNut.__init__(self,master=master, outside=outside+40,
                inset=35, frame=frame, mount=mount,
                bg=bg, nutbase=nutbase, top=top)
        self.status = status
        self.mode   = mode
        self.center = (outside+44)/2
        self.r      = (outside/2)-4
        ## First Fill in the center
        self.r1=self.canv.create_oval(self.center-self.r,
                self.center-self.r, self.center+self.r,
                self.center+self.r, fill=self.vdbase,
                outline=self.dbase, width=1)
        self.update()  ## The rest is dependent on the on/off state

    def update(self):
        self.canv.delete('lever')   ## Remove any previous toggle lever
        direction = POINT_UP
        if (self.mode == MODE_UK and self.status == STATUS_ON) or \
           (self.mode == MODE_US and self.status == STATUS_OFF):
            direction = POINT_DOWN
        # Now update the status
        if direction == POINT_UP:   ❶
            ## Draw the toggle lever
```

The callout **call constructors for base classes** points to the two `__init__` lines.

```
                self.p1=self.canvas.create_polygon(self.center-self.r,
                    self.center, self.center-self.r-3,
                    self.center-(4*self.r), self.center+self.r+3,
                    self.center-(4*self.r),  self.center+self.r,
                    elf.center,  fill=self.dbase,
                    outline=self.vdbase, tags="lever")
            centerx = self.center
            centery = self.center - (4*self.r)
            r = self.r + 2
            ## Draw the end of the lever
            self.r2=self.canv.create_oval(centerx-r, centery-r,
                    centerx+r, centery+r, fill=self.base,
                    outline=self.vdbase, width=1, tags="lever")
            centerx = centerx - 1
            centery = centery - 3
            r = r / 3
            ## Draw the highlight
            self.r2=self.canv.create_oval(centerx-r, centery-r,
                    centerx+r, centery+r, fill=self.vlbase,
                    outline=self.lbase, width=2, tags="lever")
        else:
            ## Draw the toggle lever
            self.p1=self.canv.create_polygon(self.center-self.r,
                    self.center,  self.center-self.r-3,
                    self.center+(4*self.r), self.center+self.r+3,
                    self.center+(4*self.r), self.center+self.r,
                    self.center, fill=self.dbase,
                    outline=self.vdbase, tags="lever")
            centerx = self.center
            centery = self.center + (4*self.r)
            r = self.r + 2
            ## Draw the end of the lever
            self.r2=self.canv.create_oval(centerx-r, centery-r,
                    centerx+r, centery+r, fill=self.base,
                    outline=self.vdbase, width=1, tags="lever")
            centerx = centerx - 1
            centery = centery - 3
            r = r / 3
            ## Draw the highlight
            self.r2=self.canv.create_oval(centerx-r, centery-r,
                    centerx+r, centery+r, fill=self.vlbase,
                    outline=self.lbase, width=2, tags="lever")
        self.canv.update_idletasks()

class TestSwitches(Frame, GUICommon):
    def __init__(self, parent=None):
        Frame.__init__(self)
        self.pack()
        self.make_widgets()

    def make_widgets(self):
        # List of metals to create
        metals = (Color.BRONZE, Color.CHROME, Color.BRASS)
        # List of switches to display, with sizes and other attributes
        switches = [(NUT_POINT, 0, STATUS_OFF, MODE_US),
```

```
                    (NUT_FLAT,1, STATUS_ON,  MODE_US),
                    (NUT_FLAT,0, STATUS_ON,  MODE_UK),
                    (NUT_POINT, 0, STATUS_OFF, MODE_UK)]
        # Iterate for each metal type
        for metal in metals:
            mframe = Frame(self, bg="slategray2")
            mframe.pack(anchor=N, expand=YES, fill=X)
            # Iterate for each of the switches
            for top, mount, state, mode in switches:
                ToggleSwitch(mframe,
                        mount=mount, outside=20,
                        nutbase=metal, mode=mode,
                        bg="slategray2", top=top,
                        status=state).frame.pack(side=LEFT,
                                        expand=YES,
                                        padx=2, pady=6)
if __name__ == '__main__':
  TestSwitches().mainloop()
```

Code comments

1 `direction` determines if the toggle is up or down. Since this may be changed programmatically, it provides simple animation in the GUI.

Running this code displays the window in figure 7.5.

Figure 7.5 Toggle switches

7.2.3 Building a MegaWidget

Now that we have mastered creating objects and subclassing to create new behavior and appearance, we can start to create some even more complex widgets, which will result ultimately in more efficient GUIs, since the code required to generate them will be quite compact. First, we need to collect all of the class definitions for LED, HexNut, Nut and ToggleSwitch in a single class library called Components.py.

Next, we are going to create a new class, `SwitchIndicator`, which displays a toggle switch with an LED indicator above the switch, showing the on/off state of the switch. Everything is contained in a single frame that can be placed simply on a larger GUI. Here is the code to construct the composite widget:

Example_7_6.py

```
from Tkinter     import *
from Common      import *
from Components   import *

class SwitchIndicator:
    def __init__(self, master, outside=70, bg=Color.PANEL,
            metal=Color.CHROME, mount=1, frame=1,
            shape=ROUND, top=NUT_POINT, mode=MODE_US, status=1):
        self.frame = Frame(master, bg=bg)
        self.frame.pack(anchor=N, expand=YES, fill=X)

        self.led = LED(self.frame, width=outside, height=outside,
                status=status, bg=bg, shape=shape,
                outline=metal)
        self.led.frame.pack(side=TOP)

        self.switch = ToggleSwitch(self.frame, mount=mount,
                outside=outside, nutbase=metal,
                mode=mode, bg=bg, top=top,
                status=status)
        self.switch.frame.pack(side=TOP)
        self.update()

    def update(self):
        self.led.update()
        self.switch.update()

class TestComposite(Frame):
    def __init__(self, parent=None):
        Frame.__init__(self)
        self.pack()
        self.make_widgets()

    def make_widgets(self):
        # List of switches to display,
        # with sizes and other attributes
        switches = [(NUT_POINT, 0, STATUS_OFF, MODE_US),
                    (NUT_FLAT,1, STATUS_ON,  MODE_US),
                    (NUT_FLAT,0, STATUS_ON,  MODE_UK),
                    (NUT_POINT, 0, STATUS_OFF, MODE_UK)]

        frame = Frame(self, bg="gray80")
        frame.pack(anchor=N, expand=YES, fill=X)

        for top, mount, state, mode in switches:
            SwitchIndicator(frame,
                    mount=mount,
                    outside=20,
                    metal=Color.CHROME,
                    mode=mode,
                    bg="gray80",
                    top=top,
                    status=state).frame.pack(side=LEFT,
```

```
                                        expand=YES,
                                        padx=2,
                                        pady=6)

if __name__ == '__main__':
    TestComposite().mainloop()
```

You can see from this example that the test code is beginning to exceed the size of the code needed to construct the widget; this is not an unusual situation when building Python code! If you run Example_7_6.py the following switches shown in figure 7.6 are displayed:

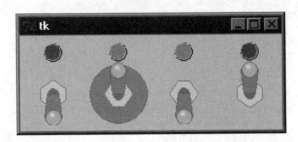

Figure 7.6 Composite Switch/Indicator Widgets

Note The two switches on the left are US switches while the two on the right are UK switches. American and British readers may be equally confused with this if they have never experienced switches on the opposite side of the Atlantic Ocean.

In the preceding examples we have simplified the code by omitting to save the instances of the objects that we have created. This would not be very useful in real-world applications. In future examples we will save the instance in the class or a local variable. Changing our code to save the instance has a side effect that requires us to separate the instantiation and the call to the Packer in our examples. For example, the following code:

```
for top, mount, state, mode in switches:
    SwitchIndicator(frame, mount=mount, outside=20, metal=Color.CHROME,
                    mode=mode, bg="gray80",top=top,
                    status=state).frame.pack(side=LEFT,
                                     expand=YES, padx=2, pady=6)
```

becomes:

```
idx = 0
for top, mount, state, mode in switches:
    setattr(self, 'swin%d' % idx, None)
    var = getattr(self, 'swin%d' % idx)
    var = SwitchIndicator(frame,
                          mount=mount,
                          outside=20,
                          metal=Color.CHROME,
                          mode=mode,
                          bg="gray80",
```

```
                        top=top,
                        status=state)
        var.frame.pack(side=LEFT, expand=YES,
                        padx=2, pady=6)
        idx = idx + 1
```

This code is not quite so elegant, but it allows access to the methods of the instance:

```
self.swin0.turnon()
self.swin3.blinkon()
```

There will be several examples of using composite widgets and inherited methods in examples in later chapters.

7.3 Summary

In this chapter we have seen how we can build classes to define quite complex GUI objects and that these can be instantiated so that they exhibit quite different appearance even though the underlying behavior of the objects is quite similar. I have demonstrated the use of mixin classes to encapsulate common properties within related classes, and I have given you some insight into the way that Python handles multiple-inheritance.

CHAPTER 8

Dialogs and forms

This chapter presents examples of a wide range of designs for dialogs and forms. If you are not in the business of designing and developing forms for data entry, you could possibly expend a lot of extra energy. It's not that this subject is difficult, but as you will see in "Designing effective graphics applications" on page 338, small errors in design quickly lead to ineffective user interfaces.

The term *dialog* is reasonably well understood, but *form* can be interpreted in several ways. In this chapter the term is used to describe any user interface which collects or displays information and which may allow modification of the displayed values. The way the data is formatted depends very much on the type of information being processed. A dialog may be interpreted as a simple form. We will see examples from several application areas; the volume of example code may seem a little overwhelming at first, but it is unlikely that you would ever need to use *all* of the example types within a single application—pick and choose as appropriate.

We begin with standard dialogs and typical fill-in-the-blank forms. More examples demonstrate ways to produce effective forms without writing a lot of code. The examples will provide you with some readily-usable templates that may be used in your own applications. Many of the standard form methods will be used again in examples in later chapters.

Pmw widgets will be used extensively in the examples since these widgets encapsulate a lot of functionality and allow us to construct quite complex interfaces with a relatively small amount of code. The use and behavior of these widgets are documented in more detail in "Pmw reference: Python megawidgets" on page 542.

8.1 Dialogs

Dialogs are really just special cases of *forms*. In general, dialogs present warning or error messages to the user, ask questions or collect a limited number of values from the user (typically one value). You could argue that all forms are dialogs, but we don't need an argument! Normally dialogs are *modal*: they remain displayed until dismissed. Modality can be application-wide or system-wide, although you must take care to make sure that system-modal dialogs are reserved for situations that must be acknowledged by the user before any other interaction is possible.

Note   Exercise care in selecting when to use a modal dialog to get input from the user. You'll have many opportunities to use other methods to get input from the user and using too many dialogs can be annoying to the user. A typical problem is an application that always asks "Are you sure you want to..." on almost every operation. This can be a valuable technique for novice users, but an expert soon finds the dialogs frustrating. It is important to provide a means to switch off such dialogs for expert users.

Tkinter provides a `Dialog` module, but it has the disadvantage of using X bitmaps for error, warning and other icons, and these icons do not look right on Windows or MacOS. The `tkSimpleDialog` module defines `askstring`, `askinteger` and `askfloat` to collect strings, integers and floats respectively. The `tkMessageBox` module defines convenience functions such as `showinfo`, `showwarning`, `showeerror` and `askyesno`. The icons used for `tkMessageBox` are architecture-specific, so they look right on all the supported platforms.

8.1.1 Standard dialogs

Standard dialogs are simple to use. Several convenience functions are available in `tkMessageBox`, including `showerror`, `showwarning` and `askretrycancel`. The example shown here illustrates the use of just one form of available dialogs (`askquestion`). However, figure 8.1 shows all of the possible formats both for UNIX and Windows.

Example_8_1.py

```
from Tkinter import *
from tkMessageBox import askquestion
import Pmw

class App:
    def __init__(self, master):
        self.result = Pmw.EntryField(master, entry_width=8,
                           value='',
```

```
                                    label_text='Returned value:  ',
                                    labelpos=W, labelmargin=1)
                self.result.pack(padx=15, pady=15)

root = Tk()
question = App(root)

button = askquestion("Question:",                                        ❶
                "Oh Dear, did somebody\nsay mattress to Mr Lambert?",    ❷
                default=NO)
                                                                          ❸
question.result.setentry(button)

root.mainloop()
```

Code comments

❶ The first two arguments set the title and prompt (since this is a question dialog).

❷ default sets the button with the selected string to be the default action (the action associated with pressing the RETURN key).

❸ The standard dialogs return the button pressed as a string—for example, ok for the OK button, cancel for the CANCEL button.

For this example, all of the standard dialogs are presented, both for Windows and UNIX architectures (the UNIX screens have light backgrounds); the screen corresponding to Example_8_1.py is the first screen in figure 8.1.

8.1.2 Data entry dialogs

A dialog can be used to request information from the user. Let's take a quick look at how we query the user for data using the tkSimpleDialog module. Unlike many of our examples, this one is short and to the point:

Example_8_2.py

```
from Tkinter import *
from tkSimpleDialog import askinteger
import Pmw

class App:
    def __init__(self, master):
        self.result = Pmw.EntryField(master, entry_width=8,
                            value='',
                            label_text='Returned value:  ',
                            labelpos=W, labelmargin=1)
        self.result.pack(padx=15, pady=15)

root = Tk()
display = App(root)

retVal = askinteger("The Larch",                        ❶
                "What is the number of The Larch?",
                minvalue=0, maxvalue=50)                 ❷
```

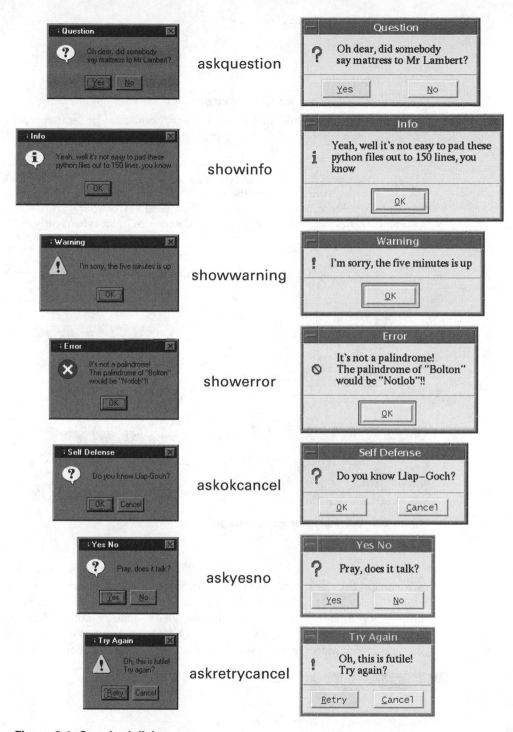

Figure 8.1 Standard dialogs

```
display.result.setentry(retVal)

root.mainloop()
```

Code comments

1 `askinteger` can be used with just two arguments: title and prompt.

2 In this case, a minimum and maximum value have been added. If the user types a value outside this range, a dialog box is displayed to indicate an error (see figure 8.1).

Note Avoid popping up dialogs whenever additional information is required from the user. If you find that the current form that is displayed frequently requires the user to supply additional information, it's very possible that your original form design is inadequate. Reserve popup dialogs for situations which occur infrequently or for near-boundary conditions.

Running Example_8_2.py displays screens similar to those shown in figure 8.2.

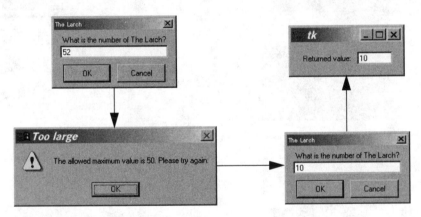

Figure 8.2 tkSimpleDialog: askinteger

Despite the warning in the note above, if you have just a *few* fields to collect from the user, you can use dialog windows. This is especially true if the application doesn't require the information every time it is run; adding the information to screens in the application adds complexity and clutters the screen. Using a dialog saves quite a bit of work, but it may not be particularly attractive, especially if you need to have more than two or three entry fields or if you need several widget types. However, this example is quite short and to the point.

Example_8_3.py

```
from   Tkinter import *
from   tkSimpleDialog import Dialog
import tkMessageBox
```

```
import Pmw

class GetPassword(Dialog):
    def body(self, master):
        self.title("Enter New Password")

        Label(master, text='Old Password:').grid(row=0, sticky=W)   ❶
        Label(master, text='New Password:').grid(row=1, sticky=W)
        Label(master, text='Enter New Password Again:').grid(row=2, sticky=W)

        self.oldpw   = Entry(master, width = 16, show='*')          ❷
        self.newpw1  = Entry(master, width = 16, show='*')
        self.newpw2  = Entry(master, width = 16, show='*')

        self.oldpw.grid(row=0, column=1, sticky=W)
        self.newpw1.grid(row=1, column=1, sticky=W)
        self.newpw2.grid(row=2, column=1, sticky=W)
        return self.oldpw

    def apply(self):
        opw  = self.oldpw.get()
        npw1 = self.newpw1.get()
        npw2 = self.newpw2.get()                                    ❸ Validate

        if not npw1 == npw2:
            tkMessageBox.showerror('Bad Password',
                    'New Passwords do not match')
        else:
            # This is where we would set the new password...
            pass

root = Tk()
dialog = GetPassword(root)
```

Code comments

❶ This example uses the grid geometry manager. The sticky attribute is used to make sure that the labels line up at the left of their grid cells (the default is to center the text in the cell). See "Grid" on page 86 for more details.

```
Label(master, text='Old Password:').grid(row=0, sticky=W)
```

❷ Since we are collecting passwords from the user, we do not echo the characters that are typed. Instead, we use the show attribute to display an asterisk for each character.

```
self.oldpw   = Entry(master, width = 16, show='*')
```

❸ When the user clicks the OK button, the apply callback gets the current data from the widgets. In a full implementation, the original password would be checked first. In our case we're just checking that the user typed the same *new* password twice and if the passwords do not match we pop up an error dialog, using showerror.

```
tkMessageBox.showerror('Bad Password',
        'New Passwords do not match')
```

Figure 8.3 illustrates the output of Example_8_3.py.

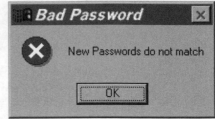

Figure 8.3 A tkSimpleDialog that is used to collect passwords. The error dialog is displayed for bad entries.

8.1.3   Single-shot forms

If your application has simple data requirements, you may need only simple forms. Many user interfaces implement a simple model:

1 Display some fields, maybe with default values.

2 Allow the user to fill out or modify the fields.

3 Collect the values from the screen.

4 Do *something* with the data.

5 Display the results obtained with the values collected.

If you think about the applications you're familiar with, you'll see that many use pretty simple, repetitive patterns. As a result, building forms has often been viewed as a rather tedious part of developing GUIs; I hope that I can make the task a little more interesting.

There *is* a problem in designing screens for applications that do not need many separate screens; developers tend to write a lot more code than they need to satisfy the needs of the application. In fact, code that supports forms often consumes more lines of code than we might prefer. Later, we will look at some techniques to reduce the amount of code that has to be written, but for now let's write the code in full.

This example collects basic information about a user and displays some of it. The example uses Pmw widgets and is a little bit longer than it needs to be, so that we can cover the basic framework now; we will leave those components out in subsequent examples.

Example_8_4.py

```
from Tkinter import *
import Pmw
import string

class Shell:
    def __init__(self, title=''):
        self.root = Tk()                    ❶
        Pmw.initialise(self.root)
        self.root.title(title)
```

```
    def doBaseForm(self, master):
        # Create the Balloon.
        self.balloon = Pmw.Balloon(master)                              ❷

        self.menuBar = Pmw.MenuBar(master, hull_borderwidth=1,
                        hull_relief = RAISED,                           ❸
                        hotkeys=1, balloon = self.balloon)
        self.menuBar.pack(fill=X)

        self.menuBar.addmenu('File', 'Exit')
        self.menuBar.addmenuitem('File', 'command',                    ❹
                    'Exit the application',
                    label='Exit', command=self.exit)
        self.menuBar.addmenu('View', 'View status')
        self.menuBar.addmenuitem('View', 'command',
                    'Get user status',
                    label='Get status',
                    command=self.getStatus)
        self.menuBar.addmenu('Help', 'About Example 8-4', side=RIGHT)
        self.menuBar.addmenuitem('Help', 'command',
                    'Get information on application',
                    label='About...', command=self.help)

        self.dataFrame = Frame(master)
        self.dataFrame.pack(fill=BOTH, expand=1)
                                                                        ❺
        self.infoFrame = Frame(self.root,bd=1, relief='groove')
        self.infoFrame.pack(fill=BOTH, expand=1, padx = 10)

        self.statusBar = Pmw.MessageBar(master, entry_width = 40,
                        entry_relief='groove',
                        labelpos = W,                                   ❻
                        label_text = '')
        self.statusBar.pack(fill = X, padx = 10, pady = 10)

        # Add balloon text to statusBar                                ❼
        self.balloon.configure(statuscommand = self.statusBar.helpmessage)

        # Create about dialog.
        Pmw.aboutversion('8.1')
        Pmw.aboutcopyright('Copyright My Company 1999'
                            '\nAll rights reserved')
        Pmw.aboutcontact(                                              ❽
            'For information about this application contact:\n' +
            '  My Help Desk\n'
            '  Phone: 800 555-1212\n'
            '  email: help@my.company.com'
            )
        self.about = Pmw.AboutDialog(master,
                        applicationname = 'Example 8-4')               ❾
        self.about.withdraw()

def exit(self):
    import sys
    sys.exit(0)
```

Code comments

1 The constructor initializes both Tk and Pmw:

```
self.root = Tk()
Pmw.initialise(self.root)
```

Note that `Pmw.initialise` is not a typo; Pmw comes from Australia!

2 We create an instance of the `Pmw.Balloon` to implement Balloon Help. Naturally, this bit could have been left out, but it is easy to implement, so we might as well include it.

```
self.balloon = Pmw.Balloon(master)
```

Actions are bound later.

3 The next few points illustrate how to construct a simple menu using Pmw components. First we create the MenuBar, associating the `balloon` and defining `hotkey` as `true` (this creates mnemonics for menu selections).

```
self.menuBar = Pmw.MenuBar(master, hull_borderwidth=1,
                   hull_relief = RAISED,
                   hotkeys=1, balloon = self.balloon)
self.menuBar.pack(fill=X)
```

Note It is important to pack each form component in the order that they are to be displayed—having a menu at the bottom of a form might be considered a little strange!

---

4 The File menu button is created with an `addmenu` call:

```
self.menuBar.addmenu('File', 'Exit')
```

The second argument to `addmenu` is the balloon help to be displayed for the menu button. We then add an item to the button using `addmenuitem`:

```
self.menuBar.addmenuitem('File', 'command',
                   'Exit the application',
                   label='Exit', command=self.exit)
```

`addmenuitem` creates an entry within the specified menu. The third argument is the help to be displayed.

5 We create a `Frame` to contain the data-entry widgets and a second frame to contain some display widgets:

```
self.dataFrame = Frame(master)
self.dataFrame.pack(fill=BOTH, expand=1)
```

6 At the bottom of the form, we create a `statusBar` to display help messages and other information:

```
self.statusBar = Pmw.MessageBar(master, entry_width = 40,
                   entry_relief=GROOVE,
                   labelpos = W,
                   label_text = '')
self.statusBar.pack(fill = X, padx = 10, pady = 10)
```

7 We bind the balloon's `statuscommand` to the `MessageBar` widget:

```
self.balloon.configure(statuscommand = self.statusBar.helpmessage)
```

⑧ We create an About . . . dialog for the application. This is definitely something we could have left out, but now that you have seen it done once, I won't need to cover it again. First, we define the data to be displayed by the dialog:

```
Pmw.aboutversion('8.1')
Pmw.aboutcopyright('Copyright My Company 1999'
                        '\nAll rights reserved')
Pmw.aboutcontact(
    'For information about this application contact:\n' +
    '  My Help Desk\n' +
    '  Phone: 800 555-1212\n' +
    '  email: help@my.company.com')
```

⑨ Then the dialog is created and withdrawn (unmapped) so that it remains invisible until required:

```
self.about = Pmw.AboutDialog(master, applicationname = 'Example 8-1')
self.about.withdraw()
```

Example_8_4.py (continued)

```
def getStatus(self):
    username  = self.userName.get()                            ⑩
    cardnumber = self.cardNumber.get()

    self.img = PhotoImage(file='%s.gif' % username)            ⑪
    self.pictureID['image'] = self.img

    self.userInfo.importfile('%s.txt' % username)             ⑫
    self.userInfo.configure(label_text = username)

def help(self):                                                ⑬
    self.about.show()

def doDataForm(self):
    self.userName=Pmw.EntryField(self.dataFrame, entry_width=8,
                    value='',
                    modifiedcommand=self.upd_username,         ⑭
                    label_text='User name:',
                    labelpos=W, labelmargin=1)
    self.userName.place(relx=.20, rely=.325, anchor=W)

    self.cardNumber = Pmw.EntryField(self.dataFrame, entry_width=8,
                    value='',
                    modifiedcommand=self.upd_cardnumber,
                    label_text='Card number:  ',
                    labelpos=W, labelmargin=1)
    self.cardNumber.place(relx=.20, rely=.70, anchor=W)

def doInfoForm(self):
    self.pictureID=Label(self.infoFrame, bd=0)
    self.pictureID.pack(side=LEFT, expand=1)

    self.userInfo = Pmw.ScrolledText(self.infoFrame,
                    borderframe=1,
                    labelpos=N,
                    usehullsize=1,
```

```
                            hull_width=270,
                            hull_height=100,
                            text_padx=10,
                            text_pady=10,
                            text_wrap=NONE)
        self.userInfo.configure(text_font = ('verdana', 8))
        self.userInfo.pack(fill=BOTH, expand=1)

    def upd_username(self):
        upname = string.upper(self.userName.get())      ⓯
        if upname:
            self.userName.setentry(upname)

    def upd_cardnumber(self):
        valid = self.cardNumber.get()
        if valid:
            self.cardNumber.setentry(valid)

if __name__ == '__main__':
    shell=Shell(title='Example 8-4')
    shell.root.geometry("%dx%d" % (400,350))
    shell.doBaseForm(shell.root)                          ⓰
    shell.doDataForm()
    shell.doInfoForm()
    shell.root.mainloop()
```

Code comments (continued)

⓾ getStatus is a placeholder for a more realistic function that can be applied to the collected data. First, we use the get methods of the Pmw widgets to obtain the content of the widgets:

```
        username   = self.userName.get()
        cardnumber = self.cardNumber.get()
```

⑪ Using username, we retrieve an image and load it into the label widget we created earlier:

```
        self.img = PhotoImage(file='%s.gif' % username)
        self.pictureID['image'] = self.img
```

⑫ Then we load the contents of a file into the ScrolledText widget and update its title:

```
        self.userInfo.importfile('%s.txt' % username)
        self.userInfo.configure(label_text = username)
```

⑬ Using the About dialog is simply a matter of binding the widget's show method to the menu item:

```
    def help(self):
        self.about.show()
```

⑭ The form itself uses two Pmw EntryField widgets to collect data:

```
        self.userName=Pmw.EntryField(self.dataFrame, entry_width=8,
                            value='',
                            modifiedcommand=self.upd_username,
                            label_text='User name:',
                            labelpos=W, labelmargin=1)
        self.userName.place(relx=.20, rely=.325, anchor=W)
```

⑮ The `modifiedcommand` in the previous code fragment binds a function to the widget to be called whenever the content of the widget changes (a `valuechanged` callback). This allows us to implement one form of validation or, in this case, to change each character to upper case:

```
upname = string.upper(self.userName.get())
if upname:
    self.userName.setentry(upname)
```

⑯ Finally, we create the root shell and populate it with the subcomponents of the form:

```
shell=Shell(title='Example 8-4')
shell.root.geometry("%dx%d" % (400,350))
shell.doBaseForm(shell.root)
shell.doDataForm()
shell.doInfoForm()
shell.root.mainloop()
```

Note that we delay calling the `doBaseForm`, `doDataForm` and `doInfoForm` methods to allow us flexibility in exactly how the form is created from the base classes.

If you run Example_8_4.py, you will see screens similar to the one in figure 8.4. Notice how the `ScrolledText` widget automatically adds scroll bars as necessary. In fact, the overall layout changes slightly to accommodate several dimension changes. The title to the `ScrolledText` widget, for example, adds a few pixels to its containing frame; this has a slight effect on the layout of the entry fields. This is one reason why user interfaces need to be completely tested.

Note   Automatic scroll bars can introduce some bothersome side effects. In figure 8.4, the vertical scroll bar was added because the number of lines exceeded the height of the widget. The horizontal scroll bar was added because the vertical scroll bar used space needed to display the longest line. If I had resized the window about 10 pixels wider, the horizontal scroll bar would not have been displayed.

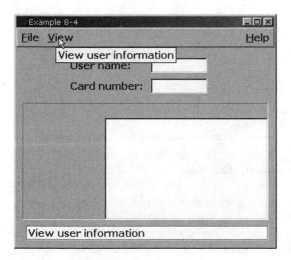

Figure 8.4 Single-shot form

8.1.4 Tkinter variables

The previous example used Pmw widgets to provide `setentry` and `get` methods to give access to the widget's content. Tk provides the ability to link the current value of many widgets (such as `text`, `toggle` and other widgets) to an application variable. Tkinter does not support this mode, instead it provides a `Variable` class which may be subclassed to give access to the `variable`, `textvariable`, `value`, and other options within the widget. Currently, Tkinter supports `StringVar`, `IntVar`, `DoubleVar` and `BooleanVar`. These objects define `get` and `set` methods to access the widget.

Example_8_5.py

```
from Tkinter import *

class Var(Frame):
    def __init__(self, master=None):
        Frame.__init__(self, master)
        self.pack()

        self.field = Entry()
        self.field.pack()

        self.value = StringVar()                          ❶
        self.value.set("Jean-Paul Sartre")               ❷
        self.field["textvariable"] = self.value          ❸

        self.field.bind('<Key-Return>', self.print_value)

    def print_value(self, event):
        print 'Value is "%s"' % self.value.get()         ❹

test = Var()
test.mainloop()
```

Code comments

❶ Remember that you cannot get directly at the Tk widget's variable; you must create a Tkinter variable. Here we create an instance of `StringVar`.

❷ Set the initial value.

❸ Bind the variable to the `textvariable` option in the widget.

❹ Extract the current value using the `get` method of the string variable.

Figure 8.5 Using Tkinter variables

If you run this example, you will see a dialog similar to figure 8.5. This is as simple a dialog as you would want to see; on the other hand, it really is not very effective, because the only way to get anything from the entry field is to press the RETURN key, and we do not give the user any information on how to use the dialog. Nevertheless, it does illustrate Tkinter variables!

Pmw provides built-in methods for setting and getting values within widgets, so you do not need to use Tkinter variables directly. In addition, `validation`, `valuechanged` (modified) and `selection` callbacks are defined as appropriate for the particular widget.

Example_8_6.py

```
from Tkinter import *
from tkSimpleDialog import Dialog
import Pmw

class MixedWidgets(Dialog):
  def body(self, master):
      Label(master, text='Select Case:').grid(row=0, sticky=W)
      Label(master, text='Select Type:').grid(row=1, sticky=W)
      Label(master, text='Enter Value:').grid(row=2, sticky=W)

      self.combo1 = Pmw.ComboBox(master,
              scrolledlist_items=("Upper","Lower","Mixed"),
              entry_width=12, entry_state="disabled",
              selectioncommand = self.ripple)
      self.combo1.selectitem("Upper")
      self.combo1.component('entry').config(bg='gray80')

      self.combo2 = Pmw.ComboBox(master, scrolledlist_items=(),
                      entry_width=12, entry_state="disabled")
      self.combo2.component('entry').config(background='gray80')

      self.entry1  = Entry(master, width = 12)

      self.combo1.grid(row=0, column=1, sticky=W)
      self.combo2.grid(row=1, column=1, sticky=W)
      self.entry1.grid(row=2, column=1, sticky=W)

      return self.combo1

  def apply(self):
      c1 = self.combo1.get()
      c2 = self.combo2.get()
      e1 = self.entry1.get()
      print c1, c2, e1

  def ripple(self, value):
      lookup = {'Upper': ("ANIMAL", "VEGETABLE", "MINERAL"),
              'Lower': ("animal", "vegetable", "mineral"),
              'Mixed': ("Animal", "Vegetable", "Mineral")}
      items = lookup[value]
      self.combo2.setlist(items)
      self.combo2.selectitem(items[0])

root = Tk()
dialog = MixedWidgets(root)
```

①
②
③
④
⑤
⑥

Code comments

① ComboBoxes are important widgets for data entry and selection. One of their most valuable attributes is that they occupy little space, even though they may give the user access to an unlimited number of selectable values.

```
      self.combo1 = Pmw.ComboBox(master,
              scrolledlist_items=("Upper","Lower","Mixed"),
```

In this case, we are just loading three values into the combo's list. Typically data may be either loaded from databases or calculated.

❷ We do not intend for the values selected in this ComboBox to be editable, so we need to disable the entry field component of the widget.

```
                entry_width=12, entry_state="disabled",
        self.combo1.component('entry').config(bg='gray80')
```

We set the background of the Entry widget to be similar to the background to give the user a clear indication that the field is not editable.

❸ This one is an unusual one. Frequently, fields on a screen are dependent on the values contained within other fields on the same screen (on other screens in some cases). So, if you change the value in the combobox, you *ripple* the values within other widgets. (Ripple is a term that I invented, but it somewhat conveys the effect you can see as the new values ripple through the interface.)

```
        selectioncommand = self.ripple)
```

Note Careless use of the ripple technique can be dangerous! Using ripple must be considered carefully, since it is quite easy to design a system which results in constant value modification if several fields are dependent on each other. Some sort of control flag is necessary to prevent a continuous loop of selectioncommand callbacks consuming CPU cycles.

See "Tkinter performance" on page 350 for other important factors you should consider when designing an application.

---

❹ We select default value from the lists or else the entry would be displayed as blank, which is probably not appropriate for a non-editable combobox.

```
        self.combo1.selectitem("Upper")
```

❺ This is our ripple callback function. The selectioncommand callback returns the value of the item selected as an argument. We use this to look up the list to be applied to the second combobox:

```
    def ripple(self, value):
        lookup = {'Upper': ("ANIMAL", "VEGETABLE", "MINERAL"),
                'Lower': ("animal", "vegetable", "mineral"),
                'Mixed': ("Animal", "Vegetable", "Mineral")}
        items = lookup[value]
```

❻ The list obtained from the lookup replaces the current list.

```
        self.combo2.setlist(items)
        self.combo2.selectitem(items[0])
```

As before, you need to select one of the values in the lists to be displayed in the widget.

If you run Example_8_6.py, you will see this simple example of rippled widgets. Part of the effect can be seen in figure 8.6.

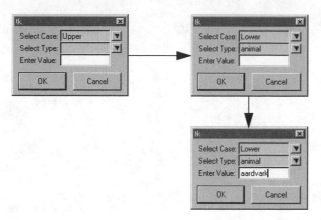

Figure 8.6 Handling
dependencies between
widgets—Ripple

8.2 A standard application framework

One of the problems with designing forms is that some features are common to most applications. What we need is a standard application framework which can be adapted to each application; this should result in moderate code reuse. Many applications fit the general form shown in figure 8.7. In addition, we need the ability to provide *busy cursors* *, attach balloon

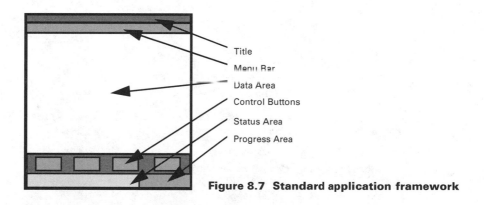

Figure 8.7 Standard application framework

help and help messages to fields, supply an about... message and add buttons with appropriate callbacks. To support these needs, I'll introduce AppShell.py, which is a fairly versatile application framework capable of supporting a wide range of interface needs. Naturally, this framework cannot be applied to all cases, but it can go a long way to ease the burden of developing effective interfaces.

---

* A busy cursor is normally displayed whenever an operation takes more than a few hundred milliseconds, it is often displayed as a watch or hourglass. In some cases the application may also inhibit button-presses and other events until the operation has completed.

Since AppShell is an important feature of several of our examples, we are going to examine the source code in detail; additionally, if you are going to use AppShell directly, or adapt it for your own needs, you need to understand its facilities and operations.

AppShell.py

```
from Tkinter import *
import Pmw
import sys, string
import ProgressBar                                                    ❶

class AppShell(Pmw.MegaWidget):
    appversion= '1.0'
    appname   = 'Generic Application Frame'
    copyright= 'Copyright YYYY Your Company. All Rights Reserved'     ❷
    contactname= 'Your Name'
    contactphone= '(999) 555-1212'
    contactemail= 'youremail@host.com'

    frameWidth= 450
    frameHeight= 320
    padx       = 5                                                    ❸
    pady       = 5
    usecommandarea= 0
    balloonhelp= 1

    busyCursor = 'watch'

    def __init__(self, **kw):
        optiondefs = (
                ('padx',    1,        Pmw.INITOPT),
                ('pady',    1,        Pmw.INITOPT),
                ('framewidth',   1, Pmw.INITOPT),                     ❹
                ('frameheight',    1,Pmw.INITOPT),
                ('usecommandarea', self.usecommandarea, Pmw.INITOPT))
        self.defineoptions(kw, optiondefs)

        self.root = Tk()
        self.initializeTk(self.root)
        Pmw.initialise(self.root)                                    ❺
        self.root.title(self.appname)
        self.root.geometry('%dx%d' % (self.frameWidth,
                                      self.frameHeight))

        # Initialize the base class
        Pmw.MegaWidget.__init__(self, parent=self.root)    ❻

        # Initialize the application
        self.appInit()

        # Create the interface
        self.__createInterface()

        # Create a table to hold the cursors for
        # widgets which get changed when we go busy
```

```
            self.preBusyCursors = None

        # Pack the container and set focus
        # to ourselves
        self._hull.pack(side=TOP, fill=BOTH, expand=YES)
        self.focus_set()
        # Initialize our options
        self.initialiseoptions(AppShell)

    def appInit(self):
        # Called before interface is created (should be overridden).
        pass

    def initializeTk(self, root):          ❼
        # Initialize platform-specific options
        if sys.platform == 'mac':
            self.__initializeTk_mac(root)
        elif sys.platform == 'win32':
            self.__initializeTk_win32(root)
        else:
            self.__initializeTk_unix(root)

    def __initializeTk_colors_common(self, root):
        root.option_add('*background', 'grey')
        root.option_add('*foreground', 'black')
        root.option_add('*EntryField.Entry.background', 'white')
        root.option_add('*MessageBar.Entry.background', 'gray85')
        root.option_add('*Listbox*background', 'white')
        root.option_add('*Listbox*selectBackground', 'dark slate blue')
        root.option_add('*Listbox*selectForeground', 'white')

    def __initializeTk_win32(self, root):
        self.__initializeTk_colors_common(root)
        root.option_add('*Font', 'Verdana 10 bold')
        root.option_add('*EntryField.Entry.Font', 'Courier 10')
        root.option_add('*Listbox*Font', 'Courier 10')

    def __initializeTk_mac(self, root):
        self.__initializeTk_colors_common(root)

    def __initializeTk_unix(self, root):
        self.__initializeTk_colors_common(root)
```

Code comments

❶ AppShell imports `ProgressBar`. Its code is not shown here, but is available online.

```
import ProgressBar
```

❷ AppShell inherits `Pmw.MegaWidget` since we are constructing a megawidget.

```
class AppShell(Pmw.MegaWidget):
    appversion= '1.0'
    appname    = 'Generic Application Frame'
    copyright= 'Copyright YYYY Your Company. All Rights Reserved'
    contactname= 'Your Name'
    contactphone= '(999) 555-1212'
    contactemail= 'youremail@host.com'
```

We then define several class variables which provide default data for the version, title and about... information. We assume that these values will be overridden.

3 Default dimensions and padding are supplied. Again we expect that the application will override these values.

```
frameWidth= 450
frameHeight= 320
padx      = 5
pady      = 5
usecommandarea= 0
balloonhelp= 1
```

usecommandarea is used to inhibit or display the command (button) area.

4 In the __init__ for AppShell, we build the options supplied by the megawidget.

```
def __init__(self, **kw):
    optiondefs = (
        ('padx',    1,       Pmw.INITOPT),
        ('pady',    1,       Pmw.INITOPT),
        ('framewidth',   1, Pmw.INITOPT),
        ('frameheight',    1,Pmw.INITOPT),
        ('usecommandarea', self.usecommandarea, Pmw.INITOPT))
    self.defineoptions(kw, optiondefs)
```

Pmw.INITOPT defines an option that is available only at initialization—it cannot be set with a configure call. (See "Pmw reference: Python megawidgets" on page 542 for more information on defining options.)

5 Now we can initialize Tk and Pmw and set the window's title and geometry:

```
self.root = Tk()
self.initializeTk(self.root)
Pmw.initialise(self.root)
self.root.title(self.appname)
self.root.geometry('%dx%d' % (self.frameWidth,
                              self.frameHeight))
```

6 After defining the options and initializing Tk, we call the constructor for the base class:

```
Pmw.MegaWidget.__init__(self, parent=self.root)
```

7 AppShell is intended to support the major Tkinter architectures; the next few methods define the colors and fonts appropriate for the particular platform.

AppShell.py (continued)

```
def initializeTk(self, root):
    # Initialize platform-specific options
    if sys.platform == 'mac':
        self.__initializeTk_mac(root)
    elif sys.platform == 'win32':
        self.__initializeTk_win32(root)
    else:
        self.__initializeTk_unix(root)

def busyStart(self, newcursor=None):          **8**
    if not newcursor:
        newcursor = self.busyCursor
```

```
        newPreBusyCursors = {}

        for component in self.busyWidgets:
            newPreBusyCursors[component] = component['cursor']
            component.configure(cursor=newcursor)
            component.update_idletasks()
        self.preBusyCursors = (newPreBusyCursors, self.preBusyCursors)

    def busyEnd(self):
        if not self.preBusyCursors:
            return
        oldPreBusyCursors = self.preBusyCursors[0]
        self.preBusyCursors = self.preBusyCursors[1]

        for component in self.busyWidgets:
            try:
                component.configure(cursor=oldPreBusyCursors[component])
            except KeyError:
                pass
            component.update_idletasks()

    def __createAboutBox(self):                    ❾
        Pmw.aboutversion(self.appversion)
        Pmw.aboutcopyright(self.copyright)
        Pmw.aboutcontact(
            'For more information, contact:\n %s\n Phone: %s\n Email: %s' %\
            (self.contactname, self.contactphone,
             self.contactemail))
        self.about = Pmw.AboutDialog(self._hull,
                          applicationname=self.appname)
        self.about.withdraw()
        return None

    def showAbout(self):
        # Create the dialog to display about and contact information.
        self.about.show()
        self.about.focus_set()

    def toggleBalloon(self):                       ❿
        if self.toggleBalloonVar.get():
            self.__balloon.configure(state = 'both')
        else:
            self.__balloon.configure(state = 'status')

    def __createMenuBar(self):                     ⓫
        self.menuBar = self.createcomponent('menubar', (), None,
                          Pmw.MenuBar,
                          (self._hull,),
                          hull_relief=RAISED,
                          hull_borderwidth=1,
                          balloon=self.balloon())
        self.menuBar.pack(fill=X)
        self.menuBar.addmenu('Help', 'About %s' % self.appname, side='right')
        self.menuBar.addmenu('File', 'File commands and Quit')

    def createMenuBar(self):
```

```
          self.menuBar.addmenuitem('Help', 'command',
                         'Get information on application',
                         label='About...', command=self.showAbout)
          self.toggleBalloonVar = IntVar()
          self.toggleBalloonVar.set(1)
          self.menuBar.addmenuitem('Help', 'checkbutton',
                         'Toggle balloon help',
                         label='Balloon help',
                         variable = self.toggleBalloonVar,
                         command=self.toggleBalloon)

          self.menuBar.addmenuitem('File', 'command', 'Quit this application',
                         label='Quit',
                         command=self.quit)
```

Code comments (continued)

8 The next few methods support setting and unsetting the busy cursor:

```
def busyStart(self, newcursor=None):
    ...
```

9 Next we define methods to support the About... functionality. The message box is created before it is used, so that it can be popped up when required.

```
def __createAboutBox(self):
    ...
```

10 Balloon help can be useful for users unfamiliar with an interface, but annoying to expert users. AppShell provides a menu option to turn off balloon help, leaving the regular status messages displayed, since they do not tend to cause a distraction.

```
def toggleBalloon(self):
    if self.toggleBalloonVar.get():
        self.__balloon.configure(state = 'both')
    else:
        self.__balloon.configure(state = 'status')
```

11 Menu bar creation is split into two member functions. __createMenuBar creates a Pmw MenuBar component and createMenuBar populates the menu with standard options, which you may extend as necessary to support your application.

AppShell.py (continued)

```
def __createBalloon(self):       12
    # Create the balloon help manager for the frame.
    # Create the manager for the balloon help
    self.__balloon = self.createcomponent('balloon', (), None,
                            Pmw.Balloon, (self._hull,))

def balloon(self):
    return self.__balloon

def __createDataArea(self):      13
    # Create a data area where data entry widgets are placed.
    self.dataArea = self.createcomponent('dataarea',
                            (), None,
```

```
                                    Frame, (self._hull,),
                                    relief=GROOVE,
                                    bd=1)
        self.dataArea.pack(side=TOP, fill=BOTH, expand=YES,
                        padx=self['padx'], pady=self['pady'])

    def __createCommandArea(self):          ⓮
        # Create a command area for application-wide buttons.
        self.__commandFrame = self.createcomponent('commandframe', (), None,
                                    Frame,
                                    (self._hull,),
                                    relief=SUNKEN,
                                    bd=1)
        self.__buttonBox = self.createcomponent('buttonbox', (), None,
                                    Pmw.ButtonBox,
                                    (self.__commandFrame,),
                                    padx=0, pady=0)
        self.__buttonBox.pack(side=TOP, expand=NO, fill=X)
        if self['usecommandarea']:
            self.__commandFrame.pack(side=TOP,
                                expand=NO,
                                fill=X,
                                padx=self['padx'],
                                pady=self['pady'])

    def __createMessageBar(self):          ⓯
        # Create the message bar area for help and status messages.
        frame = self.createcomponent('bottomtray', (), None,
                                Frame,(self._hull,), relief=SUNKEN)
        self.__messageBar = self.createcomponent('messagebar',
                                    (), None,
                                    Pmw.MessageBar,
                                    (frame,),
                                    #entry_width = 40,
                                    entry_relief=SUNKEN,
                                    entry_bd=1,
                                    labelpos=None)
        self.__messageBar.pack(side=LEFT, expand=YES, fill=X)

        self.__progressBar = ProgressBar.ProgressBar(frame,          ⓰
                                    fillColor='slateblue',
                                    doLabel=1,
                                    width=150)
        self.__progressBar.frame.pack(side=LEFT, expand=NO, fill=NONE)

        self.updateProgress(0)
        frame.pack(side=BOTTOM, expand=NO, fill=X)

        self.__balloon.configure(statuscommand = \
                        self.__messageBar.helpmessage)

    def messageBar(self):
        return self.__messageBar

    def updateProgress(self, newValue=0, newLimit=0):
        self.__progressBar.updateProgress(newValue, newLimit)
```

```
def bind(self, child, balloonHelpMsg, statusHelpMsg=None):
    # Bind a help message and/or status message to a widget.
    self.__balloon.bind(child, balloonHelpMsg, statusHelpMsg)

def interior(self):                                          ⓱
    # Retrieve the interior site where widgets should go.
    return self.dataArea

def buttonBox(self):
    # Retrieve the button box.
    return self.__buttonBox

def buttonAdd(self, buttonName, helpMessage=None,     ⓲
            statusMessage=None, **kw):
    # Add a button to the button box.
    newBtn = self.__buttonBox.add(buttonName)
    newBtn.configure(kw)
    if helpMessage:
        self.bind(newBtn, helpMessage, statusMessage)
    return newBtn
```

Code comments (continued)

⓬ The `balloon` component is created:

```
def __createBalloon(self):
    self.__balloon = self.createcomponent('balloon', (), None,
                            Pmw.Balloon, (self._hull,))
```

⓭ The `dataarea` component is simply a frame to contain whatever widget arrangement is needed for the application:

```
def __createDataArea(self):
    self.dataArea = self.createcomponent('dataarea',
                            (), None,
                            Frame, (self._hull,),
                            relief=GROOVE,
                            bd=1)
```

⓮ The `commandarea` is a frame containing a Pmw ButtonBox:

```
def __createCommandArea(self):
    self.__commandFrame = self.createcomponent('commandframe', (), None,
                            Frame,
                            (self._hull,),
                            relief=SUNKEN,
                            bd=1)
    self.__buttonBox = self.createcomponent('buttonbox', (), None,
                            Pmw.ButtonBox,
                            (self.__commandFrame,),
                            padx=0, pady=0)
```

⓯ Similarly, the `messagebar` is a frame containing a Pmw MessageBox:

```
def __createMessageBar(self):
    ...
```

⓰ To complete our major components, we create a `progressbar` component next to the messagebar:

```
        self.__progressBar = ProgressBar.ProgressBar(frame,
        ...
```

⑰ It is a Pmw convention to provide a method to return a reference to the container where widgets should be created; this method is called `interior`:

```
def interior(self):
        return self.dataArea
```

⑱ It also provides a method to create buttons within the `commandarea` and to bind balloon and status help to the button:

```
def buttonAdd(self, buttonName, helpMessage=None,
            statusMessage=None, **kw):
        newBtn = self.__buttonBox.add(buttonName)
        newBtn.configure(kw)
        if helpMessage:
                self.bind(newBtn, helpMessage, statusMessage)
        return newBtn
```

AppShell.py (continued)

```
    def __createInterface(self):          ⑲
        self.__createBalloon()
        self.__createMenuBar()
        self.__createDataArea()
        self.__createCommandArea()
        self.__createMessageBar()
        self.__createAboutBox()
        #
        # Create the parts of the interface
        # which can be modified by subclasses.
        #
        self.busyWidgets = ( self.root, )
        self.createMenuBar()
        self.createInterface()

    def createInterface(self):
        # Override this method to create the interface for the app.
        pass

    def main(self):
        self.pack()
        self.mainloop()

    def run(self):
        self.main()

class TestAppShell(AppShell):
    usecommandarea=1

    def createButtons(self):              ⑳
        self.buttonAdd('Ok',
                helpMessage='Exit',
                statusMessage='Exit',
                command=self.quit)

    def createMain(self):                 ㉑
```

```
        self.label = self.createcomponent('label', (), None,
                                Label,
                                (self.interior(),),
                                text='Data Area')
        self.label.pack()
        self.bind(self.label, 'Space taker')

    def createInterface(self):        ㉒
        AppShell.createInterface(self)
        self.createButtons()
        self.createMain()

if __name__ == '__main__':
    test = TestAppShell(balloon_state='both')
    test.run()
```

Code comments (continued)

⑲ __createInterface creates each of the standard areas and then calls the createInterface method (which is overridden by the application) to complete the population of the various areas:

```
def __createInterface(self):
    self.__createBalloon()
    self.__createMenuBar()
    self.__createDataArea()
    self.__createCommandArea()
    self.__createMessageBar()
    self.__createAboutBox()
    self.busyWidgets = ( self.root, )
    self.createMenuBar()
    self.createInterface()
```

⑳ For this example, we define just one button to exit the application; you would add all of your buttons to this method for your application.

```
def createButtons(self):
    self.buttonAdd('Ok',
               helpMessage='Exit',
               statusMessage='Exit',
               command=self.quit)
```

㉑ Again, for the purpose of illustration, the dataarea has not been populated with any more than a simple label:

```
def createMain(self):
    self.label = self.createcomponent('label', (), None,
                            Label,
                            (self.interior(),),
                            text='Data Area')
    self.label.pack()
    self.bind(self.label, 'Space taker')
```

Notice how we define balloon help for the label.

㉒ Finally, here is the createInterface method which extends AppShells method:

```
def createInterface(self):
    AppShell.createInterface(self)
```

```
        self.createButtons()
        self.createMain()
```

If you run AppShell.py, you will see a shell similar to the one in figure 8.8. Look for the `toggle` menu item in the `Help` menu to enable or disable balloon help.

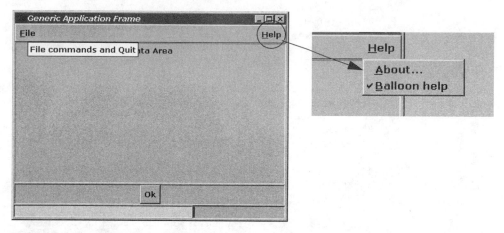

Figure 8.8 AppShell—A standard application framework

8.3 *Data dictionaries*

The forms that I have presented as examples have been coded explicitly for the material to be displayed, this becomes cumbersome when several forms are required to support an application. The solution is to use a *data dictionary* which defines fields, labels, widget types and other information. In addition, it may provide translation from database to screen and back to database, and define validation requirements, editable status and other behavior. We will see some more complete examples in "Putting it all together..." on page 311. However, the examples presented here will certainly give you a clear indication of their importance in simplifying form design.

First let's take a look at a simple data dictionary; in this case it really *is* a Python dictionary, but other data structures could be used.

datadictionary.py

```
LC      = 1       # Lowercase Key       ❶
UC      = 2       # Uppercase Key
XX      = 3       # As Is
DT      = 4       # Date Insert
ND      = 5       # No Duplicate Keys
ZP      = 6       # Pad Zeroes
ZZ      = 7       # Do Not Display
ZS      = 8       # Do Not display, but fill in with key if blank

BLANKOK = 0     # Blank is valid in this field
```

```
NONBLANK = 1   # Field cannot be blank

dataDict = {
  'crewmembers': ('crewmembers',  0.11, 0.45, 0.05, [         ❷
      ('Employee #', 'employee_no', 9, XX, 'valid_blank', NONBLANK) ❸
      ('PIN', 'pin', 4, XX, '', BLANKOK),
      ('Category', 'type', 1, UC, 'valid_category', NONBLANK),
      ('SSN #', 'ssn', 9, XX, 'valid_ssn', BLANKOK),
      ('First Name', 'firstname', 12, XX, 'valid_blank', NONBLANK),
      ('Middle Name', 'middlename', 10, XX, '', BLANKOK),
      ('Last Name', 'lastname', 20, XX, 'valid_blank', NONBLANK),
      ('Status', 'status', 1, UC, '', BLANKOK),
      ('New Hire', 'newhire', 1, UC, 'valid_y_n_blank', BLANKOK),
      ('Seniority Date', 'senioritydate', 8, XX, 'valid_blank', NONBLANK),
      ('Seniority', 'seniority', 5, XX, 'valid_blank', NONBLANK),
      ('Base', 'base', 3, UC, 'valid_base', NONBLANK),
      ('Language 1', 'lang1', 2, UC, 'valid_lang', BLANKOK),
      ('Language 2', 'lang2', 2, UC, 'valid_lang', BLANKOK),
      ('Language 3', 'lang3', 2, UC, 'valid_lang', BLANKOK),
      ('Language 4', 'lang4', 2, UC, 'valid_lang', BLANKOK),
      ('Language 5', 'lang5', 2, UC, 'valid_lang', BLANKOK),
      ('Language 6', 'lang6', 2, UC, 'valid_lang', BLANKOK)],
          'Crew Members', [0]),                                 ❹
  'crewqualifications': ('crewqualification',0.25,0.45,0.075, [
      ('Employee #', 'employee_no', 9, XX, '', BLANKOK),
      ('Equipment', 'equipment', 3, UC, '', BLANKOK),
      ('Eqpt. Code', 'equipmentcode', 1, UC, '', BLANKOK),
      ('Position', 'position', 2, UC, '', BLANKOK),
      ('Pos. Code', 'positioncode', 2, UC, '', BLANKOK),
      ('Reserve', 'reserve', 1, UC, 'valid_r_blank', BLANKOK),
      ('Date of Hire', 'hiredate', 8, UC, '', BLANKOK),
      ('End Date', 'enddate', 8, UC, '', BLANKOK),
      ('Base Code', 'basecode', 1, UC, '', BLANKOK),
      ('Manager', 'manager', 1, UC, 'valid_y_n_blank', BLANKOK)],
                  'Crew Qualifications', [0]) }
```

Code comments

❶ We define several constants to characterize the behavior of entry fields, controlling case-changing, for example:

```
LC  = 1     # Lowercase Key
UC  = 2     # Uppercase Key
XX  = 3     # As Is
...
```

❷ The first section of each entry in the dictionary defines the key, database table and layout data to customize the position of the first line, label/field position and the line spacing respectively.

```
'crewmembers': ('crewmembers',  0.11, 0.45, 0.05, [
```

❸ Each entry in the dictionary defines the label, database key, field length, entry processing, validation and whether the field may be left blank.

```
('Employee #', 'employee_no', 9, XX, 'valid_blank', NONBLANK),
('PIN', 'pin', 4, XX, '', BLANKOK),
('Category', 'type', 1, UC, 'valid_category', NONBLANK),
```

The final entry in each table defines the title and a list of indices for the primary and secondary keys (in this case, we are only using a single key):

```
'Crew Members', [0]),
```

Now let's use datadictionary.py to create an interface. We will also use AppShell to provide the framework.

Example_8_7.py

```python
from    Tkinter import *
import  Pmw
import  os
import  AppShell
from    datadictionary import *

class DDForm(AppShell.AppShell):           ❶
    usecommandarea = 1
    appname        = 'Update Crew Information'
    dictionary     = 'crewmembers'
    frameWidth     = 600
    frameHeight    = 590

    def createButtons(self):               ❷
        self.buttonAdd('Save',
                    helpMessage='Save current data',
                    statusMessage='Write current information to database',
                    command=self.unimplemented)
        self.buttonAdd('Undo',
                    helpMessage='Ignore changes',
                    statusMessage='Do not save changes to database',
                    command=self.unimplemented)
        self.buttonAdd('New',
                    helpMessage='Create a New record',
                    statusMessage='Create New record',
                    command=self.unimplemented)
        self.buttonAdd('Delete',
                    helpMessage='Delete current record',
                    statusMessage='Delete this record',
                    command=self.unimplemented)
        self.buttonAdd('Print',
                    helpMessage='Print this screen',
                    statusMessage='Print data in this screen',
                    command=self.unimplemented)
        self.buttonAdd('Prev',
                    helpMessage='Previous record',
                    statusMessage='Display previous record',
                    command=self.unimplemented)
        self.buttonAdd('Next',
                    helpMessage='Next record',
                    statusMessage='Display next record',
                    command=self.unimplemented)
        self.buttonAdd('Close',
                    helpMessage='Close Screen',
                    statusMessage='Exit',
```

```
                            command=self.unimplemented)
    def createForm(self):                                    ❸
        self.form = self.createcomponent('form', (), None,
                            Frame, (self.interior(),),)
        self.form.pack(side=TOP, expand=YES, fill=BOTH)
        self.formwidth = self.root.winfo_width()

    def createFields(self):
        self.table, self.top, self.anchor, self.incr, self.fields, \    ❹
                self.title, self.keylist = dataDict[self.dictionary]
        self.records= []
        self.dirty= FALSE
        self.changed= []
        self.newrecs= []
        self.deleted= []
        self.checkDupes = FALSE
        self.delkeys= []

        self.ypos = self.top                                 ❺
        self.recrows = len(self.records)
        if self.recrows < 1: # Create one!
            self.recrows = 1
            trec = []
            for i in range(len(self.fields)):
                trec.append(None)
                self.records.append((trec))

        Label(self.form, text=self.title, width=self.formwidth-4,    ❻
                bd=0).place(relx=0.5, rely=0.025, anchor=CENTER)
        self.lmarker = Label(self.form, text="", bd=0, width=10)
        self.lmarker.place(relx=0.02, rely=0.99, anchor=SW)
        self.rmarker = Label(self.form, text="", bd=0, width=10)
        self.rmarker.place(relx=0.99, rely=0.99, anchor=SE)

        self.current = 0
        idx = 0
        for label, field, width, proc, valid, nonblank in self.fields:    ❼
            pstr = 'Label(self.form,text="%s").place(relx=%f,rely=%f,'\
            'anchor=E)\n' % (label, (self.anchor-0.02), self.ypos)
            if idx == self.keylist[0]:
                pstr = '%sself.%s=Entry(self.form,text="",'\
                'insertbackground="yellow", width=%d+1,'\
                'highlightthickness=1)\n' % (pstr,field,width)
            else:
                pstr = '%sself.%s=Entry(self.form,text="",'\
                'insertbackground="yellow",'\
                'width=%d+1)\n' % (pstr,field,width)
            pstr = '%sself.%s.place(relx=%f, rely=%f,'
            'anchor=W)\n' % (pstr,field,(self.anchor+0.02),self.ypos)
            exec '%sself.%sV=StringVar()\n'\
            'self.%s["textvariable"] = self.%sV' % \
                            (pstr,field,field,field)
            self.ypos = self.ypos + self.incr
            idx = idx + 1
        self.update_display()
```

```
        def update_display(self):            ❽
            idx = 0
            for label, field, width, proc, valid, nonblank in self.fields:
                v=self.records[self.current][idx]
                if not v:v=""
                exec 'self.%sV.set(v)' % field
                idx = idx + 1
            if self.current in self.deleted:
                self.rmarker['text'] = 'Deleted'
            elif self.current in self.newrecs:
                self.rmarker['text'] = 'New'
            else:
                self.rmarker['text'] = ''
            if self.dirty:
                self.lmarker['text']    = "Modified"
                self.lmarker['foreground'] = "#FF3333"
            else:
                self.lmarker['text']    = ""
                self.lmarker['foreground'] = "#00FF44"
            # We'll set focus on the first widget
            label, field, width, proc, valid, nonblank = self.fields[0]
            exec 'self.%s.focus_set()' % field

    def unimplemented(self):            ❾
        pass

    def createInterface(self):
        AppShell.AppShell.createInterface(self)
        self.createButtons()
        self.createForm()
        self.createFields()

if __name__ == '__main__':
    ddform = DDForm()
    ddform.run()
```

Code comments

❶ First we define the Application class, inheriting from AppShell and overriding its class variables to set the title, width, height and other values:

```
class DDForm(AppShell.AppShell):
    usecommandarea = 1
    appname       = 'Update Crew Information'
    dictionary    = 'crewmembers'
    frameWidth    = 600
    frameHeight   = 590
```

❷ In this example, we are defining a more realistic complement of control buttons:

```
def createButtons(self):
    self.buttonAdd('Save',
                helpMessage='Save current data',
                statusMessage='Write current information to database',
                command=self.save)
    ...
```

❸ Rather than use the default megawidget interior, we create our own form component:

```
def createForm(self):
    self.form = self.createcomponent('form', (), None,
                    Frame, (self.interior(),),)
    self.form.pack(side=TOP, expand=YES, fill=BOTH)
    self.formwidth = self.root.winfo_width()
```

❹ We extract the data from the selected data dictionary element and initialize data structures:

```
def createFields(self):
    self.table, self.top, self.anchor, self.incr, self.fields, \
            self.title, self.keylist = dataDict[self.dictionary]
    self.records= []
    self.dirty= FALSE
```

❺ This example does not interface with any database, but we still need to create a single empty record even for this case. We create one empty entry for each field:

```
self.ypos = self.top
self.recrows = len(self.records)
if self.recrows < 1: # Create one!
    self.recrows = 1
    trec = []
    for i in range(len(self.fields)):
        trec.append(None)
        self.records.append((trec))
```

❻ Although we are not going to be able to save any information input to the form, we still define markers at the left- and right-bottom of the screen to indicate when a record has been modified or added:

```
Label(self.form, text=self.title, width=self.formwidth-4,
        bd=0).place(relx=0.5, rely=0.025, anchor=CENTER)
self.lmarker = Label(self.form, text="", bd=0, width=10)
self.lmarker.place(relx=0.02, rely=0.99, anchor=SW)
self.rmarker = Label(self.form, text="", bd=0, width=10)
self.rmarker.place(relx=0.99, rely=0.99, anchor=SE)
```

❼ This is where we create the label/field pairs which make up our interface. We give the user a visual clue that a field is the key by increasing the highlight thickness:

```
for label, field, width, proc, valid, nonblank in self.fields:
    pstr = 'Label(self.form,text="%s").place(relx=%f,rely=%f,'\
    'anchor=E)\n' % (label, (self.anchor-0.02), self.ypos)
    if idx == self.keylist[0]:
        pstr = '%sself.%s=Entry(self.form,text="",'\
        'insertbackground="yellow", width=%d+1,'\
        'highlightthickness=1)\n' % (pstr,field,width)
    else:
        ...
```

Note In this application we have chosen to use highlightthickness to provide a visual clue to the user that the field contains the key to the data. You might choose one of several other methods to get this effect, such as changing the background color or changing the borderwidth.

---

8 The `update_display` method is responsible for setting the markers to indicate new, deleted and modified records:

```
def update_display(self):
    idx = 0
    for label, field, width, proc, valid, nonblank in self.fields:
        v=self.records[self.current][idx]
        if not v:v=""
        exec 'self.%sV.set(v)' % field
        idx = idx + 1
    if self.current in self.deleted:
        ...
```

9 The methods bound to the control buttons do nothing in our example, but they are required for Python to run the application:

```
def unimplemented(self):
    pass
```

Running Example_8_7.py will display a screen similar to figure 8.9. Notice that the layout could be improved if the fields were individually placed, or if more than one field were placed on a single line, but that would obviate the simplicity of using a data dictionary.

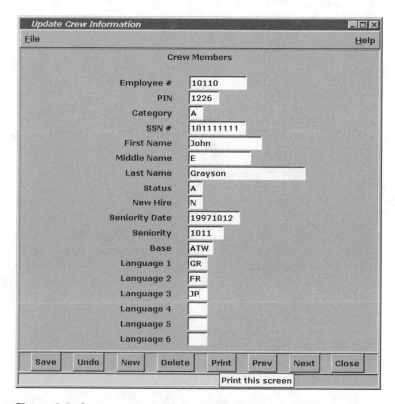

Figure 8.9 A screen created from a data dictionary

8.4 Notebooks

Notebooks (sometimes referred to as *style* or *property sheets*) have become a common motif for user interfaces. One large advantage is that they allow the form designer to display a large number of entry fields without overwhelming the user. Additionally, the fields can be arranged in related groupings, or less-important fields can be separated from fields which are frequently changed.

The next example demonstrates the use of notebooks, data dictionaries and AppShell to present the same basic data in Example_8_7.py on three separate notebook panes. datadictionary.py has been rearranged as datadictionary2.py, but it will not be presented here (the previous dictionary has been divided into one section for each pane of the notebook).

Example_8_9.py

```
from    Tkinter import *
import Pmw
import os
import AppShell
from    datadictionary2 import *

class DDNotebook(AppShell.AppShell):
    usecommandarea = 1
    appname       = 'Update Crew Information'
    dictionary    = 'crewmembers'
    frameWidth    = 435
    frameHeight   = 520

    def createButtons(self):
        self.buttonAdd('Save',
                    helpMessage='Save current data',
                    statusMessage='Write current information to database',
                    command=self.save)
        self.buttonAdd('Close',
                    helpMessage='Close Screen',
                    statusMessage='Exit',
                    command=self.close)

    def createNotebook(self):
        self.notebook = self.createcomponent('notebook', (), None,
                                  Pmw.NoteBookR, (self.interior(),),)     ❶
        self.notebook.pack(side=TOP, expand=YES, fill=BOTH, padx=5, pady=5)
        self.formwidth = self.root.winfo_width()

    def addPage(self, dictionary):
        table, top, anchor, incr, fields, \
             title, keylist = dataDict[dictionary]
        self.notebook.add(table, label=title)                              ❷
        self.current = 0
        ypos = top
        idx = 0

        for label, field, width, proc, valid, nonblank in fields:          ❸
            pstr = 'Label(self.notebook.page(table).interior(),'\
```

```
                        'text="%s").place(relx=%f,rely=%f, anchor=E)\n' % \
                            (label, (anchor-0.02), ypos)
                if idx == keylist[0]:
                    pstr = '%sself.%s=Entry(self.notebook.page(table).\
                            `interior(), text="",insertbackground="yellow"',
                            'width=%d+1, highlightthickness=1)\n' % \
                                        (pstr,field,width)
                else:
                    pstr = '%sself.%s=Entry(self.notebook.page(table).\
                            `interior(), text="", insertbackground="yellow",'
                        'width=%d+1)\n' % (pstr,field,width)
            pstr = '%sself.%s.place(relx=%f, rely=%f,'\
                'anchor=W)\n' % (pstr,field, (anchor+0.02),ypos)
            exec '%sself.%sV=StringVar()\n'\
                'self.%s["textvariable"] = self.%sV' % (pstr,field,field,field)
            ypos = ypos + incr
            idx = idx + 1

    def createPages(self):                ❹
        self.addPage('general')
        self.addPage('language')
        self.addPage('crewqualifications')
        self.update_display()

    def update_display(self):
        pass

    def save(self):
        pass
    def close(self):
        self.quit()

    def createInterface(self):
        AppShell.AppShell.createInterface(self)
        self.createButtons()
        self.createNotebook()
        self.createPages()

if __name__ == '__main__':
    ddnotebook = DDNotebook()
    ddnotebook.run()
```

Code comments

❶ Creating a notebook within the AppShell is simply a case of creating a Pmw NoteBookR component.

```
def createNotebook(self):
    self.notebook = self.createcomponent('notebook', (), None,
                            Pmw.NoteBookR, (self.interior(),),)
    self.notebook.pack(side=TOP, expand=YES, fill=BOTH, padx=5, pady=5)
```

Pmw provides an alternate notebook widget, NoteBookS (see figure 8.10 on page 174 for an example). I do not recommend that you use this widget since it has a generally inferior layout.

2 The name and text displayed in the notebook tab comes directly from the data dictionary:

```
def addPage(self, dictionary):
    table, top, anchor, incr, fields, \
        title, keylist = dataDict[dictionary]
    self.notebook.add(table, label=title)
```

3 Loading the fields from the data dictionary is similar to the previous example:

```
for label, field, width, proc, valid, nonblank in fields:
    pstr = 'Label(self.notebook.page(table).interior(),'\
        'text="%s").place(relx=%f,rely=%f, anchor=E)\n' % \
        (label, (anchor-0.02), ypos)
    ...
```

4 The pages are tagged with the dictionary key:

```
def createPages(self):
    self.addPage('general')
    self.addPage('language')
    self.addPage('crewqualifications')
    self.update_display()
```

Figure 8.10 shows the result of running Example_8_9.py. Notice how the fields are much less cluttered and that they now have clear logical groupings.

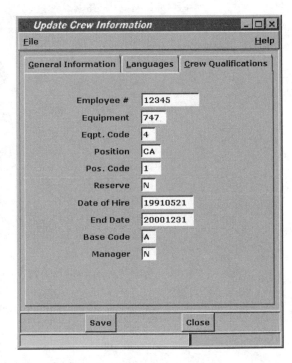

Figure 8.10 Notebooks

8.5 Browsers

Browsers have become a popular motif for navigating information that is, or can be, organized as a hierarchy. Good examples of browsers include the Preferences editor in Netscape and Windows Explorer. The advantage of browsers is that branches of the typical tree display can be expanded and collapsed, resulting in an uncluttered display, even though the volume of data displayed can be quite high.

As an example, we are going to develop a simple image browser which will display all of the images in a particular directory. Tk, and therefore Tkinter, supports three image formats: GIF, PPM (truecolor), and XBM. To extend the capability of the example, we will use PIL from Secret Labs A.B. to build the images. This does not add a great deal of complexity to the example, as you will see when we examine the source code.

The browser uses several icons to represent various file types; for the purpose of this example we are using a mixture of icons created for this application. They are similar in style to those found in most current window systems.

The tree browser class is quite general and can readily be made into a base class for other browsers.

Example_8_10.py

```
from    Tkinter import *
import Pmw
import os
import AppShell
import Image, ImageTk                              ❶

path = "./icons/"
imgs = "./images/"

class Node:                                          ❷
    def __init__(self, master, tree, icon=None,
            openicon=None, name=None, action=None):
        self.master, self.tree = master, tree
        self.icon = PhotoImage(file=icon)
        if openicon:
            self.openicon = PhotoImage(file=openicon)
        else:
            self.openicon = None

        self.width, self.height = 1.5*self.icon.width(), \
                        1.5*self.icon.height()
        self.name = name
        self.var = StringVar()                       ❸
        self.var.set(name)
        self.text = Entry(tree, textvariable=self.var, bg=tree.bg,
                bd=0, width=len(name)+2, font=tree.font,
                fg=tree.textcolor, insertwidth=1,
                highlightthickness=1,                ❹
                highlightbackground=tree.bg,
                selectbackground="#044484",
                selectborderwidth=0,
                selectforeground='white')
```

```
        self.action = action
        self.x = self.y = 0   #drawing location
        self.child = []
        self.state = 'collapsed'
        self.selected = 0

    def addChild(self, tree, icon=None, openicon=None, name=None,      ❺
            action=None):
        child = Node(self, tree, icon, openicon, name, action)
        self.child.append(child)
        self.tree.display()
        return child

    def deleteChild(self, child):
        self.child.remove(child)
        self.tree.display()

    def textForget(self):
        self.text.place_forget()
        for child in self.child:
            child.textForget()

    def deselect(self):
        self.selected = 0
        for child in self.child:
            child.deselect()

    def boxpress(self, event=None):                                    ❻
        if self.state == 'expanded':
            self.state = 'collapsed'
        elif self.state == 'collapsed':
            self.state = 'expanded'
        self.tree.display()

    def invoke(self, event=None):                                      ❼
        if not self.selected:
            self.tree.deselectall()
            self.selected = 1
            self.tree.display()
            if self.action:
                self.action(self.name)
        self.name = self.text.get()
        self.text.config(width=len(self.name)+2)
```

Code comments

❶ We begin by importing PIL modules:

```
import Image, ImageTk
```

❷ The Node class defines the subordinate tree and the open and closed icons associated with the node.

```
class Node:
    def __init__(self, master, tree, icon=None,
            openicon=None, name=None, action=None):
        ...
```

❸ Each node has a Tkinter variable assigned to it since we are going to allow the nodes to be renamed (although code to use the new name is not provided in the example):

```
self.name = name
self.var = StringVar()
self.var.set(name)
self.text = Entry(tree, textvariable=self.var, bg=tree.bg,
```

❹ The Entry widget does not display a highlight by default. To indicate that we are editing the filename, we add a highlight.

❺ When we construct the hierarchy of nodes later, we will use the addChild method in the Node class:

```
def addChild(self, tree, icon=None, openicon=None, name=None,
        action=None):
    child = Node(self, tree, icon, openicon, name, action)
    self.child.append(child)
    self.tree.display()
    return child
```

This creates an instance of Node and appends it to the child list.

❻ The boxpress method toggles the state of nodes displayed in the browser; clicking on + expands the node, while clicking on − collapses the node.

```
def boxpress(self, event=None):
    if self.state == 'expanded':
        self.state = 'collapsed'
    elif self.state == 'collapsed':
        self.state = 'expanded'
    self.tree.display()
```

❼ If the node is not currently selected, invoke supports an action assigned to either clicking or double-clicking on a node in the tree. For example, it might open the file using an appropriate target.

```
def invoke(self, event=None):
    if not self.selected:
        self.tree.deselectall()
        self.selected = 1
        self.tree.display()
        if self.action:
            self.action(self.name)
    self.name = self.text.get()
    self.text.config(width=len(self.name)+2)
```

Example_8_10.py (continued)

```
def displayIconText(self):                    ❽
    tree, text = self.tree, self.text
    if self.selected and self.openicon:
        self.pic = tree.create_image(self.x, self.y,
                            image=self.openicon)
    else:
        self.pic = tree.create_image(self.x, self.y,
                            image=self.icon)

    text.place(x=self.x+self.width/2, y=self.y, anchor=W)
```

```
            text.bind("<ButtonPress-1>", self.invoke)
            tree.tag_bind(self.pic, "<ButtonPress-1>", self.invoke, "+")
            text.bind("<Double-Button-1>", self.boxpress)
            tree.tag_bind(self.pic, "<Double-Button-1>",
                    self.boxpress, "+")

    def displayRoot(self):
        if self.state == 'expanded':
            for child in self.child:
                child.display()
        self.displayIconText()

    def displayLeaf(self):                                    9
        self.tree.hline(self.y, self.master.x+1, self.x)
        self.tree.vline(self.master.x, self.master.y, self.y)
        self.displayIconText()

    def displayBranch(self):                                  10
        master, tree = self.master, self.tree
        x, y = self.x, self.y
        tree.hline(y, master.x, x)
        tree.vline(master.x, master.y, y)
        if self.state == 'expanded' and self.child != []:
            for child in self.child:
                child.display()
            box = tree.create_image(master.x, y,
                            image=tree.minusnode)
        elif self.state == 'collapsed' and self.child != []:
            box = tree.create_image(master.x, y,
                            image=tree.plusnode)
        tree.tag_bind(box, "<ButtonPress-1>", self.boxpress, "+")
        self.displayIconText()

    def findLowestChild(self, node):                          11
        if node.state == 'expanded' and node.child != []:
            return self.findLowestChild(node.child[-1])
        else:
            return node

    def display(self):
        master, tree = self.master, self.tree
        n = master.child.index(self)
        self.x = master.x + self.width
        if n == 0:
            self.y = master.y + (n+1)*self.height
        else:
            previous = master.child[n-1]
            self.y = self.findLowestChild(previous).y + self.height

        if master == tree:
            self.displayRoot()
        elif master.state == 'expanded':
            if self.child == []:
                self.displayLeaf()
            else:
                self.displayBranch()
```

```
                    tree.lower('line')

        class Tree(Canvas):
            def __init__(self, master, icon, openicon, treename, action,
                    bg='white', relief='sunken', bd=2,
                    linecolor='#808080', textcolor='black',
                    font=('MS Sans Serif', 8)):
                Canvas.__init__(self, master, bg=bg, relief=relief, bd=bd,
                        highlightthickness=0)
                self.pack(side='left', anchor=NW, fill='both', expand=1)

                self.bg, self.font= bg, font
                self.linecolor, self.textcolor= linecolor, textcolor
                self.master = master
                self.plusnode = PhotoImage(file=os.path.join(path, 'plusnode.gif'))
                self.minusnode = PhotoImage(file=os.path.join(path, 'minusnode.gif'))
                self.inhibitDraw = 1                        ⓬
                self.imageLabel = None
                self.imageData = None
                self.child = []
                self.x = self.y = -10

                self.child.append( Node( self, self, action=action,
                            icon=icon, openicon=openicon, name=treename) )

            def display(self):
                if self.inhibitDraw: return
                self.delete(ALL)
                for child in self.child:
                    child.textForget()
                    child.display()

            def deselectall(self):
                for child in self.child:
                    child.deselect()

            def vline(self, x, y, y1):                      ⓭
                for i in range(0, abs(y-y1), 2):
                    self.create_line(x, y+i, x, y+i+1, fill=self.linecolor,
                            tags='line')

            def hline(self, y, x, x1):
                for i in range(0, abs(x-x1), 2):
                    self.create_line(x+i, y, x+i+1, y, fill=self.linecolor,
                            tags='line')
```

Code comments (continued)

❽ displayIconText displays the open or closed icon and the text associated with the node, and it binds single- and double-button-clicks to the text field:

```
        def displayIconText(self):
            tree, text = self.tree, self.text
            if self.selected and self.openicon:
                self.pic = tree.create_image(self.x, self.y,
                                image=self.openicon)
```

```
...
...
        text.bind("<ButtonPress-1>", self.invoke)
        tree.tag_bind(self.pic, "<ButtonPress-1>", self.invoke, "+")
        text.bind("<Double-Button-1>", self.boxpress)
        tree.tag_bind(self.pic, "<Double-Button-1>",
                      self.boxpress, "+")
```

9 displayLeaf draws a horizontal and vertical line connecting the icon with the current place in the tree:

```
def displayLeaf(self):
    self.tree.hline(self.y, self.master.x+1, self.x)
    self.tree.vline(self.master.x, self.master.y, self.y)
    self.displayIconText()
```

10 Similarly, displayBranch draws the lines and an open or closed box:

```
def displayBranch(self):
    master, tree = self.master, self.tree
    x, y = self.x, self.y
    tree.hline(y, master.x, x)
    tree.vline(master.x, master.y, y)
    if self.state == 'expanded' and self.child != []:
        for child in self.child:
            child.display()
        box = tree.create_image(master.x, y,
                        image=tree.minusnode)
    elif self.state == 'collapsed' and self.child != []:
        box = tree.create_image(master.x, y,
                        image=tree.plusnode)
    tree.tag_bind(box, "<ButtonPress-1>", self.boxpress, "+")
    self.displayIconText()
```

11 findLowestChild is a recursive method that finds the lowest terminal child in a given branch:

```
def findLowestChild(self, node):
    if node.state == 'expanded' and node.child != []:
        return self.findLowestChild(node.child[-1])
    else:
        return node
```

12 We define a flag called inhibitDraw to prevent the tree from being redrawn every time we add a node. This speeds up the time it takes to construct a complex tree by saving many CPU cycles:

```
        self.inhibitDraw = 1
```

13 vline and hline are simple routines to draw vertical and horizontal lines:

```
def vline(self, x, y, y1):
    for i in range(0, abs(y-y1), 2):
        self.create_line(x, y+i, x, y+i+1, fill=self.linecolor,
                    tags='line')
```

Example_8_10.py (continued)

```
class ImageBrowser(AppShell.AppShell):
    usecommandarea=1
```

```
        appname = 'Image Browser'
        def createButtons(self):
            self.buttonAdd('Ok',
                        helpMessage='Exit',
                        statusMessage='Exit',
                        command=self.quit)

        def createMain(self):
            self.panes = self.createcomponent('panes', (), None,
                                    Pmw.PanedWidget,
                                    (self.interior(),),
                                    orient='horizontal')
            self.panes.add('browserpane', min=150, size=160)
            self.panes.add('displaypane', min=.1)

            f = os.path.join(path, 'folder.gif')
            of = os.path.join(path, 'openfolder.gif')
            self.browser = self.createcomponent('browse', (), None,
                                    Tree,
                                    (self.panes.pane('browserpane'),),
                                    icon=f,
                                    openicon=of,
                                    treename='Multimedia',
                                    action=None)
            self.browser.pack(side=TOP, expand=YES, fill=Y)

            self.datasite = self.createcomponent('datasite', (), None,
                                    Frame,
                                    (self.panes.pane('displaypane'),))

            self.datasite.pack(side=TOP, expand=YES, fill=BOTH)

            f  = os.path.join(path, 'folder.gif')                    ⓮
            of = os.path.join(path, 'openfolder.gif')
            gf = os.path.join(path, 'gif.gif')
            jf = os.path.join(path, 'jpg.gif')
            xf = os.path.join(path, 'other.gif')

            self.browser.inhibitDraw = 1

            top=self.browser.child[0]                                 ⓯
            top.state='expanded'
            jpeg=top.addChild(self.browser, icon=f, openicon=of,
                        name='Jpeg',action=None)
            gif=top.addChild(self.browser, icon=f, openicon=of,
                        name='GIF',    action=None)
            other=top.addChild(self.browser, icon=f, openicon=of,
                        name='Other', action=None)

            imageDir = { '.jpg': (jpeg, jf), '.jpeg': (jpeg, jf),    ⓰
                    '.gif': (gif, gf), '.bmp':  (other, xf),
                    '.ppm': (other, xf)}

            files = os.listdir(imgs)                                 ⓱
            for file in files:
                r, ext = os.path.splitext(file)
```

```
            cont, icon = imageDir.get(ext, (None, None))
            if cont:
                cont.addChild(self.browser, icon=icon,
                           name=file, action=self.showMe)
        self.browser.inhibitDraw = 0
        self.browser.display()
        self.panes.pack(side=TOP, expand=YES, fill=BOTH)

    def createImageDisplay(self):
        self.imageDisplay = self.createcomponent('image', (), None,
                           Label,
                           (self.datasite,))
        self.browser.imageLabel = self.imageDisplay
        self.browser.imageData= None
        self.imageDisplay.place(relx=0.5, rely=0.5, anchor=CENTER)

    def createInterface(self):
        AppShell.AppShell.createInterface(self)
        self.createButtons()
        self.createMain()
        self.createImageDisplay()

    def showMe(self, dofile):
        if self.browser.imageData: del self.browser.imageData
        self.browser.imageData = ImageTk.PhotoImage(\
                    Image.open('%s%s' % \
                        (imgs, dofile)))
        self.browser.imageLabel['image'] = self.browser.imageData

if __name__ == '__main__':
    imageBrowser = ImageBrowser()
    imageBrowser.run()
```

⑱

Code comments (continued)

⑭ We define all of the icons that may be displayed for each file type:

```
f  = os.path.join(path, 'folder.gif')
of = os.path.join(path, 'openfolder.gif')
gf = os.path.join(path, 'gif.gif')
jf = os.path.join(path, 'jpg.gif')
xf = os.path.join(path, 'other.gif')
```

⑮ Now the root of the tree is created and we populate the root with the supported image types:

```
top=self.browser.child[0]
top.state='expanded'
jpeg=top.addChild(self.browser, icon=f, openicon=of,
            name='Jpeg',action=None)
...
```

⑯ We create a dictionary to provide translation from file extensions to an appropriate image type and icon (dictionaries are an efficient way of determining properties of an object which have varied processing requirements).

```
imageDir = { '.jpg': (jpeg, jf), '.jpeg': (jpeg, jf),
            '.gif': (gif, gf), '.bmp': (other, xf),
            '.ppm': (other, xf)}
```

⑰ We scan the disk, finding all files with recognizable extensions and add the nodes to the tree:

```
files = os.listdir(imgs)
for file in files:
    r, ext = os.path.splitext(file)
    cont, icon = imageDir.get(ext, (None, None))
    if cont:
        cont.addChild(self.browser, icon=icon,
                            name=file, action=self.showMe)
```

This code would probably be a little more complex in reality; I can see a couple of potential problems as I'm writing this (I could write "I leave this as an exercise for you to identify problems with this code").

⑱ Once the tree has been built, we reset the `inhibitDraw` flag and display the tree:

```
self.browser.inhibitDraw = 0
self.browser.display()
```

That probably seems like a lot of code, but the resulting browser provides a highly-acceptable interface. In addition, users will understand the interface's navigation and it is readily adaptable to a wide range of data models.

Running Example_8_10.py (with a Python built with PIL) will display a screen similar to the one in figure 8.11.

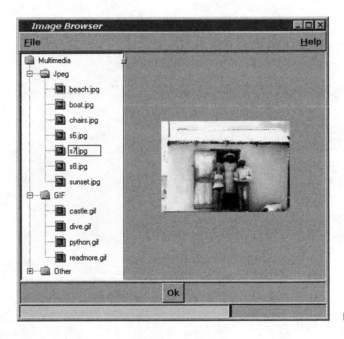

Figure 8.11 Image browser

8.6 Wizards

Windows 95/98/NT users have become familiar with wizard interfaces since they have become prevalent with installation and configuration tools. Wizards guide the user through a sequence of steps, and they allow forward and backward navigation. In many respects they are similar to Notebooks, except for their ordered access as opposed to the random access of the Notebook.

This example illustrates a wizard that supports software installation. WizardShell.py is derived from AppShell.py, but it has sufficient differences to preclude inheriting AppShell's properties. However, much of the code is similar to AppShell and is not presented here; the complete source is available online.

WizardShell.py

```python
from Tkinter import *
import Pmw
import sys, string

class WizardShell(Pmw.MegaWidget):
    wizversion= '1.0'
    wizname    = 'Generic Wizard Frame'
    wizimage= 'wizard.gif'

    panes      = 4                                          ❶

    def __init__(self, **kw):
        optiondefs = (
                ('framewidth',    1,          Pmw.INITOPT),
                ('frameheight',   1,          Pmw.INITOPT))
        self.defineoptions(kw, optiondefs)

        # setup panes                                       ❷
        self.pCurrent = 0
        self.pFrame = [None] * self.panes

    def wizardInit(self):
        # Called before interface is created (should be overridden).
        pass
                                                            ❸
    def __createWizardArea(self):
        self.__wizardArea = self.createcomponent('wizard',(), None,
                                    Frame, (self._hull,),
                                    relief=FLAT, bd=1)
        self.__illustration = self.createcomponent('illust',(), None,
                                     Label,(self.__wizardArea,))
        self.__illustration.pack(side=LEFT, expand=NO, padx=20)
        self.__wizimage = PhotoImage(file=self.wizimage)
        self.__illustration['image'] = self.__wizimage

        self.__dataArea = self.createcomponent('dataarea',(), None,
                                    Frame,(self.__wizardArea,),
                                    relief=FLAT, bd=1)

        self.__dataArea.pack(side=LEFT, fill = 'both', expand = YES)
```

```
                    self.__wizardArea.pack(side=TOP, fill=BOTH, expand=YES)

        def __createSeparator(self):
            self.__separator = self.createcomponent('separator',(), None,
                                    Frame,(self._hull,),
                                    relief=SUNKEN,
                                    bd=2, height=2)
            self.__separator.pack(fill=X, expand=YES)

        def __createCommandArea(self):
            self.__commandFrame = self.createcomponent('commandframe',(), None,
                                    Frame,(self._hull,),
                                    relief=FLAT, bd=1)
            self.__commandFrame.pack(side=TOP, expand=NO, fill=X)

        def interior(self):
            return self.__dataArea

        def changePicture(self, gif):
            self.__wizimage = PhotoImage(file=gif)
            self.__illustration['image'] = self.__wizimage

        def buttonAdd(self, buttonName, command=None, state=1):     ❹
            frame = Frame(self.__commandFrame)
            newBtn = Button(frame, text=buttonName, command=command)
            newBtn.pack()
            newBtn['state'] = [DISABLED,NORMAL][state]
            frame.pack(side=RIGHT, ipadx=5, ipady=5)
            return newBtn

        def __createPanes(self):                                   ❺
            for i in range(self.panes):
                self.pFrame[i] = self.createcomponent('pframe',(), None,
                                    Frame,(self.interior(),),
                                    relief=FLAT, bd=1)
                if not i == self.pCurrent:
                    self.pFrame[i].forget()
                else:
                    self.pFrame[i].pack(fill=BOTH, expand=YES)

        def pInterior(self, idx):                                  ❻
            return self.pFrame[idx]

        def next(self):                                            ❼
            cpane = self.pCurrent
            self.pCurrent = self.pCurrent + 1
            self.prevB['state'] = NORMAL
            if self.pCurrent == self.panes - 1:
                self.nextB['text']    = 'Finish'
                self.nextB['command'] = self.done
            self.pFrame[cpane].forget()
            self.pFrame[self.pCurrent].pack(fill=BOTH, expand=YES)

        def prev(self):
            cpane = self.pCurrent
            self.pCurrent = self.pCurrent - 1
```

```
                    if self.pCurrent <= 0:
                        self.pCurrent = 0
                        self.prevB['state'] = DISABLED
                    if cpane == self.panes - 1:
                        self.nextB['text']    = 'Next'
                        self.nextB['command'] = self.next
                    self.pFrame[cpane].forget()
                    self.pFrame[self.pCurrent].pack(fill=BOTH, expand=YES)

            def done(self):
                #to be Overridden
                pass

            def __createInterface(self):
                self.__createWizardArea()
                self.__createSeparator()
                self.__createCommandArea()
                self.__createPanes()
                self.busyWidgets = ( self.root, )
                self.createInterface()

    class TestWizardShell(WizardShell):
        def createButtons(self):
            self.buttonAdd('Cancel',     command=self.quit)          ❽
            self.nextB = self.buttonAdd('Next', command=self.next)
            self.prevB = self.buttonAdd('Prev', command=self.prev, state=0)

        def createMain(self):
            self.w1 = self.createcomponent('w1', (), None,
                                    Label,(self.pInterior(0),),
                                    text='Wizard Area 1')
            self.w1.pack()
            self.w2 = self.createcomponent('w2', (), None,
                                    Label,(self.pInterior(1),),
                                    text='Wizard Area 2')
            self.w2.pack()

        def createInterface(self):
            WizardShell.createInterface(self)
            self.createButtons()
            self.createMain()

        def done(self):                 ❾
            print 'All Done'

    if __name__ == '__main__':
        test = TestWizardShell()
        test.run()
```

Code comments

❶ WizardShell uses AppShell's class variables, adding panes to define the number of discrete steps to be presented in the wizard.

```
        class WizardShell(Pmw.MegaWidget):
            panes      = 4
```

❷ We initialize an empty pane for each step and initialize for the first step:

```
self.pCurrent = 0
self.pFrame = [None] * self.panes
```

❸ The main WizardArea is created:

```
def __createWizardArea(self):
    ...
def __createSeparator(self):
    ...
def __createCommandArea(self):
    ...
```

Then, a Separator and a CommandArea are added.

❹ buttonAdd is slightly more comprehensive than AppShell's since we have to enable and disable the next and prev buttons as we move through the sequence:

```
def buttonAdd(self, buttonName, command=None, state=1):
    frame = Frame(self.__commandFrame)
    newBtn = Button(frame, text=buttonName, command=command)
    newBtn.pack()
    newBtn['state'] = [DISABLED,NORMAL][state]
    frame.pack(side=RIGHT, ipadx=5, ipady=5)
    return newBtn
```

❺ Now we create a pane for each step, packing the current frame and forgetting all others so that they are not displayed:

```
def __createPanes(self):
    for i in range(self.panes):
        self.pFrame[i] = self.createcomponent('pframe',(), None,
                                   Frame,(self.interior(),),
                                   relief=FLAT, bd=1)
        if not i == self.pCurrent:
            self.pFrame[i].forget()
        else:
            self.pFrame[i].pack(fill=BOTH, expand=YES)
```

❻ Similar to the convention to define an interior method, we define the pInterior method to give access to individual panes in the wizard:

```
def pInterior(self, idx):
    return self.pFrame[idx]
```

❼ The next and prev methods forget the current pane and pack the next pane, changing the state of buttons as appropriate and changing the labels as necessary:

```
def next(self):
    cpane = self.pCurrent
    self.pCurrent = self.pCurrent + 1
    self.prevB['state'] = NORMAL
    if self.pCurrent == self.panes - 1:
        self.nextB['text']    = 'Finish'
        self.nextB['command'] = self.done
    self.pFrame[cpane].forget()
    self.pFrame[self.pCurrent].pack(fill=BOTH, expand=YES)
```

❽ Unlike AppShell, we have to store references to the control buttons so that we can manipulate their state and labels:

```
class TestWizardShell(WizardShell):
    def createButtons(self):
        self.buttonAdd('Cancel',    command=self.quit)
        self.nextB = self.buttonAdd('Next', command=self.next)
        self.prevB = self.buttonAdd('Prev', command=self.prev, state=0)
```

9 The done method is clearly intended to be overridden!

```
    def done(self):
        print 'All Done'
```

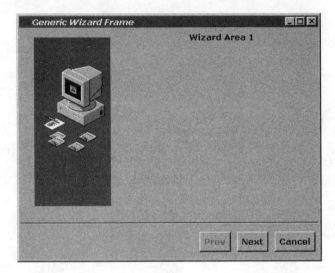

Figure 8.12 Wizard

If you run wizardshell.py, you'll see the basic shell shown in figure 8.12. Now we need to populate the wizard. Here is an example installation sequence:

Example_8_11.py

```
from Tkinter import *
import Pmw
import sys, string
import WizardShell

class Installer(WizardShell.WizardShell):
    wizname = 'Install Widgets'
    panes= 4

    def createButtons(self):
        self.buttonAdd('Cancel',    command=self.quit, state=1)
        self.nextB = self.buttonAdd('Next', command=self.next, state=1)
        self.prevB = self.buttonAdd('Prev', command=self.prev, state=0)

    def createTitle(self, idx, title):                              ❶
        label = self.createcomponent('l%d' % idx, (), None,
                        Label,(self.pInterior(idx),),
                        text=title,
```

```
                                   font=('verdana', 18, 'bold', 'italic'))
        label.pack()
        return label

    def createExplanation(self, idx):                              ❷
        text = self.createcomponent('t%d' % idx, (), None,
                            Text,(self.pInterior(idx),),
                            bd=0, wrap=WORD, height=6)
        fd = open('install%d.txt' % (idx+1))
        text.insert(END, fd.read())
        fd.close()
        text.pack(pady=15)

    def createPanelOne(self):
        self.createTitle(0, 'Welcome!')
        self.createExplanation(0)

    def createPanelTwo(self):                                      ❸
        self.createTitle(1, 'Select Destination\nDirectory')
        self.createExplanation(1)
        frame = Frame(self.pInterior(1), bd=2, relief=GROOVE)
        self.entry = Label(frame, text='C:\\Widgets\\WidgetStorage',
                            font=('Verdana', 10))
        self.entry.pack(side=LEFT, padx=10)
        self.btn   = Button(frame, text='Browse...')
        self.btn.pack(side=LEFT, ipadx=5, padx=5, pady=5)
        frame.pack()

    def createPanelThree(self):
        self.createTitle(2, 'Select Components')
        self.createExplanation(2)
        frame = Frame(self.pInterior(2), bd=0)
        idx = 0
        for label, size in [('Monkey','526k'),('Aardvark','356k'),
                    ('Warthog','625k'),
                    ('Reticulated Python','432k')]:
            ck  = Checkbutton(frame).grid(row=idx, column=0)
            lbl = Label(frame, text=label).grid(row=idx, column=1,
                                    columnspan=4, sticky=W)
            siz = Label(frame, text=size).grid(row=idx, column=5)
            idx = idx + 1
        frame.pack()

    def createPanelFour(self):
        self.createTitle(3, 'Finish Installation')
        self.createExplanation(3)

    def createInterface(self):
        WizardShell.WizardShell.createInterface(self)
        self.createButtons()
        self.createPanelOne()
        self.createPanelTwo()
        self.createPanelThree()
        self.createPanelFour()

    def done(self):                    ❹
```

```
      print 'This is where the work starts!'

if __name__ == '__main__':
  install = Installer()
  install.run()
```

Code comments

1 We begin by defining some routines to perform common tasks. Each of the wizard panes has a title:

```
def createTitle(self, idx, title):
    label = self.createcomponent('l%d' % idx, (), None,
                      Label, (self.pInterior(idx),),
                      text=title,
                      font=('verdana', 18, 'bold', 'italic'))
    label.pack()
    return label
```

2 Wizards need to supply concise and clear directions to the user; this routine formats the information appropriately using a regular Tkinter Text widget—the text is read from a file:

```
def createExplanation(self, idx):
    text = self.createcomponent('t%d' % idx, (), None,
                      Text, (self.pInterior(idx),),
                      bd=0, wrap=WORD, height=6)
    fd = open('install%d.txt' % (idx+1))
    text.insert(END, fd.read())
    fd.close()
    text.pack(pady=15)
```

3 Each pane in the wizard is constructed separately—here is an example:

```
def createPanelTwo(self):
    self.createTitle(1, 'Select Destination\nDirectory')
    self.createExplanation(1)
    frame = Frame(self.pInterior(1), bd=2, relief=GROOVE)
    self.entry = Label(frame, text='C:\\Widgets\\WidgetStorage',
                      font=('Verdana', 10))
    self.entry.pack(side=LEFT, padx=10)
    self.btn   = Button(frame, text='Browse...')
    self.btn.pack(side=LEFT, ipadx=5, padx=5, pady=5)
    frame.pack()
```

4 This example is still a bit of a cheat because the done function still does not do very much! (However, I'm sure that you've got the idea by now!)

Figure 8.13 shows the sequence supported by the wizard. Screens such as these will clearly give a polished image for an installation program.

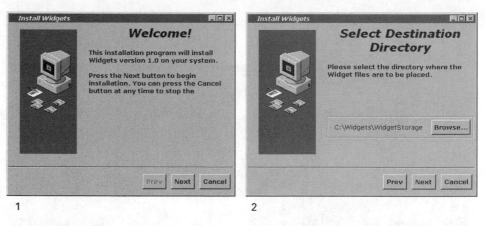

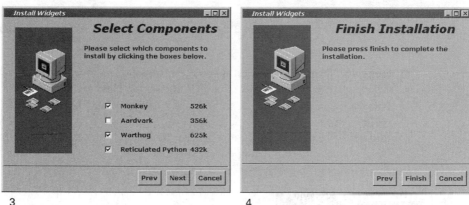

Figure 8.13 An installation wizard

8.7 Image maps

The final topic in this chapter presents an input technique which is typically used with web pages; image maps associate actions with clickable areas on an image. You could argue that this topic belongs in "Panels and machines" on page 199, but I am including it here since it is a viable method for getting input from the user.

If you take a look at "Building an application" on page 18 again, you will remember how a simple calculator was constructed using button widgets to bind user input to calculator functions. The application could be reworked using an image map; the major motivation for this would be to increase the realism of the interface by presenting an image of the calculator rather than a drawing.

One of the problems of creating image maps is that without a tool to define the targets for the map, it can be a time-consuming task to measure and input all of the coordinates. Take a look at figure 8.14. The area around each of the buttons (the targets for this case) have been out-

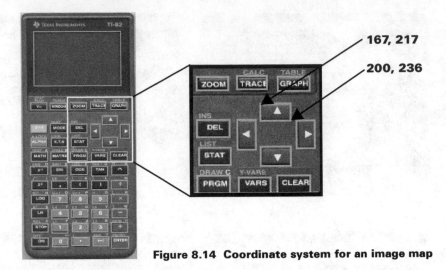

Figure 8.14 Coordinate system for an image map

lined in gray. The enlarged section shows the arrow keys in a little more detail. For each target, we need to determine the x-y coordinate of the top-left-hand corner and the x-y coordinate of the bottom-right-hand corner; together they define the rectangular area containing the button.

The next example demonstrates how a simple tool can be constructed to first collect the coordinates of rectangular areas on an image, and then to generate a simple program to test the image map. This example supports only rectangular targets; you may wish to extend it to support polygonal and other target shapes.

Example_8_12.py

```python
from Tkinter import *
import sys, string
class MakeImageMap:

    def __init__(self, master, file=None):
        self.root = master
        self.root.title("Create Image Map")
        self.rubberbandBox = None
        self.coordinatedata = []
        self.file = file

        self.img = PhotoImage(file=file)
        self.width  = self.img.width()
        self.height = self.img.height()

        self.canvas = Canvas(self.root, width=self.width,
                         height=self.height)
        self.canvas.pack(side=TOP, fill=BOTH, expand=0)
        self.canvas.create_image(0,0,anchor=NW, image=self.img)

        self.frame1 = Frame(self.root, bd=2, relief=RAISED)
        self.frame1.pack(fill=X)
```

❶

```
            self.reference = Entry(self.frame1, width=12)
            self.reference.pack(side=LEFT, fill=X, expand=1)
            self.add = Button(self.frame1, text='Add', command=self.addMap)
            self.add.pack(side=RIGHT, fill=NONE, expand=0)
            self.frame2 = Frame(self.root, bd=2, relief=RAISED)
            self.frame2.pack(fill=X)
            self.done = Button(self.frame2, text='Build ImageMap',
                      command=self.buildMap)
            self.done.pack(side=TOP, fill=NONE, expand=0)               ❷

            Widget.bind(self.canvas, "<Button-1>", self.mouseDown)
            Widget.bind(self.canvas, "<Button1-Motion>", self.mouseMotion)
            Widget.bind(self.canvas, "<Button1-ButtonRelease>", self.mouseUp)

      def mouseDown(self, event):                                       ❸
            self.startx = self.canvas.canvasx(event.x)
            self.starty = self.canvas.canvasy(event.y)

      def mouseMotion(self, event):                                     ❹
            x = self.canvas.canvasx(event.x)
            y = self.canvas.canvasy(event.y)

            if (self.startx != event.x)  and (self.starty != event.y) :
                  self.canvas.delete(self.rubberbandBox)
                  self.rubberbandBox = self.canvas.create_rectangle(
                        self.startx, self.starty, x, y, outline='white',width=2)
                  self.root.update_idletasks()                          ❺

      def mouseUp(self, event):                                         ❻
            self.endx = self.canvas.canvasx(event.x)
            self.endy = self.canvas.canvasy(event.y)
            self.reference.focus_set()
            self.reference.selection_range(0, END)

      def addMap(self):                                                 ❼
            self.coordinatedata.append(self.reference.get(),
                              self.startx, self.starty,
                              self.endx, self.endy)

      def buildMap(self):                                               ❽
            filename = os.path.splitext(self.file)[0]
            ofd = open('%s.py' % filename, 'w')
            ifd = open('image1.inp')                                    ❾
            lines = ifd.read()
            ifd.close()
            ofd.write(lines)

            for ref, sx,sy, ex,ey in self.coordinatedata:               ❿
                  ofd.write("    self.iMap.addRegion(((%5.1f,%5.1f),"
                        "(%5.1f,%5.1f)), '%s')\n" % (sx,sy, ex,ey, ref))

            ofd.write('\n%s\n' % ('#'*70))                              ⓫
            ofd.write('if __name__ == "__main__":\n')
            ofd.write('    root = Tk()\n')
            ofd.write('    root.title("%s")\n' % self.file)
            ofd.write('    imageTest = ImageTest(root, width=%d, height=%d,'
```

```
                    'file="%s")\n' % (self.width, self.height, self.file))
        ofd.write('    imageTest.root.mainloop()\n')
        ofd.close()
        self.root.quit()

if __name__ == '__main__':
    file = sys.argv[1]
    root = Tk()
    makeImageMap = MakeImageMap(root, file=file)
    makeImageMap.root.mainloop()
```

Code comments

❶ The first task is to determine the size of the image to be mapped. Since we want to display the image on a canvas, we cannot just load the image, because the canvas will not resize to fit the image. Therefore, get the size of the image and size the canvas appropriately:

```
self.img = PhotoImage(file=file)
self.width  = self.img.width()
self.height = self.img.height()
```

❷ Our tool implements a simple graphic selection rectangle to show the selected target area. We bind functions to mouse button press and release and also to mouse motion:

```
Widget.bind(self.canvas, "<Button-1>", self.mouseDown)
Widget.bind(self.canvas, "<Button1-Motion>", self.mouseMotion)
Widget.bind(self.canvas, "<Button1-ButtonRelease>", self.mouseUp)
```

❸ mouseDown converts the x- and y-screen coordinates of the mouse button press to coordinates relative to the canvas, which corresponds to the image coordinates:

```
def mouseDown(self, event):
    self.startx = self.canvas.canvasx(event.x)
    self.starty = self.canvas.canvasy(event.y)
```

❹ mouseMotion continuously updates the size of the selection rectangle with the current coordinates:

```
def mouseMotion(self, event):
    x = self.canvas.canvasx(event.x)
    y = self.canvas.canvasy(event.y)

    if (self.startx != event.x)  and (self.starty != event.y) :
        self.canvas.delete(self.rubberbandBox)
        self.rubberbandBox = self.canvas.create_rectangle(
            self.startx, self.starty, x, y, outline='white',width=2)
```

❺ Each time we update the selection rectangle, we have to call update_idletasks to display the changes. Doing a drag operation such as this causes a flood of events as the mouse moves, so we need to make sure that the screen writes get done in a timely fashion:

```
self.root.update_idletasks()
```

❻ When the mouse button is released, we convert the coordinates of the finishing location and set focus to the entry widget to collect the identity of the map:

```
def mouseUp(self, event):
    self.endx = self.canvas.canvasx(event.x)
    self.endy = self.canvas.canvasy(event.y)
    self.reference.focus_set()
    self.reference.selection_range(0, END)
```

7 Once the map ID has been entered, clicking the `Add` button adds the ID and the map coordinates to the list of map entries:

```
def addMap(self):
        self.coordinatedata.append(self.reference.get(),
                       self.startx, self.starty,
                       self.endx, self.endy)
```

8 When the `Build` button is pressed, we generate a Python file to test the image map:

```
def buildMap(self):
        filename = os.path.splitext(self.file)[0]
        ofd = open('%s.py' % filename, 'w')
```

9 The first section of the code is boilerplate, so it can be read in from a file:

```
        ifd = open('image1.inp', 'r')
        lines = ifd.readlines()
        ifd.close()
        ofd.writelines(lines)
```

10 Then we generate an entry for each map collected previously:

```
        for ref, sx,sy, ex,ey in self.coordinatedata:
            ofd.write("    self.iMap.addRegion(((%5.1f,%5.1f),"
                    "(%5.1f,%5.1f)), '%s')\n" % (sx,sy, ex,ey, ref))
```

11 Finally, we add some code to launch the image map:

```
        ofd.write('\n%s\n' % ('#'*70))
        ofd.write('if __name__ == "__main__":\n')
        ofd.write('    root = Tk()\n')
        ofd.write('    root.title("%s")\n' % self.file)
        ofd.write('    imageTest = ImageTest(root, width=%d, height=%d,'
               'file="%s")\n' % (self.width, self.height, self.file))
        ofd.write('    imageTest.root.mainloop()\n')
        ofd.close()
```

All you have to do is supply a GIF file and then drag the selection rectangle around each of the target regions. Give the region an identity and click the Add button. When you have identified all of the regions, click the Build button.

Note This example illustrates how Python can be used to generate code from input data. Python is so easy to use and debug that it can be a valuable tool in building complex systems. If you take a little time to understand the structure of the target code, you can write a program to generate that code. Of course, this only works if you have to produce lots of replicated code segments, but it can save you a lot of time and effort!

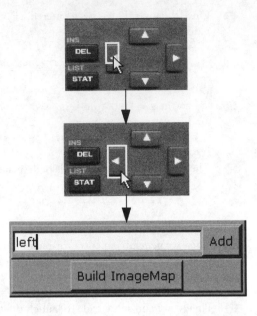

Figure 8.15 Creating an image map

Let's take a quick look at the code generated by the tool.

Calculator.py

```python
from Tkinter import *
from imagemap import *
class ImageTest:

    def hit(self, event):
        self.infoVar.set(self.iMap.getRegion(event.x, event.y))

    def __init__(self, master, width=0, height=0, file=None):
        self.root = master
        self.root.option_add('*font', ('verdana', 12, 'bold'))
        self.iMap = ImageMap()

        self.canvas = Canvas(self.root, width=width, height=height)
        self.canvas.pack(side="top", fill=BOTH, expand='no')

        self.img = PhotoImage(file=file)
        self.canvas.create_image(0,0,anchor=NW, image=self.img)
        self.canvas.bind('<Button-1>', self.hit)
        self.infoVar = StringVar()
        self.info = Entry(self.root, textvariable=self.infoVar)
        self.info.pack(fill=X)

        self.iMap.addRegion((( 61.0,234.0),( 96.0,253.0)), 'mode')
        self.iMap.addRegion(((104.0,234.0),(135.0,250.0)), 'del')
```

```
                self.iMap.addRegion((( 19.0,263.0),( 55.0,281.0)), 'alpha')
                self.iMap.addRegion((( 63.0,263.0),( 96.0,281.0)), 'x-t-phi')
                self.iMap.addRegion(((105.0,263.0),(134.0,281.0)), 'stat')
# ----- Some lines removed for brevity--------------
                self.iMap.addRegion((( 24.0,467.0),( 54.0,488.0)), 'on')
                self.iMap.addRegion((( 64.0,468.0),( 97.0,486.0)), '0')
                self.iMap.addRegion(((104.0,469.0),(138.0,486.0)), '.')
                self.iMap.addRegion(((185.0,469.0),(220.0,491.0)), 'enter')

if __name__ == "__main__":
    root = Tk()
    root.title("calculator.gif")
    imageTest = ImageTest(root, width=237, height=513,file="calculator.gif")
    imageTest.root.mainloop()
```

It's really quite simple. The image map uses the `ImageMap` class. This class can be readily extended to support regions other than rectangles:

imagemap.py

```
class Region:                                    ❶
    def __init__(self, coords, ref):
        self.coords = coords
        self.ref    = ref

    def inside(self, x, y):                       ❷
        isInside = 0
        if self.coords[0][0] <= x <= self.coords[1][0] and \
            self.coords[0][1] <= y <= self.coords[1][1]:
                isInside = 1
        return isInside

class ImageMap:
    def __init__(self):
        self.regions = []
        self.cache   = {}

    def addRegion(self, coords, ref):
        self.regions.append(Region(coords, ref))

    def getRegion(self, x, y):
        try:                                      ❸
            return self.cache[(x,y)]
        except KeyError:
            for region in self.regions:           ❹
                if region.inside(x, y) == 1:
                    self.cache[(x,y)] = region
                    return region.ref
            return None
```

Code comments

❶ The `Region` class provides a container for the target regions:
```
class Region:
    def __init__(self, coords, ref):
```

```
        self.coords = coords
        self.ref    = ref
```

② Detecting when a button press occurs within a region is a simple test:

```
def inside(self, x, y):
    isInside = 0
    if self.coords[0][0] <= x <= self.coords[1][0] and \
        self.coords[0][1] <= y <= self.coords[1][1]:
            isInside = 1
    return isInside
```

③ When we attempt to find a region, we first look in the cache that is accumulated from previous lookups:

```
def getRegion(self, x, y):
    try:
        return self.cache[(x,y)]
```

④ If it is not in the cache, we have to search each of the regions in turn; we cache the map if we find it:

```
    except KeyError:
        for region in self.regions:
            if region.inside(x, y) == 1:
                self.cache[(x,y)] = region
                return region.ref
```

Figure 8.16 Running calculator.py

Figure 8.16 shows calculator.py in action.

8.8   Summary

This chapter has covered several types of forms and dialogs, ranging from simple fill-in-the-blank dialogs through browsers and wizards to image-mapping techniques. I hope that you will find sufficient material here so you can create forms appropriate for your own applications.

CHAPTER 9

Panels and machines

This chapter is where Tkinter gets to be FUN! (Maybe I should find a hobby!) Network management applications have set a standard for graphical formats; many hardware device manufacturers supply a software front-panel display showing the current state of LEDs, connectors and power supply voltages—anything that has a measurable value. In general, such devices are SNMP-capable, although other systems exist. This model may be extended to subjects which have no mechanical form—even database applications can have attractive interfaces. The examples presented in this chapter should be useful for an application developer needing a framework for alternative user interfaces.

9.1 Building a front panel

Let's construct a hypothetical piece of equipment. The task is to present a front-panel display of a switching system (perhaps an ATM switch or a router) to an administrator. The display will show the current state of the interfaces, line cards, processors and other components. For the purposes of the example, we shall assume that the device is SNMP-capable and that the code to poll the devices agent and to receive and process traps will be developed independently from the GUI.

If this were not a hypothetical device, you would have either the equipment itself or some technical specifications for the device to work from. For this example, we can dream up almost anything! Figure 9.1 shows a line drawing for the equipment. The device has two power supplies, each with a power connector and an on/off switch along with an LED showing the status of the power supply (off, on or failed). There are nine empty card slots, which will be populated with a variety of cards, and there are passive decorations such as the air-intake screens and chassis-mounting screws. The card slots will be populated with a switch card, a processor card, an eight-port 10Base-T Ethernet card*, a four-port FDDI card†, a two-channel T3 access card‡ and four high-speed serial cards. I'm not sure what this device is going to do, who will be configuring it, or who will be paying for it, but it should be fun conjuring it up!

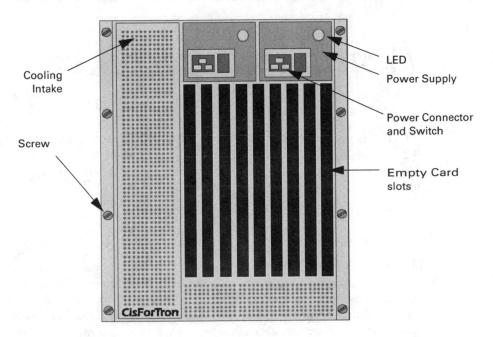

Figure 9.1 Hypothetical router/switch chassis

---

* The most widely installed Ethernet local area networks (LANs) use ordinary telephone twisted-pair wire. When used on Ethernet, this carrier medium is known as 10BASE-T. 10BASE-T supports Ethernet's 10 Mbps transmission speed.

† FDDI is a standard for data transmission on fiber optic lines in a local area network that can extend in range up to 200 km (124 miles).

‡ The T-3 line, a variant of the T-carrier system introduced by the Bell System in the USA in the 1960s, provides 44.736 Mbps. It is commonly used by internet service providers (ISPs).

Each of the cards has LEDs, connectors and passive components such as buttons, card-pullers and locking screws. Sounds like a lot? It is not as difficult as it may seem, on first analysis, and once the basic components have been built, you will observe a great deal of code reuse.

9.2 Modularity

In section 7.2 on page 129 we started to develop a class library of components such as LEDs, switches and other devices. In this chapter we are going to use an expanded library of indicators, connectors and panel devices. We will also make use of the built-in status methods of the composite widgets, which was only briefly noted in the previous examples. We will also introduce the topic of *navigation* in the GUI, (see "Navigation" on page 300) since our front panel should provide the administrator access to functionality bound to each of the graphical elements on the panel. A good example of such a binding is to warp the user to the list of alarms associated with an LED on the display or a configuration screen to allow him to set operational parameters for a selected port.

If you look again at figure 9.1, it is possible to identify a number of graphical components that must be developed to build the front panel. Although the configuration of each of the cards has not been revealed at this point, there are some "future" requirements for components to be displayed on the card which drives the following list:

1 A chassis consisting of the rack-mount extensions and base front panel along with passive components such as mounting screws.
2 Card slots which may be populated with a variety of cards.
3 A number of cards consisting of LEDs, connectors and other active devices along with the card front to mount the devices and other passive components such as card pullers and labels.
4 Power supply modules containing connectors, switches and LEDs.
5 Passive components such as the air-intake screens and the logo.
6 LEDs, connectors (J-45*, BNC†, FDDI‡, J-25, J-50 and power) and power switches.

9.3 Implementing the front panel

Some preparation work needs to be done to convert the notional front panel to a working system. In particular, it is necessary to calculate the sizes of screen components based on some scaling factors, since the majority of panels are much larger than typical computer screens. As the reader will observe in the following example code, the author tends to work with relative positioning on a *canvas*. This is a somewhat more difficult approach to widget placement

---

* J connectors are typically used for serial connections. The number of pins available for connection is indicated by the suffix of the connector. Common connectors are J-9, J-25, and J-50.

† A Bayonet Neil-Concelman (BNC) connector is a type of connector used to connect using coaxial cable.

‡ FDDI connectors are used to connect fiber-optic lines and to normally connect a pair of cables, one for reception and one for transmission.

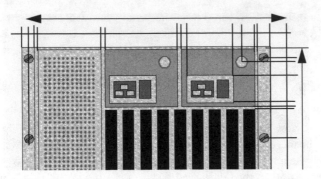

Figure 9.2 Making router/switch chassis measurements

when contrasted with using the *pack* or *grid* geometry managers. However, precise placement of graphical objects requires the precision of the *place* geometry manager.

The approach I took to implement this panel was to take a drawing of the panel and to perform some basic measurements. In figure 9.2, lines have been drawn marking the key dimensions that are needed to recreate a graphic representation. Making measurements on a drawing can be easier than performing the measurements on a real device. Overall width and height are measured in some standard units (such as inches or centimeters) and then the relative size of each of the rectangular objects and the relative offset of one corner of the object must be calculated. The offset is used for the placer calls in the code. The selected corner is the anchor for this call. It may appear to be a lot of work, but it takes just a few minutes to get the required information.

The example extends the class library to provide a number of new graphical elements; in the listings that follow, elements that have already been presented have been eliminated.

Components_1.py

```
from Tkinter    import *
from GUICommon import *
from Common     import *

class Screen(GUICommon):
    def __init__(self, master, bg=Color.PANEL, height=1, width=1):
        self.screen_frame = Frame(master, width=width, height=height,
                bg=bg, bd=0)
        self.base = bg
        self.set_colors(self.screen_frame)
        radius = 4    # radius of an air hole
        ssize  = radius*3  # spacing between holes

        rows = int(height/ssize)
        cols = int(width/ssize)

        self.canvas = Canvas(self.screen_frame, height=height, width=width,
                bg=bg, bd=0, highlightthickness=0)

        self.canvas.pack(side=TOP, fill=BOTH, expand=NO)

        y = ssize - radius#
        for r in range(rows):
            x0 = ssize -radius
            for c in range(cols):
                x = x0 + (ssize*c)
```

❶ creating an instance

❷ Optimizing performance

```
                    self.canvas.create_oval(x-radius, y-radius,
                                 x+radius, y+radius,
                                 fill=self.dbase,
                                 outline=self.lbase)
            y = y + ssize

class PowerConnector:
    def __init__(self, master, bg=Color.PANEL):
        self.socket_frame = Frame(master, relief="raised", width=60,
                        height=40,  bg=bg, bd=4)

        inside=Frame(self.socket_frame, relief="sunken", width=56,
                    height=36, bg=Color.INSIDE, bd=2)
        inside.place(relx=.5, rely=.5, anchor=CENTER)

        ground=Frame(inside, relief="raised", width=6, height=10,
                    bg=Color.CHROME, bd=2)
        ground.place(relx=.5, rely=.3, anchor=CENTER)

        p1=Frame(inside, relief="raised", width=6, height=10,
                bg=Color.CHROME, bd=2)
        p1.place(relx=.25, rely=.7, anchor=CENTER)

        p2=Frame(inside, relief="raised", width=6, height=10,
                bg=Color.CHROME, bd=2)
        p2.place(relx=.75, rely=.7, anchor=CENTER)

class PowerSwitch(GUICommon):
    def __init__(self, master, label='I   0', base=Color.PANEL):
        self.base = base
        self.set_colors(master)
```

③ Calculating colors

```
        self.switch_frame = Frame(master, relief="raised", width=45,
                        height=28, bg=self.vlbase, bd=4)
        switch = Frame(self.switch_frame, relief="sunken", width=32,
                    height=22, bg=self.base, bd=2)
        switch.place(relx=0.5, rely=0.5, anchor=CENTER)

        lbl=Label(switch, text=label, font=("Verdana", 10, "bold"),
                fg='white', bd=0, bg=self.dbase)
        lbl.place(relx=0.5, rely=0.5, anchor=CENTER)

class PowerSupply(GUICommon):
    def __init__(self, master, width=160, height=130, bg=Color.PANEL,
            status=STATUS_ON):
        self.base = bg
        self.set_colors(master)

        self.psu_frame = Frame(master, relief=SUNKEN, bg=self.dbase, bd=2,
                        width=width, height=height)

        Label(self.psu_frame, text='DC OK', fg='white',
            bg=self.dbase, font=('Verdana', 10, 'bold'),bd=0).place(relx=.8,
                        rely=.15, anchor=CENTER)

        self.led = LED(self.psu_frame, height=12, width=12, shape=ROUND,
                bg=self.dbase)
```

```
                    self.led.led_frame.place(relx=0.8, rely=0.31, anchor=CENTER)

                    lsub = Frame(self.psu_frame, width=width/1.2, height=height/2,
                                 bg=self.dbase, bd=1, relief=GROOVE)
                    lsub.place(relx=0.5, rely=0.68, anchor=CENTER)

                    pwr=PowerConnector(lsub)
                    pwr.socket_frame.place(relx=0.30, rely=0.5, anchor=CENTER)
                    sw=PowerSwitch(lsub)
                    sw.switch_frame.place(relx=0.75, rely=0.5, anchor=CENTER)

class Screw(GUICommon):
    def __init__(self, master, diameter=18, base="gray40", bg=Color.PANEL):
        self.base = base

        basesize = diameter+6
        self.screw_frame = Frame(master, relief="flat", bg=bg, bd=0,
                            highlightthickness=0)
        self.set_colors(self.screw_frame)

        canvas=Canvas(self.screw_frame, width=basesize, height=basesize,
                      highlightthickness=0, bg=bg, bd=0)
        center = basesize/2
        r = diameter/2
        r2 = r - 4.0

        canvas.create_oval(center-r, center-r, center+r, center+r,
                           fill=self.base, outline=self.lbase)
        canvas.create_rectangle(center-r2, center-0.2,
                                center+r2, center+0.2,
                                fill=self.dbase, width=0)
        canvas.create_rectangle(center-0.2, center-r2,
                                center+0.2, center+r2,
                                fill=self.dbase, width=0)
        canvas.pack(side="top", fill='x', expand='no')

class CardBlank(GUICommon):
    def __init__(self, master=None, width=20, height=396,
             appearance="raised", bd=2, base=Color.CARD):
        self.base = base
        self.set_colors(master)
        self.card_frame=Frame(master, relief=appearance, height=height,
                         width=width, bg=base, bd=bd)

        top_pull = CardPuller(self.card_frame, CARD_TOP, width=width)
        top_pull.puller_frame.place(relx=.5, rely=0, anchor=N)

        bottom_pull = CardPuller(self.card_frame, CARD_BOTTOM, width=width)
        bottom_pull.puller_frame.place(relx=.5, rely=1.0,anchor=S)
```

Code comments

❶ In some of the earlier examples we used Tkinter's internal reference to the instance of the widgets, so the following was possible:

```
Button(parent, text='OK').pack(side=LEFT)
```

The structure of the code for this example requires that we make sure that instances of objects are unique. Each widget must keep references to its child widgets.

```
self.screen_frame = Frame(master, width=width, height=height,
                          bg=bg, bd=0)
```

This creates a specific instance of `screen_frame` within `self`.

2 The air-intake screen illustrates the ease with which repeated graphical objects may be created. It also highlights the importance of careful code construction—it is easy to forget that Python is an interpreted language and it is important to ensure that code is constructed in a way that optimizes execution.

```
y = ssize - radius
for r in range(rows):
    x0 = ssize -radius
    for c in range(cols):
        x = x0 + (ssize*c)
        self.canvas.create_oval(x-radius, y-radius,
                    x+radius, y+radius,
                    fill=self.dbase,
                    outline=self.lbase)
    y = y + ssize
```

Some additional code might be appropriate here, since the first air intake is the "tall" by "narrow" case, but the lower intake has an opposite aspect. The loop could be improved by having the outer loop iterate over largest dimension to reduce some of the math operations in the inner loop. Of course, this would increase the code complexity and for many operations might be unnecessary, but is worth considering. Remember that a good C or C++ would optimize loops for you; *you* are Python's optimizer!

3 `GUICommon.set_colors` has been extended to pass a widget to provide access to `winfo` early in the initializer.

```
def __init__(self, master, label='I   0', base=Color.PANEL):
    self.base = base
    self.set_colors(master)
```

In this case, the master container widget and base color have been passed in the constructor and are used to set the color variants for the object.

Components_1.py (continued)

```
class CardPuller(GUICommon):

    def __init__(self, master, torb, width=20):
        self.base = master['background']
        self.set_colors(master)
        self.puller_frame=Frame(master, width=width, height=32,
                    bg=self.lbase, relief='flat')

        Frame(self.puller_frame, width=width/8, height=8,
            bg=self.dbase).place(relx=1.0, rely=[1.0,0][torb],
                            anchor=[SE,NE][torb])

        Frame(self.puller_frame, width=width/3, height=24,
            bg=self.vdbase).place(relx=1.0, rely=[0,1.0][torb],
```

4

5

```
                              anchor=[NE,SE][torb])

        Screw(self.puller_frame, diameter=10, base=self.base,
             bg=self.lbase).screw_frame.place(relx=0.3, rely=[0.2,0.8][torb],
                              anchor=CENTER)

class Chassis:
    def __init__(self, master):
        self.outer=Frame(master, width=540, height=650,
                   borderwidth=2, bg=Color.PANEL)
        self.outer.forget()                                    ❻

        self.inner=Frame(self.outer, width=490, height=650,
                   borderwidth=2, relief=RAISED, bg=Color.PANEL)
        self.inner.place(relx=0.5, rely=0.5, anchor=CENTER)

        self.rack = Frame(self.inner, bd=2, width=325, height=416,
                   bg=Color.CHASSIS)
        self.rack.place(relx=0.985, rely=0.853, anchor=SE)

        incr = 325/9
        x = 0.0                                       ❼ Creating blank cards
        for i in range(9):
            card =CardBlank(self.rack, width=incr-1, height=414)
            card.card_frame.place(x=x, y=0, anchor=NW)
            x = x + incr

        self.img = PhotoImage(file='images/logo.gif')
        self.logo=Label(self.outer, image=self.img, bd=0)
        self.logo.place(relx=0.055, rely=0.992, anchor=SW)

        for x in [0.02, 0.98]:
            for y in [0.0444, 0.3111, 0.6555, 0.9711]:
                screw = Screw(self.outer, base="gray50")
                screw.screw_frame.place(relx=x, rely=y, anchor=CENTER)

        self.psu1 = PowerSupply(self.inner)
        self.psu1.psu_frame.place(relx=0.99, rely=0.004, anchor=NE)
        self.psu2 = PowerSupply(self.inner)
        self.psu2.psu_frame.place(relx=0.65, rely=0.004, anchor=NE)

        self.psu2.led.turnoff()                       ❽ Deactivating LED

        screen1 = Screen(self.inner, width=150, height=600, bg=Color.PANEL)
        screen1.screen_frame.place(relx=0.16, rely=0.475, anchor=CENTER)
        screen2 = Screen(self.inner, width=330, height=80, bg=Color.PANEL)
        screen2.screen_frame.place(relx=0.988, rely=0.989, anchor=SE)
```

Code comments (continued)

❹ In the CardPuller class we obtain the base color from the parent widget, rather than passing it in the constructor.

```
def __init__(self, master, torb, width=20):
    self.base = master['background']
    self.set_colors(master)
```

⑤ We index into a list to obtain the y-coordinate and the anchor-position for the `place` call. This valuable technique is used in many examples throughout the book.

```
bg=self.dbase).place(relx=1.0, rely=[1.0,0][torb],
                     anchor=[SE,NE][torb])
```

⑥ If widgets are created in a complex GUI, there can be some somewhat ugly effects to the display if the window is realized. One of these effects is that with the pack or grid geometry managers, the widgets are readjusted several times as additional widgets are created. Another effect is that it takes longer to draw the widgets, since the system redraws the widgets several times as widget configurations change. The solution is to delay the realization of the outer container of the widget hierarchy:

```
self.outer.forget()
```

⑦ The loop populates the card rack with blank cards:

```
incr = 325/9
x = 0.0
for i in range(9):
    card =CardBlank(self.rack, width=incr-1, height=414)
    card.card_frame.place(x=x, y=0, anchor=NW)
    x = x + incr
```

⑧ Finally, we change the state of one of the LEDs on the display. You'll learn more about this later.

```
self.psu2.led.turnoff()
```

Since the front panel will be built incrementally, for the purpose of illustration, a separate module, FrontPanel_1.py, is used to create the device.

FrontPanel.py

```
#! /bin/env/python

from Tkinter   import *
from Components_1 import *
from GUICommon  import *
from Common   import *

class Router(Frame):
  def __init__(self, master=None):
      Frame.__init__(self, master)
      Pack.config(self)
      self.createChassis()

  def createChassis(self):
      self.chassis = Chassis(self)
      # Realize the outer frame (which
      # was forgotten when created)
      self.chassis.outer.pack(expand=0)        ❶ Realize the frame

if __name__ == '__main__':
  root = Router()
  root.master.title("CisForTron")
  root.master.iconname("CisForTron")
  root.mainloop()
```

Code comments

1 If you examine the __init__ method for each of the frames in the various classes in Components_1.py, you will notice that there are no geometry-management calls. It would have been possible to pass the location to place the object or simply pack the object within the constructor, but the style of coding used here allows the user to have more control over widget geometry. This is especially true for the chassis frame; this widget was explicitly forgotten so that the screen updates are made before the chassis is realized. This improves performance considerably when a large number of graphic objects need to be drawn.

```
self.chassis.outer.pack(expand=0)
```

Here, the chassis frame is packed, realizing the widget and drawing the contained widgets. It does make a difference!

When FrontPanel.py is run, the screen shown in figure 9.3 is displayed. This display draws remarkably fast, even though we have to construct each of the air-screen holes individually. For highly computational or memory-intensive graphics which depict purely passive components, it is probably better to use GIF or bitmap images. Some aspects of this are discussed in "GIF, BMP and overlays" on page 215. Notice how we use the intrinsic three-dimensional properties of the widgets to create some depth in the display. In general, it is best to avoid trying to totally mimic the actual device and produce some level of abstraction.

Let's create one of the cards that will populate the chassis. The T3 Access card has four BNC connectors (two pairs of Rx/Tx connectors), four LEDs for each pair of BNC connectors, and some identifying labels. Every card in the chassis has a power (PWR) and fault (FLT) LED.

Figure 9.3 Basic router chassis

Here is the code to construct a BNC connector:

Components.py (fragment)

```
class BNC(GUICommon):                                              ❶
    def __init__(self, master, status=0, diameter=18,
            port=-1, fid=''):
        self.base = master['background']
        self.hitID = fid
        self.status=status
        self.blink        = 0
        self.blinkrate    = 1
        self.on           = 0
        self.onState      = None
        self.Colors       = [None, Color.CHROME, Color.ON,
                             Color.WARN, Color.ALARM, '#00ffdd']

        basesize = diameter+6
        self.bnc_frame = Frame(master, relief="flat", bg=self.base,
                        bd=0, highlightthickness=0, takefocus=1)
        self.bnc_frame.pack(expand=0)
        self.bnc_frame.bind('<FocusIn>', self.focus_in)           ❷
        self.bnc_frame.bind('<FocusOut>', self.focus_out)

        self.canvas=Canvas(self.bnc_frame, width=basesize,
                     height=basesize, highlightthickness=0,
                     bg=self.base, bd=0)
        center = basesize/2
        r = diameter/2
        self.pins=self.canvas.create_rectangle(0, center+2, basesize-1,
                              10, fill=Color.CHROME)
        self.bnc=self.canvas.create_oval(center-r, center-r,
                           center+r, center+r,
                           fill=Color.CHROME,
                           outline="black")
        r = r-3
        self.canvas.create_oval(center-r, center-r, center+r, center+r,
                     fill=Color.INSIDE, outline='black')
        r = r-2
        self.canvas.create_oval(center-r, center-r, center+r, center+r,
                     fill=Color.CHROME)
        r = r-3
        self.canvas.create_oval(center-r, center-r, center+r, center+r,
                     fill=Color.INSIDE, outline='black')

        self.canvas.pack(side=TOP, fill=X, expand=0)
        if self.hitID:
            self.hitID = '%s.%d' % (self.hitID, port)
            for widget in [self.bnc_frame]:
                widget.bind('<KeyPress-space>', self.panelMenu)
                widget.bind('<Button-1>', self.panelMenu)
            for widget in [self.canvas]:
                widget.bind('<1>', self.panelMenu)

    def focus_in(self, event):
        self.last_bg= self.canvas.itemcget(self.bnc, 'fill')
```

```
            self.canvas.itemconfig(self.bnc, fill=Color.HIGHLIGHT)
            self.update()

        def focus_out(self, event):
            self.canvas.itemconfig(self.bnc, fill=self.last_bg)
            self.update()

        def update(self):                                    ❸
            # First do the blink, if set to blink
            if self.blink:
                if self.on:
                    if not self.onState:
                        self.onState = self.status
                        self.status  = STATUS_OFF
                        self.on      = 0
                    else:
                        if self.onState:
                            self.status = self.onState     # Current ON color
                            self.on = 1
            # now update the status
            self.canvas.itemconfig(self.bnc,  fill=self.Colors[self.status])
            self.canvas.itemconfig(self.pins, fill=self.Colors[self.status])
            self.bnc_frame.update_idletasks()
            if self.blink:
                self.bnc_frame.after(self.blinkrate * 1000, self.update)
```

Code comments

❶ This example uses the GUICommon mixin class to define basic methods for widget state manipulation.

```
class BNC(GUICommon):
```

❷ Here we bind callbacks to FocusIn and FocusOut events.

```
self.bnc_frame.bind('<FocusIn>', self.focus_in)
self.bnc_frame.bind('<FocusOut>', self.focus_out)
```

This binds the focus_in and focus_out functions to the widget so that if we tab into the widget or click the widget, we highlight it and enable the functions to be accessed.

❸ All of the graphical objects (LEDs, BNC, J and FDDI connectors) define a specific update method to change the appearance of the widget based upon current status. We need specialized methods to allow us to update the color of particular areas within the composite. This method is also responsible for blinking the widget at one-second intervals.

```
def update(self):
    # First do the blink, if set to blink
    if self.blink:
        if self.on:
            if not self.onState:
                self.onState = self.status
                self.status  = STATUS_OFF
                self.on      = 0
            else:
                if self.onState:
                    self.status = self.onState     # Current ON color
```

```
                self.on = 1
        # now update the status
        self.canvas.itemconfig(self.bnc,  fill=self.Colors[self.status])
        self.canvas.itemconfig(self.pins, fill=self.Colors[self.status])
        self.bnc_frame.update_idletasks()
        if self.blink:
                self.bnc_frame.after(self.blinkrate * 1000, self.update)
```

Now, we complete the example by defining the layout of the T3 Access card:

```
class StandardLEDs(GUICommon):                        ❶
    def __init__(self, master=None, bg=Color.CARD):
        for led, label, xpos, ypos, state in [('flt', 'Flt', 0.3, 0.88, 1),
                                              ('pwr', 'Pwr', 0.7, 0.88, 2)]:
                setattr(self, led, LED(self.card_frame,shape=ROUND,width=8,
                    status=state, bg=bg))
                getattr(self, led).led_frame.place(relx=xpos,rely=ypos,
                                                        anchor=CENTER)
                Label(self.card_frame,text=label,font=("verdana", 4),
                    fg="white",bg=bg).place(relx=xpos,rely=(ypos+0.028),
                                                anchor=CENTER)


class T3AccessCard(CardBlank,StandardLEDs):            ❷
    def __init__(self, master, width=1, height=1):
        CardBlank.__init__(self, master=master, width=width, height=height)
        bg=master['background']
        StandardLEDs.__init__(self, master=master, bg=bg)
        for port, lbl, tag, ypos in [ (1,'RX1','T3AccessRX', 0.30),
                                      (2,'TX1','T3AccessTX', 0.40),       ❸
                                      (3,'RX2','T3AccessRX', 0.65),
                                      (4,'TX2','T3AccessRX', 0.75)]:

                setattr(self, 'bnc%d' % port, BNC(self.card_frame,
                                            fid=tag,port=port))
                getattr(self, 'bnc%d' % port).bnc_frame.place(relx=0.5,   ❹
                                            rely=ypos,anchor=CENTER))
                Label(self.card_frame,text=lbl,
                    font=("verdana", 6), fg="white",
                    bg=bg).place(relx=0.5,rely=(ypos+0.045),anchor=CENTER)

        for led, lbl, xpos, ypos, state in [('rxc','RXC',0.3,0.18,2)
                                            ('oos','OOS',0.7,0.18,1)
                                            ('flt','FLT',0.3,0.23,1)
                                            ('syn','SYN',0.7,0.23,2)
                                            ('rxc','RXC',0.3,0.53,2)
                                            ('oos','OOS',0.7,0.53,1)
                                            ('flt','FLT',0.3,0.58,1)
                                            ('syn','SYN',0.7,0.58,2)]:
                setattr(self, led, LED(self.card_frame,shape=ROUND,width=8,
                                status=state, bg=bg))
                getattr(self, led).led_frame.place(relx=xpos,rely=ypos,
                                                    anchor=CENTER)
                Label(self.card_frame,text=lbl,
                    font=("verdana", 4), fg="white",
                    bg=bg).place(relx=xpos,rely=(ypos+0.028),anchor=CENTER)
```

Code comments

1 We add one class to draw the LEDs that appear on each card in the rack:

```
class StandardLEDs(GUICommon):
```

2 The T3 access card inherits from the CardBlank and StandardLEDs classes which are explicitly constructed:

```
class T3AccessCard(CardBlank,StandardLEDs):
    def __init__(self, master, width=1, height=1):
        CardBlank.__init__(self, master=master, width=width,
                           height=height) bg=master['background']
        StandardLEDs.__init__(self, master=master, bg=bg)
```

3 Readers who have been observing my coding style will have noticed a definite pattern; I like to create objects from lists of tuples! This example is no exception:

```
for port, lbl, tag, ypos in [ (1,'RX1','T3AccessRX', 0.30),
                               (2,'TX1','T3AccessTX', 0.40),
                               (3,'RX2','T3AccessRX', 0.65),
                               (4,'TX2','T3AccessRX', 0.75)]:
```

Python's ability to unpack a tuple contained in a list of tuples provides a mechanism to compress the amount of code required to achieve a desired effect.

4 The arguments unpacked from the tuple are substituted in `setattr` and `getattr` calls:

```
setattr(self, 'bnc%d' % port, BNC(self.card_frame,
fid=tag,port=port))
getattr(self, 'bnc%d' % port).bnc_frame.place(relx=0.5,
rely=ypos,anchor=CENTER))
Label(self.card_frame,text=lbl,
font=("verdana", 6), fg="white",
bg=bg).place(relx=0.5,rely=(ypos+0.045),anchor=CENTER)
```

This style of coding results in tight code. It may be a little difficult to read initially, but it is still an efficient way of creating graphic elements in a loop.

As the last step to adding the T3 card, we must modify the loop that generates blank cards to add one of the T3 Access cards:

```
for i in range(9):
    if i == 4:
        card =T3AccessCard(self.rack, width=incr-1, height=414)
    else:
        card =CardBlank(self.rack, width=incr-1, height=414)
    card.card_frame.place(x=x, y=0, anchor=NW)
    x = x + incr
```

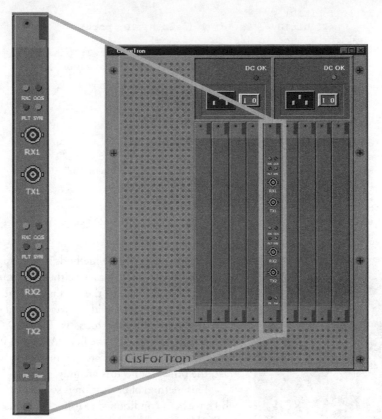

**Figure 9.4
T3 access card**

Figure 9.5 Populated chassis

Running FrontPanel2.py will display the screen shown in figure 9.4. The next step is a little scary. Creating the additional graphic elements and placing them on the cards does not require a lot of code. The code will not be presented here, it may be obtained online. If you run FrontPanel_3.py, you will see the screen in figure 9.5.

A few more words of explanation about the code presented earlier: We are attaching a menu operation to the widget. Access to the menu will be from the keyboard, using the *spacebar* or by clicking with the mouse.

```
    if self.hitID:
        self.hitID = '%s.%d' % (self.hitID, port)
        for widget in [self.bnc_frame]:
            widget.bind('<KeyPress-space>', self.panelMenu)
            widget.bind('<Button-1>', self.panelMenu)
        for widget in [self.canvas]:
            widget.bind('<1>', self.panelMenu)
```

We define the focus_in and focus_out methods.

```
def focus_in(self, event):
    self.last_bg= self.canvas.itemcget(self.bnc, 'fill')
    self.canvas.itemconfig(self.bnc, fill=Color.HIGHLIGHT)
    self.update()

def focus_out(self, event):
    self.canvas.itemconfig(self.bnc, fill=self.last_bg)
    self.update()
```

Figure 9.6 Widget focus

The purpose of these methods is to change the highlight color of the widgets as we either click on them with the mouse or navigate to them using the tab key. As we navigate from widget to widget, we display a highlight to show the user where the focus is. Figure 9.6 shows the effect of tabbing through the field. Although it's less obvious without color, the selected connector is blue; in contrast, the other connectors are gray.

This method of navigation is somewhat alien to users who have been conditioned to using the mouse to navigate GUIs. However, the ability to select tiny graphic objects is valuable and it can change a user's opinion of a product markedly. Without naming names, I have seen network management systems which required the user to click on graphic elements no more than 2mm square!

Components_3.py contains some additional code to animate the display to show the effect of status changes. Basically, each class that defines objects which can display status appends the instance to a widget list:

```
st_wid.append(self)    # register for animation
```

We then bind the animate function to the logo:

```
self.img = PhotoImage(file='logo.gif')
self.logo=Label(self.outer, image=self.img, bd=0)
self.logo.place(relx=0.055, rely=0.992, anchor=SW)
self.logo.bind('<Button-1>', self.animate)
```

The animate function is quite simple:

```
def animate(self, event):
    import random
    choice = random.choice(range(0, len(st_wid)-1))
```

```
op       = random.choice(range(0, len(ops)-1))

pstr = 'st_wid[%d].%s()' % (choice, ops[op])
self.cobj = compile(pstr, 'inline', 'exec')
self.rack.after(50, self.doit)

def doit(self):
  exec(self.cobj)
  self.rack.after(50, self.animate(None))
```

If you run FrontPanel_3.py and click on the logo, you will activate the animation. Of course, it is difficult to depict the result of this in a black-and-white printed image, but you should be able to discern differences in the shading of the controls on the panels–especially the J45 connectors on the fourth panel from the left in figure 9.7.

Of course, there is quite a lot of work to turn a panel such as this into a functional system. You would probably use a periodic SNMP poll of the device to get the state of each of the components and set the LEDs appropriately. In addition, you might monitor the content of the card rack to detect changes in hardware, if the device supports "hot pull" cards. Finally, menus might be added to the ports to give access to configuration utilities.

Figure 9.7 Animated widgets

9.4 GIF, BMP and overlays

The panels and machines introduced in the previous section used *drawn* interfaces. With a little effort, it is possible to produce a panel or machine that closely resembles the actual device. In some cases, it is necessary to have a little artistic flair to produce a satisfactory result, so an alternate approach must be used. Sometimes, it can be easier to use photographs of the device to produce a totally accurate representation of it; this is particularly true if the device is large. In this section I will provide you with a number of techniques to merge photographic images with GUIs.

Let's begin by taking a look at the front panel of the Cabletron SmartSwitch 6500 shown in figure 9.8. If you contrast the magnified section in this figure with the components in figure 9.6, you may notice that the drawn panel shows clearer detail, particularly for text labels. However, if you consider the amount of effort required to develop code to precisely place the components on the panels, the photo image is much easier. In addition, the photo image reproduces every detail, no matter how small or complex, and it has strong three-dimensional features which are time-consuming to recreate with drawn panels.

Figure 9.8 EC6110 Switch. The Highlighted area is magnified.
Photo courtesy Cabletron Systems

The task of creating modular panels is somewhat easier than creating similar panels with drawn components. Constructing a system with images requires the following steps:

1 Photograph the device with an empty card rack, if possible.

2 Photograph the device with cards inserted (singly, if possible) at the same scale.

3 Crop the card images so that they *exactly* define a card face.

4 Create a class for each card type, loading appropriate graphics and overlays for active components (LEDs, annunciators, etc.) and navigable components (connectors, buttons, etc.).

5 Create a chassis population based on configuration.

6 Write the rest of the supporting code.

In the following code, just a sample of the code will be presented. The full source code may be obtained online.

Components_4.py

```
class C6C110_CardBlank(GUICommon):
    def __init__(self, master=None, width=10, height=10,
            appearance=FLAT, bd=0):
        self.card_frame=Frame(master, relief=appearance, height=height,
                    width=width, bd=bd, highlightthickness=0)

class C6C110_ENET(C6C110_CardBlank):
    def __init__(self, master, slot=0):
```

```
                self.img = PhotoImage(file='images/6c110_enet.gif')
                setattr(glb, 'img%d % slot, self.img)
                self.width  = self.img.width()
                self.height = self.img.height()
```
①
```
                C6C110_CardBlank.__init__(self, master=master, width=self.width,
                                height=self.height)
```
```
                xypos = [(10,180),(10,187),
                            (10,195),(10,203),
                            (10,210),(10,235),
                            (10,242)]
```
② **LED Positions**
```
                self.canvas = Canvas(self.card_frame, width=self.width,
                                bd=0,highlightthickness=0,
                                height=self.height,selectborderwidth=0)
                self.canvas.pack(side="top", fill=BOTH, expand='no')
                self.canvas.create_image(0,0,anchor=NW,
                                image=eval('glb.img%d' % slot))
```
③

④
```
                for i, y in [(0, 0.330), (1, 0.619)]:
                    setattr(self, 'j%d' % i, Enet10baseT(self.card_frame,
                            fid="10Base-T-%d" % i, port=i, orient=HW_LEFT,
                            status=STATUS_OFF, xwidth=15, xheight=12))
                    getattr(self, 'j%d' % i).j45_frame.place(relx=0.52,
                            rely=y, anchor=CENTER)
```
⑤
```
                for i in range(len(xypos)):
                    xpos,ypos = xypos[i]
                    setattr(self, 'led%d' % (i+1), CLED(self.card_frame,
                            self.canvas, shape=ROUND, width=4, status=STATUS_ON,
                            relx=xpos, rely=ypos))
```
⑥ **Create LEDs**
```
    class C6C110_Chassis:
        def __init__(self, master):
            self.outer=Frame(master, borderwidth=0, bg=Color.PANEL)
            self.outer.forget()

            self.img = PhotoImage(file='images/6c110_chassis.gif')
            self.width  = self.img.width()
            self.height = self.img.height()

            self.canvas = Canvas(self.outer, width=self.width,
                            height=self.height,selectborderwidth=0)
            self.canvas.pack(side="top", fill=BOTH, expand='no')
            self.canvas.create_image(0,0,anchor=NW, image=self.img)

            self.rack = Frame(self.outer, bd=0, width=self.width-84,
                            height=self.height-180,
                            bg=Color.CHASSIS, highlightthickness=0)
            self.rack.place(relx=0.081, rely=0.117, anchor=NW)

            x = 0.0
            for i in range(12):
                if i in [0,1,2,3,4,5]:
                    card =C6C110_FDDI(self.rack, slot=i)
```
⑦

```
    elif i in [6,7,8,9]:
        card =C6C110_ENET(self.rack, slot=i)
    else:
        card =C6C110_PSU(self.rack, slot=i)
    card.card_frame.place(x=x, y=0, anchor=NW)
    x = x + card.width
```

Code comments

1 Most of the code resembles that for drawn panel components. The code is a little shorter, since it is not necessary to build as many components.

```
self.img = PhotoImage(file='images/6c110_enet.gif')
setattr(glb, 'img%d % slot, self.img)
self.width  = self.img.width()
self.height = self.img.height()
```

In the __init__ method, we create a PhotoImage instance. It is important that this reference remains within scope. If the image gets garbage-collected, you'll see an empty background field where you had hoped to have an image. The size of the image is obtained (in pixels) in order to construct the panels.

2 As might be expected, we build a list of tuples to contain the calculated positions of the LEDs.

```
xypos = [(10,180),(10,187),
...
```

3 All borders, highlights, and selectionborders must be zero-width to ensure that the panels can be butted together.

```
self.canvas = Canvas(self.card_frame, width=self.width,
            bd=0,highlightthickness=0,
            height=self.height,selectborderwidth=0)
```

4 The image is created on the base canvas using the stored PhotoImage.

```
self.canvas.create_image(0,0,anchor=NW,
            image=eval('glb.img%d' % slot))
```

5 The J45 connectors are drawn *over* the connectors depicted in the image; this adds navigation and status properties to the otherwise passive devices.

```
for i, y in [(0, 0.330), (1, 0.619)]:
    setattr(self, 'j%d' % i, Enet10baseT(self.card_frame,
        fid="10Base-T-%d" % i, port=i, orient=HW_LEFT,
        status=STATUS_OFF, xwidth=15, xheight=12))
    getattr(self, 'j%d' % i).j45_frame.place(relx=0.52,
        rely=y, anchor=CENTER)
```

The size of the connector is passed in the constructor; this adds functionality to the J45 connectors shown earlier in the chapter.

6 The LEDs are drawn on the canvas at their designated location. Note that these use the CLED class, not the LED class, because these LEDs are drawn directly on the canvas and not within a Frame. If the LED class had been used, we would have experienced problems in attempting to fill the rectangular frame associated with the widget and the background color.

```
for i in range(len(xypos)):
    xpos,ypos = xypos[i]
    setattr(self, 'led%d' % (i+1), CLED(self.card_frame,
```

```
                self.canvas, shape=ROUND, width=4, status=STATUS_ON,
            relx=xpos, rely=ypos))
```

Note also that we pass both the enclosing `card_frame` and the `canvas` to the constructor. This facilitates accessing the `after` method of the Widget base class to implement flashing.

❼ Finally, we populate the card rack. For the purpose of illustration, two of the FDDI cards have been replaced with Ethernet cards. Although this does not make much sense for this ATM switch, it demonstrates the ease with which the cards may be arranged.

```
x = 0.0
for i in range(12):
    if i in [0,1,2,3,4,5]:
        card =C6C110_FDDI(self.rack, slot=i)
    elif i in [6,7,8,9]:
        card =C6C110_ENET(self.rack, slot=i)
    else:
        card =C6C110_PSU(self.rack, slot=i)
    card.card_frame.place(x=x, y=0, anchor=NW)
    x = x + card.width
```

Note that the actual card width is used to determine the placement of the next card, and not a calculated increment, as in the earlier example.

Running EC6110.py displays the screen shown at the right of figure 9.9. The screen at the left of this figure illustrates the unpopulated rack. As in the earlier example, provision has been made to animate the components. Clicking anywhere on the enclosing chassis activates the animated display; this is not presented here and is left for you to try.

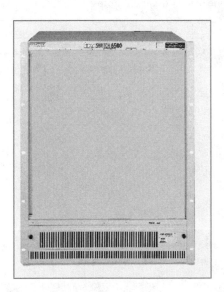 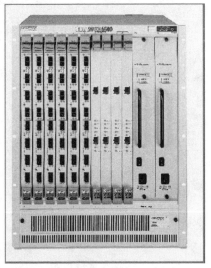

Figure 9.9 Cardrack implemented with GIF panels and overlaid components

9.5 *And now for a more complete example*

Figure 9.10
Digital multimeter

The previous examples have illustrated the overall methods for developing GUI representation of panels and other devices. To further develop this theme we will look at a simple but quite useful example.

Many digital multimeters have serial interfaces which allow connection to a computer. I own a RadioShack 22-168A multimeter, which is shown in figure 9.10. The meter has 24 ranges that provide AC/DC voltage and current measurements, resistance, capacitance, frequency counting and other functions. The meter implements a simple serial protocol which allows the currently-displayed value to be polled. Using a simple encoding scheme the current range selection can be deduced.

Implementing a GUI to display the current state of the meter's display is not particularly difficult. It is displaying the range that has been selected that introduces a challenge. One solution would be to display just the LCD panel at the top of the meter and then display the current range as text, either in the LCD or elsewhere. However this does not attempt to achieve photorealism and does not make for a particularly interesting example for you, the reader!

The solution we are going to implement is to animate the selector knob on the meter so that it reflects the actual appearance of the meter to the user. This requires quite a lot of work, but, as you will see later, it results in an attractive GUI.

These are the steps that we will go through to prepare a series of overlaid GIF images for the selector, as illustrated in figure 9.11:

1. Obtain the base image with the selector at one position.
2. Crop the selector as a rectangular selection.
3. Retouch the image to remove the pixels surrounding the selector.
4. Fill the background with a distinct color.
5. Rotate the image 15 degrees.
6. Crop the image to the same size as the original selection.
7. Save the image as a transparent GIF image, using the colormap entry corresponding to the surroundings of the selector as the transparent color (the last image in the series, figure 9.11(7), demonstrates the effect of displaying the overlaid image).

You have probably judged me as criminally insane to propose generating **24** rotated GIF images simply to show an accurate view of the actual multimeter. Perhaps you are right, but please reserve your final judgement until after you have seen the finished result!

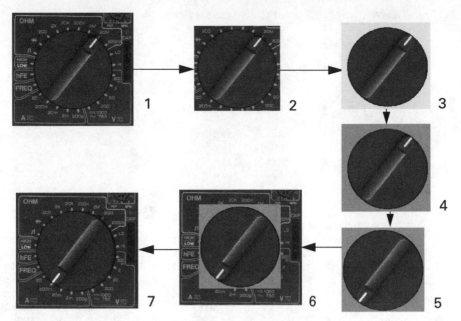

Figure 9.11 Steps to generate rotated selector images

Note As I began to develop this example, I encountered a problem with the serial communications to the multimeter. While investigating this problem I wanted to continue developing the GUI. I did this by building a simple test harness to simulate input from the device. I am going to present development of this example by showing the test version first and then adding serial communications later. This technique is valuable to get an application started, since it is possible to simulate input from devices even if they are not available for your use (or too expensive for your boss to sign a purchase requisition so that you can get your hands on one!).

Here is the code to implement the test version of the multimeter. First, we begin with the data file, defining the meter's ranges, control tables, labels, and other key data.

Example_9_1_data.py

```
# Tag  Run RFlag  Units  Key
PRIMARY_DATA = [                        ❶
  ('DI', 1, 'OL',  'mV',  'di'),
  ('DI', 0, '',    'mV',  'di'),
  ('OH', 1, 'OL.', 'Ohm', 'oh200o'),
  ('OH', 0, '4',   'Ohm', 'oh200o'),
  ('OH', 1, '.OL', 'KOhm','oh2ko'),    ❷
  ('OH', 0, '2',   'KOhm','oh2ko'),
  ('OH', 1, 'O.L', 'KOhm','oh20ko'),
...
  ('CA', 0, '2',   'nF',  'calo'),
```

```
                   ('CA',  0, '2',    'uF',     'cahi'),
                   ('DC',  0, '4',    'mV',     'dc200mv'),
                   ('DC',  0, '2',    'V',      'dc2v'),
                   ('DC',  0, '3',    'V',      'dc20v'),
                   ('DC',  0, '4',    'V',      'dc200v'),
                   ('DC',  0, '',     'V',      'dc1000v'),
              ...
                   ('AC',  0, '4',    'V',      'ac200v'),
              ...
                   ('FR',  0, '2',    'Hz',     'frh'),
                   ('FR',  0, '2',    'KHz',    'frk'),
                   ('FR',  0, '2',    'MHz',    'frm'),
                   ('HF',  0, '',     '',       'hfe'),
                   ('LO',  0, '',     '',       'logic'),
                   ('XX',  0, '',     '',       'cont')]
```

```
SECONDARY_DATA = {
# Key        m  u  A  m  V  k  M  O  n  u  F  M  K  Hz AC Control, Label
'di':       (0, 0, 0, 0, 0, 0, 0, 0, 0, 0, 0, 0, 0, 0, 0, 'diode', 'DIO'),
'oh200o':   (0, 0, 0, 0, 0, 0, 0, 1, 0, 0, 0, 0, 0, 0, 0, '200Ohm', ''),
'oh2ko':    (0, 0, 0, 0, 0, 1, 0, 1, 0, 0, 0, 0, 0, 0, 0, '2KOhm', ''),
'oh20ko':   (0, 0, 0, 0, 0, 1, 0, 1, 0, 0, 0, 0, 0, 0, 0, '20KOhm', ''),
'oh200ko':  (0, 0, 0, 0, 0, 1, 0, 1, 0, 0, 0, 0, 0, 0, 0, '200KOhm', ''),
'oh2mo':    (0, 0, 0, 0, 0, 0, 1, 1, 0, 0, 0, 0, 0, 0, 0, '2MOhm', ''),
'oh20mo':   (0, 0, 0, 0, 0, 0, 1, 1, 0, 0, 0, 0, 0, 0, 0, '20MOhm', ''),
....
'frh':      (0, 0, 0, 0, 0, 0, 0, 0, 0, 0, 0, 0, 0, 1, 0, 'freq', 'FREQ'),
'frk':      (0, 0, 0, 0, 0, 0, 0, 0, 0, 0, 0, 0, 1, 1, 0, 'freq', 'FREQ'),
'frm':      (0, 0, 0, 0, 0, 0, 0, 0, 0, 0, 0, 1, 0, 1, 0, 'freq', 'FREQ'),
'hfe':      (0, 0, 0, 0, 0, 0, 0, 0, 0, 0, 0, 0, 0, 0, 0, 'hfe', 'HFE'),
'logic':    (0, 0, 0, 0, 0, 0, 0, 0, 0, 0, 0, 0, 0, 0, 0, 'logic', 'LOGI'),
'cont':     (0, 0, 0, 0, 0, 0, 0, 0, 0, 0, 0, 0, 0, 0, 0, 'cont', '')}

TESTDATA = ['DI    OL    mV', 'DI    OL    mV', 'DI    OL    mV',
            'DI    OL    mV', 'DI    OL    mV', 'DI    OL    mV',
            'DI  0422    mV', 'DI  0022    mV', 'DI  0003    mV',
            'DI  0001    mV', 'DI  0004    mV', 'DI  0001    mV',
            'DI  0001    mV', 'DI  0001    mV', 'DI  0892    mV',
...
            'OH    OL.  Ohm', 'OH    OL.  Ohm', 'OH    OL.  Ohm',
            'OH    OL.  Ohm', 'OH    OL.  Ohm', 'OH  007.8 Ohm',
            'OH  014.7 Ohm', 'OH  001.1 Ohm', 'OH  116.3 Ohm',
            'OH  018.3 Ohm', 'OH  002.9 Ohm', 'OH  003.0 Ohm',
            'OH    OL.  Ohm', 'OH    .OL KOhm', 'OH    .OL KOhm',
            'OH    .OL KOhm', 'OH    .OL KOhm', 'OH -0.010KOhm',
            'OH  0.085KOhm', 'OH  0.001KOhm', 'OH  0.001KOhm',
            'OH  0.047KOhm', 'OH  0.410KOhm', 'OH  0.277KOhm',
...
            'CA  0.000  nF', 'CA  0.000  nF', 'CA  0.000  nF',
            'CA  0.000  nF', 'CA  0.000  nF', 'CA  0.000  uF',
            'CA  0.000  uF', 'CA  0.000  uF', 'CA  0.000  uF',
            'DC  034.1  mV', 'DC  025.6  mV', 'DC  063.5  mV',
            'DC  072.3  mV', 'DC  040.7  mV', 'DC  017.5  mV',
            'DC  005.2  mV', 'DC  0.005   V', 'DC  0.002   V',
            'DC  0.001   V', 'DC  0.001   V', 'DC  0.001   V',
```

```
...
          'FR  0.000 KHz', 'FR  0.001 KHz', 'FR  0.001 KHz',
          'FR  0.002 KHz', 'FR  0.000 KHz', 'FR  0.001 KHz',
          'FR  0.001 KHz', 'FR  0.000 KHz', 'HF  0000      ',
          'HF  0000      ', 'HF  0000      ', 'HF  0000      ',
          'HF  0000      ', 'HF  0000      ', 'HF  0000      ',
          'HF  0000      ', 'LO     rdy    ', 'LO     rdy    ',
          'LO     rdy    ', 'LO     rdy    ', 'LO     rdy    ',
          'LO     rdy    ', 'LO - rdy     ' ]

PANEL_LABELS = [ (225,  80, 'Arial',  'M',  'mhz'),
                 (240,  80, 'Arial',  'K',  'khz'),
                 (255,  80, 'Arial',  'Hz', 'hz'),
                 (225,  95, 'Arial',  'm',  'ma'),
                 (240,  95, 'Symbol', 'm',  'ua'),
                 (255,  95, 'Arial',  'A',  'a'),
                 (240, 110, 'Arial',  'm',  'mv'),
                 (255, 110, 'Arial',  'V',  'v'),
                 (225, 125, 'Arial',  'K',  'ko'),
                 (240, 125, 'Arial',  'M',  'mo'),
                 (255, 125, 'Symbol', 'W',  'o'),
                 (225, 140, 'Arial',  'n',  'nf'),
                 (240, 140, 'Symbol', 'm',  'uf'),
                 (255, 140, 'Arial',  'F',  'f'),
                 (50,  110, 'Arial',  'AC', 'ac')]
```

Code comments

1 The first list defines the ranges that the meter is capable of supporting, stored as tuples. The Tag determines the category of the reading:

```
# Tag  Run RFlag Units  Key
PRIMARY_DATA = [
  ('DI', 1, 'OL', 'mV',  'di'),
  ('DI', 0, '',   'mV',  'di'),
```

The Key is used to get the data that controls annunciators on the screen.

2 The over limit indicator is encoded (by changing the decimal point) to indicate the range that is currently selected.

```
  ('OH', 1, '.OL', 'KOhm', 'oh2ko'),
  ('OH', 1, 'O.L', 'KOhm', 'oh20ko'),
```

Most of the ranges have an over limit value.

3 The Key in PRIMARY_DATA is used to access a row in the SECONDARY_DATA dictionary which defines which of the annunciators are to be "turned on" on the display:

```
# Key      m u A m V k M O n u F M K Hz AC Control, Label
'di':     (0, 0, 0, 0, 0, 0, 0, 0, 0, 0, 0, 0, 0, 0, 0, 'diode', 'DIO'),
'oh200o': (0, 0, 0, 0, 0, 0, 0, 1, 0, 0, 0, 0, 0, 0, 0, '200Ohm', ''),
```

4 TESTDATA captures data in the format defined by the serial protocol for the meter. This data was captured directly from the meter using a data capture program (which was also used to debug the problem mentioned above).

```
TESTDATA = ['DI    OL    mV', 'DI    OL    mV', 'DI    OL    mV',
            'DI    OL    mV', 'DI    OL    mV', 'DI    OL    mV',
```

```
              'DI  0422   mV', 'DI  0022   mV', 'DI  0003   mV',
              'DI  0001   mV', 'DI  0004   mV', 'DI  0001   mV',
              'DI  0001   mV', 'DI  0001   mV', 'DI  0892   mV',
```

The data is sent as a 14-character string. The first two characters (Tag) determine the category. The position of the decimal point, in conjunction with the units, determines the range.

Here is the main code to support the application:

Example_9_1.py

```python
from Common  import *
from Tkinter import *
from Example_9_1_data import *
import sys, time, string

class MeterServer:
    def __init__(self):
        # Open up the serial port
        pass

    def poll(self):
        import random
        choice = random.choice(range(0, len(TESTDATA)-1))
        return TESTDATA[choice]

class MultiMeter:
    def __init__(self, master):
        self.root = master
        self.root.title("Digital Multimeter")
        self.root.iconname('22-168a')

        self.holdVal  = '0.0'
        self.curRange = None
        self.lineOpen = FALSE

        self.canvas = Canvas(self.root, width=300, height=694)
        self.canvas.pack(side="top", fill=BOTH, expand='no')

        self.img = PhotoImage(file='images/multimeter.gif')
        self.canvas.create_image(0,0,anchor=NW, image=self.img)
        self.buildRule()

        self.root.update()
        self.root.after(5, self.buildSymbols)
        self.dataReady = FALSE
        self.root.after(5, self.buildScanner)
        self.multimeter = MeterServer()
        self.root.after(500, self.doPoll)

    def buildSymbols(self):
        for x, y, font, txt, tag in PANEL_LABELS:
            self.canvas.create_text(x, y, text=txt,
                        font=(font, 12),
                        fill="gray75",
```

①

②

③

```
                                anchor = CENTER,
                                tags=tag)

        def buildRule(self):
            self.canvas.create_line(75,150, 213,150,
                            width=1,fill="#333377")
            self.Xincr = 140.0/40.0
            self.X = x = 75
            self.X1 = 213
            y = 150
            lbli = 0

            for i in range(40):
                lbl = ''
                if i in [0,9,19,29,39]:
                    h    = 6
                    lbl  = `lbli`
                    lbli = lbli + 5
                elif i in [5,14,24,34]:
                    h = 4
                else:
                    h = 2
                    self.canvas.create_line(x,y, x,y-h,
                                width=1,fill="#333377")

                if lbl:
                    self.canvas.create_text(x, y-5, text=lbl,
                                font=("Arial", 6),
                                fill="#333377",
                                anchor = S),
                x = x + self.Xincr

        def startAnimation(self):
            self.animX = self.X
            self.action = TRUE
            self.root.after(30, self.animate)
```

_____

Code comments

❶ The test version of our code does not initialize the serial interface:

```
def __init__(self):
    # Open up the serial port
    pass
```

❷ The poll method retrieves a random entry from the TESTDATA list, simulating a poll of the meter:

```
def poll(self):
    import random
    choice = random.choice(range(0, len(TESTDATA)-1))
    return TESTDATA[choice]
```

❸ This section of code illustrates how to arrange for an operation to occur as a background task. The methods buildSymbols and buildScanner are set up to run as callbacks after a few milliseconds.

```
        self.root.after(5, self.buildSymbols)
```

```
        self.dataReady = FALSE
        self.root.after(5, self.buildScanner)
        self.multimeter = MeterServer()
        self.root.after(500, self.doPoll)
```

buildScanner converts the GIF files to photo images and this is a time-consuming task. By moving the initialization to the background, we can display the base GUI immediately (although the user has to wait for all of the images to load before proceeding).

4 buildRule constructs tickmarks used by the multimeter to indicate the currently measured value relative to full-scale deflection of the selected range and to animate a graphic when the value is over range.

Example_9_1.py (continued)

```
def animate(self):                        5
    if self.action:
        self.canvas.create_line(self.animX,155, self.animX,167,
                        width=2,fill="#333377",
                        tags='anim')
        self.animX = self.animX + self.Xincr
        if self.animX > self.X1:
            self.animX= self.X
            self.canvas.delete('anim')
            self.root.after(30, self.animate)
    else:
        self.canvas.delete('anim')

def stopAnimation(self):
    self.action = FALSE

def buildScanner(self):                   6
    self.primary_lookup = {}
    for key, hasr, rfmt, un, sec in PRIMARY_DATA:
        if not self.primary_lookup.has_key(key):
            self.primary_lookup[key] = []
            self.primary_lookup[key].append((hasr, rfmt, un, sec))

    keys = SECONDARY_DATA.keys()
    for key in keys:
        img = SECONDARY_DATA[key][-2]
        try:
            if getattr(self, 'i%s' % key):
                pass    # Already done...
        except:
            setattr(self, 'i%s' % key,
                PhotoImage(file="images/%s.gif" % img))
    self.dataReady = TRUE

def doPoll(self):
    if self.dataReady:
        result = self.multimeter.poll()
        if result:
            self.updateDisplay(result)
    self.root.after(1000, self.doPoll)

def getRange(self, tag, val, units):          7
```

```python
        matchlist = self.primary_lookup[tag]
        if not matchlist: return None
        gotIndex = None
        gotOpenLine = FALSE
        for hasr, rfmt, un, sec in matchlist:
            if hasr and (string.find(val, 'L') >= 0):
                if rfmt == string.strip(val):
                    gotIndex = sec
                    gotOpenLine = TRUE
            else:
                decimal = string.find(val, '.')
                if decimal > 0:
                    if rfmt == `decimal`:
                        gotIndex = sec
                else:
                    if not rfmt:  # No decimals
                        gotIndex = sec
            if gotIndex:
                if not string.strip(units) == string.strip(un):
                    gotIndex = None
            if gotIndex:
                break
        return (gotIndex, gotOpenLine)

    def updateDisplay(self, result):
        self.canvas.delete('display')
        tag   = result[:2]
        val   = result[3:9]
        units = result [9:13]
        # display the hold value
        redraw = FALSE
        try:
            hold = string.atof(self.holdVal)
            nval = string.atof(val)
            if hold <= 0.0:
                if nval < 0.0:
                    if nval < hold:
                        self.holdVal = val
                        redraw = TRUE
                else:
                    hold = 0.0
            if hold >= 0.0 and not redraw:
                if nval >= 0.0:
                    if nval > hold:
                        self.holdVal = val
                        redraw = TRUE
                else:
                    self.holdVal = '0.0'
                    redraw = TRUE
        except ValueError:
            self.holdVal = '0.0'
            redraw = TRUE

        if redraw:
            self.canvas.delete('holdval')
```

⚫8

```
                self.canvas.create_text(263, 67, text=self.holdVal,
                              font=("Digiface", 16),
                              fill="#333377",
                              anchor = E,
                              tags="holdval")

        range, openline = self.getRange(tag, val, units)
        if range:      # Change the control to reflect the range
            if not self.curRange == range:
                self.curRange = range
                self.canvas.delete('control')
                self.canvas.create_image(146, 441,anchor=CENTER,
                        image=getattr(self, 'i%s' % range).
                        tags="control")
                self.holdVal = '0.0'  # reset
            if openline:
                self.startAnimation()
            else:
                self.stopAnimation()

            # Now we will update the units symbols on the display
            ma,ua,a,mv,v,ko,mo,o,nf,uf,f,mhz,khz,hz,ac, ctrl, lbl = \
                                    SECONDARY_DATA[range]

            for tag in ['ma','ua','a','mv','v','ko','mo','o',
                    'nf','uf','f','mhz','khz','hz','ac']:
                self.canvas.itemconfig(tag,
                        fill=['gray75','#333377'][eval(tag)])
                # Update the label field if there is one
                self.canvas.delete('label')
                if lbl:
                    self.canvas.create_text(55, 150, text=lbl,
                                    font=("Arial", 12),
                                    fill="#333377",
                                    anchor = CENTER,
                                    tags="label")

            # Finally, display the value
            self.canvas.create_text(214, 100, text=val,
                            font=("Digiface", 48),
                            fill="#333377",
                            anchor = E,
                            tags="display")

if __name__ == '__main__':
    root = Tk()
    multimeter = MultiMeter(root)
    multimeter.root.mainloop()
```

⑨

⑩

Code comments (continued)

❺ The `animate` method displays a rapidly increasing row of vertical bars which reset when they reach the right-hand side of the display.

❻ `buildScanner` builds a dictionary from PRIMARY_DATA to provide the primary lookup for the messages received from the meter. The GIF images are also loaded as PhotoImages.

❼ `getRange` parses the message received from the meter to determine the range and value to be displayed.

❽ The meter holds the highest (or lowest) value measured. This code displays this data. The code is longer than we might expect because we have to be able to detect the most positive or the most negative value.

❾ In this section of code, we change the overlaid selector knob position if the range has changed. Note that the previous image, tagged as `control`, is deleted first.

❿ Finally, we update the annunciators according to the currently selected range. To simplify this, we fill the text stroke with either a very light or dark gray.

If we run Example_9_1.py we will observe the display shown in figure 9.12. As each value is displayed, the range selector is animated to indicate the range for the value. An example of the display is shown in figure 9.13.

To complete the example, we simply need to add asynchronous support to connect the multimeter. This makes use of a Python extension module, siomodule, which is readily available from the Python language site (http://www.python.org), with one small change to support an idiosyncrasy of the meter's handshake protocol, but more about that in a moment. Extension modules are covered in detail in a later section, "Putting it all together..." on page 311. This module makes use of a commercial dll, which has been made available for general use (see "Siomodule" on page 625 for details). The necessary code changes are in Example_9_2.py:

Figure 9.12 Simulating measurements

Figure 9.13 Range selector animation

Example_9_2.py

```
from crilib import *
import sys, regex, serial, time, string, os
IGNORE = '\n\r'

class RS232(serial.Port):
    def __init__(self):
        serial.Port.__init__(self)
```

❶ Load serial

❷ Init UART

```
        def open(self, cfg):
            self.debug = cfg['debug']
            self._trace('RS232.open')
            cfg['cmdsEchoed']   = FALSE
            cfg['cmdTerm']      = '\r'                      ③  Setup params
            cfg['rspTerm']      = '\r'
            cfg['rspType']      = serial.RSP_TERMINATED
            serial.Port.open(self, cfg)

class MeterServer:
    def __init__(self):
        # Open up the serial port
        try:
            d = serial.PortDict()                          ④  Connection
            d['port']      = serial.COM1
            d['baud']      = serial.Baud1200
            d['parity']    = serial.NoParity
            d['dataBits']  = serial.WordLength7
            d['stopBits']  = serial.TwoStopBits
            d['timeOutMs'] = 1500                          ⑤
            d['rspTerm']   = IGNORE
            d['rtsSignal'] = 'C'                           ⑥
            d['debug']     = FALSE
            self.fd = RS232()
            self.fd.open(d)
        except:
            print 'Cannot open serial port (COM1)'
            sys.exit()

    def poll(self):
        try:
            line = self.fd.write('D\r')
            # OK, read the serial line (wait maximum of 1500 mSec)  ⑦
            inl = self.fd.readTerminated()
            return inl
        except:
            return 'XX    Off     '                        ⑧
```

Code comments

① The serial module wraps the sio module, which is a dll.

```
from crilib import *
import sys, serial, time, string, os
```

crilib contains simple constants.

② This time we have to initialize the UART (Universal Asynchronous Receiver Transmitter):

```
def __init__(self):
    serial.Port.__init__(self)
```

③ The terminators for the serial protocol are defined. Although we are not turning debug on for this example, the necessary initializers are given to help you reuse the code.

④ The communication parameters for the UART are set.

```
            d['port']      = serial.COM1
            d['baud']      = serial.Baud1200
```

```
d['parity']    = serial.NoParity
d['dataBits']  = serial.WordLength7
d['stopBits']  = serial.TwoStopBits
```

Note the somewhat unusual format and slow communication speed. However, the meter is a quite simple device, and not very expensive, so we can make an exception here.

⑤ The read is blocking, which is unusual for a GUI. Since there are no user controls on the display, we do not need to worry about exposing the event loop. So, if the meter failed to respond to a request for data, we might lock up for a a second or so.

⑥ This is where the meter's unusual handshaking protocol is handled. This is the reason I constructed the test version of the code, because I could not get the device to respond to the poll request initially. I had to use a software datascope to monitor the control lines on the serial interface to determine what the device needed to communicate. Unusually, it required Request-To-Send (RTS) to go *low* before it would send anything. The serial module, as obtained from the Python FTP site, has RTS strapped high. A simple change fixes this problem. Here we force RTS low.

```
d['rtsSignal'] = 'C'
```

⑦ The meter has to be polled to get the current value measured.

```
line = self.fd.write('D\r')
```

⑧ If the poll times out, we assume that the multimeter is switched off and we fabricate a message to show an appropriate value on the display.

```
return 'XX    Off      '
```

The minimal changes to serial.py are shown here:

serial.py (changes only)

```
    def __init__(self):
        self._dict = {}
...
        self._dict['rspType'] = RSP_BEST_EFFORT
        self._dict['rspFixedLen'] = 0
        self._dict['rtsSignal'] = 'S'
        self._dict['dtrSignal'] = 'S'
...
    def __setitem__(self, key, value):
...
        elif key == 'debug' or key == 'cmdsEchoed':
            if type(value) != IntType:
                raise AttributeError, 'must be a boolean value'
        elif key == 'rtsSignal':
            if not value[:1] in 'CS':
                raise AttributeError, 'Illegal rtsSignal value'
        elif key == 'dtrSignal':
            if not value[:1] in 'CS':
                raise AttributeError, 'Illegal dtrSignal value'

        self._dict[key] = value
...
    def open(self, cfg):
```

```
        self._chkSioExec(SioRxClear, (port,))
        self._chkSioExec(SioDTR, (port, cfg['dtrSignal'][:1]))
        self._chkSioExec(SioRTS, (port, cfg['rtsSignal'][:1]))
        self._chkSioExec(SioFlow, (port, 'N'))
```

Running Example_9_2.py displays the multimeter. Since there are no changes to the display methods, the display is indistinguishable from the one shown in figure 9.12, so it will not be shown here.

9.6 *Virtual machines using POV-Ray*

Of course, some applications may not have a physical device; for these cases, it is possible to create ray-traced images (using Persistence of Vision POV-Ray, or other rendering systems, for example) to create virtual machines.

Figure 9.14 shows an example of a ray-traced GUI which has been used in a commercial application. This employs the same overlay technique used to develop the front panel shown in figure 9.9, except that the image was completely fabricated. The application that this GUI supported was intended to be used by airline pilots, and so the display is constructed to be similar to some of the radio stacks encountered in aircraft. The GUI has a strong three-dimensional content, with shadows and highlights. All of this is computer generated by POV-Ray. The text, LEDs and navigable buttons are overlaid Tkinter widgets. The important feature to note is that the application has nothing to do with radio stacks; it is really a database access application. This is an application with punch!

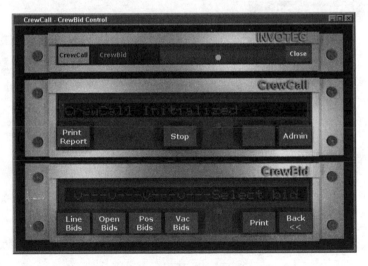

Figure 9.14 Ray-traced user interface
Photo courtesy INVOTEC, Inc.

9.6.1 And now for something completely different... #10 The Example

I'm sorry! I had to use that title. The last example is going to illustrate just how unusual a user interface can become. Readers who are familiar with popular computer games such as Myst and Riven will share with me their love of ray-traced user interfaces. This is a simplistic version of such an interface. I'm not going to detail the development of ray-traced images, as many texts cover the subject. Let's start with the basic image shown in figure 9.15.

Figure 9.15 Base scene generated with POV-Ray

The figure looks best in color, so you may want to obtain the image online. Since you may wish to solve the simple puzzle presented by this example, I will present only a fragment of the code for the application. We are using the overlay techniques presented in this chapter to bind functionality to the two "buttons" in the display. This requires special handling, since the two "buttons" need to take focus, show a highlight when they have focus, and receive button-down events. The following code excerpt manages these buttons.

Example_9_3.py

```
class Machine:
    def __init__(self, master):
        self.root = master
...
        self.b1 = self.canvas.create_oval(216,285, 270,340, fill="",
                        outline='#226644', width=3, tags='b_1')
        self.canvas.tag_bind(self.b1, "<Any-Enter>", self.mouseEnter)
        self.canvas.tag_bind(self.b1, "<Any-Leave>", self.mouseLeave)

        self.b2 = self.canvas.create_oval(216,355, 270,410, fill="",
                        outline='#772244', width=3, tags='b_2')
```

❶

```python
            self.canvas.tag_bind(self.b2, "<Any-Enter>", self.mouseEnter)
            self.canvas.tag_bind(self.b2, "<Any-Leave>", self.mouseLeave)
            Widget.bind(self.canvas, "<1>", self.mouseDown)

            self.buttonAction = {'b_1': self.b1_action,
                                 'b_2': self.b2_action}

    def mouseDown(self, event):
        # See if we're on a button. If we are, it
        # gets tagged as CURRENT for by Tk.
        if event.widget.find_withtag(CURRENT):
            tags = self.canvas.gettags('current')
            if '_' in tags[0]:
                self.buttonAction[tags[0]]()

    def mouseEnter(self, event):
        # The CURRENT tag is applied to
        # The object the cursor is over.
        tags = self.canvas.gettags('current')
        usetag= tags[0]
        self.lastcolor = self.canvas.itemcget(usetag, 'outline')
        self.canvas.itemconfig(usetag,outline=Color.HIGHLIGHT)
        self.canvas.itemconfig(usetag,fill=self.lastcolor)

    def mouseLeave(self, event):
        tags = self.canvas.gettags('current')
        usetag= tags[0]
        self.canvas.itemconfig(usetag, outline=self.lastcolor)
        self.canvas.itemconfig(usetag,fill="")

    def b1_action(self):
        if self.inSet:
            value = eval(self.digits[self.curDigit])
            value = value + 1
            exec('%s = value' % self.digits[self.curDigit])
            self.makeTime()
            self.displaySet()

    def b2_action(self):
        if not self.inSet:
            self.inSet = TRUE
            self.displaySet()
            self.root.after(1000, self.displayTime)
        else:
            self.curDigit = self.curDigit + 1
            if self.curDigit > 3:
                self.inSet = FALSE
                self.canvas.delete('settag')
                self.mouseLeave(None)
                self.doCountdown()
```

2

3

4

5

6

7

Code comments

1 We create two circles surrounding the spheres on the display, colored to match the existing display. Note that the circle has no fill color, and is thus transparent.

```
                        self.b1 = self.canvas.create_oval(216,285, 270,340, fill="",
                                       outline='#226644', width=3, tags='b_1')
```

2 The transparent fill on the circle has a side effect: a transparent object does not receive button events, so we bind enter and leave events to the line drawn for the circle.

```
            self.canvas.tag_bind(self.b2, "<Any-Enter>", self.mouseEnter)
            self.canvas.tag_bind(self.b2, "<Any-Leave>", self.mouseLeave)
            Widget.bind(self.canvas, "<1>", self.mouseDown)
```

We also bind left-mouse-button to the whole canvas. Note that we use the `bind` method of the mixin `Widget` to bind the event.

3 `self.buttonAction` is a very simple dispatcher:

```
            self.buttonAction = {'b_1': self.b1_action,
                                 'b_2': self.b2_action}
```

4 `mouseDown` dispatches to the appropriate function using the tag of the canvas item receiving the event:

```
        def mouseDown(self, event):
            if event.widget.find_withtag(CURRENT):
                tags = self.canvas.gettags('current')
                if '_' in tags[0]:
                    self.buttonAction[tags[0]]()
```

5 `mouseEnter` fills the circle with a color so that it can receive button events:

```
        def mouseEnter(self, event):
            tags = self.canvas.gettags('current')
            usetag= tags[0]
            self.lastcolor = self.canvas.itemcget(usetag, 'outline')
            self.canvas.itemconfig(usetag,outline=Color.HIGHLIGHT)
            self.canvas.itemconfig(usetag,fill=self.lastcolor)
```

6 `mouseLeave` removes the fill as the cursor leaves the button:

```
        def mouseLeave(self, event):
            tags = self.canvas.gettags('current')
            usetag= tags[0]
            self.canvas.itemconfig(usetag, outline=self.lastcolor)
            self.canvas.itemconfig(usetag,fill="")
```

7 Finally, when certain conditions have been met, we call `mouseLeave` directly to remove the highlight, even if the cursor is over the canvas item:

```
                    self.canvas.delete('settag')
                    self.mouseLeave(None)
```

If you run Example_9_3.py and work out the sequence, you should see a display similar to the one shown in figure 9.16.

Figure 9.16 Running the puzzle

9.7 Summary

The material in this chapter may seem to be very inappropriate for uses other than mechanical devices. Yet there is no reason that information about a system which has no real "front panel" cannot be given an abstract interface. If combinations of the techniques presented in this chapter are used, quite complex devices can be displayed to present status indicators and input devices for users. I hope that you have fun with these examples–there is something very satisfying about generating representations of devices.

C H A P T E R   1 0

Drawing blobs and rubber lines

Despite the title, this chapter covers some of the techniques used to build drawing tools and interfaces which allow the user to create and move objects around in a GUI. The chapter is not meant to be a *complete* guide to developing a new "paint" tool, but I will provide you with some useful templates for drawing objects on a canvas, using rubber lines and rearranging objects on a canvas. You have already seen the effect of drawing items on a canvas in earlier chapters—this chapter reveals a little more detail on how to create and maintain drawn objects.

      Some of the examples are Tkinter adaptations of Tk demonstration programs; they may be used as an additional guide to converting Tcl/Tk scripts to Tkinter. I have avoided the temptation to completely rework the code, since a side-by-side comparison would reveal how well Tkinter supports Tk.

10.1 Drawing on a canvas

We have already encountered several examples of objects drawn on canvases. However, these objects were drawn to represent physical objects on front panels and to create images programmatically. Now we need to allow the user to create drawn objects on the canvas.

Almost all drawing operations define a *bounding box* which encloses the object. The bounding box is expressed as a pair of *x/y* coordinates at the top-left and bottom-right corners. Lines are special cases; they have a start and end coordinate which does not have to correspond to the coordinates of its bounding box. The bounding box for a line will always be the top-left and bottom-right coordinates. It is important to note that Tk does not guarantee that the bounding box *exactly* bounds the object, so some allowances may have to be made in critical code. This is illustrated in figure 10.1.

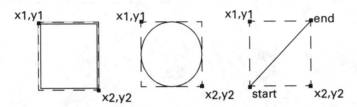

Figure 10.1 Bounding boxes for rectangles, ovals, and lines

Curved lines (not arcs) are defined as a series of straight lines, each with its own bounding box. Although we will see the application of these object types in some of the examples, they really require special consideration.

Let's start with a very simple drawing program, inspired by one of the examples in Douglas A. Young's *The X Window System: Programming and Applications with Xt*. This example allows the user to draw lines, rectangles and ovals on a canvas and then select each of these objects. The original example was written in C using X Window, so I have obviously Tkinterized it. It does not allow editing of the resulting drawn objects, so it is somewhat akin to drawing on soft paper with a very hard pencil!

draw.py

```
from    Tkinter import *
import Pmw, AppShell, math

class Draw(AppShell.AppShell):
    usecommandarea = 1
    appname       = 'Drawing Program - Version 1'
    frameWidth    = 800
    frameHeight   = 600

    def createButtons(self):
        self.buttonAdd('Close', helpMessage='Close Screen',
                    statusMessage='Exit', command=self.close)
```

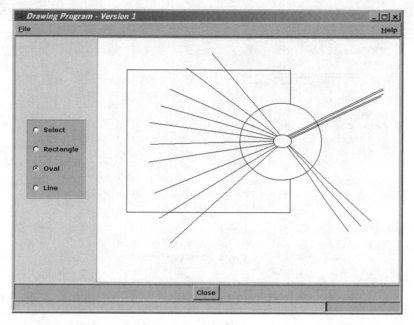

Figure 10.2 A very simple drawing program

```python
def createBase(self):
    self.width  = self.root.winfo_width()-10
    self.height = self.root.winfo_height()-95
    self.command= self.createcomponent('command', (), None,
        Frame, (self.interior(),), width=self.width*0.25,
        height=self.height, background="gray90")
    self.command.pack(side=LEFT, expand=YES, fill=BOTH)

    self.canvas = self.createcomponent('canvas', (), None,
        Canvas, (self.interior(),), width=self.width*0.73,
        height=self.height, background="white")
    self.canvas.pack(side=LEFT, expand=YES, fill=BOTH)

    Widget.bind(self.canvas, "<Button-1>", self.mouseDown)
    Widget.bind(self.canvas, "<Button1-Motion>", self.mouseMotion)
    Widget.bind(self.canvas, "<Button1-ButtonRelease>", self.mouseUp)

    self.radio = Pmw.RadioSelect(self.command, labelpos = None,
        buttontype = 'radiobutton', orient = VERTICAL,
        command = self.selectFunc, hull_borderwidth = 2,
        hull_relief = RIDGE,)
    self.radio.pack(side = TOP, expand = 1)

    self.func = {}
    for text, func in (('Select', None),
                       ('Rectangle', self.drawRect),
                       ('Oval', self.drawOval),
                       ('Line', self.drawLine)):
```

```
                self.radio.add(text)
                self.func[text] = func
            self.radio.invoke('Rectangle')

    def selectFunc(self, tag):
        self.currentFunc = self.func[tag]

    def mouseDown(self, event):
        self.currentObject = None                                        ❸
        self.lastx = self.startx = self.canvas.canvasx(event.x)
        self.lasty = self.starty = self.canvas.canvasy(event.y)
        if not self.currentFunc:
            self.selObj = self.canvas.find_closest(self.startx,         ❹
                                          self.starty)[0]
            self.canvas.itemconfig(self.selObj, width=2)
            self.canvas.lift(self.selObj)

    def mouseMotion(self, event):
        self.lastx = self.canvas.canvasx(event.x)
        self.lasty = self.canvas.canvasy(event.y)
        if self.currentFunc:
            self.canvas.delete(self.currentObject)
            self.currentFunc(self.startx, self.starty,                  ❺
                        self.lastx, self.lasty,
                        self.foreground, self.background)

    def mouseUp(self, event):
        self.lastx = self.canvas.canvasx(event.x)
        self.lasty = self.canvas.canvasy(event.y)
        self.canvas.delete(self.currentObject)
        self.currentObject = None
        if self.currentFunc:
            self.currentFunc(self.startx, self.starty,
                        self.lastx, self.lasty,
                        self.foreground, self.background)
        else:
            if self.selObj:
                self.canvas.itemconfig(self.selObj, width=1)

    def drawLine(self, x, y, x2, y2, fg, bg):                           ❻
        self.currentObject = self.canvas.create_line(x,y,x2,y2,
                                  fill=fg)

    def drawRect(self, x, y, x2, y2, fg, bg):
        self.currentObject = self.canvas.create_rectangle(x, y,
                                  x2, y2, outline=fg, fill=bg)

    def drawOval(self, x, y, x2, y2, fg, bg):
        self.currentObject = self.canvas.create_oval(x, y, x2, y2,
                                  outline=fg, fill=bg)

    def initData(self):
        self.currentFunc   = None
        self.currentObject = None
        self.selObj    = None
        self.foreground   = 'black'
```

```
            self.background   = 'white'

    def close(self):
        self.quit()

    def createInterface(self):
        AppShell.AppShell.createInterface(self)
        self.createButtons()
        self.initData()
        self.createBase()

if __name__ == '__main__':
    draw = Draw()
    draw.run()
```

Code comments

1 This example is completely pointer-driven so it relies on binding functionality to mouse events. We bind click, movement and release to appropriate member functions.

```
Widget.bind(self.canvas, "<Button-1>", self.mouseDown)
Widget.bind(self.canvas, "<Button1-Motion>", self.mouseMotion)
Widget.bind(self.canvas, "<Button1-ButtonRelease>", self.mouseUp)
```

2 This simple example supports three basic shapes. We build `Pmw.RadioSelect` buttons to link each of the shapes with an appropriate drawing function. Additionally, we define a selection option which allows us to click on the canvas without drawing.

3 The `mouseDown` method deselects any currently selected object. The event returns x- and y-coordinates for the mouse-click as screen coordinates. The `canvasx` and `canvasy` methods of the `Canvas` widget convert these screen coordinates into coordinates relative to the canvas.

```
def mouseDown(self, event):
    self.currentObject = None
    self.lastx = self.startx = self.canvas.canvasx(event.x)
    self.lasty = self.starty = self.canvas.canvasy(event.y)
```

Converting the x- and y-coordinates to canvas coordinates is a step that is often forgotten when first coding canvas-based applications. Figure 10.3 illustrates what this means.

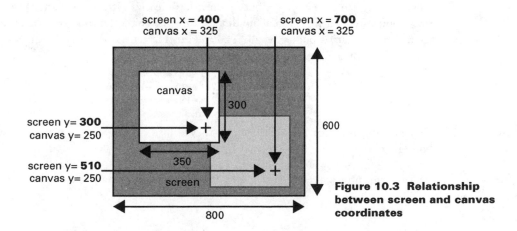

Figure 10.3 Relationship between screen and canvas coordinates

When the user clicks on the canvas, the click effectively goes through to the desktop and these coordinates are returned in the event. Converting to canvas coordinates returns the coordinates relative to the canvas origin, regardless of where the canvas is on the screen.

4 If no drawing function is selected, we are in select mode, and we search to locate the nearest object on the canvas and select it. This method of selection may not be appropriate for all drawing applications, since the method will always find an object, no matter where the canvas is clicked. This can lead to some confusing behavior in certain complex diagrams, so the selection model might require direct clicking on an object to select it.

```
if not self.currentFunc:
    self.selObj = self.canvas.find_closest(self.startx,
                                            self.starty))
    self.canvas.itemconfig(self.selObj, width=2)
    self.canvas.lift(self.selObj)
```

Having selected the object, we thicken its outline and raise (`lift`) it to the top of the drawing stack, as shown in figure 10.4.

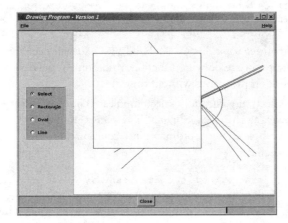

Figure 10.4 Selecting an object on a canvas

5 As the mouse is moved (with the button down), we receive a stream of motion events. Each of these represents a change in the bounding box for the object. Having converted the x- and y-coordinates to canvas points, we `delete` the existing canvas object and redraw it using the current function and the new bounding box.

```
self.canvas.delete(self.currentObject)
self.currentFunc(self.startx, self.starty,
                 self.lastx, self.lasty,
                 self.foreground, self.background)
```

6 The drawing methods are quite simple; they're just creating canvas primitives within the bounding box.

```
def drawLine(self, x, y, x2, y2, fg, bg):
    self.currentObject = self.canvas.create_line(x,y,x2,y2,
                                                  fill=fg)
```

10.1.1 Moving canvas objects

The selection of objects in the first example simply raises them in the display stack. If you were to raise a large object above smaller objects you could quite possibly prevent access to those objects. Clearly, we need to provide a more useful means of manipulating the drawn objects. Typically, draw tools move objects in response to a mouse drag. Adding this to the example is very easy. Here are the modifications which have been applied to draw.py:

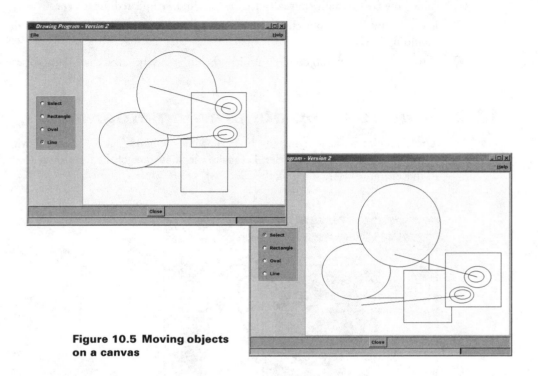

Figure 10.5 Moving objects on a canvas

draw2.py

```
def mouseMotion(self, event):
    cx = self.canvas.canvasx(event.x)                          ❶
    cy = self.canvas.canvasy(event.y)
    if self.currentFunc:
        self.lastx = cx                                        ❷
        self.lasty = cy
        self.canvas.delete(self.currentObject)
        self.currentFunc(self.startx, self.starty,
                self.lastx, self.lasty,
                self.foreground, self.background)
    else:
        if self.selObj:
```

```
            self.canvas.move(self.selObj, cx-self.lastx,
                                          cy-self.lasty)
            self.lastx = cx
            self.lasty = cy
```

Code comments

1 We need to store the x- and y-coordinates in intermediate variables, since we need to determine how far the mouse moved since the last time we updated the screen.

2 If we are drawing the object, we use the x- and y-coordinates as the second coordinate of the bounding box.

3 If we are moving the object, we calculate the difference between the current location and the last bounding box location.

10.2 A more complete drawing program

The examples so far demonstrate basic drawing methods, but a realistic drawing program must supply many more facilities. Let's take a look at some of the features that we are adding in this example before studying the code:

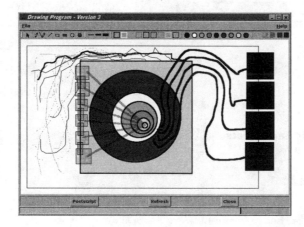

Figure 10.6 Drawing program: extended features

1 A Toolbar to give access to a number of specific drawing tools and options:

- Drawing tools for freehand curves, smoothed curves, straight (rubber) lines, open and filled rectangles, and open and filled ovals.
- Provision to set the color of the line or outline of a drawn object.
- Provision to set the width of the line or outline of a drawn object.
- Provision to set the fill color of an object.
- A limited number of stipple masks (to allow variable transparency).

2 Holding down the SHIFT key draws rectangles and ovals as squares and circles respectively.

3 An option to generate a PostScript file rendering the current content of the canvas.

4 A refresh option to repaint the screen.

5 Balloon help (provided through AppShell, which was introduced on page 155).

Here is the source to support the functionality:

draw3.py

```python
from   Tkinter import *
import Pmw, AppShell, math, time, string

class ToolBarButton(Label):
    def __init__(self, top, parent, tag=None, image=None, command=None,
                 statushelp='', balloonhelp='', height=21, width=21,
                 bd=1, activebackground='lightgrey', padx=0, pady=0,
                 state='normal', bg='grey'):
        Label.__init__(self, parent, height=height, width=width,
                       relief='flat', bd=bd, bg=bg)
        self.bg = bg
        self.activebackground = activebackground
        if image != None:
            if string.split(image, '.')[1] == 'bmp':
                self.Icon = BitmapImage(file='icons/%s' % image)
            else:
                self.Icon = PhotoImage(file='icons/%s' % image)
        else:
            self.Icon = PhotoImage(file='icons/blank.gif')
        self.config(image=self.Icon)

        self.tag = tag
        self.icommand = command
        self.command  = self.activate
        self.bind("<Enter>",          self.buttonEnter)
        self.bind("<Leave>",          self.buttonLeave)
        self.bind("<ButtonPress-1>",   self.buttonDown)
        self.bind("<ButtonRelease-1>", self.buttonUp)
        self.pack(side='left', anchor=NW, padx=padx, pady=pady)

        if balloonhelp or statushelp:
            top.balloon().bind(self, balloonhelp, statushelp)
            self.state = state

    def activate(self):
        self.icommand(self.tag)

    def buttonEnter(self, event):
        if self.state != 'disabled':
            self.config(relief='raised', bg=self.bg)

    def buttonLeave(self, event):
        if self.state != 'disabled':
            self.config(relief='flat', bg=self.bg)

    def buttonDown(self, event):
        if self.state != 'disabled':
            self.config(relief='sunken', bg=self.activebackground)
```

❶

❷

```
        def buttonUp(self, event):
            if self.state != 'disabled':
                if self.command != None:
                    self.command()
                time.sleep(0.05)
                self.config(relief='flat', bg=self.bg)

class Draw(AppShell.AppShell):
    usecommandarea = 1
    appname       = 'Drawing Program - Version 3'
    frameWidth    = 840
    frameHeight   = 600

    def createButtons(self):
        self.buttonAdd('Postscript',
                helpMessage='Save current drawing (as PostScript)',
                statusMessage='Save drawing as PostScript file',
                command=self.ipostscript)
        self.buttonAdd('Refresh', helpMessage='Refresh drawing',
                statusMessage='Redraw the screen', command=self.redraw)
        self.buttonAdd('Close', helpMessage='Close Screen',
                statusMessage='Exit', command=self.close)

    def createBase(self):
        self.toolbar = self.createcomponent('toolbar', (), None,
                Frame, (self.interior(),), background="gray90")
        self.toolbar.pack(fill=X)

        self.canvas = self.createcomponent('canvas', (), None,
                Canvas, (self.interior(),), background="white")
        self.canvas.pack(side=LEFT, expand=YES, fill=BOTH)

        Widget.bind(self.canvas, "<Button-1>", self.mouseDown)
        Widget.bind(self.canvas, "<Button1-Motion>", self.mouseMotion)
        Widget.bind(self.canvas, "<Button1-ButtonRelease>", self.mouseUp)
        self.root.bind("<KeyPress>", self.setRegular)
        self.root.bind("<KeyRelease>", self.setRegular)

    def setRegular(self, event):
        if event.type == '2' and event.keysym == 'Shift_L':
            self.regular = TRUE
        else:
            self.regular = FALSE

    def createTools(self):
        self.func = {}
        ToolBarButton(self, self.toolbar, 'sep', 'sep.gif',
                width=10, state='disabled')
        for key, func, balloon in [
                ('pointer',    None,                'Edit drawing'),
                ('draw',       self.drawFree,       'Draw freehand'),
                ('smooth',     self.drawSmooth,     'Smooth freehand'),
                ('line',       self.drawLine,       'Rubber line'),
                ('rect',       self.drawRect,       'Unfilled rectangle'),
                ('frect',      self.drawFilledRect, 'Filled rectangle'),
                ('oval',       self.drawOval,       'Unfilled oval'),
```

❸

❹

```
                  ('foval',        self.drawFilledOval, 'Filled oval')]:
               ToolBarButton(self, self.toolbar, key, '%s.gif' % key,
                       command=self.selectFunc, balloonhelp=balloon,
                       statushelp=balloon)
               self.func[key] = func

    def createLineWidths(self):
        ToolBarButton(self, self.toolbar, 'sep', 'sep.gif', width=10,
                   state='disabled')
        for width in ['1', '3', '5']:
            ToolBarButton(self, self.toolbar, width, 'tline%s.gif' % \
                   width, command=self.selectWidth,
                   balloonhelp='%s pixel linewidth' % width,
                   statushelp='%s pixel linewidth' % width)

    def createLineColors(self):
    def createFillColors(self):
    def createPatterns(self):

# --- Code Removed -------------------------------------------------------
```

Code comments

❶ The ToolBarButton class implements a simple iconic button. A bitmap or PhotoImage may be used for the icon.

❷ We establish bindings for the Label widget, since we have to create our own button-press animation when the user clicks on the button or places the cursor over the button.

❸ Forcing rectangles to be squares and ovals to be circles is achieved by binding a <Keypress> event to the root window. When we receive the callback, we have to check that the SHIFT key is pressed and set a flag accordingly.

```
        self.root.bind("<KeyPress>", self.setRegular)
        self.root.bind("<KeyRelease>", self.setRegular)
    def setRegular(self, event):
        if event.type == '2' and event.keysym == 'Shift_Left':
            self.regular = TRUE
```

❹ We create a dispatch table for the various drawn object types, with a display name, function, and Balloon help text.

❺ The method to create each group of toolbar buttons is essentially the same, so some of the code has been removed for brevity.

draw3.py (continued)

```
    def selectFunc(self, tag):
        self.curFunc = self.func[tag]
        if self.curFunc:
            self.canvas.config(cursor='crosshair')
        else:
            self.canvas.config(cursor='arrow')

    def selectWidth(self, tag):
    def selectBackground(self, tag):
    def selectForeground(self, tag):
```

```
        def selectPattern(self, tag):

# --- Code Removed --------------------------------------------------

    def mouseDown(self, event):
        self.curObject = None
        self.canvas.dtag('drawing')
        self.lineData = []
        self.lastx = self.startx = self.canvas.canvasx(event.x)
        self.lasty = self.starty = self.canvas.canvasy(event.y)
        if not self.curFunc:
            self.selObj = self.canvas.find_closest(self.startx,
                                          self.starty)[0]
            self.savedWidth = string.atoi(self.canvas.itemcget( \
                        self.selObj, 'width'))
            self.canvas.itemconfig(self.selObj,
                            width=self.savedWidth + 2)
            self.canvas.lift(self.selObj)

    def mouseMotion(self, event):
        curx = self.canvas.canvasx(event.x)
        cury = self.canvas.canvasy(event.y)
        prevx = self.lastx
        prevy = self.lasty
        if self.curFunc:
            self.lastx = curx
            self.lasty = cury

            if self.regular and self.canvas.type('drawing') in \
                ['oval','rectangle']:
                dx    = self.lastx - self.startx
                dy    = self.lasty - self.starty
                delta = max(dx, dy)
                self.lastx = self.startx + delta
                self.lasty = self.starty + delta
                self.curFunc(self.startx, self.starty, self.lastx,
                        self.lasty, prevx, prevy, self.foreground,
                        self.background, self.fillStyle, self.lineWidth,None)

            else:
                if self.selObj:
                    self.canvas.move(self.selObj, curx-prevx, cury-prevy)
                    self.lastx = curx
                    self.lasty = cury

    def mouseUp(self, event):
        self.prevx = self.lastx
        self.prevy = self.lasty
        self.lastx = self.canvas.canvasx(event.x)
        self.lasty = self.canvas.canvasy(event.y)
        if self.curFunc:
            if self.regular and self.canvas.type('drawing') in \
                ['oval','rectangle']:
                dx    = self.lastx - self.startx
                dy    = self.lasty - self.starty
                delta = max(dx, dy)
```

7

8

```
                    self.lastx = self.startx + delta          8   ↑      7   ↑
                    self.lasty = self.starty + delta
                self.curFunc(self.startx, self.starty, self.lastx,
                    self.lasty, self.prevx, self.prevy, self.foreground,
                    self.background, self.fillStyle, self.lineWidth,
                    self.lineData)
                self.storeObject()
        else:
            if self.selObj:
                self.canvas.itemconfig(self.selObj,
                                    width=self.savedWidth)

    def drawLine(self,x,y,x2,y2,x3,y3,fg,bg,fillp,wid,ld):               9
        self.canvas.delete(self.curObject)
        self.curObject = self.canvas.create_line(x,y,x2,y2,fill=fg,
                tags='drawing',stipple=fillp,width=wid)

    def drawFree(self,x,y,x2,y2,x3,y3,fg,bg,fillp,wid,ld):
        self.drawFreeSmooth(x,y,x2,y2,x3,y3,FALSE,fg,bg,fillp,wid,ld)

    def drawSmooth(self,x,y,x2,y2,x3,y3,fg,bg,fillp,wid, ld):
        self.drawFreeSmooth(x,y,x2,y2,x3,y3,TRUE,fg,bg,fillp,wid,ld)

    def drawFreeSmooth(self,x,y,x2,y2,x3,y3,smooth,fg,bg,fillp,
                wid,ld):
        if not ld:
            for coord in [[x3, y3, x2, y2], [x2, y2]][smooth]:
                self.lineData.append(coord)
                ild = self.lineData
        else:
            ild = ld
        if len(ild) > 2:
            self.curObject = self.canvas.create_line(ild, fill=fg,
                stipple=fillp, tags='drawing', width=wid, smooth=smooth)

    def drawRect(self,x,y,x2,y2,x3,y3,fg,bg,fillp,wid,ld):
        self.drawFilledRect(x,y,x2,y2,x3,y3,fg,'',fillp,wid,ld)

    def drawFilledRect(self,x,y,x2,y2,x3,y3,fg,bg,fillp,wid,ld):
        self.canvas.delete(self.curObject)
        self.curObject = self.canvas.create_rectangle(x,y,x2,y2,
                outline=fg, tags='drawing',fill=bg,
                stipple=fillp,width=wid)

    def drawOval(self,x,y,x2,y2,x3,y3,fg,bg,fillp,wid,ld):
        self.drawFilledOval(x,y,x2,y2,x3,y3,fg,'',fillp,wid,ld)

    def drawFilledOval(self,x,y,x2,y2,x3,y3,fg,bg,fillp,wid,ld):
        self.canvas.delete(self.curObject)
        self.curObject = self.canvas.create_oval(x,y,x2,y2,outline=fg,
                fill=bg,tags='drawing',stipple=fillp,width=wid)
```

Code comments (continued)

6 Each of the select callbacks uses the `tag` attached to each of the toolbar buttons to look up the function, line width, or other property of a button (Some of the code has been removed).

```
def selectFunc(self, tag):
    self.curFunc = self.func[tag]
    if self.curFunc:
        self.canvas.config(cursor='crosshair')
    else:
        self.canvas.config(cursor='arrow')
```

A cursor is also selected, appropriate for the current operation.

7 The mouse callbacks are similar to those in the earlier two examples.

8 This code implements the squaring or rounding of rectangles and ovals if the appropriate flags have been set.

9 The draw methods are quite similar to earlier examples with the addition of storing a list of line segments (for curved lines), smoothing and object attributes.

draw3.py (continued)

```
def storeObject(self):
    self.objects.append(( self.startx, self.starty, self.lastx,
            self.lasty, self.prevx, self.prevy, self.curFunc,
            self.foreground, self.background, self.fillStyle,
            self.lineWidth, self.lineData ))
```
10

```
def redraw(self):
    self.canvas.delete(ALL)
    for startx, starty, lastx, lasty, prevx, prevy, func, \
        fg, bg, fill, lwid, ld,  in self.objects:
        self.curObject = None
        func(startx, starty, lastx, lasty, prevx, prevy,
                fg, bg, fill, lwid, ld)
```
11

```
def initData(self):
    self.curFunc       = self.drawLine
    self.curObject     = None
    self.selObj        = None
    self.lineData      = []
    self.savedWidth    = 1
    self.objects       = []
    self.foreground    = 'black'
    self.background    = 'white'
    self.fillStyle     = None
    self.lineWidth     = 1
    self.regular       = FALSE

def ipostscript(self):                **12**
    postscript = self.canvas.postscript()
    fd = open('drawing.ps', 'w')
    fd.write(postscript)
    fd.close()

def close(self):
    self.quit()

def createInterface(self):
    AppShell.AppShell.createInterface(self)
    self.createButtons()
```

```
        self.initData()
        self.createBase()
        self.createTools()
        self.createLineWidths()
        self.createLineColors()
        self.createFillColors()
        self.createPatterns()

if __name__ == '__main__':
    draw = Draw()
    draw.run()
```

Code comments (continued)

10 The purpose of storeObject is to store a list of object descriptors in the order in which they were created, so that the drawing can be refreshed in the correct order.

11 redraw deletes all of the current objects and recreates them, with all original attributes and tags.

12 Tk canvases have a wonderful ability to create a PostScript representation of themselves (it is a pity that the rest of the widgets cannot do this). As a result, we are able to output a file containing the PostScript drawing, which can be printed or viewed with the appropriate software.

10.3 *Scrolled canvases*

Frequently, the size of a drawing exceeds the available space on the screen. To provide a larger canvas, we must scroll the canvas under a viewing area. Handling scrollbars in some windowing systems (X Window, for example) can require a moderate amount of code. Tkinter (Tk) makes scroll operations relatively easy to code. Take a look at this example, which was reworked directly from a Tk example.

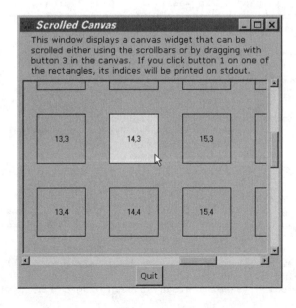

Figure 10.7 Managing a scrolled canvas

```
from Tkinter import *

class ScrolledCanvas:
    def __init__(self, master, width=500, height=350):
        Label(master, text="This window displays a canvas widget "
                "that can be scrolled either using the scrollbars or "
                "by dragging with button 3 in the canvas. If you "
                "click button 1 on one of the rectangles, its indices "
                "will be printed on stdout.",
                wraplength="4i", justify=LEFT).pack(side=TOP)
        self.control=Frame(master)
        self.control.pack(side=BOTTOM, fill=X, padx=2)
        Button(self.control, text='Quit', command=master.quit).pack()

        self.grid = Frame(master)
        self.canvas = Canvas(master, relief=SUNKEN, borderwidth=2,
                        scrollregion=('-11c', '-11c', '50c', '20c'))
        self.hscroll = Scrollbar(master, orient=HORIZONTAL,
                        command=self.canvas.xview)
        self.vscroll = Scrollbar(master, command=self.canvas.yview)

        self.canvas.configure(xscrollcommand=self.hscroll.set,
                        yscrollcommand=self.vscroll.set)

        self.grid.pack(expand=YES, fill=BOTH, padx=1, pady=1)
        self.grid.rowconfigure(0, weight=1, minsize=0)
        self.grid.columnconfigure(0, weight=1, minsize=0)
        self.canvas.grid(padx=1, in_=self.grid, pady=1, row=0,
                    column=0, rowspan=1, columnspan=1, sticky='news')
        self.vscroll.grid(padx=1, in_=self.grid, pady=1, row=0,
                    column=1, rowspan=1, columnspan=1, sticky='news')
        self.hscroll.grid(padx=1, in_=self.grid, pady=1, row=1,
                    column=0, rowspan=1, columnspan=1, sticky='news')
        self.oldFill = None

        bg = self.canvas['background']
        for i in range(20):
            x = -10 + 3*i
            y = -10
            for j in range(10):
                self.canvas.create_rectangle('%dc'%x, '%dc'%y,
                        '%dc'%(x+2), '%dc'%(y+2), outline='black',
                        fill=bg, tags='rect')
                self.canvas.create_text('%dc'%(x+1), '%dc'%(y+1),
                            text='%d,%d'%(i,j), anchor=CENTER,
                            tags=('text', 'rect'))
                y = y + 3
        self.canvas.tag_bind('rect', '<Any-Enter>', self.scrollEnter)
        self.canvas.tag_bind('rect', '<Any-Leave>', self.scrollLeave)
        self.canvas.bind_all('<1>', self.scrollButton)
        self.canvas.bind('<3>',
                lambda e, s=self: s.canvas.scan_mark(e.x, e.y))
        self.canvas.bind('<B3-Motion>',
                lambda e, s=self: s.canvas.scan_dragto(e.x, e.y))
```

```
    def scrollEnter(self, event):
        id = self.canvas.find_withtag(CURRENT)[0]
        if 'text' in self.canvas.gettags(CURRENT):
            id = id-1
        self.canvas.itemconfigure(id, fill='SeaGreen1')

    def scrollLeave(self, event):
        id = self.canvas.find_withtag(CURRENT)[0]
        if 'text' in self.canvas.gettags(CURRENT):
            id = id-1
        self.canvas.itemconfigure(id, fill=self.canvas['background'])

    def scrollButton(self, event):
        ids = self.canvas.find_withtag(CURRENT)
        if ids:
            id = ids[0]
            if not 'text' in self.canvas.gettags(CURRENT):
                id = id+1
            print 'You clicked on %s' % \
                self.canvas.itemcget(id, 'text')

if __name__ == '__main__':
    root = Tk()
    root.option_add('*Font', 'Verdana 10')
    root.title('Scrolled Canvas')
    scroll = ScrolledCanvas(root)
    root.mainloop()
```

④

Code comments

① We create the canvas with a 61cm×31cm scroll region which clearly will not fit in a 500×350 (pixels) window. The horizontal and vertical bars are created and bound directly to the position method of the canvas.

```
self.canvas = Canvas(master, relief=SUNKEN, borderwidth=2,
                     scrollregion=('-11c', '-11c', '50c', '20c'))
self.hscroll = Scrollbar(master, orient=HORIZONTAL,
                         command=self.canvas.xview)
self.vscroll = Scrollbar(master, command=self.canvas.yview)
```

② The scroll bars are set to track the canvas:

```
self.canvas.configure(xscrollcommand=self.hscroll.set,

                      yscrollcommand=self.vscroll.set)
```

③ Setting up the bindings to pan the canvas when the right mouse button is clicked and dragged is surprisingly easy–we just bind the click to the scan_mark method and the drag to scan_dragto.

```
self.canvas.bind('<3>',
                 lambda e, s=self: s.canvas.scan_mark(e.x, e.y))
self.canvas.bind('<B3-Motion>',
                 lambda e, s=self: s.canvas.scan_dragto(e.x, e.y))
```

④ Finally, the ScrollButton callback is worthy of a brief note. It illustrates the ease of using tags to identify objects:

```
ids = self.canvas.find_withtag(CURRENT)
```

```
if ids:
    id = ids[0]
    if not 'text' in self.canvas.gettags(CURRENT):
        id = id+1
    print 'You clicked on %s' % \
        self.canvas.itemcget(id, 'text')
```

First we find all the ids with the CURRENT tag (this will be either the rectangle or the text field at its center). We only care about the first tag.

Then, we check to see if it is the text object. If it is not, the next id will be the text object, since we defined the rectangle first.

Last, we get the text object's contents which give the row-column coordinates.

10.4 *Ruler-class tools*

Another common drawing tool is a ruler. This can be used to provide tab stops or other constraint graphics. It also illustrates some of the aspects of drag-and-drop from within an application. This example was also recoded from a Tk example.

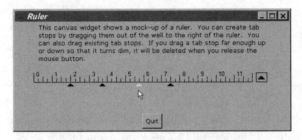

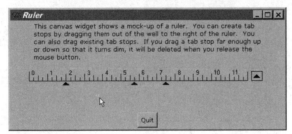

Figure 10.8 A simple ruler tool

ruler.py

```
from Tkinter import *

class Ruler:
    def __init__(self, master, width='14.8c', height='2.5c'):
        Label(master, text="This canvas widget shows a mock-up of a "
                "ruler.  You can create tab stops by dragging them out "
                "of the well to the right of the ruler.  You can also "
                "drag existing tab stops. If you drag a tab stop far "
```

```
                    "enough up or down so that it turns dim, it will be "
                    "deleted when you release the mouse button.",
                    wraplength="5i", justify=LEFT).pack(side=TOP)
        self.ctl=Frame(master)
        self.ctl.pack(side=BOTTOM, fill=X, padx=2, pady=2)
        Button(self.ctl, text='Quit', command=master.quit).pack()
        self.canvas = Canvas(master, width=width, height=height,
                        relief=FLAT, borderwidth=2)
        self.canvas.pack(side=TOP, fill=X)

        c = self.canvas
        self.grid    = '0.25c'
        self.left    = c.winfo_fpixels('1c')
        self.right   = c.winfo_fpixels('13c')
        self.top     = c.winfo_fpixels('1c')
        self.bottom  = c.winfo_fpixels('1.5c')
        self.size    = c.winfo_fpixels('.2c')
        self.normalStyle    = 'black'
        self.activeStyle    = 'green'
        self.activeStipple  = ''
        self.deleteStyle    = 'red'
        self.deleteStipple  = 'gray25'

        c.create_line('1c', '0.5c', '1c', '1c', '13c', '1c',
                    '13c', '0.5c', width=1)
        for i in range(12):
            x = i+1
            c.create_line('%dc'%x, '1c', '%dc'%x, '0.6c', width=1)
            c.create_line('%d.25c'%x, '1c', '%d.25c'%x,
                        '0.8c', width=1)
            c.create_line('%d.5c'%x, '1c', '%d.5c'%x,
                        '0.7c', width=1)
            c.create_line('%d.75c'%x, '1c', '%d.75c'%x,
                        '0.8c', width=1)
            c.create_text('%d.15c'%x, '.75c', text=i, anchor=SW)

        wellBorder = c.create_rectangle('13.2c', '1c', '13.8c',
                            '0.5c', outline='black',
                            fill=self.canvas['background'])
        wellTab = self.mkTab(c.winfo_pixels('13.5c'),
                    c.winfo_pixels('.65c'))
        c.addtag_withtag('well', wellBorder)
        c.addtag_withtag('well', wellTab)

        c.tag_bind('well', '<1>',
                lambda e, s=self: s.newTab(e.x, e.y))
        c.tag_bind('tab',  '<1>',
                lambda e, s=self: s.selectTab(e.x, e.y))
        c.bind('<B1-Motion>',
                lambda e, s=self: s.moveTab(e.x, e.y))
        c.bind('<Any-ButtonRelease-1>', self.releaseTab)

    def mkTab(self, x, y):
        return self.canvas.create_polygon(x, y, x+self.size,
                            y+self.size, x-self.size, y+self.size)
```

①

②

```
def newTab(self, x, y):
    newTab = self.mkTab(x, y)
    self.canvas.addtag_withtag('active', newTab)
    self.canvas.addtag_withtag('tab', newTab)
    self.x = x
    self.y = y
    self.moveTab(x, y)

def selectTab(self, x, y):
    self.x = self.canvas.canvasx(x, self.grid)
    self.y = self.top + 2
    self.canvas.addtag_withtag('active', CURRENT)
    self.canvas.itemconfig('active', fill=self.activeStyle,
                    stipple=self.activeStipple)
    self.canvas.lift('active')

def moveTab(self, x, y):
    tags = self.canvas.find_withtag('active')
    if not tags: return
    cx = self.canvas.canvasx(x, self.grid)
    cy = self.canvas.canvasx(y)
    if cx < self.left:
        cx = self.left
    if cx > self.right:
        cx = self.right
    if cy >= self.top and cy <= self.bottom:
        cy = self.top+2
        self.canvas.itemconfig('active', fill=self.activeStyle,
                        stipple=self.activeStipple)
    else:
        cy = cy-self.size-2
        self.canvas.itemconfig('active', fill=self.deleteStyle,
                        stipple=self.deleteStipple)
    self.canvas.move('active', cx-self.x, cy-self.y)
    self.x = cx
    self.y = cy

def releaseTab(self, event):
    tags = self.canvas.find_withtag('active')
    if not tags: return
    if self.y != self.top+2:
        self.canvas.delete('active')
    else:
        self.canvas.itemconfig('active', fill=self.normalStyle,
                        stipple=self.activeStipple)
        self.canvas.dtag('active')

if __name__ == '__main__':
    root = Tk()
    root.option_add('*Font', 'Verdana 10')
    root.title('Ruler')
    ruler = Ruler(root)
    root.mainloop()
```

❸
❹
❺
❻
❼
❽
❾
❿

Code comments

① This example illustrates how dimensions may be specified in any valid Tkinter distance and converted to pixels (in this case as a floating point number),

```
self.right    = c.winfo_fpixels('13c')
```

② Similarly, we can create an object using absolute measurements (in this case, centimeters). This can be useful if you are working directly from a drawing and you have a ruler!

```
c.create_line('1c', '0.5c', '1c', '1c', '13c', '1c',
              '13c', '0.5c', width=1)
```

③ Tkinter sometimes hides the capability of the underlying Tk function. In this case we are adding two tags, active and tab, to the newly-created object newTab.

```
newTab = self.mkTab(x, y)
self.canvas.addtag_withtag('active', newTab)
self.canvas.addtag_withtag('tab', newTab)
```

The addtag_withtag method hides the fact that the withtag argument applies to both tags and ids, which are being passed here.

④ moveTab has a lot of work to do, since the user can create new tabs, as well as move and delete existing ones. If I weren't following Ousterhout's example, I would probably reduce the complexity here.

⑤ The ruler arranges to snap the tab to the nearest 0.25 cm (self.grid). The canvasx method takes an optional argument, which defines the resolution with which the conversion to canvas coordinates is to be made.

```
cx = self.canvas.canvasx(x, self.grid)
```

⑥ If the pointer moves between the top and bottom range of the ruler, we snap the vertical position of the tab and fill it with a distinctive color so that it is readily identified.

```
cy = self.top+2
self.canvas.itemconfig('active', fill=self.activeStyle,
                       stipple=self.activeStipple)
```

⑦ If we have moved outside the bounds of top and bottom, we push it out further and fill it with a distinctive color stippling so that it becomes a ghost.

```
cy = cy-self.size-2
self.canvas.itemconfig('active', fill=self.deleteStyle,
                       stipple=self.deleteStipple)
```

⑧ As with moving the tab, releasing it requires multiple actions.

⑨ If the tab is marked for deletion (it isn't at the snapped-to y-value) the object is deleted.

```
if self.y != self.top+2:
    self.canvas.delete('active')
```

⑩ Otherwise, we fill the tab with a normal color and delete the active tag.

```
self.canvas.itemconfig('active', fill=self.normalStyle,
                       stipple=self.activeStipple)
self.canvas.dtag('active')
```

10.5 *Stretching canvas objects*

A common operation for drawing programs is stretching an existing object. This requires us to provide grab handles which the user can click and drag to resize the object. Before we add resize operations to our drawing example, let's take a look at a slightly simpler example which was also converted from Tk. This little program allows you to experiment with the two attributes that determine the shape of an arrow, width and arrowshape. You might find this a useful tool if you ever want to create arrows with a distinctive shape.

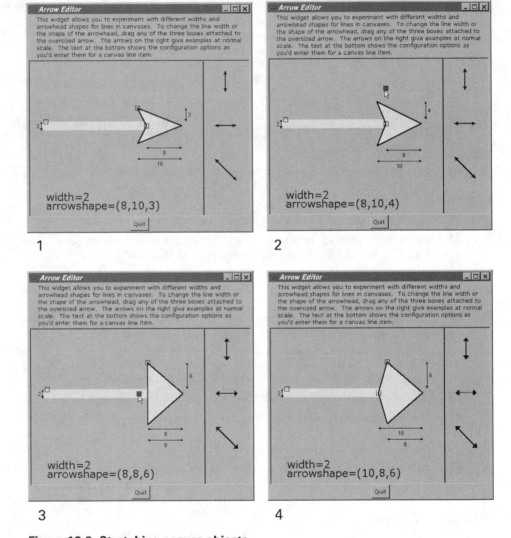

Figure 10.9 Stretching canvas objects

arrow.py

```python
from Tkinter import *

class ArrowEditor:
    def __init__(self, master, width=500, height=350):
        Label(master, text="This widget allows you to experiment "
                "with different widths and arrowhead shapes for lines "
                "in canvases.  To change the line width or the shape "
                "of the arrowhead, drag any of the three boxes "
                "attached to the oversized arrow. The arrows on the "
                "right give examples at normal scale.  The text at "
                "the bottom shows the configuration options as you'd "
                "enter them for a canvas line item.",
                wraplength="5i", justify=LEFT).pack(side=TOP)
        self.control=Frame(master)
        self.control.pack(side=BOTTOM, fill=X, padx=2)
        Button(self.control, text='Quit', command=master.quit).pack()
        self.canvas = Canvas(master, width=width, height=height,
                        relief=SUNKEN, borderwidth=2)
        self.canvas.pack(expand=YES, fill=BOTH)

        self.a    = 8     # Setup default values
        self.b    = 10
        self.c    = 3
        self.width= 2
        self.motionProc = None
        self.x1   = 40
        self.x2   = 350
        self.y    = 150
        self.smallTips= (5,5,2)
        self.bigLine= 'SkyBlue2'
        self.boxFill= ''
        self.activeFill = 'red'

        self.arrowSetup()    # Draw default arrow
        self.canvas.tag_bind('box', '<Enter>', lambda e, s=self:
                        s.canvas.itemconfig(CURRENT, fill='red'))
        self.canvas.tag_bind('box', '<Leave>', lambda e, s=self:
                        s.canvas.itemconfig(CURRENT, fill=''))
        self.canvas.tag_bind('box1', '<1>', lambda e, s=self:
                        s.motion(s.arrowMove1))
        self.canvas.tag_bind('box2', '<1>', lambda e, s=self:
                        s.motion(s.arrowMove2)   )
        self.canvas.tag_bind('box3', '<1>', lambda e, s=self:
                        s.motion(s.arrowMove3))
        self.canvas.tag_bind('box', '<B1-Motion>', lambda e,
                        s=self: s.motionProc(e))
        self.canvas.bind('<Any-ButtonRelease-1>', lambda e,
                    s=self: s.arrowSetup())

    def motion(self, func):
        self.motionProc = func
```

❶

```
def arrowMove1(self, event):
    newA = (self.x2+5-int(self.canvas.canvasx(event.x)))/10
    if newA < 0: newA = 0
    if newA > 25: newA = 25
    if newA != self.a:
        self.canvas.move("box1", 10*(self.a-newA), 0)
        self.a = newA

def arrowMove2(self, event):
    newB = (self.x2+5-int(self.canvas.canvasx(event.x)))/10
    if newB < 0: newB = 0
    if newB > 25: newB = 25
    newC = (self.y+5-int(self.canvas.canvasx(event.y)+ \
            5*self.width))/10
    if newC < 0: newC = 0
    if newC > 20: newC = 20
    if newB != self.b or newC != self.c:
        self.canvas.move("box2", 10*(self.b-newB),
                    10*(self.c-newC))
        self.b = newB
        self.c = newC

def arrowMove3(self, event):
    newW = (self.y+2-int(self.canvas.canvasx(event.y)))/5
    if newW < 0: newW = 0
    if newW > 20: newW = 20
    if newW != self.width:
        self.canvas.move("box3", 0, 5*(self.width-newW))
        self.width = newW

def arrowSetup(self):
    tags = self.canvas.gettags(CURRENT)
    cur = None
    if 'box' in tags:
        for tag in tags:
            if len(tag) == 4 and tag[:3] == 'box':
                cur = tag
                break
    self.canvas.delete(ALL)
    self.canvas.create_line(self.x1, self.y, self.x2, self.y,
                    width=10*self.width,
                    arrowshape=(10*self.a, 10*self.b,  10*self.c),
                    arrow='last', fill=self.bigLine)
    xtip = self.x2-10*self.b
    deltaY = 10*self.c+5*self.width
    self.canvas.create_line(self.x2, self.y, xtip, self.y+deltaY,
                    self.x2-10*self.a, self.y, xtip, self.y-deltaY,
                    self.x2, self.y, width=2, capstyle='round',
                    joinstyle='round')
    self.canvas.create_rectangle(self.x2-10*self.a-5, self.y-5,
                        self.x2-10*self.a+5, self.y+5,
                        fill=self.boxFill, outline='black',
                        tags=('box1', 'box'))
    self.canvas.create_rectangle(xtip-5, self.y-deltaY-5,
                        xtip+5, self.y-deltaY+5,
                        fill=self.boxFill, outline='black',
```

```
                            tags=('box2', 'box'))
            self.canvas.create_rectangle(self.x1-5,
                            self.y-5*self.width-5, self.x1+5,
                            self.y-5*self.width+5, fill=self.boxFill,
                            outline='black', tags=('box3', 'box'))
        if cur:
            self.canvas.itemconfig(cur, fill=self.activeFill)
        self.canvas.create_line(self.x2+50, 0, self.x2+50,
                1000, width=2)

        tmp = self.x2+100
        self.canvas.create_line(tmp, self.y-125, tmp, self.y-75,
                        width=self.width, arrow='both',
                        arrowshape=(self.a, self.b, self.c))
        self.canvas.create_line(tmp-25, self.y, tmp+25, self.y,
                        width=self.width, arrow='both',
                        arrowshape=(self.a, self.b, self.c))
        self.canvas.create_line(tmp-25, self.y+75, tmp+25, self.y+125,
                        width=self.width, arrow='both',
                        arrowshape=(self.a, self.b, self.c))

        tmp = self.x2+10
        self.canvas.create_line(tmp, self.y-5*self.width, tmp,
                        self.y-deltaY, arrow='both', arrowshape=self.smallTips)
        self.canvas.create_text(self.x2+15, self.y-deltaY+5*self.c,
                        text=self.c, anchor=W)
        tmp = self.x1-10
        self.canvas.create_line(tmp, self.y-5*self.width, tmp,
                        self.y+5*self.width, arrow='both',
                        arrowshape=self.smallTips)
        self.canvas.create_text(self.x1-15, self.y,
                        text=self.width, anchor=E)
        tmp = self.y+5*self.width+10*self.c+10
        self.canvas.create_line(self.x2-10*self.a, tmp, self.x2, tmp,
                        arrow='both', arrowshape=self.smallTips)
        self.canvas.create_text(self.x2-5*self.a, tmp+5,
                        text=self.a, anchor=N)
        tmp = tmp+25
        self.canvas.create_line(self.x2-10*self.b, tmp, self.x2, tmp,
                        arrow='both', arrowshape=self.smallTips)
        self.canvas.create_text(self.x2-5*self.b, tmp+5,
                        text=self.b, anchor=N)

        self.canvas.create_text(self.x1, 310, text="width=%d" % \
                        self.width, anchor=W, font=('Verdana', 18))
        self.canvas.create_text(self.x1, 330,
                        text="arrowshape=(%d,%d,%d)" % \
                        (self.a, self.b, self.c),
                        anchor=W, font=('Verdana', 18))

if __name__ == '__main__':
    root = Tk()
    root.option_add('*Font', 'Verdana 10')
    root.title('Arrow Editor')
    arrow = ArrowEditor(root)
    root.mainloop()
```

Code comments

❶ This example has to create many bindings:

  1 An `<Enter>` callback to color the grab handle.

  2 A `<Leave>` callback to remove the added color.

  3 A `<Button-1>` (`<1>`) callback for each of the grab handles.

  4 A `<B1-Motion>` callback for a common callback for each of the grabs.

  5 An `<Any-ButtonRelease-1>` callback to process the final location of the grab.

❷ The responsibility of each of the three `arrowMove` methods is to validate that the value is within bounds and then draw the grab at the current location.

❸ Since we have three separate boxes (`box1`, `box2` and `box3`) we need to implement a simple search algorithm within the tags to determine which box created the event:

```
if 'box' in tags:
    for tag in tags:
        if len(tag) == 4 and tag[:3] == 'box':
            cur = tag
            break
```

❹ We then create a line using the supplied `width` and the appropriate `arrowshape` values.

The remainder of the code is responsible for updating the values of the dimensions on the screen and drawing the example arrows. Since this example illustrates 1-to-1 translation of Tk to Tkinter, I have not attempted to optimize the code. I am certain that some of the code can be made more succinct.

10.6 *Some finishing touches*

We are going to extend the capability of draw3.py to add some additional functionality and provide some features that may be useful if you use this example as a template for your own code. This is what has been added:

  1 Menu options to create New drawings and Open existing ones.

  2 A Menu option to save drawings with a supplied filename (Save As).

  3 A Menu option to save an existing drawing to its file (Save).

  4 A Move operation to allow an object to be moved about the canvas.

  5 Stretch operations with eight grab handles.

The following code example is derived from draw3.py, which was presented on page 245. I have removed much of the common code, so that this example is not too long, but note that this example has a *lot* to do!

draw4.py

```
from   Tkinter import *
import Pmw, AppShell, math, time, string, marshal
from cursornames import *
from toolbarbutton import ToolBarButton                    ❶
from tkFileDialog import *
```

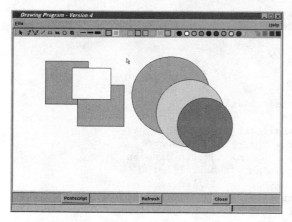
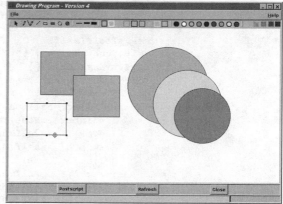
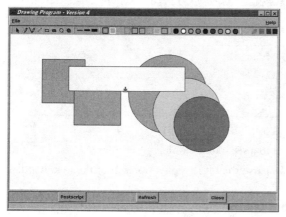
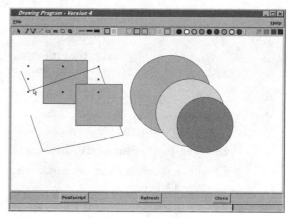

Figure 10.10 Adding movement and stretching to the drawing program

```
transDict = { 'bx': 'boundX', 'by': 'boundY',
        'x':  'adjX',    'y':  'adjY',
        'S':  'uniqueIDINT' }

class Draw(AppShell.AppShell):

# --- Code Removed -----------------------------------------------------

    def createMenus(self):
        self.menuBar.deletemenuitems('File')
        self.menuBar.addmenuitem('File', 'command', 'New drawing',
                    label='New', command=self.newDrawing)
        self.menuBar.addmenuitem('File', 'command', 'Open drawing',
                    label='Open...', command=self.openDrawing)
        self.menuBar.addmenuitem('File', 'command', 'Save drawing',
                    label='Save', command=self.saveDrawing)
        self.menuBar.addmenuitem('File', 'command', 'Save drawing',
                    label='SaveAs...', command=self.saveAsDrawing)
        self.menuBar.addmenuitem('File', 'separator')
```

❷

SOME FINISHING TOUCHES   *263*

```
        self.menuBar.addmenuitem('File', 'command', 'Exit program',
                      label='Exit', command=self.quit)

    def createTools(self):
        self.func     = {}
        self.transFunc = {}                              ❸
        ToolBarButton(self, self.toolbar, 'sep', 'sep.gif',
                    width=10, state='disabled')
        for key, func, balloon in [
             ('pointer', None, 'Edit drawing'),
             ('draw',    self.drawFree, 'Draw freehand'),
             ('smooth',  self.drawSmooth, 'Smooth freehand'),
             ('line',    self.drawLine, 'Rubber line'),
             ('rect',    self.drawRect, 'Unfilled rectangle'),
             ('frect',   self.drawFilledRect, 'Filled rectangle'),
             ('oval',    self.drawOval, 'Unfilled oval'),
             ('foval',   self.drawFilledOval, 'Filled oval')]:
             ToolBarButton(self, self.toolbar, key, '%s.gif' % key,
                         command=self.selectFunc, balloonhelp=balloon,
                         statushelp=balloon)
             self.func[key]      = func
             self.transFunc[func] = key

# --- Code Removed ------------------------------------------------------
```

Code comments

❶ The ToolBarButton class has been moved to a separate module.

❷ transDict is going to be used when we parse the tags assigned to each of the grab handles.
See ❻ below.

❸ transFunc is created as a reverse-lookup, so that we can find the key associated with a particular function.

draw4.py (continued)

```
    def mouseDown(self, event):
        self.curObject = None
        self.canvas.dtag('drawing')
        self.lineData = []
        self.lastx = self.startx = self.canvas.canvasx(event.x)
        self.lasty = self.starty = self.canvas.canvasy(event.y)
        self.uniqueID = 'S*%d' % self.serial              ❹
        self.serial = self.serial + 1

        if not self.curFunc:
            if event.widget.find_withtag(CURRENT):
                tags = self.canvas.gettags(CURRENT)
                for tag in tags:
                    if tag[:2] == 'S*':
                        objectID = tag                    ❺
                if 'grabHandle' in tags:
                    self.inGrab = TRUE
                    self.releaseGrab = FALSE
```

```
                              self.uniqueID = objectID
                  else:
                              self.inGrab = FALSE
                              self.addGrabHandles(objectID, 'grab')
                              self.canvas.config(cursor='fleur')
                              self.uniqueID = objectID
          else:
                  self.canvas.delete("grabHandle")
                  self.canvas.dtag("grabHandle")
                  self.canvas.dtag("grab")

    def mouseMotion(self, event):
        curx = self.canvas.canvasx(event.x)
        cury = self.canvas.canvasy(event.y)
        prevx = self.lastx
        prevy = self.lasty
        if not self.inGrab and self.curFunc:
            self.lastx = curx
            self.lasty = cury
            if self.regular and self.curFunc in \
                [self.func['oval'], self.func['rect'],
                 self.func['foval'],self.func['frect']]:
                    dx    = self.lastx - self.startx
                    dy    = self.lasty - self.starty
                    delta = max(dx, dy)
                    self.lastx = self.startx + delta
                    self.lasty = self.starty + delta
            self.curFunc(self.startx, self.starty, self.lastx,
                        self.lasty, prevx, prevy, self.foreground,
                        self.background, self.fillStyle, self.lineWidth,None)
        elif self.inGrab:
            self.canvas.delete("grabbedObject")
            self.canvas.dtag("grabbedObject")
            tags = self.canvas.gettags(CURRENT)
            for tag in tags:
                if '*' in tag:
                    key, value = string.split(tag, '*')
                    var = transDict[key]
                    setattr(self, var, string.atoi(value))
            self.uniqueID = 'S*%d' % self.uniqueIDINT
            x1, y1, x2, y2, px, py, self.growFunc, \
                fg, bg, fill, lwid, ld= self.objects[self.uniqueID]
            if self.boundX == 1 and self.adjX:
                x1 =  x1 + curx-prevx
            elif self.boundX == 2 and self.adjX:
                x2 =  x2 + curx-prevx
            if self.boundY == 1 and self.adjY:
                y1 = y1 + cury-prevy
            elif self.boundY == 2 and self.adjY:
                y2 = y2 + cury-prevy
            self.growFunc(x1,y1,x2,y2,px,py,fg,bg,fill,lwid,ld)
            self.canvas.addtag_withtag("grabbedObject",
                              self.uniqueID)
            self.storeObject(x1,y1,x2,y2,px,py,self.growFunc,
                        fg,bg,fill,lwid,ld)
```

```
                    self.lastx = curx
                    self.lasty = cury
            else:
                    self.canvas.move('grab', curx-prevx, cury-prevy)
                    self.lastx = curx
                    self.lasty = cury

    def mouseUp(self, event):
            self.prevx = self.lastx
            self.prevy = self.lasty
            self.lastx = self.canvas.canvasx(event.x)
            self.lasty = self.canvas.canvasy(event.y)
            if self.curFunc:
                    if self.regular and self.curFunc in \
                        [self.func['oval'], self.func['rect'],
                         self.func['foval'],self.func['frect']]:
                            dx = self.lastx - self.startx
                            dy = self.lasty - self.starty
                            delta = max(dx, dy)
                            self.lastx = self.startx + delta
                            self.lasty = self.starty + delta
                    self.curFunc(self.startx, self.starty, self.lastx,
                                self.lasty, self.prevx, self.prevy, self.foreground,
                                self.background, self.fillStyle, self.lineWidth,
                                self.lineData)
                    self.inGrab = FALSE
                    self.releaseGrab = TRUE
                    self.growFunc = None
                    self.storeObject(self.startx, self.starty, self.lastx,
                                self.lasty, self.prevx, self.prevy, self.curFunc,
                                self.foreground, self.background, self.fillStyle,
                                self.lineWidth, self.lineData)
            else:
                if self.inGrab:
                        tags = self.canvas.gettags(CURRENT)
                        for tag in tags:
                            if '*' in tag:
                                    key, value = string.split(tag, '*')
                                    var = transDict[key]
                                    setattr(self, var, string.atoi(value))
                        x1,y1,x2,y2, px, py, self.growFunc, \
                                fg,bg,fill,lwid,ld = self.objects[self.uniqueID]
                        if self.boundX == 1 and self.adjX:
                            x1 =  x1 + self.lastx-self.prevx
                        elif self.boundX == 2 and self.adjX:
                            x2 =  x2 + self.lastx-self.prevx
                        if self.boundY == 1 and self.adjY:
                            y1 = y1 + self.lasty-self.prevy
                        elif self.boundY == 2 and self.adjY:
                            y2 = y2 + self.lasty-self.prevy
                        self.growFunc(x1,y1,x2,y2,px,py,fg,bg,fill,lwid,ld)
                        self.storeObject(x1,y1,x2,y2,px,py,self.growFunc,
                                    fg,bg,fill,lwid,ld)
                        self.addGrabHandles(self.uniqueID, self.uniqueID)
                if self.selObj:
```

6

7

8

```
                    self.canvas.itemconfig(self.selObj,
                                 width=self.savedWidth)
            self.canvas.config(cursor='arrow')

    def addGrabHandles(self, objectID, tag):
        self.canvas.delete("grabHandle")
        self.canvas.dtag("grabHandle")
        self.canvas.dtag("grab")
        self.canvas.dtag("grabbedObject")

        self.canvas.addtag("grab", "withtag", CURRENT)
        self.canvas.addtag("grabbedObject", "withtag", CURRENT)
        x1,y1,x2,y2 = self.canvas.bbox(tag)
        for x,y, curs, tagBx, tagBy, tagX, tagY in [
             (x1,y1,TLC,         'bx*1','by*1','x*1','y*1'),
             (x2,y1,TRC,         'bx*2','by*1','x*1','y*1'),
             (x1,y2,BLC,         'bx*1','by*2','x*1','y*1'),
             (x2,y2,BRC,         'bx*2','by*2','x*1','y*1'),
             (x1+((x2-x1)/2),y1,TS, 'bx*0','by*1','x*0','y*1'),
             (x2,y1+((y2-y1)/2),RS, 'bx*2','by*0','x*1','y*0'),
             (x1,y1+((y2-y1)/2),LS, 'bx*1','by*0','x*1','y*0'),
             (x1+((x2-x1)/2),y2,BS, 'bx*0','by*2','x*0','y*1')]:
             ghandle = self.canvas.create_rectangle(x-2,y-2,x+2,y+2,
                     outline='black', fill='black', tags=('grab',
                     'grabHandle', tagBx, tagBy, tagX,
                     tagY,'%s'%objectID))
             self.canvas.tag_bind(ghandle, '<Any-Enter>',
                     lambda e, s=self, c=curs: s.setCursor(e,c))
             self.canvas.tag_bind(ghandle, '<Any-Leave>',
                     self.resetCursor)
             self.canvas.lift("grab")

# --- Code Removed ----------------------------------------------------
```

9

10

Code comments (continued)

④ Each of the objects drawn on the canvas is identified by a unique identity, which is attached to the object as a tag. Here we construct an identity:

```
self.uniqueID = 'S*%d' % self.serial
self.serial = self.serial + 1
```

⑤ Here we use the tags to get the identity of a drawn object from one of the grab handles or the object itself:

```
for tag in tags:
    if tag[:2] == 'S*':
        objectID = tag
```

Then, we determine if we have grabbed a grab handle (which all contain a `grabhandle` tag) or an object, in which case we change the cursor to indicate that the object is moveable.

⑥ This is where we parse the tags attached to the grab handles. The grab handles are encoded with information about their processing; this reduces the amount of code needed to support stretching the objects. The tags are attached in step ⑩ below.

```
for tag in tags:
    if '*' in tag:
```

```
key, value = string.split(tag, '*')
var = transDict[key]
setattr(self, var, string.atoi(value))
```

This requires a little more explanation. Take a look at figure 10.11. Each of the grab handles at the four corners modifies the bounding box. The *x*- or *y*-value is associated with either `BB1` or `BB2`. So, for example, the bottom-left grab handle is tagged with `bx*1` and `by*2`. Additionally, the four median grab handles are constrained to stretch one side of the bounding box at a time, so we encode (as a boolean value) the axis that is free (`x*1 y*0` indicates that the x-axis is free).

7 Since we need to know the current dimensions of an object's bounding box as we grow or move the object, we store that data each time the callback is invoked.

8 When the mouse is released, we have to recalculate the bounding box and store the object's data. This code is similar to the code for mouse movement shown in **6**.

9 In `addGrabHandles` we begin by removing all existing grab handles from the display, along with the associated tags.

10 To construct the grab handles, we first get the current bounding box. Then we construct the handles using data contained in a list. The tags are constructed to provide the associations noted in step **6** above.

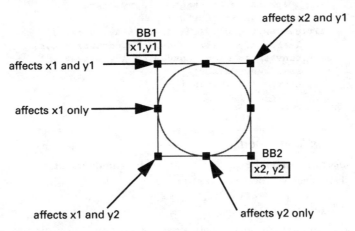

Figure 10.11 Grab handles and their association with the bounding-box coordinates

draw4.py (continued)

```
x1,y1,x2,y2 = self.canvas.bbox(tag)

for x,y, curs, tagBx, tagBy, tagX, tagY in [

    (x1,y1,TLC,        'bx*1','by*1','x*1','y*1'),

    (x2,y1,TRC,        'bx*2','by*1','x*1','y*1'),

    ---- code removed -----
```

```
                    ghandle = self.canvas.create_rectangle(x-2,y-2,x+2,y+2,
                        outline='black', fill='black', tags=('grab',
                        'grabHandle','%s'%tagBx,'%s'%tagBy,'%s'%tagX,
                        '%s'%tagY,'%s'%objectID))

    def storeObject(self, x1,y1,x2,y2,px,py,func,fg,bg,fill,lwid,ld):
        self.objects[self.uniqueID] = ( x1,y1,x2,y2,px,py,func,fg,bg,
                        fill,lwid,ld )

    def redraw(self):
        self.canvas.delete(ALL)
        keys = self.objects.keys()
        keys.sort()
        for key in keys:
            startx, starty, lastx, lasty, prevx, prevy, func, \
                fg, bg, fill, lwid , ld= self.objects[key]
            self.curObject = None
            self.uniqueID = key
            func(startx, starty, lastx, lasty, prevx, prevy,
                fg, bg, fill, lwid, ld)

    def newDrawing(self):
        self.canvas.delete(ALL)
        self.initData()

    def openDrawing(self):
        ofile = askopenfilename(filetypes=[("PTkP Draw", "ptk"),
                        ("All Files", "*")])
        if ofile:
            self.currentName = ofile
            self.initData()
            fd = open(ofile)
            items = marshal.load(fd)
            for i in range(items):
                self.uniqueID, x1,y1,x2,y2,px,py,cfunc, \
                        fg,bg,fill,lwid,ld = marshal.load(fd)
                self.storeObject(x1,y1,x2,y2,px,py,self.func[cfunc],
                        fg,bg,fill,lwid,ld)
            fd.close()
        self.redraw()

    def saveDrawing(self):
        self.doSave()

    def saveAsDrawing(self):
        ofile = asksaveasfilename(filetypes=[("PTkP Draw", "ptk"),
                        ("All Files", "*")])
        if ofile:
            self.currentName = ofile
            self.doSave()

    def doSave(self):
        fd = open(self.currentName, 'w')
        keys = self.objects.keys()
        keys.sort()
```

⑪

⑫

```
          marshal.dump(len(keys), fd)
          for key in keys:
              startx, starty, lastx, lasty, prevx, prevy, func, \
                  fg, bg, fill, lwid , ld= self.objects[key]
              cfunc = self.transFunc[func]
              marshal.dump((key, startx, starty, lastx, lasty, prevx, \
                      prevy, cfunc, fg, bg, fill, lwid , ld), fd)
          fd.close()

    def initData(self):
        self.curFunc = self.drawLine
        self.growFunc = None
        self.curObject = None
        self.selObj = None
        self.lineData= []
        self.savedWidth = 1
        self.savedCursor = None
        self.objects = {}      # Now a dictionary
        self.foreground = 'black'
        self.background = 'white'
        self.fillStyle = None
        self.lineWidth = 1
        self.serial = 1000
        self.regular = FALSE
        self.inGrab = FALSE
        self.releaseGrab = TRUE
        self.currentName = 'Untitled'

# --- Code Removed ------------------------------------------------------------
```

(12) (margin annotation)

Code comments (continued)

(11) To load an existing file, we use the standard `tkFileDialog` dialogs to obtain the filename. We then *unmarshal** the contents of the file to obtain the stored object dictionary and then simply redraw the screen.

```
          fd = open(ofile)
          items = marshal.load(fd)
          for i in range(items):
              self.uniqueID, x1,y1,x2,y2,px,py,cfunc, \
                      fg,bg,fill,lwid,ld = marshal.load(fd)
              self.storeObject(x1,y1,x2,y2,px,py,self.func[cfunc],
                      fg,bg,fill,lwid,ld)
```

Because it is not possible to marshal member functions of classes (`self.func`), we store the key to the function and use the reverse-lookup created in **3** to obtain the corresponding method.

---

* Marshaling is a method of serializing arbitrary Python data in a form that may be written and read to simple files. Not all Python types can be marshaled and other methods such as pickle or shelve (to store a database object) may be used. It is adequate to provide persistence for our relatively simple dictionary.

⑫ doSave implements the writing of the marshaled data to a file. Figure 10.12 illustrates the tkFileDialog used to get the file name. Note that the dialogs are native dialogs for the particular architecture upon which Tk is running at release 8.0 and above.

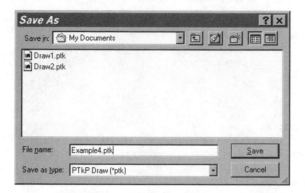

Figure 10.12 Save As dialog

10.7 *Speed drawing*

In general, creating canvas objects is relatively efficient and rarely causes a performance problem. However, for very complex drawings, you may notice a delay in drawing the canvas. This is particularly noticeable when the display contains a large number of objects or when they contain complex line segments.

One way of improving drawing performance is to draw the canvas as an image. The Python Imaging Library, which was introduced briefly in chapter 5 on page 89, has the facility to draw directly to a GIF file. We will use this facility to draw a quite challenging image. I always found Mandelbrot diagrams, now generally referred to as fractals, fascinating. While I was looking at Douglas A. Young's *The X Window System: Programming and Applications with Xt*, I noticed the fractal on the cover. Here is an adaptation of the fractal in Python, Tkinter and PIL.

fractal.py

```
from    Tkinter import *
import Pmw, AppShell, Image, ImageDraw, os

class Palette:
  def __init__(self):
      self.palette = [(0,0,0), (255,255,255)]

  def getpalette(self):
      # flatten the  palette
      palette = []
      for r, g, b in self.palette:
          palette = palette + [r, g, b]
      return palette
```

```
            def loadpalette(self, cells):
                import random
                for i in range(cells-2):
                    self.palette.append((
                        random.choice(range(0, 255)),    # red
                        random.choice(range(0, 255)),    # green
                        random.choice(range(0, 255))))   # blue

    class Fractal(AppShell.AppShell):
        usecommandarea = 1
        appname       = 'Fractal Demonstration'
        frameWidth    = 780
        frameHeight   = 580

        def createButtons(self):
            self.buttonAdd('Save',
                        helpMessage='Save current image',
                        statusMessage='Write current image as "out.gif"',
                        command=self.save)
            self.buttonAdd('Close',
                        helpMessage='Close Screen',
                        statusMessage='Exit',
                        command=self.close)

        def createDisplay(self):
            self.width  = self.root.winfo_width()-10
            self.height = self.root.winfo_height()-95
            self.form = self.createcomponent('form', (), None,
                                Frame, (self.interior(),),
                                width=self.width,
                                height=self.height)
            self.form.pack(side=TOP, expand=YES, fill=BOTH)
            self.im = Image.new("P", (self.width, self.height), 0)
            self.d = ImageDraw.ImageDraw(self.im)
            self.d.setfill(0)
            self.label = self.createcomponent('label', (), None,
                                Label, (self.form,),)
            self.label.pack()

        def initData(self):
            self.depth = 20
            self.origin = -1.4+1.0j
            self.range = 2.0
            self.maxDistance = 4.0
            self.ncolors = 256
            self.rgb = Palette()
            self.rgb.loadpalette(255)
            self.save = FALSE

        def createImage(self):
            self.updateProgress(0, self.height)
            for y in range(self.height):
                for x in range(self.width):
                    z = 0j
                    k = complex(self.origin.real + \
```

```
                        float(x)/float(self.width)*self.range,
                        self.origin.imag - \
                        float(y) / float(self.height)*self.range)
            # calculate z = (z +k) * (z + k) over and over
            for iteration in range(self.depth):
                    real_part = z.real + k.real
                    imag_part = z.imag + k.imag
                    del z
                    z = complex(real_part * real_part - imag_part * \
                            imag_part, 2 * real_part * imag_part)
                    distance  = z.real * z.real + z.imag * z.imag
                    if distance >= self.maxDistance:
                            cidx = int(distance % self.ncolors)
                            self.pixel(x, y, cidx)                    ❸
                            break
                self.updateProgress(y)
        self.updateProgress(self.height, self.height)
        self.im.putpalette(self.rgb.getpalette())
        self.im.save("out.gif")                                      ❹
        self.img = PhotoImage(file="out.gif")
        self.label['image'] = self.img

    def pixel(self, x, y, color):                                    ❺
        self.d.setink(color)
        self.d.point((x, y))

    def save(self):
        self.save = TRUE
        self.updateMessageBar('Saved as "out.gif"')

    def close(self):
        if not self.save:
            os.unlink("out.gif")
        self.quit()

    def createInterface(self):
        AppShell.AppShell.createInterface(self)
        self.createButtons()
        self.initData()
        self.createDisplay()

if __name__ == '__main__':
    fractal = Fractal()
    fractal.root.after(10, fractal.createImage())
    fractal.run()
```

Code comments

❶ The Palette class is responsible for creating a random palette (loadpalette) and generating an RGB list for inclusion in the GIF image (getpalette).

❷ We create a new image, specifying pixel mode (P), and we instantiate the ImageDraw class, which provides basic drawing functions to the image. We fill the image with black, initially with the setfill method.

```
self.im = Image.new("P", (self.width, self.height), 0)
self.d = ImageDraw.ImageDraw(self.im)
self.d.setfill(0)
```

3 At the center of the computational loop, we select a color and set the corresponding pixel to that color.

```
cidx = int(distance % self.ncolors)
self.pixel(x, y, cidx)
```

4 When complete, we add the palette to the image, save it as a GIF file, and then load the image as a Tkinter `PhotoImage`.

```
self.im.putpalette(self.rgb.getpalette())
self.im.save("out.gif")
self.img = PhotoImage(file="out.gif")
self.label['image'] = self.img
```

5 The pixel method is very simple. We set the color of the ink and place the pixel at the specified x, y coordinate.

```
def pixel(self, x, y, color):
    self.d.setink(color)
    self.d.point((x, y))
```

Running fractal.py on a moderately fast workstation will generate an 800×600 pixel image in about 2-3 minutes. If you are interested, you will find slowfractal.py online. This version is written using Tkinter canvas methods and it takes *considerably* longer to complete.

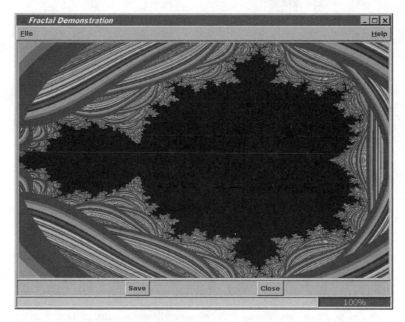

Figure 10.13 Generating fractals

10.8 Summary

This is another important chapter for those readers who want to manipulate objects on a screen. Whether building a drawing program or a drafting system of a UML editor, the principles are similar and you will find many of the techniques are readily transferable.

One thing is very important when designing interfaces such as these: think carefully about the range of pointing devices that may be used with your program. While it is quite easy to drag an object to resize it when you are using a mouse, it may not be as easy if the user has a trackball or is using one of the embedded keyboard mouse buttons.

C H A P T E R   1 1

Graphs and charts

There was a time when the term *graphics* included graphs; this chapter reintroduces this meaning. Although graphs, histograms and pie charts may not be appropriate for all applications, they do provide a useful means of conveying a large amount of information to the viewer. Examples will include linegraphs, histograms, and pie charts to support classical graphical formats. More complex graph examples will include threshold alarms and indicators.

11.1   Simple graphs

Let's start by constructing a very simple graph, without trying to make a graph class or adding too many features, so we can see how easy it can be to add a graph to an application. We'll add more functionality later.

simpleplot.py

```
from Tkinter import *
root = Tk()
root.title('Simple Plot - Version 1')
```

```
canvas = Canvas(root, width=450, height=300, bg = 'white')
canvas.pack()

Button(root, text='Quit', command=root.quit).pack()

canvas.create_line(100,250,400,250, width=2)          ● Draw axes
canvas.create_line(100,250,100,50,  width=2)

for i in range(11):                                    ❶
    x = 100 + (i * 30)
    canvas.create_line(x,250,x,245, width=2)
    canvas.create_text(x,254, text='%d'% (10*i), anchor=N)

for i in range(6):                                     ● Draw y
    y = 250 - (i * 40)                                   ticks
    canvas.create_line(100,y,105,y, width=2)
    canvas.create_text(96,y, text='%5.1f'% (50.*i), anchor=E)

for x,y in [(12, 56), (20, 94), (33, 98), (45, 120), (61, 180),
        (75, 160), (98, 223)]:                         ● Draw data
    x = 100 + 3*x                                        points
    y = 250 - (4*y)/5
    canvas.create_oval(x-6,y-6,x+6,y+6, width=1,
                outline='black', fill='SkyBlue2')

root.mainloop()
```

Code comments

❶ Here we add the ticks and labels for the x-axis. Note that the values used are hard-coded—we have made little provision for reuse!

```
for i in range(11):
    x = 100 + (i * 30)
    canvas.create_line(x,250,x,245, width=2)
    canvas.create_text(x,254, text='%d'% (10*i), anchor=N)
```

Notice how we have set this up to increment *x* in units of 10.

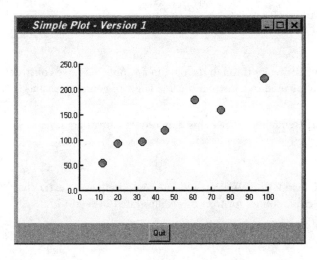

Figure 11.1 Simple two-dimensional graph

This small amount of code produces an effective graph with little effort as you can see in figure 11.1. We can improve this graph easily by adding lines connecting the dots as shown in figure 11.2.

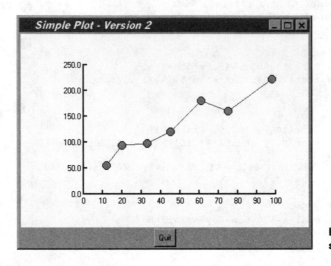

Figure 11.2 Adding lines to a simple graph

simpleplot2.py

```
scaled = []
for x,y in [(12, 56), (20, 94), (33, 98), (45, 120), (61, 180),
       (75, 160), (98, 223)]:
  scaled.append(100 + 3*x, 250 - (4*y)/5)

canvas.create_line(scaled, fill='royalblue')

for x,y in scaled:
  canvas.create_oval(x-6,y-6,x+6,y+6, width=1,
              outline='black', fill='SkyBlue2')
```

❶
❷
❸

Code comments

❶ So that we do not have to iterate through the data in a simple loop, we construct a list of x-y coordinates which may be used to construct the line (a list of coordinates may be input to the `create_line` method).

❷ We draw the line first. Remember that items drawn on a canvas are layered so we want the lines to appear under the blobs.

❸ Followed by the blobs.

Here come the Ginsu knives! We can add line smoothing at no extra charge! If we turn on smoothing we get cubic splines for free; this is illustrated in figure 11.3.

CHAPTER 11   GRAPHS AND CHARTS

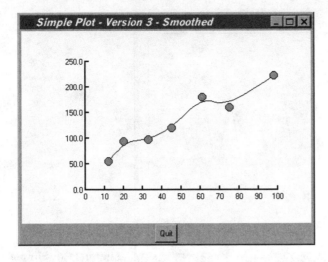

Figure 11.3 Smoothing the line

```
canvas.create_line(scaled, fill='black', smooth=1)
```

I don't think that needs an explanation!

11.2 A graph widget

The previous examples illustrate that it is quite easy to produce simple graphs with a small amount of code. However, when it is necessary to display several graphs on the same axes, it is cumbersome to produce code that will be flexible enough to handle all situations. Some time ago Konrad Hinsen made an effective graph widget available to the Python community. The widget was intended to be used with NumPy.* With his permission, I have adapted it to make it usable with the standard Python distribution and I have extended it to support additional display formats. An example of the output is shown in figure 11.4. In the following code listing, I have removed some repetitive code. You will find the complete source code online.

```
from Tkinter import *
from Canvas import Line, CanvasText
import string, math
from utils import *
from math import pi
```

---

* NumPy is Numeric Python, a specialized collection of additional modules to facilitate numeric computation where performance is needed.

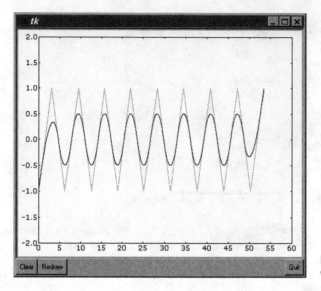

Figure 11.4 Simple graph widget: lines only

```
class GraphPoints:
    def __init__(self, points, attr):
        self.points = points
        self.scaled = self.points
        self.attributes = {}
        for name, value in self._attributes.items():
            try:
                value = attr[name]
            except KeyError: pass
            self.attributes[name] = value

    def boundingBox(self):
        return minBound(self.points),  maxBound(self.points)

    def fitToScale(self, scale=(1,1), shift=(0,0)):
        self.scaled = []
        for x,y in self.points:
            self.scaled.append(((scale[0]*x)+shift[0],\
                               (scale[1]*y)+shift[1])

class GraphLine(GraphPoints):
    def __init__(self, points, **attr):
        GraphPoints.__init__(self, points, attr)

    _attributes = {'color':  'black',
                   'width':         1,
                   'smooth':        0,
                   'splinesteps': 12}

    def draw(self, canvas):
        color  = self.attributes['color']
        width  = self.attributes['width']
        smooth = self.attributes['smooth']
```

1
2
3
4
5

```
            steps   = self.attributes['splinesteps']
            arguments = (canvas,)

            if smooth:
                for i in range(len(self.points)):
                    x1, y1 = self.scaled[i]
                    arguments = arguments + (x1, y1)
            else:
                for i in range(len(self.points)-1):
                    x1, y1 = self.scaled[i]
                    x2, y2 = self.scaled[i+1]
                    arguments = arguments + (x1, y1, x2, y2)

            apply(Line, arguments, {'fill': color, 'width': width,
                          'smooth': smooth,
                          'splinesteps': steps})

class GraphSymbols(GraphPoints):
    def __init__(self, points, **attr):
        GraphPoints.__init__(self, points, attr)

    _attributes = {'color': 'black',
                   'width': 1,
                   'fillcolor': 'black',
                   'size': 2,
                   'fillstyle': '',
                   'outline': 'black',
                   'marker': 'circle'}

    def draw(self, canvas):
        color   = self.attributes['color']
        size    = self.attributes['size']
        fillcolor = self.attributes['fillcolor']
        marker  = self.attributes['marker']
        fillstyle = self.attributes['fillstyle']
        self._drawmarkers(canvas, self.scaled, marker, color,
                   fillstyle, fillcolor, size)

    def _drawmarkers(self, c, coords, marker='circle',
            color='black', fillstyle='', fillcolor='',size=2):
        l = []
        f = eval('self._' +marker)
        for xc, yc in coords:
            id = f(c, xc, yc, outline=color, size=size,
                   fill=fillcolor, fillstyle=fillstyle)
            if type(id) is type(()):
                for item in id: l.append(item)
            else:
                l.append(id)
        return l

    def _circle(self, c, xc, yc, size=1, fill='',
            outline='black', fillstyle=''):
        id = c.create_oval(xc-0.5, yc-0.5, xc+0.5, yc+0.5,
                   fill=fill, outline=outline,
                   stipple=fillstyle)
```

```
        c.scale(id, xc, yc, size*5, size*5)    ⚑ ⑧    ⚑ ⑪
        return id

# --- Code Removed ------------------------------------------------------------
```

Code comments

❶ The GraphPoints class defines the points and attributes of a single plot. As you will see later, the attributes that are processed by the constructor vary with the type of line style. Note that the `self._attributes` definitions are a requirement for subclasses.

❷ `boundingBox` returns the top-left and bottom-right coordinates by scanning the coordinates in the points data. The convenience functions are in utils.py.

❸ `fitToScale` modifies the coordinates so that they fit within the scale determined for all of the lines in the graph.

```
def fitToScale(self, scale=(1,1), shift=(0,0)):
    self.scaled = []
    for x,y in self.points:
        self.scaled.append(((scale[0]*x)+shift[0],\
                            (scale[1]*y)+shift[1])
```

Note that we supply tuples for `scale` and `shift`. The first value is for x and the second is for y.

❹ The GraphLine class defines methods to draw lines from the available coordinates.

❺ The `draw` method first extracts the appropriate arguments from the attributes dictionary.

❻ Depending on whether we are doing smoothing, we supply start-end-coordinates for line segments (unsmoothed) or a sequence of coordinates (smoothed).

❼ We then `apply` the arguments and the keywords to the canvas `Line` method. Remember that the format of the `Line` arguments is really:

```
Line(*args, **keywords)
```

❽ `GraphSymbols` is similar to `GraphLine`, but it outputs a variety of filled shapes for each of the x-y coordinates.

❾ The `draw` method calls the appropriate marker routine through the generic `_drawmarkers` method:

```
self._drawmarkers(canvas, self.scaled, marker, color,
                      fillstyle, fillcolor, size)
```

❿ `_drawmarkers` evaluates the selected marker method, and then it builds a list of the symbols that are created.

```
f = eval('self._' +marker)
for xc, yc in coords:
    id = f(c, xc, yc, outline=color, size=size,
            fill=fillcolor, fillstyle=fillstyle)
```

⑪ I have included just one of the shapes that can be drawn by the graph widget. The full set are in the source code available online.

```
    def _dot(self, c, xc, yc, ... ):
    def _square(self, c, xc, yc, ... ):
    def _triangle(self, c, xc, yc, ... ):
    def _triangle_down(self, c, xc, yc, ... ):
    def _cross(self, c, xc, yc, ... ):
    def _plus(self, c, xc, yc, ... ):

# --- Code Removed ---------------------------------------------------

class GraphObjects:
    def __init__(self, objects):
        self.objects = objects

    def boundingBox(self):
        c1, c2 = self.objects[0].boundingBox()
        for object in self.objects[1:]:
            c1o, c2o = object.boundingBox()
            c1 = minBound([c1, c1o])
            c2 = maxBound([c2, c2o])
        return c1, c2

    def fitToScale(self, scale=(1,1), shift=(0,0)):
        for object in self.objects:
            object.fitToScale(scale, shift)

    def draw(self, canvas):
        for object in self.objects:
            object.draw(canvas)

class GraphBase(Frame):
    def __init__(self, master, width, height,
            background='white', **kw):
        apply(Frame.__init__, (self, master), kw)
        self.canvas = Canvas(self, width=width, height=height,
                    background=background)
        self.canvas.pack(fill=BOTH, expand=YES)
        border_w = self.canvas.winfo_reqwidth() - \
                string.atoi(self.canvas.cget('width'))
        border_h = self.canvas.winfo_reqheight() - \
                string.atoi(self.canvas.cget('height'))
        self.border = (border_w, border_h)
        self.canvas.bind('<Configure>', self.configure)
        self.plotarea_size = [None, None]
        self._setsize()
        self.last_drawn = None
        self.font = ('Verdana', 10)

    def configure(self, event):
        new_width = event.width-self.border[0]
        new_height = event.height-self.border[1]
        width = string.atoi(self.canvas.cget('width'))
        height = string.atoi(self.canvas.cget('height'))
        if new_width == width and new_height == height:
```

12

13

14

15

16

```
                return
        self.canvas.configure(width=new_width, height=new_height)
        self._setsize()
        self.clear()
        self.replot()

    def bind(self, *args):
        apply(self.canvas.bind, args)

    def _setsize(self):
        self.width = string.atoi(self.canvas.cget('width'))
        self.height = string.atoi(self.canvas.cget('height'))
        self.plotarea_size[0] = 0.97 * self.width
        self.plotarea_size[1] = 0.97 * -self.height
        xo = 0.5*(self.width-self.plotarea_size[0])
        yo = self.height-0.5*(self.height+self.plotarea_size[1])
        self.plotarea_origin = (xo, yo)

    def draw(self, graphics, xaxis = None, yaxis = None):
        self.last_drawn = (graphics, xaxis, yaxis)
        p1, p2 = graphics.boundingBox()
        xaxis = self._axisInterval(xaxis, p1[0], p2[0])
        yaxis = self._axisInterval(yaxis, p1[1], p2[1])
        text_width = [0., 0.]
        text_height = [0., 0.]

        if xaxis is not None:
            p1 = xaxis[0], p1[1]
            p2 = xaxis[1], p2[1]
            xticks = self._ticks(xaxis[0], xaxis[1])
            bb = self._textBoundingBox(xticks[0][1])
            text_height[1] = bb[3]-bb[1]
            text_width[0] = 0.5*(bb[2]-bb[0])
            bb = self._textBoundingBox(xticks[-1][1])
            text_width[1] = 0.5*(bb[2]-bb[0])
        else:
            xticks = None
        if yaxis is not None:
            p1 = p1[0], yaxis[0]
            p2 = p2[0], yaxis[1]
            yticks = self._ticks(yaxis[0], yaxis[1])
            for y in yticks:
                bb = self._textBoundingBox(y[1])
                w = bb[2]-bb[0]
                text_width[0] = max(text_width[0], w)
                h = 0.5*(bb[3]-bb[1])
                text_height[0] = h
                text_height[1] = max(text_height[1], h)
        else:
            yticks = None
        text1 = [text_width[0], -text_height[1]]
        text2 = [text_width[1], -text_height[0]]
        scale = ((self.plotarea_size[0]-text1[0]-text2[0]) / \
                 (p2[0]-p1[0]),
                 (self.plotarea_size[1]-text1[1]-text2[1]) / \
```

```
                        (p2[1]-p1[1]))
            shift = ((-p1[0]*scale[0]) + self.plotarea_origin[0] + \
                    text1[0],
                    (-p1[1]*scale[1]) + self.plotarea_origin[1] + \
                    text1[1])
            self._drawAxes(self.canvas, xaxis, yaxis, p1, p2,
                        scale, shift, xticks, yticks)
            graphics.fitToScale(scale, shift)
            graphics.draw(self.canvas)

# --- Code Removed -------------------------------------------------
```

Code comments (continued)

⑫ The GraphObjects class defines the collection of graph symbologies for each graph. In particular, it is responsible for determining the common bounding box for all of the lines.

⑬ `fitToScale` scales each of the lines to the calculated bounding box.

⑭ Finally, the `draw` method renders each of the graphs in the composite.

⑮ `GraphBase` is the base widget class which contains each of the composites. As you will see later, you may combine different arrangements of graph widgets to produce the desired effect.

⑯ An important feature of this widget is that it redraws whenever the parent container is resized. This allows the user to shrink and grow the display at will. We bind a `configure` event to the `configure` callback.

plot.py (continued)

```
        self.canvas.bind('<Configure>', self.configure)
if __name__ == '__main__':
    root = Tk()
    di = 5.*pi/5.
    data = []

    for i in range(18):                                                 ⑰
        data.append((float(i)*di,
                    (math.sin(float(i)*di)-math.cos(float(i)*di))))
    line  = GraphLine(data, color='gray', smooth=0)
    linea = GraphLine(data, color='blue', smooth=1, splinesteps=500)

    graphObject = GraphObjects([line, linea])                           ⑱

    graph = GraphBase(root, 500, 400, relief=SUNKEN, border=2)
    graph.pack(side=TOP, fill=BOTH, expand=YES)                         ⑲

    graph.draw(graphObject, 'automatic', 'automatic')

    Button(root, text='Clear',  command=graph.clear).pack(side=LEFT)
    Button(root, text='Redraw', command=graph.replot).pack(side=LEFT)
    Button(root, text='Quit',   command=root.quit).pack(side=RIGHT)

    root.mainloop()
```

⑰ Using the graph widget is quite easy. First, we create the line/curve that we wish to plot:

```
for i in range(18):
    data.append((float(i)*di,
                 (math.sin(float(i)*di)-math.cos(float(i)*di))))
line  = GraphLine(data, color='gray', smooth=0)
linea = GraphLine(data, color='blue', smooth=1, splinesteps=500)
```

⑱ Next we create the `GraphObject` which does the necessary scaling:

```
graphObject = GraphObjects([line, linea])
```

⑲ Finally, we create the graph widget and associate the `GraphObject` with it:

```
graph  = GraphBase(root, 500, 400, relief=SUNKEN, border=2)
graph.pack(side=TOP, fill=BOTH, expand=YES)
graph.draw(graphObject, 'automatic', 'automatic')
```

11.2.1 Adding bargraphs

Having developed the basic graph widget, it is easy to add new types of visuals. Bargraphs, sometimes called *histograms*, are a common way of presenting data, particularly when it is intended to portray the magnitude of the data, since the bars have actual volume as opposed to perceived volume under-the-curve. Figure 11.5 shows some typical bargraphs, in some cases combined with line graphs. Note that it is quite easy to set up multiple instances of the graph widget.

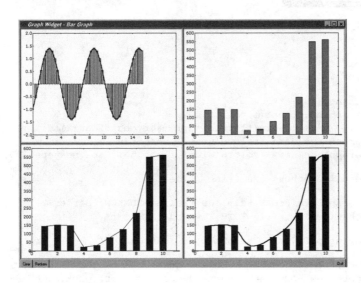

Figure 11.5 Adding bar graphs to the graph widget

plot2.py

```
from Tkinter import *
from Canvas import Line, CanvasText, Rectangle
```

```
class GraphPoints:

# --- Code Removed ------------------------------------------------------

def fitToScale(self, scale=(1,1), shift=(0,0)):
        self.scaled = []
        for x,y in self.points:
            self.scaled.append(((scale[0]*x)+shift[0],\
                                 (scale[1]*y)+shift[1])
        self.anchor = scale[1]*self.attributes.get('anchor', 0.0)\    ❶
                            + shift[1]

# --- Code Removed ------------------------------------------------------

class GraphBars(GraphPoints):
    def __init__(self, points, **attr):
        GraphPoints.__init__(self, points, attr)
        _attributes = {'color': 'black',
                       'width': 1,
                       'fillcolor': 'yellow',          ❷
                       'size': 3,
                       'fillstyle': '',
                       'outline': 'black'}

    def draw(self, canvas):
        color    = self.attributes['color']
        width    = self.attributes['width']
        fillstyle = self.attributes['fillstyle']
        outline  = self.attributes['outline']
        spread   = self.attributes['size']
        arguments = (canvas,)
        p1, p2   = self.boundingBox()
        for i in range(len(self.points)):
            x1, y1 = self.scaled[i]
            canvas.create_rectangle(x1-spread, y1, x1+spread,     ❸
                            self.anchor, fill=color,
                            width=width, outline=outline,
                            stipple=fillstyle)

# --- Code Removed ------------------------------------------------------

if __name__ == '__main__':
    root = Tk()
    root.title('Graph Widget - Bar Graph')

    di = 5.*pi/40.
    data = []
    for i in range(40):
        data.append((float(i)*di,
                    (math.sin(float(i)*di)-math.cos(float(i)*di))))
    line1  = GraphLine(data, color='black', width=2,
                smooth=1)
    line1a = GraphBars(data[1:], color='blue', fillstyle='gray25',     ❹
                anchor=0.0)

    line2 = GraphBars([(0,0),(1,145),(2,151),(3,147),(4,22),(5,31),
```

```
                    (6,77),(7,125),(8,220),(9,550),(10,560),(11,0)],
                color='green', size=10)

    line3 = GraphBars([(0,0),(1,145),(2,151),(3,147),(4,22),(5,31),
                (6,77),(7,125),(8,220),(9,550),(10,560),(11,0)],
                color='blue', size=10)
    line3a = GraphLine([(1,145),(2,151),(3,147),(4,22),(5,31),
                (6,77),(7,125),(8,220),(9,550),(10,560)],
                color='black', width=1, smooth=0)

    line4 = GraphBars([(0,0),(1,145),(2,151),(3,147),(4,22),(5,31),
                (6,77),(7,125),(8,220),(9,550),(10,560),(11,0)],
                color='blue', size=10)
    line4a = GraphLine([(1,145),(2,151),(3,147),(4,22),(5,31),
                (6,77),(7,125),(8,220),(9,550),(10,560)],
                color='black', width=2, smooth=1)

    graphObject  = GraphObjects([line1a, line1])
    graphObject2 = GraphObjects([line2])
    graphObject3 = GraphObjects([line3a, line3])
    graphObject4 = GraphObjects([line4, line4a])

    f1 = Frame(root)
    f2 = Frame(root)

    graph  = GraphBase(f1, 500, 350, relief=SUNKEN, border=2)
    graph.pack(side=LEFT, fill=BOTH, expand=YES)
    graph.draw(graphObject, 'automatic', 'automatic')

    graph2= GraphBase(f1, 500, 350, relief=SUNKEN, border=2)
    graph2.pack(side=LEFT, fill=BOTH, expand=YES)
    graph2.draw(graphObject2, 'automatic', 'automatic')

    graph3= GraphBase(f2, 500, 350, relief=SUNKEN, border=2)
    graph3.pack(side=LEFT, fill=BOTH, expand=YES)
    graph3.draw(graphObject3, 'automatic', 'automatic')

    graph4= GraphBase(f2, 500, 350, relief=SUNKEN, border=2)
    graph4.pack(side=LEFT, fill=BOTH, expand=YES)
    graph4.draw(graphObject4, 'automatic', 'automatic')

    f1.pack()
    f2.pack()

# --- Code Removed -----------------------------------------------------------
```

Code comments

❶ There's not much to explain here; I think that the changes are fairly self-explanatory. However, anchor is worthy of a brief note. In the case of the sine/cosine curve, we want the bars to start on zero. This is the anchor value. If we don't set it, we'll draw from the x-axis regardless of its value.

```
    self.anchor = scale[1]*self.attributes.get('anchor', 0.0) + shift[1]
```

❷ The bargraph has some slightly different options that need to be set.

❸ The bargraph simply draws a rectangle for the visual.

❹ Defining the data is similar to the method for lines. Note that I have omitted the first data point so that it does not overlay the y-axis:

```
line1a = GraphBars(data[1:], color='blue', fillstyle='gray25',
anchor=0.0)
```

11.2.2 Pie charts

As Emeril Lagasse* would say, "Let's kick it up a notch!" Bargraphs were easy to add, and adding pie charts is not much harder. Pie charts seem to have found a niche in management reports, since they convey certain types of information very well. As you will see in figure 11.6, I have added some small details to add a little extra punch. The first is to scale the pie chart if it is drawn in combination with another graph—this prevents the pie chart from getting in the way of the axes (I do not recommend trying to combine pie charts and bar graphs, however). Secondly, if the height and width of the pie chart are unequal, I add a little decoration to give a three-dimensional effect.

There is a problem with Tk release 8.0/8.1. A stipple is ignored for arc items, if present, when running under Windows; the figure was captured under UNIX. Here are the changes to create pie charts:

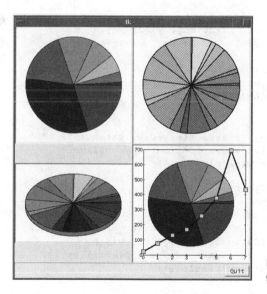

Figure 11.6 Adding pie charts to the graph widget

---

* Emeril Lagasse is a popular chef/proprietor of restaurants in New Orleans and Las Vegas in the USA. He is the exhuberant host of a regular cable-television cooking show. The audience join Emeril loudly in shouting "Bam! Let's kick it up a notch!" as he adds his own Essence to his creations.

plot3.py

```
# --- Code Removed -------------------------------------------------

class GraphPie(GraphPoints):
    def __init__(self, points, **attr):
        GraphPoints.__init__(self, points, attr)

        _attributes = {'color': 'black',
                       'width': 1,
                       'fillcolor': 'yellow',
                       'size': 2,
                       'fillstyle': '',
                       'outline': 'black'}

    def draw(self, canvas, multi):
        width    = self.attributes['width']
        fillstyle = self.attributes['fillstyle']
        outline  = self.attributes['outline']
        colors   = Pmw.Color.spectrum(len(self.scaled))        ❶
        arguments = (canvas,)

        x1 = string.atoi(canvas.cget('width'))
        y1 = string.atoi(canvas.cget('height'))
        adj = 0
        if multi: adj = 15
        xy  = 25+adj, 25+adj, x1-25-adj, y1-25-adj            ❷
        xys = 25+adj, 25+adj+10, x1-25-adj, y1-25-adj+10
        tt = 0.0
        i = 0
        for point in self.points:
            tt = tt + point[1]
        start = 0.0
        if not x1 == y1:
            canvas.create_arc(xys, start=0.0, extent=359.99,   ❸
                        fill='gray60', outline=outline,
                        style='pieslice')

        for point in self.points:
            x1, y1 = point
            extent = (y1/tt)*360.0
            canvas.create_arc(xy, start=start, extent=extent,  ❹
                        fill=colors[i], width=width,
                        outline=outline, stipple=fillstyle,
                        style='pieslice')
            start = start + extent
            i = i+1

class GraphObjects:
    def __init__(self, objects):
        self.objects  = objects
        self.multiple = len(objects)-1                         ❺

# --- Code Removed -------------------------------------------------
```

```
        def draw(self, canvas):
            for object in self.objects:
                object.draw(canvas, self.multiple)        ❻

    # --- Code Removed -------------------------------------------------

    if __name__ == '__main__':
      root = Tk()
      root.title('Graph Widget - Piechart')

      pie1    = GraphPie([(0,21),(1,77),(2,129),(3,169),(4,260),(5,377),
                      (6,695),(7,434)])

      pie2    = GraphPie([(0,5),(1,22),(2,8),(3,45),(4,22),
                      (5,9),(6,40),(7,2),(8,56),(9,34),
                      (10,51),(11,43),(12,12),(13,65),(14,22),
                      (15,15),(16,48),(17,16),(18,45),(19,19),
                      (20,33)], fillstyle='gray50', width=2)

      pie3    = GraphPie([(0,5),(1,22),(2,8),(3,45),(4,22),
                      (5,9),(6,40),(7,2),(8,56),(9,34),
                      (10,51),(11,43),(12,12),(13,65),(14,22),
                      (15,15),(16,48),(17,16),(18,45),(19,19),
                      (20,33)])

      pieline4  = GraphLine([(0,21),(1,77),(2,129),(3,169),(4,260),
                      (5,377),(6,695),(7,434)], width=3)
      pielines4 = GraphSymbols([(0,21),(1,77),(2,129),(3,169),(4,260),
                      (5,377),(6,695),(7,434)],
                      marker='square', fillcolor='yellow')

      graphObject1 = GraphObjects([pie1])
      graphObject2 = GraphObjects([pie2])
      graphObject3 = GraphObjects([pie3])
      graphObject4 = GraphObjects([pie1, pieline4, pielines4])

      f1 = Frame(root)
      f2 = Frame(root)

      graph1= GraphBase(f1, 300, 300, relief=SUNKEN, border=2)
      graph1.pack(side=LEFT, fill=BOTH, expand=YES)
      graph1.draw(graphObject1)

    # --- Code Removed -------------------------------------------------
```

Code comments

❶ The pie chart implementation assigns a spectrum of colors to the slices of the pie, one color value per slice. This gives a reasonable appearance for a small number of slices.

```
        colors  = Pmw.Color.spectrum(len(self.scaled))
```

❷ This code adjusts the position of the pie chart for cases where we are displaying the pie chart along with other graphs:

```
        adj = 0
        if multi: adj = 15
```

```
xy  = 25+adj, 25+adj, x1-25-adj, y1-25-adj
xys = 25+adj, 25+adj+10, x1-25-adj, y1-25-adj+10
```

The shadow disc (xys) is used if the pie chart is being displayed as a tilted disc.

❸ The shadow is drawn as a pie slice with an almost complete circular slice:

```
if not x1 == y1:
    canvas.create_arc(xys, start=0.0, extent=359.99,
            fill='gray60', outline=outline, style='pieslice')
```

❹ As in the case of adding bar graphs, adding pie charts requires a specialized draw routine.

❺ The scaling factors are determined by the presence of multiple graphs in the same widget.

❻ self.multiple is passed down to the graph object's draw method.

As you have seen in these examples, adding a new graph type is quite easy and it produces some reasonably attractive graphs. I hope that you can make use of them and perhaps create new visual formats for the Python community.

11.3 *3-D graphs*

If you have a large amount of data and that data follows a pattern that encourages examining the graphs on the same axes (same scale), there are a number of ways to display the graphs. One way is to produce a series of separate graphs and then present them side by side. This is good if you want to examine the individual graphs in detail, but it does not readily demonstrate the relationship between the graphs. To show the relationship you can produce a single diagram with all of the plots superimposed using different symbols, line styles, or combinations of both. However, there is often a tendency for the lines to become entangled or for symbols to be drawn on top of each other. This can produce very confusing results.

I always like to solve these problems by producing three-dimensional graphs. They allow the viewer to get a sense of the topology of the data as a whole, often highlighting features in the data that may be difficult to discern in other formats. The next example illustrates such a graph (see figure 11.7). I have taken a few shortcuts to reduce the overall amount of code. For example, I have made no provision for modifying the orientation of the axes or the viewing position. I'll leave that as an exercise for the enthusiastic reader!

3dgraph.py

```
from    Tkinter import *
import Pmw, AppShell, math

class Graph3D(AppShell.AppShell):
    usecommandarea = 1
    appname       = '3-Dimensional Graph'
    frameWidth    = 800
    frameHeight   = 650

    def createButtons(self):
        self.buttonAdd('Print',
                helpMessage='Print current graph (PostScript)',
                statusMessage='Print graph as PostScript file',
                command=self.iprint)
```

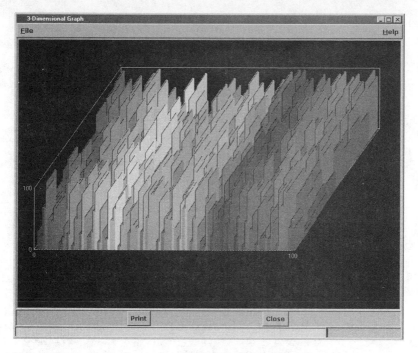

Figure 11.7 three-dimensional graphical display

```
        self.buttonAdd('Close',
                  helpMessage='Close Screen',
                  statusMessage='Exit',
                  command=self.close)

    def createBase(self):
        self.width  = self.root.winfo_width()-10
        self.height = self.root.winfo_height()-95
        self.canvas = self.createcomponent('canvas', (), None,
              Canvas, (self.interior(),), width=self.width,
              height=self.height, background="black")
        self.canvas.pack(side=TOP, expand=YES, fill=BOTH)

        self.awidth  = int(self.width  * 0.68)
        self.aheight = int(self.height * 0.3)
        self.hoffset = self.awidth  / 3
        self.voffset = self.aheight +3
        self.vheight = self.voffset / 2
        self.hrowoff = (self.hoffset / self.rows)
        self.vrowoff = self.voffset / self.rows
        self.xincr   = float(self.awidth) / float(self.steps)
        self.xorigin = self.width/3.7
        self.yorigin = self.height/3
        self.yfactor = float(self.vheight) / float(self.maxY-self.minY)

        self.canvas.create_polygon(self.xorigin, self.yorigin,
              self.xorigin+self.awidth, self.yorigin,
```

```
                self.xorigin+self.awidth-self.hoffset,self.yorigin+self.voffset,
                self.xorigin-self.hoffset, self.yorigin+self.voffset,
                self.xorigin, self.yorigin, fill='', outline=self.lineColor)

        self.canvas.create_rectangle(self.xorigin, self.yorigin-self.vheight,
                self.xorigin+self.awidth, self.yorigin,
                fill='', outline=self.lineColor)

        self.canvas.create_polygon(self.xorigin, self.yorigin,
         self.xorigin-self.hoffset, self.yorigin+self.voffset,
         self.xorigin-self.hoffset, self.yorigin+self.voffset-self.vheight,
         self.xorigin, self.yorigin-self.vheight,
         fill='', outline=self.lineColor)

        self.canvas.create_text(self.xorigin-self.hoffset-5,
                self.yorigin+self.voffset, text='%d' % self.minY,
                fill=self.lineColor, anchor=E)
        self.canvas.create_text(self.xorigin-self.hoffset-5,
                self.yorigin+self.voffset-self.vheight, text='%d' % \
                self.maxY, fill=self.lineColor, anchor=E)

        self.canvas.create_text(self.xorigin-self.hoffset,
                self.yorigin+self.voffset+5, text='%d' % self.minX,
                fill=self.lineColor, anchor=N)
        self.canvas.create_text(self.xorigin+self.awidth-self.hoffset,
                self.yorigin+self.voffset+5, text='%d' % self.maxX,
                fill=self.lineColor, anchor=N)

    def initData(self):
        self.minY =    0
        self.maxY = 100
        self.minX =    0
        self.maxX = 100
        self.steps = 100
        self.rows =   10
        self.spectrum = Pmw.Color.spectrum(self.steps, saturation=0.8,
                                intensity=0.8, extraOrange=1)
        self.lineColor = 'gray80'
        self.lowThresh =   30
        self.highThresh =   70

    def transform(self, base, factor):
        rgb = self.winfo_rgb(base)
        retval = "#"
        for v in [rgb[0], rgb[1], rgb[2]]:
            v = (v*factor)/256
            if v > 255: v = 255
            if v < 0:   v = 0
            retval = "%s%02x" % (retval, v)
        return retval

    def plotData(self, row, rowdata):
        rootx  = self.xorigin - (row*self.hrowoff)
        rooty  = self.yorigin + (row*self.vrowoff)
        cidx   = 0
        lasthv = self.maxY*self.yfactor
```

❷

```
                xadj    = float(self.xincr)/4.0
                lowv    = self.lowThresh*self.yfactor
                for datum in rowdata:
                    lside = datum*self.yfactor
                    color = self.spectrum[cidx]
                    if datum <= self.lowThresh:
                        color = self.transform(color, 0.8)
                    elif datum >= self.highThresh:
                        color = self.transform(color, 1.2)

                    self.canvas.create_polygon(rootx, rooty, rootx, rooty-lside,
                            rootx-self.hrowoff, rooty-lside+self.vrowoff,
                            rootx-self.hrowoff, rooty+self.vrowoff,
                            rootx, rooty, fill=color, outline=color,
                            width=self.xincr)
                    base = min(min(lside, lasthv), lowv)
                    self.canvas.create_line(rootx-xadj, rooty-lside,
                            rootx-xadj-self.hrowoff, rooty-lside+self.vrowoff,
                            rootx-xadj-self.hrowoff, rooty+self.vrowoff-base,
                            fill='black', width=1)
                    lasthv = lowv = lside

                    cidx = cidx + 1
                    rootx = rootx + self.xincr

    def makeData(self, number, min, max):
        import random
        data = []
        for i in range(number):
            data.append(random.choice(range(min, max)))
            return data

    def demo(self):
        for i in range(self.rows):
            data = self.makeData(100, 4, 99)
            self.plotData(i, data)
            self.root.update()

    def close(self):
        self.quit()

    def createInterface(self):
        AppShell.AppShell.createInterface(self)
        self.createButtons()
        self.initData()
        self.createBase()

if __name__ == '__main__':
    graph = Graph3D()
    graph.root.after(100, graph.demo)
    graph.run()
```

Code comments

1 Despite the complex diagram, the code is quite simple. Much of the code is responsible for drawing the frame and text labels.

2 You may have seen the `transform` method used in "Adding a hex nut to our class library" on page 131. Its purpose is to calculate a lighter or darker color intensity when given a color.

```
def transform(self, base, factor):
```

3 The transformed color is used to highlight values which exceed a high threshold and to deaccentuate those below a lower threshold.

4 For this example, we generate ten rows of random data.

Because the data was generated randomly, the effect is quite busy. If data is supplied from topological sources, the plot may be used to provide a surface view. Figure 11.8 illustrates the kind of three-dimensional plot that can be produced with such data.

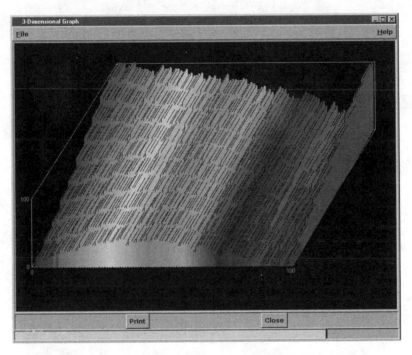

Figure 11.8 Using the 3-D to present topological data

11.4 *Strip charts*

In this final section we are going to look briefly at using strip charts to display data coming from a source of continuously changing data. Such displays will typically build a plot incrementally as the data is made available or polled at some time interval, and then they reset the chart when the maximum space has been filled.

Strip charts are an ideal medium for displaying performance data; data from sensors, such as temperature, speed, or humidity; data from more abstract measurements (such as the average number of items purchased per hour by each customer in a grocery store); and other types of data. They also can be used as a means of setting thresholds and triggering alarms when those thresholds have been reached.

The final example implements a weather monitoring system utilizing METAR* data. This encoded data may be obtained via FTP from the National Weather Service in the United States and from similar authorities around the globe. We are not going to enter a long tutorial about how to decode METARs, since that would require a chapter of its own. For this example, I am not even going to present the source code (there is *really* too much to use the space on the printed page). The source code is available online and it may be examined to determine how a simple FTP poll may be made to gather data continuously.

Take a look at figure 11.9 which shows the results of collecting the data from Tampa Bay, Florida (station *KTPA*), for about nine hours, starting at about 8:00 a.m. EST. The graphs depict temperature, humidity, altimeter (atmospheric pressure), visibility, wind speed, wind direction, clouds over 10,000 feet and clouds under 25,000 feet.

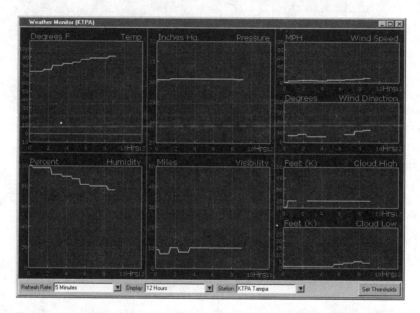

Figure 11.9 Strip chart display with polled meteorological data

---

* If you are a weather buff or a private pilot, you will be familiar with the automated, encoded weather observations that are posted at many reporting stations, including major airports, around the world. Updated on an hourly basis (more frequently if there are rapid changes in conditions), they contain details of wind direction and speed, temperature, dewpoints, atmospheric pressure, cloud cover and other data important to aviation in particular.

The presentation for the strip chart is intended to be similar to an oscilloscope or some other piece of equipment. Normally reverse-video is not the best medium for presenting data; this may be one of the exceptions.

The example code implements a threshold setting which allows the user to set values which trigger an alarm or warning when values are above or below the selected threshold. Take a look at figure 11.10 which shows how thresholds can be set on the data. This data comes from my home airport (Providence, in Warwick, Rhode Island) and it shows data just before a thunderstorm started.

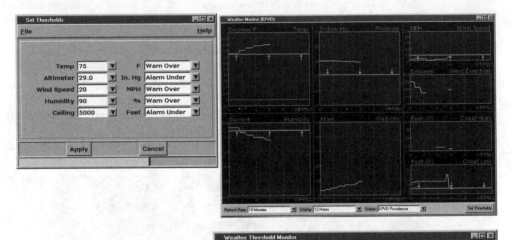

Figure 11.10 Setting thresholds on data values

If you look at figure 11.11 you can observe how the cloud base suddenly dropped below 5000 feet and triggered the threshold alarm.

If you do use this example please do not set the update frequency to a high rate. The data on the National Oceanic and Atmospheric Administration (NOAA) website is important for many pilots—leave the bandwidth for them!

11.5 Summary

Drawing graphs may not be necessary for many applications, but the ability to generate attractive illustrations from various data sources may be useful in some cases. While there are several general-purpose plotting systems available to generate graphs from arbitrary data, there is something satisfying about creating the code yourself.

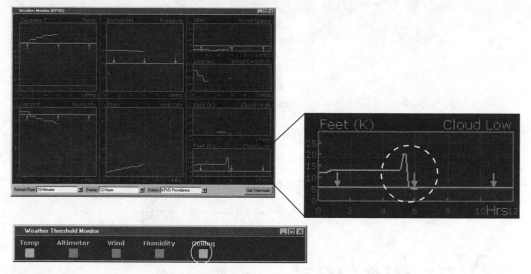

Figure 11.11 Alarm and warning thresholds

CHAPTER 12

Navigation

All successful GUIs provide a consistent and convenient means of navigation between their graphical elements. This short chapter covers each of these methods in detail. Some advanced navigation methods will be discussed to provide a guide to the topic. From the methods presented, you should be able to identify appropriate patterns for your application and apply the methods.

12.1 Introduction: navigation models

This chapter is all about *focus*. Specifically, *keyboard focus*, which is at the widget level and determines where keyboard events are delivered. *Window focus* is strictly a feature of the *window manager*, which is covered in more detail in "The window manager" on page 306.

There are normally two focus models:

Pointer   When a widget contains the *pointer*, all keyboard events are directed to the widget.

Explicit   The user must click on the widget to tab from widget to widget to set focus on a particular widget.

There are advantages and disadvantages for both models. Many users like the pointer model, since a simple movement of the mouse positions the pointer and requires no clicking. However, if the mouse is accidentally moved, the keyboard events may be directed to an unintended widget. The explicit model requires the user to click on every window and widget that focus is to be directed to. However, even if the pointer moves out of the widget, keyboard events are directed to it. On Win32 and MacOS, *explicit* focus is the default, whereas on UNIX, *pointer* focus is the default.

Tk (and therefore Tkinter) implements an explicit model within a given top-level shell, regardless of how the window manager is configured. However, within the application, the window manager is capable of overriding focus to handle system-level operations, so focus can be lost.

12.2 *Mouse navigation*

Most computer users are familiar with using the mouse to select actions and objects on the screen. However, there are times when stopping keyboard input to move the mouse is inconvenient; a *touch typist* will lose station and have to reestablish it before continuing. Therefore, it is usually a good idea to provide a sensible series of tab groups which allow the user to move from widget to widget and area to area in the GUI. This is discussed in more detail in the next section.

When the mouse is used to select objects, you need to consider some important human factors:

1 Widget alignment is important. If widgets are arranged aimlessly on the screen, additional dexterity is needed to position the mouse. Widgets arranged in rows and columns typically allow movement in one or two axes to reposition the pointer.

2 The clickable components of a widget need to be big enough to ensure that the user does not have to reposition the pointer to hit a target. However, this may interfere with the GUI's visual effectiveness.

3 Ensure that there is space between widgets so that the user cannot accidentally choose an adjacent widget.

4 Remember that not all pointing devices are equal. While a mouse can be easy to use to direct the pointer to a clickable area, some of the mouse buttons (the little buttons embedded in the keyboard on certain laptop computers) can be difficult to control.

Unless Tkinter (Tk) is directed to obey strict Motif rules, it has a useful property that allows it to change the visual attributes of many widgets as the pointer enters the widgets. This can provide valuable feedback to the user that a widget has been located.

12.3 *Keyboard navigation: "mouseless navigation"*

It is easy to forget to provide alternate navigation methods. If you, as the programmer, are used to using the mouse to direct focus, you may overlook mouseless navigation. However, there are times when the ability to use Tab or Arrow keys to get around a GUI are important.

There may be times when the mouse is unavailable (I've had problems with a cat sleeping on my desk and leaving mouse-jamming hairs!) or when an application is intended to be deployed in a hostile environment where a mouse just would not survive.

This method of navigation does require some discipline in how your GUI is created. The order in which focus moves *between* and *within* groups is determined by the order in which widgets are created. So careless maintenance of a GUI can result in erratic behavior, with focus jumping all over the screen. Also, some widgets cannot accept focus (if they are disabled, for instance) and others bind the navigation keys internally (the Text widget allows you to enter Tab characters, for instance).

It is also important to remember that the pointer always directs events (such as Enter, Leave and Button1) to the widget under it, regardless of where the keyboard focus is set. Thus, you may have to change focus to a widget if it does not take keyboard focus itself.

12.4 *Building navigation into an application*

Let's look at a simple example which allows you to discover how widgets behave in the focus models and under certain states. Widgets with the takefocus option set to true are placed in the window's tab group and focus moves from one widget to the next as the TAB key is pressed. If the widget's highlightthickness is at least one pixel, you will see which widget currently has focus. One thing to note is that there is somewhat less control of the navigation model under Tkinter. This is not normally a problem, but X Window programmers may find the restrictions limiting.

Example_12_1.py

```
from Tkinter import *

class Navigation:
    def __init__(self, master):

        frame = Frame(master, takefocus=1, highlightthickness=2,    ➊
                highlightcolor='blue')
        Label(frame, text='   ').grid(row=0, column=0,sticky=W)
        Label(frame, text='   ').grid(row=0, column=5,sticky=W)

        self.B1 = self.mkbutton(frame, 'B1', 1)
        self.B2 = self.mkbutton(frame, 'B2', 2)
        self.B3 = self.mkbutton(frame, 'B3', 3)
        self.B4 = self.mkbutton(frame, 'B4', 4)

        frame2 = Frame(master, takefocus=1, highlightthickness=2,
                highlightcolor='green')
        Label(frame2, text='   ').grid(row=0, column=0,sticky=W)
        Label(frame2, text='    ').grid(row=0, column=4,sticky=W)
        self.Disable = self.mkbutton(frame2, 'Disable', 1, self.disable)
        self.Enable  = self.mkbutton(frame2, 'Enable', 2, self.enable)
        self.Focus   = self.mkbutton(frame2, 'Focus', 3, self.focus)

        frame3 = Frame(master, takefocus=1, highlightthickness=2,
                highlightcolor='yellow')
        Label(frame3, text='   ').grid(row=0, column=0,sticky=W)
        Label(frame2, text='    ').grid(row=0, column=4,sticky=W)
```

```
            self.text = Text(frame3, width=20, height=3, highlightthickness=2)
            self.text.insert(END, 'Tabs are valid here')
            self.text.grid(row=0, col=1, columnspan=3)                          ❷

            frame.pack(fill=X, expand=1)
            frame2.pack(fill=X, expand=1)
            frame3.pack(fill=X, expand=1)

    def mkbutton(self, frame, button, column, action=None):                     ❸
            button = Button(frame, text=button, highlightthickness=2)
            button.grid(padx=10, pady=6, row=0, col=column, sticky=NSEW)
            if action:
                button.config(command=action)
            return button

    def disable(self):
            self.B2.configure(state=DISABLED, background='cadetblue')
            self.Focus.configure(state=DISABLED, background='cadetblue')

    def enable(self):
            self.B2.configure(state=NORMAL, background=self.B1.cget('background'))
            self.Focus.configure(state=NORMAL,
                                   background=self.B1.cget('background'))

    def focus(self):
            self.B3.focus_set()

root = Tk()
root.title('Navigation')
top = Navigation(root)
quit = Button(root, text='Quit', command=root.destroy)
quit.pack(side=BOTTOM, pady=5)

root.mainloop()
```

Code comments

❶ To show where keyboard focus is, we must give the highlight size, since the default for a Frame is 0. The color is also set so that it is easy to see.

❷ The Text widget also requires highlightthickness to be set. Text widgets are in the class of widgets that do not propagate TAB characters so you cannot navigate *out* of a Text widget using the TAB key (you must use CTRL-TAB).

❸ Buttons are window-system dependent. On Win32, buttons show their highlight as a dotted line, whereas Motif widgets require you to set the highlight width. If your application is targeted solely for Win32, you could omit the highlightthickness option.

Let's run the code in example 12.1 and see how TAB-key navigation works:
Each time you press the TAB key, the focus will move to the next widget in the group. To reverse the traversal, use the SHIFT-TAB key. In the second frame in figure 12.1, you can see that the frame is showing a highlight. Tkinter gets the order of the widgets right if you make sure that the widgets are presented to the geometry manager in the order that you want to navigate. If you do not take care, you will end up with the focus jumping all over the GUI as you attempt to navigate.

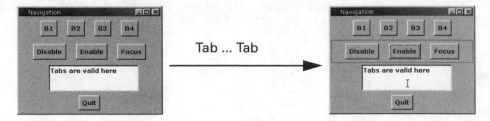

Figure 12.1 Using the Tab key to select a frame

Once you have focus, you can activate the widget using the SPACE bar (this is the default SELECT key, certainly for Win32 and Motif) or you can click on any widget using the pointer. Notice in figure 12.2 that the Enable button shows that it has been traversed to using TAB key, but that we select Disable with the pointer. Keyboard focus remains with the Enable button, so pressing the SPACE key will re-enable the buttons.

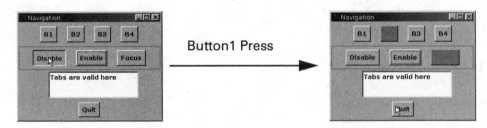

Figure 12.2 Demonstrating the difference between keyboard and pointer focus

Text widgets use TAB keys as separators, so the default binding does not cause traversal out of the widget. In figure 12.3 you can see that tabs are inserted into the text. To move out of the widget we must use CTRL-TAB which is not bound to the Text widget.

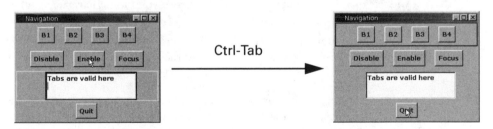

Figure 12.3 Using CONTROL-TAB to navigate out of a Text widget

12.5 *Image maps*

In "Image maps" on page 191, we looked at an implementation of image maps. It used pointer clicks to detect regions on the image and to select mapped areas. This technique cannot support mouseless operation, so if this is necessary, you have some work to do.

One solution is to overlay the image with objects that can take focus, then you can tab from object to object. This does work (the application shown on page 232 uses this technique to place buttons over button images on a ray-traced image), but it does require much more planning and code.

12.6 **Summary**

This chapter is another illustration of the fact that an application developer should consider its end-users carefully. If you are developing an application for a single group of users on uniform hardware platforms, then it may not be necessary to think about providing alternate means for navigating the GUIs. However, if you have no control of the end-user's environment you can change their perception of your application greatly by allowing alternate navigation models.

The window manager

Even though it is possible to build applications that have no direct communication with the window manager, it is useful to have an understanding of the role that the window manager (wm) has in X Window, Win32 and MacOS environments. This chapter covers some of the available wm facilities and presents examples of their use.

13.1   What is a window manager?

If you already know the answer to that question, you may want to skip ahead. It is perfectly possible to develop complex GUI-based applications without knowing *anything* about the window manager. However, many of the attributes of the displayed GUI are determined by the window manager.

Window managers exist in one form or another for each of the operating systems; examples are *mwm* (Motif), *dtwm* (CDE) and *ovwm* (OpenView). In the case of Win32, the window manager is just part of the operating system rather than being a separate application. The main functions that window managers typically support are these:

1 Management of windows (obviously!): placement, sizing, iconizing and maximizing, for example.

2 Appearance and behavior of windows and the relationship of windows in an application.

3 Management of one or more screens.

4 Keyboard focus control.

5 Window decoration: titles, controls, menus, size and position controls.

6 Icons and icon management (such as iconboxes and system tray).

7 Overall keybindings (before application bindings).

8 Overall mouse bindings.

9 Root-window menus.

10 Window stacking and navigation.

11 Default behavior and client resources (.XDefaults).

12 Size and position negotiation with windowing primitives (geometry managers).

13 Device configuration: mouse double-click time, keyboard repeat and movement thresholds, for example.

Not all window managers support the same features or behave in the same way. However, Tkinter supports a number of window-manager-related facilities which may support your application. Naturally, the names of the facilities are oriented to Tk, so you may not recognize other manager's names immediately.

13.2 Geometry methods

Geometry methods are used to position and size windows and to set resize behavior. It is important to note that these are *requests* to the window manager to allocate a given amount of space or to position the window at a particular screen position. There is no guarantee that the window manager will observe the request, since overriding factors may prevent it from happening. In general, if you get no apparent effect from geometry methods, you are probably requesting something that the window manager cannot grant or you are requesting it at the wrong time (either before window realization or too late).

You normally apply window manager methods to the TopLevel widget.

To control the size and position of a window use geometry, giving a single string as the argument in the format:

```
widthxheight+xoffset+yoffset
root.geometry('%dx%d+%d+%d' % (width, height, x, y))
```

Note that it is valid to supply either *widthxheight* or *+xoffset+yoffset* as separate arguments if you just want to set those parameters.

Without arguments, self.geometry() returns a string in the format shown above.

In general, you should issue `geometry` requests at most only once when a window is first drawn. It is not good practice to change the position of windows under program control; such positioning should be left for the user to decide using the window manager controls.

Setting the minimum and maximum dimensions of a window is often a good idea. If you have designed an application which has a complex layout, it may be inappropriate to provide the user with the ability to resize the window. In fact, it may be *impossible* to maintain the integrity of a GUI if you do not limit this ability. However, Tkinter GUIs using the `Pack` or `Grid` geometry managers are much easier to configure than equivalent X window GUIs.

```
window.maxsize(width, height)
window.minsize(width, height)
```

`window.minsize()` and `window.maxsize()` with no arguments return a tuple `(width, height)`.

You may control the resize capability using the `resizable` method. The method takes two boolean flags; setting either the `width` or `height` flags to `false` inhibits the resizing of the corresponding dimension:

```
resizable(1, 0)          # allow width changes only
resizable(0, 0)          # do not allow resizing in either dimension
```

13.3 *Visibility methods*

Window managers usually provide the ability to iconify windows so that the user can declutter the workspace. It is often appropriate to change the state of the window under program control. For example, if the user requests a window which is currently iconified, we can `deiconify` the window on his behalf. For reasons which will be explained in "Programming for performance" on page 348, it is usually better to draw complex GUIs with the window hidden; this results in faster window-creation speeds.

To iconify a window, use the `iconify` method:

```
root.iconify()
```

To hide a window, use the `withdraw` method:

```
self.toplevel.withdraw()
```

You can find out the current state of a window using the `state` method. This returns a string which is one of the following values: `normal` (the window is currently realized), `iconic` (the window has been iconified), `withdrawn` (the window is hidden), or `icon` (the window is an icon).

```
state = self.toplevel.state()
```

If a window has been iconified or withdrawn, you may restore the window with the `deiconify` method. It is not an error to deiconify a window that is currently displayed. Make sure that the window is placed on top of the window stack by calling `lift` as well.

```
self.deiconify()
self.lift()
```

13.4 *Icon methods*

The icon methods are really only useful with X Window window managers. You have limited control over icons with most window managers.

To set a two-color icon, use `iconbitmap`:

```
self.top.iconbitmap(myBitmap)
```

To give the icon a name *other* than the window's title, use `iconname`:

```
self.top.iconname('Example')
```

You can give the window manager a hint about where you want to position the icon (however, the window manager may place the icon in an `iconbox` if one is defined or wherever else it wishes):

```
self.root.iconposition(10,200)
```

If you want a color bitmap, you must create a `Label` with an image and then use `iconwindow`:

```
self.label = Label(self, image=self.img)
self.root.iconwindow(self.label)
```

13.5 *Protocol methods*

Window managers that conform to the ICCCM* conventions support a number of protocols:

- `WM_DELETE_WINDOW`   The window is about to be deleted.
- `WM_SAVE_YOURSELF`   Saves client data.
- `WM_TAKE_FOCUS`   The window has just gained focus.

You normally will use the first protocol to clean up your application when the user has chosen the exit window menu option and destroyed the window without using the application's Quit button:

```
self.root.protocol(WM_DELETE_WINDOW, self.cleanup)
```

In Python 1.6, the `WM_DELETE_WINDOW` protocol will be bound to the window's `destroy` method by default.

---

* ICCCM stands for Inter-Client Communication Conventions Manual, which is a manual for client communication in the X environment. This pertains to UNIX systems, but Tk emulates the behavior on all platforms.

WM_SAVE_YOURSELF is less commonly encountered and is usually sent before a WM_DELETE_WINDOW is sent. WM_TAKE_FOCUS may be used by an application to allow special action to be taken when focus is gained (perhaps a polling cycle is executed more frequently when a window has focus, for example).

13.6 *Miscellaneous wm methods*

There are several window manager methods, many of which you may never need to look at. They are documented in "Inherited methods" on page 433. However, you might find a few of them useful.

To raise or lower a window in the window stack, use `lift` and `lower` (you cannot use "raise" since that is a Python keyword):

```
self.top.lift()                          # Bring to top of stack
self.top.lift(name)                       # Lift on top of 'name'

self.top.lower(self.spam)                 # Lower just below self.spam
```

To find which screen your window is on (this is really only useful for X Window), use:

```
screen = self.root.screen()
print screen
  :0.1
```

Note *Win32 readers* The numbers returned refer to the *display* and *screen* within that display. X window is capable of supporting multiple display devices on the same system.

Putting it all together...

Part 3 covers a number of topics. Not all relate directly to Tkinter, or even Python, necessarily. In chapter 14 we begin by looking at building extensions to Python. Extensions can be an effective way of adding new functionality to Python or they may be used to boost performance to correct problems when you're using native Python.

Chapter 15 looks at debugging techniques for Python and Tkinter applications, and chapter 16 examines GUI design. Both of these areas can be problematic to programmers, particularly those who are new to GUI applications.

Chapter 17 looks at techniques to get optimum performance from applications. This area can have a dramatic impact on whether your users will like or dislike the interface you have designed.

In chapter 18 we examine threads and other asynchronous techniques. This is only an introduction to the subject, but it may provide a starting point for readers who are interested in this topic.

Finally, chapter 19 documents some methods to package and distribute Python and Tkinter applications. While it's not exhaustive, it should help programmers to deliver a Python application without involving the end user in setting up complex systems.

CHAPTER 14

Extending Python

Python is readily extensible using a well-defined interface and build scheme. In this chapter, I will show you how to build interfaces to external systems as well as existing extensions. In addition, we will look at maintaining extensions from one Python revision to another. We'll also discuss the choice between embedding Python within an application or developing a freestanding Python application.

The documentation that comes with Python is a good source of information on this topic, so this chapter will attempt not to repeat this information. My goal is to present the most important points so that you can easily build an interface.

14.1 *Writing a Python extension*

Many Python programmers will never have a need to extend Python; the available library modules satisfy a wide range of requirements. So, unless there are special requirements, the standard, binary distributions are perfectly adequate.

In some cases, writing an extension in C or C++ may be necessary:

1 When computational demands (intensive numeric operations, for example) make Python code inefficient.

2 Where access to third-party software is required. This might be through some API (Application Program Interface) or a more complex interface.*

3 To provide access to legacy software which does not lend itself to conversion to Python.

4 To control external devices through mechanisms similar to items 2 and 3 above.

Note Writing an extension for Python means that you must have the full source for the Python interpreter and access to a C or C++ compiler (if you are going to work with Windows, I recommend that you use Microsoft's Visual C++ version 5 or later). Unless you are going to interface a library API or have severe performance problems, you may wish to avoid building an extension altogether. See "Programming for performance" on page 348 for some ideas to improve the performance of Python code.

Let's begin by looking at a simple example which will link a C API to Python (we will look at C++ later). For the sake of simplicity, let's assume that the API implements several statistical functions. One of these functions is to determine the minimum, average and maximum values within four supplied real numbers. From the Python code, we are going to supply the values as discrete arguments and return the result as a tuple. Don't worry if this sounds like a trivial task for Python–this is just a simple example!.

Here's what we want to do from the Python side:

```
import statistics
.....
minimum, average, maximum = statistics.mavm(1.3, 5.5, 6.6, 8.8)
.....
```

We start by creating the file statisticsmodule.c. The accepted naming-convention for extension modules is *module*module.c (this will be important later if we want to create dynamic loading modules).

All extension modules must include the Python API by including `Python.h`. This also includes several standard C-include files such as `stdio.h`, `string.h` and `stdlib.h`. Then we define the C functions that will support our API.

The source code will look something like this:

statisticsmodule1.c

```
#include "Python.h"
static PyObject *
stats_mavm(self, args)
  PyObject *self, *args;
```

---

* If you need to provide a Python interface to a library, you may wish to take a look at SWIG (See "SWIG" on page 625), which provides a very convenient way of building an interface. In some cases it is possible for SWIG to develop an interface from an include file alone. This obviously saves effort and time.

```
{
    double          value[4], total;
    double          minimum =  1E32;
    double          maximum = -1E32;
    int             i;

    if (!PyArg_ParseTuple (args, "dddd", &value[0], &value[1],
                                          &value[2], &value[3]))        ④

        return NULL;

    for (i=0; i<4; i++)
    {
        if (value[i] < minimum)
            minimum = value[i];                     ⑤
        if (value[i] > maximum)
            maximum = value[i];
        total = total + value[i];
    }

    return Py_BuildValue("(ddd)", minimum, total/4, maximum) ;      ⑥
}
static PyMethodDef statistics_methods[] = {
    {"mavm",     stats_mavm, METH_VARARGS,  "Min, Avg, Max"},       ⑦
    {NULL, NULL} };

DL_EXPORT(void)
initstatistics()
{                                                                  ⑧
  Py_InitModule("statistics", statistics_methods);
}
```

Code comments

① As mentioned earlier, all extension modules must include the Python API definitions.

② All interface items are Python objects, so we define the function to return a PyObject.

③ Similarly, the instance and arguments, args, are PyObjects.

④ The Python API provides a function to parse the arguments, converting Python objects into C entities:

```
if (!PyArg_ParseTuple (args, "dddd", &value[0], &value[1],
                                      &value[2], &value[3]))

        return NULL;
```

PyArg_ParseTuple parses the args object using the supplied format string. The available options are explained in "Format strings" on page 321. Note that you must supply the *address* of the variables into which parsed values are to be placed.

⑤ Here we process our data. As you will note, this is *really* difficult!

⑥ In a manner similar to PyArg_ParseTuple, Py_BuildValue creates Python objects from C entities. The formats have the same meaning.

```
return Py_BuildValue("(ddd)", minimum, total/4, maximum)
```

In this case, we create a tuple as our return object.

7 All interface modules must define a *methods table*, whose function is to associate Python function names with their equivalent C functions

```
static PyMethodDef statistics_methods[] = {
        {"mavm",      stats_mavm, METH_VARARGS,  "Min, Avg, Max"},
        {NULL, NULL} };
```

METH_VARARGS defines how the arguments are to be presented to the parser. The documentation field is optional. Notice the naming convention for the methods table. Although this can take any name, it is usually a good idea to follow the convention.

8 The methods table must be registered with the interpreter in an initialization function. When the module is first imported, the initstatistics() function is called.

```
DL_EXPORT(void) initstatistics()
{
   Py_InitModule("statistics", statistics_methods);
}
```

Again, the naming convention must be followed, because Python will attempt to call initmodulename for each module imported.

14.2 *Building Python extensions*

Before you can use the Python extension, you have to compile and link it. Here, you have several choices, depending on whether the target system is UNIX or Windows (sorry, I am not covering Macintosh extensions).

Basically, we can make the module a permanent part of the Python interpreter so that it is always available, or we can link it dynamically. Dynamic linking is not available on all systems, but it works well for many UNIX systems and for Windows. The advantage to loading dynamically is that you do not need to modify the interpreter to extend Python.

14.2.1 Linking an extension statically in UNIX

Linking an extension statically in UNIX is quite simple to do. If you have not already configured and built Python, do so as described in "Building and installing Python, Tkinter" on page 610. Copy your module (in this case, statisticsmodule.c) to the Modules directory. Then, add on line at the end of Modules/Setup.local (you may add some comments, too, if you wish):

```
*static*
statistics statisticsmodule.c
```

If your module requires additional libraries, such as an API, add **-lxxx** flags at the end of the line. Note that the *static* flag is really only required if the preceding modules have been built as shared modules by including the *shared* flag.

Now, simply invoke **make** in the top-level Python directory to rebuild the **python** executable in that directory.

14.2.2 Linking an extension statically in Windows

Linking an extension statically in Windows is a little more involved than the case for UNIX, but it is quite easy if you follow the steps. If you have not yet built Python, do so as described in "Building and installing Python, Tkinter" on page 610.

First, edit PC/config.c. You will find a comment:

```
/* -- ADDMODULE MARKER 1 -- */
extern void PyMarshal_Init();
extern void initimp();
extern void initstatistics();
extern void initwprint();
```

Add an `extern` reference for the `init` function. Then locate the second comment:

```
/* -- ADDMODULE MARKER 2 -- */
        /* This module "lives in" with marshal.c */
        {"marshal", PyMarshal_Init},
        /* This lives it with import.c */
        {"imp", initimp},
        /* Statistics module (P-Tk-P) */
        {"statistics", initstatistics},
        /* Window Print module */
        {"wprint", initwprint},
```

Add the module name and its `init` function.

Next, edit PC/python15.dsp. Near the end you should find an entry for **typeobject.c**:

```
SOURCE=..\Objects\typeobject.c
# End Source File
#
# Begin Source File
SOURCE=..\Modules\statisticsmodule.c
# End Source File
#
# Begin Source File
SOURCE=..\Modules\wprintmodule.c
# End Source File
```

Insert the lines for `statisticsmodule.c`.

Lastly, open the workspace PCbuild/pcbuild.dsw in VC++, select the appropriate configuration (see "Building and installing Python, Tkinter" on page 610) and build the projects.

14.2.3 Building a dynamic module in UNIX

There are several styles of generating dynamically-loadable modules. I'm just going to present a method that works for Solaris, but all UNIX systems derived from SVR4 should provide similar interfaces. All the work is done in the makefile, so no code changes should be needed. As with static linking, build and install Python first so that libraries and other such items are in place.

makefile_dyn

```
SRCS=          statisticsmodule.c
CFLAGS=        -DHAVE_CONFIG_H          ❶
C=             cc

# Symbols used for using shared libraries
SO=            .so
LDSHARED=      ld -G                    ❷

OBJS=          statisticsmodule.o
PYTHON_INCLUDE=  -I/usr/local/include/python1.5 \      ❸
                 -I/usr/local/lib/python1.5/config
statistics:  $(OBJS)                                   ❹
             $(LDSHARED) $(OBJS)
             -Bdynamic -o statisticsmodule.so

statisticsmodule.o:    statisticsmodule.c              ❺
                       $(C) -c $(CFLAGS) $(PYTHON_INCLUDE) \
                       statisticsmodule.c
```

Code comments

❶ CFLAGS defines HAVE_CONFIG_H (among other things, this defines the mode of dynamic loading). Not all architectures need this, but define it anyway.

❷ LDSHARED defines the ld command line needed to generate shared libraries. This will vary with different architectures.

❸ PYTHON_INCLUDE defines the path for Python.h and the installed config.h.

❹ The target for the link might need libraries to be supplied for more complex modules. The -lxxx flags would be placed right after the $(OBJS).

❺ The compile rule is quite simple; just add the CFLAGS and PYTHON_INCLUDE variables.

14.2.4 Building a dynamic module in Windows

Once again, building a dynamic module in Windows is quite involved. It does require you to edit some files which contain comments such as **DO NOT EDIT**, but despite that, it works! As with static linking, build and install Python first so that libraries and other such items are in place.

First, create a directory in the top-level Python directory, at the same level as Modules, Parser and so on. Give it the same name as your module.

Next, copy all of the files necessary to support your module into this directory; for our example, we need only statisticsmodule.c.

Then, in the *PC* directory of the standard Python distribution, you will find a directory called example_nt. Copy example.def, example.dsp, example.dsw and example.mak into the module directory, renaming the files with your module name as the prefix.

Edit each of these files, changing the references to **example** to your module name. You will need to make over 50 changes to the make file. As you make the changes, note the paths to the Python library (which is python15.lib in this case). If this does not match your installed library, the best way to correct it is to delete it from the project and then add it in again.

Finally, select the Debug or Release configuration and then choose the Build menu option Build statistics.dll to build the dll.

14.2.5 Installing dynamic modules

To install dynamic modules, you can do one of three things. You can place the module.so or module.dll anywhere that is defined in the PYTHONPATH environment variable, you may add its path into the sys.path list at runtime, or you may copy it into the installed .../ python/lib/**lib-dynload** directory. All three methods achieve the same effect, but I usually place *dll* files right with python.exe on Windows and I put .so files in lib-dynload for UNIX. You may make your own choice.

14.2.6 Using dynamic modules

There are no differences in the operation and use of modules that are linked statically with the interpreter and those that are linked dynamically. The only thing that you may experience is a error if you forget to put the files in the right directory or to add the path to PYTHONPATH!

```
Python 1.5.2b2 (#17, Apr  7 1999, 13:25:13) [C] on sunos5
Copyright 1991-1995 Stichting Mathematisch Centrum, Amsterdam
>>> import statistics
>>> statistics.mavm(1.3, 5.5, 6.6, 8.8)
(1.3, 5.55, 8.8)
>>>
```

14.3 *Using the Python API in extensions*

The mavm routine in the previous example is really rather tame. Let's change the input to a list and perform the same operations on it.

statisticsmodule2.c

```
#include "Python.h"

static PyObject *
stats_mavm(self, args)
  PyObject *self, *args;
{
  double    total   =  0.0;
  double    minimum =  1E31;
  double    maximum = -1E31;
  int       i, len;
  PyObject       *idataList =  NULL;          ❶
  PyFloatObject *f  =  NULL;
  double        df;

  if (!PyArg_ParseTuple (args, "O", &idataList))     ❷
      return NULL;

  /* check first to make sure we've got a list */
```

```
    if (!PyList_Check(idataList))
    {
        PyErr_SetString(PyExc_TypeError,                    ❸
                "input argument must be a list");
        return NULL;
    }
    len = PyList_Size(idataList);                           ❹

    for (i=0; i<len; i++)
    {
        f = (PyFloatObject *)PyList_GetItem(idataList, i);  ❺
        df = PyFloat_AsDouble(f);                           ❻
        if (df < minimum)
            minimum = df;
#-------------------------------Remaining code removed-----------
```

Code comments

❶ We need to define a Python object for the list that is being passed in as an argument and a `PyFloatObject` (a subtype of `PyObject`) to receive the items in the list.

❷ We are now receiving a single object (as opposed to discrete values in the previous example).

❸ We check that the object is indeed a list. This actually introduces a shortcoming—we cannot pass a tuple containing the values. If there *is* an error, we use `PyErr_SetString` to generate `PyExc_TypeError` with a specific error message.

❹ List objects have a `length` attribute, so we get it.

❺ We get each item in the list.

❻ For each item we convert the `PyFloat` to a C `double`. The rest of the code has been removed; you have seen it before.

This example only scratches the surface of what can be done with the Python API. A good place to find examples of its use is in the `Modules` directory in the Python source. One reason that this topic is important is that Python is very good at creating and manipulating strings, especially if they involve lists, tuples, or dictionaries. A very realistic scenario is the ability to use Python to create such data structures and then to use use C to further process the entries, using API calls inside an iterator. In this way, C can provide the speed for critical operations and Python can provide the power to handle data succinctly.

14.4 *Building extensions in C++*

Python is a C-based interpreter. Although it's possible to adjust the source so that it would compile as C++, it would be a large undertaking. This means that calling C++ functions from this C base introduces some special problems. However, if you are able to link Python with the C++ compiler (linker), the problems are reduced.

Clearly, many C++ class libraries can support Python systems. The trick is to leave Python essentially unchanged and provide a wrapper which gives access to the class library. If you can use dynamic linking for extension modules, this is quite a painless experience. If you *must* link statically, you may be facing some challenges.

Because of the great variability of each architecture's C++ compilers, I am not going to try to provide a cookbook to solve the various problems. However, I *am* going to present some code fragments that have worked for Solaris.

To get a module to compile with C++, you need to define the Python API as a C segment to the C++ compiler:

```
extern "C" {
#include "Python.h"
}
```

Then, the init function must be given the same treatment:

```
extern "C" {
  DL_EXPORT(void)
  initstatistics()
  {
      Py_InitModule("statistics", statistics_methods);
  }
}
```

14.5 *Format strings*

Format strings provide a mechanism to specify the conversion of Python types passed as arguments to the extension routines. The items in the string must match, in number and type, the addresses supplied in the `PyArg_ParseTuple()` call. Although the type of the arguments is checked with the format string, the supplied addresses are not checked. Consequently, errors here can have a disastrous effect on your application.

Since Python supports long integers of arbitrary length, it is possible that the values cannot be stored in `C long integers`; in all cases where the receiving field is too small to store the value, the most significant bits are silently truncated.

The characters |, :, and ; have special meaning in format strings.

"|" This indicates that the remaining arguments in the Python argument list are optional. The C variables corresponding to optional arguments must be initialized to their default value since `PyArg_ParseTuple` leaves the variables corresponding to absent arguments unchanged.

":" The list of format units ends here; the string after the colon is used as the function name in error messages.

";" The list of format units ends here; the string after the colon is used as the error message instead of the default error message.

Table 14.1 Format strings for PyArg_ParseTuple( )

Format unit	Python type	C type	Description
s	string	char *	Convert a Python string to a C pointer to a character string. The address you pass must be a character pointer; you do not supply storage. The C string is null-terminated. The Python string may not contain embedded nulls and it cannot be None. If it does or is, a TypeError exception is raised.
s#	string	char *, int	Stores into two C variables, the first one being a pointer to a character string, the second one being its length. The Python string may have embedded nulls.
z	string or None	char *	Similar to s, but the Python object may also be None, in which case the C pointer is set to NULL.
z#	string or None	char *, int	Similar to s#.
b	integer	char	Convert a Python integer to a tiny int, stored in a C char.
h	integer	short int	Convert a Python integer to a C short int.
i	integer	int	Convert a Python integer to a plain C int.
l	integer	long int	Convert a Python integer to a C long int.
c	string of length 1	char	Convert a Python character, represented as a string of length 1, to a C char.
f	float	float	Convert a Python floating point number to a C float.
d	float	double	Convert a Python floating point number to a C double.
D	complex	Py_complex	Convert a Python complex number to a C Py_complex structure.
O	object	PyObject *	Store a Python object (without conversion) in a C object pointer. The C interface receives the actual object that was passed. The object's reference count is not increased.
O!	object	typeobject, PyObject *	Store a Python object in a C object pointer. This is similar to O, but it takes two C arguments: the first is the address of a Python-type object specifying the required type, and the second is the address of the C variable (of type PyObject *) into which the object pointer is stored. If the Python object does not have the required type, a TypeError exception is raised.

Table 14.1   Format strings for PyArg_ParseTuple( ) (continued)

Format unit	Python type	C type	Description
O&	object	function, variable	Convert a Python object to a C variable through a converter function. This takes two arguments: the first is a function, the second is the address of a C variable (of arbitrary type), cast to void *. The converter function is called as follows: status = function(object, variable); where object is the Python object to be converted and variable is the void * argument that was passed to PyArg_ConvertTuple(). The returned status should be 1 for a successful conversion and 0 if the conversion has failed. If conversion fails, the function should raise an exception.
S	string	PyStringObject *	Similar to O, but it expects that the Python object is a string object. It raises a TypeError exception if the object is not a string object.
(items)	sequence	matching items	The object must be a Python sequence whose length is the number of format units in items. The C arguments must correspond to the individual format units in items. Format units for sequences may be nested.

To return values to the Python program that called the extension, we use Py_BuildValue, which uses similar format strings to PyArg_ParseTuple. Py_BuildValue has a couple of differences. First, the arguments in the call are values, not addresses. Secondly, it does not create a tuple unless there are two or more format units, or if you enclose the empty or single format unit in parentheses.

Table 14.2   Format strings for Py_BuildValue()

Format unit	C type	Python type	Description
s	char *	string	Convert a null-terminated C string to a Python object. If the C string pointer is NULL, None is returned.
s#	char *, int	string	Convert a C string and its length to a Python object. If the C string pointer is NULL, the length is ignored and None is returned.
z	char *	string or None	Same as "s". If the C string pointer is NULL, None is returned.
z#	char *, int	string or None	Same as "s#". If the C string pointer is NULL, None is returned.

Table 14.2   Format strings for Py_BuildValue() (continued)

Format unit	C type	Python type	Description
i	int	integer	Convert a plain C int to a Python integer object.
b	char	integer	Same as i.
h	short int	integer	Same as i.
l	long int	integer	Convert a C long int to a Python integer object.
c	char	string of length 1	Convert a C int representing a character to a Python string of length 1.
d	double	float	Convert a C double to a Python floating point number.
f	float	float	Same as d.
O	PyObject *	object	Pass a Python object incrementing its reference count. If the object passed in is a NULL pointer, it is assumed that this was caused because the call producing the argument found an error and set an exception. Therefore, Py_BuildValue() will return NULL but it does not raise an exception. If no exception has been raised, PyExc_SystemError is set.
S	PyObject *	object	Same as O.
N	PyObject *	object	Similar to O, except that the reference count is not incremented.
O&	function, variable	object	Convert variable to a Python object through a converter function. The function is called with variable (which should be compatible with void *) as its argument and it should return a new Python object, or NULL if an error occurred.
(items)	matching items	tuple	Convert a sequence of C values to a Python tuple with the same number of items.
[items]	matching items	list	Convert a sequence of C values to a Python list with the same number of items.
{items}	matching items	dictionary	Convert a sequence of C values to a Python dictionary. Each consecutive pair of C values adds one item to the dictionary, using the first value as the key and the second as the value.

14.6 *Reference counts*

You may have noticed a couple of mentions of reference counts in the previous format string descriptions: If you are new to Python, and especially if you are new to extension writing and the Python API, this may be an important area to study.

The Python documentation for extensions and the API provides an excellent picture of what is entailed, and you want to see a full explanation, I recommend that you study the Python documentation.

Most API functions have a return value of type `PyObject *`. This is a pointer to an arbitrary Python object. All Python objects have similar base behavior and may be represented by a single C type. You cannot declare a variable of type `PyObject`; you can only declare `PyObject *` pointers to the actual storage. All `PyObjects` have a reference count.

This is where we need to take special care! When an object's reference count becomes zero, it will be deconstructed. If the object contains references to other objects, then *their* reference counts are decremented. If their reference count becomes zero, then they too will be deconstructed.

Problems usually occur when the interface extracts an object from a list and then uses that reference for a while (or worse, passes the reference back to the caller). In a similar fashion, a `Py_DECREF()` call before passing data to the caller will result in disaster.

The Python documentation recommends that extensions use the API functions that have a `PyObject`, `PyNumber`, `PySequence` or `PyMapping` prefix, since these operations always increment the reference count. It is the caller's responsibility to call `Py_DECREF()` when no further reference is required.

Here's a general rule of thumb: If you are writing a Python extension and you repeatedly get a crash when you either return a value or exit your application, you've got the reference counts wrong.

14.7 *Embedding Python*

When it is necessary to add Python functionality to a C or C++ application, it is possible to embed the Python interpreter. This can be invaluable if you need to create Python objects within a C program or, perhaps, use dictionaries as a data structure. It is also possible to combine extending and embedding within the same application.

The Python documentation provides full documentation for the API, and you should reference this material for details. All you need to use the API is to call `Py_Initialize()` once from your application before using API calls.

Once the interpreter has been initialized, you may execute Python strings using `PyRun_SimpleString()` or you may execute complete files with `PyRun_SimpleFile()`. Alternatively, you can use the Python API to exercise precise control over the interpreter.

Here is a simple example that illustrates a way that Python functionality may be accessed from C. We will access a dictionary created using a simple Python script from C. This provides a powerful mechanism for C programs to perform *hashed lookups* of data without the need to implement specific code. Most of the code runs entirely in C code, which means that performance is good.

dictionary.c

```
#include <stdio.h>
#include <string.h>
#include <stdlib.h>
#include "Python.h"
```

```c
PyObject *rDict = NULL; /* Keep these global */
PyObject *instanceDict;
/*
**    Initializes the dictionary
**    Returns TRUE if successful, FALSE otherwise
*/
int
initDictionary(char *name)
{
   PyObject *importModule;
   int retval = 0;

   /*   **************** Initialize interpreter ******************   */
   Py_Initialize();

/* Import a borrowed reference to the dict Module   */
   if ((importModule = PyImport_ImportModule("dict")))
   {
        /* Get a borrowed reference to the dictionary instance */
        if ((instanceDict = PyObject_CallMethod(importModule, "Dictionary",
                              "s", name)))
        {
            /* Store a global reference to the dictionary */
            rDict = PyObject_GetAttrString(instanceDict, "dictionary");
            if (rDict != NULL)
                retval = 1;
        }
        else
        {
            printf("Failed to initialize dictionary\n");
        }
   }
   else
   {
        printf("import of dict failed\n");
   }
   return (retval);
}
/*
**    Finalizes the dictionary
**    Returns TRUE
*/
int
exitDictionary(void)
{
   /*   **************** Finalize interpreter ******************   */
   Py_Finalize();
   return (1);
}
/*
**    Returns the information in buffer (which caller supplies)
*/
void
getInfo(char *who, char *buffer)
{
```

```
        PyObject *reference;
        int    birthYear;
        int    deathYear;
        char *birthPlace;
        char *degree;
        *buffer = '\0';

        if (rDict)
        {
            if ((reference = PyDict_GetItemString( rDict, who )))
            {
                if (PyTuple_Check(reference))
                {
                    if (PyArg_ParseTuple(reference, "iiss",
                        &birthYear, &deathYear, &birthPlace, &degree))
                    {
                        sprintf(buffer,
                "%s was born at %s in %d. His degree is in %s.\n",
                        who, birthPlace, birthYear, degree);
                        if (deathYear > 0)
                            sprintf((buffer+strlen(buffer)),
                "He died in %d.\n", deathYear);
                    }
                }
            }
            else
                strcpy(buffer, "No information\n");
        }
        return;
    }

    main()
    {
        static char  buf[256];
        initDictionary("Not Used");
        getInfo("Michael Palin", buf);
        printf(buf);
        getInfo("Spiny Norman", buf);
        printf(buf);
        getInfo("Graham Chapman", buf);
        printf(buf);
        exitDictionary();
    }
```

(5)

(6)

(7)

Code comments

(1) This example is meant to represent a long-term lookup service, so we hang on to the references from call to call to reduce overhead.

(2) We import the module dict.py. The PyImport_ImportModule call is entirely analogous to the Python statement import dict.

(3) We create an instance of the dictionary using PyObject_CallMethod. Now, although instantiating a class is not really calling a method, Python's implementation makes it a method call in effect. Here is the short Python module, dict.py:

```
class Dictionary:
    def __init__(self, name=None):
        self.dictionary = {
                'Graham Chapman':   (1941, 1989, 'Leicester', 'Medicine'),
                'John Cleese':      (1939, -1, 'Weston-Super-Mare', 'Law'),
                'Eric Idle':        (1943, -1, 'South Shields', 'English'),
                'Terry Jones':      (1942, -1, 'Colwyn Bay', 'English'),
                'Michael Palin':    (1943, -1, 'Sheffield', 'History'),
                'Terry Gilliam': (1940, -1, 'Minneapolis', 'Political Science'),
                }
```

4 Then we get the reference to `self.dictionary` and store it for later use.

5 `PyDict_GetItemString(rDict, who)` is equivalent to the statement:

```
tuple = self.dictionary[who]
```

6 This is a bit of paranoid code: we check that we really retrieved a tuple.

7 Finally, we unpack the tuple using the format string.

To compile and link you would use something like this (on Win32):

```
cl -c dictionary.c -I\pystuff\python-1.5.2\Include \
        -I\pystuff\python-1.5.2\PC -I.
link dictionary.obj \pystuff\python-1.5.2\PCbuild\python15.lib \
        -out:dict.exe
```

If you run dict.exe, you'll see output similar to figure 14.1.

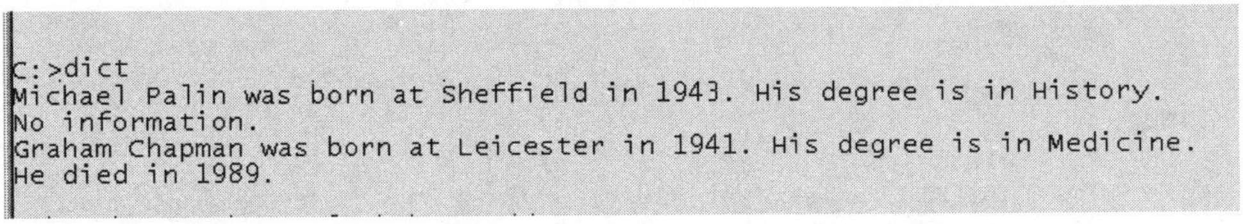

```
C:>dict
Michael Palin was born at Sheffield in 1943. His degree is in History.
No information.
Graham Chapman was born at Leicester in 1941. His degree is in Medicine.
He died in 1989.
```

Figure 14.1 Python embedded in a C application

14.8 *Summary*

You may never need to build a Python extension or embed Python in an application, but in some cases it is the only way to interface with a particular system or develop code economically. Although the information contained in this chapter is accurate at the time of writing, I suggest that you visit www.python.org to obtain information about the current release.

C H A P T E R   1 5

Debugging applications

Debugging is a tricky area. I know that I'm going to get some stern comments from some of my readers, but I'm going to make a statement that is bound to inflame some of them. Python is easy to debug if you insert `print` statements at strategic points in suspect code.

Not that some excellent debug tools aren't available, including IDLE, which is Python's emerging IDE, but as we shall see later there are some situations where debuggers get in the way and introduce artifacts.

In this chapter we will look at some simple techniques that really work and I'll offer some suggestions for readers who have not yet developed a method for debugging their applications.

15.1 Why print statements?

Debugging a simple Python program using a debugger rarely causes problems—you can happily single-step through the code, printing out data as changes are made, and you can make changes to data values to experiment with known values. When you are working with GUIs, networked applications or any code where timed events occur, it is difficult to predict the *exact* behavior of the application. This is why: for GUIs, a mainloop dispatches events in a particular timing sequence; for network applications there are timed events (in particular, *time-outs* which may be short enough to occur while single-stepping).

Since many of the applications that I have worked on have fallen into these categories, I have developed a method which usually avoids the pitfalls I have described. I say *usually* because even though adding print statements to an application only *slightly* increases the overall execution time, it still has an effect on CPU usage, ouput either to a file or stdout and the overall size of the code.

By all means try the tools that are available—they are very good. If you get results that have you totally confused, discouraged, or angry, try print statements!

15.2 *A simple example*

Many of the examples in this book use try ... except clauses to trap errors in execution. This is a good way of writing solid code, but it can make life difficult for the programmer if there are errors, since an error will cause Python to branch to the except section when an error occurs, possibly masking the real problem.

Python has one downside to testing a program: even though the syntax may be correct when Python compiles to bytecode, it may not be correct at runtime. Hence we need to locate and fix such errors. I have doctored one of the examples used earlier in the book to introduce a couple of runtime errors. This code is inside a try ... except clause with no defined exception; this is not a particularly good idea, but it does help the example, because it is really difficult to find the location of the error.

Let's try running debug1.py:

```
C:> python debug1.py
An error has occurred!
```

To add insult to injury, we still get part of the expected output, as shown in figure 15.1.

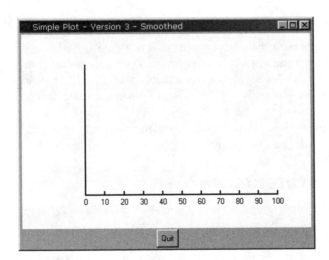

Figure 15.1 Debugging stage one

To start debugging, we have two alternatives: we can put `print` statements in the code to find out where we last executed successfully, or we can disable the `try ... except`. To do this, quickly edit the file like this:

```
        if 1:
#           try:
#----------Code removed-----------------------------------------
#           except:
#               print 'An error has occurred!'
```

Putting in the `if 1:` and commenting out the `except` clause means that you don't have to redo the indentation—which would probably cause even *more* errors. Now, if you run debug2.py, you'll get the following result:

```
C:> python debug2.py
Traceback (innermost last):
  File "debug2.py", line 41, in ?
    main()
  File "debug2.py", line 23, in main
    canvas.create_line(100,y,105,y, width=2)
NameError: y
```

So, we take a look at the section of code and see the following:

```
for i in range(6):
    x = 250 - (i + 40)
    canvas.create_line(100,y,105,y, width=2)
    canvas.create_text(96,y, text='%5.1f'% (50.*i), anchor=E)
```

Okay, it's my fault! I cut and pasted some of the code and left x as the variable. So I'll change the x to y and reinstate the `try ... except` (that's *obviously* the only problem!).

Now, let's run debug3.py:

```
C:> python debug3.py
```

No errors, but the screen is nothing like I expect—take a look at figure 15.2! Clearly the y-axis is not being created correctly, so let's print out the values that are being calculated:

```
for i in range(6):
    y = 250 - (i + 40)
    print "i=%d, y=%d" %(i, y)
    canvas.create_line(100,y,105,y, width=2)
    canvas.create_text(96,y, text='%5.1f'% (50.*i), anchor=E)
```

Now run debug4.py:

```
C:> python debug4.py
i=0, y=210
i=1, y=209
i=2, y=208
i=3, y=207
i=4, y=206
i=5, y=205
```

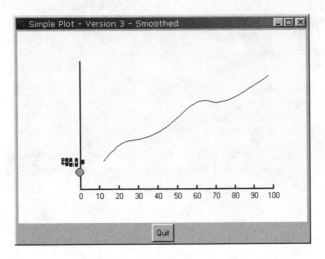

Figure 15.2 Debugging stage two

That's not what I meant! Decrementing 1 pixel at a time will not work!. If you look at the line of code before the `print` statement, you will see that I meant to *multiply* by 40 not just add 40. So let's make the changes and run debug5.py:

```
C:> python debug5.py
```

No errors, again, but not the result I expected (see figure 15.3) the "blobs" are supposed to be on the line. Let's look at the bit of code that's supposed to plot the points:

```
scaled = []
for x,y in [(12, 56), (20, 94), (33, 98), (45, 120), (61, 180),
        (75, 160), (98, 223)]:
    scaled.append(100 + 3*x, 250 - (4*y)/5)
```

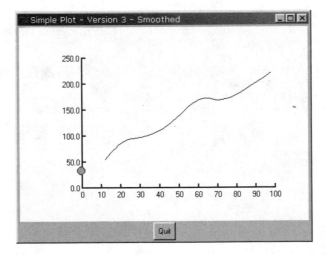

Figure 15.3 Debugging, stage three

That *looks* Okay, but let's check it out:

```
scaled = []
    for x,y in [(12, 56), (20, 94), (33, 98), (45, 120), (61, 180),
            (75, 160), (98, 223)]:
        s = 100 + 3*x, 250 - (4*y)/5
        print "x,y = %d,%d" % (s[0], s[1])
        scaled.append(s)
```

Now, run debug6.py:

```
C:> python debug6.py
x,y - 136,206
x,y - 160,175
x,y - 199,172
x,y - 235,154
x,y - 283,106
x,y - 325,122
x,y - 394,72
```

Yes, that looks right (blast!). We need to look further:

```
canvas.create_line(scaled, fill='black', smooth=1)

for xs,ys in scaled:
    canvas.create_oval(x-6,y-6,x+6,y+6, width=1,
                        outline='black', fill='SkyBlue2')
```

I'll save you any more pain on this example. Obviously it was contrived and I'm not usually so careless. I meant to use xs and xy as the *scaled* coordinates, but I used x and y in the canvas.create_oval method. Since I had used x and y earlier, I did not get a NameError, so we just used the *last* values. I'm sure that you will take my word that if the changes are made, the code will now run!

15.3 How to debug

The ability to debug is really as important as the ability to code. Some programmers have real problems in debugging failing code, particularly when the code is complex. The major skill in debugging is to *ignore the unimportant* and *focus on the important*. The secondary skill is to learn how to gain the major skill.

Really, you want to confirm that the code is producing the values you expect and following the paths you expect. This is why using print statements (or using a debugger where appropriate) to show the actual values of variables, pointers and the like is a good idea. Also, putting *tracers* into your code to show which statements are being executed can quickly help you focus on problem areas.

If you are proficient with an editor such as emacs it is really easy to insert debugging statements into your code. If you have the time and the inclination, you can build your code so that it is ready to debug. Add statements which are only executed when a variable has been set. For example:

```
...
if debug > 2:
    print('location: var=%d, var2=%s' % (var, var2)
```

Clearly, you could add more detail, timestamps and other data that may help you if you encounter problems when you start running your code. Planning for the need to debug is often easier at the time you write the code than when you have pressure to deliver.

15.4 *A Tkinter explorer*

In "Building an application" on page 18 I suggested a technique for hiding access to a debug window. This often works well, since you have immediate access to the tool, usually without restarting the application. I'm including an example here (the code is available online) which pops up if an error is output to `stderr`. Then you can look at the source, change variables in the `namespace` or even launch another copy of the application to check it out. Here are a series of screenshots:

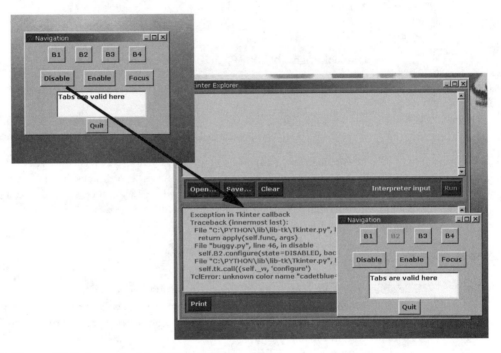

Figure 15.4 An embedded debug tool

Then, open up the source in the top window and look for the error:

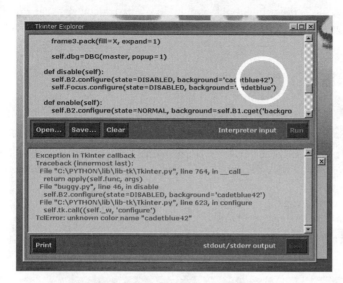

Figure 15.5 Locating the code error

If we correct the error and then click Run, we execute another copy of the application and we can see that the problem has been corrected. The window at the top-left-hand corner of figure 15.6 shows how this looks.

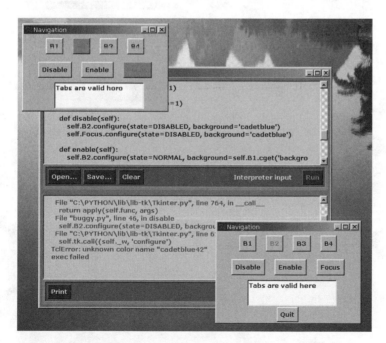

Figure 15.6 Executing a second version of the application

15.5 pdb

If you like to type, this is the debug tool for you! pdb is a basic debugger that will allow you to set breakpoints, get data values and examine the stack, to name but a few of its facilities. Its drawback is that you have to input a lot of data to get to a particular point of interest and when the time comes to do it again, you have to enter the information again!

This tool isn't for everyone, but if your debug style fits pdb, then it will probably work for you.

15.6 IDLE

IDLE is an emerging IDE for Python. It has some limitations which will reduce as time goes by and its usage increases. You can already see demands for various types of functionality on the Python news group. This will continue to grow as more users find out what is needed in the tool. Make sure that you obtain the latest code rather than using the code packaged in Python 1.5.2—many changes and bug fixes have been made recently.

I have included a screenshot of an IDLE session to give you an idea of what is provided. Try the tool and decide if it will meet your expectations.

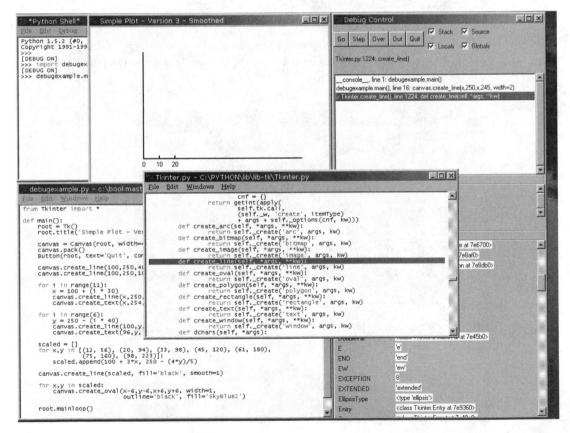

Figure 15.7 Debugging with IDLE

15.7 DDD

DDD is a graphic front-end debugger for a number of languages. It uses a modified version of pdb and has a wide range of support from programmers. Again, I have included an example session, and I leave it to you to decide if it will be useful to you!

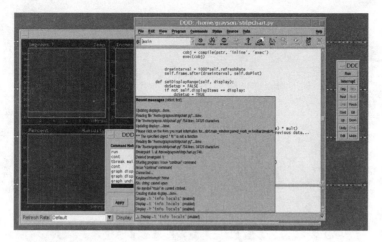

Figure 15.8 Debugging with DDD

C H A P T E R   1 6

Designing effective graphics applications

A graphical user interface has become an expected part of most applications which have direct communication with users. This chapter describes the essentials of good GUI design—but keep in mind that this area is highly subjective, of course. Some considerations of font and color schemes will be covered, along with size, ergonomic and other human factors. Finally, alternatives for GUI design will be suggested, introducing photo-realism, virtual reality and other emerging techniques.

Established standards for interface design are noted in the bibliography. Many companies have internal design standards which may be in conflict with established standards; the life of a GUI programmer is not always easy and aesthetics may succumb to standards in some cases.

If one thing should be selected as the major determinant of good GUI design, it is probably *simplicity*. An elegant interface will display the minimum information necessary to guide the user into inputting data and observing output. As we shall see, there may be cases where a little added complexity enhances an interface, but in general, *keep it simple*.

16.1 The elements of good interface design

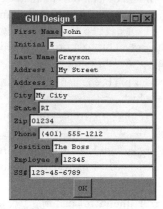

Figure 16.1 An inferior interface

User interfaces are really rather simple: display a screen, have the user input data and click on a button or two and show the user the result of their actions. This appears to be easy, but unless you pay attention to detail, the end user's satisfaction with the application can be easily destroyed by a badly designed GUI. Of course, appreciation of GUI's is highly subjective and it is almost impossible to satisfy everyone. We are going to develop a number of example interfaces in this chapter and examine their relative merits. The source code for the examples will not be presented in the text, but it is available online if you want to reproduce the examples or use them as templates for your own interfaces. You can see many more examples of Tkinter code throughout the book! If you do use the supplied source code, please make sure that only the *good* examples are used.

Take a look at the first GUI (figure 16.1). You may not believe me, but I have seen GUIs similar to this one in commercial applications. This screen does all that it is intended to do—and nothing more—but without any concern for the end user or for human factors. You may wish to examine this example again after we have discussed how to construct a better GUI.

Even though I said that this is an inferior GUI, this type of screen can be acceptable in certain contexts; if all that is needed is a simple screen to input debug information for an application, the amount of code necessary to support this screen is quite small. However, don't inflict this type of screen on an end user; especially if they are expected to pay money for it!

So let's take a quick look at the screen's faults before we determine how the screen could be improved.

1 Jagged label/entry boundary is visually taxing, causing the user to scan randomly in the GUI.

2 Poor choice of font: Courier is a fixed pitch serif font. In this case it does not have sufficient weight or size to allow easy visual scanning.

3 Although the contrast between the black letters and the white background in the entry fields is good, the contrast between the frame and the label backgrounds is too great and makes for a stark interface.

4 Crowded fields make it difficult for the user to locate labels and fields.

5 Fields have arbitrary length. This provides no clues to the user to determine the length of data that should be input.

6 Poor grouping of data: the Position, Employee # type of data have more to do with the name of the individual than the address of the individual and should be grouped accordingly.

Let's attempt to correct some of the problems with figure 16.1 and see if we can improve the interface. Figure 16.2 shows the result of changing some of the attributes of the GUI.

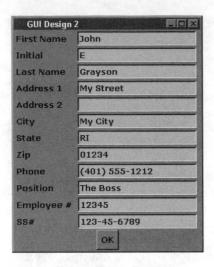

Figure 16.2   A better interface

1 This interface uses the grid manager; the previous interface used the pack manager (see "Grid" on page 86 for details of the geometry managers). This has corrected the jagged alignment of the labels and fields.

2 The font has been changed to a larger sans serif font which improves readability when compared to the previous example, but see "Choosing fonts" on page 343.

3 The background color of the entry fields has been changed to narrow the contrast between the labels and fields.

4 A small amount of padding has been applied around the fields to make scanning easier.

The interface is better, but it can still be improved more. Arranging the fields in logical groups and setting the size of some of the fields to an appropriate width will assist the user to fill in the information. Also, grouping some of the fields on the same line will result in a less vertically-linear layout, which fits scan patterns better since we tend to scan horizontally better than we scan vertically—that is how we learned to read, after all. This may not apply to cultures where printed characters are read vertically, however.

The next example implements the points discussed above.

The GUI in figure 16.3 is beginning to show signs of improvement since the fields are grouped logically and the width of the entries matches the data widths that they support. The Position entry has been replaced by a ComboBox (a Pmw widget) which allows the user to select from a list of available options (see figure 16.4).

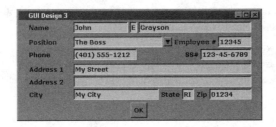

Figure 16.3 A GUI showing logical field grouping

We can improve the interface further by breaking appropriate fields into subfields. For example, social security numbers always have a 3-2-4 format. We can handle this situation in two ways:

1 Use three separate fields for each of the subfields.

2 Use a smart widget that automatically formats the data to insert the hyphens in the data. Smart widgets are discussed in "Formatted (smart) widgets" on page 117.

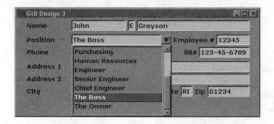

Figure 16.4   ComboBox widget

Figure 16.5 shows our example with the fields split into appropriate subfields.

Unfortunately, this change has now cluttered our interface and the composition is now rather confusing to the end user. We have to make a further adjustment to separate the logical field groups and to help the user to navigate the interface. In figure 16.6, we introduce whitespace between the three groups.

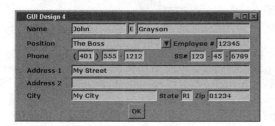

Figure 16.5   Splitting fields into sub-fields

This achieves the desired effect, but we can improve the effect further by drawing a graphic around each of the logical groups. This can be achieved in a number of ways:

1 Use available 3-D graphic relief options with containers. Tkinter frames allow `sunken`, `raised`, `groove` and `ridge`, for example.

2 Draw a frame around the group. This is commonly seen in Motif GUIs, usually with an accompanying label in the frame.

3 Arrange for the background color of the exterior of the frame to be displayed in a different color from the inside of the frame. Note that this kind of differentiation is suitable for only a limited range of interface types.

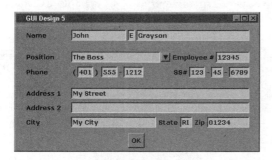

Figure 16.6 Separating logical groups with whitespace

Figure 16.7 illustrates the application of a 3-D graphic groove in the frame surrounding the grouped fields.

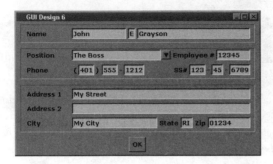

Figure 16.7 Logical groups framed with a 3-D graphic

16.2 *Human factors*

Extensive documents on Human Factor Engineering describe GUI design in scientific terms (see the Reference section). In particular, font choice may be based on calculating the arc subtended by a character from a point 20 inches from the character (the viewing position). While I have worked on projects where it was necessary to actually measure these angles to confirm compliance with specifications, it is not usually necessary to be *so* precise.

When designing an application that includes a GUI, you should consider the following human factors:

1 Ensure that the application meets the end user's expectations. If a paper system is currently being used, the GUI application should mimic at least some of that operation, for example.

2 Keep the interface simple and only request necessary data from the user; accordingly, only display pertinent data.

3 Select fonts that make the interface work effectively. Use as few different fonts as possible within a single screen.

4 Lay out the information in a logical sequence, grouping areas where appropriate, so that the user is led through the information in a smooth fashion, not jumping between key areas.

5 Use color sparingly and to achieve a specific purpose. For example, use color to highlight fields that must be entered by the user as opposed to optional fields.

6 Provide multiple navigation methods in the GUI. It is not always appropriate to require navigation to be mouse-based; tabbing from field to field within a form may be more natural to users than clicking on each field to enter data. Provide both so the user may choose.

7 Ensure consistency in your application. Function keys and control-key combinations should result in similar actions throughout a single application and between applications in a suite.

8 Some platforms may have GUI style guides that constrain the design. These should be adhered to, even if it means developing platform-specific versions.

9 Provide help wherever possible. *Balloon help** can be useful for beginning users but may be annoying to experts. Consequently it is important to provide the user with a means of turning off such facilities.

10 The UI should be intuitive so that it is not necessary to provide documentation. Careful field labeling, clues to input format and clear validation schemes can go a long way to achieve this goal.

11 Whenever possible, test the UI with end users. Building prototypes in Python is easy, so take advantage of this and get feedback from the target audience for your work.

16.2.1 Choosing fonts

Choosing an appropriate font for a GUI is important to ensure that an interface is effective. Readability is an important factor here. A font that is highly readable when displayed at a screen resolution of 640 x 480 may be too small to read when displayed at a resolution of 1024 x 768 or greater. The size of the font should, therefore, be either calculated based on the screen resolution or selected by the end user. However, in the latter case, you should ensure that the end user is given a range of fonts that the application can display without changing screen layouts or causing overflows, overlaps or other problems.

Font selection can be crucial to achieving an effective interface. In general, *serif* † fonts should be avoided. Most of us are used to reading serif fonts on printed material (in fact, the body of this book is set in Adobe Garamond, a font with a light serif) since we believe that we are able to recognize word forms faster in serif as opposed to sans serif fonts. Unfortunately, many serif fonts do not display as clearly on screens as they do when printed, since the resolution of most printers is better than that of displays.

Take a look at figure 16.8. This shows a screen grab, at 1024×768 resolution, of Times New Roman and Verdana fonts in three point sizes. The sans serif font results in a crisper image, although the overall width of the text is greater. In most cases, it is easier to select `Arial`.

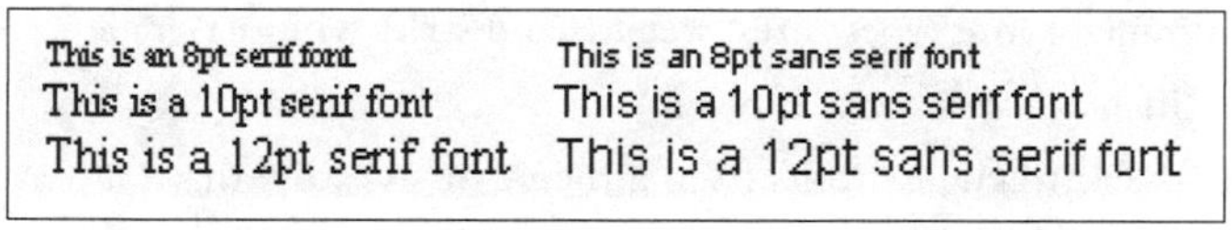

This is an 8pt serif font   This is an 8pt sans serif font
This is a 10pt serif font   This is a 10pt sans serif font
This is a 12pt serif font   This is a 12pt sans serif font

Figure 16.8 Comparing Serif and Sans Serif Fonts

---

* Balloon help is displayed when the cursor is placed over a field or control without moving it for a short time. The help may be displayed as a message in the status area of a window, if it has one, or in a popup balloon close to the field or control.

† A serif font is one in which each of the letters contain small artistic flourishes that appear to give the glyphs ledges and feet. Common serif fonts include Times, Bookman, Palatino, and Garamond. A sans serif font is one that does not contain these extra flourishes. Common sans serif fonts are Helvetica, Arial, Geneva, Gothic, and Swiss.

or `Verdana` for Windows and `Helvetica` for UNIX and MacOS, since these fonts are usually installed on their respective systems. Figure 16.9 illustrates these fonts.

This is Arial   **This Arial Bold**
This is Verdana   **This is Verdana Bold**
This is Switzerland **This is Switzerland Bold**

Figure 16.9   Arial, Verdana and Switzerland Fonts

Now let's take a look at what can happen if a font is selected that is just not meant to be used for a GUI. The fonts used in this GUI look great when printed, but when displayed on the screen, they produce the effect shown in figure 16.10. Although the weight of the font is adequate, it just does not look right on the screen.

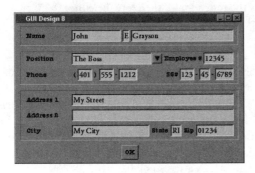

Figure 16.10 The effect of selecting the wrong font

In summary:

1 Choose sans serif fonts wherever possible.

2 Use a minimum of font types, sizes, weights and styles within a single screen.

3 Allow for different screen sizes, if possible.

4 If the user is able to choose fonts from a theme or style, use that font, even if the result offends aesthetics.

16.2.2   Use of color in graphical user interfaces

The process of selecting color schemes for a GUI is highly subjective. In many cases it is best to allow the end user complete control over the colors that will be used within an application. The current trend in systems (Windows and UNIX CDE) is to allow the user to select a theme or scheme and then apply the selected colors, extrapolating alternate colors as appropriate. If you design your GUI to look good using just shades of gray and then calculate colors based upon the user-selected scheme, the GUI will probably work well. That way the user is allowed the privilege to select bizarre combinations of colors; after all, who are we to judge?

The basic rules to be followed with color are these:

1 If you need to distinguish a graphic item, select color as the last method.

2 Use color to draw the user to the most important features on the screen.

3 Remember that your user might be color blind* and might not perceive color contrast in the same way as you do.

4 Create optimal contrast between your graphic components. You should avoid 100% contrast in most cases.†

5 Avoid reverse video (light on dark) except where you must draw attention to a graphic component. A good example of reverse video is to indicate a validation error in an input field.

As an illustration of how color selection can become a problem, take a look at figure 16.11. Although it is not possible to see the direct effect of color on the page, the color scheme chosen is quite pleasing, in warm tones of brown, olive green and cream. However, an application with GUIs implemented with these colors would prove tiring in practice, though it might look good for a short demonstration. The major problem is the use of low-contrast reverse video in the entry fields. Incidentally, the colors used in this application were adapted from a commercial application; I'm sure the designer was proud of the result that had been produced.

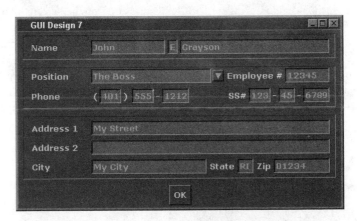

Figure 16.11 Problems with color combinations

---

* It is relatively easy to design color use to accommodate individuals with color-blindness. Do not use primary colors; mix each color with varying amounts of red, green, and blue so that the overall chrominance varies. The overall effect will not appear greatly different for individuals with normal color vision, but it will appear distinct for those with color blindness. If you have an application which is in a mission critical environment and might be used by individuals with color blindness, it may be prudent to have your GUI checked out by someone with less-than-perfect vision.

† Not all monitors display black on white as clearly as they display black on grey (or some other light color combination). Try black on 90% gray, for example. (Note that 90% gray is really 90% white and 10% black).

16.2.3 Size considerations

Apart from the need to ensure that a GUI works at different screen resolutions, consideration must be made to determine whether the user is permitted to change the size of the displayed GUI. Having designed a well-proportioned screen, it can be difficult to allow the user to change the size of the display at will. In many cases it is better to disallow resizing of the screen rather than attempting to maintain an effective GUI regardless of what the user requests (see "Geometry methods" on page 307 for details about how to do this).

In the examples presented earlier in this chapter, resizing was handled by assigning one field on each line to stretch if the window was made larger. This is generally appropriate, but it may result in strange screen appearances. Shrinking a window is much harder to handle and may be impossible.

If the screen does not contain scrolled widgets (text, lists, etc.), it is probably better to fix the size of the window and maintain optimal layout.

16.3 Alternative graphical user interfaces

The elements of GUI design described above are appropriate for most applications, but a specific application might need to break the rules to achieve a desired effect. Let me present a case study. I was contracted to develop a crew-scheduling system for an airline's pilots. Most of the airline's administrators are, or have been pilots, so I wanted to design an interface that would have impact for such individuals. Figure 16.12 illustrates one of the screens that was delivered. This interface breaks many of the rules that have been presented above, but it was highly acclaimed by the airline. For readers who have not sat in the cockpit of an airplane, the interface is made to resemble a communication stack (radios) in an airplane. In this interface, the main displays utilize reverse video and a pixel font which is not uncommon in systems of this type. The panel is ray-traced to provide an extreme 3-D appearance (this technique was covered in "Virtual machines using POV-Ray" on page 232). Although it's not apparent in the black-and-white illustration, the interface contains many colored elements. Again, this is consistent with the systems that are being mimicked.

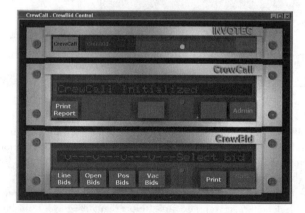

Figure 16.12 An interface for targeted users

CHAPTER 16 EFFECTIVE GRAPHICS APPLICATIONS

Here are some suggestions to help you choose an appropriate interface for an application:

1 If a manual system already exists for the application you are about to implement, and it uses paper forms, try to use elements of the system in the GUI. An order entry system would be a good example.

2 If the end user is familiar with a certain display and the application presents some aspects of that display, use familiar shapes, colors and navigation methods. The front-panel of a device controlled with SNMP is a good example.

3 If the application supports a device with a numeric keypad, and users are familiar with it or are trained to use the keypad, provide a graphical representation of the keypad in your interface. Maybe there will be a touch-screen in the future.

4 If the end user is used to interacting with a control panel, without a keyboard, consider how the user can navigate using methods which are natural to them; consider using touch-screen input, for example.

16.4 Summary

Some of the information in this chapter is somewhat subjective. Some fairly-well accepted rules are applied to human factor engineering which you should always consider when designing an application. Using tiny or huge fonts, for example, will immediately invoke a judgement by your user—you want your user to approve of your design. However, that does not mean that you *must* follow guidelines rigidly; some of the best user interfaces break some of the rules.

C H A P T E R   1 7

Programming for performance

Current computer systems have a great capability to support interpreter-based applications such as the Python/Tkinter applications that are presented in this book. This chapter provides both arguments to refute skeptical readers and evidence to support converted readers; it includes case studies to illustrate real-world applications. Since Tkinter is a good example of how effective C extensions to Python can be, I'll introduce extension-building methods to mitigate adverse performance for complex applications.

17.1 *Everyday speedups*

If you are conscientious, there is no reason for Python to perform badly. Unfortunately, you can do many things to guarantee that your application will not present the user with acceptable performance and responsiveness. However, you may be able to produce Python programs that rival the performance of compiled C++ if you work hard to avoid a number of key problem areas.

17.1.1 Program organization

You can do a number of things to make sure that your application performs well. Let's start with how you organize your code. Regardless of how you start your application and whether it is intended to run on UNIX, Win32 or MacOS, you need to make sure that the first bit of Python code is *short*. If you invoke the Python interpreter (on UNIX) using:

```
#! /usr/bin/env python
```

as the first line of a script on UNIX, all of the subsequent lines will be parsed and compiled every time you run your application. Although the script is translated to bytecode, no byte-code (.pyc or .pyo) file will be created. This means that you have to go through the parser each time you invoke your program. So, you must construct your application so that you parse the minimum number of Python statements each time you invoke the application. Let's suppose you have constructed your application to have a structure something like this:

```
from    Tkinter import *
from    tkSimpleDialog import Dialog
import tkMessageBox
import Pmw

class MyClass(Dialog):
  def body(self, master):
  ...

def amethod(self):
  ...

root = Tk()
instance = MyClass(root)
```

Sure, there aren't too many lines of code here, but *your* application might have thousands of lines. So, let's name the module myApplicationReal.py and change the last two lines to look like this:

```
def myApplicationReal():
  root = Tk()
  instance = MyClass(root)
```

Then, create a short Python script called myApplication, and insert the following lines:

```
#! /usr/bin/env python

import myApplicationReal
myApplicationReal.myApplicationReal()
```

This will use either myApplicationReal.pyc or myApplicationReal.pyo if they exist, or it will create them if they do not. This guarantees an improvement in start-up time for any large application. Incidentally, you can use the same file for Win32 also. If you construct a batch file called myApp.bat that contains the following lines, you can use the same module for UNIX and Win32:

```
python myApplication
```

Alternatively, you can pass a `.pyc` or `.pyo` file to the Python interpreter directly. On UNIX, the following script may be used:

```
#! /bin/sh
exec python script.pyo ${1+"$*"}
```

This technique may not be very effective for Win32 since the time taken to launch a batch file and start the Python interpreter may negate the increase in speed when using a `.pyo` file. However, if you set Explorer's file type to execute Python when a `.py` file is double-clicked, then you do not need a batch file at all.

17.1.2 Using the Python optimizer

If you invoke Python with the optimize command-line option set (`-O`), the compiler will generate optimized bytecode. This means that the bytecode is optimized to run faster. It does so by eliminating some of the bytecode instructions (eliminating SET_LINENO from function calls and suppressing `assert` statements). It really depends on how many function calls and `assert` statements are in your code. However, it is still worth using this option to increase your application's invocation speed even a few percentage points.

17.1.3 Examining code

Python has an unusual property: if you leave new code alone for a couple of days you can usually return to it and reduce its size. There are often opportunities to collapse code, flatten loops, or eliminate unnecessary operations. What you are doing is reducing the number of bytecode operations. This is generally possible without reducing the ability to maintain the code, so it is worth doing.

17.2 Tkinter performance

The performance of a GUI can make or break an application. Users have subconscious expectations about how fast something should happen. Even simple interfaces, such as you might see on an Automated Teller Machine (ATM), have response times set for various operations (usually feedback for every keypress, such as a beep or acknowledgment is less than two seconds and transactions are completed within ten seconds). Consistency is also important. If a GUI normally does something in one second, a user will often react adversely if it occasionally takes two or three seconds—often prompting them to repeat the button press or key entry.

However, never try to optimize an application before your application is running. What you think may be slow code might perform well in the final version. If a loop is only executed a small number of times, the effort to improve its performance may result in your overlooking more important problems.

17.2.1 Keep it short!

If you can reduce the number of lines of code in your program without reducing someone's ability to maintain it, then you will improve performance. Take a look at this simple example:

```
self.label = Label(frame, text='Password:', fg='black')
self.label.pack(side=LEFT, padx=10)
```

If you do not need to keep the instance of the label around, because you are not going to change its content, background color or other attributes, you can allow Tkinter to create an internal instance for you:

```
Label(frame, text='Password:', fg='black').pack(side=LEFT, padx=10)
```

17.2.2 Eliminate local variables

Another thing to watch for is local variables being unnecessarily assigned, particularly if this occurs within a loop (this is not an important factor if it occurs only once). This is particularly important if you are going to create many attribute variables in an instance. If you don't intend to use them again, don't create them. By scanning your code you may occasionally find an opportunity to save a few CPU cycles. Of course, this applies to regular Python programs, too. Take a look at this code:

```
...
localx = event.x
localy = event.y

...
canvas.create_text(localx, localy, text='here', ...)
```

The intent was good, but if you do not need to reuse the data, collapse the code:

```
...
canvas.create_text(event.x, event.y, text='here', ...)
```

However, local variables are not all bad. If you have an invariant subexpression or attribute reference within a loop, it may pay to take a local copy before entering the loop. Compare:

```
for i in range(30):
    self.list[i] = (self.attr2 * i) + self.attr2
```

with:

```
l = self.list
a1 = self.attr1
a2 = self.attr2
for i in range(30):
    l[i] = (a1 * i) + a2
```

17.2.3 Keep it simple

This point may be *too* obvious, but remember that a simple GUI usually initializes faster and consumes fewer system resources. Some programmers (particularly if they are true engineers) have a tendency to design GUIs for complex systems that expose every possible variable-data item within the system in a few dense screens. If you arrange the data in several screens, with just a few highly-related items in each, the application will respond faster for the user even though the underlying code still has to perform the same operations.

Avoid ripple in your applications if at all possible (ripple was introduced on page 154). Badly-designed interdependence between fields can consume a lot of system resources and the user will find it has limited value.

17.2.4 Fast initialization

It is important that your screens are drawn as quickly as possible. Users often judge an application by its response times; in some cases, flawless applications are viewed as *buggy* if the users experience long delays with no apparent progress after they have selected an operation. In some of the examples, I've included comments about delaying the packing of Frame widgets until the widgets contained within them have been completed. The purpose of doing this is to prevent the negotiation, which is inherent in the way that the geometry managers operate, from happening on-screen every time a new widget is added. If you delay the negotiation until all widgets have been created, you will see much better performance at startup

17.2.5 Throttling events

Window systems generate a lot of events for certain types of actions. Two such actions are moving the mouse and holding down the SHIFT key (if your system is configured to auto-repeat held keys). Try running Example_6_2.py and try those actions—you may be surprised at the rate at which the events are generated. If all you are interested in is the x/y location of the mouse and little computation is being triggered, then it is not a problem. However, if each event triggers redrawing a complex object, then you may have a performance problem.

You can do a number of things to handle a high rate of arrivals:

1 *Throttle* the events so that the code responds to fewer occurrences; this may be done using a timer so that updates are performed every few hundred milliseconds, for example. Alternatively, you may use a *counter*, so that every ten events are processed, as an example. The latter method is more difficult to implement and it usually requires a combination of a timer and a counter.

2 Reduce the drawing overhead. If the events are the result of a mouse drag, for example, you may be able to simplify what is drawn until the mouse is released. As an example, draw an outline or ghost of the object while the drag is in progress.

3 Suppress unrelated events. For example, dragging an object may cause a number of events to be generated as you cross other objects. Unless they are related to the drag, they might as well be ignored.

17.3 *Python techniques*

One or two techniques have already been suggested in "Everyday speedups" on page 348. In this section, we'll look at some Python-specific coding methods that usually result in more efficient code. However, before you go into every application that you've written already, be aware that you should not make changes unless there are grounds to do so. If you don't see a problem, don't correct it! See "Application profiling" on page 357 to learn how you can identify bottlenecks in your applications. If this technique identifies places to improve your code, then go ahead.

Most of the suggestions in this section are pretty straightforward. You may also find useful suggestions by reading the Python news group (see "Python News Group" on page 626).

17.3.1 Importing modules

You can execute an `import` statement almost anywhere in your program. Conventionally, most `import` statements occur at the start of the program. Sometimes you may want to delay the import of a module that is required infrequently until there is a need for it. Python handles repeated imports of the same module properly, but there is a slight cost when this occurs. If possible, avoid repeatedly importing the same module. Let's look at a hypothetical example:

Example_17_1.py

```
import time
start = time.time()

def splitter():
  import string
  list = string.split('A B C D E F G H', ' ')

for i in range(123456):
  splitter()

print time.time() - start
```

Compare this with:

Example_17_2.py

```
import time
import string

start = time.time()

def splitter():
  list = string.split('A B C D E F G H', ' ')

for i in range(123456):
  splitter()

print time.time() - start
```

If you run Example_17_1.py and then Example_17_2.py a few times, you will find that Example_17_2.py runs more than twice as fast as Example_17.1.py. By the way, don't try to do an `if not stringLoaded: import string; stringLoaded = TRUE` construct within the `splitter` function. It will not work because of scoping; the `string` module reference gets removed each time the function returns.

17.3.2 Concatenating strings

Until recent releases of Python, the documentation did not spell out the use of formatted strings, so strings were frequently concatenated like this:

```
longString = part1 + ' ' + part2 + ' ' + part3
```

It's more efficient to do this with formatted strings:

```
longString = '%s %s %s' % (part1, part2, part3)
```

It is *much* faster, because all of the work happens in C code. Depending on the type of concatenation you are doing, you should see at least 25 percent improvement using format strings.

17.3.3 Getting nested loops right

This point has been mentioned before, and most seasoned programmers have encountered this issue at least once, but it is still worth mentioning again. When you have to iterate over a multi-dimensional object, make sure that the less-rapidly changing index is to the *outside* of the loop. Let's look at a two-dimensional array with 100 columns and 25,000 rows. It really does matter which way you access it:

```
l = []
for row in range(25000):
    for col in range(100):
        l.append('%d.%d' % (row, col))
```

runs about 20 percent slower than:

```
l = []
for col in range(100):
    for row in range(25000):
        l.append('%d.%d' % (row, col))
```

However Guido van Rossum showed me this trick which beats that one by *another* 20 percent:

```
rowrange = range(100)
for col in range(25000):
    for row in rowrange:
        l.append('%d.%d' % (row, col))
```

This achieves the performance boost because integers in the range -1 to 100 are cached and are considerably faster. 25000 loops from 0 to 99 result in 24999 integer allocations, whereas 100 loops from 0 to 24999 result in 100*24999 allocations.

17.3.4 Eliminate module references

Every time you use a module reference, you incur a small overhead. If the references are within a loop, then some benefits can be gained. Contrast:

```
import time, string
start = time.time()

for i in range(5000):
    strtime = time.asctime(time.localtime(time.time()))
    lname = string.lower('UPPER')

print time.time() - start
```

with:

```
import time, string
start = time.time()

asct      = time.asctime
ltime     = time.localtime
now       = time.time
lower     = string.lower
for i in range(5000):
    strtime = asct(ltime(now()))
    lname = lower('UPPER')

print time.time() - start
```

Although the second form has more code, it runs a little faster. In a real application with reasonable constructs, the improvement can be worthwhile.

17.3.5 Use local variables

Now, there's a contradiction! Earlier I was encouraging you not to use local variables, but if you do it right, you can get another performance boost, because *local* variables are accessed faster than *global* variables.

If we recode the last example to use a function so that the variables are local, we see another small performance boost:

```
import time, string
start = time.time()

def local():
    asct      = time.asctime
    time      = time.localtime
    now       = time.time
    lower     = string.lower

    for i in range(20000):
        strtime = asct(ltime(now()))
    lname = lower('UPPER')
ocal()
print time.time() - start
```

Similarly, you may improve performance if you do a method lookup outside a loop. Compare:

```
r = []
for item in biglist:
    r.append(item)
```

with:

```
r = []
a = r.append
for item in biglist:
    a(item)
```

You can get similar speedups by caching built-in functions (such as `len`) or globals (such as other functions defined in the same modules) in local variables.

17.3.6   Using exceptions

The *exception* mechanism can be a valuable tool to improve performance. Although Python release 1.5.2 has now superseded the following tip by adding new functionality, the principle still applies.

This example looks at using dictionaries. Dictionaries are valuable Python tools since they usually give applications a program boost when there is a need to access data using a *key*. However, dictionaries used to have a problem: if you tried to access a dictionary entry that did not exist, you got a `KeyError`. This required programmers to check whether keys existed using:

```
if dictionary.has_key(key):
    ...
```

If the key *usually* exists, it is generally better to use an exception to trap occasional KeyErrors:

```
try:
    value = dictionary[key]
except KeyError:
    doErrorStuff()
```

In the current version of Python, you may not need to do any of this; use the `get` dictionary method:

```
value = dictionary.get(key, value_to_use_if_not_defined)
```

17.3.7   Using map, filter and reduce

Python supports three built-in functions which allow lists to be manipulated. The advantage of using these functions is that you push much of the looping overhead into C code, with an attendant improvement in performance.

`map(function, sequence)` applies `function` to each item in the list and returns the resultant values in a new list. Here is a simple example that changes all *Y* characters to *K*s in a list of strings:

```
from string import maketrans, translate

def Y2K(instr):
    return translate(instr, maketrans('yY', 'kK'))

list = ['thirty', 'Year 2000', 'century', 'yellow']
print map(Y2K, list)

C:> python map.py
['thirtk', 'Kear 2000', 'centurk', 'kellow']
```

You can also use map to combine several lists into a list of tuples. Using the previous example:

```
print map(None, list, map(Y2K, list))
```

```
C:> python map.py
[('thirty', 'thirtk'), ('Year 2000', 'Kear 2000'), ('century', 'centurk'),
('yellow', 'kellow')]
```

filter(function, sequence) returns a sequence that contains all items for which function returned true. Here is a simple example that selects any item that ends in a seven or is divisible by seven:

```
def func(n):
    return `n`[-1] == '7' or ( n % 7 == 0 ) # Cocoricos!

print filter(func, range(1,50))

C:> python filter.py
[7, 14, 17, 21, 27, 28, 35, 37, 42, 47, 49]
```

Finally, reduce(function, sequence) returns a single item constructed by successively applying two items in the sequence as arguments to function. It is very useful as a means of summing a sequence of numbers. We can extend the previous example like this:

```
...
def sum(n1, n2):
    return n1 + n2

seq = filter(func, range(1,50))
print reduce(sum, seq)

C:> python reduce.py
135
```

You can even better the performance by replacing the sum function with operator.add. The operator module provides a set of functions, implemented in C, which correspond to the intrinsic Python operators:

```
import operator
# ....
print reduce(operator.add, seq)
```

However, it is important to note that map, filter, and reduce are generally *slower* than inline code when the function is a lambda expression or a function constructed expressly to be used by one of these methods.

17.4 Application profiling

Python has a basic profiling module which allows you to learn where bottlenecks occur in your code. If you do find a point in the code where you spend a lot of time, or execute frequently, you may have a candidate for improvement.

Using the profile module is quite easy and requires minimal changes to your code. Essentially, you have to invoke your application through the profiler. If your application was started by invoking a function start, you would only have to add two lines:

```
import profile
profile.run('start()')
```

When the application exits from start, the profiler prints a report on all the functions and execution times. Let's take a look at one of the earlier examples in the book. In "Speed drawing" on page 271, we developed a fractal program. This is highly compute-bound, but we can probably make some improvements. To profile the code, we just add the additional profiler statements:

```
if __name__ == '__main__':
    def start():
        fractal = Fractal()
        fractal.root.after(10, fractal.createImage())
        fractal.run()

import profile
profile.run('start()')
```

When you exit the application, a screenful of statistics fly by—you will have to redirect the output to read it! Part of the output is shown here:

```
655511 function calls (655491 primitive calls) in 419.062 CPU seconds
  Ordered by: standard name

  ncalls  tottime  percall  cumtime  percall filename:lineno(function)
       2    0.000    0.000    0.003    0.002 <string>:1(after)
       1    0.000    0.000    0.001    0.001 <string>:1(after_cancel)
       1    0.000    0.000    0.002    0.002 <string>:1(after_idle)
       1    0.000    0.000    0.001    0.001 <string>:1(bind)
       2    0.000    0.000    0.003    0.002 <string>:1(bind_class)
       1    0.000    0.000    0.000    0.000 <string>:1(focus_set)
       1    0.000    0.000   20.476   20.476 <string>:1(mainloop)
       1    0.000    0.000    0.001    0.001 <string>:1(overrideredirect)
       1    0.000    0.000    0.000    0.000 ImageDraw.py:24(__init__)
  214194   22.624    0.000   22.624    0.000 ImageDraw.py:34(setink)
       1    0.000    0.000    0.000    0.000 ImageDraw.py:39(setfill)
  214194   20.578    0.000   20.578    0.000 ImageDraw.py:51(point)
       1    0.152    0.152    0.152    0.152 ImageFile.py:194(_save)
       1    0.000    0.000    0.465    0.465 p_fractal.py:55(initData)
       1  287.474  287.474  394.599  394.599 p_fractal.py:65(createImage)
       1    0.135    0.135    0.135    0.135 p_fractal.py:8(getpalette)
  214194   49.528    0.000   92.730    0.000 p_fractal.py:96(pixel)
       0    0.000             0.000           profile:0(profiler)
```

You can see three routines that are called over 200,000 times each, and notice that almost all the time is spent in createImage (which is not surprising). However, there is really too much output in a default run to be very useful.

Fortunately, the profiler can also be run in a mode where the statistics are collected in a file which may be analyzed at your leisure. You also have considerable control over the output format. To illustrate this, we need to make a small modification. In this case we will print the entries for the 20 top cumulative times:

```
import profile
profile.run('start()', 'profile_results')

import pstats
p = pstats.Stats('profile_results')
p.sort_stats('cumulative').print_stats(20)
```

Now, when we run p_fractal.py again, we get the following output when the application exits:

```
Tue Oct 05 12:14:25 1999    profile_results
        655779 function calls (655759 primitive calls) in 374.967 CPU seconds
   Ordered by: cumulative time
   List reduced from 289 to 20 due to restriction <20>
    ncalls  tottime  percall  cumtime  percall filename:lineno(function)
         1    0.003    0.003  374.969  374.969 profile:0(start())
         1    0.000    0.000  374.966  374.966 python:0(279.C.32)
         1    0.000    0.000  374.966  374.966 p_fractal.py:116(start)
         1  271.083  271.083  366.943  366.943 p_fractal.py:65(createImage)
    214194   47.581    0.000   87.823    0.000 p_fractal.py:96(pixel)
    214194   21.319    0.000   21.319    0.000 c:\py15\PIL\ImageDraw.py:34(setink)
    214194   18.923    0.000   18.923    0.000 c:\py15\PIL\ImageDraw.py:51(point)
         1    0.000    0.000    5.590    5.590 c:\Bookmaster\examples\common\AppShell.py:296(run)
         1    0.000    0.000    5.590    5.590 c:\Bookmaster\examples\common\AppShell.py:291(main)
         1    0.000    0.000    5.589    5.589 <string>:1(mainloop)
         1    5.264    5.264    5.589    5.589 c:\py15\lib-lib-tk\Tkinter.py:486(mainloop)
       489    0.345    0.001    5.301    0.011 c:\Bookmaster\examples\common\ProgressBar.py:50(update)
       488    0.072    0.000    5.288    0.011 c:\Bookmaster\examples\common\AppShell.py:248(updateProgress)
       488    0.073    0.000    5.217    0.011 c:\Bookmaster\examples\common\ProgressBar.py:44(updateProgress)
         1    0.001    0.001    2.423    2.423 c:\Bookmaster\examples\common\AppShell.py:33(__init__)
      1467    0.381    0.000    1.950    0.001 c:\py15\lib-lib-tk\Tkinter.py:1222(itemconfigure)
      1956    1.841    0.001    1.841    0.001 c:\py15\lib-lib-tk\Tkinter.py:1058(_do)
   490/489    1.800    0.004    1.804    0.004 c:\py15\lib-lib-tk\Tkinter.py:449(update_idletasks)
         1    0.000    0.000    1.567    1.567 c:\py15\lib-lib-tk\Tkinter.py:1767(__init__)
         1    1.567    1.567    1.567    1.567 c:\py15\lib-lib-tk\Tkinter.py:1717(__init__)
```

If you take a look at the output, you can see the three drawing-related routines that we saw earlier. They are responsible for about 20 percent of the overall cumulative time, so you can see that little of anything we have control over will *really* improve this application. However, your application might have many more opportunities for improvement.

You may also use some very simple benchmarking techniques to determine if a piece of code may be optimized by taking a particular approach. You just have to time a sequence of code. For example:

```
import time
...
def function():
   ...

start = time.clock(); function(); print round(time.clock() - start, 3)
```

Always use `time.clock()` for benchmarking, since it provides CPU time, as opposed to elapsed time

17.5 *Python extensions*

In "Extending Python" on page 313, we looked at building Python extensions, primarily as a way of extending functionality. In the area of performance improvements, extensions can be used to replace interpreted Python with compiled C. You first need to profile your application, as shown above. If you find candidate routines, you may be able to rewrite them in C. Remember that some of the power of Python comes from its high-level constructs. Sometimes it is difficult to reproduce such facilities in C—in fact the C-code may end up being less efficient than Python.

There are, however, plenty of places where adding an extension module to alleviate a bottleneck is worthwhile. Moderate floating-point operations, trigonometric operations and matrix operations are good candidates. In certain cases, complex dictionary processes may be faster to implement as C-calling-Python rather than pure Python.

17.6 Summary

Remember the first rule of working on application performance: do *nothing* unless you, or your users, detect a problem. You can quickly expend a great deal of effort to get relatively insignificant improvements when the same time may be better spent on working on interface ergonomics. Your users will frequently find attention to details in the interface more rewarding. However, if you *do* find a performance problem, I hope that you find these suggestions helpful.

CHAPTER 18

Threads and asynchronous techniques

Applications frequently have a need to process actions as parallel tasks or to perform time-consuming operations. This chapter covers threads and other techniques that support background processing. This area of programming for Python and Tkinter poses special problems that must be solved to prevent system hangs and unexpected behavior. It is also a difficult area to debug, since problems usually occur when the system is running at full speed, outside of any debugger or without debug `print` statements.

18.1 Threading

Threads provide a means to allow multiple tasks, or threads, to share a global data space. Sometimes they are referred to as *lightweight processes*, but I think that can be a little misleading; if you regard threads as subprocesses of the same process, it might be easier to understand how they are related.

Python provides two threading interfaces. The `thread` module provides low-level primitives to facilities to control and synchronize threads. The `threading` module is a higher-level interface which is built on top of the `thread` module.

Using threads in a Python-only environment (without involving a GUI) can be quite straightforward. However, adding Tkinter (or CORBA or ILU) can introduce some special problems. Such systems rely on a mainloop to dispatch events received from a number of stimuli, and threads can complicate the design of your code dramatically.

18.1.1 Non-GUI threads

Let's begin by looking at a simple example which does *not* involve a GUI, or at least not directly. This example is a skeleton for a server which accepts a number of requests to process data (the requests may come from a client with a GUI). In particular, the requestors do not expect to get data returned to them, or at most they accept a success/failure return code.

thread1.py

```
import thread, time

class Server:
    def __init__(self):
        self._dispatch = {}
        self._dispatch['a'] = self.serviceA         ❶
        self._dispatch['b'] = self.serviceB
        self._dispatch['c'] = self.serviceC
        self._dispatch['d'] = self.serviceD

    def service(self, which, qual):                 ❷
        self._dispatch[which](qual)

    def serviceA(self, argin):                       ❸
        thread.start_new_thread(self.engine, (argin,'A'))

    def serviceB(self, argin):
        thread.start_new_thread(self.engine, (argin,'B'))

    def serviceC(self, argin):
        thread.start_new_thread(self.engine, (argin,'C'))

    def serviceD(self, argin):
        thread.start_new_thread(self.engine, (argin,'D'))

    def engine(self, arg1, arg2):                    ❹
        for i in range(500):
            print '%s%s%03d' % (arg1, arg2, i),      ❺
            time.sleep(0.0001)
        print

server = Server()

server.service('a', '88')       # These calls simulate receipt of
server.service('b', '12')       # requests for service.
server.service('c', '44')
server.service('d', '37')

time.sleep(30.0)                                     ❻
```

Code comments

1 The constructor creates a simple dispatch dictionary that will be used to select a particular method to be called.

2 The `service` method is the dispatcher for this skeleton server. Naturally, a real implementation would be more complex.

3 Each of the four service methods start the same method in a new thread, passing the input argument and an identifier.

```
def serviceA(self, argin):
    thread.start_new_thread(self.engine, (argin,'B'))
```

Note that `start_new_thread` expects arguments to the method to be supplied as a tuple.

4 The example service engine is pretty simple; it just loops and prints to `stdout`.

5 The call `time.sleep(0.0001)` is important because it ensures that the thread blocks for a very short time, allowing other threads to run. See below for further notes on this subject.

6 The call to `time.sleep` as the final line of the example is also very important for reasons that will be explained below.

If you run thread1.py, you'll see output to `stdout` which should look something like figure 18.1. The output is ugly, but it can be used to illustrate a few points about threads and the way that the code layout can affect behavior.

Figure 18.1 Output from running thread1.py

This example starts four threads that loop 500 times, printing a few characters in each iteration. Depending on the way that the scheduler is implemented for the operating system in use, each process will receive a finite timeslice in which to execute. In a non-threaded system, doing input/output operations will suspend the process until the operation completes, thereby allowing other processes to run. With threads, we have a similar situation except that other threads within the process run when a thread does I/O. However, printing to stdout does not qualify as blocking I/O (at least when running simple Python scripts), so the thread continues to process instructions until it ends its timeslice or actually does some blocking I/O.

If you look at the fragment of output shown in figure 18.1, you will see that when the example is run with the short sleep after each print, we switch to the next thread and do one print. The result is that the output cycles in blocks of four prints, one from each thread, as shown within the gray boxes in figure 18.1.

```
12B492 44C492 37D492 88A493 12B493 44C493 37D493
495 12B495 44C495 37D495 88A496 12B496 44C496 37D4
88A498 12B498 44C498 37D498 88A499 12B499 44C499
```

Figure 18.2 Effect of running threads with a sleep after each print

If you remove the time.sleep call after the print statement, you will change the example's runtime behavior. Running the example again will produce output similar to the fragment shown in figure 18.3. Notice how one of the threads has completed the loop during a timeslice and that the next thread outputs characters sequentially.

```
12B484 12B485 12B486 12B487 12B488 12B489 12B490
495 12B496 12B497 12B498 12B499
6 88A347 88A348 88A349 88A350 88A351 88A352 88A35
```

Figure 18.3 Effect of running threads without sleeping after each print

The last time.sleep call is very important. There is no mainloop in this program since there is no GUI; if you omit the sleep, the main thread will exit, and the child threads will be killed. This problem can be infuriating when you first start programming threads. Nothing seems to work and until you realize that the main thread is just exiting, you will run the application repeatedly—sometimes getting variable results.

Now, this very simplistic example relies on the fact that data sharing between the threads is not an issue. In fact, we're lucky that it works at all. If you look at the engine method, you'll notice the for loop. The controlled variable, i, might appear to be shared between the threads, but in reality it is not; each thread creates a new reference to the controlled variable, since local variables on a thread's stack are thread-local. It is probably not a good idea to rely on such features to build threaded applications—there are too many rules to be followed and broken.

The problem, stated simplistically, is that you cannot predict when a thread will get *preempted** and if this happens when you're halfway through a series of instructions which make

---

* When a running process is stopped to allow another process to run (a *process exchange*), it is normally refered to as having been "preempted."

up an *atomic** operation, the result of another thread executing the same code path can be disastrous. If it is important that threads maintain *atomic* operations, you need to use *locks* (*semaphores* or *mutexes*†) to prevent another thread from gaining access to shared data. You can find some examples of locking in the standard Python distribution in the Demo/threads directory.

18.1.2 GUI threads

The decision to use threads with a GUI must be made with some caution. In general, a system that uses threads must ensure that the GUI is updated from within the main thread, which includes the mainloop. The following example is an adaptation of wpi.py, of one of the threading examples in the standard Python distribution. The example has a main thread which creates a GUI and starts the mainloop, and a thread which continuously calculates successive digits of pi. In addition, the example uses Tkinter's event loop to update the GUI periodically.

thread2.py

```
# Display digits of pi in a window, calculating in a separate thread.
# Compare with wpi.py in Demo/threads/wpi.py.

import sys
import time
import thread
from Tkinter import *

class ThreadExample:
   def __init__(self, master=None):
        self.ok            = 1
        self.digits        = []
        self.digits_calculated = 0
        self.digits_displayed  = 0
        self.master        = master

        thread.start_new_thread(self.worker_thread, ())        ❶

        self.frame = Frame(master, relief=RAISED, borderwidth=2)
        self.text = Text(self.frame, height=26, width=50)
        self.scroll = Scrollbar(self.frame, command=self.text.yview)
        self.text.configure(yscrollcommand=self.scroll.set)
        self.text.pack(side=LEFT)
        self.scroll.pack(side=RIGHT, fill=Y)
        self.frame.pack(padx=4, pady=4)
        Button(master, text='Close', command=self.shutdown).pack(side=TOP)

        self.master.after(100, self.check_digits)             ❷

   def worker_thread(self):
        k, a, b, a1, b1 = 21, 41, 11, 121, 41
        while self.ok:
```

---

* Atomic operations complete in their entirety before any other process or thread can follow the same code path.

† Mutual exclusion locks.

```
            # Next approximation
            p, q, k = k*k, 21*k+11, k+11
            a, b, a1, b1 = a1, b1, p*a+q*a1, p*b+q*b1
            # Print common digits
            d, d1 = a/b, a1/b1
        while d == d1:
            self.digits.append(`int(d)`)
            a, a1 = 10l*(a%b), 10l*(a1%b1)
            d, d1 = a/b, a1/b1
        time.sleep(0.001)                              ❸

    def shutdown(self):                                ❹
        self.ok =0
        self.master.after(100, self.master.quit)

    def check_digits(self):
        self.digits_calculated = len(self.digits)
        diff = self.digits_calculated - self.digits_displayed
        ix = self.digits_displayed
        for i in range(diff):
            self.text.insert(END, self.digits[ix+i])
        self.digits_displayed = self.digits_calculated
        self.master.title('%d digits of pi' % self.digits_displayed)

        self.master.after(100, self.check_digits)      ❺

root = Tk()
root.option_readfile('optionDB')
example = ThreadExample(root)
root.mainloop()
```

Code comments

❶ The worker_thread, which continuously updates digits of pi, is started up as before, with start_new_thread.

❷ We are using after to place a timed event on the event queue. Using this technique allows a delay without blocking the mainloop.

❸ Again, a small sleep is added at the end of the worker_thread's loop to ensure that the mainloop gets to spin (see below for more detail).

❹ To ensure an orderly shutdown of the application, we set the ok flag, which will cause the worker_thread to exit and wait for 100 ms before killing the GUI. A more realistic application might need additional methods.

❺ after events are one-shot events; you must put an event back on the queue if the timed event is to be repetitive.

If you run thread2.py, you will see a screen similar to figure 18.4. Digits are appended to the text widget at approximately 100ms intervals. You may wish to experiment and comment out the sleep in the worker_thread. When you run the code, you will see that the application takes much longer to respond to a click on the Close button—the worker_thread gets a complete timeslice to run before getting suspended, so the event queue for GUI events gets drained less frequently.

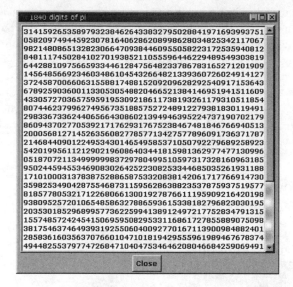

Figure 18.4 Threaded GUI application

With one thread going, we can try adding another thread. Since this example is not really very useful directly, we can make it do something pretty useless to illustrate multiple threads. We'll just change the color of the Close button every 100 milliseconds with random colors. Here are the changes that have to be made to the code:

thread3.py

```
import time, thread, random
from Tkinter import *

class ThreadExample:
  def __init__(self, master=None):
# --------Code Removed-------------------------------------------------

      self.btn.pack(side=TOP, pady=5)

      thread.start_new_thread(self.worker_thread2, ())

      self.master.after(100, self.check_digits)

  def worker_thread1(self):
# --------Code Removed-------------------------------------------------

  def worker_thread2(self):
      while self.ok:
          self.btn.configure(background=self.color())
          time.sleep(0.1)

  def color(self):
      rc = random.choice
      return '#%02x%02x%02x' % (rc(range(0,255)), rc(range(0,255)),
                      rc(range(0,255)))

# --------Code Removed-------------------------------------------------
```

There are two points to note: The second thread is started *after* the widgets have been created. If the thread had been started at the same time as the first thread, the Close button would not have been created. This would have prevented the second thread from running, but it would not have caused an application failure. This important feature of threading may be used to your advantage in designing applications if it's used reasonably. Also note that the 100 ms sleep in worker_thread2 is used to time the period of the thread and not just to release the thread.

If you run thread3.py, you will see the same basic screen which is displayed by running thread2.py, but the Close button will change color rapidly.

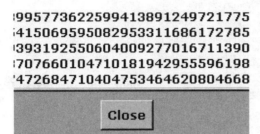

Figure 18.5 **Random color changes in a thread**

Python provides a higher-level interface, threading, which takes care of many of the details of getting threads to cooperate. It also removes the need to add sleep calls to make sure that threads release control to other threads. To illustrate how this may be used, we can convert thread3.py to the threading module.

thread4.py

```
from threading import *

class ThreadExample:
    def __init__(self, master=None):
        self.ok         = 1
# --------Code Removed-------------------------------------------------
        self.master     = master

        self.thread1= Thread(target=self.worker_thread1)      ➊
        self.thread2= Thread(target=self.worker_thread2)

# --------Code Removed-------------------------------------------------

        self.master.after(100, self.check_digits)
        self.thread1.start()                                  ➋
        self.thread2.start()

    def worker_thread1(self):
# --------Code Removed-------------------------------------------------
###     time.sleep(0.001)                  ➌

# --------Code Removed-------------------------------------------------
```

Code comments

1 We create a thread object for each of the worker threads. Note that this does not *start* the thread; that must be done later.

2 Once the GUI has been created, we start the threads.

3 Note that the short `sleep` in `worker_thread1` has been commented out.

If you run thread4.py, you will see output similar to thread3.py. Interestingly, the `threading` implementation runs 30 percent faster than the `thread` version.

18.2 "after" processing

The `after` method has been used frequently in examples, including the `threading` examples above, to provide simple alarm callbacks. For X window programmers, `after` is similar to `XtAppAddTimeOut`. `after_idle` is similar to `XtAppAddWorkProc`, which provides a simple mechanism to define a background task which is executed when there are no events in the event queue (with the exception of pending `after` events).

Here is a simple example which illustrates using `after_idle` to implement a busy cursor which is displayed when the system is processing a long operation. Before starting the operation, the application displays a `watch` cursor* and registers a work process. When the `after_idle` callback is invoked, the cursor changes back to the normal one.

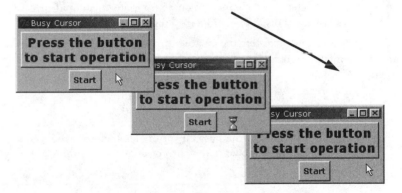

Figure 18.6 Using after_idle to implement a busy cursor

busy_cursor.py

```
import time
from Tkinter import *

class AfterIdleExample:
```

---

* On Win32, the `watch` cursor will display the current cursor selected for the `watch`.

```
        def __init__(self, master=None):
            self.master      = master
            self.frame = Frame(master, relief=RAISED, borderwidth=2)
            Label(self.frame, text='Press the button\nto start operation').pack()
            self.frame.pack(padx=4, pady=4)
            Button(master, text='Start', command=self.startOP).pack(side=TOP)

        def startOP(self):
            self.displayBusyCursor()
            time.sleep(10.0)  # simulate a long operation

        def displayBusyCursor(self):
            self.master.configure(cursor='watch')                        ❶
            self.master.update()
            self.master.after_idle(self.removeBusyCursor)                ❷


        def removeBusyCursor(self):
            self.master.configure(cursor='arrow')                        ❸

root = Tk()
root.option_readfile('optionDB2')
root.title('Busy Cursor')
AfterIdleExample(root)
root.mainloop()
```

Code comments

❶ displayBusyCursor changes the cursor to an appropriate cursor and then calls update to make sure that the cursor is displayed before the long operation starts.

❷ The after_idle method registers the removeBusyCursor which will be called when the event queue is empty. There is no opportunity for the mainloop to spin until after the sleep has ended.

❸ All that removeBusyCursor has to do is restore the cursor.

Note   In a full implementation, the busy cursor implementation would be more general so you should probably get the current cursor and store it so that you can restore the same cursor.

Another method can be used to process asynchronous operations. Unfortunately, in the current release of Tcl/Tk, this currently works only for UNIX. In Tk version 8.0, support for Win32 was suddenly withdrawn for createfilehandler which is equivalent to XtAppAddInput in the X Window world. It allows you to bind a callback which is run when a file-class operation occurs. This currently works for sockets. I would normally exclude a method which is exclusive to a particular operating system, but this one is useful enough to warrant inclusion.

Many applications have requirements to respond to an external event, such as receiving data on a socket. You have several choices in implementing a system, but normally you would choose either to block, waiting for input; or poll, on a periodic basis, until data is received. Now, when a GUI is involved, you clearly cannot block unless that occurs within a thread.

However, you may not be willing or able to use a thread or you may be running on a system which does not support threads. In this case, using `createfilehandler` provides a convenient mechanism.

As an illustration, we're going to look at a simple client/server which implements a time server. This might be used as some kind of monitor to make sure that critical components in an application are operating. Every minute, the server sends a timestamp on a given port. The client just displays this information in the example. To keep the code shorter, I've implemented the client and server in the same file:

client_server.py

```
from Tkinter import *
import sys, socket, time

class Server:
    def __init__(self):
        host = socket.gethostbyname(socket.gethostname())
        addr = host, 5000
        s = socket.socket(socket.AF_INET, socket.SOCK_DGRAM)
        s.bind('', 0)
        while 1:
            time.sleep(60.0)
            s.sendto(time.asctime(time.localtime(time.time())), addr)

class GUIClient:
    def __init__(self, master=None):
        self.master      = master
        self.master.title('Time Service Client')
        self.frame = Frame(master, relief=RAISED, borderwidth=2)
        self.text = Text(self.frame, height=26, width=50)
        self.scroll = Scrollbar(self.frame, command=self.text.yview)
        self.text.configure(yscrollcommand=self.scroll.set)
        self.text.pack(side=LEFT)
        self.scroll.pack(side=RIGHT, fill=Y)
        self.frame.pack(padx=4, pady=4)
        Button(master, text='Close', command=self.master.quit).pack(side=TOP)

        self.socket = socket.socket(socket.AF_INET, socket.SOCK_DGRAM)
        self.socket.bind('', 5000)

        tkinter.createfilehandler(self.socket, READABLE, self.ihandler)

        self.master.after(5000, self.doMark)

    def ihandler(self, sock, mask):
        data, addr = sock.recvfrom(256)
        self.text.insert(END, '%s\n' % data)

    def doMark(self):
        self.text.insert(END, 'waiting...\n')
        self.master.after(5000, self.doMark)

if len(sys.argv) < 2:
    print 'select -s (server) or -c (client)'
```

❶

❷

❸

```
        sys.exit(2)
if sys.argv[1] == '-s':
    server=Server()
elif sys.argv[1] == '-c':
    root = Tk()
    example = GUIClient(root)
    root.mainloop()
```

Code comments

❶ I've made very little mention of sockets in this book, and some readers may not be familiar with this facility. A brief mention here is warranted. Here we are setting up to send a message over a socket, which is a basic network facility available on most operating systems. Essentially, we connect to a numbered port on a particular host system, and then we send and receive messages using either the UDP (datagram) or TCP (stream) protocols. In this example we are using datagrams*.

❷ The client side of the example sets up a socket using the same port as the server, and then it registers the filehandler which will be called when one of three events occur on the socket. The possible values for the event mask are READABLE, which occurs when a socket receives data; WRITABLE, which occurs when a socket is written to and EXCEPTION, which occurs when any error occurs. We set up an after callback to write text to the window every five seconds.

❸ The handler for the file event is very simple. The mask argument specifies the type of file operation that resulted in the call, so a single handler could act for all types of file operations.

To run the example, first start the server as a separate process:

```
% python client_server.py -s &
```

Then start the client process:

```
% python client_server.py -c
```

Figure 18.7 shows the screen you can see when the example is run.

---

* The UDP protocol is a *connectionless* protocol in which packets are sent into the network for delivery to a particular host with a specified port. No confirmation is sent to the sender that the packet has been received and no mechanism for automatic retransmission of messages exists if there are problems. Thus, there is no guarantee that a datagram will be delivered to it's destination. Datagrams are normally used for noncritical messages, typically within a LAN to avoid costly connection overhead.

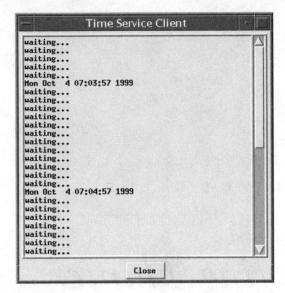

Figure 18.7 Time-server client

18.3 Summary

This chapter has been a minor introduction into the topic of threads and asynchronous techniques. In particular, the reader is directed to the Python documentation information on the `threading` module which provides a higher-level threading interface to the `thread` module shown here. There a many alternatives in this area and it really depends on the exact nature of your application to determine the best solution. The material here should serve as a simple introduction.

C H A P T E R   1 9

Distributing Tkinter applications

If you follow the Python news group for a few weeks, you will see at least one question being raised repeatedly: "How do I distribute Python applications?". In this chapter we will look at some options for UNIX and Win32. UNIX is relatively easy to handle, but Win32 has several possible solutions.

19.1 General issues in distributing applications

The main issue in distributing and installing a Python application is making sure that the end user has all of the components that are required for the application to run. You have several alternatives in deciding how to achieve this, but you first have to make sure that most of these components are present on the end user's system:

1 Python executable (*python, python.exe*).

2 Launcher for your application (*xxx* script for UNIX, *xxx.bat* for Win32).

3 Python shared-object files (*xxx.so*) for UNIX, dynamic load libraries (*xxx.dll*) for Win32.

4   Extension libraries (*Python/Lib/lib-dynload/xxx.[so|dll]*).

5   Python library files (*Python/Lib/xxx.py*).

6   Application-specific Python library files (*appropriate location*).

7   Tcl/Tk runtime (*Tcl/bin*, *Tcl/lib*, *Tk/bin*, */Tk/lib* etc.).

8   Pmw (*Python/Lib/Pmw*).

9   Any other extensions, data files, or databases that your application requires.

One decision you will have to make is whether you will handle the distribution of Python and/or Tcl/Tk separately, either leaving it to the end user to install these items independently, or distributing them with your application. In general, the latter method is preferable, since Python is still expanding in popularity and currently will not be installed on many of the end users' systems. Of course, we fully expect this to change in the future!

If you do decide to distribute Python and Tcl/Tk with your application, you have another decision to make—whether to install them *publicly* so that the end user has easy access to Python and/or Tcl/Tk, or *locally* so that they are accessed through your application. It is usually possible to install them publicly, although for Win32 it is often easier to use a local installation.

Finally, you must consider the architectures that your application is going to support. If you are targeting Win32 exclusively, then your task is quite simple. However, there are multiple UNIX architectures, which are normally supported by building from source. You probably do not want to be responsible for these builds, so you will have to consider supplying binaries for specific platforms. This is a totally different problem which requires careful consideration of both business and technical issues. It is beyond the scope of a short section such as this one..

19.2 *Distributing UNIX applications*

Supporting your application is usually a simple task once you have access to a built Python and Tcl/Tk. In general, UNIX end users are capable of building and installing both of these so you may be able to simply require your end users to take care of them. Then your application installation may be as simple as extracting files from a tar file and editing the users' environments appropriately. For the moment, let's assume that this is the case, so we will concentrate on getting your application up and running.

First, we need an executable to start your application. Our aim here is to use a minimal Python script to get into your application's main module (remember that a Python script will be interpreted every time you invoke it, so you want to keep the script simple; see "Everyday speedups" on page 348).

Here is an example of a minimal script:

```
#!/usr/bin/env python
import myapplication
myapplication.main()
```

There are some cases where you cannot use `#!/usr/bin/env python`, so you might have to give an explicit path such as `/usr/local/bin/python`. One small reminder: the space in the first form is meant to be there; it is not uncommon for UNIX folks to unconsciously translate the space into a slash. Next, you might need to add a little bit more to make this work. The script assumes that the environment variable PYTHONPATH has been set and it includes paths to .../Python/Lib and wherever MyApplication.py is installed. You may not want to modify the user's environment, but you can do that within your script:

```
#!/usr/bin/env python

import sys
sys.path.insert(0, '/opt/yourapp/lib')

import myapplication
myapplication.main()
```

Clearly some refinements can be made, but this scheme works well in practice.

19.3 *Distributing Win32 applications*

I think that this is much more problematic when compared to the UNIX case. You have several alternatives. I will advocate the simplest case, since the others do require interaction with the registry, which really implies that you will use an installation tool such as InstallShield, which automates the process of installing and registering the application components. More important, it perhaps makes provisions to install an *uninstaller* which removes the registry information and the installed files, usually without user intervention.

The decisions that have to be made for Win32 are similar to those for UNIX. The need to use a minimal script to get the application running is still present. The real problem is that Win32 will open an MS-DOS window when launching a Python script from a clickable file. With a little bit of encouragement, this can be avoided.

First, let's decide how we are going to package the application. For this example we will make a freestanding Win32 application, with everything that we need to support our application installed in a single directory (which can be called anything we wish). We are *not* going to make modifications to the registry and we want a single icon on the desktop which the user double-clicks to start the application.

Let's first take a look at the contents of the top-level directory, which is shown in figure 19.1. In this directory we have installed the Python executables (python.exe and pythonw.exe), the system dll files (_tkinter.pyd, python15.dll, tcl80.dll and tk80.dll) and the application-specific dll files (such as btrieve.dll and sio.pyd). We also have the standard Python's Lib directory, which contains Pmw* (and might contain application-specific files).

---

* Pmw is not part of the standard Python distribution. You must download Pmw from http://www.dscpl.com.au/pmw/.

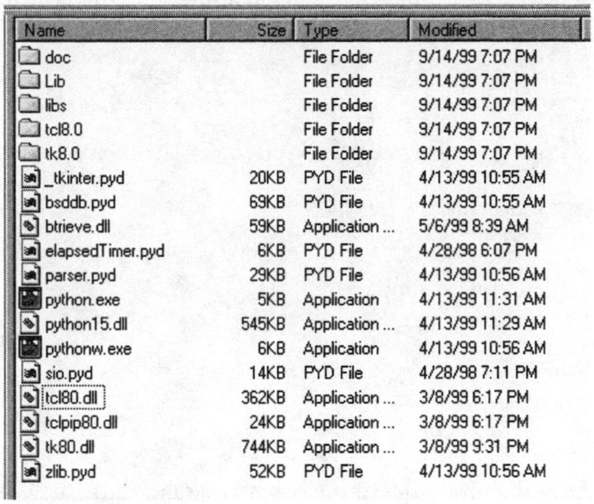

Name	Size	Type	Modified
doc		File Folder	9/14/99 7:07 PM
Lib		File Folder	9/14/99 7:07 PM
libs		File Folder	9/14/99 7:07 PM
tcl8.0		File Folder	9/14/99 7:07 PM
tk8.0		File Folder	9/14/99 7:07 PM
_tkinter.pyd	20KB	PYD File	4/13/99 10:55 AM
bsddb.pyd	69KB	PYD File	4/13/99 10:55 AM
btrieve.dll	59KB	Application ...	5/6/99 8:39 AM
elapsedTimer.pyd	6KB	PYD File	4/28/98 6:07 PM
parser.pyd	29KB	PYD File	4/13/99 10:56 AM
python.exe	5KB	Application	4/13/99 11:31 AM
python15.dll	545KB	Application ...	4/13/99 11:29 AM
pythonw.exe	6KB	Application	4/13/99 10:56 AM
sio.pyd	14KB	PYD File	4/28/98 7:11 PM
tcl80.dll	362KB	Application ...	3/8/99 6:17 PM
tclpip80.dll	24KB	Application ...	3/8/99 6:17 PM
tk80.dll	744KB	Application ...	3/8/99 9:31 PM
zlib.pyd	52KB	PYD File	4/13/99 10:56 AM

Figure 19.1 Contents of C:\python

Tcl is also installed in the toplevel directory containing the directory structure shown in figure 19.2:

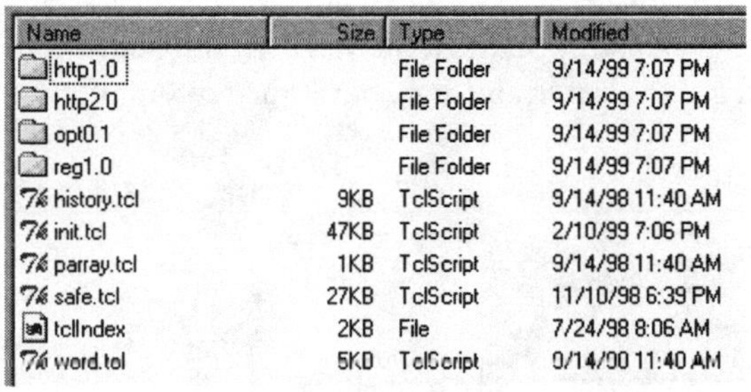

Name	Size	Type	Modified
http1.0		File Folder	9/14/99 7:07 PM
http2.0		File Folder	9/14/99 7:07 PM
opt0.1		File Folder	9/14/99 7:07 PM
reg1.0		File Folder	9/14/99 7:07 PM
history.tcl	9KB	TclScript	9/14/98 11:40 AM
init.tcl	47KB	TclScript	2/10/99 7:06 PM
parray.tcl	1KB	TclScript	9/14/98 11:40 AM
safe.tcl	27KB	TclScript	11/10/98 6:39 PM
tclIndex	2KB	File	7/24/98 8:06 AM
word.tcl	5KB	TclScript	9/14/98 11:40 AM

Figure 19.2 Contents of the Tcl directory

Similarly the Tk directory is installed in the python directory as shown in figure 19.3:

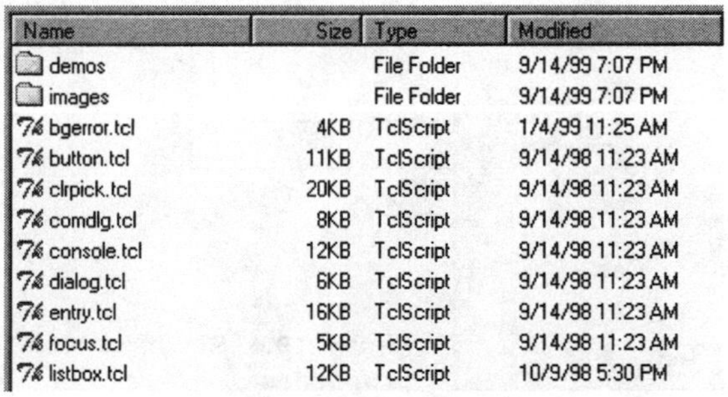

Name	Size	Type	Modified
demos		File Folder	9/14/99 7:07 PM
images		File Folder	9/14/99 7:07 PM
bgerror.tcl	4KB	TclScript	1/4/99 11:25 AM
button.tcl	11KB	TclScript	9/14/98 11:23 AM
clrpick.tcl	20KB	TclScript	9/14/98 11:23 AM
comdlg.tcl	8KB	TclScript	9/14/98 11:23 AM
console.tcl	12KB	TclScript	9/14/98 11:23 AM
dialog.tcl	6KB	TclScript	9/14/98 11:23 AM
entry.tcl	16KB	TclScript	9/14/98 11:23 AM
focus.tcl	5KB	TclScript	9/14/98 11:23 AM
listbox.tcl	12KB	TclScript	10/9/98 5:30 PM

**Remainder of directory not shown

Figure 19.3 Contents of Tk directory

Now, we need to create a batch file which sets environment variables and invokes our application's short Python script:

start.bat

```
set PYTHONPATH=C:\PYTHON\LIB;C:\PYTHON;c:\MyApplication\Common
set TCL_LIBRARY=C:\PYTHON\TCL8.0
set TK_LIBRARY=C:\PYTHON\TK8.0
c:\Python\pythonw startApp.py
```

The Python script can't get much simpler:

startApp.py

```python
import myApplication
myApplication.main()
```

Now, we need to change the properties of the batch program, start.bat. We right mouse-button click on start.bat and select Properties:

Then we set the working directory to the directory containing MyApplication.py, choose Minimized from the Run combobox and check Close on exit. These options are shown in figure 19.4. If you want to change the icon to something specific for your application, click the Change Icon... button and select an icon. Be careful to choose an icon that you ship with your application, and make sure that it is installed in the right place.

Now, when you double-click on the Start.bat file you'll get just your application with no MS-DOS window. You will get an icon in the Start bar at the bottom of the screen for your open window.

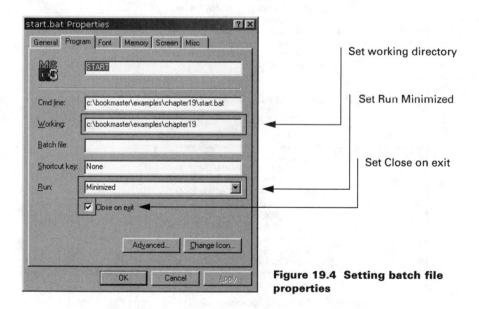

Figure 19.4 Setting batch file properties

Clearly, there are other ways to achieve this effect, and if you scan the Python news group (see "Python News Group" on page 626) you will find other suggestions on how to do this quite frequently.

19.4 *Python distribution tools*

A number of tools are available to an application developer and more are being developed. I am not going to cover these tools here, since there are such wide application targets to be covered.

One of the tools worth looking at is freeze, which wraps your Python application and all of the necessary support modules in an embedded C-program. To date, I have not found a need to use it, but I am certain that it may be a solution for some of you.

Another tool is SqueezeTool, which squeezes a Python application and all of its support modules into a single, compressed package. You can find more details in the "References" section (see "PythonWorks" on page 626).

There is also a Distutils special interest group (SIG) for people who are working to develop tools to distribute Python applications, both with and without C extensions, to all platforms. By the time this book is available, the early versions of these tools will have undergone considerable testing. Take a look at http://www.python.org/sigs/distutils-sig/ for the latest information on this interesting development.

PART 4

Appendices

A P P E N D I X   A

Mapping Tk to Tkinter

This appendix details the mapping of Tk commands and arguments into Tkinter methods and options. The order of the mappings somewhat follows the sequence presented in a reference guide published by Paul Raines and Jeff Trainer for Tcl/Tk (*Tcl/Tk is a Nutshell: A Desktop Quick Reference* is published by O'Reilly and Associates, Inc.). The mappings do not contain any Tcl information, however. I assume that you want to directly translate Tk directives into Tkinter. In many cases, there may be better means of implementing a Tcl/Tk code sequence in Tkinter. Tkinter implements many of the Tk commands as inherited widget methods, which may cause some initial confusion for Tcl/Tk programmers.

General Tk widget information

All widgets are created with:

```
widget = Widget(master [, option=value [, option=value]])
```

where *Widget* is the Tkinter class of widget desired (such as Button) and *widget* is the instance. Widget configuration options may be passed as arguments to the creation call. Options begin with a keyword and are always followed by a value or a string. After creation, options may be changed using the `configure` method and accessed using the `cget` method. Optionally, access may be references to the dictionary keys in the widget (value = `widget['option']` or `widget['option']` = value).

Some of the common widget options supported by multiple widgets are described here and to keep this appendix brief, they are not repeated with the individual widget options.. For options that take screen units, values are in pixels unless an optional one-letter suffix modifier is present. c (cm), i (inch), m (mm), or p (points).

Table A.1 Standard widget options

Tk	Tkinter
-activebackground color	activebackground=color
-activeborderwidth width	activeborderwidth=width
-activeforeground color	activeforeground=color
-anchor anchorPos	anchor=anchorPos
-background color	background=color
-bitmap bitmap	bitmap=bitmap
-borderwidth width	borderwidth=width
-command tclCommand	command=pythonCommand
-cursor cursor	cursor=cursor
-disabledforeground color	disabledforeground=color
-exportselection boolean	exportselection=boolean
-font font	font=font
-foreground color	foreground=color
-height height|textChars	height=height|textChars
-highlightbackground color	highlightbackground=color
-highlightcolor color	highlightcolor=color
-highlightthickness width	highlightthickness=width
-image image	image=image
-insertbackground color	insertbackground=color
-insertborderwidth width	insertborderwidth=width
-insertofftime milliseconds	insertofftime=milliseconds
-insertontime milliseconds	insertontime=milliseconds
-insertwidth width	insertwidth=width
-jump boolean	jump=boolean
-justify left|center|right	justify=LEFT|CENTER|RIGHT
-orient horizontal|vertical	orient=HORIZONTAL|VERTICAL
-padx width	padx=width
-pady height	pady=height
-relief flat|groove|raised|ridge|sunken	relief=FLAT|GROOVE|RAISED|RIDGE|SUNKEN|SOLID
-repeatdelay milliseconds	repeatdelay=milliseconds
-repeatinterval milliseconds	repeatinterval=milliseconds

Table A.1   Standard widget options (continued)

Tk	Tkinter
-selectbackground color	selectbackground=color
-selectborderwidth width	selectborderwidth=width
-selectforeground color	selectforeground=color
-setgrid boolean	setgrid=boolean
-state normal|disabled|active	state=NORMAL|DISABLED|ACTIVE
-takefocus focusType	takefocus=focusType
-text string	text=string
-textvariable variable	textvariable=variable
-troughcolor color	troughcolor=color
-underline index	underline=index
-width width|textChars	width=width|textChars
-wraplength length	wraplength=length
-xscrollcommand cmdPrefix	xscrollcommand=command
-yscrollcommand cmdPrefix	yscrollcommand=command

Table A.2   Tk special variables

Tk	Tkinter
tk_library	Not available
tk_patchLevel	Not available
tkPriv	Not available
tk_strictMotif	window.tk_strictMotif(boolean)
tk_version	TkVersion

The Canvas widget

Table A.3   Canvas widget standard options

Tk	Tkinter
-background color	background=color
-borderwidth width	borderwidth=width
-cursor cursor	cursor=cursor
-height height	height=height
-highlightbackground color	highlightbackground=color

Table A.3 Canvas widget standard options (continued)

Tk	Tkinter
-highlightcolor color	highlightcolor=color
-highlightthickness number	highlightthickness=number
-insertbackground color	insertbackground=color
-insertborderwidth width	insertborderwidth=width
-insertofftime milliseconds	insertofftime=milliseconds
-insertontime milliseconds	insertontime=milliseconds
-insertwidth width	insertwidth=width
-relief flat|groove|raised|ridge|sunken	relief=FLAT|GROOVE|RAISED|RIDGE|SUNKEN|SOLID
-selectbackground color	selectbackground=color
-selectborderwidth width	selectborderwidth=width
-selectforeground color	selectforeground=color
-takefocus focusType	takefocus=focusType
-width width	width=width
-xscrollcommand tclCommand	xscrollcommand=pythonCommand
-yscrollcommand tclCommand	yscrollcommand=pythonCommand

Table A.4 Canvas widget-specific options

Tk	Tkinter
-closeenough float	closeenough=float
-confine boolean	confine=boolean
-scrollregion corners	scrollregion=(x1,y1,x2,y2)
-xscrollincrement distance	xscrollincrement=distance
-yscrollincrement distance	yscrollincrement=distance

Table A.5 Canvas methods

Tk	Tkinter
canvas addtag above tagOrId	canvas.addtag_above(newtag, tagOrId)
canvas addtag all	canvas.addtag_all(newtag)
canvas addtag below tagOrId	canvas.addtag_below(newtag, tagOrId)

Table A.5   Canvas methods (continued)

Tk	Tkinter
canvas addtag closest x y [halo] [start]	canvas.addtag_closest(newtag, x, y, [, halo] [, start])
canvas addtag enclosed x1 y1 x2 y2	canvas.addtag_enclosed(newtag, x1, y1, x2, y2)
canvas addtag overlapping x1 y1 x2 y2	canvas.addtag_overlapping(newtag, x1, y1, x2, y2)
canvas addtag withtag tagOrId	canvas.addtag_withtag(newtag, tagOrId)
canvas bbox tagOrId [tagOrId ...]	canvas.bbox(tagOrId [, tagOrId ...])
canvas bind tagOrId [sequence [command]]	canvas.tag_bind(tagOrId [, sequence [, command]])
canvas canvasx screenx [gridspacing]	canvas.canvasx(screenx [, gridspacing])
canvas canvasy screeny [gridspacing]	canvas.canvasy(screeny [, gridspacing])
canvas coords tagOrId [x0 y0 ...]	canvas.coords(tagOrId [, x0, y0 ...])
canvas create **TYPE** x y [x y ...] [option value ...]	canvas.create_**TYPE**(x, y, [, x, y ...] [, option=value ...])
canvas dchars tagOrId first [last]	canvas.dchars(tagOrId, first [, last])
canvas delete [tagOrId ...]	canvas.delete([tagOrId ...])
canvas dtag tagOrId [tagToDelete]	canvas.dtag(tagOrId [, tagToDelete])
canvas find above tagOrId	canvas.find_above(tagOrId)
canvas find all	canvas.find_all()
canvas find below tagOrId	canvas.find_below(tagOrId)
canvas find closest x y [halo] [start]	canvas.find_closest(x, y, [, halo] [, start])
canvas find enclosed x1 y1 x2 y2	canvas.find_enclosed(x1, y1, x2, y2)
canvas find overlapping x1 y1 x2 y2	canvas.find_overlapping(x1, y1, x2, y2)
canvas find withtag tagOrId	canvas.find_withtag(tagOrId)
canvas focus tagOrId	canvas.focus(tagOrId)
canvas gettags tagOrId	canvas.gettags(tagOrId)
canvas icursor tagOrId index	canvas.icursor(tagOrId, index)
canvas index tagOrId index.	canvas.index(tagOrId, index)
canvas insert tagOrId beforeThis string	canvas.insert(tagOrId, string)
canvas itemcget tagOrId option	canvas.itemcget(tagOrId, option)
canvas itemconfigure tagOrId [option value ...]	canvas.itemconfigure(tagOrId [, option=value ...])
canvas lower(tagOrId [belowThis]	canvas.lower(tagOrId [, belowThis])
canvas move tagOrId xAmount yAmount	canvas.move(tagOrId, xAmount, yAmount)
canvas postscript [option value ...]	canvas.postscript([option=value ...])

Table A.5   Canvas methods (continued)

Tk	Tkinter
canvas raise tagOrId [aboveThis]	canvas.tkraise(tagOrId, [, aboveThis])
canvas scale tagOrId xOrigin yOrigin xScale yScale	canvas.scale(tagOrId, xOrigin, yOrigin, xScale, yScale)
canvas scan mark x y	canvas.scan_mark(x, y)
canvas scan dragto x y	canvas.scan_dragto(x, y)
canvas select adjust tagOrId index	canvas.select_adjust(tagOrId, index)
canvas select clear	canvas.select_clear()
canvas select from tagOrId index	canvas.select_from(tagOrId, index)
canvas select item	canvas.select_item()
canvas select to tagOrId index	canvas.select_to(tagOrId, index)
canvas type tagOrId	canvas.type(tagOrId)
canvas xview args	canvas.xview(args)
canvas xview moveto fraction	canvas.xview_moveto(fraction)
canvas xview scroll number units|pages	canvas.xview_scroll(number, UNITS|PAGES)
canvas yview args	canvas.yview(args)
canvas yview moveto fraction	canvas.yview_moveto(fraction)
canvas yview scroll number units|pages	canvas.yview_scroll(number, UNITS|PAGES)

Canvas item types

Table A.6   Create arc

Tk	Tkinter
canvas create arc x1 y1 x2 y2 [option value ...]	canvas.create_arc(x1, y1, x2, y2, [, option=value ...])

Table A.7   Arc options

Tk	Tkinter
-extent degrees	extent=degrees
-fill color	fill=color
-outline color	outline=color
-outlinestipple bitmap	outlinestipple=bitmap
-start degrees	start=degrees

Table A.7   Arc options (continued)

Tk	Tkinter
-stipple bitmap	stipple=bitmap
-style pieslice|chord|arc	style=PIESLICE|CHORD|ARC
-tags tagList	tags=tagList
-width outlineWidth	width=outlineWidth

Table A.8   Create bitmap

Tk	Tkinter
canvas create bitmap x y [option value ...]	canvas.create_bitmap(x, y, [, option=value ...])

Table A.9   Bitmap options

Tk	Tkinter
-anchor anchorPos	anchor=anchorPos
-background color	background=color
-bitmap bitmap	bitmap=bitmap
-foreground color	foreground=color
-tags tagList	tags=tagList

Table A.10   Create image

Tk	Tkinter
canvas create image x y [option value ...]	canvas.create_image(x, y, [, option=value ...])

Table A.11   Image options

Tk	Tkinter
-anchor anchorPos	anchor=anchorPos
-image image	image=image
-tags tagList	tags=tagList

THE CANVAS WIDGET

Table A.12   Create line

Tk	Tkinter
canvas create line x1 y1 ... xN yN [option value ...]	canvas.create_line(x1, y1, ... xN, yN, [option=value ...])

Table A.13   Line options

Tk	Tkinter
-arrow none|first|last|both	arrow=NONE|FIRST|LAST|BOTH
-arrowshape shape	arrowshape=shape
-capstyle butt|projecting|round	capstyle=BUTT|PROJECTING|ROUND
-fill color	fill=color
-joinstyle bevel|miter|round	joinstyle=BEVEL|MITER|ROUND
-smooth boolean	smooth=boolean
-splinesteps number	splinesteps=number
-stipple bitmap	stipple=bitmap
-tags tagList	tags=tagList
-width outlineWidth	width=outlineWidth

Table A.14   Create oval

Tk	Tkinter
canvas create oval x1 y1 x2 y2 [option value ...]	canvas.create_oval(x1, y1, x2, y2 [, option=value ...])

Table A.15   Oval options

Tk	Tkinter
-fill color	fill=color
-outline color	outline=color
-stipple bitmap	stipple=bitmap
-tags tagList	tags=tagList
-width outlineWidth	width=outlineWidth

Table A.16   Create polygon

Tk	Tkinter
canvas create polygon x1 y1 ... xN yN [option value ...]	canvas.create_polygon(x1, y1, ... xN, yN, [option=value ...])

Table A.17   Polygon options

Tk	Tkinter
-fill color	fill=color
-outline color	outline=color
-smooth boolean	smooth=boolean
-splinesteps number	splinesteps=number
-stipple bitmap	stipple=bitmap
-tags tagList	tags=tagList
-width outlineWidth	width=outlineWidth

Table A.18   Create rectangle

Tk	Tkinter
canvas create rectangle x1 y1 x2 y2 [option value ...]	canvas.create_rectangle(x1, y1, x2, y2 [, option=value ...])

Table A.19   Rectangle options

Tk	Tkinter
-fill color	fill=color
-outline color	outline=color
-stipple bitmap	stipple=bitmap
-tags tagList	tags=tagList
-width outlineWidth	width=outlineWidth

Table A.20   Create text

Tk	Tkinter
canvas create text x y [option value ...]	canvas.create_text(x, y, [, option=value ...])

Table A.21   Text options

Tk	Tkinter
-anchor anchorPos	anchor=anchorPos
-fill color	fill=color
-font font	font=font
-justify left|right|center	justify=LEFT|RIGHT|CENTER
-stipple bitmap	stipple=bitmap
-tags tagList	tags=tagList
-text string	text=string
-width lineLength	width=lineLength

Table A.22   Create window

Tk	Tkinter
canvas create window x y [option value ...]	canvas.create_window(x, y, [, option=value ...])

Table A.23   Window options

Tk	Tkinter
-anchor anchorPos	anchor=anchorPos
-height height	height=height
-tags tagList	tags=tagList
-width width	width=width

Table A.24 Canvas Postscript options

Tk	Tkinter
-height height	height=height
-width width	width=width
-window pathName	window=pathName
-colormap varName	colormap=varName
-colormode color|grey|mono	colormode='color'|'grey'|'mono'
-file fileName	file=fileName
-fontmap varName	fontmap=varName
-height size	height=size
-pageanchor anchor	pageanchor=anchor
-pageheight size	pageheight=size
-pagewidth size	pagewidth=size
-pagex position	pagex=position
-pagey position	pagey=position
-rotate boolean	rotate=boolean
-width size	width=size
-x position	x=position
-y position	y=position

The Entry widget

Table A.25 Entry widget standard options

Tk	Tkinter
-background color	background=color
-borderwidth width	borderwidth=width
-cursor cursor	cursor=cursor
-exportselection boolean	exportselection=boolean
-font font	font=font
-foreground color	foreground=color
-highlightbackground color	highlightbackground=color
-highlightcolor color	highlightcolor=color
-highlightthickness width	highlightthickness=width
-insertbackground color	insertbackground=color
-insertborderwidth width	insertborderwidth=width
-insertofftime milliseconds	insertofftime=milliseconds

Table A.25 Entry widget standard options (continued)

Tk	Tkinter
-insertontime milliseconds	insertontime=milliseconds
-insertwidth width	insertwidth=width
-justify left|center|right	justify LEFT|CENTER|RIGHT
-relief flat|groove|raised|ridge|sunken	relief=FLAT|GROOVE|RAISED|RIDGE|SUNKEN|SOLID
-selectbackground color	selectbackground=color
-selectborderwidth width	selectborderwidth=width
-selectforeground color	selectforeground=color
-state NORMAL|DISABLED|ACTIVE	state=NORMAL|DISABLED|ACTIVE
-takefocus focusType	takefocus=focusType
-textvariable variable	textvariable=variable
-width width	width=width
-xscrollcommand tclCommand	xscrollcommand=pythonCommand

Table A.26 Entry widget-specific options

Tk	Tkinter
-show char	show=char

Table A.27 Entry indices

Tk	Tkinter
number	number | (start, end)
anchor	ANCHOR
end	END
insert	INSERT
sel.first	SEL_FIRST
sel.last	SEL_LAST
@x-coord	"@x"

Table A.28 Entry widget methods

Tk	Tkinter
entry bbox index	entry.bbox(index)
entry delete first [last]	entry.delete(first [, last])
entry get	entry.get()
entry icursor index	entry.icursor(index)
entry index index	entry.index(index)
entry insert index string	entry.insert(index, string)
entry scan mark args	entry.scan_mark(args)
entry scan dragto args	entry.scan_dragto(args)
entry selection adjust index	entry.selection_adjust(index)
entry selection clear	entry.selection_clear()
entry selection from index	entry.selection_from(index)
entry selection present	entry.selection_ present()
entry selection range start end	entry.selection_range(start, end)
entry selection to index	entry.selection_to(index)
entry xview moveto fraction	entry.xview_moveto(fraction)
entry xview scroll number units|pages	entry.xviewscroll(number, units|pages)

The Listbox widget

Table A.29 Listbox widget standard options

Tk	Tkinter
-background color	background=color
-borderwidth width	borderwidth=width
-cursor cursor	cursor=cursor
-exportselection boolean	exportselection=boolean
-font font	font=font
-foreground color	foreground=color
-height height	height=height
-highlightbackground color	highlightbackground=color
-highlightcolor color	highlightcolor=color
-highlightthickness width	highlightthickness=width
-relief flat|groove|raised|ridge|sunken	relief=FLAT|GROOVE|RAISED|RIDGE|SUNKEN|SOLID
-selectbackground color	selectbackground=color

Table A.29 Listbox widget standard options (continued)

Tk	Tkinter
-selectborderwidth width	selectborderwidth=width
-selectforeground color	selectforeground=color
-setgrid boolean	setgrid=boolean
-takefocus focusType	takefocus=focusType
-width width	width=width
-xscrollcommand tclCommand	xscrollcommand=pythonCommand
-yscrollcommand tclCommand	yscrollcommand=pythonCommand

Table A.30 Listbox widget-specific options

Tk	Tkinter
-selectmode single|browse |multiple|extended	selectmode=SINGLE|BROWE |MULTIPLE|EXTENDED

Table A.31 Listbox indices

Tk	Tkinter
number	number or (start, end)
active	ACTIVE
anchor	ANCHOR
end	END
@x,y	"@x,y"

Table A.32 Listbox widget methods

Tk	Tkinter
listbox activate index	listbox.activate(index)
listbox bbox index	listbox.bbox(index)
listbox curselection	listbox.curselection()
listbox delete index1 [index2]	listbox.delete(index1 [, index2])
listbox get index1 [index2]	listbox.get(index1 [, index2])
listbox index index	listbox.index(index)
listbox insert index [element ...]	listbox.insert(index [, element ...])
listbox nearest y	listbox.nearest(y)

Tk	Tkinter
listbox scan mark args	listbox.scan_mark(args)
listbox scan dragto args	listbox.scan_dragto(args)
listbox see index	listbox.see(index)
listbox selection anchor index	listbox.selection_anchor(index)
listbox selection clear first [last]	listbox.selection_clear(first [, last])
listbox selection includes index	listbox.selection_includes(index)
listbox selection set first [last]	listbox.selection_set(first [, last])
listbox size	listbox.size()
listbox xview index	listbox.xview(index)
listbox xview moveto fraction	listbox.xview_moveto(fraction)
listbox xview scroll number units|pages	listbox.xview_scroll(number, units|pages)
listbox yview index	listbox.yview(index)
listbox yview moveto fraction	listbox.yview_moveto(fraction)
listbox yview scroll number units|pages	listbox.yview_scroll(number, units|pages)

The Menu widget

Table A.33   Menu widget standard options

Tk	Tkinter
-activebackground color	activebackground=color
-activeborderwidth width	activeborderwidth=width
-activeforeground color	activeforeground=color
-background color	background=color
-borderwidth width	borderwidth=width
-cursor cursor	cursor=cursor
-disabledforeground color	disabledforeground=color
-font font	font=font
-foreground color	foreground=color
-relief flat|groove|raised|ridge|sunken	relief=FLAT|GROOVE|RAISED|RIDGE|SUNKEN|SOLID

Table A.34 Menu widget-specific options

Tk	Tkinter
-postcommand tclCommand	postcommand=pythonCommand
-selectcolor color	selectcolor=color
-tearoff boolean	tearoff=boolean
-tearoffcommand tclCommand	tearoffcommand=pythonCommand
-title string	title=string
-type type	type=type

Table A.35 Entry types

Tk	Tkinter
cascade	cascade
checkbutton	checkbutton
command	command
radiobutton	radiobutton
separator	separator

Table A.36 Menu indices

Tk	Tkinter
number	number or (start, end)
active	ACTIVE
last	LAST
none	NONE
@y-coord	"@y"
matchPattern	matchPattern

Table A.37 Menu widget methods

Tk	Tkinter
menu activate index	menu.activate(index)
menu add cascade	menu.add_cascade(option=value...)
menu add checkbutton	menu.add_checkbutton(option=value...)

Table A.37 Menu widget methods (continued)

Tk	Tkinter
menu add command	menu.add_command(option=value...)
menu add radiobutton	menu.add_radiobutton(option=value...)
menu add separator	menu.add_separator(option=value...)
menu clone newMenuName [cloneType]	
menu delete index1 [index2]	menu.delete(index1 [, index2])
menu entrycget index option	menu.entrycget(index, option)
menu entryconfigure index [option value ...]	menu.entryconfigure(index [, option=value ...])
menu index index	menu.index(index)
menu insert index type [option value ...]	menu.insert.(index, type [, option=value ...])
menu insert index cascade [option value ...]	menu.insert_cascade(index [, option=value ...])
menu insert index checkbutton [option value ...]	menu.insert_checkbutton(index [, option=value ...])
menu insert index command [option value ...]	menu.insert_command(index [, option=value ...])
menu insert index radiobutton [option value ...]	menu.insert_radiobutton(index [, option=value ...])
menu insert index separator [option value ...]	menu.insert_separator(index [, option=value ...])
menu invoke index	menu.invoke(index)
menu post x y	menu.post(x, y)
menu postcascade index	menu.postcascade(index)
menu type index	menu.type(index)
menu unpost	menu.unpost()
menu yposition index	menu.yposition(index)

Table A.38 Additional Menu options

Tk	Tkinter
-accelerator string	accelerator=string
-command tclCommand	command=pythonCommand
-columnbreak value	columnbreak=value
-hidemargin value	hidemargin=value
-indicatoron boolean	indicatoron=boolean
-label string	label=string

Table A.38   Additional Menu options (continued)

Tk	Tkinter
-menu pathName	menu=pathName
-offvalue value	offvalue=value
-onvalue value	onvalue=value
-selectcolor color	selectcolor=color
-selectimage image	selectimage=image
-value value	value=value
-variable variable	variable=variable

The Text widget

Table A.39   Text widget standard options

Tk	Tkinter
-background color	background=color
-borderwidth width	borderwidth=width
-cursor cursor	cursor=cursor
-exportselection boolean	exportselection=boolean
-font font	font=font
-foreground color	foreground=color
-height height	height=height
-highlightbackground color	highlightbackground=color
-highlightcolor color	highlightcolor=color
-highlightthickness width	highlightthickness=width
-insertbackground color	insertbackground=color
-insertborderwidth width	insertborderwidth=width
-insertofftime milliseconds	insertofftime=milliseconds
-insertontime milliseconds	insertontime=milliseconds
-insertwidth width	insertwidth=width
-padx width	padx=width
-pady height	pady=height
-relief flat|groove|raised|ridge|sunken	relief=FLAT|GROOVE|RAISED|RIDGE|SUNKEN|SOLID
-selectbackground color	selectbackground=color
-selectborderwidth width	selectborderwidth=width
-selectforeground color	selectforeground=color

Table A.39   Text widget standard options (continued)

Tk	Tkinter
-setgrid boolean	setgrid=boolean
-state NORMAL|DISABLED|ACTIVE	state=NORMAL|DISABLED|ACTIVE
-takefocus focusType	takefocus=focusType
-width width	width=width
-xscrollcommand tclCommand	xscrollcommand=pythonCommand
-yscrollcommand tclCommand	yscrollcommand=pythonCommand

Table A.40   Text widget-specific options

Tk	Tkinter
-spacing1 size	spacing1=size
-spacing2 size	spacing2=size
-spacing3 size	spacing3=size
-tabs tabList	tabs=tabList
-wrap none|char|word	wrap=NONE|CHAR|WORD

Text indices

Table A.41   Base text indices

Tk	Tkinter
line.char	line.char
@x,y	"@x,y"
end	END
mark	mark
tag	tag
pathName (embedded window)	window
imageName (embedded window)	imageName

Table A.42　Text index modifiers

Tk	Tkinter
+ count chars	'+ count chars'
- count chars	'- count chars'
+ count lines	'+ count lines'
- count lines	'- count lines'
linestart	'linestart'
lineend	'lineend'
wordstart	'wordstart'
wordend	'wordend'

Table A.43　Text tag standard options

Tk	Tkinter
-background color	background=color
-borderwidth width	borderwidth=width
-font font	font=font
-foreground color	foreground=color
-justify left|center|right	justify LEFT|CENTER|RIGHT
-relief flat|groove|raised|ridge|sunken	relief=FLAT|GROOVE|RAISED|RIDGE|SUNKEN|SOLID

Table A.44　Text tag specific options

Tk	Tkinter
-bgstipple bitmap	bgstipple=bitmap
-fgstipple bitmap	fgstipple=bitmap
-lmargin1 size	lmargin1=size
-lmargin2 size	lmargin2=size
-offset size	offset=size
-overstrike boolean	overstrike=boolean
-rmargin size	rmargin=size
-tabs tabList	tabs=tabList
-underline boolean	underline=boolean

Table A.45   Text embedded window options

Tk	Tkinter
-align top|center|bottom|baseline	align=TOP|CENTER|BOTTOM|BASELINE
-create script	create=script
-padx width	padx=width
-pady height	pady=height
-stretch boolean	stretch=boolean
-window pathName	window=window

Table A.46   Text embedded image options

Tk	Tkinter
-align top|center|bottom|baseline	align=TOP|CENTER|BOTTOM|BASELINE
-image image	image=image
-name imageName	name=imageName
-padx width	padx=width
-pady height	pady=height

Table A.47   Text widget methods

Tk	Tkinter
text bbox index	text.bbox(index)
text compare index1 op index2	text.compare(index1, op, index2)
text delete index1 [index2]	text.delete(index1 [, index2])
text dlineinfo index	text.dlineinfo(index)
text dump [switches] index1 [index2]	text.dump(index1 [, index2] [, option=value ...])
text get index1 [index2]	text.get(index1 [, index2])
text image cget index option	text.image_cget(index, option)
text image configure index [option [value [option value ...]]]	text.image_configure(index [, option=value ...])
text image create index [option value ...]	text.image_create(index [, option value ...])
text image names	text.image_names()
text index index	text.index(index)
text insert index [string [tagList string tagList ...]]	text.insert(index [, string [, tagList, string, tagList ...]])
text mark gravity markName [left|right]	text.mark_gravity(markName [LEFT|RIGHT])

Table A.47   Text widget methods (continued)

Tk	Tkinter
text mark names	text.mark_names()
text mark next | previous index	No mapping
text mark set markName index	text.mark_set(markName, index)
text mark unset markName [markName ...]	text.mark_unset(markName [, markName ...])
text scan mark x y	text.scan_mark(x, y)
text scan dragto x y	text.scan_dragto(x, y)
text search [switches] pattern index [stopIndex]	text.search(pattern, index, [, stopIndex] [, switches])
text see index	text.see(index)
text tag add tagName index1 [index2]	text.tag_add(tagName, index1 [, index2])
text tag bind tagName [sequence [script]]	text.tag_bind(tagName, sequence, script [, '+'])
text tag cget tagName option	text.tag_cget(tagName, option)
text tag configure tagName [option [value [option value ...]]]	text.tag_configure(tagName [, option=value ...])
text tag delete tagName [tagName ...]	text.tag_delete(tagName [, tagName ...])
text tag lower tagName [belowThis]	text.tag_lower(tagName [, belowThis])
text tag names [index]	text.tag_names([index])
text tag nextrange tagName index1 [index2]	text.tag_nextrange(tagName, index1 [, index2])
text tag prevrange tagName index1 [index2]	text.tag_prevrange(tagName, index1 [, index2])
text tag raise tagName [aboveThis]	text.tag_raise(tagName [, aboveThis])
text tag ranges tagName	text.tag_ranges(tagName)
text tag remove tagName index1 [index2]	text.tag_remove(tagName, index1 [, index2])
text window cget index option	text.window_cget(index, option)
text window configure index [option [value [option value ...]]]	text.window_configure(index [, option=value ...])
text window create index [option value ...]	text.window_create(index [, option=value ...])
text window names	text.window_names()
text xview	text.xview()
text xview moveto fraction	text.xview_moveto(fraction)
text xview scroll number units|pages	text.xview_scroll(number, units|pages)
text yview	text.yview()
text yview moveto fraction	text.yview_moveto(fraction)
text yview scroll number units|pages	text.yview_scroll(number, units|pages)
text yview [-pickplace] index	text.yview_pickplace(index)

The Button widget

Table A.48   Button widget standard options

Tk	Tkinter
-activebackground color	activebackground=color
-activeforeground color	activeforeground=color
-anchor anchorPos	anchor=anchorPos
-background color	background=color
-bitmap bitmap	bitmap=bitmap
-borderwidth width	borderwidth=width
-command tclCommand	command=pythonCommand
-cursor cursor	cursor=cursor
-disabledforeground color	disabledforeground=color
-font font	font=font
-foreground color	foreground=color
-height height	height=height
-highlightbackground color	highlightbackground=color
-highlightcolor color	highlightcolor=color
-highlightthickness width	highlightthickness=width
-image image	image=image
-justify left|center|right	justify=LEFT|CENTER|RIGHT
-padx width	padx=width
-pady height	pady=height
-relief flat|groove|raised|ridge|sunken	relief=FLAT|GROOVE|RAISED|RIDGE|SUNKEN|SOLID
-state normal|disabled|active	state=NORMAL|DISABLED|ACTIVE
-takefocus focusType	takefocus=focusType
-text string	text=string
-textvariable variable	textvariable=variable
-underline index	underline=index
-width width	width=width
-wraplength length	wraplength=length

Table A.49   Button widget-specific options

Tk	Tkinter
-default normal|disabled|active	default=NORMAL|DISABLED|ACTIVE

Table A.50 Button methods

Tk	Tkinter
button flash	button.flash()
button invoke	button.invoke()

The Checkbutton widget

Table A.51 Checkbutton widget standard options

Tk	Tkinter
-activebackground color	activebackground=color
-activeforeground color	activeforeground=color
-anchor anchorPos	anchor=anchorPos
-background color	background=color
-bitmap bitmap	bitmap=bitmap
-borderwidth width	borderwidth=width
-command tclCommand	command=pythonCommand
-cursor cursor	cursor=cursor
-disabledforeground color	disabledforeground=color
-font font	font=font
-foreground color	foreground=color
-height height	height=height
-highlightbackground color	highlightbackground=color
-highlightcolor color	highlightcolor=color
-highlightthickness width	highlightthickness=width
-image image	image=image
-justify left|center|right	justify LEFT|CENTER|RIGHT
-padx width	padx=width
-pady height	pady=height
-relief flat|groove|raised|ridge|sunken	relief=FLAT|GROOVE|RAISED|RIDGE|SUNKEN|SOLID
-state normal|disabled|active	state=NORMAL|DISABLED|ACTIVE
-takefocus focusType	takefocus=focusType
-text string	text=string
-textvariable variable	textvariable=variable
-underline index	underline=index

Table A.51   Checkbutton widget standard options (continued)

Tk	Tkinter
-width width	width=width
-wraplength length	wraplength=length

Table A.52   Checkbutton widget-specific options

Tk	Tkinter
-indicatoron boolean	indicatoron=boolean
-offvalue value	offvalue=value
-onvalue value	onvalue=value
-selectcolor color	selectcolor=color
-selectimage image	selectimage=image
-variable variable	variable=variable

Table A.53   Checkbutton methods

Tk	Tkinter
checkbutton deselect	checkbutton.deselect()
checkbutton flash	checkbutton.flash()
checkbutton invoke	checkbutton.invoke()
checkbutton select	checkbutton.select()
checkbutton toggle	checkbutton.toggle()

The Frame widget

Table A.54   Frame widget standard options

Tk	Tkinter
-borderwidth width	borderwidth=width
-cursor cursor	cursor=cursor
-height height	height=height
-highlightbackground color	highlightbackground=color
-highlightcolor color	highlightcolor=color
-highlightthickness width	highlightthickness=width

Tk	Tkinter
-relief flat|groove|raised|ridge|sunken	relief=FLAT|GROOVE|RAISED|RIDGE|SUNKEN|SOLID
-takefocus focusType	takefocus=focusType
-width width	width=width

Table A.55   Frame widget-specific options

Tk	Tkinter
-background color	background=color
-class name	class=name
-colormap colormap	colormap=colormap
-container boolean	container=boolean
-visual visual	visual=visual

The Label widget

Table A.56   Label widget standard options

Tk	Tkinter
-anchor anchorPos	anchor=anchorPos
-background color	background=color
-bitmap bitmap	bitmap=bitmap
-borderwidth width	borderwidth=width
-cursor cursor	cursor=cursor
-font font	font=font
-foreground color	foreground=color
-height height	height=height
-highlightbackground color	highlightbackground=color
-highlightcolor color	highlightcolor=color
-highlightthickness width	highlightthickness=width
-image image	image=image
-justify left|center|right	justify LEFT|CENTER|RIGHT
-padx width	padx=width
-pady height	pady=height

Table A.56   Label widget standard options (continued)

Tk	Tkinter
-relief flat|groove|raised|ridge|sunken	relief=FLAT|GROOVE|RAISED|RIDGE|SUNKEN|SOLID
-takefocus focusType	takefocus=focusType
-text string	text=string
-textvariable variable	textvariable=variable
-underline index	underline=index
-width width	width=width
-wraplength length	wraplength=length

The Menubutton widget

Table A.57   Menubutton widget standard options

Tk	Tkinter
-activebackground color	activebackground=color
-activeforeground color	activeforeground=color
-anchor anchorPos	anchor=anchorPos
-background color	background=color
-bitmap bitmap	bitmap=bitmap
-borderwidth width	borderwidth=width
-cursor cursor	cursor=cursor
-disabledforeground color	disabledforeground=color
-font font	font=font
-foreground color	foreground=color
-height height	height=height
-highlightbackground color	highlightbackground=color
-highlightcolor color	highlightcolor=color
-highlightthickness width	highlightthickness=width
-image image	image=image
-justify left|center|right	justify=LEFT|CENTER|RIGHT
-padx width	padx=width
-pady height	pady=height
-relief flat|groove|raised|ridge|sunken	relief=FLAT|GROOVE|RAISED|RIDGE|SUNKEN|SOLID
-state normal|disabled|active	state=NORMAL|DISABLED|ACTIVE
-takefocus focusType	takefocus=focusType

Table A.57   Menubutton widget standard options (continued)

Tk	Tkinter
-text string	text=string
-textvariable variable	textvariable=variable
-underline index	underline=index
-width width	width=width
-wraplength length	wraplength=length

Table A.58   Menubutton widget-specific options

Tk	Tkinter
-direction direction	direction=direction
-indicatoron boolean	indicatoron=boolean
-menu pathName	menu=pathName

The Message widget

Table A.59   Message widget standard options

Tk	Tkinter
-anchor anchorPos	anchor=anchorPos
-background color	background=color
-borderwidth width	borderwidth=width
-cursor cursor	cursor=cursor
-font font	font=font
-foreground color	foreground=color
-highlightbackground color	highlightbackground=color
-highlightcolor color	highlightcolor=color
-highlightthickness width	highlightthickness=width
-justify left|center|right	justify=LEFT|CENTER|RIGHT
-padx width	padx=width
-pady height	pady=height
-relief flat|groove|raised|ridge|sunken	relief=FLAT|GROOVE|RAISED|RIDGE|SUNKEN|SOLID
-takefocus focusType	takefocus=focusType
-text string	text=string

Table A.59   Message widget standard options (continued)

Tk	Tkinter
-textvariable variable	textvariable=variable
-width width	width=width

Table A.60   Message widget-specific options

Tk	Tkinter
-aspect integer	aspect=integer

The Radiobutton widget

Table A.61   Radiobutton widget standard options

Tk	Tkinter
-activebackground color	activebackground=color
-activeforeground color	activeforeground=color
-anchor anchorPos	anchor=anchorPos
-background color	background=color
-bitmap bitmap	bitmap=bitmap
-borderwidth width	borderwidth=width
-command tclCommand	command=pythonCommand
-cursor cursor	cursor=cursor
-disabledforeground color	disabledforeground=color
-font font	font=font
-foreground color	foreground=color
-height height	height=height
-highlightbackground color	highlightbackground=color
-highlightcolor color	highlightcolor=color
-highlightthickness width	highlightthickness=width
-image image	image=image
-justify left|center|right	justify=LEFT|CENTER|RIGHT
-padx width	padx=width
-pady height	pady=height
-relief flat|groove|raised|ridge|sunken	relief=FLAT|GROOVE|RAISED|RIDGE|SUNKEN|SOLID

Table A.61   Radiobutton widget standard options (continued)

Tk	Tkinter
-state normal|disabled|active	state=NORMAL|DISABLED|ACTIVE
-takefocus focusType	takefocus=focusType
-text string	text=string
-textvariable variable	textvariable=variable
-underline index	underline=index
-width width	width=width
-wraplength length	wraplength=length

Table A.62   Radiobutton widget-specific options

Tk	Tkinter
-indicatoron boolean	indicatoron=boolean
-selectcolor color	selectcolor=color
-selectimage image	selectimage=image
-value value	value=value
-variable variable	variable=variable

Table A.63   Radiobutton widget methods

Tk	Tkinter
radiobutton deselect	radiobutton.deselect()
radiobutton flash	radiobutton.flash()
radiobutton invoke	radiobutton.invoke()
radiobutton select	radiobutton.select()

The Scale widget

Table A.64   Scale widget standard options

Tk	Tkinter
-activebackground color	activebackground=color
-background color	background=color
-borderwidth width	borderwidth=width

Table A.64 Scale widget standard options (continued)

Tk	Tkinter
-cursor cursor	cursor=cursor
-font font	font=font
-foreground color	foreground=color
-highlightbackground color	highlightbackground=color
-highlightcolor color	highlightcolor=color
-highlightthickness width	highlightthickness=width
-orient horizontal|vertical	orient=HORIZONTAL|VERTICAL
-relief flat|groove|raised|ridge|sunken	relief=FLAT|GROOVE|RAISED|RIDGE|SUNKEN|SOLID
-repeatdelay milliseconds	repeatdelay=milliseconds
-repeatinterval milliseconds	repeatinterval=milliseconds
-state normal|disabled	state=NORMAL|DISABLED|ACTIVE
-takefocus focusType	takefocus=focusType
-troughcolor color	troughcolor=color

Table A.65 Scale widget-specific options

Tk	Tkinter
-bigincrement number	bigincrement=number
-command tclCommand	command=pythonCommand
-digits integer	digits=integer
-from number	from=number
-label string	label=string
-length size	length=size
-resolution number	resolution=number
-showvalue boolean	showvalue=boolean
-sliderlength size	sliderlength=size
-sliderrelief relief	sliderrelief=relief
-tickinterval number	tickinterval=number
-to number	to=number
-variable variable	variable=variable
-width width	width=width

Table A.66   Scale widget methods

Tk	Tkinter
scale coords [value]	scale.coords([value])
scale get [x y]	scale.get()
scale identify x y	scale.identify(x, y)
scale set value	scale.set(value)

The Scrollbar widget

Table A.67   Scrollbar widget standard options

Tk	Tkinter
-activebackground color	activebackground=color
-background color	background=color
-borderwidth width	borderwidth=width
-cursor cursor	cursor=cursor
-highlightbackground color	highlightbackground=color
-highlightcolor color	highlightcolor=color
-highlightthickness width	highlightthickness=width
-jump boolean	jump=boolean
-orient horizontal|vertical	orient=HORIZONTAL|VERTICAL
-relief flat|groove|raised|ridge|sunken	relief=FLAT|GROOVE|RAISED|RIDGE|SUNKEN|SOLID
-repeatdelay milliseconds	repeatdelay=milliseconds
-repeatinterval milliseconds	repeatinterval=milliseconds
-takefocus focusType	takefocus=focusType
-troughcolor color	troughcolor=color

Table A.68   Scrollbar widget-specific options

Tk	Tkinter
-activerelief number	activerelief=number
-command tclCommandPrefix	command=pythonCommandPrefix
-elementborderwidth width	elementborderwidth=width
-width width	width=width

Table A.69   Scrollbar widget methods

Tk	Tkinter
scrollbar activate [element]	scrollbar.activate(element)
scrollbar delta deltaX deltaY	scrollbar.delta(deltaX, deltaY)
scrollbar fraction x y	scrollbar.fraction(x, y)
scrollbar get	scrollbar.get()
scrollbar identify x y	scrollbar.identify(x, y)
scrollbar set first last	scrollbar.set(first, last)

The Toplevel widget

Table A.70   Toplevel widget standard options

Tk	Tkinter
-borderwidth width	borderwidth=width
-cursor cursor	cursor=cursor
-height height	height=height
-highlightbackground color	highlightbackground=color
-highlightcolor color	highlightcolor=color
-highlightthickness width	highlightthickness=width
-relief flat|groove|raised|ridge|sunken	relief=FLAT|GROOVE|RAISED|RIDGE|SUNKEN|SOLID
-takefocus focusType	takefocus=focusType
-width width	width=width

Table A.71   Toplevel widget-specific options

Tk	Tkinter
-background color	background=color
-class string	class=string
-colormap colormap	colormap=colormap
-container boolean	container=boolean
-menu pathName	menu=pathName
-use windowID	use=windowID
-screen screen	screen=screen
-visual visual	visual=visual

The Image class

Table A.72 Image methods

Tk	Tkinter
image create type [name] [options value ...]	image = PhotoImage|BitmapImage([option=value ...])
image delete name	del(image)
image height name	image.height()
image names	image_names()
image type name	image.type()
image types	image_types()
image width name	image_width()

The bitmap image type

Table A.73 Bitmap options

Tk	Tkinter
-background color	background=color
-data string	data=string
-file fileName	file=fileName
-foreground color	foreground=color
-maskdata string	maskdata=string
-maskfile fileName	maskfile=fileName

The PhotoImage type

Table A.74 PhotoImage options

Tk	Tkinter
-data string	data=string
-file fileName	file=fileName
-format formatName	format=formatName
-height number	height=number
-palette paletteSpec	palette=paletteSpec
-width number	width=number

Table A.75 PhotoImage methods

Tk	Tkinter
image blank	image.blank()
image copy sourceImage [option value ...]	image.copy()
image copy sourceImage [-zoom x y]	image.zoom(xscale [, yscale])
image copy sourceImage [-subsample x y]	image.subsample(xscale [, yscale])
image get x y	image.get(x, y)
image put data [-to x1 y1 x2 y2]	image.put(data [, 'to' x1 y1 x2 y2]_
image read file [option value ...]	No mapping
image redither	No mapping
image write fileName [option value ...]	image.write(fileName [, formatName] [, (x1, y1, x2, y2)])

Window information

Table A.76 Winfo methods

Tk	Tkinter
winfo allmapped window	No mapping
winfo atom [-displayof window] name	window.winfo_atom(name, [, win])
winfo atomname [-displayof window] id	window.winfo_atomname(id [, win])
winfo cells window	window.winfo_cells()
winfo children window	window.winfo_children()
winfo class window	window.winfo_class()
winfo_colormapfull window	window.winfo_colormapfull()
winfo containing [-displayof window] rootX rootY	window.winfo_containing(rootX, rootY [, win])
winfo depth window	window.winfo_depth()
winfo exists window	window.winfo_exists()
winfo fpixels window number	window.winfo_fpixels(bumber)
winfo geometry window	window.winfo_geometry()
winfo height window	window.winfo_height()
winfo id window	window.winfo_id()
winfo interps [-displayof window]	window.winfo_interps([win])
winfo ismapped window	window.winfo_ismapped()
winfo manager window	window.winfo_manager()
winfo name window	window.winfo_name()
winfo parent window	window.winfo_parent()

Table A.76 Winfo methods (continued)

Tk	Tkinter
winfo pathname [-displayof window] id	window.winfo_pathname(id, [, win])
winfo pointerx window	window.winfo_pointerx()
winfo pointerxy window	window.winfo_pointerxy()
winfo pointery window	window.winfo_pointery()
winfo pixels window number	window.winfo_pixels(number)
winfo_reqheight window	window.winfo_reqheight()
winfo reqwidth window	window.winfo_reqwidth()
winfo rgb window color	window.winfo_rgb(color)
winfo rootx window	window.winfo_rootx()
winfo rooty window	window.winfo_rooty()
winfo server window	windowwindow.winfo_server()
winfo screen window	window.winfo_screen()
winfo screencells window	window.winfo_screencells()
winfo screendepth window	window.winfo_screendepth()
winfo screenheight window	window.winfo_screenheight()
winfo screenmmheight window	window.winfo_screenmmheight()
winfo screenmmwidth window	window.winfo_screenmmwidth()
winfo screenvisual window	window.winfo_screenvisual()
winfo screenwidth window	window.winfo_screenwidth()
winfo toplevel window	window.winfo_toplevel()
winfo visual window	window.winfo_visual()
winfo visualsavailable window	window.winfo_visualsavailable()
winfo vrootheight window	window.winfo_vrootheight()
winfo vrootwidth window	window.winfo_vrootwidth()
winfo vrootx window	window.winfo_vrootx()
winfo vrooty window	window.winfo_vrooty()
winfo width window	window.winfo_width()
winfo x window	window.winfo_x()
winfo y window	window.winfo_y()

The window manager

Table A.77 wm operations

Tk	Tkinter
wm aspect window [minNumer minDenom maxNumer maxDenom]	window.wm_aspect([minNumer, minDenom, maxNumer, maxDenom])
wm client window [name]	window.wm_client([name])
wm colormapwindows window [windowList]	window.wm_colormapwindows([windowList])
wm command window [value]	window.wm_command([value])
wm deiconify window	window.wm_deiconify()
wm focusmodel window [active|passive]	window.wm_focusmodel(['active'|'passive'])
wm frame window	window.wm_frame(
wm geometry window [newGeometry]	window.wm_geometry([newGeometry])
wm grid window [baseWidth baseHeight widthInc heightInc]	window.wm_grid([baseWidth, baseHeight, widthInc, heightInc])
wm group window [pathName]	window.wm_group([pathName])
wm iconbitmap window [bitmap]	window.wm_iconbitmap([bitmap])
wm iconify window	window.wm_iconify()
wm iconmask window [bitmap]	window.wm_iconmask([bitmap])
wm iconname window [newName]	window.wm_iconname([newName])
wm iconposition window [x y]	window.wm_iconposition([x, y])
wm iconwindow window [pathName]	window.wm_iconwindow([pathName])
wm maxsize window [width height]	window.wm_maxsize([width, height])
wm minsize window [width height]	window.wm_minsize([width, height])
wm overrideredirect window [boolean]	window.wm_overrideredirect([boolean])
wm positionfrom window [program|user]	window.wm_positionfrom(['program'|'user']
wm protocol window [name] [command]	window.wm_protocol([name] [, command])
wm resizable window [widthBoolean heightBoolean]	window.wm_resizable([widthBoolean, heightBoolean])
wm sizefrom window [program|user]	window.wm_sizefrom(['program'|'user'])
wm state window	window.wm_state()
wm title window [string]	window.wm_title([string])
wm transient window [master]	window.wm_transient([master])
wm withdraw window	window.wm_withdraw()

Binding and virtual events

Table A.78 Bind and event methods

Tk	Tkinter
bind tag	widget.bind()
bind tag sequence	widget.bind('sequence')
bind tag sequence script	widget.bind('sequence', script)
bindtags window [tagList]	window.bindtags([tagList])
event add <<virtual>> sequence [sequence ...]	window.event_add(virtual, sequence [, sequence ...])
event delete <<virtual>> [sequence ...]	window.event_delete(virtual [, sequence ...])
event generate window event [-when when] [option value ...]	window.event_generate(sequence [, option=value ...])

Geometry management

The pack command

Table A.79 Pack methods

Tk	Tkinter
pack [configure] slave [slave ...] [options]	slave.pack([option=value ...])
pack forget slave [slave ...]	slave.pack_forget()
pack info slave	slave.pack_info()
pack propagate master [boolean]	master.pack_propagate([boolean])
pack slaves master	master.pack_slaves()

The place command

Table A.80 Place options

Tk	Tkinter
-anchor anchor	anchor=anchor
-bordermode inside|outside|ignore	bordermode='inside'|'outside'|'ignore'
-height size	height=size
-in master	in=master
-relheight size	relheight=size
-relwidth size	relwidth=size

Table A.80 Place options (continued)

Tk	Tkinter
-relx location	relx=location
-rely location	rely=location
-width size	width=size
-x location	x=location
-y location	y=location

Table A.81 Place methods

Tk	Tkinter
place [configure] window option value [option value ...]	window.place([option=value ...])
place forget window	window.place_forget()
place info window	window.place_info()
place slaves window	window.place_slaves()

The grid command

Table A.82 Grid options

Tk	Tkinter
-column n	column=n
-columnspan n	columnspan=n
-in other	in=other
-ipadx amount	ipadx=amount
-ipady amount	ipady=amount
-padx amount	padx=amount
-pady amount	pady=amount
-row n	row=n
-rowspan n	rowspan=n
-sticky [n][s][e][w]	sticky=[N][S][E][W]

Table A.83   Grid methods

Tk	Tkinter
grid [configure] slave [slave ...] [option value ...]	slave.grid([option=value ...])
grid bbox master [column row [column2 row2]]	master.grid_bbox([column, row [, column2, row2]])
grid columnconfigure master columnList [options]	master.grid_columnconfigure(columnList [, options])
-minsize size	minsize=size
-pad amount	pad=amount
-weight int	weight=int
grid forget slave [slave ...]	slave.grid_forget()
grid info slave	slave.grid_info()
grid location master x y	slave.grid_location(x, y)
grid propagate master [boolean]	master.grid_propagate([boolean])
grid remove slave [slave ...]	slave.grid_remove()
grid rowconfigure master rowList [options]	master.grid_rowconfigure(rowList, [, options])
grid size master	master.grid_size()
grid slaves master [-row row] [-column column]	master.grid_slaves([row] [, column])

Fonts

Table A.84   Font options

Tk	Tkinter
-family name	family=name
-size size	size=size
-weight weight	weight=weight
-slant slant	slant=slant
-underline boolean	underline=boolean
-overstrike boolean	overstrike=boolean

Table A.85 Font methods

Tk	Tkinter
font actual fontDesc [-displayof window] [option]	fontDesc.actual[option])
font configure fontname [option [value option value ...]]	fontname.configure([option=value ...])
font create [fontname [option value ...]]	font = Font([master] [, option=value ...])
font delete fontname [fontname ...]	del(fontname)
font families [-displayof window]	famililes([window])
font measure fontDesc [-displayof window] text	fontDesc.measure(text)
font metrics fontDesc [-displayof window] [metric]	fontDesc.metrics([metric])
font names	names([window])

Other Tk commands

Table A.86 Other Tk methods

Tk	Tkinter
bell [-displayof window]	window.bell([displayof=window])
clipboard clear [-displayof window]	window.clipbord_clear([displayof=window])
clipboard append [-displayof win] [-format fmt] [-type type] data	window.clipbord_clear(data [, option=value ...])
destroy [window window ...]	window.destroy()
focus [-force] window	window.focus_force()
focus [-displayof window]	window.focus_displayof()
focus -lastfor window	window.focus_lastfor()
grab current [window]	window.grab_current()
grab release window	window.grab_release()
grab set window	window.grab_set()
grab set -global window	window.grab_set_global()
grab status window	window.grab_status()
lower window [belowThis]	window.lower([belowThis])
option add pattern value [priority]	window.option_add(pattern, value, [, priority])
option clear	window.option clear()
option get window name class	window.option_get(name, class)

Table A.86 Other Tk methods (continued)

Tk	Tkinter
option readfile fileName [priority]	window.option_readfile(fileName [, priority])
raise window [aboveThis]	window.raise([aboveThis])
selection clear [-displayof window] [-selection selection]	window.selection_clear([displayof=window] [, selection=sel])
selection get [-displayof window] [-selection selection] [-type type]	window.selection_get([displayof=window] [, -selection=sel][, type=type]
selection handle [-selection sel] [-type type] [-format fmt] win cmd	window.selection_handle(cmd [, selection=sel] [, type=type] [, format= fmt]
selection own [-displayof window] [-selection selection]	window.selection_own([displayof=window] [, selection=sel])
selection own [-selection selection] [-command command] window	window.selection_own_get([selection=sel] [command= command])
send [-displayof window] [-async] interp cmd [arg arg ...]	window.send(interp, cmd [, arg ...])
tk appname [newName]	No mapping
tk scaling [-displayof window] [floatNumber]	No mapping
tkwait variable varName	window.wait_variable([window])
tkwait visibility window	window.wait_variablevisibility([window])
tkwait window window	window.wait_window([window])
tk_bisque	window.tk_bisque()
tk_chooseColor [option value ...]	Use tkColorChooser
tk_dialog topw title text bitmap default string [string ...]	Use Dialog
tk_focusNext window	window.tk_focusNext()
tk_focusPrev window	window.tk_focusPrev()
tk_focusFollowsMouse	window.tk_focusFollowsMouse()
tk_getOpenFile [option value ...]	No mapping
tk_getSaveFile [option value ...]	No mapping
tk_messageBox [option value ...]	box=MessageBox(master, text=text [, option ...])
tk_optionMenu w varName value [value ...]	menu = OptionMenu(master, varName, value [, value ...])
tk_popup menu x y [entry]	menu.tk_popup(x, y [, entry])
tk_setPalette color	window.tk_setPalette(color)
tk_setPalette name color [name color ...]	window.tk_setPalette(name=color [, name=color ...])

A P P E N D I X   B

Tkinter reference

About this appendix

The information presented in this appendix has been largely generated using Python programs that use the Tkinter module dictionary and the Tk man pages, which were parsed and edited to correspond to Python use and stored in a huge dictionary. The programs produced a large ASCII file which contained headings, text and tables ready for importing into FrameMaker, which was used to produce this book. Some of the information required manual adjustment, but the bulk of data required only formatting in FrameMaker. The scripts did not take long to develop.

You will find references to both Tcl and Tk. I have left them in the text, where appropriate, since it is worth remembering that Tkinter is, ultimately, just an interface to them and it is Tcl/Tk that determines whether supplied arguments are valid and appropriate.

Common options

Many widgets accept options which are common with other widgets. There may be small differences in the absolute values, but they are similar enough for them to be documented as a group here. In general, many of the descriptions are derived from the Tk man pages, since Tkinter provides a simple interface to the underlying Tk widgets where options are considered. However, since Tkinter provides an object-oriented wrapper to Tk, some of the descriptions required considerable modification to the Tkinter context.

425

Options shared by most widgets

Option (alias)	Description	Units	Typical	All widgets except:
background (bg)	Specifies the normal background color to use when displaying the widget.	color	'gray25' '#FF4400'	
borderwidth (bd)	Specifies a non-negative value indicating the width of the 3-D border to draw around the outside of the widget (if such a border is being drawn; the relief option typically determines this). The value may also be used when drawing 3-D effects in the interior of the widget. The value may have any of the forms acceptable to Tkinter (Tk_GetPixels).	pixel	3	
cursor	Specifies the mouse cursor to be used for the widget. The value may have any of the forms acceptable to Tkinter (Tk_GetCursor).	cursor	gumby	
font	Specifies the font to use when drawing text inside the widget.	font	'Helvetica' ('Verdana', 8)	Canvas Frame Scroll-bar Toplevel
foreground (fg)	Specifies the normal Foreground color to use when displaying the widget.	color	'black' '#FF2244'	Canvas Frame Scroll-bar Toplevel
highlightbackground	Specifies the color to display in the traversal highlight region when the widget does not have the input focus.	color	'gray30'	Menu
highlightcolor	Specifies the color to use for the traversal highlight rectangle that is drawn around the widget when it has the input focus.	color	'royalblue'	Menu
highlightthickness	Specifies a non-negative value indicating the width of the highlight rectangle to draw around the outside of the widget when it has the input focus. The value may have any of the forms acceptable to Tkinter (Tk_GetPixels). If the value is zero, no focus highlight is drawn around the widget.	pixel	2, 1m	Menu

Option (alias)	Description	Units	Typical	All widgets except:
relief	Specifies the 3-D effect desired for the widget. Acceptable values are RAISED, SUNKEN, FLAT, RIDGE, SOLID, and GROOVE. The value indicates how the interior of the widget should appear relative to its exterior; for example, RAISED means the interior of the widget should appear to protrude from the screen, relative to the exterior of the widget.	constant	RAISED GROOVE	
takefocus	Determines whether the window accepts the focus during keyboard traversal (e.g., TAB and SHIFT-TAB). Before setting the focus to a window, the traversal scripts consult the value of the takefocus option. A value of 0 means that the window should be skipped entirely during keyboard traversal. 1 means that the window should receive the input focus as long as it is viewable (it and all of its ancestors are mapped). An empty value for the option means that the traversal scripts make the decision about whether or not to focus on the window: the current algorithm is to skip the window if it is disabled, if it has no key bindings, or if it is not viewable.	boolean	1 YES	
width	Specifies an integer value indicating the desired width of the widget, in average-size characters of the widget's font. If the value is less than or equal to zero, to widget picks a size just large enough to hold its current text.	integer	32	Menu

Options shared by many widgets

Option (alias)	Description	Units	Typical	These widgets only
activebackground	Specifies the background color to use when drawing active elements. An element (a widget or portion of a widget) is active if the mouse cursor is positioned over the element and pressing a mouse button will cause some action to occur. If strict Motif compliance has been requested by setting the tk_strictMotif variable, this option will normally be ignored; the normal background color will be used instead. For some elements on Windows and Macintosh systems, the active color will only be used while mouse button 1 is pressed over the element.	color	'red' '#fa07a3'	Button Checkbutton Menu Menubutton Radiobutton Scale Scrollbar
activeforeground	Specifies the foreground color to use when drawing active elements. See above for definition of active elements.	color	'cadet- blue'	Button Checkbutton Menu Mcnubutton Radiobutton
anchor	Specifies how the information in a widget (e.g. text or a bitmap) is to be displayed in the widget. Must be one of the values N, NE, E, SE, S, SW, W, NW, or CENTER. For example, NW means to display the information so that its top-left corner is at the top-left corner of the widget.	constant		Button Checkbutton Label Menubutton Message Radiobutton
bitmap	Specifies a bitmap to display in the widget, in any of the forms acceptable to Tkinter (Tk_GetBitmap). The exact way in which the bitmap is displayed may be affected by other options such as anchor or justify. Typically, if this option is specified then it overrides other options that specify a textual value to display in the widget; the bitmap option may be reset to an empty string to re-enable a text display. In widgets that support both bitmap and image options, image will usually override bitmap.	bitmap		Button Checkbutton Label Menubutton Radiobutton

Option (alias)	Description	Units	Typical	These widgets only
command	Specifies a Python command to associate with the widget. This command is typically invoked when mouse button 1 is released over the widget. For check buttons and radio buttons the button's tkinter variable (set with the variable option) will be updated before the command is invoked.	command	setupData	Button Checkbutton Radiobutton Scale Scrollbar
disabledforeground	Specifies the foreground color to use when drawing a disabled element. If the option is specified as an empty string (which is typically the case on monochrome displays), disabled elements are drawn with the normal foreground color but they are dimmed by drawing them with a stippled fill pattern.	color	'gray50'	Button Checkbutton Menu Menubutton Radiobutton
height	Specifies the desired height for the window, in units of characters in the font given by the font option. Must be at least one.	integer	1 4	Button Canvas Checkbutton Frame Label Listbox Menubutton Radiobutton Text Toplevel
image	Specifies an image to display in the widget, which must have been created with the image create method. Typically, if the image option is specified then it overrides other options that specify a bitmap or textual value to display in the widget; the image option may be reset to an empty string to re-enable a bitmap or text display.	image		Button Checkbutton Label Menubutton Radiobutton
justify	When multiple lines of text are displayed in a widget, this option determines how the lines line up with each other. Must be one of LEFT, CENTER, or RIGHT. LEFT means that the lines' left edges all line up, CENTER means that the lines' centers are aligned, and RIGHT means that the lines' right edges line up.	constant	RIGHT	Button Checkbutton Entry Label Menubutton Message Radiobutton

Option (alias)	Description	Units	Typical	These widgets only
padx	Specifies a non-negative value indicating how much extra space to request for the widget in the X-direction. The value may have any of the forms acceptable to Tkinter (Tk_GetPixels). When computing how large a window it needs, the widget will add this amount to the width it would normally need (as determined by the width of the things displayed in the widget); if the geometry manager can satisfy this request, the widget will end up with extra internal space to the left and/or right of what it displays inside. Most widgets only use this option for padding text: if they are displaying a bitmap or image, then they usually ignore padding options.	pixel	2m 10	Button Checkbutton Label Menubutton Message Radiobutton Text
pady	Specifies a non-negative value indicating how much extra space to request for the widget in the Y-direction. The value may have any of the forms acceptable to Tkinter (Tk_GetPixels). When computing how large a window it needs, the widget will add this amount to the height it would normally need (as determined by the height of the things displayed in the widget); if the geometry manager can satisfy this request, the widget will end up with extra internal space above and/or below what it displays inside. Most widgets only use this option for padding text: if they are displaying a bitmap or image, then they usually ignore padding options.	pixel	12 3m	Button Checkbutton Label Menubutton Message Radiobutton Text
selectbackground	Specifies the background color to use when displaying selected items.	color	blue	Canvas Entry Listbox Text
selectborderwidth	Specifies a non-negative value indicating the width of the 3-D border to draw around selected items. The value may have any of the forms acceptable to Tkinter (Tk_GetPixels).	pixel	3	Canvas Entry Listbox Text
selectforeground	Specifies the foreground color to use when displaying selected items.	color	yellow	Canvas Entry Listbox Text

Option (alias)	Description	Units	Typical	These widgets only
state	Specifies one of two or three states for the widget (typically `checkbutton`): `NORMAL` and `DISABLED` or `NORMAL`, `ACTIVE` and `DISABLED`. In `NORMAL` state the widget is displayed using the foreground and background options. The `ACTIVE` state is typically used when the pointer is over the widget. In `ACTIVE` state the widget is displayed using the `activeforeground` and `active-background` options. `DISABLED` state means that the widget should be insensitive: the default bindings will refuse to activate the widget and will ignore mouse button presses. In this state the `disabledforeground` and background options determine how the widget is displayed.	constant	`ACTIVE`	Button Checkbutton Entry Menubutton Radiobutton Scale Text
text	Specifies a string to be displayed inside the widget. The way in which the string is displayed depends on the particular widget and may be determined by other options, such as `anchor` or `justify`.	string	`'Display This'`	Button Checkbutton Label Menubutton Message Radiobutton
textvariable	Specifies the name of a variable. The value of the variable is converted to a text string to be displayed inside the widget; if the variable value changes then the widget will automatically update itself to reflect the new value. The way in which the string is displayed in the widget depends on the particular widget and may be determined by other options, such as `anchor` or `justify`.	variable	`widgetContent`	Button Checkbutton Entry Label Menubutton Message Radiobutton
underline	Specifies the integer index of a character to underline in the widget. This option is used by the default bindings to implement keyboard traversal for menu buttons and menu entries. `0` corresponds to the first character of the text displayed in the widget, `1` to the next character, and so on.	integer	`2`	Button Checkbutton Label Menubutton Radiobutton

Option (alias)	Description	Units	Typical	These widgets only
wraplength	For widgets that can perform word-wrapping, this option specifies the maximum line length. Lines that would exceed this length are wrapped onto the next line, so that no line is longer than the specified length. The value may be specified in any of the standard forms for screen distances. If this value is less than or equal to 0 then no wrapping is done: lines will break only at newline characters in the text.	pixel	4i, 65	Button Checkbutton Label Menubutton Radiobutton
xscrollcommand	Specifies the prefix for a command used to communicate with horizontal scrollbars. When the view in the widget's window changes (or whenever anything else occurs that could change the display in a scrollbar, such as a change in the total size of the widget's contents), the widget will generate a command by concatenating the scroll command and two numbers. Each of the numbers is a fraction between 0 and 1, which indicates a position in the document. 0 indicates the beginning of the document, 1 indicates the end, .333 indicates a position one third of the way through the document, and so on. The first fraction indicates the first information in the document that is visible in the window, and the second fraction indicates the information just after the last portion that is visible. The command is then passed to the Tcl interpreter for execution. Typically the xScrollCommand option consists of the identity of a scrollbar widget followed by set; for example, self.x.scrollbar set will cause the scrollbar to be updated whenever the view in the window changes. If this option is not specified, then no command will be executed.	function		Canvas Entry Listbox Text

Option (alias)	Description	Units	Typical	These widgets only
yscrollcommand	Specifies the prefix for a command used to communicate with vertical scrollbars. When the view in the widget's window changes (or whenever anything else occurs that could change the display in a scrollbar, such as a change in the total size of the widget's contents), the widget will generate a command by concatenating the scroll command and two numbers. Each of the numbers is a fraction between 0 and 1, which indicates a position in the document. 0 indicates the beginning of the document, 1 indicates the end, .333 indicates a position one third of the way through the document, and so on. The first fraction indicates the first information in the document that is visible in the window, and the second fraction indicates the information just after the last portion that is visible. The command is then passed to the Tcl interpreter for execution. Typically the yScrollCommand option consists of the identity of a scrollbar widget followed by set; for example, self.y.scrollbar set will cause the scrollbar to be updated whenever the view in the window changes. If this option is not specified, then no command will be executed.	function		Canvas Entry Listbox Text

Inherited methods

Many methods are inherited from the bases classes and are available to all widgets. In addition to the methods listed here, grid, pack and place geometry manager methods are inherited by all widgets. These methods are documented separately from the widgets.

The arguments to the methods are presented in the form that Tkinter defines them. You will find a mapping to Tk commands here; typically Tk commands have the window as the first argument. Tkinter methods are applied to the current instance of a widget which may be interpreted as the window or slave or master arguments in Tk commands.

Common widget methods

after(ms, function=None, *args)

Registers a callback that is called after *ms* milliseconds. Note that this period is not guaranteed to be accurate; you must assume that the wait period is at least the given period and it can be much longer. The method returns `id` which may be used as the argument to `after_cancel` to cancel the callback.

after_cancel(id)

Cancels the specified `after` callback.

after_idle(function, *args)

Registers a callback `function` which is called when the system is idle (no more events in the event queue). The callback is called once for each call to `after_idle`.

bell(displayof=0)

Rings the bell on the display for the window and returns `None`. If the `displayof` option is omitted, the display of the application's main window is used by default. The method uses the current bell-related settings for the display, which may be modified with programs such as xset. This method also resets the screen saver for the screen. Some screen savers will ignore this, but others will reset so that the screen becomes visible again.

bind(sequence=None, function=None, add=None)

Associates event handlers with events. If add is + the binding is added to the current bindings; the default is to replace the existing binding.

bind_all(sequence=None, function=None, add=None)

Associates event handlers with events at the application level. If add is + the binding is added to the current bindings; the default is to replace the existing binding.

bind_class(className, sequence=None, function=None, add=None)

Associates event handlers with events for the specified widget class. If add is + the binding is added to the current bindings; the default is to replace the existing binding.

bindtags(tagList=None)

If bindtags is invoked without an argument, then the current set of binding tags for the widget is returned as a tuple. If the `tagList` argument is specified to `bindtags`, then it must be a proper tuple; the tags for `window` are changed to the elements of the list. The elements of `tagList` may be arbitrary strings; however, any tag starting with a dot is treated as the name of a Tk window. If no window by that name exists at the time an event is processed, then the tag is ignored for that event. The order of the elements in `tagList` determines the order in which binding scripts are executed in response to events.

cget(key)

Returns the current value of the configuration option given by `key`.

clipboard_append(string)

Appends `string` to the clipboard on the window's display.

clipboard_clear()

Claims ownership of the clipboard on the window's display and removes any previous contents.

configure(option=None)

Queries or modifies the configuration options of the widget. If no option is specified, returns a dictionary describing all of the available options for the widget. If one or more option-value pairs are specified, then the method modifies the given widget option(s) to have the given value(s); in this case the method returns None.

destroy()

Destroys the widget and removes all references from namespace.

event_add(virtual, *sequences)

Associates the virtual event virtual with the physical event sequence(s) given by the sequence arguments, so that the virtual event will trigger whenever any one of the sequences occurs. Virtual may be any string value and sequence may have any of the values allowed for the sequence argument to the bind method. If virtual is already defined, the new physical event sequences add to the existing sequences for the event.

event_delete(virtual, *sequences)

Deletes each of the sequences from those associated with the virtual event given by virtual. Virtual may be any string value and sequence may have any of the values allowed for the sequence argument to the bind method. Any sequences not currently associated with virtual are ignored. If no sequence argument is provided, all physical event sequences are removed for virtual, so that the virtual event will not trigger anymore.

event_generate(sequence, option=value...)

Generates a window event and arranges for it to be processed just as if it had come from the window system. Sequence provides a basic description of the event, such as <Shift-Button-2>. Sequence may have any of the forms allowed for the sequence argument of the bind method except that it must consist of a single event pattern, not a sequence. Option-value pairs may be used to specify additional attributes of the event, such as the x and y mouse position.

event_info(virtual=None)

Returns information about virtual events. If the virtual argument is omitted, the return value is a tuple of all the virtual events that are currently defined. If virtual is specified then the return value is a tuple whose elements are the physical event sequences currently defined for the given virtual event; if the virtual event is not defined then None is returned.

focus_displayof()

Returns the name of the focus window on the display containing the widget. If the focus window for widget's display isn't in this application, the return value is None.

focus_force()

Sets the focus of the widget's display to `self`, even if the application doesn't currently have the input focus for the display. This method should be used sparingly, if at all. In normal usage, an application should not claim the focus for itself; instead, it should wait for the window manager to give it the focus.

focus_get()

If the application currently has the input focus on the widget's display, this method returns the identity of the window with focus.

focus_lastfor()

Returns the identity of the most recent window to have the input focus among all the windows in the same top-level as `self`. If no window in that top-level has ever had the input focus, or if the most recent focus window has been deleted, then the ID of the top-level is returned. The return value is the window that will receive the input focus the next time the window manager gives the focus to the top-level.

focus_set()

If the application currently has the input focus on the widget's display, this method resets the input focus for the widget's display to `self`. If the application doesn't currently have the input focus on the widget's display, `self` will be remembered as the focus for its top-level; the next time the focus arrives at the top-level, Tk will redirect it to `self`.

getboolean(string)

Converst `string` to a boolean using Tcl's conventions.

getvar(name='PY_VAR')

Returns the value of the variable `name`.

grab_current()

Returns the identity of the current grab window in this application for window's display, or `None` if there is no such window.

grab_release()

Releases the grab on `self` if there is one; otherwise it does nothing.

grab_set()

Sets a grab on all events for the current application to `self`. If a grab was already in effect for this application on the widget's display then it is automatically released. If there is already a grab on `self` then the method does nothing.

grab_set_global()

Sets a grab on all events for the entire screen to `self`. If a grab was already in effect for this application on the widget's display then it is automatically released. If there is already a grab on `self` then the method does nothing. Be careful if you use this grab.

grab_status()

Returns None if no grab is currently set on window, local if a local grab is set on window, and global if a global grab is set.

image_names()

Returns a list containing the names of all existing images.

image_types()

Returns a list of all image types that have been created.

keys()

Returns a tuple containing the names of the options available for this widget. Use self.cget to obtain the current value for each option.

lower(belowThis=None)

Changes the widget's position in the stacking order. If the belowThis argument is omitted then the method lowers the window so that it is below all of its siblings in the stacking order (it will be obscured by any siblings that overlap it and will not obscure any siblings). If belowThis is specified then it must be the identity of a window that is either a sibling of window or the descendant of a sibling of window. In this case the lower method will insert the window into the stacking order just below belowThis (or the ancestor of belowThis that is a sibling of window); this could end up either raising or lowering the window.

mainloop

Starts processing the event loop. Nothing will be updated until this method is called and this method does not return until the quit method is called.

nametowidget(name)

Returns the widget identity corresponding to name.

option_add(pattern, value, priority = None)

Allows you to add entries to the Tk option database. pattern contains the option being specified, and it consists of names and/or classes separated by asterisks or dots, in the usual X format. value contains a text string to associate with pattern; this is the value that will be returned in calls to Tkinter (Tk_GetOption) or by invocations of the option_get method. If priority is specified, it indicates the priority level for this option; it defaults to interactive.

option_clear()

Clears the Tk option database. Default options (from the RESOURCE_MANAGER property or the .Xdefaults file) will be reloaded automatically the next time an option is added to the database or removed from it.

option_get(name, className)

Returns the value of the option specified for self under name and class. If several entries in the option database match name and class, then the method returns whichever was created with the highest priority level. If there are several matching entries at the same priority level, then it returns whichever entry was most recently entered into the option database. If there are no matching entries, then the empty string is returned.

option_readfile(fileName, priority = None)

Reads `fileName`, which should have the standard format for an X resource database such as .Xdefaults, and it adds all the options specified in that file to the option database. If *priority* is specified, it indicates the priority level at which to enter the options; priority defaults to interactive.

quit()

Exits the mainloop.

selection_clear()

Clears the selection if it is currently in this widget. If the selection isn't in this widget then the method has no effect.

selection_get()

Retrieves the value of selection from the window's display and returns it as a result.

selection_handle(handler)

Creates a handler for selection requests, such that `handler` will be executed whenever selection is owned by the window and someone attempts to retrieve it in the form given by type (e.g. type is specified in the `selection_get` method). selection defaults to PRIMARY, type defaults to STRING, and format defaults to STRING. If `handler` is empty then any existing handler for the window, type and selection is removed.

selection_own()

Causes `self` to become the new owner of selection on the window's display, returning an empty string as a result. The existing owner, if any, is notified that it has lost the selection.

selection_own_get()

Returns the identity of the window in this application that owns selection on the display containing `self`, or an empty string if no window in this application owns the selection. `selection` defaults to PRIMARY and window defaults to the root window.

send(interp, cmd, *args)

Arranges for `cmd` (and `args`) to be executed in the application named by `interp`. It returns the result or error from that command execution. `interp` may be the name of any application whose main window is on the display containing the sender's main window; it need not be within the same process. If no `args` arguments are present, then the command to be executed is contained entirely within the `cmd` argument. If one or more `args` are present, they are concatenated to form the command to be executed, just as for the `eval` command.

setvar(name='PY_VAR', value ='1')

Sets the specified variable, name, to the value supplied.

tk_bisque()

Provided for backward compatibility: it restores the application's colors to the light brown (bisque) color scheme used in Tk 3.6 and earlier versions.

tk_focusFollowsMouse()

Creates an implicit focus model: it reconfigures Tk so that the focus is set to a window whenever the mouse enters it.

tk_focusNext(), tk_focusPrev()

The *tk_focusNext* and *tk_focusPrev* methods implement a focus order among the windows of a top-level; they are used in the default bindings for TAB and SHIFT TAB, among other things.

tk_menuBar(*args)

Does nothing, since the Tk function is obsolete.

tk_setPalette(*args)

Changes the color scheme for Tk by modifying the colors of existing widgets and by changing the option database so that future widgets will use the new color scheme. If tk_setPalette is invoked with a single argument, the argument is the name of a color to use as the normal background color; tk_setPalette will compute a complete color palette from this background color.

Alternatively, the arguments to tk_setPalette may consist of any number of name-value pairs, where the first argument of the pair is the name of an option in the Tk option database and the second argument is the new value to use for that option. The following database options are currently supported:

- activeBackground
- activeForeground
- background
- disabledForeground
- foreground
- highlightBackground
- highlightColor
- insertBackground
- selectColor
- selectBackground
- selectForeground
- troughColor

tk_strictMotif(boolean=None)

boolean is set to zero by default. If an application sets it to TRUE, then Tk attempts to adhere as closely as possible to Motif look-and-feel standards. For example, active elements such as buttons and scrollbar sliders will not change color when the pointer passes over them.

tkraise(aboveThis=None) [lift(aboveThis=None)]

If the `aboveThis` argument is omitted then the method raises `self` so that it is above all of its siblings in the stacking order (it will not be obscured by any siblings and will obscure any siblings that overlap it). If `aboveThis` is specified then it must be the identity of a window that is either a sibling of the window or the descendant of a sibling of the window. In this case the `raise` method will insert `self` into the stacking order just above `aboveThis` (or the ancestor of `aboveThis` that is a sibling of the window); this could end up either raising or lowering the window.

unbind(sequence, funcid=None)

Removes any bindings for the given `sequence`. If the event handler `funcid` is given bindings for `sequence`, that handler alone will be removed.

unbind_all(sequence)

Removes all bindings for the supplied `sequence` at the application level.

unbind_class(className, sequence)

Removes all bindings for the supplied `sequence` for the specified class `className`.

update()

Processes all pending events on the event list. In particular, completes all geometry negotiation and redraws widgets as necessary. Use this method with care, since it can be a source of problems, not only by consuming CPU cycles but also by setting up potential race conditions.

update_idletasks()

Processes all pending idle events on the event list.

wait_variable(name='PY_VAR')

Waits for the value of the supplied Tkinter variable, `name`, to change. Note that the method enters a local event loop until the variable changes, so the application's mainloop continues.

wait_visibility(window=None)

Waits for the specified `window` to become visible. Note that the method enters a local event loop until the variable changes, so the application's mainloop continues.

wait_window(window=None)

Waits for the specified `window` to be destroyed. Note that the method enters a local event loop until the variable changes, so the application's mainloop continues.

Winfo methods

winfo_atom(name, displayof=0)

Returns an integer giving the integer identifier for the atom whose name is name. If no atom exists with the name name then a new one is created. If the `displayof` option is given then the atom is looked up on the `display of` window; otherwise it is looked up on the display of the application's main window.

winfo_atomname(id, displayof=0)

Returns the textual name for the atom whose integer identifier is id. If the `displayof` option is given then the identifier is looked up on the display of window; otherwise it is looked up on the display of the application's main window. This method is the inverse of the `winfo_atom` method. It generates an error if no such atom exists.

winfo_cells()

Returns an integer giving the number of cells in the color map for the window.

winfo_children()

Returns a list containing the path names of all the children of window. The list is in stacking order, with the lowest window first. Top-level windows are returned as children of their logical parents.

winfo_class()

Returns the class name for window.

winfo_colormapfull()

Returns TRUE if the colormap for the window is known to be full, FALSE otherwise. The colormap for a window is "known" to be full if the last attempt to allocate a new color on that window failed and this application hasn't freed any colors in the colormap since the failed allocation.

winfo_containing(rootX, rootY, displayof=0)

Returns the identity of the window containing the point given by rootX and rootY. rootX and rootY are specified in screen units in the coordinate system of the root window (if a virtual-root window manager is in use then the coordinate system of the virtual root window is used). If the `displayof` option is given then the coordinates refer to the screen containing the window; otherwise they refer to the screen of the application's main window. If no window in this application contains the point then None is returned. In selecting the containing window, children are given higher priority than parents and among siblings the highest one in the stacking order is chosen.

winfo_depth()

Returns an integer giving the depth of window (number of bits per pixel).

winfo_exists()

Returns TRUE if a window exists for self, FALSE if no such window exists.

winfo_fpixels(number)

Returns a floating-point value giving the number of pixels in window corresponding to the distance given by number. number may be specified in any of the forms acceptable to Tkinter

(Tk_GetScreenMM), such as `2.0c` or `1i`. The return value may be fractional; for an integer value, use `winfo_pixels`.

winfo_geometry()

Returns the geometry for window, in the form `widthxheight+x+y`. All dimensions are in pixels.

winfo_height()

Returns an integer giving window's height in pixels. When a window is first created its height will be 1 pixel; the height will eventually be changed by a geometry manager to fulfill the window's needs. If you need the true height immediately after creating a widget, invoke `update` to force the geometry manager to arrange it, or use `winfo_reqheight` to get the window's requested height instead of its actual height.

winfo_id()

Returns an integer giving a low-level platform-specific identifier for window. On Unix platforms, this is the X window identifier. Under Windows, this is the Windows HWND. On the Macintosh the value has no meaning outside Tk.

winfo_interps(displayof=0)

Returns a list whose members are the names of all Tcl interpreters (e.g. all Tk-based applications) currently registered for a particular display. If the `displayof` option is given then the return value refers to the display of window; otherwise it refers to the display of the application's main window. This may be of limited use to Tkinter applications.

winfo_ismapped()

Returns `TRUE` if `self` is currently mapped, `FALSE` otherwise.

winfo_manager()

Returns the name of the geometry manager currently responsible for `self`'s window, or an empty string if window isn't managed by any geometry manager. The name is usually the name of the Tcl method for the geometry manager, such as `pack` or `place`. If the geometry manager is a widget, such as canvases or text, the name is the widget's class, such as `canvas`.

winfo_name()

Returns window's name (i.e. its name within its parent, as opposed to its full path name).

winfo_parent()

Returns the path name of window's parent, or an empty string if window is the main window of the application.

winfo_pathname(id, displayof=0)

Returns the path name of the window whose X identifier is id. id must be a decimal, hexadecimal or octal integer and must correspond to a window in the invoking application. If the `displayof` option is given then the identifier is looked up on the display of window; otherwise it is looked up on the display of the application's main window.

winfo_pixels(number)

Returns the number of pixels in window corresponding to the distance given by `number`. `number` may be specified in any of the forms acceptable to Tkinter (`Tk_GetPixels`), such as `2.0c` or `1i`. The result is rounded to the nearest integer value; for a fractional result, use `winfo_fpixels`.

winfo_pointerx()

If the mouse pointer is on the same screen as window, returns the pointer's x coordinate, measured in pixels in the screen's root window. If a virtual root window is in use on the screen, the position is measured in the virtual root. If the mouse pointer isn't on the same screen as window then `-1` is returned.

winfo_pointerxy()

If the mouse pointer is on the same screen as window, returns a tuple with two elements, which are the pointer's x and y coordinates measured in pixels in the screen's root window. If a virtual root window is in use on the screen, the position is computed in the virtual root. If the mouse pointer isn't on the same screen as window then both of the returned coordinates are `-1`.

winfo_pointery()

If the mouse pointer is on the same screen as window, returns the pointer's y coordinate, measured in pixels in the screen's root window. If a virtual root window is in use on the screen, the position is computed in the virtual root. If the mouse pointer isn't on the same screen as window then `-1` is returned.

winfo_reqheight()

Returns an integer giving window's requested height, in pixels. This is the value used by window's geometry manager to compute its geometry.

winfo_reqwidth()

Returns an integer giving window's requested width, in pixels. This is the value used by window's geometry manager to compute its geometry.

winfo_rgb(color)

Returns a tuple containing three decimal values, which are the red, green, and blue intensities that correspond to color in the window given by window. Color may be specified in any of the forms acceptable for a color option.

winfo_rootx()

Returns an integer giving the x-coordinate, in the root window of the screen, of the upper-left corner of window's border (or window if it has no border).

winfo_rooty()

Returns an integer giving the y-coordinate, in the root window of the screen, of the upper-left corner of window's border (or window if it has no border).

winfo_screen()

Returns the name of the screen associated with window, in the form `displayName.screen-Index`.

winfo_screencells()

Returns an integer giving the number of cells in the default color map for window's screen.

winfo_screendepth()

Returns an integer giving the depth of the root window of window's screen (number of bits per pixel).

winfo_screenheight()

Returns an integer giving the height of window's screen, in pixels.

winfo_screenmmheight()

Returns an integer giving the height of window's screen, in millimeters.

winfo_screenmmwidth()

Returns an integer giving the width of window's screen, in millimeters.

winfo_screenvisual()

Returns one of the following strings to indicate the default visual class for window's screen: `directcolor`, `grayscale`, `pseudocolor`, `staticcolor`, `staticgray` or `truecolor`.

winfo_screenwidth()

Returns an integer giving the width of window's screen, in pixels.

winfo_server()

Returns a string containing information about the server for window's display. The exact format of this string may vary from platform to platform. For X servers the string has the form `XmajorRminor vendor vendorVersion` where `major` and `minor` are the version and revision numbers provided by the server (e.g. `X11R5`), `vendor` is the name of the vendor for the server and `vendorRelease` is an integer release number provided by the server.

winfo_toplevel()

Returns the identity of the top-level window containing window.

winfo_viewable()

Returns `TRUE` if window and all of its ancestors up through the nearest toplevel window are mapped. Returns `FALSE` if any of these windows are not mapped.

winfo_visual()

Returns one of the following strings to indicate the visual class for window: `directcolor`, `grayscale`, `pseudocolor`, `staticcolor`, `staticgray` or `truecolor`.

winfo_visualid()

Returns the X identifier for the visual for window.

winfo_visualsavailable(includeids=0)

Returns a list whose elements describe the visuals available for window's screen. Each element consists of a visual class followed by an integer depth. The class has the same form as returned by `winfo_visual`. The depth gives the number of bits per pixel in the visual. In addition, if the `includeids` argument is provided, then the depth is followed by the X identifier for the visual.

winfo_vrootheight()

Returns the height of the virtual root window associated with window if there is one; otherwise returns the height of window's screen.

winfo_vrootwidth()

Returns the width of the virtual root window associated with window if there is one; otherwise returns the width of window's screen.

winfo_vrootx()

Returns the x-offset of the virtual root window associated with window, relative to the root window of its screen. This is normally either zero or negative. Returns 0 if there is no virtual root window for window.

winfo_vrooty()

Returns the y-offset of the virtual root window associated with window, relative to the root window of its screen. This is normally either zero or negative. Returns 0 if there is no virtual root window for window.

winfo_width()

Returns an integer giving window's width in pixels. When a window is first created its width will be 1 pixel; the width will eventually be changed by a geometry manager to fulfill the window's needs. If you need the true width immediately after creating a widget, invoke `update` to force the geometry manager to arrange it, or use `winfo_reqwidth` to get the window's requested width instead of its actual width.

winfo_x()

Returns an integer giving the x-coordinate, in window's parent, of the upper left corner of window's border (or window if it has no border).

winfo_y()

Returns an integer giving the y-coordinate, in window's parent, of the upper left corner of window's border (or window if it has no border).

Wm methods

Description

The wm methods are used to interact with window managers in order to control such things as the title for a window, its geometry, or the increments in terms of which it may be resized. Tkinter makes these methods accessible at the root window (Tk) and with all TopLevel widgets. The wm methods can take any of a number of different forms, depending on the option argument. All of the forms expect at least one additional argument, window, which must be the path name of a top-level window.

Tkinter defines synonyms for wm methods, although you are free to use the wm_ prefix if you wish. The legal forms for the wm methods follow.

aspect(minNumer=None, minDemon=None, maxNumer=None, maxDenom=None)

If minNumer, minDenom, maxNumer, and maxDenom are all specified, then they will be passed to the window manager and the window manager should use them to enforce a range of acceptable aspect ratios for window. The aspect ratio of window (width/length) will be constrained to lie between minNumer/minDenom and maxNumer/maxDenom.

If minNumer, etc., are all unspecified, then any existing aspect ratio restrictions are removed. If minNumer, etc., are specified, then the method returns None. Otherwise, it returns a tuple containing four elements, which are the current values of minNumer, minDenom, maxNumer and maxDenom (if no aspect restrictions are in effect, then None is returned).

client(name=None)

If name is specified, this method stores name (which should be the name of the host on which the application is executing) in window's WM_CLIENT_MACHINE property for use by the window manager or session manager. If name isn't specified, the method returns the last name set in a wm_client method for window. If name is specified as an empty string, the method deletes the WM_CLIENT_MACHINE property from window. This method is only useful for X systems.

colormapwindows(*windowList)

Used to manipulate the WM_COLORMAP_WINDOWS property, which provides information to the window managers about windows that have private colormaps. If windowList isn't specified, the method returns a list whose elements are the names of the windows in the WM_COLORMAP_WINDOWS property. If windowList is specified, it consists of a list of window path names; the method overwrites the WM_COLORMAP_WINDOWS property with the given windows and returns None. This method is only useful for X systems.

The WM_COLORMAP_WINDOWS property should normally contain a list of the internal windows within window whose colormaps differ from their parents. The order of the windows in the property indicates a priority order: the window manager will attempt to install as many colormaps as possible from the head of this list when window gets the colormap focus. If window is not included among the windows in windowList, Tk implicitly adds it at the end of the WM_COLORMAP_WINDOWS property, so that its colormap is lowest in priority. If wm_colormapwindows is not invoked, Tk will automatically set the property for each toplevel window to all the internal windows whose colormaps differ from their parents, followed by the top-level itself; the order of the internal windows is undefined. See the ICCCM documentation for more information on the `WM_COLORMAP_WINDOWS` property.

command(callback=None)

Specifies a `callback` to associate with the button. This callback is typically invoked when mouse button 1 is released over the button window. This method is only useful for X systems.

deiconify()

Arranges for window to be displayed in normal (non-iconified) form. This is done by mapping the window. If the window has never been mapped then this method will not map the window, but it will ensure that when the window is first mapped it will be displayed in deiconified form. Returns `None`.

focusmodel(model=None)

If active or passive is supplied as an optional `model` argument to the method, then it specifies the focus model for window. In this case the method returns an empty string. If no additional argument is supplied, then the method returns the current focus model for window. An active focus model means that window will claim the input focus for itself or its descendants, even at times when the focus is currently in some other application. Passive means that window will never claim the focus for itself: the window manager should give the focus to window at appropriate times. However, once the focus has been given to window or one of its descendants, the application may re-assign the focus among window's descendants. The focus model defaults to passive, and Tk's focus method assumes a passive model of focusing.

frame()

If window has been reparented by the window manager into a decorative frame, the method returns the platform-specific window identifier for the outermost frame that contains window (the window whose parent is the root or virtual root). If window hasn't been reparented by the window manager then the method returns the platform specific window identifier for window. This method is only useful for X systems.

geometry(newGeometry=None)

If `newGeometry` is specified, then the geometry of window is changed and an empty string is returned. Otherwise the current geometry for window is returned (this is the most recent geometry specified either by manual resizing or in a `wm_geometry` call). `newGeometry` has the form =widthxheight+-x+-y, where any of =, widthxheight, or +-x+-y may be omitted. Width and height are positive integers specifying the desired dimensions of window. If window is gridded then the dimensions are specified in grid units; otherwise they are specified in pixel units. x and y specify the desired location of window on the screen, in pixels. If x is preceded by +, it specifies the number of pixels between the left edge of the screen and the left edge of window's border; if preceded by - then x specifies the number of pixels between the right edge of the screen and the right edge of window's border. If y is preceded by + then it specifies the number of pixels between the top of the screen and the top of window's border; if y is preceded by - then it specifies the number of pixels between the bottom of window's border and the bottom of the screen. If newGeometry is specified as an empty string then any existing user-specified geometry for window is cancelled, and the window will revert to the size requested internally by its widgets.

group(pathName=None)

If pathname is specified, it gives the path name for the leader of a group of related windows. The window manager may use this information, for example, to unmap all of the windows in a group when the group's leader is iconified. pathName may be specified as an empty string to remove window from any group association. If pathname is specified then the method returns an empty string; otherwise it returns the path name of window's current group leader, or an empty string if window isn't part of any group.

iconbitmap(bitmap=None)

If bitmap is specified, then it names a bitmap in the standard forms accepted by Tkinter (Tk_GetBitmap). This bitmap is passed to the window manager to be displayed in window's icon, and the method returns an empty string. If bitmap is not specified, then any current icon bitmap is cancelled for window. If bitmap is specified then the method returns an empty string. Otherwise it returns the name of the current icon bitmap associated with window, or an empty string if window has no icon bitmap.

wm_iconify()

Arrange for window to be iconified. It window hasn't yet been mapped for the first time, this method will arrange for it to appear in the iconified state when it is eventually mapped.

iconmask(bitmap=None)

If bitmap is specified, then it names a bitmap in the standard forms accepted by Tkinter (Tk_GetBitmap). This bitmap is passed to the window manager to be used as a mask in conjunction with the iconbitmap option: where the mask has zeroes no icon will be displayed; where it has ones, the bits from the icon bitmap will be displayed. If bitmap is not specified, then any current icon mask is cancelled for window (this is equivalent to specifying a bitmap of all ones). If bitmap is specified then the method returns an empty string. Otherwise it returns the name of the current icon mask associated with window, or an empty string if no mask is in effect.

iconname(newName=None)

If newName is specified, then it is passed to the window manager; the window manager should display newName inside the icon associated with window. In this case an empty string is returned as result. If newName isn't specified then the method returns the current icon name for window, or an empty string if no icon name has been specified (in this case the window manager will normally display the window's title, as specified with the wm_title call).

iconposition(x=None, y=None)

If x and y are specified, they are passed to the window manager as a hint about where to position the icon for window. In this case an empty string is returned. If x and y are specified as empty strings then any existing icon position hint is cancelled. If neither x nor y is specified, then the method returns a tuple containing two values, which are the current icon position hints (if no hints are in effect then `None` is returned).

iconwindow(pathName=None)

If `pathname` is specified, it is the path name for a window to use as icon for window; when window is iconified then `pathname` will be mapped to serve as icon, and when window is de-iconified then `pathname` will be unmapped again. If `pathname` is specified as an empty string then any existing icon window association for window will be cancelled. If the `pathname` argument is specified then an empty string is returned. Otherwise the method returns the path name of the current icon window for window, or an empty string if there is no icon window currently specified for window. Button press events are disabled for window as long as it is an icon window; this is needed in order to allow window managers to "own" those events.

Note: Not all window managers support the notion of an icon window.

maxsize(width=None, height=None)

If `width` and `height` are specified, they give the maximum permissible dimensions for window. For gridded windows the dimensions are specified in grid units; otherwise they are specified in pixel units. The window manager will restrict the window's dimensions to be less than or equal to `width` and `height`. If `width` and `height` are specified, then the method returns `None`. Otherwise it returns a tuple with two elements, which are the maximum width and height currently in effect. The maximum size defaults to the size of the screen. If resizing has been disabled with the `wm_resizable` method, then this method has no effect. See the sections on geometry management: "Grid" section on page 492, "Pack" section on page 511 and "Place" section on page 516 for more information.

minsize(width=None, height=None)

If `width` and `height` are specified, they give the minimum permissible dimensions for window. For gridded windows the dimensions are specified in grid units; otherwise they are specified in pixel units. The window manager will restrict the window's dimensions to be greater than or equal to `width` and `height`. If `width` and `height` are specified, then the method returns `None`. Otherwise it returns a tuple with two elements, which are the minimum width and height currently in effect. The minimum size defaults to one pixel in each dimension. If resizing has been disabled with the `wm_resizable` method, then this method has no effect. See the sections on geometry management: "Grid" section on page 492, "Pack" section on page 511 and "Place" section on page 516 for more information.

overrideredirect(boolean=None)

If `boolean` is specified, it must have a proper boolean form and the override-redirect flag for window is set to that value. If `boolean` is not specified then `TRUE` or `FALSE` is returned to indicate whether the override-redirect flag is currently set for window. Setting the override-redirect flag for a window causes it to be ignored by the window manager; among other things, this means that the window will not be reparented from the root window into a decorative frame and the user will not be able to manipulate the window using the normal window manager mechanisms.

positionfrom(who=None)

If who is specified, it must be either program or user, or an abbreviation of one of these two. It indicates whether window's current position was requested by the program or by the user. Many window managers ignore program-requested initial positions and ask the user to manually position the window; if user is specified then the window manager should position the window at the given place without asking the user for assistance.

If who is specified as an empty string, then the current position source is cancelled. If who is specified, then the method returns an empty string. Otherwise it returns user or window to indicate the source of the window's current position, or an empty string if no source has been specified yet. Most window managers interpret no source as equivalent to program. Tk will automatically set the position source to user when a wm_geometry method is invoked, unless the source has been set explicitly to program.

protocol(name=None, function=None)

This method is used to manage window manager protocols such as WM_DELETE_WINDOW. Name is the name of an atom corresponding to a window manager protocol, such as WM_DELETE_WINDOW or WM_SAVE_YOURSELF or WM_TAKE_FOCUS. If both name and function are specified, then function is associated with the protocol specified by name. name will be added to window's WM_PROTOCOLS property to tell the window manager that the application has a protocol handler for name, and function will be invoked in the future whenever the window manager sends a message to the client for that protocol. In this case the method returns an empty string.

If name is specified but function isn't, then the current function for name is returned, or an empty string is returned if there is no handler defined for name. If function is specified as an empty string then the current handler for name is deleted and it is removed from the WM_PROTOCOLS property on window; an empty string is returned.

Lastly, if neither name nor function is specified, the method returns a list of all the protocols for which handlers are currently defined for window. Tk always defines a protocol handler for WM_DELETE_WINDOW, even if you haven't asked for one with wm protocol. If a WM_DELETE_WINDOW message arrives when you haven't defined a handler, then Tk handles the message by destroying the window for which it was received.

resizable(width=None, height=None)

This method controls whether or not the user may interactively resize a top level window. If width and height are specified, they are boolean values that determine whether the width and height of window may be modified by the user. In this case the method returns an empty string. If width and height are omitted then the method returns a list with two FALSE/TRUE elements that indicate whether the width and height of window are currently resizable. By default, windows are resizable in both dimensions. If resizing is disabled, then the window's size will be the size from the most recent interactive resize or wm_geometry call. If there has been no such operation then the window's natural size will be used.

sizefrom(who=None)

If who is specified, it must be either program or user, or an abbreviation of one of these two. It indicates whether window's current size was requested by the program or by the user. Some window managers ignore program-requested sizes and ask the user to manually size the window; if user is specified then the window manager should give the window its specified size without asking the user for assistance.

If who is specified as an empty string, then the current size source is cancelled. If who is specified, then the method returns an empty string. Otherwise it returns user or window to indicate the source of the window's current size, or an empty string if no source has been specified yet. Most window managers interpret no source as equivalent to program.

state()

Specifies one of three states for the button: NORMAL, ACTIVE, or DISABLED. In NORMAL state the button is displayed using the foreground and background options. ACTIVE state is typically used when the pointer is over the button. In active state the button is displayed using the activeForeground and activeBackground options. DISABLED state means that the button should be insensitive: the default bindings will refuse to activate the widget and will ignore mouse button presses. In this state the disabledForeground and background options determine how the button is displayed.

title(string=None)

If string is specified, then it will be passed to the window manager for use as the title for window (the window manager should display this string in window's title bar). If string isn't specified then the method returns the current title for the window. The title for a window defaults to its name.

transient(master=None)

If master is specified, then the window manager is informed that window is a transient window (such as a pull-down menu) working on behalf of master (where master is the identity for a top-level window). Some window managers will use this information to manage window specially. If master is specified as an empty string then window is marked as not being a transient window any more. If master is specified, then the method returns an empty string. Otherwise the method returns the path name of window's current master or an empty string if window isn't currently a transient window.

withdraw()

Arranges for the window to be withdrawn from the screen. This causes the window to be unmapped and forgotten about by the window manager. If the window has never been mapped, then this method causes the window to be mapped in the withdrawn state. Not all window managers appear to know how to handle windows that are mapped in the withdrawn state.

Note: It sometimes seems to be necessary to withdraw a window and then re-map it (such as with wm deiconify) to get some window managers to pay attention to changes in window attributes such as group.

Bitmap class

Description

A bitmap is an image whose pixels can display either of two colors or be transparent. A bitmap image is defined by four things: a background color, a foreground color, and two bitmaps, called the source and the mask. Each of the bitmaps specifies 0/1 values for a rectangular array of pixels, and the two bitmaps must have the same dimensions. For pixels where the mask is zero, the image displays nothing, producing a transparent effect. For other pixels, the image displays the foreground color if the source data is 1 and the background color if the source data is 0.

Inheritance

Inherits from Image.

Shared options

Option	Default
background	None
foreground	"black"

Options specific to Bitmap

Option (alias)	Description	Units	Typical
data	Specifies the contents of the source bitmap as a string. The string must adhere to X11 bitmap format (e.g., as generated by the bitmap program). If both the data and file options are specified, the data option takes precedence.	string	
file	filename gives the name of a file whose contents define the source bitmap. The file must adhere to X11 bitmap format (e.g., as generated by the bitmap program).	string	'icon.xbm'
maskdata	Specifies the contents of the mask as a string. The string must adhere to X11 bitmap format (e.g., as generated by the bitmap program). If both the maskdata and maskfile options are specified, the mask-data option takes precedence.	string	
maskfile	filename gives the name of a file whose contents define the mask. The file must adhere to X11 bitmap format (e.g., as generated by the bitmap program).	string	"imask.xbm"

Methods

Bitmap(option...)

Creates a bitmap instance using option-value pairs in `option`.

cget(option)

Returns the current value of the configuration option given by `option`. `option` may have any of the values accepted by the bitmap constructor.

configure(option=value...)

Queries or modifies the configuration options for the image. If no `option` is specified, returns a dictionary describing all of the available options for `imageName`. If `option` is specified with no value, then the command returns a dictionary describing the one named `option` (this dictionary will be identical to the corresponding sublist of the value returned if no option is specified). If one or more option-value pairs are specified, then the method modifies the given option(s) to have the given value(s); in this case the method returns an empty string. `option` may have any of the values accepted by the bitmap constructor.

height()

Returns an integer giving the height of the image in pixels.

type()

Returns the type of image as a string (the value of the `type` argument to image create when the image was created).

width()

Returns an integer giving the width of the image in pixels.

Button

Description

The button class defines a new window and a button widget. Additional options, described below, may be specified in the method call or in the option database to configure aspects of the button such as its colors, font, text, and initial relief. The button method returns the identity of the new widget. At the time this method is invoked, the button's parent must exist.

A button is a widget that displays a textual string, bitmap or image. If text is displayed, it must all be in a single font, but it can occupy multiple lines on the screen (if it contains new-lines or if wrapping occurs because of the `wrapLength` option) and one of the characters may optionally be underlined using the `underline` option. It can display itself in either of three different ways, according to the state option: it can be made to appear raised, sunken, or flat; and it can be made to flash. When a user invokes the button (by pressing mouse button 1 with the cursor over the button), then the activate callback specified in the `command` option is invoked.

Inheritance

Button inherits from `Widget`.

Shared options

Option (alias)	Default
activebackground	SystemButtonFace
activeforeground	SystemButtonText
anchor	center
background (bg)	SystemButtonFace
bitmap	
borderwidth (bd)	2
command	
cursor	
disabledforeground	SystemDisabledText
font	(('MS', 'Sans', 'Serif'), '8')
foreground (fg)	SystemButtonText
height	0
highlightbackground	SystemButtonFace
highlightcolor	SystemWindowFrame
highlightthickness	1
image	
justify	center
padx	1
pady	1
relief	raised
state	normal
takefocus	
text	
textvariable	
underline	-1
width	0
wraplength	0

Options specific to Button

Option (alias)	Description	Units	Typical	Default
default	Specifies one of three states for the default ring (button): NORMAL, ACTIVE, or DISABLED. In ACTIVE state, the button is drawn with the platform-specific appearance for a default button. In NORMAL state, the button is drawn with the platform-specific appearance for a non-default button, leaving enough space to draw the default button appearance. The NORMAL and ACTIVE states will result in buttons of the same size. In DISABLED state, the button is drawn with the non-default button appearance without leaving space for the default appearance. The DISABLED state may result in a smaller button than the ACTIVE state.	constant	NORMAL "disabled"	disabled

Methods

flash()

Flashes the button. This is accomplished by redisplaying the button several times, alternating between active and normal colors. At the end of the flash the button is left in the same normal/active state as when the method was invoked. This method is ignored if the button's state is disabled.

invoke()

Invokes the callback associated with the button, if there is one. The return value is the return value from the callback, or an empty string if no callback is associated with the button. This method is ignored if the button's state is disabled.

tkButtonDown(*ignored)
tkButtonEnter(*ignored)
tkButtonInvoke(*ignored)
tkButtonLeave(*ignored)
tkButtonUp(*ignored)

These methods are really only useful if you are writing your own event-handling for buttons. Their function is to set the button's appearance as if the default actions had occurred. They may also be useful in simulating user interaction with a GUI.

Canvas

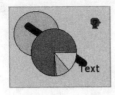

Description

The Canvas class defines a new window and creates an instance of a canvas widget. Additional options, described below, may be specified in the method call or in the option database to configure aspects of the canvas such as its colors and 3-D relief. The `canvas` method returns the identity of the new widget. At the time this method is invoked, the canvas's parent must exist.

Canvas widgets implement structured graphics. A canvas displays any number of items, which may be things like rectangles, circles, lines, and text. Items may be manipulated (e.g. moved or re-colored) and callbacks may be associated with items in much the same way that the `bind` method allows callbacks to be bound to widgets. For example, a particular callback may be associated with the `<Button-1>` event so that the callback is invoked whenever Button-1 is pressed with the mouse cursor over an item. This means that items in a canvas can have behaviors defined by the Tkinter functions bound to them.

Inheritance

Canvas inherits from `Widget`.

Shared options

Option (alias)	Default
background (bg)	SystemButtonFace
borderwidth (bd)	0
cursor	
height	7c
highlightback-ground	SystemButtonFace
highlightcolor	SystemWindowFrame
highlightthickness	2
relief	flat
selectbackground	SystemHighlight
selectborderwidth	1
selectforeground	SystemHighlightText
takefocus	
width	10c
xscrollcommand	

Options specific to Canvas

Option (alias)	Description	Units	Typical	Default
closeenough	Specifies a floating-point value indicating how close the mouse cursor must be to an item before it is considered to be "inside" the item. Defaults to 1.0.	float	0.5	1
confine	Specifies a boolean value that indicates whether or not it should be allowable to set the canvas's view outside the region defined by the scrollregion argument. Defaults to TRUE, which means that the view will be constrained within the scroll region.	boolean	FALSE 1	1
insertback-ground	Specifies the color to use as background in the area covered by the insertion cursor. This color will normally override either the normal background for the widget (or the selection background if the insertion cursor happens to fall in the selection).	color	'yel-low'	SystemBut-tonText
insertborder-width	Specifies a non-negative value indicating the width of the 3-D border to draw around the insertion cursor. The value may have any of the forms acceptable to Tkinter (Tk_GetPixels).	pixel	2	0
insertofftime	Specifies a non-negative integer value indicating the number of milliseconds the insertion cursor should remain "off" in each blink cycle. If this option is zero then the cursor doesn't blink—it is on all the time.	integer	250	300
insertontime	Specifies a non-negative integer value indicating the number of milliseconds the insertion cursor should remain "on" in each blink cycle.	integer	175	600
insertwidth	Specifies a value indicating the total width of the insertion cursor. The value may have any of the forms acceptable to Tkinter (Tk_GetPixels). If a border has been specified for the insertion cursor (using the insertBorderWidth option), the border will be drawn inside the width specified by the insertWidth option.	pixel	2	2
scrollregion	Specifies a list with four coordinates describing the left, top, right, and bottom coordinates of a rectangular region. This region is used for scrolling purposes and is considered to be the boundary of the information in the canvas. Each of the coordinates may be specified in any of the forms given in the COORDINATES section below.	list	(10,10, 200,250	

Option (alias)	Description	Units	Typical	Default
xscrollincrement	Specifies an increment for horizontal scrolling, in any of the usual forms permitted for screen distances. If the value of this option is greater than zero, the horizontal view in the window will be constrained so that the canvas x coordinate at the left edge of the window is always an even multiple of xscrollincrement; furthermore, the units for scrolling (e.g., the change in view when the left and right arrows of a scrollbar are selected) will also be xscrollincrement. If the value of this option is less than or equal to zero, then horizontal scrolling is unconstrained.	distance	10m 200	0
yscrollcommand	Specifies the prefix for a command used to communicate with vertical scrollbars. This option is treated in the same way as the xScrollCommand option, except that it is used for vertical scrollbars and is provided by widgets that support vertical scrolling. See the description of xScrollCommand for details on how this option is used.	function		
yscrollincrement	Specifies an increment for horizontal scrolling, in any of the usual forms permitted for screen distances. If the value of this option is greater than zero, the horizontal view in the window will be constrained so that the canvas y coordinate at the top edge of the window is always an even multiple of yscrollincrement; furthermore, the units for scrolling (e.g., the change in view when the top and bottom arrows of a scrollbar are selected) will also be yscrollincrement. If the value of this option is less than or equal to zero, then horizontal scrolling is unconstrained.	distance	10m 200	0

Methods

addtag_above(newtag, tagOrId)

Adds newtag to the item just above the one given by tagOrId in the display list. If tagOrId denotes more than one item, then the topmost of these items in the display list is used.

addtag_all(newtag)

Adds newtag to all the items in the canvas.

addtag_below(newtag, tagOrId)

Adds newtag to the item just below the one given by tagOrId in the display list. If tagOrId denotes more than one item, then the lowest of these items in the display list is used.

addtag_closest(newtag, x, y, halo=None, start=None)

Adds newtag to the item closest to the point given by *x* and *y*. If more than one item is at the same closest distance (meaning two items overlap the point), then the top-most of these items (the last one in the display list) is used. If halo is specified, then it must be a non-negative value. Any item closer than halo to the point is considered to overlap it. The start argument may be used to step circularly through all the closest items. If start is specified, it names an item using a tag or id (if by tag, it selects the first item in the display list with the given tag). Instead of selecting the top-most closest item, this form will select the top-most closest item that is below start in the display list; if no such item exists, then the selection behaves as if the start argument had not been specified.

addtag_enclosed(newtag, x1, y1, x2, y2)

Adds newtag to all the items completely enclosed within the rectangular region given by x1, y1, x2, and y2. x1 must be no greater than x2 and y1 must be no greater than y2.

addtag_overlapping(newtag, x1, y1, x2, y2)

Adds newtag to all the items that overlap or are enclosed within the rectangular region given by x1, y1, x2, and y2. x1 must be no greater than x2 and y1 must be no greater than y2.

addtag_withtag(newtag, tagOrId)

Adds newtag to all the items given by tagOrId.

bbox(tagOrId), bbox()

Returns a tuple with four elements giving an approximate bounding box for all the items named by the tagOrId arguments. The tuple is in the order x1,y1,x2,y2 such that the drawn areas of all the named elements are within the region bounded by x1 on the left, x2 on the right, y1 on the top, and y2 on the bottom. The return value may overestimate the actual bounding box by a few pixels. If no items match any of the tagOrId arguments or if the matching items have empty bounding boxes (i.e. they have nothing to display) then an empty string is returned.

canvasx(screenx, gridspacing=None)

Given a window x-coordinate in the canvas screenx, this method returns the canvas x-coordinate that is displayed at that location. If gridspacing is specified, then the canvas coordinate is rounded to the nearest multiple of gridspacing units.

canvasy(screeny, gridspacing=None)

Given a window y-coordinate in the canvas screeny, this method returns the canvas y-coordinate that is displayed at that location. If gridspacing is specified, then the canvas coordinate is rounded to the nearest multiple of gridspacing units.

coords(tagOrId, x0, y0, x1, y1, ..., xn, yn)

Queries or modifies the coordinates that define an item. If no coordinates are specified, this method returns a tuple whose elements are the coordinates of the item named by tagOrId. If coordinates are specified, then they replace the current coordinates for the named item. If tagOrId refers to multiple items, then the first one in the display list is used.

The following methods create canvas *items* but are documented as separate "widgets" to allow their attributes and behavior to be addressed more fully, although they are not discrete widgets in reality.

create_arc(*)

See "Canvas Arc" on page 468.

create_bitmap(*)

See "Canvas Arc" on page 468.

create_image(*)

See "Canvas Arc" on page 468.

create_line(*)

See "Canvas line" on page 472.

create_oval(*)

See "Canvas Arc" on page 468.

create_polygon(*)

See "Canvas Arc" on page 468.

create_rectangle(*)

See "Canvas Arc" on page 468.

create_text(*)

See "Canvas Arc" on page 468.

create_window(*)

See "Canvas Arc" on page 468.

dchars(tagOrId, first=0, last=first)

For each item given by tagOrId, deletes the characters in the range given by first and last, inclusive. If some of the items given by tagOrId don't support text operations, then they are ignored. first and last are indices of characters within the item(s) as described in INDICES above. If last is omitted, it defaults to first. This method returns None.

delete(tagOrId)

Deletes each of the items given by each tagOrId, and returns an empty string.

dtag(tagOrId, tagToDelete)

For each of the items given by tagOrId, deletes the tag given by tagToDelete from the list of those associated with the item. If an item doesn't have the tag tagToDelete then the item is unaffected by the method. If tagToDelete is omitted then it defaults to tagOrId. This method returns None.

find_above(tagOrId)

Finds the item just after (above) the one given by tagOrId in the display list. If tagOrId denotes more than one item, then the last (top-most) of these items in the display list is used.

find_all()

Returns a list containing the identities of all the items in the canvas.

find_below(tagOrId)

Returns the item just before (below) the one given by tagOrId in the display list. If tagOrId denotes more than one item, then the first (lowest) of these items in the display list is used.

find_closest(x, y, halo=None, start=None)

Returns the item closest to the point given by x and y. If more than one item is at the same closest distance (meaning two items overlap the point), then the top-most of these items (the last one in the display list) is used. If halo is specified, then it must be a non-negative value. Any item closer than halo to the point is considered to overlap it. The start argument may be used to step circularly through all the closest items. If start is specified, it names an item using a tag or ID (if by tag, it selects the first item in the display list with the given tag). Instead of selecting the top-most closest item, this form will select the top-most closest item that is below start in the display list; if no such item exists, then the selection behaves as if the start argument had not been specified. This method will always return an item if there are one or more items on the canvas.

find_enclosed(x1, y1, x2, y2)

Returns a list containing the identities of all the items completely enclosed within the rectangular region given by x1, y1, x2, and y2. x1 must be no greater then x2 and y1 must be no greater than y2.

find_overlapping(x1, y1, x2, y2)

Returns a list containing the identities of all the items that overlap or are enclosed within the rectangular region given by x1, y1, x2, and y2. x1 must be no greater then x2 and y1 must be no greater than y2.

find_withtag(tagOrId)

Returns a list containing the identities of all the items given by tagOrId.

focus(tagOrId)

Sets the keyboard focus for the canvas widget to the item given by tagOrId. If tagOrId refers to several items, then the focus is set to the first such item in the display list that supports the insertion cursor. If tagOrId doesn't refer to any items, or if none of them support the insertion cursor, then the focus isn't changed. If tagOrId is an empty string, then the focus item is reset so that no item has the focus. If tagOrId is not specified then the method returns the ID for the item that currently has the focus, or an empty string if no item has the focus.

Once the focus has been set to an item, the item will display the insertion cursor and all keyboard events will be directed to that item. The focus item within a canvas and the focus window on the screen (set with the focus method) are totally independent; a given item doesn't actually have the input focus unless (a) its canvas is the focus window and (b) the item is the focus item within the canvas. In most cases it is advisable to follow the focus widget method with the focus method to set the focus window to the canvas (if it wasn't there already).

gettags(tagOrId)

Returns a list whose elements are the tags associated with the item given by tagOrId. If tagOrId refers to more than one item, then the tags are returned from the first such item in the display list. If tagOrId doesn't refer to any items, or if the item doesn't contain tags, then an empty string is returned.

icursor(tagOrId, index)

Sets the position of the insertion cursor for the item(s) given by tagOrId to just before the character whose position is given by index. If some or all of the items given by tagOrId don't support an insertion cursor then this method has no effect on them.

Note: The insertion cursor is only displayed in an item if that item currently has the keyboard focus (see the widget method focus, below), but the cursor position may be set even when the item doesn't have the focus. This method returns None.

index(tagOrId, Index)

Returns an integer giving the numerical index within tagOrId corresponding to index. index gives a textual description of the desired position (such as end). The return value is guaranteed to lie between 0 and the number of characters within the item, inclusive. If tagOrId refers to multiple items, then the index is processed in the first of these items that supports indexing operations (in display list order).

insert(tagOrId, beforeThis, string)

For each of the items given by tagOrId, if the item supports text insertion then string is inserted into the item's text just before the character whose index is beforeThis. This method returns None.

itemcget(tagOrId, option)

Returns the current value of the configuration option for the item given by tagOrId whose name is option. This method is similar to the cget widget method except that it applies to a particular item rather than the widget as a whole. option may have any of the values accepted by the create widget method when the item was created. If tagOrId is a tag that refers to more than one item, the first (lowest) such item is used.

itemconfigure(tagOrId, options)

This method is similar to the configure widget method except that it modifies item-specific options for the items given by tagOrId instead of modifying options for the overall canvas widget. If no option is specified, it returns a dictionary describing all of the available options for the first item given by `tagOrId`. If `option` is specified with no value, then the method returns a dictionary describing the one named option (this list will be identical to the corresponding sublist of the value returned if no option is specified). If one or more option-value pairs are specified, then the method modifies the given widget option(s) to have the given value(s) in each of the items given by `tagOrId`; in this case the method returns `None`. The options and values are the same as those permissible in the `create` widget method when the item(s) were created; see the sections describing individual item types below for details on the legal options.

move(tagOrId, xAmount, yAmount)

Moves each of the items given by `tagOrId` in the canvas coordinate space by adding `xAmount` to the x-coordinate of each point associated with the item and `yAmount` to the y-coordinate of each point associated with the item. This method returns `None`.

postscript(options)

Generates a Postscript representation for part or all of the canvas. If the `file` option is specified then the Postscript is written to a file and an empty string is returned; otherwise the Postscript is returned as the result of the method. If the interpreter that owns the canvas is marked as safe, the operation will fail because safe interpreters are not allowed to write files. If the channel option is specified, the argument denotes the name of a channel already opened for writing. The Postscript is written to that channel, and the channel is left open for further writing at the end of the operation. The Postscript is created in Encapsulated Postscript form using version 3.0 of the Document Structuring Conventions.

Note: By default Postscript is only generated for information that appears in the canvas's window on the screen. If the canvas is freshly created it may still have its initial size of 1×1 pixel so nothing will appear in the Postscript. To get around this problem either invoke the `update` method to wait for the canvas window to reach its final size, or else use the `width` and `height` options to specify the area of the canvas to print. The option-value argument pairs provide additional information to control the generation of Postscript. The following options are supported:

Option	Value (type)	Description
colormap	varName (array)	VarName must be the name of an array variable that specifies a color mapping to use in the Postscript. Each element of `varName` must consist of Postscript code to set a particular color value (e.g. `1.0 1.0 0.0 setrgbcolor`). When outputting color information in the Postscript, Tk checks to see if there is an element of `varName` with the same name as the color. If so, Tk uses the value of the element as the Postscript command to set the color. If this option hasn't been specified, or if there isn't an entry in `varName` for a given color, then Tk uses the red, green, and blue intensities from the X color.
colormode	mode (string)	Specifies how to output color information. Mode must be either `color` (for full color output), gray (convert all colors to their gray-scale equivalents) or `mono` (convert all colors to black or white).
file	fileName (string)	Specifies the name of the file in which to write the Postscript. If this option isn't specified then the Postscript is returned as the result of the command instead of being written to a file.

Option	Value (type)	Description
fontmap	varName (array)	VarName must be the name of an array variable that specifies a font mapping to use in the Postscript. Each element of varName must consist of a Tcl list with two elements, which are the name and point size of a Postscript font. When outputting Postscript commands for a particular font, Tk checks to see if varName contains an element with the same name as the font. If there is such an element, then the font information contained in that element is used in the Postscript. Otherwise Tk attempts to guess what Postscript font to use. Tk's guesses generally only work for well-known fonts such as Times and Helvetica and Courier, and only if the X font name does not omit any dashes up through the point size. For example, -Courier-Bold-R-Normal-*-120-* will work but *CourierBoldRNormal*120* will not; Tk needs the dashes to parse the font name.
height	height (distance)	Specifies the height of the area of the canvas to print. Defaults to the height of the canvas window.
pageanchor	constant	Specifies which point of the printed area of the canvas should appear over the positioning point on the page (which is given by the pagex and pagey options). For example, pageanchor n means that the top center of the area of the canvas being printed (as it appears in the canvas window) should be over the positioning point. Defaults to center.
pageheight	height (distance)	Specifies that the Postscript should be scaled in both x and y so that the printed area is size high on the Postscript page. size consists of a floating-point number followed by c for centimeters, i for inches, m for millimeters, or p or nothing for printer's points (1/72 inch). Defaults to the height of the printed area on the screen. If both pageheight and pagewidth are specified then the scale factor from pagewidth is used (non-uniform scaling is not implemented).
pagewidth	width (distance)	Specifies that the Postscript should be scaled in both x and y so that the printed area is size wide on the Postscript page. size has the same form as for pageheight. Defaults to the width of the printed area on the screen. If both pageheight and pagewidth are specified then the scale factor from pagewidth is used (non-uniform scaling is not implemented).
pagex	position (integer)	position gives the x-coordinate of the positioning point on the Postscript page, using any of the forms allowed for pageheight. Used in conjunction with the pagey and pageanchor options to determine where the printed area appears on the Postscript page. Defaults to the center of the page.
pagey	position (integer)	position gives the y-coordinate of the positioning point on the Postscript page, using any of the forms allowed for pageheight. Used in conjunction with the pagex and pageanchor options to determine where the printed area appears on the Postscript page. Defaults to the center of the page.
rotate	boolean (boolean)	boolean specifies whether the printed area is to be rotated 90 degrees. In non-rotated output the x-axis of the printed area runs along the short dimension of the page ("portrait" orientation); in rotated output the x-axis runs along the long dimension of the page ("landscape" orientation). Defaults to non-rotated.
width	width (distance)	Specifies the width of the area of the canvas to print. Defaults to the width of the canvas window.
x	position (integer)	Specifies the x-coordinate of the left edge of the area of the canvas that is to be printed, in canvas coordinates, not window coordinates. Defaults to the coordinate of the left edge of the window.

Option	Value (type)	Description
y	position (integer)	Specifies the y-coordinate of the top edge of the area of the canvas that is to be printed, in canvas coordinates, not window coordinates. Defaults to the coordinate of the top edge of the window.

scale(tagOrId, xOrigin, yOrigin, xSc)

Rescale all of the items given by tagOrId in canvas coordinate space. xOrigin and yOrigin identify the origin for the scaling operation and xScale and yScale identify the scale factors for x- and y-coordinates, respectively (a scale factor of 1.0 implies no change to that coordinate). For each of the points defining each item, the x-coordinate is adjusted to change the distance from xOrigin by a factor of xScale. Similarly, each y-coordinate is adjusted to change the distance from yOrigin by a factor of yScale. This method returns None.

scan_dragto(x, y)

Computes the difference between its x and y arguments (which are typically mouse coordinates) and the x and y arguments to the last scan_mark call for the widget. It then adjusts the view by 10 times the difference in coordinates. This method is typically associated with mouse motion events in the widget, to produce the effect of dragging the canvas at high speed through its window. The return value is an empty string.

scan_mark(x, y)

Records x and y and the canvas's current view; used in conjunction with later scan_dragto calls. Typically this method is associated with a mouse button press in the widget and x and y are the coordinates of the mouse. It returns None.

select_adjust(tagOrId, index)

Locates the end of the selection in tagOrId nearest to the character given by index, and adjusts that end of the selection to be at index (i.e. including but not going beyond index). The other end of the selection is made the anchor point for future select_to calls. If the selection isn't currently in tagOrId then this method behaves the same as the select_to widget method. Returns None.

select_clear()

Clears the selection if it is in this widget. If the selection isn't in this widget then the method has no effect. Returns None.

select_from(tagOrId, index)

Sets the selection anchor point for the widget to be just before the character given by index in the item given by tagOrId. This method doesn't change the selection; it just sets the fixed end of the selection for future select_to calls. Returns None.

select_item()

Returns the ID of the selected item, if the selection is in an item in this canvas. If the selection is not in this canvas then an empty string is returned.

select_to(tagOrId, index)

Sets the selection to consist of those characters of `tagOrId` between the selection anchor point and `index`. The new selection will include the character given by `index`; it will include the character given by the anchor point only if `index` is greater than or equal to the anchor point. The anchor point is determined by the most recent `select_adjust` or `select_from` call for this widget. If the selection anchor point for the widget isn't currently in `tagOrId`, then it is set to the same character given by `index`. Returns `None`.

tag_bind(tagOrId, sequence=None, function=None, add=None)

Associates `function` with all the items given by `tagOrId` so that whenever the event sequence given by `sequence` occurs for one of the items, the `function` will be invoked. This widget method is similar to the `bind` method except that it operates on items in a canvas rather than entire widgets. If all arguments are specified then a new binding is created, replacing any existing binding for the same sequence and `tagOrId` (if the first character of `function` is + then `function` augments an existing binding rather than replacing it). In this case the return value is an empty string. If `function` is omitted then the method returns the function associated with `tagOrId` and `sequence` (an error occurs if there is no such binding). If both `function` and `sequence` are omitted then the method returns a list of all the sequences for which bindings have been defined for `tagOrId`.

The only events for which bindings may be specified are those related to the mouse and keyboard (such as `Enter`, `Leave`, `ButtonPress`, `Motion`, and `KeyPress`) or virtual events. `Enter` and `Leave` events trigger for an item when it becomes the current item or ceases to be the current item; note that these events are different than `Enter` and `Leave` events for windows.

Mouse-related events are directed to the current item, if any. Keyboard related events are directed to the focus item, if any. If a virtual event is used in a binding, that binding can trigger only if the virtual event is defined by an underlying mouse-related or keyboard-related event. It is possible for multiple bindings to match a particular event. This could occur, for example, if one binding is associated with the item's ID and another is associated with one of the item's tags. When this occurs, all of the matching bindings are invoked. A binding associated with the `ALL` tag is invoked first, followed by one binding for each of the item's tags (in order), followed by a binding associated with the item's ID. If there are multiple matching bindings for a single tag, then only the most specific binding is invoked.

A "break" string returned by an event handler terminates that handler and skips any remaining handlers for the event, just as for the `bind` method. If bindings have been created for a canvas window using the `bind` method, then they are invoked in addition to bindings created for the canvas's items using the `bind` widget call. The bindings for items will be invoked before any of the bindings for the window as a whole.

tag_lower(tagOrId, belowThis)

Moves all of the items given by `tagOrId` to a new position in the display list just before the item given by `belowThis`. If `tagOrId` refers to more than one item then all are moved but the relative order of the moved items will not be changed. `belowThis` is a tag or ID; if it refers to more than one item then the first (lowest) of these items in the display list is used as the destination location for the moved items.

Note: This method has no effect on window items. Window items always obscure other item types, and the stacking order of window items is determined by the `raise` and lower methods, not the raise and lower widget methods for canvases. This method returns None.

tag_raise(tagOrId, aboveThis)

Moves all of the items given by tagOrId to a new position in the display list just after the item given by aboveThis. If tagOrId refers to more than one item then all are moved but the relative order of the moved items will not be changed. aboveThis is a tag or ID; if it refers to more than one item then the last (topmost) of these items in the display list is used as the destination location for the moved items.

Note: This method has no effect on window items. Window items always obscure other item types, and the stacking order of window items is determined by the raise and lower methods, not the raise and lower widget methods for canvases. This method returns None.

tag_unbind(tagOrId, sequence, funcId=None)

Removes the association of the event sequence with the event handler funcId for all the items given by tagOrId. If funcId is supplied the handler will be destroyed.

type(tagOrId)

Returns the type of the item given by tagOrId, such as rectangle or text. If tagOrId refers to more than one item, then the type of the first item in the display list is returned. If tagOrId doesn't refer to any items at all then an empty string is returned.

xview_moveto(fraction)

Adjusts the view in the window so that fraction of the total width of the canvas is off-screen to the left. Fraction is a fraction between 0 and 1.

xview_scroll(number, what)

This command shifts the view in the window left or right according to number and what. number must be an integer. what must be either UNITS or PAGES. If what is UNITS, the view adjusts left or right in units of the xScrollIncrement option, if it is greater than zero, or in units of one-tenth the window's width otherwise. If what is PAGES then the view adjusts in units of nine-tenths the window's width. If number is negative, information farther to the left becomes visible; if it is positive, then information farther to the right becomes visible.

yview_moveto(fraction)

Adjusts the view in the window so that fraction of the canvas's area is off-screen to the top. fraction is a fraction between 0 and 1.

yview_scroll(number, what)

Adjusts the view in the window up or down according to number and what. number must be an integer. what must be either UNITS or PAGES. If what is UNITS, the view adjusts up or down in units of the yScrollIncrement option, if it is greater than zero, or in units of one-tenth the window's height otherwise. If what is PAGES then the view adjusts in units of nine-tenths the window's height. If number is negative then higher information becomes visible; if it is positive then lower information becomes visible.

Canvas Arc

Description

Items of type arc appear on the display as arc-shaped regions. An arc is a section of an oval delimited by two angles (specified by the start and extent options) and is displayed in one of several ways (specified by the style option).

Inheritance

Inherits from Widget, Canvas.

Shared options

Option	Default
fill	Transparent
width	1

Options specific to Arc

Option (alias)	Description	Units	Typical	Default
extent	Specifies the size of the angular range occupied by the arc. The arc's range extends for degrees degrees counter-clockwise from the starting angle given by the start option. degrees may be negative. If it is greater than 360 or less than –360, then degrees modulo 360 is used as the extent.	degrees	10.0	
outline	color specifies a color to use for drawing the arc's outline; it may have any of the forms accepted by Tkinter (Tk_GetColor). This option defaults to black. If color is specified as an empty string then no outline is drawn for the arc.	color	RED 'black'	'black'
outlinestipple	Indicates that the outline for the arc should be drawn with a stipple pattern; bitmap specifies the stipple pattern to use. If the outline option hasn't been specified then this option has no effect. If bitmap is an empty string (the default), then the outline is drawn in a solid fashion.	bitmap	'gray12'	None
start	Specifies the beginning of the angular range occupied by the arc. degrees is given in units of degrees measured counter-clockwise from the three-o'clock position; it may be either positive or negative.	degrees	0.0	0.0

Option (alias)	Description	Units	Typical	Default
stipple	Indicates that the arc should be filled in a stipple pattern; bitmap specifies the stipple pattern to use.	bitmap	'gray25'	None
style	Specifies how to draw the arc. If type is PIESLICE (the default) then the arc's region is defined by a section of the oval's perimeter plus two line segments, one each between the center of the oval and each end of the perimeter section. If type is CHORD then the arc's region is defined by a section of the oval's perimeter plus a single line segment connecting the two end points of the perimeter section. If type is ARC then the arc's region consists of a section of the perimeter alone. In this last case the fill option is ignored.	con-stant	CHORD 'arc'	PIESLICE
tags	Specifies a set of tags to apply to the item. TagList consists of a tuple of tag names, which replace any existing tags for the item.	tuple	('tag1', 'arc')	None

Methods

create_arc(x0, y0, x1, y1, *options)

The arguments x0, y0, x1, and y1 give the coordinates of two diagonally opposite corners of a rectangular region enclosing the oval that defines the arc. After the coordinates there may be any number of option-value pairs, each of which sets one of the configuration options for the item. These same option value pairs may be used in itemconfigure method calls to change the item's configuration.

delete(item)

Deletes an arc item.

coords(item, x0, y0, x1, y1)

Queries or modifies the coordinates that define an item. If no coordinates are specified, this command returns a list whose elements are the coordinates of the item named by item. If coordinates are specified, then they replace the current coordinates for the named item. If item refers to multiple items, then the first one in the display list is used.

itemconfigure(item, *options)

Modifies the options for one or more arc items.

Canvas bitmap

Description

Items of type `bitmap` appear on the display as images with two colors, foreground and background.

Inheritance

Inherits from `Widget`, `Canvas`.

Shared options

Option	Default
anchor	CENTER
background	transparent
foreground	"black"

Options specific to Bitmap

Option (alias)	Description	Units	Typical	Default
bitmap	Specifies the bitmap to display in the item. `bitmap` may have any of the forms accepted by Tkinter (`Tk_GetBitmap`).	bitmap	'info'	
tags	Specifies a set of tags to apply to the item. `TagList` consists of a tuple of tag names, which replace any existing tags for the item. `TagList` may be empty.	tuple	('tag1', 'bit-map')	None

Methods

create_bitmap(x, y, *options)

The arguments x and y specify the coordinates of a point used to position the bitmap on the display (using the `anchor` option). After the coordinates there may be any number of option-value pairs, each of which sets one of the configuration options for the item. These same option-value pairs may be used in `itemconfigure` calls to change the item's configuration.

delete(item)

Deletes a bitmap `item`

coords(item, x, y)

Queries or modifies the coordinates that define an `item`. If no coordinates are specified, this command returns a list whose elements are the coordinates of the item named by `item`. If coordinates are specified, then they replace the current coordinates for the named `item`. If `item` refers to multiple items, then the first one in the display list is used.

itemconfigure(item, *options)

Modifies the options for one or more bitmap items.

Canvas image

Description

Items of type `image` are used to display images on a canvas.

Inheritance

Inherits from `Widget`, `Canvas`.

Shared options

Option	Default
anchor	CENTER

Options specific to Image

Option	Description	Units	Typical	Default
image	Specifies the name of the image to display in the item. This image must have been created previously with the `create_image` method.	image	`'scene.gif'`	
tags	Specifies a set of tags to apply to the item. TagList consists of a tuple of tag names, which replace any existing tags for the item. TagList may be empty.	tuple	`('tag1', 'img')`	None

Methods

create_image(x, y, *options)

The arguments x and y specify the coordinates of a point used to position the image on the display (using the anchor option). After the coordinates there may be any number of option-value pairs, each of which sets one of the configuration options for the item. These same option-value pairs may be used in itemconfigure calls to change the item's configuration.

delete(item)

Deletes an image item.

coords(item, x, y)

Queries or modifies the coordinates that define an item. If no coordinates are specified, this command returns a list whose elements are the coordinates of the item named by item. If coordinates are specified, then they replace the current coordinates for the named item. If item refers to multiple items, then the first one in the display list is used.

itemconfigure(item, *options)

Modifies the options for one or more image items.

Canvas line

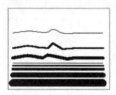

Description

Items of type line appear on the display as one or more connected line segments or curves.

Inheritance

Inherits from Widget, Canvas.

Shared options

Option	Default
fill	"black"
width	1

Options specific to Line

Option	Description	Units	Typical	Default
arrow	Indicates whether or not arrowheads are to be drawn at one or both ends of the line. where must have one of the values None (for no arrowheads), FIRST (for an arrowhead at the first point of the line), last (for an arrowhead at the last point of the line), or both (for arrowheads at both ends).	constant	FIRST 'last'	None
arrowshape	This option indicates how to draw arrowheads. The shape argument must be a tuple with three elements, each specifying a distance in any of the forms acceptable to Tkinter. The first element of the list gives the distance along the line from the neck of the arrowhead to its tip. The second element gives the distance along the line from the trailing points of the arrowhead to the tip, and the third element gives the distance from the outside edge of the line to the trailing points. If this option isn't specified then Tk picks a "reasonable" shape.	tuple	(6,8,3)	(8,10,3)
capstyle	Specifies the ways in which caps are to be drawn at the endpoints of the line. The style may have any of the forms (BUTT, PROJECTING, or ROUND). Where arrowheads are drawn the cap style is ignored.	constant	BUTT 'round'	BUTT
joinstyle	Specifies the ways in which joints are to be drawn at the vertices of the line. The style may have any of the forms (BEVEL, MITER, or ROUND). If the line only contains two points then this option is irrelevant.	constant	DEVEL 'miter'	ROUND
smooth	The value must be a boolean. It indicates whether or not the line should be drawn as a curve. If so, the line is rendered as a set of parabolic splines: one spline is drawn for the first and second line segments, one for the second and third, and so on. Straight-line segments can be generated within a curve by duplicating the end-points of the desired line segment.	boolean	1 FALSE	FALSE
splinesteps	Specifies the degree of smoothness desired for curves: each spline will be approximated with number line segments. This option is ignored unless the smooth option is true.	integer	20	12

Option	Description	Units	Typical	Default
stipple	Indicates that the line should be filled in a stipple pattern; bitmap specifies the stipple pattern to use, in any of the forms accepted by Tkinter (Tk_GetBitmap). If bitmap is an empty string (the default), then filling is done in a solid fashion.	bitmap	'gray25'	None
tags	Specifies a set of tags to apply to the item. TagList consists of a tuple of tag names, which replace any existing tags for the item. TagList may be empty.	tuple	('tag1', 'line')	None

Methods

create_line(x0, y0, x1, y1, ..., xn, yn, *options)

The arguments x0 through yn give the coordinates for a series of two or more points that describe a series of connected line segments. After the coordinates there may be any number of option-value pairs, each of which sets one of the configuration options for the item. These same option-value pairs may be used in itemconfigure calls to change the item's configuration.

delete(item)

Deletes a line item.

coords(item, x0, y0, x1, y1, ..., xn, yn)

Queries or modifies the coordinates that define an item. If no coordinates are specified, this command returns a list whose elements are the coordinates of the item named by item. If coordinates are specified, then they replace the current coordinates for the named item. If item refers to multiple items, then the first one in the display list is used.

itemconfigure(item, *options)

Modifies the options for one or more line items.

Canvas oval

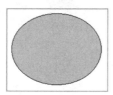

Description

Items of type oval appear as circular or oval regions on the display. Each oval may have an outline, a fill, or both.

Inheritance

Inherits from Widget, Canvas.

Shared options

Option	Default
fill	transparent
width	1

Options specific to Oval

Option	Description	Units	Typical	Default
outline	color specifies a color to use for drawing the oval's outline. If color is an empty string then no outline will be drawn for the oval.	color	RED 'black'	'black'
stipple	Indicates that the oval should be filled in a stipple pattern; bitmap specifies the stipple pattern to use. If the fill option hasn't been specified then this option has no effect. If bitmap is an empty string (the default), then filling is done in a solid fashion.	bitmap	'gray25'	None
tags	Specifies a set of tags to apply to the item. TagList consists of a tuple of tag names, which replace any existing tags for the item. TagList may be empty.	tuple	('tag1', 'oval')	None

Methods

create_oval(x0, y0, x1, y1, *options)

The arguments x0, y0, x1, and y1 give the coordinates of two diagonally opposite corners of a rectangular region enclosing the oval. The oval will include the top and left edges of the rectangle, not the lower or right edges. If the region is square then the resulting oval is circular; otherwise it is elongated in shape. After the coordinates there may be any number of option-value pairs, each of which sets one of the configuration options for the item. These same option-value pairs may be used in itemconfigure method calls to change the item's configuration.

delete(item)

Deletes an oval item.

coords(item, x0, y0, x1, y1)

Queries or modifies the coordinates that define an item. If no coordinates are specified, this command returns a list whose elements are the coordinates of the item named by item. If coordinates are specified, then they replace the current coordinates for the named item. If item refers to multiple items, then the first one in the display list is used.

itemconfigure(item, *options)

Modifies the options for one or more oval items.

Canvas polygon

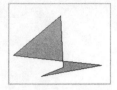

Description

Items of type `polygon` apear as polygonal or curved-filled regions on the display.

Inheritance

Inherits from `Widget`, `Canvas`.

Shared options

Option	Default
fill	transparent
width	1

Options specific to Polygon

Option	Description	Units	Typical	Default
outline	color specifies a color to use for drawing the polygon's outline. If color is an empty string then no outline will be drawn for the polygon.	color	BLUE 'black'	'black'
smooth	boolean must have one of the forms accepted by Tkinter. It indicates whether or not the polygon should be drawn with a curved perimeter. If so, the outline of the polygon becomes a set of parabolic splines, one spline for the first and second line segments, one for the second and third, and so on. Straight-line segments can be generated in a smoothed polygon by duplicating the end-points of the desired line segment.	boolean	1 FALSE	FALSE
splinesteps	Specifies the degree of smoothness desired for curves: each spline will be approximated with number line segments. This option is ignored unless the smooth option is true.	integer	20	12
stipple	Indicates that the polygon should be filled in a stipple pattern; bitmap specifies the stipple pattern to use. If the fill option hasn't been specified then this option has no effect. If bitmap is an empty string (the default), then filling is done in a solid fashion.	bitmap	'gray25'	None
tags	Specifies a set of tags to apply to the item. TagList consists of a tuple of tag names, which replace any existing tags for the item. TagList may be empty.	tuple	('tag1', 'poly')	None

Methods

create_polygon(x0, y0, x1, y1, ..., xn, yn, *options)

The arguments x0 through yn specify the coordinates for three or more points that define a closed polygon. The first and last points may be the same; whether they are or not, Tk will draw the polygon as a closed polygon. After the coordinates there may be any number of option-value pairs, each of which sets one of the configuration options for the item. These same option-value pairs may be used in itemconfigure method calls to change the item's configuration.

delete(item)

Deletes a polygon item.

coords(item, x0, y0, x1, y1, ..., xn, yn)

Queries or modifies the coordinates that define an item. If no coordinates are specified, this command returns a list whose elements are the coordinates of the item named by item. If coordinates are specified, then they replace the current coordinates for the named item. If item refers to multiple items, then the first one in the display list is used.

itemconfigure(item, *options)

Modifies the options for one or more polygon items.

Canvas rectangle

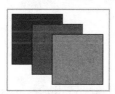

Description

Items of type rectangle appear as rectangular regions on the display. Each rectangle may have an outline, a fill, or both.

Inheritance

Inherits from Widget, Canvas.

Shared options

Option	Default
fill	transparent
width	1

Options specific to Rectangle

Option	Description	Units	Typical	Default
outline	color specifies a color to use for drawing the rectangle's outline. If color is an empty string then no outline will be drawn for the rectangle.	color	RED 'black'	'black'
stipple	Indicates that the rectangle should be filled in a stipple pattern; bitmap specifies the stipple pattern to use. If the fill option hasn't been specified then this option has no effect. If bitmap is an empty string (the default), then filling is done in a solid fashion.	bitmap	'gray25'	None
tags	Specifies a set of tags to apply to the item. TagList consists of a tuple of tag names, which replace any existing tags for the item. TagList may be empty.	tuple	('tag1', 'rect')	None

Methods

create_rectangle(x0, y0, x1, y1, *options)

The arguments x0, y0, x1, and y1 give the coordinates of two diagonally opposite corners of the rectangle (the rectangle will include its upper and left edges but not its lower or right edges). After the coordinates there may be any number of option-value pairs, each of which sets one of the configuration options for the item. These same option-value pairs may be used in itemconfigure method calls to change the item's configuration.

delete(item)

Deletes a rectangle item.

coords(item, x0, y0, x1, y1)

Queries or modifies the coordinates that define an item. If no coordinates are specified, this command returns a list whose elements are the coordinates of the item named by item. If coordinates are specified, then they replace the current coordinates for the named item. If item refers to multiple items, then the first one in the display list is used.

itemconfigure(item, *options)

Modifies the options for one or more rectangle items.

Canvas text

Canvas Text

Description

A text item displays a string of characters on the screen in one or more lines. Text items support indexing and selection, along with the following text-related canvas widget methods: dchars, focus, icursor, index, insert, and select.

Inheritance

Inherits from `Widget`, `Canvas`.

Shared options

Option	Default
anchor	CENTER
fill	transparent
width	1

Options specific to Text

Option	Description	Units	Typical	Default
font	Specifies the font to use for the text item. FontName may be any string acceptable to Tkinter. If this option isn't specified, it defaults to a system-dependent font.	font	'Ver-dana'	(('MS', 'Sans', 'Serif'), '8')
justify	Specifies how to justify the text within its bounding region. Must be one of the values LEFT, RIGHT, or CENTER. This option will only matter if the text is displayed as multiple lines.	constant	RIGHT	LEFT
stipple	Indicates that the text should be filled in a stipple pattern; bitmap specifies the stipple pattern to use. If the fill option hasn't been specified then this option has no effect. If bitmap is an empty string (the default), then filling is done in a solid fashion.	bitmap	'gray25'	None
tags	Specifies a set of tags to apply to the item. TagList consists of a tuple of tag names, which replace any existing tags for the item. TagList may be empty.	tuple	('tag1', 'text')	None
text	string specifies the characters to be displayed in the text item. Newline characters cause line breaks. The characters in the item may also be changed with the insert and delete methods.	string	'Hello'	None

Methods

create_text(x, y, *options)

The arguments x and y specify the coordinates of a point used to position the text on the display. After the coordinates there may be any number of option-value pairs, each of which sets one of the configuration options for the item. These same option-value pairs may be used in `itemconfigure` method calls to change the item's configuration.

delete(item)

Deletes a text `item`.

coords(item, x0, y0)

Queries or modifies the coordinates that define an `item`. If no coordinates are specified, this command returns a list whose elements are the coordinates of the item named by `item`. If coordinates are specified, then they replace the current coordinates for the named `item`. If `item` refers to multiple items, then the first one in the display list is used.

itemconfigure(item, *options)

Modifies the options for one or more text items.

Canvas window

Description

Items of type `window` cause a particular window to be displayed at a given position on the canvas.

Inheritance

Inherits from `Widget`, `Canvas`.

Shared options

Option	Default
anchor	CENTER
height	window height
width	window width

Options specific to Window

Option	Description	Units	Typical	Default
tags	Specifies a set of tags to apply to the item. TagList consists of a tuple of tag names, which replace any existing tags for the item. TagList may be empty.	tuple	('tag1', 'win')	None
window	Specifies the window to associate with this item. The window specified must either be a child of the canvas widget or a child of some ancestor of the canvas widget. The window may not refer to a top-level window.	window	mywin	None

Methods

create_window(x, y, *options)

The arguments x and y specify the coordinates of a point used to position the window on the display. After the coordinates there may be any number of option-value pairs, each of which sets one of the configuration options for the item. These same option-value pairs may be used in itemconfigure method calls to change the item's configuration.

delete(item)

Deletes a window item.

coords(item, x0, y0)

Queries or modifies the coordinates that define an item. If no coordinates are specified, this command returns a list whose elements are the coordinates of the item named by item. If coordinates are specified, then they replace the current coordinates for the named item. If item refers to multiple items, then the first one in the display list is used.

itemconfigure(item, *options)

Modifies the options for one or more window items.

Checkbutton

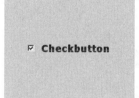

Description

The Checkbutton class defines a new window and creates an instance of a checkbutton widget. Additional options, described below, may be specified in the method call or in the option database to configure aspects of the checkbutton such as its colors, font, text, and initial relief. The checkbutton method returns the identity of the new widget. At the time this method is invoked, the checkbutton's parent must exist.

A checkbutton is a widget that displays a textual string, bitmap, or image and a square called an indicator. If text is displayed, it must all be in a single font, but it can occupy multiple lines on the screen (if it contains newlines or if wrapping occurs because of the wrapLength option) and one of the characters may optionally be underlined using the underline option. A checkbutton has all of the behavior of a simple button, including the following: it can display itself in either of three different ways, according to the *state* option; it can be made to appear raised, sunken, or flat; it can be made to flash; and it invokes a callback whenever mouse button 1 is clicked over the checkbutton. In addition, checkbuttons can be selected. If a checkbutton is selected then the indicator is normally drawn with a selected appearance, and a Tkinter variable associated with the checkbutton is set to a particular value (normally 1). Under UNIX, the indicator is drawn with a sunken relief and a special color. Under Windows, the indicator is drawn with a check markinside.

If the checkbutton is not selected, then the indicator is drawn with a deselected appearance, and the associated variable is set to a different value (typically 0). Under UNIX, the indicator is drawn with a raised relief and no special color. Under Windows, the indicator is drawn without a checkmark inside.

The on and off values stored in the checkbutton may be modified with options on the command line or in the option database. Configuration options may also be used to modify the way the indicator is displayed (or whether it is displayed at all). By default a checkbutton is configured to select and deselect itself on alternate button clicks. In addition, each checkbutton monitors its associated variable and automatically selects and deselects itself when the variable's value changes to and from the button's on value.

Inheritance

Checkbutton inherits from `Widget`.

Shared options

Option (alias)	Default
activebackground	SystemButtonFace
activeforeground	SystemWindowText
anchor	center
background (bg)	SystemButtonFace
bitmap	
borderwidth (bd)	2
command	
cursor	
disabledforeground	SystemDisabledText
font	(('MS', 'Sans', 'Serif'), '8')
foreground (fg)	SystemWindowText
height	0
highlightbackground	SystemButtonFace
highlightcolor	SystemWindowFrame
highlightthickness	1
image	
justify	center
padx	1
pady	1
relief	flat
state	normal
takefocus	
text	
textvariable	

Option (alias)	Default
underline	-1
width	0
wraplength	0

Options specific to Checkbutton

Option (alias)	Description	Units	Typical	Default
indicatoron	Specifies whether or not the indicator should be drawn. Must be a proper boolean value. If FALSE, the relief option is ignored and the widget's relief is always sunken if the widget is selected and raised otherwise.	Boolean	0 TRUE	1
offvalue	Specifies the value to store in the widgets's associated variable whenever this button is deselected. Defaults to 0.	string	0 off	0
onvalue	Specifies the value to store in the widget's associated variable whenever this button is selected. Defaults to 1.	string	1 On	1
selectcolor	Specifies a background color to use when the widget (usually a check or radio button) is selected. If indicatoron is TRUE then the color applies to the indicator. Under Windows, this color is used as the background for the indicator regardless of the select state. If indicatoron is FALSE, this color is used as the background for the entire widget, in place of background or activeBackground, whenever the widget is selected. If specified as an empty string then no special color is used for displaying when the widget is selected.	color	"red"	System-Window
selectimage	Specifies an image to display (in place of the image option) when the widget (typically a checkbutton) is selected. This option is ignored unless the image option has been specified.	image	"red-cross"	
variable	Specifies name of a Tkinter variable to contain the content and set the content of the widget.	variable	myVari-able	

Methods

deselect()

Deselects the checkbutton and sets the associated variable to its off value.

flash()

Flashes the checkbutton. This is accomplished by redisplaying the checkbutton several times, alternating between active and normal colors. At the end of the flash the checkbutton is left in the same normal/active state as when the method was invoked. This method is ignored if the checkbutton's state is disabled.

invoke()

Does just what would have happened if the user invoked the checkbutton with the mouse: toggles the selection state of the button and invokes the callback associated with the check-button, if there is one. The return value is the return value from the callback, or an empty string if no callback is associated with the checkbutton. This method is ignored if the check-button's state is disabled.

select()

Selects the checkbutton and sets the associated variable to its on value.

toggle()

Toggles the selection state of the button, redisplaying it and modifying its associated variable to reflect the new state.

Entry

Description

The Entry class defines a new window and creates an instance of an entry widget. Additional options, described below, may be specified in the method call or in the option database to configure aspects of the entry such as its colors, font, and relief. The entry method returns the identity of the new widget. At the time this method is invoked, the entry's parent must exist.

An entry is a widget that displays a one-line text string and allows that string to be edited using methods described below, which are typically bound to keystrokes and mouse actions. When first created, an entry's string is empty. A portion of the entry may be selected as described below. If an entry is exporting its selection (see the exportSelection option), then it will observe the standard *X11* protocols for handling the selection; entry selections are available as type STRING.

Entries also observe the standard Tk rules for dealing with the input focus. When an entry has the input focus it displays an insertion cursor to indicate where new characters will be inserted.

Entries are capable of displaying strings that are too long to fit entirely within the widget's window. In this case, only a portion of the string will be displayed; commands described below may be used to change the view in the window.

Entries use the standard xScrollCommand mechanism for interacting with scrollbars (see the description of the xScrollCommand option for details). They also support scanning, as described below.

Inheritance

Entry inherits from Widget.

Shared options

Option (alias)	Default
background (bg)	SystemWindow
borderwidth (bd)	2
cursor	xterm
font	(('MS', 'Sans', 'Serif'), '8')
foreground (fg)	SystemWindowText
highlightbackground	SystemButtonFace
highlightcolor	SystemWindowFrame
highlightthickness	0
justify	left
relief	sunken
selectbackground	SystemHighlight
selectborderwidth	0
selectforeground	SystemHighlightText
state	normal
takefocus	
textvariable	
width	20
xscrollcommand	

Options specific to Entry

Option	Description	Units	Typical	Default
exportselection	Specifies whether or not a selection in the widget should also be the X selection. The value may have any of the forms accepted by `Tcl_GetBoolean`, such as true, false, 0, 1, yes, or no. If the selection is exported, then selecting in the widget deselects the current X selection, selecting outside the widget deselects any widget selection, and the widget will respond to selection retrieval requests when it has a selection. The default is usually for widgets to export selections.	boolean	0 YES	1
insertbackground	Specifies the color to use as background in the area covered by the insertion cursor. This color will normally override either the normal background for the widget or the selection background if the insertion cursor happens to fall in the selection.	color	'yellow'	SystemWindowText
insertborderwidth	Specifies a non-negative value indicating the width of the 3-D border to draw around the insertion cursor. The value may have any of the forms acceptable to Tkinter (`Tk_GetPixels`).	pixel	2	0
insertofftime	Specifies a non-negative integer value indicating the number of milliseconds the insertion cursor should remain "off" in each blink cycle. If this option is zero then the cursor doesn't blink—it is on all the time.	integer	250	300
insertontime	Specifies a non-negative integer value indicating the number of milliseconds the insertion cursor should remain "on" in each blink cycle.	integer	175	600
insertwidth	Specifies a value indicating the total width of the insertion cursor. The value may have any of the forms acceptable to Tkinter (`Tk_GetPixels`). If a border has been specified for the insertion cursor (using the `insertBorderWidth` option), the border will be drawn inside the width specified by the `insertWidth` option.	pixel	2	2

Option	Description	Units	Typical	Default
show	If this option is specified, then the true contents of the entry are not displayed in the window. Instead, each character in the entry's value will be displayed as the first character in the value of this option, such as *. This is useful, for example, if the entry is to be used to enter a password. If characters in the entry are selected and copied elsewhere, the information copied will be what is displayed, not the true contents of the entry.	character	"*"	

Methods

delete(first, last=None)

Deletes one or more elements of the entry. `first` is the index of the first character to delete, and `last` is the index of the character just after the last one to delete. If `last` isn't specified it defaults to `first+1`, meaning a single character is deleted. This method returns `None`.

get()

Returns the entry's string.

icursor(index)

Arranges for the insertion cursor to be displayed just before the character given by `index`. Returns `None`.

index(index)

Adjusts the view in the window so that the character given by `index` is displayed at the left edge of the window.

insert(index, string)

Inserts the characters of `string` just before the character indicated by `index`. Returns `None`.

scan_dragto(x)

Computes the difference between its x argument and the x argument to the last `scan_mark` method call for the widget. It then adjusts the view left or right by 10 times the difference in x-coordinates. This command is typically associated with mouse motion events in the widget, to produce the effect of dragging the entry at high speed through the window. The return value is an empty string.

scan_mark(x)

Records x and the current view in the entry window; it is used in conjunction with later `scan_dragto` method. Typically this command is associated with a mouse button press in the widget. It returns an empty string.

selection_adjust(index)

Locates the end of the selection nearest to the character given by index, and adjusts that end of the selection to be at index (meaning including but not going beyond index). The other end of the selection is made the anchor point for future select to commands. If the selection isn't currently in the entry, then a new selection is created to include the characters between index and the most recent selection anchor point, inclusive. Returns an empty string.

selection_clear()

Clears the selection if it is in this widget. If the selection isn't in this widget then the method has no effect. Returns None.

selection_from(index)

Sets the selection anchor point to just before the character given by index. Doesn't change the selection. Returns None.

selection_present()

Returns TRUE if characters are selected in the entry, FALSE if nothing is selected.

selection_range(start, end)

Sets the selection to include the characters starting with the one indexed by start and ending with the one just before end. If end refers to the same character as start or an earlier one, then the entry's selection is cleared.

selection_to(index)

If index is before the anchor point, sets the selection to the characters from index up to but not including the anchor point. If index is the same as the anchor point, does nothing. If index is after the anchor point, sets the selection to the characters from the anchor point up to but not including index. The anchor point is determined by the most recent select from or select adjust command in this widget. If the selection isn't in this widget then a new selection is created using the most recent anchor point specified for the widget. Returns None.

xview(index)

Adjusts the view in the window so that the character given by index is displayed at the left edge of the window.

xview_moveto(fraction)

Adjusts the view in the window so that the character fraction of the way through the text appears at the left edge of the window. fraction must be a fraction between 0 and 1.

xview_scroll(number, what)

Shifts the view in the window left or right according to number and what. number must be an integer. what must be either UNITS or PAGES or an abbreviation of one of these. If what is UNITS, the view adjusts left or right by number average-width characters on the display; if it is

PAGES then the view adjusts by number screenfuls. If number is negative then characters farther to the left become visible; if it is positive then characters farther to the right become visible.

Font class

Inheritance

Inherits from None.

Description

The Font class provides several facilities for dealing with fonts, such as defining named fonts and inspecting the actual attributes of a font. The class defines several methods.

Shared options

None.

Options specific to Font

Option	Description	Units	Typical	Default
family	The case-insensitive font family name. Tk guarantees to support the font families named Courier (a monospaced "typewriter" font), Times (a serifed "newspaper" font), and Helvetica (a sans-serif "European" font). The most closely matching native font family will automatically be substituted when one of the above font families is used. The name may also be the name of a native, platform-specific font family; in that case it will work as desired on one platform but may not display correctly on other platforms. If the family is unspecified or unrecognized, a platform-specific default font will be chosen.	string	'Times'	'MS'
font	Font specifier in X-font format or as a (family, size, style) tuple.	font	'MS'	(('MS', 'Sans', 'Serif') , '8')
overstrike	The value is a boolean flag that specifies whether a horizontal line should be drawn through the middle of characters in this font. The default value for overstrike is false.	Boolean	1 FALSE	FALSE
size	The desired size of the font. If the size argument is a positive number, it is interpreted as a size in points. If size is a negative number, its absolute value is interpreted as a size in pixels. If a font cannot be displayed at the specified size, a nearby size will be chosen. If size is unspecified or zero, a platform-dependent default size will be chosen.	integer	12, -16	

Option	Description	Units	Typical	Default
slant	The amount the characters in the font are slanted away from the vertical. Valid values for slant are roman and italic. A roman font is the normal, upright appearance of a font, while an italic font is one that is tilted some number of degrees from upright. The closest available slant to the one specified will be chosen. The default slant is roman.	constant	ITALIC	NORMAL
underline	The value is a boolean flag that specifies whether characters in this font should be underlined.	Boolean	TRUE 0	FALSE
weight	The nominal thickness of the characters in the font. The value NORMAL specifies a normal weight font, while BOLD specifies a bold font. The closest available weight to the one specified will be chosen.	constant	BOLD	NORMAL

Methods

actual(option=None)

Returns information about the the actual attributes that are obtained when font is used on the window's display; the actual attributes obtained may differ from the attributes requested due to platform-dependant limitations, such as the availability of font families and pointsizes. If option is omitted, returns all actual font attributes as a dictionary. If option is specified, returns the value of that attribute.

cget(option)

Queries the desired attribute, option, for the current font.

configure(**options)

Queries or modifies the desired attributes for the current font. If no option is specified, returns a dictionary describing all the options and their values for fontname. If a single option is specified with no value, then it returns the current value of that attribute. If one or more option-value pairs are specified, then the method modifies the given named font to have the given values; in this case, all widgets using that font will redisplay themselves using the new attributes for the font.

copy()

Returns a copy of the actual font.

measure(text)

Measures the amount of space the string text would use in the given font when displayed in the current font. The return value is the total width in pixels of text, not including the extra pixels used by highly exagerrated characters such as cursive "f." If the string contains newlines or tabs, those characters are not expanded or treated specially when measuring the string.

metrics(*options)

Returns information about the metrics (the font-specific data), for font when it is used on window's display. If option is specified, returns the value of that metric; if it is omitted, the return value is a dictionary of all the metrics and their values.

Functions

families(root=None)

The return value is a list of all the available font families.

names(root=None)

The return value is a list of all the named fonts that are currently defined.

Frame

Description

The Frame class defines a new window and creates an instance of a frame widget. Additional options, described below, may be specified in the method call or in the option database to configure aspects of the frame such as its background color and relief. The frame command returns the path name of the new window.

A frame is a simple widget. Its primary purpose is to act as a spacer or container for complex window layouts. The only features of a frame are its background color and an optional 3-D border to make the frame appear raised or sunken.

Inheritance

Frame inherits from Widget.

Shared options

Option (alias)	Default
background (bg)	SystemButtonFace
borderwidth (bd)	0
cursor	
height	0
highlightbackground	SystemButtonFace
highlightcolor	SystemWindowFrame
highlightthickness	0
relief	flat
takefocus	0
width	0

Options specific to Frame

Option	Description	Units	Typical	Default
class	Specifies a class for the window. This class will be used when querying the option database for the window's other options, and it will also be used later for other purposes such as bindings. The class option may not be changed with the con- figure method. Note that because class is a reserved word, _class must be used with Tkinter.	class		Frame
colormap	Specifies a colormap to use for the window. The value may be either NEW, in which case a new col- ormap is created for the window and its children, or the name of another window (which must be on the same screen and have the same visual as pathName), in which case the new window will use the colormap from the specified window. If the colormap option is not specified, the new win- dow uses the same colormap as its parent. This option may not be changed with the configure method.	colormap	NEW myWindow	
container	The value must be a boolean. If TRUE, it means that this window will be used as a container in which some other application will be embedded (for example, a Tkinter toplevel can be embedded using the use option). The window will support the appropriate window manager protocols for things like geometry requests. The window should not have any children of its own in this application. This option may not be changed with the configure method.	boolean	TRUE 0	0
visual	Specifies visual information for the new window in any of the forms accepted by winfo.visual. If this option is not specified, the new window will use the same visual as its parent. The visual option may not be modified with the configure method.	visual	monochrome	

Methods

There are no Frame methods, other than common widget methods such as configure.

Grid geometry manager

Inheritance

Inherits from None.

Description

Grid is used to communicate with the grid geometry manager that arranges widgets in rows and columns inside of another window, called the geometry master (or master window).

Shared options

None.

Options specific to Grid

Option	Description	Units	Typical	Default
column	Insert the slave so that it occupies the nth column in the grid. Column numbers start with 0. If this option is not supplied, then the slave is arranged just to the right of previous slave specified on this call to grid, or column 0 if it is the first slave. For each x that immediately precedes the slave, the column position is incremented by one. Thus the x represents a blank column for this row in the grid.	integer	1 4	0
columnspan	Insert the slave so that it occupies n columns in the grid.	integer	2	1
in_	Insert the slave(s) in the master window supplied.	widget	myWin	None
ipadx	The amount specifies how much horizontal internal padding to leave on each side of the slave(s). This space is added inside the slave(s) border. The amount must be a valid screen distance, such as 2 or .5c.	distance	5m	0
ipady	The amount specifies how much vertical internal padding to leave on on the top and bottom of the slave(s). This space is added inside the slave(s) border.	distance	3m	0
minsize (row, column)	The minsize option sets the minimum size, in screen units, that will be permitted for this row/column.	integer	25	None
pad	Specifies the number of screen units that will be added to the largest window contained completely in that column when the grid geometry manager requests a size from the containing window.	integer	5	0
padx	The amount specifies how much horizontal external padding to leave on each side of the slave(s), in screen units. This space is added outside the slave(s) border.	distance	5	0
pady	The amount specifies how much vertical external padding to leave on the top and bottom of the slave(s), in screen units. This space is added outside the slave(s) border.	distance	5	0
row	Insert the slave so that it occupies the nth row in the grid. Row numbers start with 0. If this option is not supplied, then the slave is arranged on the same row as the previous slave specified on this call to grid, or the first unoccupied row if this is the first slave.	integer	3	Same row

Option	Description	Units	Typical	Default
rowspan	Insert the slave so that it occupies n rows in the grid. The default is one row.	integer	4	Same row
sticky	If a slave's cell is larger than its requested dimensions, this option may be used to position (or stretch) the slave within its cell. Style is a string that contains zero or more of the characters N, S, E or W. The string can optionally contain spaces or commas, but they are ignored. Each letter refers to a side (north, south, east, or west) that the slave will "stick" to. If both N and S (or E and W) are specified, the slave will be stretched to fill the entire height (or width) of its cavity. The sticky option subsumes the combination of anchor and fill that is used by pack.	string	EW	CEN-TER
weight (row/column)	The weight option sets the relative weight for apportioning any extra spaces among rows/columns. A weight of zero (0) indicates the column will not deviate from its requested size. A column whose weight is two will grow at twice the rate as a column of weight one when extra space is allocated to the layout.	integer	2	0

Methods

grid(option=value, ...)

Use the grid manager for self.

grid_bbox(column=None, row=None, col2=None, row2=None)

With no arguments, the bounding box (in pixels) of the grid is returned. The return value consists of four integers. The first two are the pixel offset from the master window (x then y) of the top-left corner of the grid, and the second two integers are the width and height of the grid, also in pixels. If a single column and row is specified in the method call, then the bounding box for that cell is returned, where the top left cell is numbered from zero. If both column and row arguments are specified, then the bounding box spanning the rows and columns indicated is returned.

grid_columnconfigure(index, options...)

Queries or sets the column properties of the index column of the geometry master, master. The valid options are minsize, weight and pad.

grid_configure(options...)

The arguments consist of pairs of arguments that specify how to manage the slaves.

grid_forget()

Removes self from grid for its master and unmaps their windows. The slave will no longer be managed by the grid geometry manager. The configuration options for that window are forgotten, so that if the slave is managed once more by the grid geometry manager, the initial default settings are used.

grid_info()

Returns a list whose elements are the current configuration state of the slave. The first two elements of the tuple are in master where master is the slave's master

grid_location(x, y)

Given x and y values in screen units relative to the master window, the column and row number at that x and y location is returned. For locations that are above or to the left of the grid, -1 is returned.

grid_propagate(flag=_noarg_)

If flag has a true boolean value such as 1 or ON then propagation is enabled for self. If flag has a false boolean value then propagation is disabled for self. If flag is omitted then the command returns FALSE or TRUE to indicate whether propagation is currently enabled for self. Propagation is enabled by default.

grid_rowconfigure(index, options...)

Queries or sets the row properties of the index row of the geometry master, master. The valid options are minsize, weight and pad.

grid_remove()

Removes slave from grid for its master and unmaps the window. The slave will no longer be managed by the grid geometry manager. However, the configuration options for that window are remembered, so if the slave is managed once more by the grid geometry manager, the previous values are retained.

grid_size()

Returns the size of the grid (in columns then rows) for master. The size is determined either by the slave occupying the largest row or column, or the largest column or row with a minsize, weight, or pad that is non-zero.

grid_slaves(row=None, column=None)

If no options are supplied, a list of all of the slaves in master are returned, with the most recently managed first. Option can be either row or column which causes only the slaves in the row (or column) specified by value to be returned.

Label

Description

The Label class defines a new window and creates an instance of a label widget. Additional options, described below, may be specified in the method call or in the option database to configure aspects of the label such as its colors, font, text, and initial relief. The `label` method returns the identity of the new widget. At the time this method is invoked, the label's parent must exist.

A label is a widget that displays a textual string, bitmap or image. If text is displayed, it must all be in a single font, but it can occupy multiple lines on the screen (if it contains newlines or if wrapping occurs because of the `wrapLength` option) and one of the characters may optionally be underlined using the `underline` option. The label can be manipulated in a few simple ways, such as changing its relief or text, using the standard widget options.

Inheritance

Label inherits from `Widget`.

Shared options

Option (alias)	Default
anchor	center
background (bg)	SystemButtonFace
bitmap	
borderwidth (bd)	2
cursor	
font	(('MS', 'Sans', 'Serif'), '8')
foreground (fg)	SystemButtonText
height	0
highlightbackground	SystemButtonFace
highlightcolor	SystemWindowFrame
highlightthickness	0
image	
justify	center
padx	1
pady	1
relief	flat
takefocus	0
text	
textvariable	
underline	-1
width	0
wraplength	0

Methods

There are no `label` methods, other than common widget methods such as `configure`.

Listbox

Description

The Listbox class defines a new window and creates an instance of a listbox widget. Additional options, described below, may be specified in the method call or in the option database to configure aspects of the listbox such as its colors, font, text, and relief. The `listbox` method returns the identity of the new widget. At the time this method is invoked, the listbox's parent must exist.

A listbox is a widget that displays a list of strings, one per line. When first created, a new listbox has no elements. Elements may be added or deleted using the methods described below. In addition, one or more elements may be selected as described below.

If a listbox is exporting its selection (see the `exportSelection` option), then it will observe the standard X11 protocols for handling the selection. Listbox selections are available as type `STRING`; the value of the selection will be the text of the selected elements, with newlines separating the elements.

It is not necessary for all the elements to be displayed in the listbox window at once; commands described below may be used to change the view in the window. Listboxes allow scrolling in both directions using the standard `xScrollCommand` and `yScrollCommand` options. They also support scanning, as described below.

Inheritance

Listbox inherits from `Widget`.

Shared options

Option (alias)	Default
background (bg)	SystemButtonFace
borderwidth (bd)	2
cursor	
font	(('MS', 'Sans', 'Serif'), '8')
foreground (fg)	SystemButtonText
height	10
highlightbackground	SystemButtonFace
highlightcolor	SystemWindowFrame
highlightthickness	1
relief	sunken
selectbackground	SystemHighlight
selectborderwidth	1
selectforeground	SystemHighlightText
takefocus	

Option (alias)	Default
width	20
xscrollcommand	

Options specific to Listbox

Option	Description	Units	Typical	Default
exportselection	Specifies whether or not a selection in the widget should also be the X selection. The value may have any of the forms accepted by Tcl_GetBoolean, such as true, false, 0, 1, yes, or no. If the selection is exported, then selecting in the widget deselects the current X selection, selecting outside the widget deselects any widget selection, and the widget will respond to selection retrieval requests when it has a selection. The default is usually for widgets to export selections.	boolean	0 YES	1
selectmode	Specifies one of several styles for manipulating the selection. The value of the option may be arbitrary, but the default bindings expect it to be either SINGLE, BROWSE, MULTIPLE, or EXTENDED; the default value is BROWSE.	constant	SINGLE "browse"	browse
setgrid	Specifies a boolean value that determines whether this widget controls the resizing grid for its top-level window. This option is typically used in text widgets, where the information in the widget has a natural size (the size of a character) and it makes sense for the window's dimensions to be integral numbers of these units. These natural window sizes form a grid. If the setGrid option is set to true then the widget will communicate with the window manager so that when the user interactively resizes the top-level window that contains the widget, the dimensions of the window will be displayed to the user in grid units and the window size will be constrained to integral numbers of grid units. See the section "Gridded geometry mamagement" in the wm entry in the Tkman pages for more details.	boolean	NO 1	0
yscrollcommand	Specifies the prefix for a command used to communicate with vertical scrollbars. This option is treated in the same way as the xScrollCommand option, except that it is used for vertical scrollbars and is provided by widgets that support vertical scrolling. See the description of xScrollCommand for details on how this option is used.	function		

Methods

activate(index)

Sets the active element to the one indicated by index. If index is outside the range of elements in the listbox then the closest element is activated. The active element is drawn with an underline when the widget has the input focus, and its index may be retrieved with the index active.

bbox(index)

Returns a list of four numbers describing the bounding box of the text in the element given by index. The first two elements of the list give the x and y coordinates of the upper-left corner of the screen area covered by the text (specified in pixels relative to the widget) and the last two elements give the width and height of the area, in pixels. If no part of the element given by index is visible on the screen, or if index refers to a non-existent element, then the result is None; if the element is partially visible, the result gives the full area of the element, including any parts that are not visible.

curselection()

Returns a list containing the numerical indices of all of the elements in the listbox that are currently selected. If no elements are selected in the listbox then an empty string is returned.

delete(first, last=None)

Deletes one or more elements of the listbox. first and last are indices specifying the first and last elements in the range to delete. If last isn't specified it defaults to first, for example, a single element is deleted.

get(first, last=None)

If last is omitted, returns the contents of the listbox element indicated by first, or an empty string if first refers to a non-existent element. If last is specified, the method returns a list whose elements are all of the listbox elements between first and last, inclusive. Both first and last may have any of the standard forms for indices.

index(index)

Adjusts the view in the window so that the element given by index is displayed at the top of the window.

insert(index, *elements)

Inserts zero or more new elements in the list just before the element given by index. If index is specified as END then the new elements are added to the end of the list. Returns None.

nearest(y)

Given a y-coordinate within the listbox window, this method returns the index of the (visible) listbox element nearest to that y-coordinate.

scan_dragto(x, y)

This method computes the difference between its x and y arguments (which are typically mouse coordinates) and the x and y arguments to the last scan_mark call for the widget. It then adjusts the view by 10 times the difference in coordinates. This method is typically associated with mouse motion events in the widget, to produce the effect of dragging the list at high speed through its window. The return value is an empty string.

scan_mark(x, y)

Records x and y and the listbox's current view; used in conjunction with later scan_dragto calls. Typically this method is associated with a mouse button press in the widget and x and y are the coordinates of the mouse. It returns None.

see(index)

Adjusts the view in the listbox so that the element given by index is visible. If the element is already visible then the method has no effect; if the element is near one edge of the window then the listbox scrolls to bring the element into view at the edge; otherwise the listbox scrolls to center the element.

selection_anchor(index)

Sets the selection anchor to the element given by index.

selection_clear(first, last=None)

If any of the elements between first and last (inclusive) are selected, they are deselected. The selection state is not changed for elements outside this range.

selection_includes(index)

Returns TRUE if the element indicated by index is currently selected, FALSE if it isn't.

selection_set(first, last=None)

Selects all of the elements in the range between first and last, inclusive, without affecting the selection state of elements outside that range.

size()

Returns an integer indicating the total number of elements in the listbox.

xview_moveto(fraction)

Adjusts the view in the window so that fraction of the the total width of the listbox is off-screen to the left. fraction is a fraction between 0 and 1.

xview_scroll(number, what)

This command shifts the view in the window left or right according to number and what. number must be an integer. what must be either UNITS or PAGES or an abbreviation of one of these. If what is UNITS, the view adjusts left or right by number character units (the width of the 0 character) on the display; if it is PAGES then the view adjusts by number screenfuls. If number is negative then characters farther to the left become visible; if it is positive then characters farther to the right become visible.

yview_moveto(fraction)

Adjusts the view in the window so that `fraction` of the the total height of the listbox is off-screen to the top. `fraction` is a fraction between 0 and 1.

yview_scroll(number, what)

This command adjusts the view in the window up or down according to `number` and `what`. `number` must be an integer. `what` must be either UNITS or PAGES. If `what` is UNITS, the view adjusts up or down by `number` lines; if it is PAGES then the view adjusts by `number` screenfuls. If `number` is negative then earlier elements become visible; if it is positive then later elements become visible.

Menu

| Button | Cascade | Checkbutton | Radiobutton |

Description

The Menu class defines a new top-level window and creates an instance of a menu widget. Additional options, described below, may be specified in the method call or in the option database to configure aspects of the menu such as its colors and font. The `menu` method returns the identity of the new widget. At the time this method is invoked, the menu's parent must exist.

Inheritance

Menu inherits from `Widget`.

Shared options

Option (alias)	Default
activebackground	SystemHighlight
activeforeground	SystemHighlightText
background (bg)	SystemMenu
borderwidth (bd)	1
cursor	arrow
disabledforeground	SystemDisabledText
font	('Georgia', '8')
foreground (fg)	SystemMenuText
relief	flat
takefocus	0

Options specific to Menu

Option	Description	Units	Typical	Default
activeborderwidth	Specifies a non-negative value indicating the width of the 3-D border drawn around active elements. The value may have any of the forms acceptable to Tkinter (Tk_GetPixels). This option is typically only available in widgets displaying more than one element at a time (such as menus but not buttons).	pixel	2, 1m	1
postcommand	If this option is specified then it provides a Tkinter command to execute each time the menu is posted. The command is invoked by the widget before posting the menu. Note that in 8.0 on Macintosh and Windows, all commands in a menu system are executed before any are posted. This is due to the limitations in the individual platforms's menu managers.	command	display-Menu	
selectcolor	Specifies a background color to use when the widget (usually a check or radio-button) is selected. If indicatoron is TRUE then the color applies to the indicator. Under Windows, this color is used as the background for the indicator regardless of the select state. If indicatoron is FALSE, this color is used as the background for the entire widget, in place of background or activeBackground, whenever the widget is selected. If specified as an empty string then no special color is used for displaying when the widget is selected.	color	"red"	SystemMenu-Text
tearoff	This option must have a proper boolean value, which specifies whether or not the menu should include a tear-off entry at the top. If so, it will exist as entry 0 of the menu and the other entries will number starting at 1. The default menu bindings arrange for the menu to be torn off when the tear-off entry is invoked.	boolean	TRUE 0	1

Option	Description	Units	Typical	Default
tearoffcommand	If this option has a non-empty value, then it specifies a Tkinter command to invoke whenever the menu is torn off. The actual command will consist of the value of this option, followed by a space, followed by the name of the menu window, followed by a space, followed by the name of the torn-off menu window.	command	myTearoff	
title	The string will be used to title the window created when a shell is created or a menu is torn off. For menus, if the title is NULL, then the window will have the title of the menubutton or the text of the cascade item from which this menu was invoked.	string	"Widget Table"	
type	This option can be one of MENUBAR, TEAROFF, or NORMAL, and it is set when a menu is created. While the string returned by the configuration database will change if this option is changed, this does not affect the menu widget's behavior. This is used by the cloning mechanism and is not normally set outside of the Tk library.	constant	NORMAL	normal

Methods

add_cascade(options...)

Adds a new cascade to the bottom of the menu.

add_checkbutton(options...)

Adds a new checkbutton to the bottom of the menu.

add_command(options...)

Adds a new command to the bottom of the menu.

add_radiobutton(options...)

Adds a new radiobutton to the bottom of the menu.

add_separator(options...)

Adds a new separator to the bottom of the menu.

delete(index1, index2=None)

Deletes all of the menu entries between index1 and index2 inclusive. If index2 is omitted then it defaults to index1. Attempts to delete a tear-off menu entry are ignored (instead, you should change the tearOff option to remove the tear-off entry).

entrycget(index, option)

Returns the current value of a configuration option for the entry given by index. option may have any of the values accepted by the add method.

entryconfigure(index, options...)

This method is similar to the configure command, except that it applies to the options for an individual entry index, whereas configure applies to the options for the menu as a whole. options may have any of the values accepted by the add widget method. If options are specified, options are modified as indicated in the method and the method returns None. If no options are specified, it returns a list describing the current options for entry index.

index(index)

Returns the numerical index corresponding to index, or None if index was specified as None.

insert_cascade(index, options...)

Same as the add method except that it inserts the new cascade entry just before the entry given by index, instead of appending to the end of the menu. options arguments have the same interpretation as for the add method. It is not possible to insert new menu entries before the tear-off entry, if the menu has one.

insert_checkbutton(index, options...)

Same as the add method except that it inserts the new checkbutton entry just before the entry given by index, instead of appending to the end of the menu. options arguments have the same interpretation as for the add method. It is not possible to insert new menu entries before the tear-off entry, if the menu has one.

insert_command(index, options...)

Same as the add method except that it inserts the new command entry just before the entry given by index, instead of appending to the end of the menu. options arguments have the same interpretation as for the add method. It is not possible to insert new menu entries before the tear-off entry, if the menu has one.

insert_radiobutton(index, options...)

Same as the add method except that it inserts the new radiobutton entry just before the entry given by index, instead of appending to the end of the menu. options arguments have the same interpretation as for the add method. It is not possible to insert new menu entries before the tear-off entry, if the menu has one.)

insert_separator(index, options...)

Same as the add method except that it inserts the new separator entry just before the entry given by index, instead of appending to the end of the menu. options arguments have the same interpretation as for the add method. It is not possible to insert new menu entries before the tear-off entry, if the menu has one.

invoke(index)

Invokes the action of the menu entry `index`. If the menu entry is disabled then nothing happens. If the entry has a callback associated with it then the result of that callback is returned as the result of the `invoke` widget call. Otherwise the result is an empty string.

Note: Invoking a menu entry does not automatically unpost the menu; the default bindings normally take care of this before invoking the `invoke` widget call.

post(x, y)

Arranges for the menu to be displayed on the screen at the root-window coordinates given by x and y. These coordinates are adjusted, if necessary, to guarantee that the entire menu is visible on the screen. This method normally returns None. If the `postCommand` option has been specified, then its value is executed as a callback before posting the menu and the result of that script is returned as the result of the `post` method. If an error returns while executing the method, then the error is returned without posting the menu.

With the exception of `tk_popup`, the following methods are really only useful if you are writing your own event handling for menus. Their function is to set the state of menu elements as if the default actions had occurred. They may also be useful in simulating user interaction with a GUI.

tk_bindForTraversal()
tk_firstMenu()
tk_getMenuButtons()
tk_invokeMenu()
tk_mbButtonDown()
tk_mbPost()
tk_mbUnpost()
tk_nextMenu(count)
tk_nextMenuEntry(count)

tk_popup(x, y, entry="")

Posts a menu at a given position on the screen and configures Tk so that the menu and its cascaded children can be traversed with the mouse or the keyboard. x and y are the root coordinates at which to display the menu. If entry is omitted or is an empty string, the menu's upper left corner is positioned at the given point. Otherwise entry gives the index of an entry in menu and the menu will be positioned so that the entry is positioned over the given point.

tk_traverseToMenu(char)
tk_traverseWithinMenu(char)

type(index)

Returns the type of the menu entry given by `index`. This is the type argument passed to the `add` method when the entry was created, such as `command` or `separator`, or `tearoff` for a tear-off entry.

unpost()

Unmaps the window so that it is no longer displayed. If a lower-level cascaded menu is posted, unpost that menu. Returns an empty string. This method does not work on Windows and Macintosh, as those platforms have their own way of unposting menus.

yposition(index)

Returns an integer giving the y-coordinate within the menu window of the top-most pixel in the entry specified by index.

Menubutton

Description

The Menubutton class defines a new window and creates an instance of a menubutton widget. Additional options, described below, may be specified in the method call or in the option database to configure aspects of the menubutton such as its colors, font, text, and initial relief. The menubutton method returns the identity of the new widget. At the time this method is invoked, the menubuttons's parent must exist.

A menubutton is a widget that displays a textual string, bitmap, or image and is associated with a menu widget. If text is displayed, it must all be in a single font, but it can occupy multiple lines on the screen (if it contains newlines or if wrapping occurs because of the wrapLength option) and one of the characters may optionally be underlined using the underline option.

In normal usage, pressing mouse button 1 over the menubutton causes the associated menu to be posted just underneath the menubutton. If the mouse is moved over the menu before releasing the mouse button, the button release causes the underlying menu entry to be invoked. When the button is released, the menu is unposted. Menubuttons are typically organized into groups called menu bars that allow scanning: if the mouse button is pressed over one menubutton (causing it to post its menu) and the mouse is moved over another menubutton in the same menu bar without releasing the mouse button, then the menu of the first menubutton is unposted and the menu of the new menubutton is posted instead.

There are several interactions between menubuttons and menus; see the menu entry for information on various menu configurations, such as pulldown menus and option menus.

Inheritance

Menubutton inherits from Widget.

Shared options

Option (alias)	Default
activebackground	SystemButtonFace
activeforeground	SystemButtonText
anchor	center
background (bg)	SystemButtonFace
bitmap	
borderwidth (bd)	2
cursor	
disabledforeground	SystemDisabledText
font	(('MS', 'Sans', 'Serif'), '8')
foreground (fg)	SystemButtonText
height	0
highlightbackground	SystemButtonFace
highlightcolor	SystemWindowFrame
highlightthickness	0
image	
justify	center
padx	4p
pady	3p
relief	flat
state	normal
takefocus	0
text	
textvariable	
underline	-1
width	0
wraplength	0

Options specific to Menubutton

Option (alias)	Description	Units	Typical	Default
direction	Specifies where the menu is going to pop up. ABOVE tries to pop the menu above the menubutton. BELOW tries to pop the menu below the menubutton. LEFT tries to pop the menu to the left of the menubutton. RIGHT tries to pop the menu to the right of the menu button. FLUSH pops the menu directly over the menubutton.	constant	FLUSH "above"	below
indicatoron	Specifies whether or not the indicator should be drawn. Must be a proper boolean value. If FALSE, the relief option is ignored and the widget's relief is always sunken if the widget is selected; otherwise, it is raised.	Boolean	0 TRUE	0
menu	Specifies the pathname of the menu associated with a menubutton. The menu must be a child of the menubutton.	string	subMenu-Action	

Methods

menubutton(options...)

options determine the exact behavior of the menubutton method.

cget(option)

Returns the current value of the configuration option.

configure(options...)

Queries or modifies the configuration options of the widget. If no option is specified, returns a dictionary describing all of the available options for the menubutton. If option is specified with no value, then the command returns a dictionary describing the one named option. If one or more option-value pairs are specified, then the method modifies the given widget option(s) to have the given value(s); in this case the method returns an empty string. options may have any of the values accepted by the menubutton method.

Message

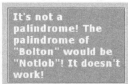

It's not a palindrome! The palindrome of "Bolton" would be "Notlob"! It doesn't work!

Description

The Message class defines a new window and creates an instance of a message widget. Additional options, described below, may be specified in the method call or in the option database to configure aspects of the message such as its colors, font, text, and initial relief. The message method returns the identity of the new widget. At the time this method is invoked, the message's parent must exist.

A message is a widget that displays a textual string. A message widget has three special features. First, it breaks up its string into lines in order to produce a given aspect ratio for the window. The line breaks are chosen at word boundaries wherever possible (if not even a single word will fit on a line, then the word will be split across lines). Newline characters in the string will force line breaks; they can be used, for example, to leave blank lines in the display.

The second feature of a message widget is justification. The text may be displayed left-justified (each line starts at the left side of the window), centered on a line-by-line basis, or right-justified (each line ends at the right side of the window).

The third feature of a message widget is that it handles control characters and non-printing characters specially. Tab characters are replaced with enough blank space to line up on the next 8-character boundary. Newlines cause line breaks. Other control characters (ASCII code less than 0×20) and characters not defined in the font are displayed as a four-character sequence \xhhh where hh is the two-digit hexadecimal number corresponding to the character. In the unusual case where the font doesn't contain all of the characters in 0123456789abcdefx then control characters and undefined characters are not displayed at all.

Inheritance

Message inherits from Widget.

Shared options

Option (alias)	Default
anchor	center
background (bg)	SystemButtonFace
borderwidth (bd)	2
cursor	
font	(('MS', 'Sans', 'Serif'), '8')
foreground (fg)	SystemButtonText
highlightbackground	SystemButtonFace
highlightcolor	SystemWindowFrame
highlightthickness	0
justify	left
padx	-1
pady	-1
relief	flat
takefocus	0
text	
textvariable	
width	0

Options specific to Message

Option (alias)	Description	Units	Typical	Default
aspect	Specifies a non-negative integer value indicating the desired aspect ratio for the text. The aspect ratio is specified as 100*width/height. 100 means the text should be as wide as it is tall, 200 means the text should be twice as wide as it is tall, 50 means the text should be twice as tall as it is wide, and so on. Used to choose line length for text if the width option isn't specified. Defaults to 150.	integer	50 75	150

Methods

message(options...)

options determine the exact behavior of the message method.

cget(option)

Returns the current value of the configuration option.

configure(options...)

Queries or modifies the configuration options of the widget. If no option is specified, returns a dictionary describing all of the available options for the menubutton. If option is specified with no value, then the command returns a dictionary describing the one named option. If one or more option-value pairs are specified, then the method modifies the given widget option(s) to have the given value(s); in this case the method returns an empty string. options may have any of the values accepted by the message method.

OptionMenu class

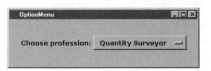

Description

This class instantiates an option menubutton with an associated menu. Together they allow the user to select one of the values given by the value arguments. The current value will be stored in the Tkinter variable whose name is given in the constructor and it will also be displayed as the label in the option menubutton. The user can click on the menubutton to display a menu containing all of the values and thereby select a new value. Once a new value is selected, it will be stored in the variable and appear in the option menubutton. The current value can also be changed by setting the variable.

Inheritance

Inherits from Menubutton.

Shared options

None.

Options specific to Widget

None.

Methods

OptionMenu(master, variable, value, *values)

Creates an instance of `OptionMenu`. `master` is the parent widget, and `variable` is the identity of the Tkinter variable. `value` is the default value and `values` is a list of values to be inserted in the optionmenu's menu.

Pack geometry manager

Description

The `pack` method is used to communicate with the Packer, a geometry manager that arranges the children of a parent by packing them in order around the edges of the parent.

Inheritance

Inherits from None. Pack does not inherit from anything.

Shared options

None.

Options specific to Pack

Option	Description	Units	Typical	Default
after	Value must be another window. Use its master as the master for the slaves, and insert the slaves just after other in the packing order.	widget	label	
before	Value must be another window. Use its master as the master for the slaves, and insert the slaves just before other in the packing order.	widget	self.entry	
expand	Specifies whether the slaves should be expanded to consume extra space in their master. Boolean may have any proper boolean value, such as 1 or NO.	boolean	YES	0
fill	If a slave's parcel is larger than its requested dimensions, this option may be used to stretch the slave.	constant	X 'both'	NONE
in_	Insert the slave(s) at the end of the packing order for the master window given by value.	widget	container	parent

Option	Description	Units	Typical	Default
ipadx	Amount specifies how much horizontal internal padding to leave on each side of the slave(s). Amount must be a valid screen distance, such as 2 or .5c.	distance	2	0
ipady	Amount specifies how much vertical internal padding to leave on each side of the slave(s).	distance	1m	0
padx	Amount specifies how much horizontal external padding to leave on each side of the slave(s).	distance	3	0
pady	Amount specifies how much vertical external padding to leave on each side of the slave(s).	distance	'2m'	0
side	Specifies which side of the master the slave(s) will be packed against. Must be LEFT, RIGHT, TOP, or BOTTOM.	constant	LEFT 'top'	TOP

Methods

pack(option=value, ...)

The arguments consist of pairs of arguments that specify how to manage the slaves.

pack_forget()

Removes self from the packing order for its master and unmaps its windows. The slave will no longer be managed by the Packer.

pack_info()

Returns a dictionary whose elements are the current configuration state of self in the same option-value form that might be specified to pack_configure.

pack_propagate(flag=_noarg_)

If flag has a true boolean value such as 1 or ON then propagation is enabled for self. If flag has a FALSE boolean value then propagation is disabled for master. If flag is omitted then the command returns FALSE or TRUE to indicate whether propagation is currently enabled for master. Propagation is enabled by default.

pack_slaves()

Returns a list of IDs for all of the slaves in the packing order for master. The order of the slaves in the list is the same as their order in the packing order. If master has no slaves then None is returned.

PhotoImage class

Description

A photo is an image whose pixels can display any color or be transparent. A photo image is stored internally in full color (24 bits per pixel), and is displayed using dithering if necessary.

Image data for a photo image can be obtained from a file or a string, or it can be supplied from C code through a procedural interface. At present, only GIF and PPM/PGM formats are supported, but an interface exists to allow additional image file formats to be added easily. A photo image is transparent in regions where no image data has been supplied.

Inheritance

Inherits from Image.

Shared options

Option	Default
width	requested width
height	requested height

Options specific to PhotoImage

Option	Description	Units	Typical	Default
data	Specifies the contents of the image as a string. The format of the string must be one of those for which there is an image file format handler that will accept string data (currently GIF). If both the data and file options are specified, the file option takes precedence.	string		
file	filename gives the name of a file that is to be read to supply data for the photo image. The file format must be one of those for which there is an image file format handler that can read data (currently GIF, PGM and PPM).	string	"icon.gif'	
format	Specifies the name of the file format for the data specified with the data or file option.	string		
gamma	Specifies that the colors allocated for displaying this image in a window should be corrected for a non-linear display with the specified gamma exponent value. (The intensity produced by most CRT displays is a power function of the input value, to a good approximation; gamma is the exponent and is typically around 2). The value specified must be greater than zero. The default value is 1 (no correction). In general, values greater than 1 will make the image lighter, and values less than 1 will make it darker.	float	1.2	1.0

Option	Description	Units	Typical	Default
palette	Specifies the resolution of the color cube to be allocated for displaying this image, and thus the number of colors used from the colormaps of the windows where it is displayed. The `palette-spec` string may be either a single decimal number, specifying the number of shades of gray to use, or three decimal numbers separated by slashes (/), specifying the number of shades of red, green and blue to use, respectively. If the first form (a single number) is used, the image will be displayed in monochrome (i.e., grayscale).	integer or string	'255/220/ 125'	system dependent

Methods

PhotoImage(option...)

Creates a photo instance using option-value pairs in `option`.

blank()

Blank the image; that is, set the entire image to have no data, so it will be displayed as transparent, and the background of whatever window it is displayed in will show through.

cget(option)

Returns the current value of the configuration option given by `option`. `option` may have any of the values accepted by the photoimage constructor.

configure(option=value...)

Queries or modifies the configuration options for the image. If no `option` is specified, returns a dictionary describing all of the available options for the image. If `option` is specified with no value, then the command returns a dictionary describing the one named `option` (this dictionary will be identical to the corresponding sublist of the value returned if no option is specified). If one or more option-value pairs are specified, then the method modifies the given option(s) to have the given value(s); in this case the method returns an empty string. `option` may have any of the values accepted by the photoimage constructor.

copy()

Copies the current image. Note the Tkinter method simplifies the Tk command which allows copying of a region within the image.

get(x, y)

Returns the color of the pixel at coordinates (x,y) in the image as a tuple of three integers between 0 and 255, representing the red, green and blue components respectively.

height()

Returns an integer giving the height of the image in pixels.

put(data, to=None)

Sets pixels in the image to the colors specified in `data`. `data` is used to form a two-dimensional array of pixels that are then copied into the image. `data` is structured as a list of horizontal rows, from top to bottom, each of which is a list of colors, listed from left to right. Each color may be specified by name (e.g., blue) or in hexadecimal form (e.g., #2376af). The `to` option can be used to specify the bounding box to be affected. If the tuple contains only x1 and y1, the area affected has its top-left corner at (x1,y1) and is the same size as the array given in `data`. If all four coordinates are given, they specify diagonally opposite corners of the affected rectangle, and the array given in `data` will be replicated as necessary in the x and y directions to fill the rectangle.

subsample(x, y = None)

Reduces the image in size by using only every *x*th pixel in the x direction and *y*th pixel in the y direction. Negative values will cause the image to be flipped about the y or x axes, respectively. If y is not given, the default value is the same as x.

type()

Returns the type of image as a string (the value of the type argument to `image create` when the image was created).

width()

Returns an integer giving the width of the image in pixels.

write(filename, options...)

Writes image data from the image to a `file` named filename. The following `options` may be specified:

Option	Type	Description
format	string	Specifies the name of the image file format handler to be used to write the data to the file. Specifically, this subcommand searches for the first handler whose name matches an initial substring of format-name and which has the capability to write an image file. If this option is not given, this subcommand uses the first handler that has the capability to write an image file.
from_coords	tuple	Specifies a rectangular region of `imageName` to be written to the image file. If only x1 and y1 are specified, the region extends from (x1,y1) to the bottom-right corner of the image. If all four coordinates are given, they specify diagonally opposite corners of the rectangular region. The default, if this option is not given, is the whole image.

zoom(x, y = None)

Magnifies the image by a factor of x in the x direction and y in the y direction. If y is not given, the default value is the same as x. With this option, each pixel in the source image will be expanded into a block of x × y pixels in the new image, all the same color. x and y must be greater than 0.

Place geometry manager

Description

The Placer is a geometry manager for Tk. It provides simple fixed placement of windows, where you specify the exact size and location of one window, called the slave, within another window, called the master. The Placer also provides rubber-sheet placement, where you specify the size and location of the slave in terms of the dimensions of the master, so that the slave changes size and location in response to changes in the size of the master. Lastly, the Placer allows you to mix these styles of placement so that, for example, the slave has a fixed width and height but it is centered inside the master.

Inheritance

Inherits from None. Place does not inherit from anything.

Shared options

None.

Options specific to Place

Option	Description	Units	Typical	Default
anchor	Value specifies which point of window is to be positioned at the (x,y) location selected by the x, y, relx, and rely options. The anchor point is in terms of the outer area of the window including its border, if any. Thus if where is SE then the lower-right corner of window's border will appear at the given (x,y) location in the master.	constant	N SE	NW
bordermode	mode determines the degree to which borders within the master are used in determining the placement of the slave. The default and most common value is INSIDE. In this case the Placer considers the area of the master to be the innermost area of the master, inside any border: an option of x 0 corresponds to an x-coordinate just inside the border and an option of rel-width 1.0 means the window will fill the area inside the master's border. If mode is OUTSIDE then the Placer considers the area of the master to include its border; this mode is typically used when placing the window outside its master, as with the options x 0 y 0 anchor NE. Lastly, mode may be specified as IGNORE, in which case borders are ignored: the area of the master is considered to be its official X area, which includes any internal border but no external border. A bordermode of ignore is probably not very useful.	constant	OUTSIDE	INSIDE

Option	Description	Units	Typical	Default
height	value specifies the height for window in screen units. The height will be the outer dimension of the window including its border, if any. If no `height` or `relheight` option is specified, then the height requested internally by the window will be used.	integer	134	Natu-ral size
in_	value specifes the identity of the window relative to which window is to be placed. Master must either be window's parent or a descendant of window's parent. In addition, master and window must both be descendants of the same top-level window. These restrictions are necessary to guarantee that window is visible whenever master is visible.	widget	fred	parent
relheight	value specifies the height for window. In this case the height is specified as a floating-point number relative to the height of the master: 0.5 means window will be half as high as the master, 1.0 means window will have the same height as the master, and so on. If both `height` and `relheight` are specified for a slave, their values are summed. For example, `relheight 1.0 height 2` makes the slave 2 pixels shorter than the master.	float	0.45	1.0
relwidth	value specifies the width for window. In this case the width is specified as a floating-point number relative to the width of the master: 0.5 means window will be half as wide as the master, 1.0 means window will have the same width as the master, and so on. If both `width` and `relwidth` are specified for a slave, their values are summed. For example, `relwidth 1.0 width 5` makes the slave 5 pixels wider than the master.	float	0.5	1.0
relx	location specifies the x-coordinate within the master window of the anchor point for window. In this case the location is specified in a relative fashion as a floating-point number: 0.0 corresponds to the left edge of the master and 1.0 corresponds to the right edge of the master. `location` need not be in the range 0.0 - 1.0. If both `x` and `relx` are specified for a slave then their values are summed. For example, `relx 0.5 x 2` positions the left edge of the slave 2 pixels to the left of the center of its master.	float	0.66	0.0
rely	location specifies the y-coordinate within the master window of the anchor point for window. In this case the value is specified in a relative fashion as a floating-point number: 0.0 corresponds to the top edge of the master and 1.0 corresponds to the bottom edge of the master. `location` need not be in the range 0.01.0. If both `y` and `rely` are specified for a slave then their values are summed. For example, `rely 0.5 x 3` positions the top edge of the slave 3 pixels below the center of its master.	float	0.34	0.0

Option	Description	Units	Typical	Default
x	`location` specifies the x-coordinate within the master window of the anchor point for window. The location is specified in screen units and need not lie within the bounds of the master window.	integer	105	0
width	`size` specifies the width for window in screen units (i.e. any of the forms accepted by Tkinter (`Tk_GetPixels`)). The width will be the outer width of the window including its border, if any. If `size` is empty, or if no `width` or `relwidth` option is specified, then the width requested internally by the window will be used.	integer	125	natural width
y	`location` specifies the y-coordinate within the master window of the anchor point for window. The location is specified in screen units and need not lie within the bounds of the master window.	integer	88	0

Methods

place(option=value, ...)

The arguments consist of one or more option-value pairs that specify the way in which `self`'s geometry is managed. If the Placer is already managing `self`, then the option-value pairs modify the configuration for its window. In this form the `place` method returns `None` as the result.

place_forget()

The `place_forget` method causes the Placer to stop managing the geometry of window. As a side effect of this method `self` will be unmapped so that it doesn't appear on the screen. If `self` isn't currently managed by the Placer then the method has no effect.

place_info()

The `place_info` method returns a dictionary giving the current configuration of the window. The dictionary consists of option-value pairs in exactly the same form as might be specified to the `place` method. If the configuration of a window has been retrieved with `place_info`, that configuration can be restored later by first using `place_forget` to erase any existing information for the window and then invoking `place` with the saved information.

place_slaves()

The `place_slaves` method returns a list of all the slave windows for which `self` is the master. If there are no slaves for `self` then `None` is returned.

Radiobutton

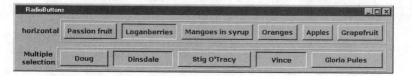

Description

The Radiobutton class defines a new window and creates an instance of a radiobutton widget. Additional options, described below, may be specified in the method call or in the option database to configure aspects of the radiobutton such as its colors, font, text, and initial relief. The `radiobutton` method returns the identity of the new widget. At the time this command is invoked, the radiobutton's parent must exist.

A radiobutton is a widget that displays a textual string, bitmap or image and a diamond or circle called an indicator. If text is displayed, it must all be in a single font, but it can occupy multiple lines on the screen (if it contains newlines or if wrapping occurs because of the `wrapLength` option), and one of the characters may optionally be underlined using the `underline` option.

A radiobutton has all of the behavior of a simple button: it can display itself in either of three different ways, according to the state option; it can be made to appear raised, sunken, or flat; it can be made to flash; and it invokes a Tcl command whenever mouse button 1 is clicked over the checkbutton. In addition, radiobuttons can be selected.

If a radiobutton is selected, the indicator is normally drawn with a selected appearance, and a Tkinter variable associated with the radiobutton is set to a particular value (normally 1). Under UNIX, the indicator is drawn with a sunken relief and a special color. Under Windows, the indicator is drawn with a round mark inside.

If the radiobutton is not selected, then the indicator is drawn with a deselected appearance, and the associated variable is set to a different value (typically 0). Under UNIX, the indicator is drawn with a raised relief and no special color. Under Windows, the indicator is drawn without a round mark inside.

Typically, several radiobuttons share a single variable and the value of the variable indicates which radiobutton is to be selected. When a radiobutton is selected it sets the value of the variable to indicate that fact; each radiobutton also monitors the value of the variable and automatically selects and deselects itself when the variable's value changes.

Configuration options may also be used to modify the way the indicator is displayed (or whether it is displayed at all). By default a radiobutton is configured to select itself on button clicks.

Inheritance

Radiobutton inherits from `Widget`.

Shared options

Option (alias)	Default
activebackground	SystemButtonFace
activeforeground	SystemWindowText
anchor	center
background (bg)	SystemButtonFace
bitmap	
borderwidth (bd)	2
command	
cursor	
disabledforeground	SystemDisabledText
font	(('MS', 'Sans', 'Serif'), '8')
foreground (fg)	SystemWindowText
height	0
highlightbackground	SystemButtonFace
highlightcolor	SystemWindowFrame
highlightthickness	1
image	
justify	center
padx	1
pady	1
relief	flat
state	normal
takefocus	
text	
textvariable	
underline	-1
width	0
wraplength	0

Options specific to Radiobutton

Option	Description	Units	Typical	Default
indicatoron	Specifies whether or not the indicator should be drawn. Must be a proper boolean value. If FALSE, the relief option is ignored and the widget's relief is always sunken if the widget is selected; otherwise, it is raised.	Boolean	0 TRUE	1

Option	Description	Units	Typical	Default
selectcolor	Specifies a background color to use when the widget (usually a check or radiobutton) is selected. If indicatoron is TRUE then the color applies to the indicator. Under Windows, this color is used as the background for the indicator regardless of the select state. If indicatoron is FALSE, this color is used as the background for the entire widget, in place of background or activeBackground, whenever the widget is selected. If specified as an empty string then no special color is used for displaying when the widget is selected.	color	"red"	SystemWindow
selectimage	Specifies an image to display (in place of the image option) when the widget (typically a checkbutton) is selected. This option is ignored unless the image option has been specified.	image	"redcross"	
value	Specifies the value to store in the button's associated Tkinter variable whenever this button is selected.	string	0 "Power"	
variable	Specifies the name of a Tkinter variable to contain the content and set the content of the widget.	variable	myVariable	selectedButton

Methods

deselect()

Deselects the radiobutton and sets the associated variable to an empty string. If this radiobutton was not currently selected, the method has no effect.

flash()

Flashes the radiobutton. This is accomplished by redisplaying the radiobutton several times, alternating between active and normal colors. At the end of the flash the radiobutton is left in the same normal/active state as when the method was invoked. This method is ignored if the radiobutton's state is disabled.

invoke()

Does just what would have happened if the user invoked the radiobutton with the mouse: selects the button and invokes its associated callback, if there is one. The return value is the return value from the callback, or an empty string if no callback is associated with the radiobutton. This method is ignored if the radiobutton's state is disabled.

select()

Selects the radiobutton and sets the associated variable to the value corresponding to this widget.

Scale

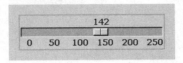

Description

The Scale class defines a new window and creates an instance of a scale widget. Additional options, described below, may be specified in the method call or in the option database to configure aspects of the scale such as its colors, orientation, and relief. The `scale` method returns the identity of the new widget. At the time this command is invoked, the scale's parent must exist.

A scale is a widget that displays a rectangular trough and a small slider. The trough corresponds to a range of real values (determined by the `from`, `to`, and `resolution` options), and the position of the slider selects a particular real value. The slider's position (and hence the scale's value) may be adjusted with the mouse or keyboard. Whenever the scale's value is changed, a callback is invoked (using the `command` option) to notify other interested widgets of the change. In addition, the value of the scale can be linked to a Tkinter variable (using the `variable` option), so that changes in either are reflected in the other.

Three annotations may be displayed in a scale widget: a label appearing at the top right of the widget (top left for horizontal scales), a number displayed just to the left of the slider (just above the slider for horizontal scales), and a collection of numerical tick marks just to the left of the current value (just below the trough for horizontal scales). Each of these three annotations may be enabled or disabled using the configuration options.

Inheritance

Scale inherits from `Widget`.

Shared options

Option (alias)	Default
activebackground	SystemButtonFace
background (bg)	SystemButtonFace
borderwidth (bd)	2
command	
cursor	
font	(('MS', 'Sans', 'Serif'), '8')
foreground (fg)	SystemButtonText
highlightbackground	SystemButtonFace
highlightcolor	SystemWindowFrame

Option (alias)	Default
highlightthickness	2
relief	flat
state	normal
takefocus	
width	15

Options specific to Scale

Option	Description	Units	Typical	Default
bigincrement	Some interactions with the scale widget cause its value to change by "large" increments; this option specifies the size of the large increments. If specified as 0, the large increments default to 1/10 the range of the scale.	integer	60	0
digits	An integer specifying how many significant digits should be retained when converting the value of a scale widget to a string. If the number is less than or equal to zero, then the scale picks the smallest value that guarantees that every possible slider position prints as a different string.	integer	2	0
from	A real value corresponding to the left or top end of the scale widget.	float	0.0	0
label	A string to display as a label for a scale widget. For vertical scales the label is displayed just to the right of the top end of the scale. For horizontal scales the label is displayed just above the left end of the scale. If the option is specified as an empty string, no label is displayed.	string	Power Level	
length	Specifies the desired long dimension of the scale in screen units (i.e. any of the forms acceptable to `winfo.pixels`). For vertical scales this is the scale's height; for horizontal scales it is the scale's width.	distance	150 1i	100
orient	For widgets that can lay themselves out with either a horizontal or vertical orientation, such as scrollbars, this option specifies which orientation should be used. Must be either HORIZONTAL or VERTICAL or an abbreviation of one of these.	constant	VERTICAL "vertical"	vertical
repeatdelay	Specifies the number of milliseconds a button or key must be held down before it begins to auto-repeat. Used, for example, on the up- and down-arrows in scrollbars.	integer	300	300

Option	Description	Units	Typical	Default
repeatinterval	Used in conjunction with repeatDelay: once auto-repeat begins, this option determines the number of milliseconds between auto repeats.	integer	100	100
resolution	A real value specifying the resolution for a scale widget. If this value is greater than zero then the scale's value will always be rounded to an even multiple of this value, as will tick marks and the endpoints of the scale. If the value is less than zero then no rounding occurs. Defaults to 1 (i.e., the value will be integral).	float	2.0 10.0	1
showvalue	Specifies a boolean value indicating whether or not the current value of a scale widget is to be displayed.	boolean	TRUE 0	1
sliderlength	Specfies the size of a slider, measured in screen units along the slider's long dimension. The value may be specified in any of the forms acceptable to winfo.pixels.	distance	140 2i	30
sliderrelief	Specifies the relief to use when drawing the slider, such as raised or sunken.			raised
tickinterval	Must be a real value. Determines the spacing between numerical tick marks displayed below or to the left of the slider. If it is 0, no tick marks will be displayed.	float	0 5.0	0
to	Specifies a real value corresponding to the right or bottom end of the scale. This value may be either less than or greater than the from option.	float	25.0 -30.0	100
troughcolor	Specifies the color to use for the rectangular trough areas in widgets such as scrollbars and scales.	color	'gray40'	System-Scroll-bar
variable	Specifies name of a Tkinter variable to contain the content and set the content of the widget.	variable	myVariable	

Methods

coords(value=None)

Returns a tuple whose elements are the x and y coordinates of the point along the centerline of the trough that corresponds to value. If value is omitted then the scale's current value is used.

get()

Returns the current value of the scale.

identify(x, y)

Returns a string indicating what part of the scale lies under the coordinates given by x and y. A return value of SLIDER means that the point is over the slider; TROUGH1 means that the point is over the portion of the slider above or to the left of the slider; and TROUGH2 means that the point is over the portion of the slider below or to the right of the slider. If the point isn't over one of these elements, an empty string is returned.

set(value)

This method is invoked to change the current value of the scale, and hence the position at which the slider is displayed. Value gives the new value for the scale. The method has no effect if the scale is disabled.

Scrollbar

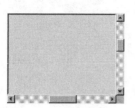

Description

The Scrollbar class defines a new window and creates an instance of a scrollbar widget. Additional options, described below, may be specified in the method call or in the option database to configure aspects of the scrollbar such as its colors, orientation, and relief. The scrollbar method returns the identity of the new widget. At the time this command is invoked, the scrollbar's parent must exist.

A scrollbar is a widget that displays two arrows, one at each end of the scrollbar, and a slider in the middle portion of the scrollbar. It provides information about what is visible in an associated window that displays a document of some sort (such as a file being edited or a drawing). The position and size of the slider indicate which portion of the document is visible in the associated window.

For example, if the slider in a vertical scrollbar covers the top third of the area between the two arrows, it means that the associated window displays the top third of its document. Scrollbars can be used to adjust the view in the associated window by clicking or dragging with the mouse.

Inheritance

Scrollbar inherits from Widget.

Shared options

Option (alias)	Default
activebackground	SystemButtonFace
background (bg)	SystemButtonFace
borderwidth (bd)	0
command	

Option (alias)	Default
cursor	
highlightbackground	SystemButtonFace
highlightcolor	SystemWindowFrame
highlightthickness	0
relief	sunken
takefocus	
width	16

Options specific to Scrollbar

Option	Description	Units	Typical	Default
activerelief	Specifies the relief to use when displaying the element that is active, if any. Elements other than the active element are always displayed with a raised relief.	constant	SUNKEN	raised
elementborderwidth	Specifies the width of borders drawn around the internal elements of a scrollbar (the two arrows and the slider). The value may have any of the forms acceptable to winfo.pixels. If this value is less than zero, the value of the borderwidth option is used in its place.	distance	10 1m	-1
jump	For widgets with a slider that can be dragged to adjust a value, such as scrollbars, this option determines when notifications are made about changes in the value. The option's value must be a boolean of the form accepted by Tcl_GetBoolean. If the value is false, updates are made continuously as the slider is dragged. If the value is true, updates are delayed until the mouse button is released to end the drag; at that point a single notification is made (the value "jumps" rather than changing smoothly).	boolean	TRUE NO	0
orient	For widgets that can lay themselves out with either a horizontal or vertical orientation, such as scrollbars, this option specifies which orientation should be used. Must be either HORIZONTAL or VERTICAL or an abbreviation of one of these.	constant	VERTICAL "verti-cal"	vertical
repeatdelay	Specifies the number of milliseconds a button or key must be held down before it begins to auto-repeat. Used, for example, on the up- and down-arrows in scrollbars.	integer	300	300

Option	Description	Units	Typical	Default
repeatinterval	Used in conjunction with repeatDelay: once auto-repeat begins, this option determines the number of milliseconds between auto repeats.	integer	100	100
troughcolor	Specifies the color to use for the rectangular trough areas in widgets such as scrollbars and scales.	color	'gray40'	System-Scroll-bar

Methods

activate(element)

Marks the element indicated by element as active, which causes it to be displayed as specified by the activeBackground and activeRelief options. The only element values understood by this method are ARROW1, SLIDER, or ARROW2. If any other value is specified then no element of the scrollbar will be active. If element is not specified, the method returns the name of the element that is currently active, or an empty string if no element is active.

delta(deltaX, deltaY)

Returns a real number indicating the fractional change in the scrollbar setting that corresponds to a given change in slider position. For example, if the scrollbar is horizontal, the result indicates how much the scrollbar setting must change to move the slider deltaX pixels to the right (deltaY is ignored in this case). If the scrollbar is vertical, the result indicates how much the scrollbar setting must change to move the slider pixels down. The arguments and the result may be zero or negative.

fraction(x, y)

fraction is a real number between 0 and 1. The widget should adjust its view so that the point given by fraction appears at the beginning of the widget. If fraction is 0 it refers to the beginning of the document. 1.0 refers to the end of the document, 0.333 refers to a point one-third of the way through the document, and so on.

get()

Returns the scrollbar settings in the form of a list whose elements are the arguments to the most recent set widget method.

identify(x, y)

Returns the name of the element under the point given by x and y (such as ARROW1), or an empty string if the point does not lie in any element of the scrollbar. x and y must be pixel coordinates relative to the scrollbar widget.

set(first, last)

This method is invoked by the scrollbar's associated widget to tell the scrollbar about the current view in the widget. The method takes two arguments, each of which is a real fraction between 0 and 1. The fractions describe the range of the document that is visible in the associated widget. For example, if `first` is 0.2 and `last` is 0.4, it means that the first part of the document visible in the window is 20% of the way through the document, and the last visible part is 40% of the way through.

Text

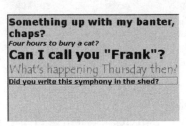

Description

The Text class defines a new window and creates an instance of a text widget. Additional options, described below, may be specified in the method call or in the option database to configure aspects of the text such as its default background color and relief. The `text` method returns the path name of the new window.

A text widget displays one or more lines of text and allows that text to be edited. Text widgets support four different kinds of annotations on the text: tags, marks, embedded windows and embedded images. Tags allow different portions of the text to be displayed with different fonts and colors. In addition, Tcl commands can be associated with tags so that scripts are invoked when particular actions such as keystrokes and mouse button presses occur in particular ranges of the text.

The second form of annotation consists of marks, which are floating markers in the text. Marks are used to keep track of various interesting positions in the text as it is edited.

The third form of annotation allows arbitrary windows to be embedded in a text widget.

The fourth form of annotation allows Tk images to be embedded in a text widget.

Many of the widget commands for texts take one or more indices as arguments. An index is a string used to indicate a particular place within a text, such as a place to insert characters or one endpoint of a range of characters to delete.

Inheritance

Text inherits from `Widget`.)

Shared options

Option (alias)	Default
background (bg)	SystemWindow
borderwidth (bd)	2
cursor	xterm
font	(('MS', 'Sans', 'Serif'), '8')
foreground (fg)	SystemWindowText
height	24
highlightbackground	SystemButtonFace
highlightcolor	SystemWindowFrame
highlightthickness	0

Option (alias)	Default
padx	1
pady	1
relief	sunken
selectbackground	SystemHighlight
selectborderwidth	0
selectforeground	SystemHighlightText
state	normal
takefocus	
width	80
xscrollcommand	

Options specific to Text

Option	Description	Units	Typical	Default
exportselection	Specifies whether or not a selection in the widget should also be the X selection. The value may have any of the forms accepted by `Tcl_GetBoolean`, such as `true`, `false`, `0`, `1`, `yes`, or `no`. If the selection is exported, then selecting in the widget deselects the current X selection, selecting outside the widget deselects any widget selection, and the widget will respond to selection retrieval requests when it has a selection. The default is usually for widgets to export selections.	boolean	0 YES	1
insertbackground	Specifies the color to use as background in the area covered by the insertion cursor. This color will normally override either the normal background for the widget or the selection background if the insertion cursor happens to fall in the selection.	color	'yellow'	System-Window-Text
insertborderwidth	Specifies a non-negative value indicating the width of the 3-D border to draw around the insertion cursor. The value may have any of the forms acceptable to Tkinter (`Tk_GetPixels`).	pixel	2	0
insertofftime	Specifies a non-negative integer value indicating the number of milliseconds the insertion cursor should remain "off" in each blink cycle. If this option is zero then the cursor doesn't blink: it is on all the time.	integer	250	300
insertontime	Specifies a non-negative integer value indicating the number of milliseconds the insertion cursor should remain "on" in each blink cycle.	integer	175	600

Option	Description	Units	Typical	Default
insertwidth	Specifies a value indicating the total width of the insertion cursor. The value may have any of the forms acceptable to Tkinter (`Tk_GetPixels`). If a border has been specified for the insertion cursor (using the `insertBorderWidth` option), the border will be drawn inside the width specified by the `insertWidth` option.	pixel	2	2
setgrid	Specifies a boolean value that determines whether this widget controls the resizing grid for its top-level window. This option is typically used in text widgets, where the information in the widget has a natural size (the size of a character) and it makes sense for the window's dimensions to be integral numbers of these units. These natural window sizes form a grid. If the `setGrid` option is set to `true` then the widget will communicate with the window manager so that when the user interactively resizes the top-level window that contains the widget, the dimensions of the window will be displayed to the user in grid units and the window size will be constrained to integral numbers of grid units. See the section "Gridded geometry management" in the wm manual entry for more details.	boolean	NO 1	0
spacing1	Requests additional space above each text line in the widget, using any of the standard forms for screen distances. If a line wraps, this option only applies to the first line on the display. This option may be overriden with `spacing1` options in tags.	distance	2m 15	0
spacing2	For lines that wrap (so that they cover more than one line on the display) this option specifies additional space to be provided between the display lines that represent a single line of text. The value may have any of the standard forms for screen distances. This option may be overriden with `spacing2` options in tags.	distance	1m, 3	0
spacing3	Requests additional space below each text line in the widget, using any of the standard forms for screen distances. If a line wraps, this option only applies to the last line on the display. This option may be overriden with `spacing3` options in tags.	distance	3m, 14	0

Option	Description	Units	Typical	Default
tabs	Specifies a set of tab stops for the window. The option's value consists of a list of screen distances giving the positions of the tab stops. Each position may optionally be followed in the next list element by one of the keywords LEFT, RIGHT, CENTER, or NUMERIC; these all specify how to justify text relative to the tab stop. LEFT is the default; it causes the text following the tab character to be positioned with its left edge at the tab position. RIGHT means that the right edge of the text following the tab character is positioned at the tab position, and CENTER means that the text is centered at the tab position. NUMERIC means that the decimal point in the text is positioned at the tab position; if there is no decimal point then the least significant digit of the number is positioned just to the left of the tab position; if there is no number in the text then the text is right-justified at the tab position. For example, tabs=(2c, left, 4c, 6c, center) creates three tab stops at two-centimeter intervals; the first two use left justification and the third uses center justification. If the list of tab stops does not have enough elements to cover all of the tabs in a text line, then Tk extrapolates new tab stops using the spacing and alignment from the last tab stop in the list. The value of the tabs option may be overridden by -tabs options in tags. If no -tabs option is specified, or if it is specified as an empty list, then Tk uses default tabs spaced every eight (average size) characters.	string		
wrap	Specifies how to handle lines in the text that are too long to be displayed in a single line of the text's window. The value must be NONE or CHAR or WORD. A wrap mode of None means that each line of text appears as exactly one line on the screen; extra characters that don't fit on the screen are not displayed. In the other modes each line of text will be broken up into several screen lines if necessary to keep all the characters visible. In CHAR mode a screen line break may occur after any character; in WORD mode a line break will only be made at word boundaries.	constant	"char" NONE	char

Option	Description	Units	Typical	Default
yscrollcommand	Specifies the prefix for a command used to communicate with vertical scrollbars. This option is treated in the same way as the xScrollCommand option, except that it is used for vertical scrollbars and is provided by widgets that support vertical scrolling. See the description of xScrollCommand for details on how this option is used.	function		

Methods

bbox(index)

Returns a list of four elements describing the screen area of the character given by index. The first two elements of the list give the x and y coordinates of the upper-left corner of the area occupied by the character, and the last two elements give the width and height of the area. If the character is only partially visible on the screen, then the return value reflects just the visible part. If the character is not visible on the screen then the return value is an empty list.

compare(index1, op, index2)

Compares the indices given by index1 and index2 according to the relational operator given by op, and returns TRUE if the relationship is satisfied and FALSE if it isn't. op must be one of the operators <, <=, ==, >=, >, or !=. If op is == then TRUE is returned if the two indices refer to the same character; if op is < then TRUE is returned if index1 refers to an earlier character in the text than index2, and so on.

debug(boolean=None)

If boolean is specified, then it must have one of the true or false values accepted by Tcl_GetBoolean. If the value is a true one then internal consistency checks will be turned on in the B-tree code associated with text widgets. If boolean has a false value then the debugging checks will be turned off. In either case the method returns a boolean indicating whether debug is enabled. If boolean is not specified then the method returns on or off to indicate whether or not debugging is turned on. There is a single debugging switch shared by all text widgets: turning debugging on or off in any widget turns it on or off for all widgets. For widgets with large amounts of text, the consistency checks may cause a noticeable slowdown.

delete(index1, index2=None)

Deletes a range of characters from the text. If both index1 and index2 are specified, then deletes all the characters starting with the one given by index1 and stopping just before index2 (i.e. the character at index2 is not deleted). If index2 doesn't specify a position later in the text than index1 then no characters are deleted. If index2 isn't specified then the single character at index1 is deleted.

It is not allowable to delete characters in a way that would leave the text without a newline as the last character. Returns None.

dlineinfo(index)

Returns a tuple with five elements describing the area occupied by the display line containing `index`. The first two elements of the list give the x and y coordinates of the upper-left corner of the area occupied by the line, the third and fourth elements give the width and height of the area, and the fifth element gives the position of the baseline for the line, measured down from the top of the area. All of this information is measured in pixels.

If the current wrap mode is `None` and the line extends beyond the boundaries of the window, the area returned reflects the entire area of the line, including the portions that are out of the window. If the line is shorter than the full width of the window then the area returned reflects just the portion of the line that is occupied by characters and embedded windows. If the display line containing `index` is not visible on the screen then the return value is an empty list.

get(index1, index2=None)

Returns a range of characters from the text. The return value will be all the characters in the text starting with the one whose index is `index1` and ending just before the one whose index is `index2` (the character at `index2` will not be returned). If `index2` is omitted then the single character at `index1` is returned. If there are no characters in the specified range (e.g. `index1` is past the end of the file or `index2` is less than or equal to `index1`) then an empty string is returned. If the specified range contains embedded windows, no information about them is included in the returned string.

image_cget(index, option)

Returns the value of a configuration option for an embedded image. `index` identifies the embedded image, and `option` specifies a particular configuration option.

image_configure(index, options...)

Queries or modifies the configuration options for an embedded image. If no `option` is specified, returns a dictionary describing all of the available options for the embedded image at `index`. If `option` is specified with no value, then the method returns a dictionary describing the one named `option` (this dictionary will be identical to the corresponding sublist of the value returned if no option is specified).

If one or more option-value pairs are specified, then the command modifies the given option(s) to have the given value(s); in this case the command returns an empty string.

image_names()

Returns a tuple whose elements are the names of all windows currently embedded in window.

index(index)

Returns the position corresponding to `index` in the form `line.char` where `line` is the line number and `char` is the character number.

insert(index, chars, tagList, chars, tagList...)

Inserts all of the `chars` arguments just before the character at `index`. If `index` refers to the end of the text (the character after the last new line) then the new text is inserted just before the last newline instead. If there is a single `chars` argument and no `tagList`, then the new text will receive any tags that are present on both the character before and the character after the insertion point; if a tag is present on only one of these characters then it will not be applied to the new text.

If `tagList` is specified then it consists of a list of tag names; the new characters will receive all of the tags in this list and no others, regardless of the tags present around the insertion point. If multiple `chars-tagList` argument pairs are present, they produce the same effect as if a separate insert widget method had been issued for each pair, in order. The last `tagList` argument may be omitted.

mark_gravity(markName, direction=None)

If `direction` is not specified, returns LEFT or RIGHT to indicate which of its adjacent characters `markName` is attached to. If `direction` is specified, it must be LEFT or RIGHT; the gravity of `markName` is set to the given value.

mark_names()

Returns a tuple whose elements are the names of all windows currently embedded in window.

mark_set(markName, index)

Sets the mark named `markName` to a position just before the character at `index`. If `markName` already exists, it is moved from its old position; if it doesn't exist, a new mark is created.

mark_unset(mark)

Removes the mark corresponding to `mark`. The removed mark will not be usable in indices and will not be returned by future calls to `mark_names` calls. This method returns None.

scan_dragto(x, y)

Computes the difference between its *x* and *y* arguments and the x and y arguments to the last `scan_mark` call for the widget. It then adjusts the view by 10 times the difference in coordinates. This command is typically associated with mouse motion events in the widget, to produce the effect of dragging the text at high speed through the window. The return value is an empty string.

scan_mark(x, y)

Records x and y and the current view in the text window, for use in conjunction with later `scan_dragto` commands. Typically this command is associated with a mouse button press in the widget. It returns None.

see(index)

Adjusts the view in the window so that the character given by `index` is completely visible. If `index` is already visible then the method does nothing. If `index` is a short distance out of view, the method adjusts the view just enough to make `index` visible at the edge of the window. If `index` is far out of view, then the method centers `index` in the window.

tag_add(tagName, index1, index2=None)

Associates the tag `tagName` with all of the characters starting with `index1` and ending just before `index2` (the character at `index2` isn't tagged). A single method may contain any number of `index1index2` pairs. If the last `index2` is omitted then the single character at `index1` is tagged. If there are no characters in the specified range (e.g. `index1` is past the end of the file or `index2` is less than or equal to `index1`) then the command has no effect.

tag_bind(tagName, sequence, function, add=None)

Associates `function` with the tag given by `tagName`. Whenever the event sequence given by `sequence` occurs for a character that has been tagged with `tagName`, the function will be invoked.

This widget command is similar to the `bind` method except that it operates on characters in a text rather than entire widgets.

If all arguments are specified then a new binding is created, replacing any existing binding for the same `sequence` and `tagName` (if the first character of `function` is + then `function` augments an existing binding rather than replacing it). In this case the return value is an empty string. If `function` is omitted then the command returns the function associated with `tagName` and `sequence` (an error occurs if there is no such binding).

If both `function` and `sequence` are omitted then the command returns a list of all the sequences for which bindings have been defined for `tagName`.

The only events for which bindings may be specified are those related to the mouse and keyboard (such as `Enter`, `Leave`, `ButtonPress`, `Motion`, and `KeyPress`) or virtual events. Event bindings for a text widget use the CURRENT mark. An `Enter` event triggers for a tag when the tag first becomes present on the current character, and a `Leave` event triggers for a tag when it ceases to be present on the current character. `Enter` and `Leave` events can happen either because the CURRENT mark moved or because the character at that position changed.

Note that these events are different than `Enter` and `Leave` events for windows. Mouse and keyboard events are directed to the current character. If a virtual event is used in a binding, that binding can trigger only if the virtual event is defined by an underlying mouse-related or keyboard-related event. It is possible for the current character to have multiple tags, and for each of them to have a binding for a particular event sequence. When this occurs, one binding is invoked for each tag, in order from lowest priority to highest priority.

If there are multiple matching bindings for a single tag, then the most specific binding is chosen. The tag bindings will be invoked first, followed by general bindings.

tag_cget(tagName, option)

Returns the current value of the option named `option` associated with the tag given by `tagName`. `option` may have any of the values accepted by `tag_configure`.

tag_configure(tagName, options...)

This command is similar to the `configure_widget` method except that it modifies options associated with the tag given by `tagName` instead of modifying options for the overall text widget. If no `option` is specified, the command returns a dictionary describing all of the available options for `tagName`. If `option` is specified with no value, then the command returns a dictionary describing the one named option (this dictionary will be identical to the corresponding dictionary of the value returned if no option is specified).

If one or more option-value pairs are specified, then the method modifies the given option(s) to have the given value(s) in tagName; in this case the command returns an empty string.

tag_delete(*tagNames)

Deletes all tag information for each of the tagName arguments. The method removes the tags from all characters in the file and also deletes any other information associated with the tags, such as bindings and display information.

tag_lower(tagName, belowThis=None)

Changes the priority of tag tagName so that it is just lower in priority than the tag whose name is belowThis. If belowThis is omitted, then tagName's priority is changed to make it the lowest priority of all tags.

tag_names(index=None)

Returns a tuple whose elements are the names of all the tags that are active at the character position given by index. If index is omitted, then the return value will describe all of the tags that exist for the text (this includes all tags that have been named in a tag widget method call but haven't been deleted by a tag_delete method call, even if no characters are currently marked with the tag). The tuple will be sorted in order from lowest priority to highest priority.

tag_nextrange(tagName, index1, index2=None)

Searches the text for a range of characters tagged with tagName where the first character of the range is no earlier than the character at index1 and no later than the character just before index2 (a range starting at index2 will not be considered). If several matching ranges exist, the first one is chosen. The method's return value is a list containing two elements, which are the index of the first character of the range and the index of the character just after the last one in the range.

If no matching range is found then the return value is an empty string. If index2 is not given then it defaults to the end of the text.

tag_prevrange(tagName, index1, index2=None)

Searches the text for a range of characters tagged with tagName where the first character of the range is before the character at index1 and no earlier than the character at index2 (a range starting at index2 will be considered). If several matching ranges exist, the one closest to index1 is chosen. The method's return value is a list containing two elements, which are the index of the first character of the range and the index of the character just after the last one in the range.

If no matching range is found then the return value is an empty string. If index2 is not given then it defaults to the beginning of the text.

tag_raise(tagName, aboveThis=None)

Changes the priority of tag `tagName` so that it is just higher in priority than the tag whose name is `aboveThis`. If `aboveThis` is omitted, then `tagName`'s priority is changed to make it the highest priority of all tags.

tag_ranges(tagName)

Returns a tuple describing all of the ranges of text that have been tagged with `tagName`. The first two elements of the tuple describe the first tagged range in the text, the next two elements describe the second range, and so on. The first element of each pair contains the index of the first character of the range, and the second element of the pair contains the index of the character just after the last one in the range. If no characters are tagged with tag then an empty string is returned.

tag_remove(tagName, index1, index2=None)

Removes the tag `tagName` from all of the characters starting at `index1` and ending just before `index2` (the character at `index2` isn't affected). A single call may contain any number of `index1index2` pairs. If the last `index2` is omitted then the single character at `index1` is tagged. If there are no characters in the specified range (e.g. `index1` is past the end of the file or `index2` is less than or equal to `index1`) then the method has no effect. This method returns `None`.

tag_unbind(tagName, sequence, funcid=None)

Removes the association of the event `sequence` with the event handler `funcId` for all the items given by `tagOrId`. If `funcId` is supplied the handler will be destroyed.

tk_textBackspace()
tk_textIndexCloser(a, b, c)
tk_textResetAnchor(index)
tk_textSelectTo(index)

These four methods are really only useful if you are writing your own event handling for text. Their function is to set the text appearance as if the default actions had occurred. They may also be useful in simulating user interaction with a GUI.

window_cget(index, option)

Returns the value of a configuration option for an embedded window. `index` identifies the embedded window, and *option* specifies a particular configuration option.

window_configure(index, options...)

Queries or modifies the configuration options for an embedded window. If no `option` is specified, it returns a dictionary describing all of the available options for the embedded window at `index`. If `option` is specified with no value, then the method returns a dictionary describing the one named `option` (this dictionary will be identical to the corresponding dictionary of the value returned if no option is specified).

If one or more option-value pairs are specified, then the method modifies the given option(s) to have the given value(s); in this case the method returns an empty string.

window_create(index, options...)

Creates a new window annotation, which will appear in the text at the position given by index. Any number of option-value pairs may be specified to configure the annotation.

window_names()

Returns a list whose elements are the names of all windows currently embedded in window.

xview_moveto(fraction)

Adjusts the view in the window so that fraction of the horizontal span of the text is off-screen to the left. fraction is a fraction between 0 and 1.

xview_scroll(number, what)

Shifts the view in the window left or right according to number and what. number must be an integer. what must be either UNITS or PAGES or an abbreviation of one of these. If what is UNITS, the view adjusts left or right by number average-width characters on the display; if it is PAGES then the view adjusts by number screenfuls. If number is negative then characters farther to the left become visible; if it is positive then characters farther to the right become visible.

yview_moveto(fraction)

Adjusts the view in the window so that the character given by fraction appears on the top line of the window. fraction is a fraction between 0 and 1; 0 indicates the first character in the text, 0.33 indicates the character one-third of the way through the text, and so on.

yview_scroll(number, what)

Adjusts the view in the window up or down according to number and what. number must be an integer. what must be either UNITS or PAGES. If what is UNITS, the view adjusts up or down by number lines on the display; if it is PAGES then the view adjusts by number screen-fuls. If number is negative then earlier positions in the text become visible; if it is positive then later positions in the text become visible.

yview_pickplace(index)

Changes the view in the widget's window to make index visible. If the pickplace option isn't specified then index will appear at the top of the window. If pickplace is specified then the widget chooses where index appears in the window. If index is already visible somewhere in the window then the method does nothing.

If index is only a few lines off-screen above the window then it will be positioned at the top of the window. If index is only a few lines off-screen below the window then it will be positioned at the bottom of the window. Otherwise, index will be centered in the window.

The pickplace option has been made obsolete by the see widget method (see handles both x- and y-motion to make a location visible, whereas pickplace only handles motion in y).

Toplevel

Description

The Toplevel class defines a new toplevel widget (given by the `pathName` argument). Additional options, described below, may be specified in the method call or in the option database to configure aspects of the toplevel such as its background color and relief. The `toplevel` method returns the pathname of the new window.

A toplevel is similar to a frame except that it is created as a top-level window: its X parent is the root window of a screen rather than the logical parent from its pathname. The primary purpose of a toplevel is to serve as a container for dialog boxes and other collections of widgets. The only visible features of a toplevel are its background color and an optional 3-D border to make the toplevel appear raised or sunken.

Inheritance

Toplevel inherits from `BaseWidget`, `Wm`.

Shared options

Option (alias)	Default
background (bg)	SystemButtonFace
borderwidth (bd)	0
cursor	
height	0
highlightbackground	SystemButtonFace
highlightcolor	SystemWindowFrame
highlightthickness	0
relief	flat
takefocus	0
width	0

Options specific to Toplevel

Option	Description	Units	Typical	Default
class	Specifies a class for the window. This class will be used when querying the option database for the window's other options, and it will also be used later for other purposes such as bindings. The class option may not be changed with the configure method. Note that because class is a reserved word, _class must be used with Tkinter.	class		Toplevel
colormap	Specifies a colormap to use for the window. The value may be either NEW, in which case a new colormap is created for the window and its children, or the name of another window (which must be on the same screen and have the same visual as pathName), in which case the new window will use the colormap from the specified window. If the colormap option is not specified, the new window uses the same colormap as its parent. This option may not be changed with the configure method.	colormap	NEW myWindow	
container	The value must be a boolean. If TRUE, it means that this window will be used as a container in which some other application will be embedded (for example, a Tkinter toplevel can be embedded using the use option). The window will support the appropriate window manager protocols for things like geometry requests. The window should not have any children of its own in this application. This option may not be changed with the configure method.	boolean	TRUE 0	0
menu	Specifies the pathname of the menu associated with a menubutton. The menu must be a child of the menubutton.	string	subMenuAction	
screen	Specifies the screen on which to place the new window. Any valid screen name may be used, even one associated with a different display. Defaults to the same screen as its parent. This option is special in that it may not be specified via the option database, and it may not be modified with the configure method.	screen	"Default"	
use	Specifies the value to store in the widget's associated Tkinter variable whenever the widget is selected.	string		

Option	Description	Units	Typical	Default
visual	Specifies visual information for the new window in any of the forms accepted by `winfo.visual`. If this option is not specified, the new window will use the same visual as its parent. The `visual` option may not be modified with the `configure` method.	visual	monochrome	

Methods

Toplevel has standard widget methods such as `configure`.

Pmw reference: Python megawidgets

The information presented in this appendix has been largely generated, in a manner similar to appendix B, using Python programs to walk the Pmw package and the Pmw HTML documentation, which was then processed to generate a large ASCII file which contained headings, text and tables ready for importing into FrameMaker, which was used to produce this book.

AboutDialog

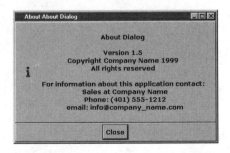

Description

This class displays a window with application, copyright and contact information.

Inheritance

AboutDialog inherits from `Pmw.MessageDialog`.

AboutDialog options

Option	Description	Units	Default
activatecommand	If this is callable, it will be called whenever the mega-widget is activated by a call to `activate()`.	function	None
applicationname	Sets the application name displayed by `AboutDialog`.	string	None
borderx	Specifies the width of the border to the left and right of the message area.	distance	20
bordery	Specifies the height of the border to the top and bottom of the message area.	distance	20
buttonboxpos	Specifies on which side of the dialog window to place the button box. Must be one of N, S, E, or W.	anchor	S
buttons	This must be a tuple or a list. It specifies the names on the buttons in the button box.	(string, ...)	('OK',)
command	Specifies a function to call whenever a button in the button box is invoked or the window is deleted by the window manager. The function is called with a single argument, which is the name of the button which was invoked, or `None` if the window was deleted by the window manager.	function	None
deactivatecommand	If this is callable, it will be called whenever the mega-widget is deactivated by a call to `deactivate()`.	function	None
defaultbutton	Specifies the default button in the button box. If the Return key is pressed when the dialog has focus, the default button will be invoked. If `defaultbutton` is `None`, there will be no default button and pressing the Return key will have no effect.	index	0
iconmargin	Specifies the space to be left around the icon, if present.	distance	20
iconpos	Determines the placement of the icon if it is to be displayed. Value must be either one of the letters N, S, E, and W or None.	anchor	W
separatorwidth	If this is greater than 0, a separator line with the specified width will be created between the button box and the child site, as a component-named separator. Since the default border of the button box and child site is raised, this option does not usually need to be set for there to be a visual separation between the button box and child site.	distance	0
title	This is the title that the window manager displays in the title bar of the window.	string	None

Components

buttonbox

This is the button box containing the buttons for the dialog. By default, it is created with the options (hull_borderwidth = 1, hull_relief = 'raised').

dialogchildsite

This is the child site for the dialog, which may be used to specialize the megawidget by creating other widgets within it. By default it is created with the options (borderwidth = 1, relief = 'raised').

hull

This acts as the body for the entire megawidget. Other components are created as children of the hull to further specialize the widget.

icon

This is the icon to display alongside the message.

message

This widget contains the text displayed within the dialog.

separator

If the separatorwidth initialization option is nonzero, the separator component is the line dividing the area between the button box and the child site.

Methods

There are no AboutDialog methods, other than inherited methods from the base classes.

Functions

aboutversion(value)

Sets the version displayed by the AboutDialog to value.

aboutcopyright(value)

Sets the copyright string displayed by the AboutDialog to value.

aboutcontact(value)

Sets the contact information displayed by the AboutDialog to value.

Balloon

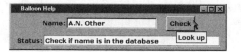

Description

This class implements a balloon help system and provides a mechanism to supply the same (or different) messages to a status area, if present. It is good practice to provide a mechanism for the user to turn off such messages if they are not required.

Inheritance

Balloon inherits from `Pmw.MegaToplevel`.

Balloon options

Option	Description	Units	Default
activatecommand	If this is callable, it will be called whenever the megawidget is activated by a call to `activate()`.	function	None
deactivatecommand	If this is callable, it will be called whenever the megawidget is deactivated by a call to `deactivate()`.	function	None
initwait	The time to wait, in milliseconds, after the pointer has entered the widget before the balloon is displayed.	milliseconds	500
state	Determines whether balloon help or status messages are displayed. May be none, balloon, status or both.	constant	'both'
statuscommand	If this is callable, it will be called whenever the status message is to be updated. This will normally be a call to a `Pmw.MessageBar`'s helpmessage method.	function	None
title	This is the title that the window manager displays in the title bar of the window.	string	None
xoffset	Horizontal offset for the balloon help widget. Starts at the bottom left-hand corner of the associated widget's bounding box.	distance	20
yoffset	Vertical offset for the balloon help widget. Starts at the bottom left-hand corner of the associated widget's bounding box.	distance	1

Components

hull

This acts as the body for the entire megawidget. Other components are created as children of the hull to further specialize the widget.

label

If the `labelpos` option is not `None`, this component is created as a text label for the mega-widget. See the `labelpos` option for details. Note that to set, for example, the text option of the label, you need to use the `label_text` component option.

Methods

bind(widget, balloonHelp, statusHelp = None)

Adds `balloonHelp` to the specified widget. If `statusHelp` is `None`, `balloonHelp` is bound as the status message. If `statusHelp` is specified, the bind message is bound to the status area for widget. If both `balloonHelp` and `statusHelp` are `None`, `bind(widget, None)` is equivalent to `unbind(widget)`.

clearstatus()

Removes any existing status message.

showstatus(statusHelp)

If `statuscommand` is defined, it is called with `statusHelp` as its argument.

tagbind(widget, tagOrItem, balloonHelp, statusHelp = None)

Similar to `bind`, this method adds `balloonHelp` to the item `tagOrItem` defined within `widget`.

tagunbind(widget, tagOrItem)

Removes any existing binding for `tagOrId` within `widget`.

unbind(widget)

Removes all `<Motion>`, `<Enter>`, `<Leave>` and `<ButtonPress>` bindings for `widget`.

ButtonBox

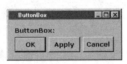

Description

This class creates a manager widget for containing buttons. One of these buttons may be specified as the default and it will be displayed with the platform-specific appearance for a default button. The buttons may be laid out either horizontally or vertically.

Inheritance

ButtonBox inherits from `Pmw.MegaWidget`.

ButtonBox options

Option	Description	Units	Default
labelmargin	If the labelpos option is not None, this specifies the distance between the label component and the rest of the megawidget.	distance	0
labelpos	Specifies where to place the label component. If not None, it should be a concatenation of one or two of the letters N, S, E and W. The first letter specifies on which side of the megawidget to place the label. If a second letter is specified, it indicates where on that side to place the label. For example, if labelpos is W, the label is placed in the center of the left-hand side; if it is WN, the label is placed at the top of the left-hand side; if it is WS, the label is placed at the bottom of the left-hand side.	anchor	None
orient	Specifies the orientation of the button box. This may be HORIZONTAL or VERTICAL.	constant	HORIZONTAL
padx	Specifies a padding distance to leave between each button in the x direction and also between the buttons and the outer edge of the button box.	distance	3
pady	Specifies a padding distance to leave between each button in the y direction and also between the buttons and the outer edge of the button box.	distance	3

Components

frame

If the label component has been created (that is, the labelpos option is not None), the frame component is created to act as the container of the buttons created by the add() and insert() methods. If there is no label component, then no frame component is created and the hull component acts as the container.

hull

This acts as the body for the entire megawidget. Other components are created as children of the hull to further specialize the widget.

label

If the labelpos option is not None, this component is created as a text label for the megawidget. See the labelpos option for details. Note that to set, for example, the text option of the label, you need to use the label_text component option.

Methods

add(name, **kw)

Adds a button to the end of the button box as a component named name. Any keyword arguments present will be passed to the constructor when creating the button. If the text keyword argument is not given, the text option of the button defaults to name. The method returns the name component widget.

alignbuttons(when = 'later')

Sets the widths of all the buttons to be the same as the width of the widest button. If when is later, this will occur when the interpreter next becomes idle; otherwise, the resizing will occur immediately.

delete(index)

Deletes the button given by index from the button box. index may have any of the forms accepted by the index() method.

index(index, forInsert = 0)

Returns the numerical index of the button corresponding to index. This may be specified in any of the following forms:

- number   Specifies the button numerically, where 0 corresponds to the left (or top) button.
- end   Indicates the right (or bottom) button.
- default   Indicates the current default button.
- name   Specifies the button named name.

If forInsert is true, end returns the number of buttons rather than the index of the last button.

insert(name, before = 0, **kw)

Adds a button just before the button specified by before, as a component named name. Any keyword arguments present will be passed to the constructor when creating the button. before may have any of the forms accepted by the index() method. To add a button to the end of the button box, use add(). The method returns the name component widget.

invoke(index = 'default', noFlash = 0)

Invokes the callback command associated with the button specified by index. Unless noFlash is true, flashes the button to indicate to the user that something happened. index may have any of the forms accepted by the index() method.

numbuttons()

Returns the number of buttons in the button box.

setdefault(index)

Sets the default button to the button given by index. This causes the specified button to be displayed with the platform-specific appearance for a default button. If index is None, there will be no default button. index may have any of the forms accepted by the index() method.

ComboBox

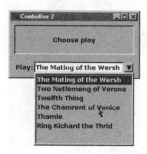

Description

This class creates an entry field and an associated scrolled listbox. When an item in the listbox is selected, it is displayed in the entry field. Optionally, the user may also edit the entry field directly.

For a simple combobox, the scrolled listbox is displayed beneath the entry field. For a dropdown combobox (the default), the scrolled listbox is displayed in a window which pops up beneath the entry field when the user clicks on an arrow button on the right of the entry field. Either style allows an optional label.

Inheritance

ComboBox inherits from Pmw.MegaWidget.

ComboBox options

Option	Description	Units	Default
autoclear	If both autoclear and history are true, clear the entry field whenever RETURN is pressed, after adding the value to the history list.	boolean	0
buttonaspect	The width of the arrow button as a proportion of the height. The height of the arrow button is set to the height of the entry widget.	float	1.0
dropdown	Specifies whether the combobox megawidget should be dropdown or simple.	boolean	1
fliparrow	If true, the arrow button is drawn upside down when the listbox is being displayed. Used only in dropdown megawidgets.	boolean	0
history	When RETURN is pressed in the entry field, the current value of the entry field is appended to the listbox if history is true.	boolean	1
labelmargin	If the labelpos option is not None, this specifies the distance between the label component and the rest of the megawidget.	distance	0

Option	Description	Units	Default
labelpos	Specifies where to place the label component. If not None, it should be a concatenation of one or two of the letters N, S, E and W. The first letter specifies on which side of the megawidget to place the label. If a second letter is specified, it indicates where on that side to place the label. For example, if labelpos is W, the label is placed in the center of the left-hand side; if it is WN, the label is placed at the top of the left-hand side; if it is WS, the label is placed at the bottom of the left-hand side.	anchor	None
listheight	The height, in pixels, of the dropdown listbox.	height	150
selectioncommand	The function to call when an item is selected.	function	None
Pmw:unique	If both unique and history are true, the current value of the entry field is not added to the listbox if it is already in the list.	boolean	1

Components

arrowbutton

In a dropdown combobox, this is the button to pop up the listbox.

entryfield

The entry field where the current selection is displayed.

hull

This acts as the body for the entire megawidget. Other components are created as children of the hull to further specialize the widget.

label

If the labelpos option is not None, this component is created as a text label for the megawidget. See the labelpos option for details. Note that to set, for example, the text option of the label, you need to use the label_text component option.

popup

In a dropdown combobox, this is the dropdown window.

scrolledlist

The scrolled listbox which displays the items to select.

Methods

get(first = None, last = None)

This is the same as the get() method of the scrolledlist component, except that if neither first nor last are specified, the value of the entry field is returned.

invoke()

If it's a dropdown combobox, displays the dropdown listbox. In a simple combobox, selects the currently selected item in the listbox, calls the `selectioncommand` and returns the result.

selectitem(index, setentry = 1)

Selects the item in the listbox specified by `index` which may be either one of the items in the listbox or the integer index of one of the items in the listbox.

size()

This method is explicitly forwarded to the scrolledlist component's `size()` method. Without this explicit forwarding, the `size()` method (aliased to `grid_size()`) of the hull would be invoked, which is probably not what the programmer intended.

ComboBoxDialog

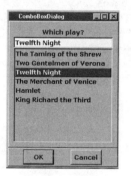

Description

A ComboBoxDialog is a convenience dialog window with a simple combobox. This is used to request the user to enter a value or make a selection from the combobox `list`.

Inheritance

ComboBoxDialog inherits from `Pmw.Dialog`.

ComboBoxDialog options

Option	Description	Units	Default
activatecommand	If this is callable, it will be called whenever the megawidget is activated by a call to `activate()`.	function	None
borderx	Specifies the width of the border to the left and right of the message area.	distance	10
bordery	Specifies the height of the border to the top and bottom of the message area.	distance	10
buttonboxpos	Specifies on which side of the dialog window to place the button box. Must be one of N, S, E or W.	anchor	S
buttons	This must be a tuple or a list. It specifies the names on the buttons in the button box.	(string, ...)	('OK',)

Option	Description	Units	Default
command	Specifies a function to call whenever a button in the button box is invoked or the window is deleted by the window manager. The function is called with a single argument, which is the name of the button which was invoked, or None if the window was deleted by the window manager.	function	None
deactivatecommand	If this is callable, it will be called whenever the megawidget is deactivated by a call to deactivate().	function	None
defaultbutton	Specifies the default button in the button box. If the RETURN key is hit when the dialog has focus, the default button will be invoked. If defaultbutton is None, there will be no default button and hitting the RETURN key will have no effect.	index	None
separatorwidth	If this is greater than 0, a separator line with the specified width will be created between the button box and the child site, as a component named separator. Since the default border of the button box and child site is raised, this option does not usually need to be set for there to be a visual separation between the button box and the child site.	distance	0
title	This is the title that the window manager displays in the title bar of the window.	string	None

Components

buttonbox

This is the button box containing the buttons for the dialog. By default it is created with the options (hull_borderwidth = 1, hull_relief = 'raised').

combobox

The widget used as the selection widget. By default, this component is a Pmw.ComboBox.

dialogchildsite

This is the child site for the dialog, which may be used to specialize the megawidget by creating other widgets within it. By default it is created with the options (borderwidth = 1, relief = 'raised').

hull

This acts as the body for the entire megawidget. Other components are created as children of the hull to further specialize the widget.

separator

If the separatorwidth initialization option is nonzero, the separator component is the line dividing the area between the button box and the child site.

Methods

This megawidget has no methods of its own. In addition, methods from the Pmw.ComboBox class are forwarded by this megawidget to the combobox component.

Counter

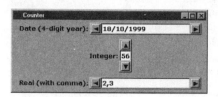

Description

This class consists of an entry field with arrow buttons to increment and decrement the value in the entry field. Standard counting types include numbers, times and dates. A user-defined counting function may also be supplied for specialized counting. Counting can be used in combination with the entry field's validation. The components may be laid out horizontally or vertically.

Each time an arrow button is pressed the value displayed in the entry field is incremented or decremented by the value of the increment option. If the new value is invalid (according to the entry field's `validate` option, perhaps due to exceeding minimum or maximum limits), the old value is restored.

When an arrow button is pressed and the value displayed is not an exact multiple of the increment, it is "truncated" up or down to the nearest increment.

Inheritance

Counter inherits from `Pmw.MegaWidget`.

Counter options

Option	Description	Units	Default
autorepeat	If `true`, the counter will continue to count up or down while an arrow button is held down.	boolean	1
buttonaspect	Specifies the width of the arrow buttons as a proportion of their height. Values less than 1.0 will produce thin arrow buttons. Values greater than 1.0 will produce fat arrow buttons.	float	1.0
datatype	Specifies how the counter should count up and down.The most general way to specify the datatype option is as a dictionary. The kind of counting is specified by the `counter` dictionary field, which may be either a function or the name of one of the standard counters described below. *Any other fields in the dictionary are passed on to the counter function as keyword arguments.	constant	'numeric'

Option	Description	Units	Default
	If datatype is not a dictionary, then it is equivalent to specifying it as a dictionary with a single counter field. For example, datatype = 'real' is equivalent to datatype = {'counter' : 'real'}.		
increment	Specifies how many units should be added or subtracted when the counter is incremented or decremented. If the currently displayed value is not a multiple of increment, the value is changed to the next multiple greater or less than the current value.	units	1
	For the number datatypes, the value of increment is a number. For the time datatype, the value is in seconds. For the date datatype, the value is in days.		
initwait	Specifies the initial delay (in milliseconds) before a depressed arrow button automatically starts to repeat counting.	milliseconds	300
labelmargin	If the labelpos option is not None, this specifies the distance between the label component and the rest of the megawidget.	distance	0
labelpos	Specifies where to place the label component. If not None, it should be a concatenation of one or two of the letters N, S, E and W. The first letter specifies on which side of the megawidget to place the label. If a second letter is specified, it indicates where on that side to place the label. For example, if labelpos is W, the label is placed in the centre of the left-hand side; if it is WN, the label is placed at the top of the left-hand side; if it is WS, the label is placed at the bottom of the left-hand side.	anchor	
orient	Specifies whether the arrow buttons should appear to the left and right of the entry field (HORIZONTAL) or above and below (VERTICAL).	constant	HORIZONTAL
padx	Specifies a padding distance to leave around the arrow buttons in the x direction.	distance	0
pady	Specifies a padding distance to leave around the arrow buttons in the y direction.	distance	0
repeatrate	Specifies the delay (in milliseconds) between automatic counts while an arrow button is held down.	milliseconds	50

* The standard counters are:

- numeric   An integer number, as accepted by string.atol()
- integer   Same as numeric.
- real   A real number, as accepted by string.atof(). This counter accepts a separator argument, which specifies the character used to represent the decimal point. The default separator is '.'.

- `time` A time specification, as accepted by `Pmw.timestringtoseconds()`. This counter accepts a `separator` argument, which specifies the character used to separate the time fields. The default separator is ':'.
- `date` A date specification, as accepted by `Pmw.datestringtojdn()`. This counter accepts a `separator` argument, which specifies the character used to separate the three date fields. The default is '/'. This counter also accepts a `format` argument, which is passed to `Pmw.datestringtojdn()` to specify the desired ordering of the fields. The default is `ymd`.

If `counter` is a function, then it will be called whenever the counter is incremented or decremented. The function is called with at least three arguments, the first three being (`text`, `factor`, `increment`), where `text` is the current contents of the entry field, `factor` is `1` when incrementing or `-1` when decrementing, and `increment` is the value of the increment megawidget option.

The other arguments are keyword arguments made up of the fields of the datatype dictionary (excluding the `counter` field). The `counter` function should return a string representing the incremented or decremented value. It should raise a `ValueError` exception if the text is invalid. In this case the bell is rung and the entry text is not changed.

Components

downarrow

The arrow button used for decrementing the counter. Depending on the value of `orient`, it will appear on the left or below the entry field. Its component group is `Arrow`.

entryfield

The entry field widget where the text is entered, displayed and validated.

frame

If the label component has been created (that is, the `labelpos` option is not `None`), the frame component is created to act as the container of the entry field and arrow buttons. If there is no label component, then no frame component is created and the hull component acts as the container. In either case the border around the container of the entry field and arrow buttons will be raised (but not around the label).

hull

This acts as the body for the entire megawidget. Other components are created as children of the hull to further specialize the widget.

label

If the `labelpos` option is not `None`, this component is created as a text label for the megawidget. See the `labelpos` option for details. Note that to set, for example, the text option of the label, you need to use the `label_text` component option.

uparrow

The arrow button used for incrementing the counter. Depending on the value of `orient`, it will appear on the right or above the entry field. Its component group is `Arrow`.

Methods

decrement()

Decrements the counter once, as if the down arrow had been pressed.

increment()

Increments the counter once, as if the up arrow had been pressed.

CounterDialog

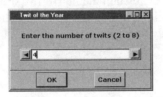

Description

A CounterDialog is a convenience dialog window with a simple counter. This is used to request the user to select a value using the up or down buttons.

Inheritance

CounterDialog inherits from `Pmw.Dialog`.

CounterDialog options

Option	Description	Units	Default
activatecommand	If this is callable, it will be called whenever the megawidget is activated by a call to `activate()`.	function	None
borderx	Specifies the width of the border to the left and right of the message area.	distance	20
bordery	Specifies the height of the border to the top and bottom of the message area.	distance	20
buttonboxpos	Specifies on which side of the dialog window to place the button box. Must be one of N, S, E or W.	anchor	S
buttons	This must be a tuple or a list. It specifies the names on the buttons in the button box.	(string, ...)	('OK',)
command	Specifies a function to call whenever a button in the button box is invoked or the window is deleted by the window manager. The function is called with a single argument, which is the name of the button which was invoked, or None if the window was deleted by the window manager.	function	None

Option	Description	Units	Default
deactivatecommand	If this is callable, it will be called whenever the megawidget is deactivated by a call to deactivate().	function	None
defaultbutton	Specifies the default button in the button box. If the RETURN key is hit when the dialog has focus, the default button will be invoked. If defaultbutton is None, there will be no default button and hitting the RETURN key will have no effect.	index	None
separatorwidth	If this is greater than 0, a separator line with the specified width will be created between the button box and the child site, as a component named separator. Since the default border of the button box and child site is raised, this option does not usually need to be set for there to be a visual separation between the button box and child site.	distance	0
title	This is the title that the window manager displays in the title bar of the window.	string	None

Components

buttonbox

This is the button box containing the buttons for the dialog. By default it is created with the options (hull_borderwidth = 1, hull_relief = 'raised').

counter

By default, this component is a Pmw.Counter.

dialogchildsite

This is the child site for the dialog, which may be used to specialize the megawidget by creating other widgets within it. By default it is created with the options (borderwidth = 1, relief = 'raised').

hull

This acts as the body for the entire megawidget. Other components are created as children of the hull to further specialize the widget.

separator

If the separatorwidth initialization option is nonzero, the separator component is the line dividing the area between the button box and the child site.

Methods

deleteentry(first, last = None)

Removes entries from the counter starting at first and ending at last. first and last are integer indices. If last is None, first will be deleted.

indexentry(index)

Returns the numerical index of the item corresponding to `index`.

insertentry(index, text)

Insers `text` at the integer position `index`.

Dialog

Description

This class creates a toplevel window composed of a button box and a child site area. The child site area can be used to specialize the megawidget by creating other widgets within it. This can be done by using this class directly or by deriving from it.

Inheritance

Dialog inherits from `Pmw.MegaToplevel`.

Dialog options

Option	Description	Units	Default
activatecommand	If this is callable, it will be called whenever the megawidget is activated by a call to `activate()`.	function	None
buttonboxpos	Specifies on which side of the dialog window to place the button box. Must be one of N, S, E or W.	anchor	S
buttons	This must be a tuple or a list. It specifies the names on the buttons in the button box.	(string, ...)	('OK',)
command	Specifies a function to call whenever a button in the button box is invoked or the window is deleted by the window manager. The function is called with a single argument, which is the name of the button which was invoked, or None if the window was deleted by the window manager.	function	None
deactivatecommand	If this is callable, it will be called whenever the megawidget is deactivated by a call to `deactivate()`.	function	None
defaultbutton	Specifies the default button in the button box. If the RETURN key is hit when the dialog has focus, the default button will be invoked. If defaultbutton is None, there will be no default button and hitting the RETURN key will have no effect.	index	None
separatorwidth	If this is greater than 0, a separator line with the specified width will be created between the button box and the child site, as a component named separator. Since the default border of the button box and child site is raised, this option does not usually need to be set for there to be a visual separation between the button box and child site.	distance	0

Option	Description	Units	Default
title	This is the title that the window manager displays in the title bar of the window.	string	None

Components

buttonbox

This is the button box containing the buttons for the dialog. By default it is created with the options (hull_borderwidth = 1, hull_relief = 'raised').

dialogchildsite

This is the child site for the dialog, which may be used to specialize the megawidget by creating other widgets within it. By default it is created with the options (borderwidth = 1, relief = 'raised').

hull

This acts as the body for the entire megawidget. Other components are created as children of the hull to further specialize the widget.

separator

If the separatorwidth initialization option is nonzero, the separator component is the line dividing the area between the button box and the child site.

Methods

interior()

Returns the child site for the dialog. This is the same as component('dialogchildsite').

invoke(index = 'default')

Invokes the command specified by the command option as if the button specified by index had been pressed. index may have any of the forms accepted by the Pmw.ButtonBox index() method.

EntryField

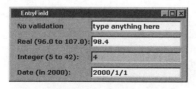

Description

This class consists of an entry widget with optional validation of various kinds. Built-in validation may be used, such as integer, real, time or date, or an external validation function may be supplied. If valid text is entered, it will be displayed with the normal background. If invalid text is entered, it is not displayed and the previously displayed text is restored. If partially valid text is entered, it will be displayed with a background color to indicate it is in error. An example of partially valid real text is '-.', which may be the first two characters of the valid string '-.5'. Some validators, such as date, have a relaxed interpretation of partial validity, which allows the user flexibility in how he enters the text.

Validation is performed early, at each keystroke or other event which modifies the text. However, if partially valid text is permitted, the validity of the entered text can be checked just before it is to be used; this is a form of late validation.

Minimum and maximum values may be specified. Some validators also accept other specifications, such as date and time formats and separators.

Validation function return values

Validation is performed by a function which takes as its first argument the entered text and returns one of three standard values, indicating whether the text is valid:

- Pmw.OK   The text is valid.
- Pmw.ERROR   The text is invalid and is not acceptable for display. In this case the entry will be restored to its previous value.
- Pmw.PARTIAL   The text is partially valid and is acceptable for display. In this case the text will be displayed using the errorbackground color.

Inheritance

EntryField inherits from Pmw.MegaWidget.

EntryField options

Option	Description	Units	Default
command	This specifies a function to call whenever the RETURN key is pressed or invoke() is called.	function	None
errorbackground	Specifies the background color to use when displaying invalid or partially valid text.	color	'pink'
extravalidators	This is a dictionary of extra validators. The keys are the names of validators which may be used in a future call to the validate option. Each value in the dictionary is a tuple of (validate_function, stringtovalue_function). The validate_function is used to implement the validation and the stringtovalue_function is used to convert the entry input into a value which can be compared with the minimum and maximum limits. These functions are as described for the validate option. If either of these is not given as a function, it is assumed to be the name of one of the other extra validators or one of the standard validators. The alias search is performed when the validate option is configured, not when the extravalidators option is configured or when the validate function is called.	dictionary	{}

Option	Description	Units	Default
	If the name of one of the extra validators is the same as one of the standard validators, the extra validator takes precedence.		
invalidcommand	This is executed when invalid text is entered and the text is restored to its previous value (that is, when the validate function returns Pmw.ERROR). It is also called if an attempt is made to set invalid text in a call to setentry().	function	self.bell
labelmargin	If the labelpos option is not None, this specifies the distance between the label component and the rest of the megawidget.	distance	0
labelpos	Specifies where to place the label component. If not None, it should be a concatenation of one or two of the letters N, S, E and W. The first letter specifies on which side of the megawidget to place the label. If a second letter is specified, it indicates where on that side to place the label. For example, if labelpos is W, the label is placed in the center of the left-hand side; if it is WN, the label is placed at the top of the left-hand side; if it is WS, the label is placed at the bottom of the left-hand side.	anchor	None
modifiedcommand	This is called whenever the content of the entry has been changed due to user action or by a call to setentry().	function	None
validate	Specifies what kind of validation should be performed on the entry input text. See below for details.	constant	None
value	Specifies the initial contents of the entry. If this text is invalid, it will be displayed with the errorbackground color and the invalidcommand function will be called. If both value and entry_textvariable options are specified in the constructor, value will take precedence.	string	' '

Validators

The most general way to specify the validate option is as a dictionary. The kind of validation is specified by the validator dictionary field, which may be the name of one of the standard validators described below, the name of a validator supplied by the extravalidators option, a function or None.

Any other dictionary fields specify other restrictions on the entered values. For all validators, the following fields may be specified:

- min   Specifies the minimum acceptable value, or None if no minimum checking should be performed. The default is None.
- max   Specifies the maximum acceptable value, or None if no maximum checking should be performed. The default is None.
- minstrict   If true, then minimum checking is strictly enforced. Otherwise, the entry input may be less than min, but it will be displayed using the errorbackground color. The default is true.

- `maxstrict` If `true`, then maximum checking is strictly enforced. Otherwise, the entry input may be more than `max`, but it will be displayed using the `errorbackground` color. The default is `true`.

If the dictionary contains a `stringtovalue` field, it overrides the normal `stringtovalue` function for the validator. The `stringtovalue` function is described below.

Other fields in the dictionary (apart from the core fields mentioned above) are passed on to the validator and `stringtovalue` functions as keyword arguments.

If `validate` is not a dictionary, then it is equivalent to specifying it as a dictionary with a single `validator` field. For example, `validate = 'real'` is equivalent to `validate = {'validator' : 'real'}` and it specifies real numbers without any minimum or maximum limits and using "." as the decimal point character.

The standard validators accepted in the `validator` field are these:

- `numeric` An integer greater than or equal to 0. Digits only. No sign.
- `hexadecimal` Hex number (with optional leading `0x`), as accepted by `string.atol(text, 16)`.
- `real` A number, with or without a decimal point and optional exponent (e or E), as accepted by `string.atof()`. This validator accepts a `separator` argument, which specifies the character used to represent the decimal point. The default separator is ".".
- `alphabetic` Consisting of the letters a-z and A-Z. In this case, `min` and `max` specify limits on the length of the text.
- `alphanumeric` Consisting of the letters a-z, A-Z and the numbers 0-9. In this case, `min` and `max` specify limits on the length of the text.
- `time` Hours, minutes and seconds, in the format `HH:MM:SS`, as accepted by `Pmw.timestringtoseconds()`. This validator accepts a `separator` argument, which specifies the character used to separate the three fields. The default separator is ":". The time may be negative.
- `date` Day, month and year, as accepted by `Pmw.datestringtojdn()`. This validator accepts a `separator` argument, which specifies the character used to separate the three fields. The default is ":". This validator also accepts a `format` argument, which is passed to `Pmw.datestringtojdn()` to specify the desired ordering of the fields. The default is `ymd`.

If `validator` is a function, then it will be called whenever the contents of the entry may have changed due to user action or by a call to `setentry()`. The function is called with at least one argument, the first one being the new text as modified by the user or `setentry()`. The other arguments are keyword arguments made up of the non-core fields of the validate dictionary.

The validator function should return `Pmw.OK`, `Pmw.ERROR` or `Pmw.PARTIAL` as described above. It should not perform minimum and maximum checking. This is done after the call, if it returns `Pmw.OK`.

The `stringtovalue` field in the dictionary may be specified as the name of one of the standard validators, the name of a validator supplied by the extravalidators option, a function or `None`.

The `stringtovalue` function is used to convert the entry input into a value which can then be compared with any minimum or maximum values specified for the validator. If the `min` or `max` fields are specified as strings, they are converted using the `stringtovalue` function. The `stringtovalue` function is called with the same arguments as the `validator` function. The `stringtovalue` function for the standard number validators convert the string to a number. Those for the standard alpha validators return the length of the string. Those for the standard `time` and `date` validators return the number of seconds and the Julian Day Number, respectively. See `Pmw.stringtoreal()`, `Pmw.timestringtoseconds()` and `Pmw.datestringtojdn()`.

If the validator has been specified as a function and no `stringtovalue` field is given, then it defaults to the standard Python `len()` function.

If `validator` is `None`, no validation is performed. However, minimum and maximum checking may be performed, according to the `stringtovalue` function. For example, to limit the entry text to a maximum of five characters:

```
Pmw.EntryField(validate = {'max' : 5})
```

The `validator` functions for each of the standard validators can be accessed this way:

```
Pmw.numericvalidator
Pmw.integervalidator
Pmw.hexadecimalvalidator
Pmw.realvalidator
Pmw.alphabeticvalidator
Pmw.alphanumericvalidator
Pmw.timevalidator
Pmw.datevalidator
```

Whenever the `validate` option is configured, the text currently displayed in the entry widget is revalidated. If it is not valid, the `errorbackground` color is set and the `invalidcommand` function is called. However, the displayed text is not modified.

Components

entry
The widget where the user may enter text. Long text may be scrolled horizontally by dragging with the middle mouse button.

hull
This acts as the body for the entire megawidget. Other components are created as children of the hull to further specialize the widget.

label
If the `labelpos` option is not `None`, this component is created as a text label for the megawidget. See the `labelpos` option for details. Note that to set, for example, the text option of the label, you need to use the `label_text` component option.

Methods

checkentry()
Checks the validity of the current contents of the entry widget. If the text is not valid, sets the background to `errorbackground` and calls the `invalidcommand` function. If a variable is

specified by the `entry_textvariable` option, this method should be called after the `set()` method of the variable is called. If this is not done in this case, the entry widget background will not be set correctly.

clear()

Removes all text from the entry widget. Equivalent to `setentry('')`.

invoke()

Invokes the command specified by the `command` option as if the RETURN key had been pressed and returns the result.

setentry(text)

Sets the contents of the entry widget to `text` and carries out validation as if the text had been entered by the user. If the text is invalid, the entry widget will not be changed and the `invalidcommand` function will be called.

valid()

Returns `true` if the contents of the entry widget are valid.

Group

Description

This megawidget consists of an interior frame with an exterior ring border and an identifying tag displayed over the top edge of the ring. The programmer can create other widgets within the interior frame.

Inheritance

Group inherits from `Pmw.MegaWidget`.

Group options

Option	Description	Units	Default
`tagindentl`	The distance from the left edge of the ring to the left side of the `tag` component.	distance	10

Components

groupchildsite

The frame which can contain other widgets to be grouped.

hull

This acts as the body for the entire megawidget. Other components are created as children of the hull to further specialize the widget.

ring

This component acts as the enclosing ring around the `groupchildsite`. The default borderwidth is 2 and the default relief is `groove`.

tag

The identifying tag displayed over the top edge of the enclosing ring. If this is `None`, no tag is displayed.

Methods

interior()

Returns the frame within which the programmer may create widgets. This is the same as `component('groupchildsite')`.

LabeledWidget

Description

This megawidget consists of an interior frame with an associated label which can be positioned on any side of the frame. The programmer can create other widgets within the interior frame.

Inheritance

LabeledWidget inherits from `Pmw.MegaWidget`.

LabeledWidget options

Option	Description	Units	Default
labelmargin	If the `labelpos` option is not `None`, this specifies the distance between the label component and the rest of the megawidget.	distance	0

Option	Description	Units	Default
labelpos	Specifies where to place the label component. If not None, it should be a concatenation of one or two of the letters N, S, E and W. The first letter specifies on which side of the megawidget to place the label. If a second letter is specified, it indicates where on that side to place the label. For example, if labelpos is W, the label is placed in the center of the left-hand side; if it is WN, the label is placed at the top of the left-hand side; if it is WS, the label is placed at the bottom of the left-hand side.	anchor	None

Components

hull

This acts as the body for the entire megawidget. Other components are created as children of the hull to further specialize the widget.

label

If the labelpos option is not None, this component is created as a text label for the megawidget. See the labelpos option for details. Note that to set, for example, the text option of the label, you need to use the label_text component option.

labelchildsite

The frame which can contain other widgets to be labelled.

Methods

interior()

Returns the frame within which the programmer may create widgets. This is the same as component('labelchildsite').

MegaArchetype

Description

This class is the basis for all Pmw megawidgets. It provides methods to manage options and component widgets.

This class is normally used as a base class for other classes. If the hullClass argument is specified, such as in the Pmw.MegaWidget and Pmw.MegaToplevel classes, a container widget is created to act as the parent of all other component widgets. Classes derived from these subclasses create other component widgets and options to implement megawidgets that can be used in applications.

If no hullClass argument is given to the constructor, no container widget is created and only the option configuration functionality is available.

Inheritance

MegaArchetype inherits from `None`.

Methods

addoptions(optionDefs)

Adds additional options for this megawidget. The `optionDefs` argument is treated in the same way as the `defineoptions()` method. This method is used by derived classes. It is only used if a megawidget should conditionally define some options, perhaps depending on the value of other options. Usually, megawidgets unconditionally define all their options in the call to `defineoptions()` and do not need to use `addoptions()`. This method may be called after the call to `defineoptions()` and before the call to `initialiseoptions()`.

cget(option)

Returns the current value of `option` (which should be in the format described in the Options section). This method is also available using object subscripting, for example `myWidget['font']`. Unlike Tkinter's `cget()`, which always returns a string, this method returns the same value and type as used when the `option` was set (except where option is a component option and the component is a Tkinter widget, in which case it returns the string returned by Tcl/Tk).

component(name)

Returns the component widget whose name is `name`. This allows the user of a megawidget to access and configure component widgets directly.

componentaliases()

Returns the list of aliases for components. Each item in the list is a tuple whose first item is the name of the alias and whose second item is the name of the component or subcomponent it refers to.

componentgroup(name)

Returns the group of the component whose name is `name` or `None` if it does not have a group.

components()

Returns a sorted list of names of the components of this megawidget.

configure (option = None, ** kw)

Queries or configures the megawidget options. If no arguments are given, returns a tuple consisting of all megawidget options and values, each as a 5-element tuple (`name`, `resourceName`, `resourceClass`, `default`, `value`). This is in the same format as the value returned by the standard Tkinter `configure()` method, except that the resource name is always the same as the option name and the resource class is the option name with the first letter capitalized.

If one argument is given, it returns the 5-element tuple for option. Otherwise, it sets the configuration options specified by the keyword arguments.

createcomponent(name, aliases, group, widgetClass, widgetArgs, ** kw)

Creates a component widget by calling `widgetClass` with the arguments given by `widgetArgs` and any keyword arguments. The `name` argument is the name by which the component will be known and must not contain the underscore character (_). The `group` argument specifies the group of the component. The `aliases` argument is a sequence of 2-element tuples, whose first item is an alias name and whose second item is the name of the component or subcomponent it is to refer to.

createlabel(parent, childCols = 1, childRows = 1)

Creates a `Label` component named `label` in the `parent` widget. This convenience method is used by several megawidgets that require an optional label. The widget must have options named `labelpos` and `labelmargin`. If `labelpos` is `None`, no label is created. Otherwise, a label is created and positioned according to the value of `labelpos` and `labelmargin`. The label is added to the `parent` using the `grid()` method, with `childCols` and `childRows` indicating how many rows and columns the label should span. Note that all other child widgets of the parent must be added to the parent using the `grid()` method. The `createlabel()` method may be called by derived classes during megawidget construction.

defineoptions(keywords, optionDefs)

Creates options for this megawidget. The `optionDefs` argument defines the options. It is a sequence of 3-element tuples, (`name`, `default`, `callback`), where `name` is the name of the option, `default` is its default value and `callback` is the function to call when the value of the option is set by a call to `configure()`. The `keywords` argument should be the keyword arguments passed in to the constructor of a megawidget. The user may override the default value of an option by supplying a keyword argument to the constructor.

This should be called before the constructor of the base class, so that default values defined in a derived class override those in a base class.

If callback is `Pmw.INITOPT`, then the option is an initialization option.

destroycomponent(name)

Removes the megawidget component called `name`. This method may be called by derived classes to destroy a megawidget component. It destroys the component widget and then removes all record of the component from the megawidget.

hulldestroyed()

Returns `true` if the Tk widget corresponding to the hull component has been destroyed.

initialiseoptions(myclass)

Checks keyword arguments and calls option callback functions. This must be called at the end of a megawidget constructor with `myClass` set to the class being defined. It checks that all keyword arguments given to the constructor have been used. If not, it raises an error indicating which arguments were unused. A keyword is defined to be used if, during the construction of a megawidget, it is defined in a call to `defineoptions()` or `addoptions()` (by the megawidget or one of its base classes); or if it references, by name, a component of the mega-widget; or if it references, by group, at least one component.

It also calls the configuration callback function for all configuration options.

This method is only effective when called by the constructor of the leaf class, that is, if `myClass` is the same as the class of the object being constructed. The method returns immediately when called by the constructors of base classes.

interior()

Returns the widget framing the interior space in which any children of this megawidget should be created. By default, this returns the hull component widget, if one was created, or `None` otherwise. A subclass should use the widget returned by `interior()` as the parent of any components or sub-widgets it creates. Megawidgets which can be further subclassed, such as `Pmw.Dialog`, should redefine this method to return the widget in which subclasses should create children. The overall containing widget is always available as the hull component.

isinitoption(option)

If `option` is an initialization option, returns `true`. Otherwise returns `false` (the `option` is a configuration option). The `option` argument must be an option of this megawidget, not an option of a component. Otherwise an exception is raised.

options()

Returns a sorted list of this megawidget's options. Each item in the list is a 3-element tuple, (`option`, `default`, `isinit`), where `option` is the name of the option, `default` is its default value and `isinit` is `true` if the option is an initialization option.

MegaToplevel

Description

This class creates a megawidget contained within a toplevel window. It may be used directly to create a toplevel megawidget or it may be used as a base class for more specialized toplevel megawidgets, such as `Pmw.Dialog`. It creates a `Toplevel` component, named `hull`, to act as the container of the megawidget. The window class name for the hull widget is set to the most-specific class name for the megawidget. Derived classes specialize this widget by creating other widget components as children of the hull widget.

The megawidget may be used as either a normal toplevel window or as a modal dialog. Use `show()` and `withdraw()` for normal use and `activate()` and `deactivate()` for modal dialog use. If the window is deleted by the window manager while being shown normally, the default behavior is to destroy the window. If the window is deleted by the window manager while the window is active (such as when it is used as a modal dialog), the window is deactivated. Use the `userdeletefunc()` and `usermodaldeletefunc()` methods to override these behaviors. Do not call `protocol()` to set the `WM_DELETE_WINDOW` window manager protocol directly if you want to use this window as a modal dialog.

The currently active windows form a stack with the most recently activated window at the top of the stack. All mouse and keyboard events are sent to this top window. When it deactivates, the next window in the stack will start to receive events.

Inheritance

MegaToplevel inherits from `Pmw.MegaArchetype`.

MegaToplevel options

Option	Description	Units	Default
activatecommand	If this is callable, it will be called whenever the megawidget is activated by a call to `activate()`.	function	None
deactivatecommand	If this is callable, it will be called whenever the megawidget is deactivated by a call to `deactivate()`.	function	None
title	This is the title that the window manager displays in the title bar of the window.	string	None

Components

hull

This acts as the body for the entire megawidget. Other components are created as children of the hull to further specialize the widget.

Methods

activate(globalMode = 0, master = None, geometry = 'centerscreenfirst)

Displays the window as a modal dialog. This means that all mouse and keyboard events go to this window and no other windows can receive any events. If you do not want to restrict mouse and keyboard events to this window, use the `show()` method instead. The `activate()` method does not return until the `deactivate()` method is called, when the window is withdrawn, the grab is released and the result is returned.

If `globalMode` is `false`, the window will grab control of the pointer and keyboard, preventing any events from being delivered to any other toplevel windows within the application. If `globalMode` is true, the grab will prevent events from being delivered to any other toplevel windows regardless of application. Global grabs should be used sparingly.

When the window is displayed, it is positioned on the screen according to geometry which may be one of the following:

- `centerscreenfirst` The window will be centered the first time it is activated. On subsequent activations it will be positioned in the same position as the last time it was displayed, even if it has been moved by the user.
- `centerscreenalway` The window will be centered on the screen (halfway across and one-third down).

- `first + spec` It is assumed that the rest of the argument (after `first`) is a standard geometry specification. The window will be positioned using this specification the first time it is activated. On subsequent activations it will be positioned in the same position as the last time it was displayed, even if it has been moved by the user. For example, `geometry = first+100+100` will initially display the window at position (100,100). Other calls to `activate()` will not change the previous position of the window.
- `spec` This is a standard geometry specification. The window will be positioned using this specification.

If the BLT Tcl extension library is present, a clock cursor will be displayed until the window is deactivated.

If the `activatecommand` option is callable, it is called just before the window begins to wait for the result.

If master is not `None`, the window will become a transient window of master. The master should be another existing toplevel window.

MegaWidget

Description

This class creates a megawidget contained within a Frame window. The class acts as the base class for megawidgets that are not contained in their own toplevel window, such as `Pmw.ButtonBox` and `Pmw.ComboBox`. It creates a `Frame` component named `hull` to act as the container of the megawidget. The window class name for the hull widget is set to the most-specific class name for the megawidget. Derived classes specialize this widget by creating other widget components as children of the hull widget.

Inheritance

MegaWidget inherits from `Pmw.MegaArchetype`.

Components

hull

This acts as the body for the entire megawidget. Other components are created as children of the hull to further specialize the widget.

Methods

destroy()

Destroys the hull component widget, including all of its children.

MenuBar

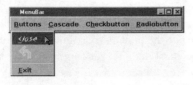

Description

This class creates a manager widget for containing menus. There are methods to add menu buttons and menus to the menu bar and for adding menu items to the menus. Menu buttons may be added to the left or right of the widget. Each menu button and menu item may have help text to be displayed by a Pmw.Balloon widget.

Inheritance

MenuBar inherits from Pmw.MegaWidget.

MenuBar options

Option	Description	Units	Default
balloon	Specifies the Pmw.Balloon widget to display the help text for menu buttons and menu items. If None, no help is displayed.	widget	None
hotkeys	Specifies if the menu is to support "hot keys", otherwise known as "accelerators". If true, the user may select menu items using the underlined character in the item's text.	boolean	1
padx	Specifies a padding distance to leave between each menu button in the x direction and also between the menu buttons and the outer edge of the menu bar.	distance	0

Components

hull

This acts as the body for the entire megawidget. Other components are created as children of the hull to further specialize the widget.

Methods

addcascademenu(menuName, submenu, help = '', traverseSpec = None, ** kw)

Adds a cascade submenu which is named submenu-menu to menu menuName. submenu must not already exist. If help is defined it is used for balloonHelp. If traverseSpec is defined it defines the underline character within the cascade which may be used as a keyboard accelerator. traverseSpec may be defined either as the character or the integer index of the character to be underlined.

addmenu(menuName, balloonHelp, statusHelp = None, side = 'left', traverseSpec = None, ** kw)

Adds a menu button and its associated menu to the menu bar. Any keyword arguments present will be passed to the constructor when creating the menu button. If the text keyword argument is not given, the text option of the menu button defaults to menuName. Each menu button is packed into the menu bar using the given side, which should be either left or right.

If the balloon option has been defined, balloonHelp and statusHelp are passed to the balloon as the help strings for the menu button. See the bind() method of Pmw.Balloon for information on how these strings may be displayed.

The menu button is created as a component named menuName-button and the menu is created as a component named menuName-menu. The method returns the menu button component widget.

addmenuitem(menuName, type, help = '', traverseSpec = None, ** kw)

Adds a menu item to the menu given by menuName. The kind of menu item is given by type and it may be one of command, separator, checkbutton, radiobutton or cascade. Any keyword arguments present will be passed to the menu when creating the menu item. See Menu for the valid options for each type. When the mouse is moved over the menu item, the string given by help will be displayed by the balloon's statuscommand.

deletemenu(menuName)

Deletes the menu named menuName. Subordinate cascade menus should be deleted before main menu items.

deletemenuitems(menuName, start = '0', end = None)

Deletes menu items from the menu named menuName. If start and end are defined it deletes items beginning at index start and ending at index end. If start is defined without end, it deletes the item at start. If neither start or end are defined it deletes all items in menuName.

disableall()

Disables all items in the menubar.

enableall()

Enables all items in the menubar.

MessageBar

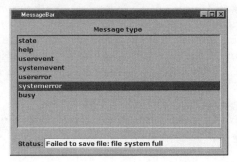

Description

This class creates a single-line message display area. Messages of several different types may be displayed. Messages are cleared after a period defined for each message type. Each message type has a priority so that if the application attempts to display more than one message at a time, the message with the highest priority will be displayed. Messages may be accompanied by a number of audible bells.

Inheritance

MessageBar inherits from Pmw.MegaWidget.

MessageBar options

Option	Description	Units	Default
labelmargin	If the labelpos option is not None, this specifies the distance between the label component and the rest of the megawidget.	distance	0
labelpos	Specifies where to place the label component. If not None, it should be a concatenation of one or two of the letters N, S, E and W. The first letter specifies on which side of the megawidget to place the label. If a second letter is specified, it indicates where on that side to place the label. For example, if labelpos is W, the label is placed in the center of the left-hand side; if it is WN, the label is placed at the top of the left-hand side; if it is WS, the label is placed at the bottom of the left-hand side.	anchor	None
messagetypes	This defines what message types are supported by the message bar and the characteristics of those message types. It is a dictionary where the key is a string specifying a message type and the value is a tuple of four integers (priority, showtime, bells, logmessage), where priority is the rank of the message type, showtime is the number of seconds to display messages of this message type, bells is the number of audible bells to ring and logmessage is a boolean specifying whether this message should be logged for retrieval later. Messages with a higher priority are displayed in preference to those with lower priority. If a high priority message times out (because it has been displayed for showtime seconds), then a lower priority message may be displayed. A showtime of 0 means that the message will never time out and it is useful for displaying messages describing the current state of the application as opposed to messages describing events. Logging is not currently implemented. The default is:	dictionary	

```
                {
                'systemerror' : (5, 10, 2, 1),
                'usererror' : (4, 5, 1, 0),
                'busy'      : (3, 0, 0, 0),
                'systemevent' : (2, 5, 0, 0),
                'userevent'  : (2, 5, 0, 0),
                'help'      : (1, 5, 0, 0),
                'state'     : (0, 0, 0, 0),
                }
```

Option	Description	Units	Default
silent	If `true`, no audible bells will sound, regardless of the value for bells defined in the `messagetypes` option.	boolean	0

Components

entry

The widget where the messages are displayed. Long messages may be scrolled horizontally by dragging with the middle mouse button.

hull

This acts as the body for the entire megawidget. Other components are created as children of the hull to further specialize the widget.

label

If the `labelpos` option is not `None`, this component is created as a text label for the megawidget. See the `labelpos` option for details. Note that to set, for example, the text option of the label, you need to use the `label_text` component option.

Methods

helpmessage(text)

A convenience method that displays `text` in the message bar according to the characteristics defined by the help message type. Equivalent to `message('help', text)`.

message(type, text)

Displays `text` in the message bar according to the characteristics defined by the `type` message type, as discussed under `messagetypes`.

resetmessages(type)

Clears the `type` message and all message types with a lower priority, except permanent messages, such as state. This is useful for clearing the busy message and any outstanding event and help messages.

MessageDialog

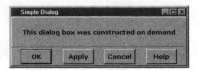

Description

A MessageDialog is a convenience dialog window containing a message widget. This is used to display multiple lines of text to the user in a transient window.

Inheritance

MessageDialog inherits from Pmw.Dialog.

MessageDialog options

Option	Description	Units	Default
activatecommand	If this is callable, it will be called whenever the megawidget is activated by a call to activate().	function	None
borderx	Specifies the width of the border to the left and right of the message area.	distance	20
bordery	Specifies the height of the border to the top and bottom of the message area.	distance	20
buttonboxpos	Specifies on which side of the dialog window to place the button box. Must be one of N, S, E or W.	anchor	S
buttons	This must be a tuple or a list. It specifies the names on the buttons in the button box.	(string, ...)	('OK',)
command	Specifies a function to call whenever a button in the button box is invoked or the window is deleted by the window manager. The function is called with a single argument, which is the name of the button which was invoked, or None if the window was deleted by the window manager.	function	None
deactivatecommand	If this is callable, it will be called whenever the megawidget is deactivated by a call to deactivate().	function	None
defaultbutton	Specifies the default button in the button box. If the RETURN key is hit when the dialog has focus, the default button will be invoked. If defaultbutton is None, there will be no default button and hitting the RETURN key will have no effect.	index	None
iconmargin	Specifies the space to be left around the icon, if present.	distance	20
iconpos	Determines the placement of the icon if it is to be displayed. Value must be either one of the letters N, S, E and W or None.	distance	None

Option	Description	Units	Default
separatorwidth	If this is greater than 0, a separator line with the specified width will be created between the button box and the child site, as a component named separator. Since the default border of the button box and child site is raised, this option does not usually need to be set for there to be a visual separation between the button box and the child site.	distance	0
title	This is the title that the window manager displays in the title bar of the window.	string	None

Components

buttonbox

This is the button box containing the buttons for the dialog. By default it is created with the options (hull_borderwidth = 1, hull_relief = 'raised').

dialogchildsite

This is the child site for the dialog, which may be used to specialize the megawidget by creating other widgets within it. By default it is created with the options (borderwidth = 1, relief = 'raised').

hull

This acts as the body for the entire megawidget. Other components are created as children of the hull to further specialize the widget.

icon

By default, this component is a Label.

message

By default, this component is a Label.

separator

If the separatorwidth initialization option is nonzero, the separator component is the line dividing the area between the button box and the child site.

Methods

This megawidget has no methods of its own.

NoteBook

Description

This widget replaces NoteBookR and NoteBookS in release 0_8_3 and later.

A notebook contains a set of tabbed pages. At any one time only one of these pages (the selected page) is visible, with the other pages being hidden "beneath" it. Another page in the notebook may be displayed by clicking on the tab attached to the page. The tabs are displayed along the top edge.

Optionally, the notebook may be displayed without tabs. In this case, another selection widget, such as `Pmw.OptionMenu`, may be used to select the pages.

Inheritance

NoteBook inherits from `Pmw.MegaArchetype`.

NoteBook options

Option	Description	Units	Default
borderwidth	The width of the border drawn around each tab and around the selected page.	integer	2
createcommand	Specifies a function to call when a page is selected for the first time. The function is called with a single argument, which is the name of the selected page, and it is called before the `raisecommand` function. This allows the creation of the page contents to be deferred until the page is first displayed.	function	None
lowercommand	Specifies a function to call when the selected page is replaced with a new selected page. The function is called with a single argument, which is the name of the previously selected page, and it is called before the `createcommand` or `raisecommand` functions.	function	None
pagemargin	The margin around the selected page inside the notebook's page border.	pixels	4
raisecommand	Specifies a function to call when a new page is selected. The function is called with a single argument, which is the name of the selected page.	function	None
tabpos	Specifies the location of the tabs. If n, tabs are created for each page and positioned at the top of the notebook. If None, no tabs are created, in which case another selection widget can be used to select pages by calling the `selectpage()` method.	string	'n'

Components

hull

This acts as the body for the megawidget. The contents of the megawidget are created as canvas items and positioned in the hull using the canvas coordinate system. By default, this component is a `Tkinter.Canvas`.

Methods

add(pagename, ** kw)

Adds a page at the end of the notebook. See the `insert()` method for full details.

delete(*pageNames)

Deletes the pages given by `pageNames` from the notebook. Each of the `pageNames` may have any of the forms accepted by the `index()` method. If the currently selected page is deleted, then the `next` page, in index order, is selected. If the `end` page is deleted, then the `previous` page is selected.

getcurselection()

Returns the name of the currently selected page.

Index(Index, forInsert = 0)

Returns the numerical index of the page corresponding to `index`. This may be specified in any of the following forms:

- `name`   Specifies the page labelled `name`.
- `number`   Specifies the page numerically, where 0 corresponds to the first page.
- `END`   Specifies the last page.
- `SELECT`   Specifies the currently selected page.

insert(pageName, before = 0, **kw)

Adds a page to the notebook as a component named `pageName`. The page is added just before the page specified by `before`, which may have any of the forms accepted by the `index()` method. If `tabpos` is not `None`, also create a tab as a component named `pageName-tab`. Keyword arguments prefixed with `page_` or `tab_` are passed to the respective constructors when creating the page or tab. If the `tab_text` keyword argument is not given, the text option of the tab defaults to `pageName`. If a page is inserted into an empty notebook, the page is selected. To add a page to the end of the notebook, use `add()`. The method returns the `pageName` component widget.

page(pageIndex)

Returns the frame component widget of the page `pageIndex`, where `pageIndex` may have any of the forms accepted by the `index()` method.

pagenames()

Returns a list of the names of the pages, in display order.

recolorborders()

Changes the color of the page and tab borders. This method is required because the borders are created as canvas polygons and hence do not respond to normal color changing techniques, such as `Pmw.Color.changecolor()`.

selectpage(page)

Selects `page` to be the currently selected page. The page will be raised and the previous selected page will be lowered.

setnaturalpagesize(pageNames = None)

Sets the width and height of the notebook to be the maximum requested width and height of all the pages. This should be called after all pages and their contents have been created. It calls `update_idletasks()` so that the width and height of the pages can be determined. This may cause the notebook to flash onto the screen at the default size before resizing to the natural size.

tab(pageIndex)

Returns the tab component widget of the page `pageIndex`, where `pageIndex` may have any of the forms accepted by the `index()` method. If `tabpos` is `None`, returns `None`.

NoteBookR

Description

NoteBookR implements the familiar *notebook* motif. The window is arranged as a series of overlaid panes with a tab which raises the corresponding pane to the top of the stack.

Inheritance

NoteBookR inherits from `Pmw.MegaWidget`.

NoteBookR options

Option	Description	Units	Default
balloon	Specifies balloon help for the widget.	string	None
ipadx	Specifies a padding distance to leave within each pane in the x direction.	distance	4
ipady	Specifies a padding distance to leave within each pane in the y direction.	distance	4

Components

hull

This acts as the body for the entire megawidget. Other components are created as children of the hull to further specialize the widget.

nbframe

By default, this component is a `Canvas`.

Methods

add(pagename, ** kw)

Adds a page at the end of the notebook. See the `insert()` method for full details.

initialise(e = None, w = 1, h = 1)

interior()

Returns the widget framing the interior space in which any children of this megawidget should be created. By default, this returns the hull component widget, if one was created, or `None` otherwise. A subclass should use the widget returned by `interior()` as the parent of any components or sub-widgets it creates. Megawidgets which can be further subclassed, such as `Pmw.Dialog`, should redefine this method to return the widget in which subclasses should create children. The overall containing widget is always available as the hull component.

lift(pagenameOrIndex)

If `pagenameOrIndex` is a string, it raises the pane with that name. If `pagenameOrIndex` is an integer, it raises the page with `index`.

pagecget(pagename, option)

Returns the value of `option` for the pane `pagename`.

pageconfigure(pagename, ** kw)

Configures the pane specified by `pagename`, where `name` is a string, specifying the name of the pane. The keyword arguments specify the new values for the options for the pane.

pages()

Returns a list of the `panes` currently defined in the notebook.

raised()

Returns the name of the pane that is currently at the top of the stack.

tkdelete(pagename)

Removes the pane and tab button for pane `pagename`.

tkraise(pagenameOrIndex)

`tkraise` is an alias for `lift`.

NoteBookS

Description

NoteBookS implements an alternative to the familiar *notebook* motif. The window is arranged as a series of overlaid panes with a tab which raises the corresponding pane to the top of the stack. NoteBookS has more precise control of options than NoteBookR.

Inheritance

NoteBookS inherits from `Pmw.MegaWidget`.

NoteBookS options

Option	Description	Units	Default
activeColor	Specifies the color of the tab and its associated pane when it is the active tab.	color	'red'
canvasColor	Specifies the background color of the canvas behind the notebook panes (normally not seen if there is at least one pane).	color	'white'
canvasHeight	Specifies the overall height of the base canvas.	height	250
canvasWidth	Specifies the overall width of the base canvas.	width	400
deactiveColor	Specifies the color of any tab that is not currently the active tab.	color	'grey'
longX	Specifies the long X dimension (see diagram below).	coord	30
longY	Specifies the long Y dimension (see diagram below).	coord	35
offsetY	Specifies the offset of the top of the tab from the top of the canvas.	distance	5
shadeColor	Specifies the color of the "shadow" effect behind each tab.	color	'#666666'
shortX	Specifies the short X dimension (see diagram below).	coord	7
shortY	Specifies the short short Y dimension (see diagram below).	coord	7
tabColor	Specifies the color of the canvas behind the tabs.	color	'blue'
tabHeight	Specifies the height of the area in which the tabs will be drawn.	height	40
textColor	The color (fill) of the text used for the tab labels	color	'black'
textFont	The font used to draw the tab labels.	font	('Helvetica, 10, normal)

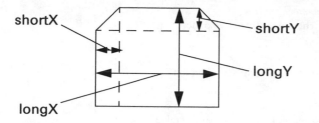

Components

containerCanvas

By default, this component is a Canvas.

hull

This acts as the body for the entire megawidget. Other components are created as children of the hull to further specialize the widget.

mainCanvas

By default, this component is a Canvas.

tabCanvas

By default, this component is a Canvas.

Methods

addPage(name)

Creates a Frame within the notebook associated with name name.

delPage(name)

Deletes the pane (Frame) associated with name name.

getPage(name)

Returns the panel (Frame) associated with name name. Does not raise the specified panel to the top of the stack.

pageNames()

Returns a list of all the page names currently defined for the notebook.

pages()

Returns a list of all the panes (Frames) currently defined for the notebook.

raisePage(name, select = 1)

Raises the pane associated with name name to the top of the stack. If select is false, do not deselect the currently active pane.

raised()

Returns the name of the currently active pane.

reBind()

Allows selection of panes by clicking on the tabs.

unBind()

Disallows selection of panes by clicking on the tabs.

OptionMenu

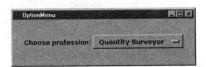

Description

This class creates an option menu which consists of a menu button and an associated menu which pops up when the button is pressed. The text displayed in the menu button is updated whenever an item is selected in the menu. The currently selected value can be retrieved from the megawidget.

Inheritance

OptionMenu inherits from `Pmw.MegaWidget`.

OptionMenu options

Option	Description	Units	Default
command	Specifies a function to call whenever a menu item is selected or the `invoke()` method is called. The function is called with the currently selected value as its single argument.	function	None
initialitem	Specifies the initial selected value. This option is treated in the same way as the index argument of the `setitems()` method.		None
items	A sequence containing the initial items to be displayed in the menu component.		()
labelmargin	If the `labelpos` option is not None, this specifies the distance between the label component and the rest of the megawidget.	distance	0
labelpos	Specifies where to place the label component. If not None, it should be a concatenation of one or two of the letters N, S, E and W. The first letter specifies on which side of the megawidget to place the label. If a second letter is specified, it indicates where on that side to place the label. For example, if `labelpos` is W, the label is placed in the center of the left-hand side; if it is WN, the label is placed at the top of the left-hand side; if it is WS, the label is placed at the bottom of the left-hand side.	anchor	None

Components

hull

This acts as the body for the entire megawidget. Other components are created as children of the hull to further specialize the widget.

label

If the labelpos option is not None, this component is created as a text label for the megawidget. See the labelpos option for details. Note that to set, for example, the text option of the label, you need to use the label_text component option.

menu

The popup menu displayed when the menu button is pressed.

menubutton

The menu button displaying the currently selected value.

Methods

get()

Returns the currently selected value.

index(index)

Returns the numerical index of the menu item corresponding to index. This may be specified in any of the following forms:

- end   Indicates the last menu item.
- name   Specifies the menu item labelled name.
- None   Specifies the currently selected menu item.

invoke (index = None)

Calling this method is the same as selecting the menu item specified by index, meaning the text displayed by the menubutton component is updated and the function specified by the command option is called. index may have any of the forms accepted by the index() method.

setitems (items, index = None)

Replaces all the items in the menu component with those specified by the items sequence. If index is not None, it sets the selected value to index, which may have any of the forms accepted by the index() method. If index is None and the textvariable option of the menubutton component is the empty string, it sets the selected value to the first value in items. If items is empty, it sets the selected value to the empty string.

If index is None and the textvariable option of the menubutton component is not the empty string, then do not set the selected value. This assumes that the variable is already (or will be) set to the desired value.

PanedWidget

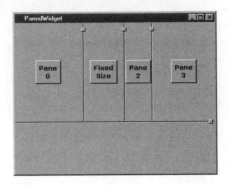

Description

This class creates a manager widget for containing resizable frames, known as panes. Each pane may act as the container for other widgets. The user may resize the panes by dragging a small rectangle (the handle) or the line between the panes (the separator).

Inheritance

PanedWidget inherits from Pmw.MegaWidget.

PanedWidget options

Option	Description	Units	Default
command	Specifies a function to be called whenever the size of any of the panes changes. The function is called with a single argument, being a list of the sizes of the panes, in order. For vertical orientation, the size is the height of the panes. For horizontal orientation, the size is the width of the panes.	function	None
orient	Specifies the orientation of the paned widget. This may be HORIZONTAL or VERTICAL. If VERTICAL, the panes are stacked above and below each other; otherwise the panes are laid out side by side.	constant	VERTICAL
separatorrelief	Specifies the relief of the line separating the panes.	constant	SUNKEN

Pane options

Option	Description	Units	Default
size	Specifies the initial size of the pane.	integer or real	0
min	Specifies the minimum size of the pane.	integer or real	0
max	Specifies the maximum size of the pane.	integer or real	100000

Components

hull

This acts as the body for the entire megawidget. Other components are created as children of the hull to further specialize the widget.

Methods

add(name, ** kw)

Adds a pane to the end of the paned widget using the component name name. This is equivalent to calling insert() with before set to the current number of panes. The method returns the name component widget.

configurepane(name, ** kw)

Configures the pane specified by name, where name is either an integer, specifying the index of the pane, or a string, specifying the name of the pane. The keyword arguments specify the new values for the options for the pane. These options are described in the Pane options section.

insert(name, before = 0, ** kw)

Adds a pane just before (that is, to the left of or above) the pane specified by before, where before is either an integer, specifying the index of the pane, or a string, specifying the name of the pane. The keyword arguments specify the initial values for the options for the new pane. These options are described in the Pane options section. To add a pane to the end of the paned widget, use add().

pane(name)

Returns the Frame pane widget for the pane specified by name, where name is either an integer, specifying the index of the pane, or a string, specifying the name of the pane.

panes()

Returns a list of the names of the panes, in display order.

remove(name)

Removes the pane specified by name, where name is either an integer, specifying the index of the pane, or a string, specifying the name of the pane.

PromptDialog

Description

A PromptDialog is a convenience dialog window that requests input from the user.

Inheritance

PromptDialog inherits from `Pmw.Dialog`.

PromptDialog options

Option	Description	Units	Default
activatecommand	If this is callable, it will be called whenever the megawidget is activated by a call to `activate()`.	function	None
borderx	Specifies the width of the border to the left and right of the message area.	distance	20
bordery	Specifies the height of the border to the top and bottom of the message area.	distance	20
buttonboxpos	Specifies on which side of the dialog window to place the button box. Must be one of N, S, E or W.	anchor	S
buttons	This must be a tuple or a list. It specifies the names on the buttons in the button box.	(string, ...)	('OK',)
command	Specifies a function to call whenever a button in the button box is invoked or the window is deleted by the window manager. The function is called with a single argument, which is the name of the button which was invoked, or None if the window was deleted by the window manager.	function	None
deactivatecommand	If this is callable, it will be called whenever the megawidget is deactivated by a call to `deactivate()`.	function	None
defaultbutton	Specifies the default button in the button box. If the RETURN key is hit when the dialog has focus, the default button will be invoked. If `defaultbutton` is None, there will be no default button and hitting the RETURN key will have no effect.	index	None
separatorwidth	If this is greater than 0, a separator line with the specified width will be created between the button box and the child site, as a component named `separator`. Since the default border of the button box and child site is raised, this option does not usually need to be set for there to be a visual separation between the button box and the child site.	distance	0
title	This is the title that the window manager displays in the title bar of the window.	string	None

Components

buttonbox

This is the button box containing the buttons for the dialog. By default it is created with the options (`hull_borderwidth` = 1, `hull_relief` = 'raised').

dialogchildsite

This is the child site for the dialog, which may be used to specialize the megawidget by creating other widgets within it. By default it is created with the options (borderwidth = 1, relief = 'raised').

entryfield

By default, this component is a Pmw.EntryField.

hull

This acts as the body for the entire megawidget. Other components are created as children of the hull to further specialize the widget.

separator

If the separatorwidth initialization option is nonzero, the separator component is the line dividing the area between the button box and the child site.

Methods

deleteentry(first, last = None)

Removes characters from the entryField starting at first and ending at last. first and last are integer indices. If last is None, first will be deleted.

indexentry(index)

Returns the numerical index of the character corresponding to index.

insertentry(index, text)

Inserts text at the integer position index.

RadioSelect

Description

This class creates a manager widget for containing buttons. The buttons may be laid out either horizontally or vertically. In single selection mode, only one button may be selected at any one time. In multiple selection mode, several buttons may be selected at the same time and clicking on a selected button will deselect it.

The buttons displayed can be either standard buttons, radio buttons or check buttons. When selected, standard buttons are displayed sunken, and radio and check buttons are displayed with the appropriate indicator color and relief.

Inheritance

RadioSelect inherits from Pmw.MegaWidget.

RadioSelect options

Option	Description	Units	Default
buttontype	Specifies the default type of buttons created by the add() method. If button, the default type is Button. If radiobutton, the default type is Radiobutton. If checkbutton, the default type is Checkbutton.	constant	None
command	Specifies a function to call when one of the buttons is clicked on or when invoke() is called.	function	None
labelmargin	If the labelpos option is not None, this specifies the distance between the label component and the rest of the megawidget.	distance	0
labelpos	Specifies where to place the label component. If not None, it should be a concatenation of one or two of the letters N, S, E and W. The first letter specifies on which side of the megawidget to place the label. If a second letter is specified, it indicates where on that side to place the label. For example, if labelpos is W, the label is placed in the center of the left-hand side; if it is WN, the label is placed at the top of the left-hand side; if it is WS, the label is placed at the bottom of the left-hand side.	anchor	None
orient	Specifies the direction in which the buttons are laid out. This may be HORIZONTAL or VERTICAL.	constant	HORIZONTAL
padx	Specifies a padding distance to leave between each button in the x direction and also between the buttons and the outer edge of the radio select widget.	distance	5
pady	Specifies a padding distance to leave between each button in the y direction and also between the buttons and the outer edge of the radio select widget.	distance	5
selectmode	Specifies the selection mode: whether a single button or multiple buttons can be selected at one time. If single, clicking on an unselected button selects it and deselects all other buttons. If multiple, clicking on an unselected button selects it and clicking on a selected button deselects it. This option is ignored if buttontype is radiobutton or checkbutton.	constant	'single'

Components

frame

If the label component has been created (that is, the labelpos option is not None), the frame component is created to act as the container of the buttons created by the add() method. If there is no label component, then no frame component is created and the hull component acts as the container.

hull

This acts as the body for the entire megawidget. Other components are created as children of the hull to further specialize the widget.

label

If the `labelpos` option is not `None`, this component is created as a text label for the mega-widget. See the `labelpos` option for details. Note that to set, for example, the text option of the label, you need to use the `label_text` component option.

Methods

add(name, ** kw)

Adds a button to the end of the radio select widget as a component named `name`, with a default type as specified by `buttontype`. Any keyword arguments present (except command) will be passed to the constructor when creating the button. If the text keyword argument is not given, the text option of the button defaults to `name`. The method returns the `name` component widget.

deleteall()

Deletes all buttons and clears the current selection.

getcurselection()

In single selection mode, returns the name of the currently selected button, or `None` if no buttons have been selected yet. In multiple selection mode, returns a list of the names of the currently selected buttons.

index(index)

Returns the numerical index of the button corresponding to index. This may be specified in any of the following forms:

- `number`   Specifies the button numerically, where 0 corresponds to the left (or top) button.
- `end`   Indicates the right (or bottom) button.
- `name`   Specifies the button named `name`.

invoke (index)

Calling this method is the same as clicking on the button specified by `index`: the buttons are displayed selected or deselected according to the selection mode and `command` is called. `index` may have any of the forms accepted by the `index()` method.

numbuttons ()

Returns the number of buttons in the radio select widget.

ScrolledCanvas

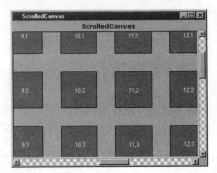

Description

This megawidget consists of a standard canvas widget with optional scrollbars which can be used to scroll the canvas. The scrollbars can be dynamic, which means that a scrollbar will only be displayed if it is necessary (if the scrollregion of the canvas is larger than the canvas).

Inheritance

ScrolledCanvas inherits from `Pmw.MegaWidget`.

ScrolledCanvas options

Option	Description	Units	Default
borderframe	A frame widget which snugly fits around the canvas, to give the appearance of a canvas border. It is created with a border so that the canvas, which is created without a border, looks like it has a border.	widget	Frame
canvasmargin	The margin around the items in the canvas. Used by the `resizescrollregion()` method.	distance	0
hscrollmode	The horizontal scroll mode. If `none`, the horizontal scrollbar will never be displayed. If `static`, the scrollbar will always be displayed. If `dynamic`, the scrollbar will be displayed only if necessary.	constant	'dynamic'
labelmargin	If the `labelpos` option is not `None`, this specifies the distance between the label component and the rest of the megawidget.	distance	0
labelpos	Specifies where to place the label component. If not `None`, it should be a concatenation of one or two of the letters N, S, E and W. The first letter specifies on which side of the megawidget to place the label. If a second letter is specified, it indicates where on that side to place the label. For example, if `labelpos` is W, the label is placed in the center of the left-hand side; if it is WN, the label is placed at the top of the left-hand side; if it is WS, the label is placed at the bottom of the left-hand side.	anchor	None
scrollmargin	The distance between the scrollbars and the enclosing canvas widget.	distance	2
usehullsize	If `true`, the size of the megawidget is determined solely by the width and height options of the hull component.	boolean	0

Option	Description	Units	Default
vscrollmode	The vertical scroll mode. If `none`, the vertical scrollbar will never be displayed. If `static`, the scrollbar will always be displayed. If `dynamic`, the scrollbar will be displayed only if necessary.	constant	`'dynamic'`

Components

borderframe

A frame widget which snugly fits around the canvas, to give the appearance of a canvas border. It is created with a border so that the canvas, which is created without a border, looks like it has a border.

canvas

The canvas widget which is scrolled by the scrollbars. If the `borderframe` option is `true`, this is created with a `borderwidth` of `0` to overcome a known problem with canvas widgets—if a widget inside a canvas extends across one of the edges of the canvas, then the widget obscures the border of the canvas. Therefore, if the canvas has no border, then this overlapping does not occur.

horizscrollbar

The horizontal scrollbar. Its component group is `Scrollbar`.

hull

This acts as the body for the entire megawidget. Other components are created as children of the hull to further specialize the widget.

label

If the `labelpos` option is not `None`, this component is created as a text label for the megawidget. See the `labelpos` option for details. Note that to set, for example, the text option of the label, you need to use the `label_text` component option.

vertscrollbar

The vertical scrollbar. Its component group is `Scrollbar`.

Methods

bbox(* args)

This method is explicitly forwarded to the canvas component's `bbox()` method. Without this explicit forwarding, the `bbox()` method (aliased to `grid_bbox()`) of the hull would be invoked, which is probably not what the programmer intended.

interior()

Returns the canvas widget within which the programmer should create graphical items and child widgets. This is the same as component('canvas').

resizescrollregion()

Resizes the scrollregion of the canvas component to be the bounding box covering all the items in the canvas plus a margin on all sides, as specified by the canvasmargin option.

ScrolledField

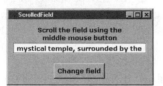

Description

This megawidget displays a single line of text. If the text is wider than the widget the user can scroll to the left and right by dragging with the middle mouse button. The text is also selectable by clicking or dragging with the left mouse button.

This megawidget can be used instead of a Label widget when displaying text of unknown width such as application status messages.

Inheritance

ScrolledField inherits from Pmw.MegaWidget.

ScrolledField options

Option	Description	Units	Default
labelmargin	If the labelpos option is not None, this specifies the distance between the label component and the rest of the megawidget.	distance	0
labelpos	Specifies where to place the label component. If not None, it should be a concatenation of one or two of the letters N, S, E and W. The first letter specifies on which side of the megawidget to place the label. If a second letter is specified, it indicates where on that side to place the label. For example, if labelpos is W, the label is placed in the center of the left-hand side; if it is WN, the label is placed at the top of the left-hand side; if it is WS, the label is placed at the bottom of the left-hand side.	anchor	None
text	Specifies the text to display in the scrolled field.	string	None

Components

entry

This is used to display the text and it allows the user to scroll and select the text. The state of this component is set to disabled, so that the user is unable to modify the text.

hull

This acts as the body for the entire megawidget. Other components are created as children of the hull to further specialize the widget.

label

If the `labelpos` option is not `None`, this component is created as a text label for the megawidget. See the `labelpos` option for details. Note that to set, for example, the text option of the label, you need to use the `label_text` component option.

Methods

This megawidget has no methods of its own.

ScrolledFrame

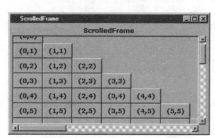

Description

This megawidget consists of a scrollable interior frame within a clipping frame. The programmer can create other widgets within the interior frame. If the frame becomes larger than the surrounding clipping frame, the user can position the frame using the horizontal and vertical scrollbars.

The scrollbars can be dynamic, which means that a scrollbar will only be displayed if it is necessary—if the frame is smaller than the surrounding clipping frame, the scrollbar will be hidden.

Inheritance

ScrolledFrame inherits from `Pmw.MegaWidget`.

ScrolledFrame options

Option	Description	Units	Default
borderframe	A frame widget which snugly fits around the clipper, to give the appearance of a border. It is created with a border so that the clipper, which is created without a border, looks like it has a border.	widget	Frame

Option	Description	Units	Default
horizflex	Specifies how the width of the scrollable interior frame should be resized relative to the clipping frame. If `fixed`, the interior frame is set to the natural width, as requested by the child widgets of the frame. If `expand` and the requested width of the interior frame is less than the width of the clipping frame, the interior frame expands to fill the clipping frame. If `shrink` and the requested width of the interior frame is more than the width of the clipping frame, the interior frame shrinks to the width of the clipping frame. If `elastic`, the width of the interior frame is always set to the width of the clipping frame.	constant	'fixed'
horizfraction	The fraction of the width of the clipper frame to scroll the interior frame when the user clicks on the horizontal scrollbar arrows.	distance	0.05
hscrollmode	The horizontal scroll mode. If `none`, the horizontal scrollbar will never be displayed. If `static`, the scrollbar will always be displayed. If `dynamic`, the scrollbar will be displayed only if necessary.	constant	'dynamic'
labelmargin	If the `labelpos` option is not None, this specifies the distance between the label component and the rest of the megawidget.	distance	0
labelpos	Specifies where to place the label component. If not None, it should be a concatenation of one or two of the letters N, S, E and W. The first letter specifies on which side of the megawidget to place the label. If a second letter is specified, it indicates where on that side to place the label. For example, if `labelpos` is W, the label is placed in the center of the left-hand side; if it is WN, the label is placed at the top of the left-hand side; if it is WS, the label is placed at the bottom of the left-hand side.	anchor	None
scrollmargin	The distance between the scrollbars and the clipping frame.	distance	2
usehullsize	If `true`, the size of the megawidget is determined solely by the width and height options of the hull component. Otherwise, the size of the megawidget is determined by the width and height of the clipper component, along with the size and/or existence of the other components, such as the label, the scrollbars and the `scrollmargin` option. All these affect the overall size of the megawidget.	boolean	0
vertflex	Specifies how the height of the scrollable interior frame should be resized relative to the clipping frame. If `fixed`, the interior frame is set to the natural height, as requested by the child widgets of the frame. If `expand` and the requested height of the interior frame is less than the height of the clipping frame, the interior frame expands to fill the clipping frame. If `shrink` and the requested height of the interior frame is more than the height of the clipping frame, the interior frame shrinks to the height of the clipping frame. If `elastic`, the height of the interior frame is always set to the height of the clipping frame.	constant	'fixed'

Option	Description	Units	Default
vertfraction	The fraction of the height of the clipper frame to scroll the interior frame when the user clicks on the vertical scrollbar arrows.	distance	0.05
vscrollmode	The vertical scroll mode. If none, the vertical scrollbar will never be displayed. If static, the scrollbar will always be displayed. If dynamic, the scrollbar will be displayed only if necessary.	constant	'dynamic'

Components

borderframe

A frame widget which snugly fits around the clipper, to give the appearance of a border. It is created with a border so that the clipper, which is created without a border, looks like it has a border.

clipper

The frame which is used to provide a clipped view of the frame component. If the border-frame option is true, this is created with a borderwidth of 0 to overcome a known problem with using place to position widgets: if a widget (in this case, the frame component) is placed inside a frame (in this case the clipper component) and it extends across one of the edges of the frame, then the widget obscures the border of the frame. Therefore, if the clipper has no border, then this overlapping does not occur.

frame

The frame within the clipper to contain the widgets to be scrolled.

horizscrollbar

The horizontal scrollbar. Its component group is Scrollbar.

hull

This acts as the body for the entire megawidget. Other components are created as children of the hull to further specialize the widget.

label

If the labelpos option is not None, this component is created as a text label for the mega-widget. See the labelpos option for details. Note that to set, for example, the text option of the label, you need to use the label_text component option.

vertscrollbar

The vertical scrollbar. Its component group is Scrollbar.

Methods

interior()

Returns the frame within which the programmer may create widgets to be scrolled. This is the same as component('frame').

reposition()

Updates the position of the frame component in the clipper and updates the scrollbar.

Usually, this method does not need to be called explicitly, since the position of the frame component and the scrollbars are automatically updated whenever the size of the frame or clipper components change or the user clicks in the scrollbars. However, if horizflex or vertflex is expand, the megawidget cannot detect when the requested size of the frame increases to greater than the size of the clipper. Therefore, this method should be called when a new widget is added to the frame (or a widget is increased in size) after the initial megawidget construction.

ScrolledListBox

Description

This megawidget consists of a standard listbox widget with optional scrollbars which can be used to scroll the listbox. The scrollbars can be dynamic, which means that a scrollbar will only be displayed if it is necessary—if the listbox does not contain enough entries, the vertical scrollbar will be automatically hidden and if the entries are not wide enough, the horizontal scrollbar will be automatically hidden.

Inheritance

ScrolledListBox inherits from Pmw.MegaWidget.

ScrolledListBox options

Option	Description	Units	Default
dblclickcommand	This specifies a function to call when mouse button 1 is double clicked over an entry in the listbox component.	function	None
hscrollmode	The horizontal scroll mode. If none, the horizontal scrollbar will never be displayed. If static, the scrollbar will always be displayed. If dynamic, the scrollbar will be displayed only if necessary.	constant	'dynamic'
items	A tuple containing the initial items to be displayed by the listbox component.	(string, ...)	()

Option	Description	Units	Default
labelmargin	If the labelpos option is not None, this specifies the distance between the label component and the rest of the megawidget.	distance	0
labelpos	Specifies where to place the label component. If not None, it should be a concatenation of one or two of the letters N, S, E and W. The first letter specifies on which side of the megawidget to place the label. If a second letter is specified, it indicates where on that side to place the label. For example, if labelpos is W, the label is placed in the center of the left-hand side; if it is WN, the label is placed at the top of the left-hand side; if it is WS, the label is placed at the bottom of the left-hand side.	anchor	None
scrollmargin	The distance between the scrollbars and the listbox widget.	distance	2
selectioncommand	This specifies a function to call when mouse button 1 is single clicked over an entry in the listbox component.	function	None
usehullsize	If true, the size of the megawidget is determined solely by the width and height options of the hull component. Otherwise, the size of the megawidget is determined by the width and height of the listbox component, along with the size and/or existence of the other components, such as the label, the scrollbars and the scrollmargin option. All of these affect the overall size of the megawidget.	boolean	0
vscrollmode	The vertical scroll mode. If none, the vertical scrollbar will never be displayed. If static, the scrollbar will always be displayed. If dynamic, the scrollbar will be displayed only if necessary.	constant	'dynamic'

Components

horizscrollbar

The horizontal scrollbar. Its component group is Scrollbar.

hull

This acts as the body for the entire megawidget. Other components are created as children of the hull to further specialize the widget.

label

If the labelpos option is not None, this component is created as a text label for the megawidget. See the labelpos option for details. Note that to set, for example, the text option of the label, you need to use the label_text component option.

listbox

The listbox widget which is scrolled by the scrollbars.

vertscrollbar

The vertical scrollbar. Its component group is `Scrollbar`.

Methods

bbox(index)

This method is explicitly forwarded to the listbox component's `bbox()` method. Without this explicit forwarding, the `bbox()` method (aliased to `grid_bbox()`) of the hull would be invoked, which is probably not what the programmer intended.

get(first = None, last = None)

This is the same as the `get()` method of the listbox component, except that if neither `first` nor `last` are specified, all list elements are returned.

getcurselection()

Returns the currently selected items of the listbox. This returns the text of the selected items, rather than their indexes as returned by `curselection()`.

setlist(items)

Replaces all the items of the listbox component with those specified by the item's sequence.

size()

This method is explicitly forwarded to the listbox component's `size()` method. Without this explicit forwarding, the size() method (aliased to grid_size()) of the hull would be invoked, which is probably not what the programmer intended.

ScrolledText

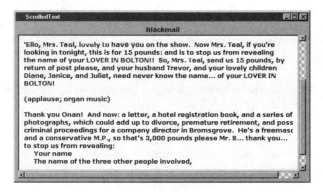

Description

This megawidget consists of a standard text widget with optional scrollbars which can be used to scroll the text widget. The scrollbars can be dynamic, which means that a scrollbar will only be displayed if it is necessary—if the text widget does not contain enough text (either horizontally or vertically), the scrollbar will be automatically hidden.

Inheritance

ScrolledText inherits from `Pmw.MegaWidget`.

ScrolledText options

Option	Description	Units	Default
borderframe	A frame widget which snugly fits around the text widget, to give the appearance of a text border. It is created with a border so that the text widget, which is created without a border, looks like it has a border.	widget	Frame
hscrollmode	The horizontal scroll mode. If none, the horizontal scrollbar will never be displayed. If `static`, the scrollbar will always be displayed. If `dynamic`, the scrollbar will be displayed only if necessary.	constant	'dynamic'
labelmargin	If the `labelpos` option is not None, this specifies the distance between the label component and the rest of the megawidget.	distance	0
labelpos	Specifies where to place the label component. If not None, it should be a concatenation of one or two of the letters N, S, E and W. The first letter specifies on which side of the megawidget to place the label. If a second letter is specified, it indicates where on that side to place the label. For example, if `labelpos` is W, the label is placed in the center of the left-hand side; if it is WN, the label is placed at the top of the left-hand side; if it is WS, the label is placed at the bottom of the left-hand side.	anchor	None
scrollmargin	The distance between the scrollbars and the text widget.	distance	2
uschullsize	If `true`, the size of the megawidget is determined solely by the `width` and `height` options of the hull component. Otherwise, the size of the megawidget is determined by the width and height of the text component, along with the size and/or existence of the other components, such as the label, the scrollbars and the `scrollmargin` option. All of these affect the overall size of the megawidget.	boolean	0
vscrollmode	The vertical scroll mode. If none, the vertical scrollbar will never be displayed. If `static`, the scrollbar will always be displayed. If `dynamic`, the scrollbar will be displayed only if necessary.	constant	'dynamic'

Components

borderframe

A frame widget which snugly fits around the text widget, to give the appearance of a text border. It is created with a border so that the text widget, which is created without a border, looks like it has a border.

horizscrollbar

The horizontal scrollbar. Its component group is `Scrollbar`.

hull

This acts as the body for the entire megawidget. Other components are created as children of the hull to further specialize the widget.

label

If the `labelpos` option is not `None`, this component is created as a text label for the megawidget. See the `labelpos` option for details. Note that to set, for example, the text option of the label, you need to use the `label_text` component option.

text

The text widget which is scrolled by the scrollbars. If the `borderframe` option is `true`, this is created with a borderwidth of `0` to overcome a known problem with text widgets: if a widget inside a text widget extends across one of the edges of the text widget, then the widget obscures the border of the text widget. Therefore, if the text widget has no border, then this overlapping does not occur.

vertscrollbar

The vertical scrollbar. Its component group is `Scrollbar`.

Methods

bbox(index)

This method is explicitly forwarded to the text component's `bbox()` method. Without this explicit forwarding, the `bbox()` method (aliased to `grid_bbox()`) of the hull would be invoked, which is probably not what the programmer intended.

clear()

Deletes all text from the text component.

exportfile(fileName)

Writes the contents of the text component to the file `fileName`.

get(first = None, last = None)

This is the same as the `get()` method of the text component, except that if neither `first` nor `last` are specified the entire contents of the text widget are returned.

importfile(fileName, where = 'end')

Reads the contents of the file `fileName` into the text component at the position given by `where`.

settext(text)

Replaces the entire contents of the text component with `text`.

SelectionDialog

Description

A SelectionDialog is a convenience dialog window with a `ScrolledList`. This is used to request the user to make a selection from the `ScrolledList`.

Inheritance

SelectionDialog inherits from `Pmw.Dialog`.

SelectionDialog options

Option	Description	Units	Default
activatecommand	If this is callable, it will be called whenever the megawidget is activated by a call to `activate()`.	function	None
borderx	Specifies the width of the border to the left and right of the message area.	distance	10
bordery	Specifies the height of the border to the top and bottom of the message area.	distance	10
buttonboxpos	Specifies on which side of the dialog window to place the button box. Must be one of N, S, E or W.	anchor	S
buttons	This must be a tuple or a list. It specifies the names on the buttons in the button box.	(string, ...)	('OK',)
command	Specifies a function to call whenever a button in the button box is invoked or the window is deleted by the window manager. The function is called with a single argument, which is the name of the button which was invoked, or None if the window was deleted by the window manager.	function	None
deactivatecommand	If this is callable, it will be called whenever the megawidget is deactivated by a call to `deactivate()`.	function	None
defaultbutton	Specifies the default button in the button box. If the RETURN key is hit when the dialog has focus, the default button will be invoked. If defaultbutton is None, there will be no default button and hitting the RETURN key will have no effect.	index	None
separatorwidth	If this is greater than 0, a separator line with the specified width will be created between the button box and the child site, as a component named separator. Since the default border of the button box and child site is raised, this option does not usually need to be set for there to be a visual separation between the button box and child site.	distance	0

Option	Description	Units	Default
title	This is the title that the window manager displays in the title bar of the window.	string	None

Components

buttonbox

This is the button box containing the buttons for the dialog. By default it is created with the options (hull_borderwidth = 1, hull_relief = 'raised').

dialogchildsite

This is the child site for the dialog, which may be used to specialize the megawidget by creating other widgets within it. By default it is created with the options (borderwidth = 1, relief = 'raised').

hull

This acts as the body for the entire megawidget. Other components are created as children of the hull to further specialize the widget.

scrolledlist

By default, this component is a Pmw.ScrolledListBox.

separator

If the separatorwidth initialization option is nonzero, the separator component is the line dividing the area between the button box and the child site.

Methods

This megawidget has no methods of its own.

TextDialog

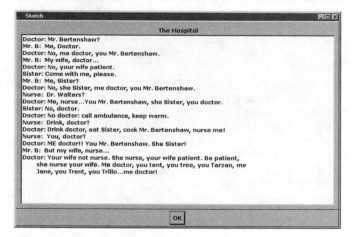

Description

A TextDialog is a convenience dialog window containing a scrolled text widget. This is used to display multiple lines of text to the user.

Inheritance

TextDialog inherits from `Pmw.Dialog`.

TextDialog options

Option	Description	Units	Default
activatecommand	If this is callable, it will be called whenever the megawidget is activated by a call to `activate()`.	function	None
borderx	Specifies the width of the border to the left and right of the message area.	distance	10
bordery	Specifies the height of the border to the top and bottom of the message area.	distance	10
buttonboxpos	Specifies on which side of the dialog window to place the button box. Must be one of N, S, E or W.	anchor	S
buttons	This must be a tuple or a list. It specifies the names on the buttons in the button box.	(string, ...)	('OK',)
command	Specifies a function to call whenever a button in the button box is invoked or the window is deleted by the window manager. The function is called with a single argument, which is the name of the button which was invoked, or None if the window was deleted by the window manager.	function	None
deactivatecommand	If this is callable, it will be called whenever the megawidget is deactivated by a call to `deactivate()`.	function	None

Option	Description	Units	Default
defaultbutton	Specifies the default button in the button box. If the RETURN key is hit when the dialog has focus, the default button will be invoked. If defaultbutton is None, there will be no default button and hitting the RETURN key will have no effect.	index	None
separatorwidth	If this is greater than 0, a separator line with the specified width will be created between the button box and the child site, as a component named separator. Since the default border of the button box and child site is raised, this option does not usually need to be set for there to be a visual separation between the button box and child site.	distance	0
title	This is the title that the window manager displays in the title bar of the window.	string	None

Components

buttonbox

This is the button box containing the buttons for the dialog. By default it is created with the options (hull_borderwidth = 1, hull_relief = 'raised').

dialogchildsite

This is the child site for the dialog, which may be used to specialize the megawidget by creating other widgets within it. By default it is created with the options (borderwidth = 1, relief = 'raised').

hull

This acts as the body for the entire megawidget. Other components are created as children of the hull to further specialize the widget.

scrolledtext

By default, this component is a Pmw.ScrolledText.

separator

If the separatorwidth initialization option is nonzero, the separator component is the line dividing the area between the button box and the child site.

Methods

This megawidget has no methods of its own.

TimeCounter

Description

A TimeCounter presents three up/down counters which act together to allow the user to input a time. Incrementing a `second` or `minute` counter past 59 will increment the `minute` or `hour` counter respectively.

Inheritance

TimeCounter inherits from `Pmw.MegaWidget`.

TimeCounter options

Option	Description	Units	Default
autorepeat	If `autorepeat` is true the up and down buttons will activate every `repeatrate` milliseconds after the `initwait` delay.	boolean	1
buttonaspect	Specifies the width of the arrow buttons as a proportion of their height. Values less than 1.0 will produce thin arrow buttons. Values greater than 1.0 will produce fat arrow buttons.	float	1.0
initwait	If `autorepeat` is true the widget will wait `initwait` milliseconds before repeatedly activating an up or down button.	milliseconds	300
labelmargin	If the `labelpos` option is not None, this specifies the distance between the label component and the rest of the megawidget.	distance	0
labelpos	Specifies where to place the label component. If not None, it should be a concatenation of one or two of the letters N, S, E and W. The first letter specifies on which side of the megawidget to place the label. If a second letter is specified, it indicates where on that side to place the label. For example, if `labelpos` is W, the label is placed in the center of the left-hand side; if it is WN, the label is placed at the top of the left-hand side; if it is WS, the label is placed at the bottom of the left-hand side.	anchor	None
max	The maximum value to be displayed by the widget. A value of 23:59:59 will result in a 24-hour time counter.	string	''
min	The minimum time to be displayed in the widget. This will normally be 00:00:00 or be left as the default.		''
padx	Specifies a padding distance to leave between each spin button in the x dimension.	distance	0
pady	Specifies a padding distance to leave between each spin button in the y dimension.	distance	0
repeatrate	If `autorepeat` is true, specifies the rate at which a button will repeatedly activate if the button is held down.	milliseconds	50
value	The initial value to be displayed in the widget.		''

Components

downhourarrow
Its component group is Arrow.

downminutearrow
Its component group is Arrow.

downsecondarrow
Its component group is Arrow.

frame
By default, this component is a Frame.

hourentryfield
By default, this component is a Pmw.EntryField.

hull
This acts as the body for the entire megawidget. Other components are created as children of the hull to further specialize the widget.

label
If the labelpos option is not None, this component is created as a text label for the mega-widget. See the labelpos option for details. Note that to set, for example, the text option of the label, you need to use the label_text component option.

minuteentryfield
By default, this component is a Pmw.EntryField.

secondentryfield
By default, this component is a Pmw.EntryField.

uphourarrow
Its component group is Arrow.

upminutearrow
Its component group is Arrow.

upsecondarrow
Its component group is Arrow.

Methods

decrement()
Decrements the time by one second.

getint()

Returns the time as an `integer`.

getstring()

Returns the time as a `string` with the format `HH:MM:SS`.

increment()

Increments the time by one second.

invoke()

If `command` is callable, it invokes `command`.

Building and installing Python, Tkinter

In general, you will not need to build Python or its components from source; binary distributions are readily available from www.python.org for several UNIX variants, Win32, and MacOS. However, if you intend to build extensions to Python you will need to obtain the sources for Python and sometimes for Tcl and Tk.

If you *do* decide to build Python, you may also want to build Tcl/Tk. The information presented here is for Python 1.5.2 and Tcl/Tk 8.0.5, which were the stable releases at the time of writing. For newer releases, you should visit the respective web pages for up-to-date information.

We will look at building everything for UNIX, Win32, and MacOS in turn.

Building for UNIX

Building Python and Tkinter for UNIX is probably the most straightforward process when compared to the other architectures. Personally, I've had only two UNIX systems that have given me trouble and the problems can be attributed to the fact that they were new systems.

Before starting, you will need to obtain the appropriate source distributions.

Obtaining source distributions

Before collecting any source, decide where you are going to store the source files. You are going to have three directories (Python, Tcl and Tk) each with their revision as a suffix. You must arrange for these directories to be at the *same* relative level on the disk (for example, all in /python_source).

Next, visit www.python.org and find the latest version of Python (you will usually find a reference to the current version in the Topics panel). This should point you to the source distribution which is currently a gzipped tar file. While on this page, find out which version of Tcl/Tk was used for the binary distribution of Python. This is the version that you will need to build Tkinter. Retrieve the Python distribution and copy the file to the location you have chosen. Extract the source as follows (substitute the current version number for the **bolded** version).

```
gunzip -c py152.tgz | tar xf -
```

Tcl/Tk may be obtained from www.scriptics.com/products/tcltk. From this page, you will find a reference to the source distribution for the current patch level. You do not have to build Tcl/Tk if you do not want to; binary distributions of Tcl/Tk are available which include libraries that may be used to build Tkinter. It is quite likely that you will find a version later than the one used for the binary distribution of Python. Normally the patches represent bug fixes and should not cause any problems. However, do not be tempted into using the very latest release (for example, if Python was originally built with 8.0.5 and there are three later versions (8.0.6, 8.1.0 and 8.2.0 available, select 8.0.6). Retrieve the two gzipped tar files and copy them to the location you have chosen. Extract the source as follows (substitute the current version number for the **bolded** version).

```
gunzip -c tcl8.0.5.tar.gz | tar xf -
gunzip -c tk8.0.5.tar.gz | tar xf -
```

You must now build Tcl, Tk and Python, in that order.

Building Tcl

Change directory to the UNIX directory in the Tcl directory. In that directory you will find a ReadMe file giving complete details for building Tcl. The following is a summary of what you need to do. Of course, certain UNIX systems have special issues, so you may need to read all of the ReadMe file or consult the web.

1 Decide where the binary and library files will be installed. We will assume that the install directory is /usr/local (the default).

2 Run the configuration script. This automatically determines the compiler options and system facilities to be used by the build.
   ```
   ./configure
   ```

3 Run the make utility to create the Tcl library.
   ```
   make
   ```

4 Install the binary and library files.
   ```
   make install
   ```

Assuming that you did not encounter errors, you may go on to build Tk.

Building Tk

Building Tk is similar to building Tcl. Change directory to the UNIX directory in the Tk directory. In that directory you will find a ReadMe file giving complete details for building Tk. The following is a summary of what you need to do.

1   You should install Tk into the same directory structure as Tcl. If you did change from the default `/usr/local` then you should use the same path for the configure script.

2   Run the configuration script. This automatically determines the compiler options and system facilities to be used by the build.
    ```
    ./configure
    ```

3   Run the `make` utility to create the Tk library.
    ```
    make
    ```

4   Install the binary and library files.
    ```
    make install
    ```

We are now ready to build Python.

Building Python

Building Python is quite similar to building Tcl or Tk. A little more work is required to configure the build to add Tkinter, which is *not* built by default. You'll find a ReadMe file at the top-level Python directory which gives full details and explains differences between different variants of UNIX. Once again, the following is a summary.

1   We will assume again that the install directory is `/usr/local` (the default). It does not have to be the same as the Tcl/Tk installation directory, but there is little reason to use a different location.

2   Run the configuration script. This automatically determines the compiler options and system facilities to be used by the build. Note that if you intend to use threading, you will have to add the `--with-thread` option to configure. Read the ReadMe file for further details and information about platform-specific issues.
    ```
    ./configure
    ```

3   Copy Modules/Setup.in to Modules/Setup. This file is used to determine which built-in modules will be added to Python. For the moment, we are concerned only with adding Tkinter. You will find many platform-specific modules that may be added or removed from the build.

4   Edit Modules/Setup and locate the line commented as:
    ```
    # The _tkinter module.
    ```

5   Follow the instructions in the file. The example shown here is appropriate for Solaris 2.5 or 2.6 (the bold sections should not be commented):

```
# The TKPATH variable is always enabled, to save you the effort.
TKPATH=:lib-tk
# The command for _tkinter is long and site-specific.  Please
# uncomment and/or edit those parts as indicated.  If you don't have a
# specific extension (e.g. Tix or BLT), leave the corresponding line
# commented out.  (Leave the trailing backslashes in!  If you
# experience strange errors, you may want to join all uncommented
```

```
# lines and remove the backslashes -- the backslash interpretation is
# done by the shell's "read" command and it may not be implemented on
# every system.

# *** Always uncomment this (leave the leading underscore in!):
_tkinter _tkinter.c tkappinit.c -DWITH_APPINIT \
# *** Uncomment and edit to reflect where your Tcl/Tk headers are:
-I/usr/local/include \
# *** Uncomment and edit to reflect where your X11 header files are:
#  -I/usr/X11R6/include \
# *** Or uncomment this for Solaris:
-I/usr/openwin/include \
# *** Uncomment and edit for Tix extension only:
#  -DWITH_TIX -ltix4.1.8.0 \
# *** Uncomment and edit for BLT extension only:
#  -DWITH_BLT -I/usr/local/blt/blt8.0-unoff/include -lBLT8.0 \
# *** Uncomment and edit for PIL (TkImaging) extension only:
#  -DWITH_PIL -I../Extensions/Imaging/libImaging  tkImaging.c \
# *** Uncomment and edit for TOGL extension only:
#  -DWITH_TOGL togl.c \
# *** Uncomment and edit to reflect where your Tcl/Tk libraries are:
-L/usr/local/lib \
# *** Uncomment and edit to reflect your Tcl/Tk versions:
-ltk8.0 -ltcl8.0 \
# *** Uncomment and edit to reflect where your X11 libraries are:
#  -L/usr/X11R6/lib \
# *** Or uncomment this for Solaris:
-L/usr/openwin/lib \
# *** Uncomment these for TOGL extension only:
#  -lGL -lGLU -lXext -lXmu \
# *** Uncomment for AIX:
#  -lld \
# *** Always uncomment this; X11 libraries to link with:
-lX11
```

6   If you wish to build modules as shared objects, uncomment the line which contains
    shared. All subsequent modules will be built as separate shared objects.

7   Save Modules/Setup. You may wish to save a copy of Modules/Setup so that you will be
    able to identify your chosen configuration in later versions of Python.

8   Run the make utility to create the Python executable and library.
    ```
    make
    ```

9   Install the binary and library files.
    ```
    make install
    ```

10 Define environment variables to reflect your chosen installation locations:
    ```
    PATH= .....:/usr/local/bin:.......
    PYTHONPATH=/usr/local/lib/python1.5
    TCL_LIBRARY=/usr/local/lib/tcl8.0
    TK_LIBRARY=/usr/local/lib/tk8.0
    ```

Building for Windows

Building Python and Tkinter for Windows is relatively straightforward, but it involves a little more editing work when compared to UNIX, particularly if you have additional modules to add to Python. Although it is possible to use Borland's C compiler to build Tcl/Tk, Python requires Microsoft Visual C++ version 5 or 6.

Obtaining source distributions

Before collecting any source, decide where you are going to store the source files. You are going to have three directories (Python, Tcl and Tk) each with their revision as a suffix. You must arrange for these directories to be at the same relative level on the disk (for example, all in C:\python_source).

Next, visit www.python.org and find the latest version of Python (you will usually find a reference to the current version in the Topics panel). This should point you to the source distribution which is currently a gzipped tar file. While on this page, find out which version of Tcl/Tk was used for the binary distribution of Python. This is the version that you will need to build Tkinter. The source for the Windows (and Macintosh) distribution is identical to the UNIX distribution, although you will probably want to retrieve the zipped version. Retrieve the Python distribution and copy the file to the location you have chosen. Assuming that you have a copy of WinZip, double click on the zip file in Explorer and extract to your chosen location.

Similarly, Tcl/Tk may be obtained from www.scriptics.com/products/tcltk. From this page, you will find a reference to the source distribution for the current patch level for Windows. It is quite likely that you will find a version *later* than the one used for the binary distribution of Python. Normally the patches represent bug fixes and should not cause any problems. However, do not be tempted into using the very latest release (for example, if Python was originally built with 8.0.5 and there are three later versions (8.0.6, 8.1.0 and 8.2.0) available, select 8.0.6). Retrieve the two zip files and copy them to the location you have chosen. Extract the source to the chosen location using WinZip.

You must now build Tcl, Tk, and Python, in that order.

Building Tcl

Change directory to the `win` directory in the `Tcl` directory. In that directory you will find a ReadMe file giving complete details for building Tcl. The following is a summary of what you need to do.

1 Decide where the binary and library files will be installed. By default Tcl installs into C:\Program Files but there is a bug in the makefile which causes the install to fail (because of the embedded space in the directory name). It is suggested that you install into C:\Tcl.

2 Copy MakeFile.vc to MakeFile. Edit MakeFile and change the paths at the beginning of the file, as appropriate for your installation and chosen install location:

```
ROOT     = ..
TOOLS32  = c:\program files\devstudio\vc
TOOLS32_rc= c:\program files\devstudio\sharedide
TOOLS16  = c:\msvc
INSTALLDIR= c:\Tcl
```

3 In an MS-DOS window, run the nmake utility to create the Tcl library.

```
nmake
```

4 Install the binary and library files.

```
nmake install
```

Assuming that you did not encounter errors, you may go on to build Tk.

Building Tk

Building Tk is similar to building Tcl. Change directory to the win directory in the Tk directory. In that directory you will find a ReadMe file giving complete details for building Tk. The following is a summary of what you need to do.

1 You should install Tk into the same directory structure as a *peer* of Tcl.

2 Copy MakeFile.vc to MakeFile. Edit MakeFile and change the paths at the beginning of the file, as appropriate for your installation and chosen install location:

```
ROOT        = ..
TOOLS32     = c:\program files\devstudio\vc
TOOLS32_rc= c:\program files\devstudio\sharedide
TCLDIR      = ..\..\tcl8.0.5
INSTALLDIR= c:\tcl
```

3 Run the nmake utility to create the Tk library.

```
nmake
```

4 Install the binary and library files.

```
nmake install
```

We are now ready to build Python.

Building Python

The current distribution of Python requires you to build with Microsoft Visual C++ 5.x (or 6.x). Once Tcl/Tk has been built, it is quite easy to complete the build.

1 In Explorer, navigate to the PCbuild directory.

2 Open the workspace pcbuild.dsw.

3 Select the Debug or Release setting (using Set Active Configuration... in the Build menu).

4 Select python15 from Select Active Project in the Project menu.

5 Select Build python_15.dll from the Build menu.

6 Select python from Select Active Project in the Project menu.

7 Select Build python.exe from the Build menu.

8 Select pythonw from Select Active Project in the Project menu.

9 Select Build pythonw.exe from the Build menu.

10 Select _tkinter from Select Active Project in the Project menu.

11 Select Build _tkinter.pyd from the Build menu.

12 Move python.exe, pythonw.exe, python15.dll and _tkinter.pyd to the directory you wish to run Python from (see "Distributing Tkinter applications" on page 374 for further details).

Building for MacOS

I have to admit that I do not build the MacOS version of Tcl/Tk or Python. I have been informed that you do not need to build Tcl/Tk for MacOS; the standard installer contains a complete Tcl/Tk installation.

Visit www.python.org and find the latest version of Python (you will usually find a reference to the current version in the Topics panel). This should point you to the source distribution page; at the time of writing, it is www.cwi.nl/~jack/macpython.html. There you will find Stuffit and BinHex versions of the source. The source for the MacOS distribution is almost identical to the UNIX distribution, although you will retrieve the Stuffit or binhex version. Retrieve the Python distribution and copy the file to the location you have chosen.

Once you have retrieved the files, follow the instructions included with the release.

APPENDIX   E

Events and keysyms

The tables in this appendix document the modifiers, event types and keysyms recognized by Tkinter (strictly Tk). Translation of keycodes is highly implementation-dependent so it is important to note that not all keys can be detected consistently across multiple architectures.

The generalized format of events is as follows:

< [modifier [' '|- modifier ...] ' '|-] [[type [qualifier] | qualifier] >

Modifiers

Modifier	Alt. 1	Alt. 2	Mask
Control			ControlMask
Shift			ShiftMask
Lock			LockMask
Meta	M		META_MASK
Alt			ALT_MASK
B1	Button1		Button1Mask
B2	Button2		Button2Mask
B3	Button3		Button3Mask
B4	Button4		Button4Mask

Modifier	Alt. 1	Alt. 2	Mask
B5	Button5		Button5Mask
Mod1	M1	Command	Mod1Mask
Mod2	M2	Option	Mod2Mask
Mod3	M3		Mod3Mask
Mod4	M4		Mod4Mask
Mod5	M5		Mod5Mask
Double			
Triple			

Event types

Event name	Alt. 1	Type	Mask
Key	KeyPress	KeyPress	KeyPressMask
KeyRelease		KeyRelease	KeyPressMask|KeyReleaseMask
Button	ButtonPress	ButtonPress	ButtonPressMask
ButtonRelease		ButtonRelease	ButtonPressMask|ButtonReleaseMask
Motion		MotionNotify	ButtonPressMask|PointerMotionMask
Enter		EnterNotify	EnterWindowMask
Leave		LeaveNotify	LeaveWindowMask
FocusIn		FocusIn	FocusChangeMask
FocusOut		FocusOut	FocusChangeMask
Expose		Expose	ExposureMask
Visibility		VisibilityNotify	VisibilityChangeMask
Destroy		DestroyNotify	StructureNotifyMask
Unmap		UnmapNotify	StructureNotifyMask
Map		MapNotify	StructureNotifyMask
Reparent		ReparentNotify	StructureNotifyMask
Configure		ConfigureNotify	StructureNotifyMask
Gravity		GravityNotify	StructureNotifyMask
Circulate		CirculateNotify	StructureNotifyMask
Property		PropertyNotify	PropertyChangeMask
Colormap		ColormapNotify	ColormapChangeMask
Activate		ActivateNotify	ActivateMask
Deactivate		DeactivateNotify	ActivateMask
MouseWheel		MouseWheelEvent	MouseWheelMask

Qualifier

Qualifier	Mask
1	ButtonPressMask
2	ButtonPressMask
3	ButtonPressMask
4	ButtonPressMask
5	ButtonPressMask
keysym	KeyPressMask

Keysyms

Not all of the possible keysyms are presented here. In fact, only the Latin-1 set is presented. This is generally the set of keys that you will bind to. If you need to bind to other key sets (such as Cyrillic or Balkan) you will find them in the Tk source code (Tk[*Release*]/generic/ks_names.h).

E.5.1 Latin-1

Keysym	Key
BackSpace	BackSpace
Tab	Tab
Linefeed	Linefeed
Clear	Clear
Return	Return
Pause	Pause
Escape	Escape
Delete	Delete
Multi_key	Multi_key
Kanji	Kanji
Home	Home
Left	Left
Up	Up
Right	Right
Down	Down
Prior	Prior
Next	Next
End	End
Begin	Begin

Keysym	Key
Win_L	Left Window
Win_R	Right Window
App	Application
Select	Select
Print	Print
Execute	Execute
Insert	Insert
Undo	Undo
Redo	Redo
Menu	Menu
Find	Find
Cancel	Cancel
Help	Help
Break	Break
Mode_switch	Mode_switch
script_switch	script_switch
Num_Lock	Num_Lock
KP_Space	Keypad Space
KP_Tab	Keypad Tab

Keysym	Key	Keysym	Key
KP_Enter	Keypad Enter	numbersign	numbersign
KP_F1	Keypad F1	dollar	dollar
KP_F2	Keypad F2	percent	percent
KP_F3	Keypad F3	ampersand	ampersand
KP_F4	Keypad F4	quoteright	quoteright
KP_Equal	Keypad Equal	parenleft	parenleft
KP_Multiply	Keypad Multiply	parenright	parenright
KP_Add	Keypad Add	asterisk	asterisk
KP_Separator	Keypad Separator	plus	plus
KP_Subtract	Keypad Subtract	comma	comma
KP_Decimal	Keypad Decimal	minus	minus
KP_Divide	Keypad Divide	period	period
KP_0 ... KP_9	Keypad 0 ... Keypad 9	slash	slash
F1 ... F35	Function 1 ... Function 35	0 ... 9	0 ... 9
L1 ... L10	L1 ... L10	colon	colon
R1 ... R15	R1 ... R15	semicolon	semicolon
Shift_L	Left Shift	less	less
Shift_R	Right Shift	equal	equal
Control_L	Left Control	greater	greater
Control_R	Right Control	question	question
Caps_Lock	Caps_Lock	at	at
Shift_Lock	Shift_Lock	A ... Z	A ... Z
Meta_L	Left Meta	bracketleft	bracketleft
Meta_R	Right Meta	backslash	backslash
Alt_L	Left Alt	bracketright	bracketright
Alt_R	Right Alt	asciicircum	asciicircum
Super_L	Left Super	underscore	underscore
Super_R	Right Super	quoteleft	quoteleft
Hyper_L	Left Hyper	a ... z	a ... z
Hyper_R	Right Hyper	braceleft	braceleft
space	space	bar	bar
exclam	exclam	braceright	braceright
quotedbl	quotedbl	asciitilde	asciitilde

A P P E N D I X   F

Cursors

The tables in this appendix illustrate the cursors available to Tkinter applications. The cursors are available on all platforms. However, certain cursors may have special meaning on some operating systems (the *watch* cursor on Win32 uses the current watch cursor defined in the system, for example).

Cursor name	Cursor	Cursor name	Cursor
X_cursor	✖	bottom_left_corner	⌞
arrow	↗	bottom_right_corner	⌟
based_arrow_down	⊤	bottom_side	↓
based_arrow_up	⊥	bottom_tee	⊥
boat	⇀	box_spiral	▣
bogosity	▦	center_ptr	♠

Cursor name	Cursor	Cursor name	Cursor
circle		fleur	
clock		gobbler	
coffee_mug		gumby	
cross		hand1	
cross_reverse		hand2	
crosshair		heart	
diamond_cross		icon	
dot		iron_cross	
dotbox		left_ptr	
double_arrow		left_side	
draft_large		left_tee	
draft_small		leftbutton	
draped_box		ll_angle	
exchange		lr_angle	

Cursor name	Cursor	Cursor name	Cursor
man		sb_h_double_arrow	
middlebutton		sb_left_arrow	
mouse		sb_right_arrow	
pencil		sb_up_arrow	
pirate		sb_v_double_arrow	
plus		shuttle	
question_arrow		sizing	
right_ptr		spider	
right_side		spraycan	
right_tee		star	
rightbutton		target	
rtl_logo		tcross	
sailboat		top_left_arrow	
sb_down_arrow		top_left_corner	

Cursor name	Cursor	Cursor name	Cursor
top_right_corner	↗	umbrella	☂
top_side	↑	ur_angle	⌐
top_tee	⊤	watch	⌚
trek	♟	xterm	I
ul_angle	⌐		

A P P E N D I X   G

References

This appendix presents sources for Python resources and some book references you may find useful for obtaining more detailed information on Python, the X Window system, Tcl/Tk and human factors engineering. For most of the resources located on the web, I have reproduced the original authors' description of the resource.

Resources

Siomodule

Sio.pyd is a DLL and is a wrapper to another DLL which is a commercial package. The maker of that package agreed to let their DLL be distributed as long as the following appears:

Serial Communications DLLs by MarshallSoft Computing, Inc.
POB 4543 Huntsville AL 35815. 205-881-4630.
Email: mike@marshallsoft.com
Web : www.marshallsoft.com

SWIG

SWIG is a software development tool that connects programs written in C, C++, and Objective-C with a variety of high-level programming languages. SWIG is primarily used with common scripting languages such as Perl, Python and Tcl/Tk, but it has also been extended to include languages such as Java, Eiffel and Guile. SWIG is most commonly used to create high-level interpreted programming environments and systems integration, and as a tool for building user interfaces. SWIG may be freely used, distributed and modified for commercial or noncommercial use.

http://www.swig.org/

NumPy

NumPy is a nickname for a package of Numerical Extensions to Python. These extensions add two powerful new types to Python: a new sequence type which implements multidimensional arrays efficiently (multiarray) and a new type of function called a universal function (ufunc) which works efficiently on the new arrays and other sequence types. These new objects give Python the number-crunching power of numeric languages like MATLAB and IDL while maintaining all of the advantages which Python has as a general-purpose programming language. It's also free, just like the rest of Python.

ftp://ftp-icf.llnl.gov/pub/python/README.html

Python News Group

comp.lang.python
comp.lang.python.announce

Python Imaging Library (PIL)

The Python Imaging Library adds an image object to your Python interpreter. You can load image objects from a variety of file formats and apply a rich set of image operations to them.

http://www.pythonware.com/downloads.htm

PythonWorks

PythonWorks is a rapid-development environment under development by PythonWare/Secret Labs AB.

http://www.pythonware.com/products/works/index.htm

Python books

1 Ascher, David and Mark Lutz. *Learning Python*. O'Reilly & Associates, 1999. ISBN: 1-56592-464-9.

2 Beazley, David. *Python Essential Reference*. New Riders, 1999. ISBN: 0-7357-090-17.

3 Harms, Daryl and Kenneth McDonald. *The Quick Python Book*. Manning Publications, 2000. ISBN: 1-884777-74-0.

4 Lundh, Fredrik. *(the eff-bot guide to) The Standard Python Library*. Electronic edition at www.fatbrain.com.

5 Lutz, Mark. *Programming Python*. O'Reilly & Associates, 1996. ISBN: 1-56592-197-6.

X Window books

6 Nye, Adrian and Tim O'Reilly. *X Toolkit Intrinsics Programming Manual for X11, Release 5 (Definitive Guides to the X Window System, Vol 4)*. O'Reilly & Associates, 1992. ISBN: 1-56592-013-9.

7 Young, Douglas. *The X Window System: Programming and Applications with Xt, OSF/Motif*, 2nd edition. Prentice-Hall, 1994. ISBN: 0-13123-803-5.

Tcl/Tk books

8 Flynt, Clifton. *Tcl/Tk for Real Programmers*. Academic Press (AP Professional), 1998. ISBN: 0-12261-205-1.

9 Foster-Johnson, Eric. *Graphical Applications with Tcl and Tk*, 2nd edition. M&T Books, 1997. ISBN: 1-55851-569-0.

10 Harrison, Mark and Michael J. McLennan. *Effective Tcl/Tk Programming: Writing Better Programs in Tcl and Tk*. Addison Wesley Longman, 1997. ISBN: 0-20163-474-0.

11 Ousterhout, John. *Tcl and the Tk Toolkit*. Addison-Wesley, 1994. ISBN: 0-20163-337-X.

12 Raines, Paul. *Tcl/Tk Pocket Reference*. O'Reilly & Associates, 1998. ISBN: 1-56592-498-3.

Human factors engineering

13 Coe, Marlana. *Human Factors for Technical Communicators*. John Wiley & Sons, 1996. ISBN: 0-47103-530-0.

14 Cooper, Alan. *About Face: The Essentials of User Interface Design*. IDG Books, 1995. ISBN 1-56884-322-4.

15 Olsen, Dan R., Jr., Dan E. Olsen and Dan R. Olsen. *Developing User Interfaces*. Morgan Kaufmann, 1998. ISBN 1-55860-418-9.

index